Diplomatic Interference and the Law

Paul Behrens

• HART •

OXFORD • LONDON • NEW YORK • NEW DELHI • SYDNEY

HART PUBLISHING
Bloomsbury Publishing Plc
Kemp House, Chawley Park, Cumnor Hill, Oxford, OX2 9PH, UK

HART PUBLISHING, the Hart/Stag logo, BLOOMSBURY and the Diana logo are trademarks of Bloomsbury Publishing Plc
First published in Great Britain 2016

First published in hardback, 2016
Paperback edition, 2018

A catalogue record for this book is available from the British Library.

Library of Congress Cataloging-in-Publication Data

Names: Behrens, Paul, author.

Title: Diplomatic interference and the law / Paul Behrens.

Description: Oxford ; Portland, Oregon : Hart Publishing Ltd, 2016. | Includes bibliographical references and index.

Identifiers: LCCN 2015049486 (print) | LCCN 2015049633 (ebook) | ISBN 9781849464369 (hardback : alk. paper) | ISBN 9781509902781 (Epub)

Subjects: LCSH: Diplomatic and consular service. | Diplomacy—Political aspects.

Classification: LCC KZ4078.B44 2016 (print) | LCC KZ4078 (ebook) | DDC 341.3/3—dc23

LC record available at http://lccn.loc.gov/2015049486

ISBN: PB: 978-1-50992-459-2
HB: 978-1-84946-436-9

Typeset by Compuscript Ltd, Shannon

To find out more about our authors and books visit www.hartpublishing.co.uk. Here you will find extracts, author information, details of forthcoming events and the option to sign up for our newsletters.

DIPLOMATIC INTERFERENCE AND THE LAW

Diplomatic interference carries considerable potential for disruption. In this context, diplomats have been accused of insulting behaviour, the funding of political parties, incitement to terrorism and even attempts to topple the host government. Reactions can be harsh: expulsions are common and, occasionally, diplomatic relations are severed altogether.

But an evaluation under international law faces challenges. Often enough, charges of interference are made when legitimate interests are involved—for instance, when diplomats criticise the human rights record of their hosts. In such cases, diplomats may be able to invoke grounds which are recognised under international law.

On the basis of more than 300 cases of alleged diplomatic interference and the practice of about 100 States and territories, *Diplomatic Interference and the Law* provides an examination of the main areas in which charges of meddling have arisen—such as lobbying activities, contacts with the opposition, propaganda, the use of threats and insults and the granting of asylum. It analyses situations in which the sovereignty of the receiving State meets competing interests and offers solutions which avoid a conflict of norms. It concludes with useful advice for foreign offices and diplomatic agents and underlines the most efficient ways of dealing with situations of alleged interference.

For my mother,
for Young-ai and Robert

Preface

At the time of writing, dark clouds have gathered on the horizon. In a short span of time, an increasing number of nations have exchanged the questionable stability of authoritarian regimes for the unquestioned instability of civil strife, and even the old spectre of conflict among sovereign States has, for the first time in years, raised its head again. Against this backdrop, the writing of a book on diplomatic interference may appear a peculiar endeavour. Diplomatic interference seems so firmly lodged at the other end of the scale that one may think of it as a *quantité négligeable.*

That, however, would not reflect its true significance. Diplomatic interference is not limited to the occasional critical remark which may be a nuisance to overly sensitive hosts. Instances in which this kind of conduct has been alleged include incitement to terrorism and violence, bribery, the issuing of threats and ultimata and attempts to topple the government of the receiving State.

Nor would it be correct to consider it a phenomenon which is entirely removed from other events in international relations, including those which may have an even more severe impact on the internal order of the receiving State. It is a sobering thought that, three years before the beginning of the armed conflict in Ukraine in 2014, a Russian diplomat was expelled from her borders amid accusations that he had cast doubt on her territorial integrity[1] and that, as early as 1995, Russian consular officers were accused of interference amid allegations that they had encouraged Crimeans to become Russian citizens.[2] Ignoring such omens comes at a price.

This study examines the concept of diplomatic interference; it analyses the rationale of its prohibition and outlines the interests on the side of the sending State and the international community which may induce diplomats to engage in conduct which their hosts consider meddling in internal affairs. It investigates the applicability of mechanisms which mediate between the competing interests and provides an overview of the main fields in which charges of interference have arisen in the past.

In so doing, it relies not only on treaty law and academic opinion in the field, but draws on instances of alleged interference which have played a

[1] See below (A.247).

[2] *Official Kremlin Int'l News Broadcast*, 'Press Briefing by Russian Federation Foreign Ministry Spokesman', 11 April 1995.

role in diplomatic history. They are employed not only as illustrations for the relevant findings, but as an indication of the direction in which customary international law moves. And there is evidence that the assessment of such instances by members of the international community contributes directly to the very concept of diplomatic interference under international law—a point which will be explored in more detail in Part II.[3]

It is for that reason that a timeline of cases of alleged interference has been included in Annex A. Reference is made to them throughout the text, and the number which they carry in the annex is often indicated in the relevant footnotes (A.186, for instance, refers to Annex A, case no 186—the 'Freedom House speech' by the British Ambassador to Uzbekistan, Craig Murray, in 2002). The cut-off point for these cases was April 2014; law and literature have been considered until July 2014.

Annex B contains excerpts of draft codes and of the work of the International Law Commission and its Special Rapporteur in the 1950s, and reference to them is made in a similar way (B.7, for instance, refers to the seventh document in Annex B—ie, Article 33 in the 1957 Draft Articles of the International Law Commission).

Annex C contains excerpts of treaties and instruments on diplomatic and consular law (a mention of C.1, for instance, is a reference to the Havana Convention on Diplomatic Officers of 1928).

The focus of this study is conduct by diplomatic agents assigned to permanent missions between States. The most pertinent treaty for these purposes is the Vienna Convention on Diplomatic Relations of 1961,[4] and mentions of the 'Vienna Convention' or the 'VCDR' are references to this instrument—as are mentions of 'the Convention', unless otherwise indicated. Likewise, articles without a treaty reference are articles of the Vienna Convention, unless a different meaning is apparent from the context.

Translations, unless otherwise marked, were done by the author.

Treaties and UN materials were reproduced with permission by the United Nations; draft codes on diplomatic law with permission by the American Society of International Law. I gratefully acknowledge their kind cooperation in this matter. I would also like to thank the National Endowment for the Humanities (Washington DC) for their help regarding the reproduction of the 'Sackville Letter' on the cover of this book.

I owe a debt of gratitude to my colleagues, Professor Craig Barker, Dr Peter Slinn and Professor András Jakab, who very generously agreed to read previous parts of this study and provided much appreciated feedback. My thanks also go to Richard Hart, former Managing Director at

[3] See Introduction to Part II, after n 4.

[4] See C.3.

Hart Publishing for agreeing to this project in the first place and to Emily Braggins, Assistant Editor at Hart Publishing, and her predecessor Rachel Turner, whose wise counsel and considerable patience had been of invaluable help throughout the production process.

And as always, my thanks go to my friends and my family, whose continued support is a source of encouragement and a light in dark times.

Paul Behrens
Edinburgh, July 2015

Contents

Abbreviations

ACHR	American Convention on Human Rights
AFDI	Annuaire Française de Droit International
All ER	All England Reports
ANC	African National Congress
APEC	Asia-Pacific Economic Cooperation
AU	African Union
Aust YBIL	Australian Yearbook of International Law
BISD	Basic Instruments and Selected Documents (GATT)
CERD	International Convention on the Elimination of All Forms of Racial Discrimination
CMLR	Common Market Law Reports
COE	Council of Europe
CRSIO	Vienna Convention on the Representation of States in their Relations with International Organizations of a Universal Character
CSM	Convention on Special Missions
ECHR	[European] Convention for the Protection of Human Rights and Fundamental Freedoms; Reports of Judgments and Decisions (of the European Court of Human Rights)
ECR	European Court Reports
ECtHR	European Court of Human Rights
EFTA	European Free Trade Association
EHRR	European Human Rights Reports
EU	European Union
EWCA (Civ)	Court of Appeal of England and Wales (Civil Division)
EWHC (QB)	High Court of England and Wales (Queen's Bench Division)
GA	United Nations General Assembly
GATT	General Agreement on Tariffs and Trade
HC	House of Commons
HRC	Human Rights Committee
IACAC	Inter-American Convention Against Corruption
ICC	International Criminal Court
ICCPR	International Covenant on Civil and Political Rights
ICESCR	International Covenant on Economic, Social and Cultural Rights
ICJ	International Court of Justice
ICTR	International Criminal Tribunal for Rwanda
ICTY	International Criminal Tribunal for the Former Yugoslavia
ILC	International Law Commission

ILM	International Legal Materials
ILR	International Law Reports
ITLOS	International Tribunal for the Law of the Sea
NGO	Non-governmental organisation
OAS	Organization of American States
OAU	Organization of African Unity
PLO	Palestine Liberation Organization
RBDI	Revue belge de droit international
RGDIP	Revue générale de droit international public
RIAA	Recueil des Sentences Arbitrales (Reports of International Arbitral Awards)
SADC	Southern African Development Community
SC	United Nations Security Council
UDHR	Universal Declaration of Human Rights
UNASUR	Union of South American Nations
UNCAC	United Nations Convention Against Corruption
UNCLOS	United Nations Convention on the Law of the Sea
UNESCO	United Nations Educational, Scientific and Cultural Organization
UNHCR	United Nations High Commissioner for Refugees
UNTAET	United Nations Transitional Administration in East Timor
UPI	United Press International
VCCR	Vienna Convention on Consular Relations
VCDR	Vienna Convention on Diplomatic Relations
Vienna Convention	Vienna Convention on Diplomatic Relations
WLR	Weekly Law Reports
YILC	Yearbook of the International Law Commission
ZaöRV	Zeitschrift für ausländisches öffentliches Recht und Völkerrecht

Table of Cases

International and Regional Bodies

EFTA Court

European Court of Human Rights and European Commission on Human Rights

European Court of Justice

Human Rights Committee

Inter-American Court of Human Rights and Inter-American Commission on Human Rights

International Arbitral Awards

International Court of Justice

International Criminal Tribunal for Rwanda

International Criminal Tribunal for the Former Yugoslavia

International Military Tribunal at Nuremberg and Subsequent Nuremberg Trials

Permanent Court of International Justice

WTO and GATT

Domestic Cases

Belgium

Canada

Netherlands

United Kingdom

Table of Treaties and Other Materials

Treaties and Other Instruments

Resolutions by International Institutions

Security Council Resolutions

General Assembly Resolutions

Unesco Resolutions

UNESCO Res IV.1.5.021, Records of the General Conference, Eighth Session 1954, Resolutions, 37 (1954) 177

UNESCO Res 4.301, Records of the General Conference, 16th Session 1970, Resolutions, 60 (1970) 177

UNESCO, Records of the General Conference, 20th session, 1978, Resolutions, 4/9.3/2, 'Declaration on Fundamental Principles Concerning the Contribution of the Mass Media to Strengthening Peace and International Understanding, to the Promotion of Human Rights and to Countering Racialism, Apartheid and Incitement to War', 100 (1978) [Mass Media Declaration] 177, 183, 189, 190

Assembly of State Parties of the International Criminal Court

Assembly of State Parties, Resolution RC/Res.6, The Crime of Aggression, Annex I (11 June 2010) 106

Other Materials

For press releases, see below (News Media)

International and Regional Materials

1968 Conference, Records, 1st Session: See United Nations, Conference on the Law of Treaties

1975 Conference, Records Vol 1: See United Nations, Conference on the Representation of States in their Relations with International Organizations

Cedeño Report: See International Law Commission, Seventh Report on unilateral acts by States, by Mr Víctor Rodríguez Cedeño,

Charter of Paris: See Conference on Security and Co-operation in Europe, Charter of Paris for a New Europe

Conference on Security and Co-operation in Europe, Charter of Paris for a New Europe (21 November 1990), 30 ILM (1991), 193 [Charter of Paris] 90

——, Document of the Copenhagen Meeting of the Conference on the Human Dimension (29 June 1990), 29 ILM (1990), 1306 [Copenhagen Document] 90

——, Final Act (Helsinki 1 August 1975), 14 ILM (1975), 1292 [Helsinki Final Act] 86, 158

Congress of Vienna, Règlement sur le rang entre les agents diplomatiques (Vienna, 19 March 1815), Annex XVII of the Acts of the Congress, 2 State Papers (1839), 179 [1815 Règlement] 34

Copenhagen Document: See Conference on Security and Co-operation in Europe, Document of the Copenhagen Meeting

Council of Europe, Charter on Professional Ethics (15 July 2005), at <https://wcd.coe.int/ViewDoc.jsp?id=1146297&Site=COE> (visited 4 April 2015) 96

——, Conference on Diplomatic Intercourse and Immunities, Vienna 2 March–14 April 1961, Official Records, Vol II: Annexes, Final Act, Vienna Convention on Diplomatic Relations, Optional Protocols, Resolutions, UN Doc A/CONF.20/14/Add.1 [Vienna Conference Records Vol 2] 37

——, Conference on the Law of Treaties, Vienna 26 March– 24 May 1968, Official Records, 1st Session: Summary records of the plenary meetings and of the meetings of the Committee of the Whole, UN Doc A/CONF.39/11 [1968 Conference, Records, 1st Session] 108

——, Conference on the Representation of States in their Relations with International Organizations, Vienna 4 February–14 March 1975, Official Records, Vol I: Summary records of the plenary meetings and of the meetings of the Committee of the Whole, UN Doc A/CONF.67/18 [1975 Conference, Records Vol 1] 73

——, General Assembly, Question of Diplomatic Asylum. Report of the Secretary-General, UN Doc A/10139 (Part I) (2 September 1975) [UN Asylum Report (Part 1)] 112, 239, 245, 246, 254, 255

——, General Assembly, Question of Diplomatic Asylum. Report of the Secretary-General, UN Doc A/10139 (Part II) (22 September 1975) [UN Asylum Report (Part 2)] 238, 239, 243

——, General Assembly, The protection of human rights and fundamental freedoms while countering terrorism, Report of the Secretary-General, UN Doc A/63/337 (28 August 2008) [UN Terrorism Report] 180

——, General Assembly, Sixth Committee, 315th Meeting, Agenda Item 58: Giving priority to the codification of the topic 'Diplomatic intercourse and immunities' in accordance with article 18 of the statute of the International Law Commission, UN Doc A/C.6/SR.315 (30 October 1952) [GA Sixth Committee, 315th Meeting] 238–39

——, General Assembly, Sixth Committee, 316th Meeting, Agenda Item 58: Giving priority to the codification of the topic 'Diplomatic intercourse and immunities' in accordance with article 18 of the statute of the International Law Commission, UN Doc A/C.6/SR.316 (31 October 1952) [GA Sixth Committee, 316th Meeting] 238–39

——, General Assembly, Sixth Committee, 1505th Meeting, Agenda Item 105: Diplomatic Asylum, UN Doc A/C.6/SR.1505 (25 November 1974) [GA Sixth Committee, 1505th Meeting] 242

——, General Assembly, Third Committee, 1079th Meeting, Agenda Item 35: Draft International Covenants on Human Rights, UN Doc A/C.3/SR.1079 (20 October 1961) [GA Third Committee, 1079th Meeting)] 178

——, High Commissioner for Refugees, Handbook on Procedures and Criteria for Determining Refugee Status under the 1951 Convention and the 1967 Protocol relating to the Status of Refugees, (Reedited Geneva, January 1992), HCR/IP/ 4/Eng/REV.1 <http://www.unhcr.org/4d93528a9.pdf> accessed 14 March 2015 [UNHCR Handbook 1992] 238

——, Human Rights Committee, General Comment No 11, Article 20 (1983) HRI/GEN/1, 11 [HRC General Comment No 11 (1983)] 178, 186

——, Human Rights Committee, General Comment No 29, State of Emergency (Article 4) (2001) CCPR/C/21/ Rev.1/Add.11 [HRC General Comment No 29 (2001)] 115

——, Human Rights Committee, General Comment No 31: The Nature of the Legal Obligations Imposed on States Parties to the Covenant (2004) UN Doc CCPR/C/21/ Rev.1/Add.13 [HRC General Comment No 31 (2004)] 250, 252

——, Security Council, Resolutions and Decisions of the Security Council 1 August 2005–31 July 2006, UN Doc S/INF/61 (New York 2006) [SC Resolutions and Decisions (2006)] 179

——, Transitional Administration in East Timor, Regulation No 2000/11 On the Organization Of Courts In East Timor, UNTAET/REG/2000/11 (6 March 2000) [Dili Court Regulation (2000/11)] 80

——, Transitional Administration in East Timor, Regulation No 2000/15 On the Establishment Of Panels With Exclusive Jurisdiction Over Serious Criminal Offences, UNTAET/REG/2000/15 (6 June 2000) [Dili Court Regulation (2000/15)] 184

——, Treaty Collection Online, Convention on the International Right of Correction (1953) <https://treaties.un.org/Pages/ViewDetails.aspx?src=IND&mtdsg_no=XVII-1&chapter=17&lang=en> accessed 9 February 2015 [UN Treaty Collection (Online), Convention on the International Right of Correction] 190

——, Treaty Collection Online, Convention on the Prevention and Punishment of the Crime of Genocide (1948) <https://treaties.un. org/Pages/ViewDetails.aspx?src=TREATY&mtdsg_no=IV-1&chapter=4&lang=en> accessed 8 February 2015 [UN Treaty Collection (Online), Genocide Convention] 81

——, Treaty Collection (Online), International Covenant on Civil and Political Rights (1966) <https://treaties.un.org/pages/viewdetails.aspx?chapter=4&src=treaty&mtdsg_no=iv-4&lang=en> accessed 7 February 2015 [UN Treaty Collection (Online), ICCPR] 178–79, 183

——, Treaty Collection (Online), International Covenant on Economic, Social and Cultural Rights https://treaties.un.org/pages/ viewdetails.aspx?chapter=4&lang=en&mtdsg_no=iv-3&src= treaty accessed 29 March 2015 [UN Treaty Collection (Online), ICESCR] 87

——, Treaty Collection (Online), International Convention concerning the Use of Broadcasting in the Cause of Peace (1936) <https://treaties.un.org/pages/LONViewDetails.aspx?src= LON&id=509&chapter=30&lang=en>> accessed 9 February 2015 [UN Treaty Collection (Online), Broadcasting Convention] 190

——, Treaty Collection (Online), International Convention for the Suppression of the Financing of Terrorism (1999) <http://treaties. un.org/pages/ViewDetails.aspx?src=TREATY&mtdsg_no=XVIII- 11&chapter=18&lang=en> accessed 1 March 2015 [UN Treaty Collection (Online), Terrorism Financing Convention] 198

——, Treaty Collection (Online), International Convention on the Elimination of All Forms of Racial Discrimination (1966) <https://treaties.un.org/Pages/ViewDetails.aspx?src=TREATY& mtdsg_no=IV-2&chapter=4&lang=en> accessed 8 February 2015 [UN Treaty Collection (Online), CERD] 179

——, Treaty Collection (Online), United Nations Convention against Corruption (2003) http://treaties.un.org/Pages/ViewDetails.aspx? mtdsg_no=XVIII-

Domestic Materials

Germany

Netherlands

United Kingdom

United States

Introduction

IN THAILAND, APRIL 2010 was a month of bloodshed. After the Red Shirts movement had managed to storm the country's National Assembly,[1] the Prime Minister declared a state of emergency in Bangkok, handing extensive powers to the military and police.[2] The situation soon escalated: Clashes between the military and protesters caused the deaths of 21 people and left 800 injured.[3] Nearly two weeks later, 85 people were injured in a grenade attack in Bangkok—a young Thai woman lost her life.[4]

That diplomats would take an interest in these events was to be expected. Nor was it surprising that the Thai government considered the situation a sensitive issue. After some diplomatic agents had accepted an invitation by Red Shirt leaders to visit the protests, the Thai Foreign Minister, Kasit Piromya, declared his 'concern',[5] and accused them of interfering with internal affairs.[6] And yet, even some members of Kasit's own party took a more relaxed view: Sukhumbhand Paribatra, governor of Bangkok and former deputy minister of foreign affairs, reportedly stated that Kasit should not have made 'a big deal' of the issue. Sukhumbhand added that he, too, had received visits from diplomats when his party had been in opposition[7] and counselled against turning the matter into a problem, since the situation was 'already sensitive'.[8]

Comments of this kind go to the core of the position of diplomatic interference in current affairs. They seem to challenge the very need for an examination of this form of conduct—or at least cast doubt about the stage at which interference becomes a matter worthy of concern. If Sukhumbhand was content to let diplomats contact members of the opposition, he might have been less generous if foreign representatives (as happened in the past)

[1] 'Thai PM Clamps Down on Protests' *Toronto Star* (Toronto, 8 April 2010).

[2] A Konglang, 'State of Emergency in Bangkok' *Sydney Morning Herald* (Sydney, 8 April 2010).

[3] 'Stand-off Continues in Bangkok' *Agence France Presse* (Paris, 12 April 2010).

[4] 'Thai Authorities say One Dead' *Agence France Presse* (Paris, 23 April 2010).

[5] 'Thai FM Draws Fence' *Agence France Presse* (Paris, 29 April 2010).

[6] G Peck, 'Demands for Martial Law' *The Scotsman* (Edinburgh, 30 April 2010).

[7] 'Thailand: Foreign Diplomats Explain' *Thai News Service* (14 May 2010).

[8] 'Diplomats Chafe at Rebukes' *The Nation* (Thailand, 13 May 2010).

had taken a more active role—if they had marched with the protesters and stormed public buildings.[9]

Is diplomatic interference therefore of relevance in the modern world? And if so—what are the tools that allow observers to decide whether a certain form of conduct qualifies as interference in internal affairs? These are questions which, by necessity, precede any attempt to reach a satisfactory assessment of diplomatic interference as a phenomenon under international law.

1. TROUBLEMAKERS AND LAWBREAKERS: WHY DIPLOMATIC INTERFERENCE MATTERS

Sukhumbhand is not the only commentator who looks at allegations of diplomatic interference with a certain equanimity. In the literature—and indeed in State practice—reference is on occasion made to the breach of diplomatic 'protocol' or 'practice' which conduct of this kind represents.[10] That invokes the concept of comity: Traditions whose breach might be seen as impolite, but not (immediately) amounting to a violation of the law. From that perspective, interfering diplomats are troublemakers, but not much more than that; and their conduct is one which might not merit deeper consideration.

The reality can be quite different.

For one, there is ample evidence that receiving States are not always prepared to take allegations of interference lightly. On numerous occasions, diplomatic agents have been expelled following accusations of this kind,[11] and when the US Ambassador to Bolivia in 1980 faced accusations of interference, part of the Bolivian army declared a 'state of emergency' in the east of the republic until he would have left the country.[12] On other occasions, alleged interference by diplomatic agents led to the severing of diplomatic relations.[13] A particularly dramatic incident occurred in 1960: When the Ghanaian diplomat Nathanial Welbeck was accused of interference in the internal affairs of the Republic of Congo and declared

[9] See for instance ch 4, at nn 145–46.

[10] *cf* Alam, 61. See also 'Angry Kenya Lashes Out' *Agence France Presse* (Paris, 26 October 2005) (reference by the Kenyan Foreign Minister to 'principle[s] of diplomatic etiquette').

[11] See among many others, the 1978 case of four Soviet diplomats, expelled from Ghana (A.39); the 1987 case of the Dutch Ambassador (van Houten), expelled from Suriname (A.82); the 1991 case of the British High Commissioner David Gladstone, expelled from Sri Lanka (A.103).

[12] *New York Times*, 'Bolivia Military Chiefs Call for Postponement' *New York Times* (New York, 10 June 1980).

[13] See on this the 2002 case of a Taiwanese diplomat in Nauru, whose alleged interference led to the (temporary) severing of diplomatic ties between the two countries (A.184).

persona non grata, attempts to enforce the expulsion order led to a gun battle, resulting in the deaths of several Congolese soldiers.[14]

It is true that in some cases, a particular sensitivity on the side of the hosts may have influenced reactions of this kind. That, however, can hardly be sufficient explanation for every case in which allegations of diplomatic interference have arisen. The incidents discussed in this book reach from diplomats who allegedly funded political parties[15] to those who engaged in revisionist accounts on international crimes,[16] from agents who reportedly encouraged acts of terrorism[17] to those who granted asylum on mission premises,[18] from diplomats who stipulated ultimata to the receiving State[19] to those who actively participated in political campaigns.[20] These are not forms of behaviour which matter only to a select few governments—their gravity is often appreciated around the world. 'In Rome', stated a journalist in 1974, 'the first thing I heard was the new nickname of the American ambassador, John Volpe. He is now derisively referred to as "Ambassador Golpe". "Golpe", the Spanish word for coup, is used in Italy …'.[21] One may assume that Ambassador Coup-d'État would have been a troubling character no matter where he had been posted.

Nor are these 'merely' political concerns without legal relevance. Even if there were no specific rules in diplomatic law on this matter, diplomatic agents, as organs of their States,[22] would still be subject to the general ban on interference by States.

The existence of this rule in international law today is not subject to reasonable doubt. While non-intervention by States[23] (except in the case of the threat or use of force) is not expressly addressed in the Charter of the United Nations,[24] it has received considerable support through multilateral and bilateral treaties,[25] the founding documents of international

[14] *The Times*, 'Congo Expels United Arab Republic Ambassador' *The Times* (London, 2 December 1960); Packham, 64.

[15] See ch 8, at n 84.

[16] See ch 7, at n 138.

[17] See ch 7, at n 118.

[18] See ch 11.

[19] See ch 10, at n 33.

[20] See ch 6, at n 1.

[21] M McGrory, 'Italians have Doubts' *Sarasota Herald-Tribune* (Sarasota, 16 November 1974).

[22] *cf* Draft Articles on State Responsibility (2001), 44, art 6, commentary, para 4.

[23] The terms 'intervention' and 'interference' are usually employed interchangeably (see eg *Armed Activities* para 165). But see ch 2, at n 52 ff.

[24] The UN Charter refers to 'intervention' only where intervention through the UN itself is concerned (art 2(7)).

[25] See eg Montevideo Convention on the Rights and Duties of States, art 8. For the inclusion of the rule in Treaties on Friendship, Commerce and Navigation, see Kunig, para 7.

organisations,[26] and numerous General Assembly Resolutions[27] (most notably the Friendly Relations Declaration),[28] so that the International Court of Justice (ICJ) was on firm ground when, in 1986, it considered the rule 'part and parcel of customary international law'.[29]

But more specific norms on non-interference do exist in diplomatic law and have existed for a long time.[30] Today, the Vienna Convention on Diplomatic Relations (VCDR), the leading legal instrument on diplomatic relations between States, provides in Article 41 that persons enjoying diplomatic privileges and immunities 'have a duty not to interfere in the internal affairs' of the receiving State, and reference to this norm and to its equivalent in customary international law has been made by the ICJ.[31] This lifts the concept of diplomatic interference out of the realm of protocol: A State whose agents commit interference, finds itself in violation of a legal obligation.

Whether it had been wise to incorporate this duty—especially in such general terms—in the text of the Convention, is a different question. Diplomatic conduct, after all, covers a wide range of activities; and charges of interference have arisen even in situations in which most sending States will feel entitled to make diplomatic representations on matters which touch upon internal affairs of the hosts.[32] These are points which will be considered in more detail in subsequent chapters,[33] but even at this stage, it is clear that questions of this kind call for a more detailed assessment of the concept than that provided by the VCDR.

At the same time, rules clothed in general terms are not without advantage to those who have to negotiate treaties. The rule against diplomatic interference for one, proved particularly successful and has been reproduced in subsequent instruments on privileges and immunities.[34]

[26] *cf* Warsaw Pact art 8; OAS Charter art 19; OAU Charter art II.

[27] See GA Res 2131 (XX) (1965), in particular para 1; GA Res 31/91 (1976), in particular paras 1–3; GA Res 32/153 (1977), paras 1 and 2; GA Res 33/74 (1978), para 1; GA Res 36/103 (1981); GA Res 40/9 (1985), in particular para 2; GA Res 44/147 (1989), in particular para 4.

[28] Friendly Relations Declaration, in particular 3rd principle.

[29] *Nicaragua*, para 202.

[30] See on this ch 1.

[31] See *Tehran Hostages Case*, para 84. In the *Asylum Case*, predating the VCDR, the ICJ noted that the decision to grant diplomatic asylum constituted prima facie 'an intervention in matters which are exclusively within the competence of that State', *Asylum Case*, paras 274, 275 (see ch 11, at n 12).

[32] In the above mentioned situation of Thailand in 2010, several foreign nationals had already become victims of the unrest in the country by the time of Kasit's criticism (see 'Thai Court Hands Down 34-year Jail Terms' *UPI* (Washington DC, 26 August 2011); 'Vic: Melbourne Man Injured' *AAP Newsfeed* (23 April 2010). Diplomats from the affected States would have had strong reasons for the observation of the situation and for a critical assessment of its development (see ch 3, ss 1.2 and 1.4).

[33] See chs 3 and 4.

[34] See ch 1, at nn 86–90.

That certainly stands as a testament to the continued importance of the norm, but the way it was approached in one of these later treaties also underlines the need for more exacting scrutiny.

The Vienna Convention on the Representation of States in their Relations with International Organizations of a Universal Character (CRSIO) includes the ban on interference in Article 77(1)2.[35] But it also imposes an obligation on sending States to recall a diplomatic agent in cases of 'grave and manifest interference'.[36] While the CRSIO has not yet entered into force,[37] the inclusion of this rule indicates that, in the eyes of its drafters, a distinction between 'grave and manifest' and 'basic' forms of interference was possible and had to be applied.[38]

And yet, when diplomats and their hosts seek clarification on the concept of interference, they face difficulties. The reason often lies in the nature of the materials which are available to those who wish to gain a better understanding of the concept. It is a point which requires further consideration; for an appreciation of the character of these difficulties allows for the development of strategies to meet them in a constructive manner.

2. IN SEARCH FOR GUIDANCE: WHO SPEAKS ABOUT DIPLOMATIC INTERFERENCE?

In a 1983 statement, the government of the Netherlands noted that there were 'no international guidelines for the application of Article 41(1) of the Vienna Convention' and doubted the very possibility of developing such guidance, since opinions on inadmissible interference varied 'from place to place and time to time'.[39] It is a defeatist view, but one which, given the disagreements which regularly arise between sending and receiving States when diplomatic agents have been accused of interference, attracts a measure of sympathy.

But it was not the line which the International Law Commission (ILC) adopted. The ILC—the body which developed the text on which today's

[35] In this particular context, the 'host State' is the State in whose territory the relevant organisation has its seat or office or in whose territory the relevant meeting of an organ or a conference is held. CRSIO art 1(15).

[36] CRSIO art 77(2)2.

[37] At the time of writing, the CRSIO has 34 State parties, UN Treaty Collection (Online), CRSIO (as of 1 January 2015). Entry into force requires the participation of 35 States (CRSIO art 89(1)).

[38] *cf* YILC (Yearbook of the International Law Commission) 1971 II/1, 327, art 75, commentary, para 2. It appears that the rule against interference as such was at that stage already seen as an emanation of customary international law. *cf* YILC 1969/I, 176, para 53 [Ustor]; also YILC 1971/I, 74, para 89 [Ushakov].

[39] Netherlands, Government Statement 1983, 308.

VCDR is based[40]—sought to provide some clarification in its commentary on the Draft Article dealing with the rule against diplomatic interference: It found, for instance, that participation in political campaigns was to be seen as a form of diplomatic interference, whereas the making of representations to protect interests of the sending State or its nationals 'in accordance with international law', was not.[41]

That, however, was as much instruction as the commentary was able to give, and the very general nature of the statement may have prompted more questions than it answered.[42] But it showed that the ILC was not willing to leave the determination of interference entirely to the circumstances of the individual case—let alone to assessment by the receving State.

In a similar vein, some scholars in the field have suggested objective parameters which would assist in the evaluation of alleged interference. And yet, what Przetacznik noted in 1976 still holds today: The extent of the duty of non-interference has received neither systematic nor exhaustive treatment.[43]

Most authors either do not elaborate on the constituent elements of interference, or limit themselves to an overview of diplomatic incidents in this area.[44] Cases of alleged interference are important[45]—but they are important because of the evaluation of the diplomatic conduct which they allow, and for that, it is not enough to refer to the fact that a receiving State has accused a diplomat of meddling. Yet when one of the leading textbooks on international law states that diplomats have 'no right whatever to take part in [the] political life' of the receiving State,[46] one may be forgiven for thinking that the literature is unduly biased in favour of the diplomatic hosts. The fact in particular that there are sometimes legitimate interests on the side of the sending State which constitute a basis for the relevant diplomatic conduct, has received scant attention.[47]

[40] See ch 1, at nn 57 ff.

[41] YILC 1958/II, 104, art 40, commentary, para 3.

[42] See on this ch 4, at n 6.

[43] Przetacznik (1976), 57, 58.

[44] See for instance Rousseau, 166, 167; Denza 464–68.

[45] See on this below, after n 65.

[46] Oppenheim (1992), 1068.

[47] That does, of course, not mean that the views of receiving States are irrelevant. On the contrary: The challenge of evaluating charges of diplomatic interference lies in the fact that receiving States, too, are typically able to rely on legitimate interests which the relevant diplomatic action may have affected (see ch 1, at n 35 and, for the evaluation of the co-existence of divergent interests, ch 4). The position of receiving States also offers a starting point for the identification of areas of sensitivity for members of the international community, and is instrumental for the determination of 'prototypes' of interference (see on this, Introduction to Part II, in particular at n 28).

The majority of the sources of international law to which Article 38(1) of the ICJ Statute makes reference, face similar restrictions.[48]

Where treaty law is concerned, reference has already been made to the rather generalised way in which the rule against interference has been phrased in the Vienna Convention.[49] Later conventions which incorporate the rule likewise fail to elaborate on the kind of activities that fall in this category.

The travaux préparatoires—the drafting efforts preceding the Convention—are more helpful.[50] But they carry difficulties of their own.

The conference records enjoy particular authority for any attempt to understand the intention of the drafters, as they contain the contributions of representatives of the negotiating States. But they render little assistance for an understanding of diplomatic interference: The relevant rule, as suggested by the ILC, was adopted without discussion.[51] The records of the ILC debates are more instructive, and reference will be made to them where this is indicated. But they must be approached with caution: It is not always clear whether the view advanced by one ILC member had the support of his colleagues.[52] Debates such as that kindled by the question whether conduct on instructions violates the rule of diplomatic non-interference, present a more complex picture, and require careful assessment.[53]

'Judicial decisions' which are named in Article 38 ICJ Statute as 'subsidiary means' for the determination of the law, have limited use in this field.[54] Situations in which courts have explored diplomatic interference are far and few between,[55] and the ICJ has that far not provided a detailed examination of the concept. A brief reference to 'diplomatic intervention' was made in the *Asylum Case* (which predates the Vienna Convention) with regard to the grant of asylum to a person under the jurisdiction of the

[48] The article provides that the International Court of Justice shall apply 'a. international conventions …; b. international custom …; c. the general principles of law recognized by civilized nations; d. … judicial decisions and the teachings of the most highly qualified publicists of the various nations, as subsidiary means for the determination of rules of law.' ICJ Statute art 38(1).

[49] See above, at nn 32 and 39.

[50] On the use of travaux préparatoires, see VCLT art 32.

[51] See on this Vienna Conference Records Vol 1, 36.

[52] The ILC commentaries are more representative of the views of the Commission as a whole; but see on their limitations above at n 42 and Annex B.7 and B.8.

[53] See ch 2, s 3.

[54] On 'teachings' as a further subsidiary means, see above at nn 44–46.

[55] That applies to international as well as domestic courts. It is of course possible that an alleged conduct of interference violates the law of the receiving State at the same time. But even if a receiving State were desirous to bring charges of this kind against a diplomatic agent, the existence of diplomatic immunity makes the emergence of a court case unlikely. (See VCDR art 31). For a rare instance in which the rule of non-interference featured in a domestic case, see ch 11, at n 87.

receiving State;[56] and in the 1980 *Tehran Hostages Case*, the ICJ expressed itself in even more general terms: It referred to interference as one of the 'abuses of [diplomatic] functions',[57] and acknowledged that it was difficult to determine exactly when the diplomatic function of observation would involve acts such as espionage or interference.[58] A 2009 application by Honduras, claiming a violation of the rule of Article 41(1) VCDR by Brazil, never reached decision stage.[59]

That leaves two sources which might provide greater insight: Customary international law and general principles of law. General principles are commonly considered to fill the gaps left by conventional and customary law,[60] and it is one of their characteristics that they can claim applicability in a multitude of scenarios. For that reason, they tend to be so abstract in nature that their usefulness for the assessment of elements of diplomatic interference is limited. They do however play a role when the meeting of the ban on interference with competing interests has to be evaluated, and it is with regard to that particular situation that reference will be made to them.[61]

But it is customary international law—that is, State practice accompanied by the belief that there is an entitlement or an obligation to adopt such practice[62]—which emerges as the most hopeful source for an approach towards the concept of diplomatic interference. In view of the history of diplomatic relations, that is not surprising. For most of its existence, it was custom, rather than treaty law, which determined the lawfulness of diplomatic conduct. The VCDR itself is, to a significant part, based on custom[63] (the rule of non-interference certainly is),[64] and its text makes express reference to the continuing force of custom where the treaty leaves gaps.[65]

The usefulness of custom lies partly in its authority and partly in its availability. Instances of State practice highlight the forms of conduct receiving States deem 'diplomatic interference', but they also show the position taken by sending States in situations of this kind. It is for that reason that frequent reference will be made to such situations throughout this study, and that a list of some 300 incidents of alleged interference is

[56] See above, n 31 and ch 1, at n 33.

[57] *Tehran Hostages Case*, para 84.

[58] ibid, para 85.

[59] *Honduras Application*, para 11. The application was eventually withdrawn, see ch 7, at n 15.

[60] Bassiouni (1990), 776.

[61] See on this ch 4, at n 95.

[62] *cf North Sea Continental Shelf* cases, para 77.

[63] *cf* Vienna Conference Records, Vol 1, 83, para 55 [Bollini Shaw (Argentina)]. See also Higgins (1985), 642; Bindschedler, 34.

[64] See ch 1, s 1 and s 2, at nn 46–56 for evidence of the existence of the prohibition of interference before the entry into force of the VCDR.

[65] VCDR, preamble, 5th operative para.

included in Annex A. They are more than mere anecdotes from the pages of diplomatic history: They indicate subject areas in which receiving States have displayed a particular sensitivity, and the interests which sending States feel entitled to protect.

But not every instance in which a host has voiced misgivings about diplomatic behaviour represents customary international law. It is, for instance, entirely possible that a receiving State has expressed a sensitivity which is not reflected in the position of other States. The assessment of instances of alleged interference in light of the requirements of customary international law is therefore indispensable, but it is at that stage that the challenges of this source manifest themselves: Customary law has, with some reason, been described by Yakembe as 'indistinct and difficult to prove'.[66] Yet without clear evidence that customary international law exists, it is not possible to reach the conclusion that certain forms of conduct do indeed violate the legal rule against interference in internal affairs.

3. SOLVING THE PUZZLE: HOW TO APPROACH DIPLOMATIC INTERFERENCE

In October 2000, the US Ambassador to Indonesia, Robert Gelbard, found himself at the centre of criticism: According to the Indonesian Minister of Defence Mahfud, he had pressured the government to select General Agus Wirahadikusumah as chief of the Indonesian army.[67] Mahfud accused Gelbard of interference and reportedly even threatened his expulsion.[68]

If a case of this kind is to be evaluated under customary law, the constituent elements of this source require investigation, including its objective element (State practice) and its subjective element (*opinio iuris*—the legal opinion underlying such practice).[69] A particular act or omission on the part of a State is thus not enough for the establishment of a rule of customary law: Such conduct must have been based on the fact that the diplomats—and, through them, the States they represent—feel legally obliged or entitled to do so.

Even then, it is not the act of one State which on its own can create customary law with effect for the international community. While it may not be necessary that every State has had a say in the formation of customary law, the ICJ did stipulate a requirement of State practice which can at least be said to be generally consistent within the international community.[70]

[66] Yakembe, 25.
[67] 'Indonesia Probes Foreign Involvement' *Agence France Presse* (Paris, 17 October 2000).
[68] Simon (2000).
[69] See above, at n 62.
[70] *Nicaragua*, para 186.

To stay with the Gelbard incident: If the relevant rule is considered to be a ban on the offering of advice on military appointments, the relevant norm could be established under customary international law, if diplomats regularly refrained from offering such advice and did so, because their States felt under a duty not to adopt this course of action.[71]

But the identification of such rules meets challenges from the outset. The clearest evidence for the existence of customary international law to this effect might exist if sending States provided reasons for refraining from particular acts (thus admitting that they had thought about adopting them in the first place), or if, after such an act had been adopted anyway, they make clear that they had been in the wrong. In international relations, such mea culpa declarations are rare.[72]

On the other hand, sending States have sometimes given instructions to their missions not to engage in particular forms of conduct. One may in this context recall the telegram which James Bell, the US Ambassador to Malaysia, received in March 1964 from the State Department. Bell's masters informed him (ahead of parliamentary elections in the receiving State) that Malaysian employees of the US embassy who intended to engage in partisan political conduct would have to resign their positions with the mission.[73] The State Department pointed out that this policy had already been adopted by the Malaysian government with regard to its own officials, and found that the United States, 'being a foreign State, should exercise even more caution in such matters'.[74]

Cases of this kind can be of particular value for the evaluation of customary international law. But these instances, too, are not all too common and do not constitute a form of material that is usually widely available.

In the vast majority of cases, difficulties arise precisely because sending and receiving States do not agree on the evaluation of the diplomatic conduct and might debate the existence of a particular rule. And yet, the fact that the receiving State has voiced its opposition, has meaning and may by itself be an important step towards the identification of customary international law.

When the ICJ in the *Nicaragua* case discussed the concept of customary international law, it referred not only to the conduct of those States that may have applied the relevant customary rule, but also to the views of

[71] On the importance of *opinio iuris* even in cases of omissions, see *Lotus* case, 28.

[72] But not unheard of. See the 1997 remarks made by the Canadian Ambassador to Mexico (Perron) which the Canadian Foreign Minister himself called 'inappropriate' (A.128). See also the apology extended by the US Ambassador to Bolivia, Goldberg, for his own remarks (A.225) and the 1979 case of the French Foreign Minister distancing himself from statements by his military attaché in Argentina, (A.41).

[73] Whiteman (1970), 144. See also, for the 1964 case of the US Ambassador to Lebanon, ch 6, at n 62.

[74] ibid, Whiteman.

other members of the international community. In order to 'deduce the existence of customary rules', the Court found, 'instances of State conduct inconsistent with a given rule should generally have been treated as breaches of that rule, not as indications of the recognition of a new rule'.[75]

That highlights the importance of State protests as a tool for the identification of customary law. An important aspect in the Gelbard case is therefore the question how receiving States have in general evaluated suggestions relating to military appointments, and whether they have regularly lodged their objections when advice of this kind had been offered.[76]

Instances of State protests are certainly much more common than cases in which States explained their failure to act, and the message they carry may be less ambiguous than that conveyed through omissions by the sending State. As such, they are an indispensable tool for any effort to identify customary rules in the field of diplomatic interference.

But protests carry their own difficulties. There are three aspects in particular which merit further investigation in that regard. The first concerns the authorship of the act, that is, the question whether statements made by a commentator in the receiving State on certain forms of diplomatic conduct can be said to be the position of that State. The second relates to the question under what circumstances negative measures by the receiving State constitute valid protests. The third relates to the requirement of generality. In that regard, evidence has to mirror the law: It would hardly be sufficient to speak of a clearly established rule under customary law if the only evidence for that is the view of only one receiving State, whose opinion may not command support within the international community.

3.1. Whose Opinion Counts? The Question of Authorship

In the conduct of diplomatic relations, it may be tempting to consider the Foreign Ministry of the receiving State the principal authority for the evaluation of diplomatic behaviour, as far as the diplomatic hosts are concerned. The Foreign Ministry does, after all, enjoy a position of significance in the field: The VCDR envisages it as the default channel through which 'official business … entrusted to the mission by the sending State shall be conducted'.[77]

However, as the criticism of Robert Gelbard by the Indonesian Minister of Defence has shown, it is not the only institution which may feel moved

[75] *Nicaragua*, 98 para 186.

[76] On the particular issue of the suggestion of appointments to the administration of the State, see ch 5, at n 26.

[77] VCDR art 41(2). See also ch 5, at n 15.

to voice its objection to particular forms of conduct. That raises the question who exactly is authorised to contribute to the evaluation of diplomatic behaviour in this field.

As unilateral acts of States,[78] protests certainly need to originate with an organ of the State. But not all organs enjoy the same status under international law. For the adoption of treaties, for instance, it has been accepted that only a select group of people are deemed, because of their office, to represent the State 'without having to produce full powers'[79]—'functional representatives' therefore, such as heads of States, heads of governments and Foreign Ministers. And the rule has proved popular beyond treaty law: Similar limitations have been suggested for the creation of State practice as part of customary international law,[80] for unilateral declarations[81] and indeed for unilateral acts themselves.[82]

But this restrictive view has also attracted criticism.

In the context of customary international law, for instance, Mendelson points out that certain administrative acts under the domestic law of a State may well bear relevance for international law (the example which he invokes, is that of a nationalisation decree).[83] Following this view, international law governs 'relations between States as a whole, not just their executives'; acts therefore of executive, legislature and judiciary are seen as forming State practice if they touch upon international relations.[84] In view of this understanding, the analogy to treaty law does not always appear entirely appropriate.

The same consideration holds true where protests are concerned. Following a perceived conduct of interference by a military attaché, a Minister of Defence might, for instance, express his misgivings by excluding the diplomat's access to military installations which he had formerly been allowed to enter.[85] Such acts have immediate effect on the diplomatic freedom of movement; but it is clear that State organs, in principle, are entitled to adopt them[86] and that sending States accept this sanction, even though the acting organ may not belong to the circle of persons who are deemed to represent the State. They are accepted not because of a mutual

78 See on this Cedeño Report 48, para 89 et seq.

79 See, for today's regulation of the matter, VCLT art 7(2).

80 See Strupp (1934), 313–15.

81 Guiding Principles (2006) art 4.

82 Eick, para 6. Protests are unilateral acts, but they do not need to fulfil all the requirements of unilateral declarations. Protests can, in particular, be inferred from the conduct of a State; unilateral declarations have to be stated in 'clear and specific terms' if they are to entail obligations for the formulating State. Guiding Principles (2006) art 7.

83 Mendelson (1998), 198.

84 ibid, 199.

85 For a 2005 case featuring entry of a restricted area by a diplomatic agent, see A.207.

86 VCDR art 26; but see also ch 4, at n 82.

agreement between sending and receiving State,[87] but as emanations of the sovereignty of the latter.

It is therefore understandable that some authors have accepted a wider circle of potential authors of State protests.[88] In the related field of unilateral declarations, the ICJ too noted that 'with increasing frequency …', persons other than heads of State, heads of government and Foreign Ministers, may be authorised to bind the State by their statements, and referred in particular to 'holders of technical ministerial portfolios exercising powers in their field of competence in the area of foreign relations' but also to 'certain officials' to whom the same considerations would apply.[89]

Even if such competence did not exist in fact, no injustice is done to a State whose representatives were aware of the unilateral acts—including protests—of State organs and allowed them to continue. In instances of this kind, the ordinary representatives of the State have created the appearance that they acquiesced in this form of conduct, and to foreign diplomats, these acts do present themselves as acts of the State.[90]

In the above named case of Robert Gelbard, a (functional) representative of the State[91] did in fact take a position on the diplomatic agent's conduct, and one which was in sharp contrast to that of the Minister of Defence. The Indonesian President Wahid refused to declare Gelbard persona non grata and stated instead that he 'should be treated with the honor accorded to a foreign envoy'.[92] Had he not acted, the criticism offered by the Indonesian Minister of Defence would, however, have stood as the act by the highest authority of the receiving State that had expressed an opinion; and the sending State would have been entitled to perceive it as a protest on the part of Indonesia.

In the majority of cases, the State organ issuing a protest will be the Foreign Ministry, and thus one of the functional representatives of the State. Yet the views of other organs—and even of non-State actors—may still be of value on a different level. They are indicative of a prevailing sensitivity in the receiving State on certain areas of diplomatic activity. But they also provide guidance for the textual interpretation of the term

[87] That would have been the case if the possibility of adopting measures of this kind had only been established through the VCDR. But these measures predate the Convention by a considerable timespan. See, on restrictions to freedom of movement, Young 144, 145 (referring to the accommodation of envoys to Byzantium in a 'special fortress').

[88] MacGibbon expresses the view that protests 'to merit treatment as a factor in the legal relations of States, must be made by, or on behalf of, a State'. MacGibbon, 294. Under the rules of State responsibility, however, protests made 'by' a State would include protests made by any author whose conduct is attributable to the State.

[89] *Armed Activities*, 27, para 47.

[90] For the acceptance of a similar rule in the law of treaties, see VCLT art 7(1)(b).

[91] See above, at n 79.

[92] Simon (2000) (paraphrasing by Simon).

'interference'—especially if the relevant actors possess particular expertise in the matter under consideration.[93]

On some occasions, diplomatic conduct has, however, encountered negative sanctions which, on the face of it, seem to originate with non-State actors, but could ultimately be traced back to the host government.

Situations of this kind occur when a newspaper upon which the government wields considerable influence, issues a reaction to diplomatic conduct.[94] They also arise when parts of the population are encouraged by the government to take action against diplomats. The Soviet Union, for instance, complained in 1967 about 'organized persecution and wild hooligan violence' against her missions in China, and there were reports that mob activities against foreign missions had been incited by Chinese authorities.[95]

But a government which chooses to act through newspapers or mob violence, does not assert its authority; it conceals it behind the principal actors. A State which allows parties which are not organs to act on its behalf, may have highlighted a sensitive area of diplomatic conduct, but that is the limit of its effect. The State in hiding deprives itself of the benefits of an official sanction.

3.2. Understanding State Sanctions: When is a Protest a Protest?

On 11 July 1988, the Nicaraguan President Ortega declared the US Ambassador to that country, Richard Melton—along with other diplomats—persona non grata.[96] Melton's interaction with the opposition was at the core of accusations that arose in this context: The Nicaraguan Foreign Minister claimed that the Ambassador had attempted 'to set up an internal front to overthrow the [g]overnment' and that he had violated the rule of non-interference as enshrined in the Vienna Convention.[97]

The following day, the Reagan administration expelled Carlos Tunnermann, the Nicaraguan Ambassador to the United States, along with seven

[93] Among non-State actors, the views of foreign relations experts and former ambassadors may carry significance in the light of the expertise of their authors. See for instance comments by a former British Ambassador on a 1989 incident involving two British diplomats in Romania, ch 4, at n 147.

[94] In 2006, for instance, it was reported that 'Myanmar's official media often accuse Western countries, particularly the United States and Britain, of interfering in the country's internal affairs and accuse the opposition party of collaborating with them', 'Myanmar Accuses British Envoy of having Secret Meetings' *Japan Economic Newswire* (25 August 2006).

[95] Murty, 502.

[96] *BBC Summary*, 'Nicaraguan President, Foreign Minister on Expulsion', 13 July 1988.

[97] L Barber and T Coone, 'Washington Expels Nicaraguan Ambassador' *Financial Times* (London, 13 July 1988).

other Nicaraguan diplomats.[98] That measure, too, was accompanied by charges against the diplomats: The US government stated that Tunnermann and a military attaché had committed 'activities and actions which constitute abuse of their privileges of residence in the United States'.[99]

On the face of it, both instances appear to involve protests by the relevant receiving States and might thus be employed as evidence for the existence of a rule of customary law whose violation the diplomatic hosts decry. The circumstances of the Tunnermann expulsion, however, raise questions as to whether this had indeed been the direction of the negative measure and, therefore, whether the objection voiced by the United States can qualify as a valid protest.

That is not so much a question about its objective appearance. On the objective side, it is clear that States can resort to a wide range of sanctions to counter instances of diplomatic misconduct—including a mere expression of 'surprise' or disapproval, declarations persona non grata, or even the severing of diplomatic ties.[100] Nor does the actual word 'protest' need to have been used when the relevant measure had been adopted.[101]

On the subjective side, however, the fact must be borne in mind that States may have a good many reasons for resorting to negative measures, and some of them may have nothing to do with the underlying diplomatic conduct. In the case of declarations persona non grata, the VCDR itself makes clear that the receiving State is not required to provide reasons for its decision[102]—which might therefore be based on no more than general difficulties between the two States. But if protests are to be taken as the method by which States evaluate the lawfulness of diplomatic conduct, then motivations which are manifestly political in character, are of little use for that purpose.[103]

In the Tunnermann case, the possibility cannot be discounted that there were explanations for the American decision other than the desire to

[98] 'Nicaragua, US Trade Diplomatic Expulsions' *Facts on File* (New York, 15 July 1988).

[99] 'United States: Defends Expulsion' *IPS* (13 July 1988).

[100] *cf Tehran Hostages Case*, para 85. See also Hill, 252 et seq.

[101] See however MacGibbon, 294 (calling for an 'element of formality' as a prerequisite for the validity of protests). But MacGibbon, too, admits the 'comparative rarity of objections to protests on grounds of form alone' (ibid, 297). More recently, the Special Rapporteur of the ILC confirmed that protests may be inferred from certain acts, and mentioned specifically the examples of 'breaking off diplomatic relations or expelling the members of a mission', Cedeño Report, 49, para 93.

[102] VCDR art 9.

[103] Special Rapporteur Rodríguez Cedeño mentioned in that regard the need for an 'intent to prevent the unilateral act being opposed from achieving recognition'. Cedeño Report, 49, para 94. It is at that stage that elements of protests and of customary international law share common ground. Customary law is based on State practice and the existence of legal opinion (see above, at n 69 and see *Asylum Case*, 286); if protests are therefore used to show that an alleged rule of customary law exists (for instance, that there is a ban on diplomatic observation of human rights standards), then the objection must be based on the view of the receiving State that the legal assessment of the situation points in that direction.

evaluate the conduct of the Nicaraguan diplomat. The fact that the sanction came one day after the Melton expulsion, that Tunnermann was of the same rank as Melton and that exactly the same number of foreign agents were expelled, suggests that the true motive may well have been the wish to retaliate—thus, a motive coloured by political considerations.

At the same time, if the receiving State issues a statement which clearly contains an assessment of diplomatic behaviour (as the United States did), it conveys the impression that it was its intention to contribute to the evaluation of such conduct; and it may then be held to its words. That is true even if reasons other than legal considerations—such as a difficult state of affairs between both States[104]—may have shaped the decision.

Even doubts about the correctness of the (factual) allegations do not necessarily deprive an express statement of its value. The characterisation of a State measure as a protest is not so much a quest for historical truth, but an endeavour to identify the position taken by the receiving State towards certain forms of diplomatic behaviour. The value of the statement lies in the fact that the receiving State has made clear that it would not tolerate conduct of the alleged kind. In this way, it may support the position taken by other members of the international community in similar situations.

It is, however, true that, in diplomatic relations, such clear legal statements are the exception, rather than the rule.[105] That raises the question whether cases in which a diplomatic agent had faced a negative sanction without the provision of specific reasons—or without the naming of any reasons at all—can be immediately dismissed from consideration. A position formed on such restrictive lines would ignore the fact that, even in instances of this kind, it may be possible to establish the intention of the receiving State with sufficient clarity from the context of the case.

The factors to be considered in that regard include the receiving State's own conduct in the past: If a host habitually resorts to a specific sanction for a certain kind of diplomatic behaviour, the inference can be made that

[104] Unfriendly relations have undoubtedly often influenced negative measures against diplomatic agents. The fact may be recalled that, on the eve of the Second Gulf War in 2003, the United States called on various States to expel Iraqi diplomats, calling them representatives of a 'corrupt and ruthless regime'. 'European Haven for Iraq Envoys' *BBC Online* (London, 21 March 2003). But this condition on its own does not prevent a receiving State from contributing to the legal assessment of diplomatic conduct. The Netherlands for instance, while forming part of the coalition that supported the United States in her campaign against Iraq, stated that Iraqi diplomats would be allowed 'to stay as long as they did not violate the terms under which they were posted in this country', ibid.

[105] They do happen: see eg, T Koh, 'The Conduct of a Diplomat' *Washington Post* (Washington DC, 14 June 1988) (letter by the Singaporean Ambassador to Washington on the 1988 Hendrickson Case, see A.90).

it conveys a negative opinion on such activities, even if it does not offer an express assessment in a specific case.[106]

In other instances, the circumstances of the situation assist in the evaluation of the reasons behind a particular sanction. The factual background may often allow for a reasonable inference that personal diplomatic conduct led to the adoption of the relevant measure. Often enough, reports provided by news media shed more light on a particular incident than official statements by the hosts.

That is not to say that an assessment on the basis of the facts of a case may not carry difficulties of its own. If the State itself has been silent on the decision, and there is a paucity of other available evidence, a genuine danger of misinterpretation may come into existence.

In other cases, it is the very abundance of material that makes it difficult to assess the position of the State. The 2001 case of the US Ambassador to Belarus (Kozak) offers an illustration. On 4 September of that year, the Belarusian President Lukashenko stated that Kozak would have to leave Minsk after the elections.[107] Lukashenko complained about 'Americans telling us what to do', referred to 'sleazy election techniques', to opposition leaders in the pay of the United States whose objective it was to remove him,[108] and to the personal involvement of Kozak in an alleged conspiracy by foreign secret services to overthrow him.[109]

It became known that the United States had indeed provided financial help to the opposition in Belarus—through the funding of websites, newspapers and opinion polls—and had supported a student resistance movement. Five leaders of the opposition had, prior to the elections, met in the US Embassy to agree on a common candidate. In a letter to a newspaper, Kozak admitted that the United States had adopted an approach towards Belarus similar to that pursued in Nicaragua in 1989–1990.[110]

Cases of this kind require careful consideration if a finding is to be reached that the receiving State intended to evaluate a particular form of diplomatic conduct. From an analytical point of view, a wealth of information can create more problems than it solves, and it may not always be

[106] A number of governments have made it clear in the past that they link a particular form of misconduct to a particular sanction. See, eg, for the United Kingdom, UK Government Report (1985), para 28; for the Netherlands and the United States, Whiteman (1970), 92, 93, referring to the Briefing Book (1965).

[107] *cf* I Traynor, 'Belarussian Foils Dictator-buster' *The Guardian* (London, 14 September 2001).

[108] S Peterson, 'US Spends Millions to Bolster Belarus Opposition' *Christian Science Monitor* (Boston MA, 10 September 2001).

[109] Traynor, n 107 above; 'Lukashenko: "Yugoslav Scenario Won't Materialize"' *Pravda Online* (Moscow, 5 September 2001).

[110] M Kozak, 'Letter' *The Guardian* (London, 25 August 2001).

clear to which form of alleged misconduct the diplomatic sanction did in fact refer.

There are, however, other aspects which may, in a given situation, allow for the conclusion that the receiving State indeed intended to react to certain forms of diplomatic behaviour. The passing of a very small interval between diplomatic activity and State sanction can be evidence pointing in this direction.[111] The adoption of negative sanctions against agents of a State with which the hosts maintain generally friendly relations, may also be of help in that regard.[112] The political disadvantages to receiving States in cases of this kind will often be considerable; but if the State still feels that there is no choice but to resort to a negative measure, the conclusion may be justified that it acted because it perceived the existence of a breach of diplomatic duties.

What these scenarios indicate is the fact that the evaluation of protests faces certain challenges, especially where the suspicion arises that objections had been based on motives other than the wish to assess a specific form of diplomatic conduct. But they also show that a reasonable inference from available evidence is often possible. The factual background of the situation, the state of relations between sending and receiving State (and, of course, clear evaluatory statements by the hosts themselves) are all strands of evidence which may allow the assessment that a negative sanction had been based on the intent to express an opinion on the lawfulness of the diplomatic conduct.

Reference to some of these cases will be made in the further course of this study. They underline the fact that protests by receiving States retain their importance for the understanding of customary international law in the field and that they have to be considered one of the principal methods for the determination of limits to diplomatic conduct.

At the same time, a protest made by one host cannot, by itself, indicate that international law has taken a clear position on the relevant matter. The possibility can, after all, not be discounted that the view of the receiving State is in no way reflective of the opinion of other members of the international community. This is an aspect which merits consideration in its own right.

[111] The Special Rapporteur of the ILC went so far as to say that a 'certain immediacy' was a required precondition for valid protests. Cedeño Report, 49, para 94. The basis for this statement is, however, not clear: It is, in particular, not apparent from the ICJ judgment in the *Anglo-Norwegian Fisheries* case, to which Rodriguez Cedeño refers.

[112] For understandable reasons, such incidents are not frequent. But they have happened. In 1977 for instance, the French President voiced his concern after a meeting between US diplomats and an official of the Communist party had occurred. Given the generally friendly state of affairs between sending and receiving State, it appears a justifiable conclusion that the measure represented a genuine objection to underlying conduct rather than a political sanction. 'Giscard scores US talks with left' *Facts on File* (New York, 9 April 1977), and see ch 6, at n 57.

3.3. From Protests to Customary Law: The Requirement of Generality

On 19 March 2007, at a time of political unrest in Zimbabwe, the Zimbabwean Minister for Foreign Affairs, Simbarashe Mumbengegwi, summoned diplomats from several Western States and the mission of the European Union and complained about their alleged support to the opposition.[113] Particular criticism appeared to be reserved for diplomats who had visited police stations and courts to check on the status of opposition leaders.[114] Mumbengegwi declared that Zimbabwe would not tolerate interference in her internal affairs, and threatened the expulsion of diplomats whose conduct was not considered correct.[115]

There is little doubt that a measure of this kind fulfils the requirements of a valid State protest. It was issued by a person who had authority to speak on behalf of the State; the summoning of diplomats is a sanction which can lawfully be employed, and there is reason to believe that the receiving State had resorted to this measure in order to issue an evaluation of the relevant diplomatic conduct—the Foreign Minister had made clear that in his view the rule against diplomatic interference as enshrined in the Vienna Convention on Diplomatic Relations, had been violated.[116]

But the reaction by the sending States and their agents was equally clear. The French Foreign Ministry defended the work of the European diplomats in Zimbabwe,[117] the Australian Foreign Minister Downer noted that it was the right of diplomatic agents to meet members of the opposition,[118] a spokesperson of the British embassy stated that threats would 'not deter the UK from speaking out against the continued misgovernance and human rights abuses in Zimbabwe'.[119] The US Ambassador Christopher Dell even walked out of the meeting,[120] and the State Department later pointed out that the United States would 'continue to speak and act steadfastly in support of the people of Zimbabwe's right to democracy'.[121]

What this incident demonstrates, is that the existence of a protest by a receiving State can be only the first step in the process of identifying customary international law. If the alleged customary rule in this situation were seen as a ban on diplomatic involvement in human rights, the

[113] B Peta, 'Zimbabwe Threatens Diplomats' *The Independent* (London, 20 March 2007); *BBC Monitoring Africa—Political*, 'Foreign Diplomats in Zimbabwe' (London, 22 March 2007).
[114] 'Fed: Downer Tips Change' *AAP Newsfeed* (21 March 2007) and Peta, n 113.
[115] 'Une expulsion d'ambassadeurs' *Agence France Presse* (Paris, 22 March 2007).
[116] 'Fed: Downer Tips Change', n 114.
[117] See 'Une expulsion d'ambassadeurs' n 115.
[118] 'Fed: Downer Tips Change', n 114.
[119] 'Foreign Diplomats in Zimbabwe', n 113.
[120] ibid.
[121] 'VOA News: Diplomatic Relations' *US Fed News* (20 March 2007).

question would arise whether such a rule can indeed command wide support within the international community.

In line with the view expressed by the ICJ in *Nicaragua*,[122] an assumption of this kind can only be made if the rule were reflected in the 'general' position of receiving States.

'Generality' indicates a somewhat lower standard than that of 'uniform' or even 'extensive' State practice.[123] At the same time, it still implies that an attitude from which the evaluation of the relevant diplomatic conduct as a breach of international law can be inferred, has been adopted across the international community. If this were not the case, it would at best be possible to speak of a local interpretation of the rule in question.

These considerations cast doubt on the significance of Mumbengegwi's protest. If anything, it appears tempting to conclude that the opinion of the international community had been better expressed through the positions taken by sending States following the accusations against their diplomats.

But even that finding is not free from doubt. It may, in particular, encounter the criticism that such an approach takes into account the views of 'Western' States only—States which share certain aspects regarding their political and cultural systems and whose positions are therefore not necessarily representative of prevailing sensitivities in other parts of the world, including the African continent.

That may be a valid point. The clearest evidence for the 'generality' in this field exists if agreement on the evaluation of a particular form of diplomatic conduct can be established for a 'representative number' of States[124]—if, in the consideration of the composition of this group, different 'political, economic and legal systems' are taken into account, as well as their geographical distribution.[125] The assumption of 'general State practice' can certainly rely on stronger grounds if States with diverse—possibly even antagonistic—systems agree in their evaluation of the relevant behaviour.

In the above mentioned case of diplomatic agents in Thailand who had met with protesters of the Red Shirt movement,[126] it was therefore

[122] See above, at n 75.

[123] These are terms which the court had at some time employed for the establishment of customary law as such (as opposed to protests as tools for its evaluation). In 1950, the ICJ still required '[c]onstant and uniform' usage as the basis of customary law, *Asylum Case*, 277. However, in the 1988 *Nicaragua* case the court found that the establishment of a rule as customary law required merely 'general[ly] … consistent' State practice, above n 70 and accompanying text.

[124] This is a term which occurs in the discussion of elements of customary international law: See *North Sea Continental Shelf* cases (Dissenting Opinion Lachs), 230. See also *North Sea Continental Shelf* cases, para 73.

[125] On these factors in the context of customary international law, see Heintschel von Heinegg, 217; *North Sea Continental Shelf* cases (Dissenting Opinion Lachs), 227.

[126] See above at n 5 and n 6.

of significance that objections to the view that such conduct constituted 'interference', came not only from a multitude of countries, but that these States represented a certain political and geographical spread: The view of an African diplomat who asserted his right to 'contact … all parties', appeared to have been shared by several diplomats from EU countries.[127] Their assessment is joined by that of States which in comparable situations have defended the right of diplomatic agents to communicate with opposition parties and factions within the receiving State.[128]

In many instances, however, a positive identification of the views even of a representative number of States may prove difficult. Not all receiving States are faced with the same kind of diplomatic conduct, and doubts inevitably arise when certain forms of diplomatic behaviour have met with sanctions of differing gravity by different hosts.

Even in situations of that kind, however, it is often possible to identify evidence which indicates that a particular position is likely to be shared by the international community as a whole. One such situation arises when, in a case of alleged interference, sending and receiving States reach the same legal assessment of the relevant conduct.

A negative sanction provided by the receiving State will usually create a difficult situation: The expulsion of a diplomat, for one, is likely to carry significant loss of face for the sending State. If, in spite of that, both States find it possible to agree on a point of law, their position will often be the affirmation of an already existing rule of customary international law.

This method of ascertaining a generally applicable rule of customary law is not new in international law. In the field of the use of force by States, one may recall the 1837 Caroline incident which stands as a landmark in the identification of customary international law on self defence. The two States concerned—Britain and the United States—disagreed on the question whether the incident (the sinking of the steamboat Caroline by the British side) fulfilled the legal requirements of self defence. At the same time, the fact that Britain accepted the requirements themselves (which the US Secretary of State had stipulated),[129] must be seen as a reflection of the general acceptance of the rule by the international community.

And the history of diplomatic relations does know of cases in which agreement between the two sides had come into existence. A 1999 incident serves as an illustration: In that year, the Deputy Prime Minister of Malaysia accused diplomatic missions of interference, claiming that foreign diplomats had offered their help to the opposition with a view to

[127] 'Diplomats Chafe at Rebukes', n 8.
[128] See on this point ch 6, at nn 12–14.
[129] See on this State Papers (1840–1841), 1138 and State Papers (1841–1842), 196 and 198.

toppling the government.[130] The accusations came after the youth wing of the ruling party in Malaysia had stated that a number of embassies, including that of the United States, were funding opposition parties.[131]

The US embassy did not deny that such activities would constitute diplomatic misconduct. But it rejected the factual assessment: An embassy spokesman noted that the mission did not provide 'funding for election-related activities in any way, shape or form'. He pointed out that the US 'strongly support[ed] democracy, and free and fair elections', but added that she did not 'interfere or take sides in elections'.[132]

Evidence for the existence of a position which is likely to be acceptable to the international community also exists, if one of the relevant States has given up an advantageous position in order to support a perceived rule of customary international law. That is the case when States adopt a negative sanction against misbehaving diplomats from friendly countries,[133] but it is also the case when a sending State disciplines its own diplomats or gives them advance warning against potential interference.[134]

Surrendering a beneficial position is, prima facie, an atypical act; but if a State nevertheless finds it necessary to resort to that measure because of its understanding of the proper fulfilment of diplomatic duties, it will often have acted in compliance with a position which is already accepted within the wider international community.

The establishment of generality is therefore not an impossible task: Mechanisms exist which at least permit the finding of evidence to the effect that there is a position, shared by States across political, cultural and geographical divides, which condemns or allows the behaviour in question.

However, even a positive conclusion on this issue does not necessarily result in a comprehensive assessment of the relevant diplomatic conduct under international law. One of the most challenging features of that task lies in the fact that there will often be more than one position which commands respect in the international community. There may be evidence that a 'representative number' of receiving States takes exception to diplomatic activities of that kind; but also evidence that a 'representative number' of sending States feels entitled to adopt such conduct. Cases in which diplomatic agents acted to defend interests of the sending State, held talks with the opposition or commented on the human rights record of their hosts, are examples of situations in which this difficulty arises.

These are questions which will be explored in the subsequent chapters. The first Part of this study seeks to establish the general understanding of

[130] 'Malaysia Accuses Diplomats' *BBC Online* (London, 24 November 1999).
[131] 'Mahathir Blasts Opposition' *Agence France Presse* (Paris, 26 November 1999).
[132] 'Malaysia Accuses Diplomats', n 130.
[133] See also above, at n 112.
[134] See also above at nn 73 and 74.

interference within the legal framework in which it exists. Following an overview of the history of diplomatic interference (chapter 1) and an examination of the concept as it appears in contemporary debate (chapter 2), the discussion will move on to competing interests in situations of alleged interference—divergent interests which may exist on the side of the sending and the receiving State (chapter 3). Chapter 4 identifies mechanisms which are capable of mediating between legitimate interests of this kind and thus allow their co-existence.

The second Part deals with specific fields in which allegations of interference typically occur. This includes activities of lobbying (chapter 5), but also instances of alleged partisanship (chapter 6) and propaganda (chapter 7). Claims of interference have also arisen when diplomats employed money and other material means to pursue their aims (chapter 8), and when they resorted to criticism and insults (chapter 9). The last two chapters are dedicated to an analysis of threatening and intimidating conduct (chapter 10) and the granting of diplomatic asylum (chapter 11).

The focus here is the rule of non-interference as it relates to diplomats of permanent missions under the VCDR. To other agents—consular officers, ad hoc diplomats etc—other regimes apply. But since the relevant rule is retained there as well,[135] instances from these fields will be included by way of illustration, where they share common ground.

The leading theme throughout this study is the search for the voice of law in situations in which receiving States feel that diplomatic agents, through interference, have overstepped the boundaries of the permitted. In light of the above considerations, and in particular of the divergent interests of sending and receiving States, the identification of the lawful way is hardly ever a binary choice.

Yet it will be shown that a careful application of the law yields a method which gives room to the legitimate views of both parties, and thus allows diplomats to pursue measures which protect their interests while refraining from undue infringement of the sovereignty of their hosts.

The result is a system whose consideration leads not only to a deeper understanding of its underlying legal structure, but also permits the formulation of guidelines which benefit sending States, their agents abroad, and their hosts around the world in equal measure.

[135] See ch 1, nn 86–90.

Part I

Towards an Understanding of Diplomatic Interference

1

Diplomatic Interference: A Historical Overview

1. DIPLOMATIC INTERFERENCE IN STATE PRACTICE

IN SEPTEMBER 1888, Lord Lionel Sackville-West, the British Minister to the United States, received a letter from a US citizen who asked for advice.[1] 1888 was election year in America: The incumbent President, the Democrat Cleveland, faced a challenge by the Republican candidate Harrison.

Sackville's correspondent, who appeared to be a naturalised American of English birth, wanted to know the Minister's opinion about Cleveland. He had his doubts about the man: The President who at some time had appeared so 'favorable and friendly' towards the 'mother land', had now adopted policies which gave ground for concern.[2]

Sackville, it appears, saw no harm in replying.[3] The political climate was currently not favourable for the old country: 'any political party which openly favored the Mother Country at the present moment would lose popularity', said the Minister, adding that the Democrats were, in his opinion, 'still desirous of maintaining friendly relations with Great Britain'.

This might have been the end of the affair, if Sackville's correspondent had been who he said he was—one Charles Murchison from Pomona who 'privately and confidentially' asked for information and promised to keep it secret. But Murchison did not exist: The letter had been written by the Californian George Osgoodby, who counted the President of the local Republican club among his acquaintances.[4]

It did not take long for Sackville's missive to find its way into the press (it was reprinted in the *New York Tribune* under the headline 'The British

[1] The letter and Sackville's reply are reproduced in Hinckley, 360, 361; 81 *State Papers* (1888–1889), 483, 484.

[2] On Cleveland's policies, see Hinckley, 359. Republicans had accused Cleveland of being too favourable to the United Kingdom—accusations which were arguably part of an effort to win over the Irish vote. See *Harpweek*, '1888. Harrison v Cleveland' 3.

[3] *cf* 'Remarks of Sir Nicholas Henderson' *Federal News Service* (Washington DC, 17 November 1988).

[4] Hinckley, 365, 366.

Lion's paw thrust into American Politics to help Cleveland').[5] The cry of 'interference' soon arose, but it was made not only by Cleveland's opponents:[6] US Secretary of State Bayard raised the question whether it was 'compatible with the dignity, security and independent sovereignty' of the United States to allow a diplomat to 'interfere in its domestic affairs by advising persons formerly his countrymen concerning their political course as citizens of the United States'.[7]

When the British government showed itself reluctant to recall Sackville, Bayard, acting on the President's instructions, told the Minister that 'it would be incompatible with the best interests and detrimental to the good relations of both governments' if he continued in his current position, and sent him his passports.[8] (It did not help Cleveland: The 1888 presidential election was decided in favour of Harrison.)[9]

Over the years, the Sackville case became the *locus classicus* of diplomatic interference[10]—due, arguably, to the comparably detailed evaluation to which the Minister's conduct was subjected. It also highlighted the consequences which conduct of this kind can generate, both for the diplomatic agent and for the receiving State. For the purposes of contemporary analysis, its outstanding significance lies in its illustration of the complexity of the assessment of diplomatic conduct in situations in which competing interests exist—a point to which this study will return.[11]

But the rule against diplomatic interference was already well established by the time of the Sackville incident. It can trace its roots to the very beginnings of permanent diplomacy. Its basis was not a conscious effort at codification—it evolved naturally and corresponded to a need. By accepting diplomats, States opened the channels of communication; but they also allowed into their territory persons whose specific aim was the promotion of foreign interests.

Some ambassadors were influential:[12] They were shrewd, blessed with a silver tongue and golden coins, and sent by powerful masters. Not all of them were unduly burdened by scruples or the good manners becoming a guest.

One of the earliest reported cases illustrates the extent to which some diplomats were willing to go to serve their sovereigns abroad. It is that of the Spanish Ambassador to England in the 1580s, Don Bernardino

[5] Reitano, 123.

[6] 'The British Minister' *The Times* (London, 25 October 1888).

[7] 'Lord Sackville' *The Times* (London, 1 November 1888).

[8] 'The Recall of Lord Sackville' *The Times* (London, 14 January 1889).

[9] Cleveland won the popular vote, but did not obtain enough votes in the electoral college.

[10] *cf* Satow (1979), 133, para 15.32; Denza, 464; Rousseau, 167.

[11] See ch 3.

[12] Gaxotte, for instance, points out that the French envoy to Sweden in 1756, Louis de Cardevac, had more influence with the Senate than Queen Louisa Ulrika: Gaxotte, 370.

de Mendoza, who was involved in the 'Throckmorton Plot'—a conspiracy to overthrow the rule of Elizabeth I.[13] The general expectation at the time was that Mendoza would be prosecuted 'with fire and sword',[14] but the government, acting on the advice of Alberico Gentili, decided to merely order his expulsion.[15]

Later cases betray the sensitivity with which receiving States considered particular diplomatic statements. After the battle of Culloden in 1746, in which the last Jacobite rising was crushed by the British government, the Dutch envoy to France, van Hoey, wrote a message to the British Secretary of State, in which he advocated a policy of mercy towards the Young Pretender and his associates.[16] The British government took exception to this and complained to States General of the Netherlands,[17] which in turn instructed van Hoey to write 'a decent and polite letter, to acknowledge his impudence, confess the fault he has committed, and beg pardon, promising to behave himself more prudently for the future'.[18]

That is not to say that Britain herself had always scrupulously abstained from conduct which was perceived as meddling. After the French revolution of February 1848 for instance—and in the middle of the storm it unleashed over Europe—the British Minister in Spain (Bulwer), was instructed by the British Foreign Secretary Palmerston to advise the Spanish government to adopt 'a legal and constitutional system'. Palmerston also thought it fit to add that the Queen of Spain would act 'wisely' if she called to her counsels 'some of the men in whom the Liberal Party places confidence'.[19] The Spanish cabinet protested 'in the most energetic manner' against this form of unwanted advice.[20]

The Bulwer incident is of particular interest because of the detailed evaluation which the British conduct received by the Spanish side. In a letter to Bulwer, the Spanish Foreign Secretary referred to 'interference'[21] on three occasions: In relation to Palmerston's conduct, in relation to Bulwer's conduct, and in relation to a list of hypothetical examples that, in his view, would constitute interference. The list included a scenario in which the Spanish government would 'in the name of humanity' demand a better treatment 'of the unfortunate people of Asia' by Britain[22]—conduct which today would be considered under the headings of human rights involvement and assistance towards the realisation of self-determination.

[13] On the Mendoza case, see Satow (1979), 179, para 21.16, and Merriman at 392 and 393.
[14] Camden, 263–64, quoted in Satow (1979), 179, para 21.16.
[15] Merriman, n 13, 393. Some good came of the affair: Gentili's *De Legationibus Libri Tres* was a result of that case. Coquillette, 55, n 266.
[16] See *The Gentleman's Magazine*, vol XVI (June 1746), 304–19.
[17] ibid, 304, 305.
[18] ibid, 319.
[19] 'Mr. Bulwer' *The Times* (London, 26 April 1848).
[20] ibid.
[21] ie, to the word in its verbal form, ibid.
[22] ibid.

Seventeen years before the Sackville case, another diplomat to the United States—the Russian Minister Catacazy—triggered charges of interference.[23] Catacazy was accused of a multitude of sins, including the hassling of Senators and Representatives and thus 'embarrass[ing] the free course of legislation'.[24] But there was also the suspicion that Cataczazy had written or inspired articles in American newspapers which were 'very abusive of the President and his administration',[25] and the US Secretary of State expressed the view that Catacazy, in his personal conversations, had been 'severe and unrestrained, and employed abusive and vituperative language toward very many persons, including several in public positions'.[26]

The Catacazy case, too, has ensured its place in the history books partly due to the fact that a fairly explicit evaluation of the Minister's conduct survives in official correspondence. Even today, such appetite for investigative enterprise is rare: Neither State stands much to gain by extended scrutiny and the inevitable chain of accusations.[27]

If anything, this attitude gained in strength in the twentieth century. But there were situations when the contours of diplomatic interference received clarification through discussions by domestic legislators. In 1931 for instance, when fear of Communist propaganda had reached a high point in British public debate,[28] Sir Austen Chamberlain drew Parliament's attention to a recent address given by a member of the Soviet Embassy in the Committee room of the House and asked the Prime Minister if the 'interference of diplomats in the internal affairs of other countries' had not led to the dismissal of these diplomats and if he did not think that diplomats should in the future refrain 'from delivering addresses of that character'.[29] The Prime Minister agreed, but showed himself reluctant to raise the matter directly with the legations.

After the Second World War however, when allegations of diplomatic interference were made by an American lawmaker, the official reply by the US administration showed a greater level of discernment. Congressman Klein complained in 1949 about propaganda in favour of the Spanish (fascist) regime, which apparently emanated from the Spanish

[23] 'The Catacazy Letters' *New York Times* (New York, 8 December 1871) (reproducing letter by the US Secretary of State to the US Minister to Russia).

[24] ibid.

[25] 'Mr Catacazy' *New York Times* (New York, 23 October 1871).

[26] 'The Catacazy Letters', n 23.

[27] Even after the Sackville case, the US envoy to Britain remarked that '[p]erhaps further comment upon these incidents is unnecessary, as it is certainly unpleasant'. 'The Recall of Lord Sackville', n 8.

[28] See on this, 'Political Notes' *The Times* (London, 15 May 1931) and 'Red Propaganda. Commons Debate To-day' *The Times* (London, 18 May 1931).

[29] HC Deb 15 June 1931, vol 253, cols 1432–33; Satow (1979), 134, para 15.32.

diplomatic mission.[30] In his reply, Assistant Secretary of State Gross affirmed the general rule that applied to diplomats of the United States themselves, to 'scrupulously … abstain from interfering in the domestic policies of the countries where they reside'. But he distinguished that from the function to create a favourable sentiment for their own government. Since American diplomats abroad engaged in that function, it would be 'embarrassing' for the State Department to object to the respective activities of the Spanish embassy as long as they did not become offensive.[31]

With this statement, Gross highlighted the fundamental difficulty that inhabits the concept of interference: What critics of the diplomatic agent call 'interference', may be considered by the sending State (and, on this occasion, even the receiving State) the fulfilment of tasks which belong to an envoy's lawful brief. Gross was one of few observers to appreciate this difficulty; but he was not able to offer a satisfactory solution: 'Offensiveness' is not a test that provides sufficient objective parameters for the evaluation of interference.

In November 1950, the ICJ had, for the first time, the opportunity to assess a situation in which accusations of interference commonly arise—the provision of diplomatic asylum on mission premises.[32] The Court found that the grant of diplomatic asylum was, prima facie, 'an intervention in matters which are exclusively within the competence' of the receiving State.[33] This reference to 'exclusivity' has some significance for the evaluation of interference: As will be seen, the question whether a matter falls squarely within the 'internal affairs' of a receiving State did occupy the ILC in its deliberations on diplomatic duties a few years later.[34]

The view of the ICJ is of note also because of its position on the rationale of the rule against intervention in the field of diplomatic asylum: It referred in that regard to the 'territorial sovereignty' of the receiving State.[35] It is a view which holds true for diplomatic interference in general: It is the sovereignty of the receiving State as an independent member of the international community which calls for limitations of diplomatic conduct which encroaches upon that right.

At the same time, the ICJ recognised that sovereign rights were not absolute. In the context of diplomatic asylum, it envisaged the possibility of 'derogations' (but noted that a 'legal basis' had to be established 'in each particular case').[36] This, too, is a point which has wider applicability: Wherever allegations of interference are concerned, there may be

30 Whiteman (1970), 145.
31 ibid.
32 *Asylum Case*, 272, 273. See ch 11, at n 9.
33 *Asylum Case*, 274.
34 See ch 2, at nn 18 ff.
35 *Asylum Case*, 272, 273.
36 ibid, 274, 275.

legitimate interests on the side of the sending State whose simultaneous application would lead to a restriction of the sovereignty of the receiving State.[37]

From the cases which have risen to prominence in the history of diplomatic interference, it appears possible to identify specific topical areas—fields which have traditionally provided more fertile ground for charges of meddling than others. Partisanship in dealing with the political affairs of the receiving State occupies a position of some significance: The cases of Sackville, Mendoza and van Hoey are all instances in which a diplomat made himself the subject of criticism after lending support to a particular faction in the receiving State.

Lobbying activities directed at the government of the receiving State have likewise met with charges of interference, as the Bulwer case demonstrates. Diplomatic conduct has furthermore triggered objections from the receiving State when it was perceived as insulting or as containing sharp criticism—the Catacazy case is by far not the only instance in which this form of conduct met with negative reactions.[38]

Charges of interference arising out of contact with the public, and in particular, propaganda activities aimed at a public audience, appear to have gained prominence only from the last century onwards—a development for which the rise in means of mass communication must be held at least partially responsible. In a similar vein, diplomatic engagement with the human rights of the receiving State appears to have become a prominent issue of contention only in the relatively recent past—although diplomatic history knows of some precursors to conduct of this kind.[39]

But what the various cases of alleged interference also reveal, is the fact that receiving States considered this form of behaviour as more than occasional infractions of protocol. They accorded significance to diplomatic interference, and they were right to do so. The consequences of diplomatic activities which arose in the field of interference, are often felt not only in relations between the two States concerned, but also within the internal organisation of the receiving State itself. The Sackville and Mendoza cases attest to that.

Since the conclusion of the Vienna Convention, incidents of alleged interference have not become less frequent—nor has the sensitivity of receiving States on this matter diminished. Some of these instances will be discussed in more detail in Part II of this book, as far as they are relevant for an understanding of the concept of interference.

The subjects which attract the attention of diplomatic agents may have changed: Today's diplomats are interested in the situation of private

[37] This aspect will be discussed in more detail in ch 3.
[38] For further instances, see ch 9.
[39] See Behrens (2014b), 193, 194.

television and radio stations,[40] they express concern about drug trafficking activities,[41] lobby for the building of power plants,[42] comment on the membership of the receiving State in an international organisation[43] and are involved in the monitoring of human rights.[44]

But the underlying methods are still recognisable: In the pursuit of their aims, diplomatic agents still approach the government or the opposition in the receiving State; they employ occasionally harsh and critical language; they are known to resort to 'megaphone diplomacy' to air their concerns instead of discussing the relevant matters behind the closed doors of the foreign office. And these forms of conduct still trigger negative reactions and accusations of 'meddling'. To that degree, the attitude of the actors involved in situations of this kind does not appear to have changed very much in the course of diplomatic history. If a change has occurred, it lies in the increasing awareness of sending States and their diplomats of the fact that the rules of diplomacy not only impose restrictions upon them, but grant them certain rights too, and that they therefore may be able to rebut charges of interference on a legal basis.[45]

2. THE CODIFICATION OF THE RULE OF NON-INTERFERENCE

At the time of the *Asylum Case*, first attempts had already been made to present the law of diplomatic relations in a systematic and comprehensive form. From the nineteenth century onwards, several sets of systematic rules on this topic were published—draft codes on diplomatic law, written by legal scholars. As private projects, their authority was limited; but several of their provisions reflected customary law as it existed at that time. That is certainly the case where the rule of non-interference is concerned, whose existence was even then supported by ample evidence—not only reactions by receiving States to conduct they perceived as interfering, but also, on occasion, admissions of wrongdoing by sending States.

One of the earliest draft codes—that by Johann Caspar Bluntschli (1868)—contained a ban on interference which was already more explicit than the equivalent provision in the VCDR (Vienna Convention on Diplomatic Relations). It linked the rule of non-interference to the

[40] See the 1995 case of Brazeal (A.111).

[41] As in the 2008 case of Patrick Duddy, A.237 and 'Xinhua World News Summary' *Xinhua* (China, 1 September 2008).

[42] See on this the 1999 case of Richard Hecklinger, A.138 and H Mehta, 'Anti-foreign Feeling Resurging' *Business Times* (Singapore, 1 December 1999).

[43] *cf* the 2001 case of Dan Coats, A.171 and 'Germany Rankled' *Agence France Presse* (Paris, 3 August 2001).

[44] See on this point below, ch 3, s 2.

[45] See for instance, ch 3 at n 66, n 83, n 94, n 103, n 197.

obligation to respect the 'independence and honour' of the receiving State and referred to some common fields of interference (provocations, threats and the making of certain promises).[46] Like Bluntschli, Pasquale Fiore's draft (1890) condemned provocations and threats; but Fiore also outlined some other emanations of interference and mentioned in particular interference with administrative or judicial authorities.[47] He also emphasised the particular difficulty caused by diplomats who intend to protect the interests of nationals of the sending State. Fiore would have given only limited space to diplomatic conduct in this regard: Diplomats could take action only ('with proper reserve') before the Foreign Ministry or help their nationals to seek justice through 'the regular channels'.[48] The draft also condemned the stirring up of conflicts between political parties and the involvement in 'intrigue to approve or disapprove' governmental acts.[49]

By comparison, later draft codes were somewhat laconic on the question. The 1925 Project of the American Institute of International Law simply stated that diplomatic agents may not 'interfere in the internal or external political life' of the receiving State;[50] similar wording was used in the Project of the International Commission of American Jurists in 1927.[51] Lord Phillimore, while not mentioning the word 'interference' in his draft code (1926), did refer to the diplomatic duty to 'consider the welfare' of the receiving State and would have prohibited acts such as engagement in conspiracies against the government of that State.[52] The Harvard Law School Draft on 'Diplomatic Privileges and Immunities' (1932)—arguably the most famous of the draft codes—made no mention of diplomatic interference at all.[53]

By that time, attempts at codification had already been undertaken. The earliest initiatives, on a multilateral level, can be traced back to the nineteenth century, but they did not refer to diplomatic obligations.[54] In 1925, a more comprehensive attempt was undertaken under the auspices of the League of Nations. The project was not successful: In 1927, it was decided that the subject of diplomatic immunities and privileges should

[46] Annex B.1, para 225 (trans).
[47] Annex B.2, para 482.
[48] ibid.
[49] ibid, para 483.
[50] Annex B.3, art 16.
[51] Annex B.4, art 16.
[52] Phillimore, 180, art 34.
[53] The draft was to exert considerable influence in other areas of diplomatic law, see Young, 176, 177. It is reproduced in Reeves, 19 ff.
[54] 1815 Règlement; see also Strupp (1911), 160 with further references.

not be retained for codification, as it seemed difficult to reach universal agreement and as it was not considered a matter of priority.[55]

In the next year, however, the Havana Convention on Diplomatic Officers was signed, which addressed various fields of diplomatic relations and ultimately entered into force with the participation of several American States. While being a relatively short instrument (the Convention has only 27 articles), the rule on non-interference was considered important enough for inclusion. Its Article 12 provides that diplomats 'may not participate in the domestic or foreign politics' of the receiving State.[56]

After the Second World War, the United Nations returned to the question of the codification of international law. In 1949, the ILC decided to include the subject of 'diplomatic intercourse and immunities' in its list of topics suitable for codification;[57] and in December 1952, the General Assembly requested the ILC to deal with the subject as a matter of priority.[58]

The Special Rapporteur on this topic, the Swedish Judge Emil Sandström, must be credited with one of the most influential contributions in this context. The draft on diplomatic privileges and immunities—28 articles and commentaries—which he submitted[59] was to form the basis of the subsequent ILC debates, which began in April 1957.[60]

Given the prominence of the rule of non-interference in the existing draft codes and the Havana Convention on Diplomatic Officers, it is somewhat surprising that the Sandström draft made no mention of it. Sandström referred to diplomatic duties in Article 27, but that article only stipulated a general obligation on diplomatic agents to conduct themselves in a manner compatible with the internal order of the receiving State and to conform to its laws and rules[61]—a separate duty, which is today enshrined in the first sentence of Article 41(1) of the Vienna Convention.

That the ban on interference formed part of the discussions at all, was due to an initiative by the Mexican ILC member, Luis Padilla Nervo, and his Cuban colleague Francisco García Amador: On 5 June 1957, Padilla Nervo introduced their joint amendment to the Rapporteur's Article 27, which

[55] League of Nations Report (1927), 2. In 1928, the League of Nations also abandoned an initiative to engage in a 'revision of the classification of diplomatic agents' when it was found that international codification of this topic would not be realisable. League of Nations Report (1928), 6. See also Secretariat Memorandum (1956), 136 ff for an examination of the work done by the Committee of Experts and its Sub-Committee.

[56] Havana Convention on Diplomatic Officers (1928), art 12. See Annex C.1.

[57] YILC (Yearbook of the International Law Commission) 1949, 49, paras 21–23 and 53, para 69.

[58] GA Res 685 (VII) (1952).

[59] Sandström Report, 9–12.

[60] YILC 1957/I, 2, para 6. For a general overview of the ILC debates in 1957 and 1958, see Bruns, 28–34.

[61] Annex B.5, art 27.

included the duty 'not to interfere in the domestic or foreign politics' of the receiving State.[62] The article was discussed in several meetings in the same month[63] and formed part of the set of draft articles which the ILC included in its Report to the General Assembly. The relevant sentence now stated that beneficiaries of diplomatic privileges and immunity 'also have a duty not to interfere in the internal affairs of that State'.[64]

What were the main points of debate in the International Law Commission?

Most of the debate on interference was taken up by questions about the authorship of the offending act—would it make sense to include cases of interference in which a diplomat had acted on instructions of the sending State? Opinions on this issue were much divided, with Special Rapporteur Sandström stating that it was that particular point which had made him refrain from including an article on 'non-intervention' in his draft.[65]

Another issue related to diplomatic interference in the 'foreign politics' of the receiving State, as the amendment had phrased it. On this point, the observation was made that it might be part of the very task of diplomats to occupy themselves with foreign policy,[66] and the reference was, in the end, scrapped.

Other members of the ILC referred to particular fields of interference—Padilla Nervo in particular mentioned 'dictatorial interference'[67] (a term which had been used in academic debate at that time).[68] The way in which he understood the concept, approaches a field of potential interference which might today best be described as the posing of threats and ultimata.

It is also possible to discern, in some contributions, a foreshadowing of the difficulty caused by the existence of legitimate, competing interests which may have an impact on allegedly interfering conduct. The ILC members Khoman and Bartos, for instance, both referred to 'interests of the sending State' which a diplomatic agent, in principle, should be able to defend.[69] In a similar vein, Sandström pointed out that it might sometimes be the 'duty' of a diplomatic agent 'to make representations in connexion with the [receiving] State's internal affairs' and referred to a case in which

[62] Annex B.6, para 55.
[63] See YILC 1957/I, 143–50 and 218–21.
[64] See Annex B.7 (art 33).
[65] YILC 1957/I, 144, para 67 [Sandström]. See ch 2, s 3.
[66] YILC 1957/I, 145, para 76 [Fitzmaurice]. See ch 2, s 2.
[67] YILC 1957/I, 145, para 83 [Padilla Nervo].
[68] Padilla Nervo himself referred to Lauterpacht (1950), 167, 168. See also Falk, 172; Q Wright, 5 (highlighting, in particular, diplomatic 'intervention').
[69] YILC 1957/I, 145, para 71 [Khoman]; YILC 1957/I, 145, para 80 [Bartos].

Sweden had made such representations to protect her interests in the Federal Republic of Germany.[70]

When the 1957 debates had come to an end, States had the opportunity to offer their views on the ILC's set of draft articles. Comments were received from 21 governments,[71] but few of them dealt with the duty of non-interference. Italy wanted a clearer distinction between the addressees of diplomatic duties;[72] Switzerland suggested putting the article in a different section of the draft.[73] But when the ILC reviewed the comments in its 1958 session, it decided to leave the text of the rule on non-interference unaltered,[74] and the norm was thus included in the final set of draft articles (now renumbered as Article 40).[75] A comment received by Yugoslavia bears observation: Its Foreign Ministry suggested, with some foresight, that the article be 'reconsidered and elaborated in more detail' since it had been 'formulated in a rather incomplete manner' and required 'as comprehensive [an] analysis as possible'.[76] But Yugoslavia did not explain what parts of the rule she had found deficient, and the ILC does not appear to have even discussed her proposal.

In December 1959, the General Assembly decided to convene a conference at Vienna to consider, on the basis of the ILC work, the matter of 'diplomatic intercourse and immunities and to embody the results of its work in an international convention'.[77] Delegates from 81 States met at the Neue Hofburg in Vienna from 2 March to 14 April 1961,[78] with the Austrian academic and member of the ILC Alfred Verdross as President of the Conference.[79]

States had made several suggestions to the conference which concerned Draft Article 40, but none of them referred to the particular rule of non-interference.[80] It was therefore not discussed in the Committee of

[70] YILC 1957/I, 149, para 34 [Sandström]. The case concerned the introduction by Germany of a 'capital levy on property', from which she did however except nationals of those States that had formerly been at war with the Third Reich. According to Sandström, Sweden had 'intervened to complain of discrimination', and this representation 'had been taken in good part', ibid.

[71] See YILC 1958/II, 111–39.

[72] YILC 1958/II, 120. Italy suggested a reference to 'all diplomatic agents' and to 'members of the administrative or technical staff'.

[73] YILC 1958/II, 128. The VCDR dispensed with the grouping of articles into sections altogether.

[74] YILC 1958/I, 181, para 7 et seq; YILC 1958/I, 249, after para 23.

[75] YILC 1958/II, 104, art 40.

[76] YILC 1958/II, 139.

[77] GA Res 1450 (XIV) (1959).

[78] Vienna Conference, 'Final Act of the United Nations Conference on Diplomatic Intercourse and Immunities', Doc A/CONF.20/10, Vienna Conference Records Vol 2, 81, paras 2–5.

[79] ibid, para 6.

[80] For references to other parts of art 40, see Albania and Czechoslovakia, Vienna Conference Records Vol 2, 43; Japan, Vienna Conference Records Vol 2, 43.

the Whole,[81] and in plenary session, paragraph 1 was 'adopted without discussion'.[82]

It was one of the last items on the agenda. One day later, on 14 April 1961, the conference concluded its business and adopted the Vienna Convention on Diplomatic Relations—with 72 votes to none and with only one abstention.[83] It entered into force on 24 April 1964, when 22 States had become party to the treaty.[84] At the time of writing, the VCDR has 190 parties,[85] making it a treaty of nearly global applicability.

And the appeal of the ban on interference (which had now been enshrined in the second sentence of Article 41(1)), was to extend far beyond the confines of the VCDR. It seems remarkable that the rule, in precisely the same wording it had received in the ILC discussions, was adopted in subsequent instruments which deal with privileges and immunities—among them the Vienna Convention on Consular Relations (VCCR) (1963),[86] the Convention on Special Missions (CSM) (1969),[87] the Convention on the Representation of States in their Relations with International Organizations of a Universal Character (CRSIO) (1975),[88] the Agreement on the Privileges and Immunities of the Special Tribunal for the Law of the Sea (1997)[89] and the Agreement on the Privileges and Immunities of the International Criminal Court (2002).[90]

But this wide acceptance of the rule masks the fact that it received the most general wording, allowing for a wide range of interpretations. This undoubtedly contributed to its success, but it comes at a price: As a guideline on forms of diplomatic conduct which are acceptable under international law, its use is limited.

That gives room for further examination. But the contemplation both of the codification history and the history of diplomatic interference in State practice retains its value for this endeavour. What it shows is that the rule against interference is, at least in this general form, well established in customary international law; and had been so long before the adoption of the VCDR.

What is more: Incidents in which accusations of interference were made throughout the centuries show the sensitivities of receiving States in this

[81] *cf* Vienna Conference Records Vol 1, 210, 211, 35th Meeting of the Committee of the Whole, 29 March 1961.
[82] ibid, 38, 10th Plenary Meeting, 13 April 1961.
[83] ibid, 47, 12th Plenary Meeting, 14 April 1961.
[84] The USSR ratified the VCDR on 25 March 1964.
[85] UN Treaty Collection (Online), VCDR (as of 1 January 2015).
[86] VCCR art 55(1)2.
[87] CSM art 47(1)2.
[88] CRSIO Art 77(1) 2 (not yet in force).
[89] Privileges Agreement ITLOS (1997) art 19(2).
[90] Privileges Agreement ICC (2002) art 24.

regard; and as these sensitivities have, on the whole, retained their significance, they are helpful in delineating the fields in which interference is likely to be perceived even today. Part II of this book will return to this issue.

Most of all, however, the examination of interference by members of the ILC (and, to a lesser degree, by other commentators) has led to the identification of difficulties in its assessment—such as the problem of interference in external matters and the existence of competing interests in cases in which interference was alleged. These are difficulties which were not resolved in the VCDR or the subsequent instruments, yet—as will be seen in the subsequent examination—their importance remains undiminished, and their consideration is indispensable for a comprehensive understanding of the concept of diplomatic interference.

2

The Concept of Diplomatic Interference Today

1. A CONCEPT WITHOUT BORDERS?

TO BACKPACKERS AROUND the world, the Fiji archipelago conjures up images of palmy beaches and seductive lagoons. But it is also a State which has been victim to upheaval throughout much of her history: Since gaining independence in 1970, the island nation has seen no fewer than four coups d'état. Following the last one, led by Commodore Frank Bainimarama in 2006, Fiji also gained a prominent place in the history of diplomatic interference—as a State that displayed particular sensitivity with regard to behaviour she considered meddling in her internal affairs.

In each of the four years following that coup, Fiji expelled at least one diplomat amid charges of interference.[1] The underlying conduct varied widely. There were rather vague accusations of 'unfriendly acts',[2] of plotting against the head of State[3] and of spreading misleading information about the putsch.[4] The expulsion of one diplomat was seen as connected to his meetings with members of the former government,[5] that of another was linked to the denial of a visa to the son of a senior Fijian official.[6] When Michael Green, the High Commissioner of New Zealand,

[1] In 2007, the High Commissioner of New Zealand (Green, A.221); in 2008, the Acting High Commissioner of New Zealand (McDonald, A.240); in 2009, the Australian High Commissioner Batley and the New Zealand diplomat Cleaver (A.249); in 2010, the Acting Australian High Commissioner Roberts (A.258).

[2] 'Fiji Expels Australia's Top Diplomat' *Associated Press* (New York, 14 July 2010).

[3] P Ligaiula, 'Fiji Expels Top New Zealand Diplomat' *Associated Press* (New York, 14 June 2007).

[4] That was one of the charges made against the High Commissioner of New Zealand as well as US Ambassador Larry Dinger (who, however, was not expelled). P Ligaiula, 'US Envoy Criticized by Fiji Military Ruler' *Associated Press State & Local Wire* (New York, 11 July 2007).

[5] 'Fiji Expels New Zealand Diplomat' *BBC Online* (London, 14 June 2007).

[6] 'Fiji Denies Backdown Over McDonald Expulsion' *New Zealand Press Association* (Wellington, 23 December 2008).

was expelled in 2007, one of the reported reasons for that decision was that he had upstaged Commodore Bainimarama at a rugby match.[7]

If Fiji's position were indicative for the general attitude adopted by receiving States in these matters, the concept of diplomatic interference would cover a wide realm, and its boundaries would be difficult to determine. Nor is that a view which should be lightly dismissed.

The rule on non-interference as enshrined in the VCDR is certainly much more general than the corresponding provision in some of the historical draft codes,[8] and the Convention did not provide a definition of the offending behaviour. In the light of this, the question may be raised whether the drafters really intended to deviate from the literal meaning of the word—a meaning which would give interference considerable scope.

Two aspects in particular are apparent from the ordinary understanding of the term: Firstly, interference relates to the introduction of a new factor into existing structures—a factor which, from the point of view of the affected parties, will usually be seen as an outside influence. Secondly, the effects of that introduction will usually be considered in a negative way—as causing a disturbance to the existing state of affairs.

The aspect of disturbance is apparent even in the etymological roots of the word—the Old French *s'entreférire* and the Latin *ferire*. The meaning of the former has been rendered as 'to strike each other'; that of the latter as 'to strike, knock, smite, hit'.[9] Today, the Oxford English Dictionary (OED) offers, as lexical definitions of the verb 'to interfere', the phrases 'to take part in something, esp without having the right to do so' and '[t]o … take part, so as to affect some action'.[10]

The concept that derives from these considerations would conceivably extend to a multitude of activities. As such, it would sit well with the views of some writers on the topic whose illustrations of diplomatic interference indicate widely varying forms of behaviour: Sen mentions the '[r]endering of aid or active assistance … in favour of a party in the national elections';[11] Rousseau goes so far as to include the organisation of a secret police and the kidnapping of dissidents who live in the receiving

[7] 'We're Not Planning a Sporting Boycott' *The New Zealand Herald* (Auckland, 6 March 2008).

[8] See ch 1, at nn 46–49.

[9] OED, 'interfere (v)', Merriam-Webster, 'interfere', Menge, 295, 'ferio'.

[10] OED, 'interfere (v)', 4 b and 5. The other meanings offered in this entry are not relevant. The full list of meanings offered for 4 b is 'to meddle with; to interpose and take part in something, esp without having the right to do so; to intermeddle', and for 5 '[t]o interpose, take part, so as to affect some action; to intervene'. The French version of the rule, which, according to article 53 VCDR, is equally authentic, has the word 's'immiscer'. For 's'immiscer', LaRousse offers a definition which again highlights the aspect of disturbance ('intervenir dans les affaires d'autrui d'une maniere inopportune'), LaRousse, 's'immiscer'.

[11] Sen (1988), 90.

State.[12] Oppenheim refers to espionage,[13] the assassination of opponents and involvement in the preparation of terrorist acts.[14]

Not everybody agrees that the understanding of 'interference' as it appears in Article 41 VCDR, has to be as extensive as the ordinary meaning of the term suggests, and there have been attempts to impose restrictions on the concept. Such attempts are not without justification if the codification history indicates that a more limited understanding had indeed been intended, or if subsequent practice adopted by the international community has accepted certain limitations.

Deviations from the ordinary meaning have been discussed in particular in relation to two aspects: Firstly, in view of the subject matter to which the allegedly interfering conduct refers, and secondly, with regard to the authorship of the act. As far as the latter point is concerned, the theory has been advanced that diplomatic interference should cover only private conduct by diplomatic agents—as opposed to acts adopted on instructions of the sending State. With regard to the former aspect, the view has been offered that the subject matter of interference embraces internal affairs of the receiving State only—a perspective which raises the question whether a distinction between 'internal' and 'external' matters is always feasible.

2. INTERNAL VERSUS EXTERNAL INTERFERENCE

In December 2001, Daniel Bernard, the French Ambassador to the United Kingdom, caused one of the more memorable incidents in the history of diplomatic relations. During a dinner party hosted by Lord Black of Crossharbour (then owner of the *Daily Telegraph* newspaper), the Ambassador reportedly stated that the troubles in the world existed because of 'that shitty little country Israel' and wondered aloud why 'the world [should] be in danger of World War Three because of those people'.[15]

It is not surprising that these remarks triggered vivid reactions in Britain and other countries. Gwynneth Dunwoody, President of Labour's Friends of Israel group, called for the Ambassador's resignation, as did a spokesman for the Israeli Prime Minister, provided the remarks had

[12] Rousseau, 167.

[13] Oppenheim (1992), 1068.

[14] ibid, 1068, 1069. The case law of the ICJ does not reveal a narrower concept either—it dealt with the concept of diplomatic interference only in very general terms. See Introduction at nn 55–58 and ch 1, at n 33.

[15] B Amiel, 'Islamists Overplay their Hand' *Daily Telegraph* (London, 17 December 2001); E MacAskill, 'Israel Seeks Head of French Envoy' *The Guardian* (London, 20 December 2001).

indeed been made.[16] The French Ambassador insisted that his words had been distorted in the media, but did not issue a full denial.[17]

The case raises the question whether interference had been committed in the receiving State to begin with. The derogatory remarks did target a third State; and this allows for the view that the 'internal affairs' of the receiving State were not affected as such.

The rule of non-interference, as originally introduced in the ILC in 1957, would have prohibited meddling in foreign affairs of the receiving State as well.[18] But doubts about the wisdom of this were expressed at a very early stage. The British member Fitzmaurice took the view that the role of diplomatic agents was 'precisely, if not to interfere, at least to concern themselves with its foreign policy'[19] (which allows for the question whether a diplomat might not sometimes have to concern himself with domestic policy as well).[20] Fitzmaurice's concern was at any rate shared by some of his colleagues;[21] and the suggestion was accepted that the wording of the provision should be referred to the Drafting Committee.[22] The draft articles which the Commission adopted in that year, made reference only to the 'internal affairs' of the receiving State; the same phrase appears in the text of the VCDR. Prima facie, this version indicates a reduction of the scope of Article 41; and this is indeed an interpretation which is sometimes expressed in the literature.[23]

There is reason to believe that such an understanding of the rule of non-interference would depart from customary international law as it existed at the time. Of the various draft codes which were then in existence, only Fiore's code contained a provision which was similarly narrow.[24] Those of the American Institute of International Law[25] and the International Commission of American Jurists ban interference both in the internal and foreign 'political life' of the receiving State.[26] Bluntschli simply speaks of meddling in the 'affaires du pays',[27] whereas Phillimore calls on diplomatic agents to 'consider the welfare of the country to which they are sent'.[28] The 1928 Havana Convention on Diplomatic Officers bans participation 'in the domestic or foreign politics' of the receiving State.[29]

16 MacAskill, ibid.
17 '"Anti-Semitic" French Envoy Under Fire' *BBC Online* (London, 20 December 2001).
18 See B.6.
19 YILC (Yearbook of the International Law Commission) 1957/I, 145, para 76 [Fitzmaurice].
20 This issue is discussed in more detail in ch 3 (see, in particular, sections 1.4 and 2).
21 YILC 1957/I, 146, para 7 [Tunkin].
22 *cf* YILC 1957/I, 149, para 42 [Padilla Nervo] and 150, para 52 [Amado].
23 Denza, 465; Richtsteig, 98.
24 Annex B.2, para 482.
25 Annex B.3, art 16.
26 Annex B.4, art 16.
27 Annex B.1, para 225.
28 Phillimore, 180, para 34.
29 Havana Convention on Diplomatic Officers (1928), art 12.

State practice at that time supported the view that States would not tolerate meddling in foreign affairs either. A 1940 case may serve as an illustration: In that year, Jacob Suritz, the Soviet Ambassador to France, was expelled after he had sent a telegram *en clair* (uncoded) to Joseph Stalin, congratulating him on foiling the plans of 'Anglo-French warmongers' and on the aggressive Soviet policy concerning Finland.[30] In this instance too, the claim could have been advanced that the diplomatic message had concerned 'merely' foreign affairs. France's reaction however was decidedly negative: After the message was initially held up by the censors, it was eventually delivered by the French *chargé d'affaires* in Moscow himself, along with a call for the withdrawal of the Soviet Ambassador.[31]

But the case highlights a fundamental problem in this field: Some issues of 'foreign policy' are considered by receiving States to lie squarely within their own domain. It is a difficulty which was recognised by some ILC members: Liang for one emphasised that,

> [a]s for the reference to 'domestic or foreign politics', logically speaking the formulation and directing of the foreign policy of a State came within the meaning of 'matters within its domestic jurisdiction'.[32]

The very character of the subject with which the diplomat is dealing, can therefore impair the clarity of the distinction. At the very least, overlaps are difficult to avoid; and this invites the consideration of a range of situations in which a prima facie external matter may have repercussions on the internal affairs of the receiving State.

First of all, there is reason to believe that Liang's view finds support in modern State practice. The shaping of foreign policy, being done by organs of the receiving State, is regularly understood by the diplomat's hosts as falling within their exclusive domain.

A 1983 incident offers an illustration. The South African Ambassador to Australia, Worrall, reportedly referred to the Australian policy towards his State as 'confrontational, prescriptive and intrusive'. The Australian foreign minister considered these remarks to exceed the limits of propriety. On the other hand, his South African counterpart pointed out that the

[30] See Oppenheim (1967), 817, fn 1; 'France: Allies v Soviets' *Time* (New York, 8 April 1940); 'France And The Soviet' *The Times* (London, 28 March 1940).

[31] For earlier instances, see, eg, the Marcoleta case (1906): Demand of recall of the Nicaraguan Minister to the USA, where the object of interference was the construction of an interoceanic canal, Moore, 497–99. See also *Foreign Service Regulations of the United States*, ch I, s 15, which simply banned participation in 'political matters of the country to which [officers of the Foreign Service] are accredited or assigned'. For a case after the adoption of the VCDR, in which an ambassador likewise made comments on matters of foreign affairs, see A.157 (case of Wu Dawei).

[32] YILC 1957/I, 147, para 14 [Liang].

Ambassador had only discussed foreign policy and not touched upon Australian domestic policy at all.[33]

But the reactions of other States in situations of this kind support the Australian view and demonstrate that there is a tendency to perceive the underlying conduct as unacceptable.[34] Nor is this position altogether difficult to understand. By referring to the work of authorities to whom the receiving State entrusts the shaping of foreign policy, the message of the diplomatic agent touches upon a significant aspect of internal affairs as well.[35]

Secondly, situations in which a diplomat makes disparaging remarks about a third State—as had reportedly happened in the Bernard case[36]—warrant similar considerations. An earlier example was provided in 1983, when the Libyan People's Bureau in Australia made available copies of a letter in which Colonel Gaddafi had called the US President Reagan a 'new world Hitler'. The letter provoked sharp criticism by the Australian Foreign Ministry, and the Australian Prime Minister, to whom the message was addressed, refused to accept it.[37]

In the literature, Richtsteig has expressed the opinion that offensive comments of this kind do in fact constitute interference in the 'internal affairs' of the receiving State since they impair the receiving State's relations with the third State.[38] But relations between two States are of course the typical example of 'foreign affairs', and there is therefore reason to be more discerning about the precise aspect that turns diplomatic conduct in this scenario into interference in internal matters.

The reason why internal matters are involved lies in the fact that the diplomatic agent forces the hand of the receiving State. Silence in the light of negative comments of this kind conveys the appearance that the host accepts the diplomatic message. Where it was previously free to adopt its own decisions in its relations with the third State, it now has little choice but to react.[39]

[33] 'Pik Botha's Response' BBC Summary (London, 30 March 1983).

[34] In 1977 for instance, the Chilean Ambassador to France reportedly voiced his regret over the fact that the French President had received the widow of Salvador Allende. The French Foreign Minister however expressed the opinion that these remarks did not conform to the customs and the duty of reserve incumbent upon ambassadors. Salmon (1996), 132; *AFDI*, 'Pratique française' (1977), 1071.

[35] *cf* also Dembinski, 232.

[36] See above, at n 15.

[37] *Aust YBIL*, 'Diplomatic and Consular Relations' (1981–1983), 505, 506. See also the 1961 case of the Polish Ambassador to the United States (ch 4, at n 70 and A.1). No official State reaction was made public in the Bernard case; but in the following year, he was posted to Algeria—a move which, in the words of one observer, was 'certainly not a promotion', 'New French Ambassador's Remarks' *The Forward* (New York, 5 September 2003); 'Diplomat Hurt by Anti-Israel Remark' *National Post* (Toronto, 4 May 2004).

[38] Richtsteig, 23.

[39] See Salmon (1996), 135, para 207.

Thirdly, the object of the diplomatic message may, because of its very nature, contain internal and external aspects.[40] A diplomatic agent might, for example, refer to a territory whose sovereignty is disputed between the receiving State and a third State;[41] or he might comment on the relationship between the receiving State and an international organisation. That too may appear to be a matter of external affairs which should not be covered by the wording of Article 41. But it is here that the overlap between foreign policies and their formulation by State organs becomes particularly clear. When, for instance, Dan Coats in 2001, at his confirmation hearing for the post of US Ambassador to Germany, indicated that his prospective hosts needed to allocate more resources to NATO, his remarks met with distinctive criticism by the German side which considered the matter 'an internal German issue'.[42] There can indeed be little doubt that budgetary issues would ordinarily be considered to fall within the internal affairs of the receiving State.

If these cases appear to support Liang's position in the ILC, it should also be noted that his concerns were shared by other members of the Commission. Padilla Nervo agreed that it was 'not always easy' to tell external policy apart from 'matters of domestic concern'.[43] Special Rapporteur Sandström suggested that the wording of Article 12 of the Havana Convention on Diplomatic Officers (which included a ban on participation in foreign politics) be used; and when, at the end of the 412th meeting, it was decided to leave the matter to the Drafting Committee, the Brazilian member Amado likewise requested the Committee to keep in mind the wording of that Article of the Havana Convention—'since that appeared to meet the point precisely'.[44]

In the discussions of the commentary on the Draft Article on non-interference, García Amador remarked that 'the concept of "internal affairs" in the article had already been interpreted by the Secretary as covering both domestic and foreign politics'.[45] There arose no opposition to this interpretation, and two members of the ILC (Scelle and Tunkin) expressed clear support for this view.[46] Tunkin added that the words 'internal order' (in the first draft of the article)[47] had to be understood not as indicating a territorial notion, but in the meaning which Article 2(7) of

[40] *cf* on this problem Asante, 261.

[41] See A.188.

[42] D Lindsey, 'US Ambassador Starts off on Stern Foot' *Christian Science Monitor* (Boston MA, 6 August 2001).

[43] YILC 1957/I, 149, para 42 [Padilla Nervo].

[44] YILC 1957/I, 149, para 40 [Sandström]; YILC 1957/I, 150, para 52 [Amado].

[45] YILC 1957/I, 220, para 76 [García Amador].

[46] YILC 1957/I, 220, para 78 [Tunkin]; YILC 1957/I, 220, para 79 [Scelle].

[47] B.6, para 55.

the UN Charter had adopted.[48] There however, reference had been made to 'matters ... within the domestic jurisdiction' of the State concerned.

This interpretation gives the phrase 'internal affairs' a rather extensive understanding; but in light of the considerations made above and corresponding State practice, it seems a preferable approach. As long as the object of the message concerns an aspect which falls within the sovereign rights of the receiving State, it affects its 'domestic jurisdiction', and can therefore not be said to be withdrawn from the concept of interference which Article 41 addresses.

That does not mean that the differentiation between internal and external matters is entirely without value. The finding in particular that a given subject involves interests of the sending State may indicate that the diplomatic agent had a strong basis for conduct which his hosts considered interference.[49]

But at this stage, the conclusion has to be that the attempt to narrow down the concept of interference through the addition of the words 'internal affairs' has not been entirely successful. The allegation that purely external affairs were concerned, is considerably weakened as soon as the receiving State can show that it had an interest in the matter, which is recognised under international law. Purely external matters might exist—if, for instance, the diplomatic message referred to debates between political parties in the sending State on topics which bear no relation at all to the receiving State. At the same time, it is rare for a receiving State to claim, in situations of this kind, that a violation of the rule of non-interference had taken place.

3. PRIVATE VERSUS OFFICIAL CONDUCT

On 28 September 2001, Antonio Bandini, the Italian Ambassador to Eritrea, was expelled—a decision which came hours after he had, as leader of a delegation of representatives of the European Union, delivered a *démarche* to the Eritrean government, which criticised human rights violations committed by that State.[50] Given those circumstances, it is not surprising that observers saw a link between the two events. Eritrea herself denied any such connection, and while she accused Bandini of interference in the country's internal affairs, the allegation was also made that the expulsion had been a 'personal matter'.[51]

This distinction between private and official conduct is at the heart of the second approach that has been suggested to narrow down the concept

48 YILC 1957/I, 220, para 78 [Tunkin], and see YILC 1957/I, 146, para 8 [Tunkin].
49 See chs 3 and 4.
50 A Last, 'Eritrea Plays Down Diplomatic Row' *BBC Online* (London, 2 October 2001).
51 ibid.

of interference. In that regard, Denza expressed the view that the meaning of 'interference' is quite different from that of 'intervention': She would see the duty of non-intervention as an obligation incumbent on the sending State not to meddle with the affairs of the receiving State; whereas non-interference would be a duty relating to the 'personal activities' of the diplomat.[52] The ILC, according to Denza, had decided that the (State) duty of non-intervention was not suitable for inclusion in a draft on diplomatic law.[53]

Not everybody agrees. Hardy finds that Article 41 'embraces, beside private acts, activities which the sending State may sanction and, indeed, officially order the diplomat to execute …',[54] and the editors of Oppenheim, when discussing diplomatic interference in internal affairs, state that it does not matter 'whether an envoy acts thus on his own account, or on instructions from his home state. If he does so, he abuses his position …'.[55]

The record of the International Law Commission certainly leaves room for a more discerning interpretation.

It is true that some members of the Commission favoured a narrower view on interference. Liang for one thought it necessary to differentiate between official acts of diplomats and those carried out in a private capacity.[56] A principal concern was the possibility that a diplomat might be accused of interference when he had merely carried out instructions of the sending State[57]—situations in which the diplomat had been no more than the 'mouthpiece of his Government'.[58]

But there was no consensus on this point. Padilla Nervo, one of the co-sponsors of the amendment which introduced the rule against interference, agreed from the outset that 'non-intervention' was a duty that addressed States. But since this intervening conduct was carried out 'through the medium' of diplomatic agents, he favoured its inclusion in the draft.[59] The Egyptian member El-Erian stated during the first debate on the article that it was a duty incumbent on diplomatic agents, 'both in

[52] Denza, 464.

[53] ibid.

[54] Hardy, 17. Some authors do in fact use the terms 'intervention' and 'interference' interchangeably: *cf* Schröder, 619; Udombana, 56 (both in the context of general international law). Salmon uses the terms interchangeably in his 1993 article on self-determination, but makes a distinction in the 1996 edition of his book on diplomatic law; Salmon (1993), 268; Salmon (1996), 129, para 197. Others refer to 'diplomatic interference' when describing acts which would be carried out on instructions by the sending State; *cf* Clarke, 192; Sanei, 825. See also Hall (1924), 344 ('Interventions, whether armed or diplomatic…'); Zelniker, 1015 ('… the duty of states to refrain from interfering in the affairs of other states').

[55] Oppenheim (1992), 1068.

[56] YILC 1957/I, 147, para 12 [Liang].

[57] See eg, YILC 1957/I, 147, para 17 [Hsu]; YILC 1957/I, 149, para 39 [Scelle].

[58] YILC 1957/I, 147, para 22 [Fitzmaurice].

[59] YILC 1957/I, 143, para 58 [Padilla Nervo]. YILC 1957/I, 148, para 30 [García Amador].

an official and in a personal capacity' to respect the political independence of the host.[60]

The ILC revisited the article 20 days later when the commentary to the provision was under discussion. At that stage, the Draft Commentary explained that persons enjoying diplomatic privileges and immunities must, 'outside their functions', not interfere in the internal affairs of their host.[61] This limitation would have been very much in line with sentiments expressed by supporters of the narrower view. But the opponents stood their ground and called for the deletion of that particular phrase.[62] The ILC followed that suggestion.[63]

When the ILC debated the article again in 1958, the supporters of the narrower view were still members of the Commission. In view of the strong opinions which they had voiced when the rule was first introduced, one would have expected some objections or a request for clarification. But the article was accepted unanimously.[64]

What is more—when the Commentary to the draft articles was discussed, Liang, who had been a strong supporter of the narrower view,[65] now illustrated diplomatic interference with an example which would hardly ever be carried out as a private endeavour: Diplomats, he found, 'might interfere in the internal affairs of a State in much more serious ways as, for example, in fomenting civil war'.[66]

State practice at the time of the ILC discussions does not suggest a more restrictive meaning of interference either. The 1848 Bulwer incident[67] was a classic example of diplomatic involvement on instructions, and the Spanish Foreign Secretary was aware of the official nature of the conduct. It did not prevent him from characterising Bulwer's conduct as 'interference'.

The expulsion of Monsignore Montagnini from France in 1906 has to be seen in the same light. Following the severance of diplomatic relations between France and the Holy See, Montagnini was the only remaining diplomat at the nunciature. He was accused of having maintained contact with the French bishops and having passed on instructions to them from the Vatican. The official nature of his conduct did not prevent the making

[60] YILC 1957/I, 148, para 24 [El-Erian]. Other members of the ILC employed examples for their understanding of diplomatic interference which are rarely done as private initiatives in the absence of instructions: eg, the issuing of ultimata, YILC 1957/I, 145, para 80 [Bartos] the subsidising of political parties YILC 1957/I, 146, para 10 [Yokota].

[61] *cf* YILC 1957/I, 220, para 74 [García Amador] and YILC 1957/I, 220, para 80 [The Chairman].

[62] YILC 1957/I, 220, para 74 [García Amador] and *cf* YILC 1957/I, 220, para 77 [Tunkin].

[63] YILC 1957/I, 220, para 80, [The Chairman].

[64] YILC 1958/I, 181, para 7 [Chairman].

[65] See YILC 1957/I, 147, para 12 [Liang].

[66] YILC 1958/I, 250, para 27 [Liang].

[67] See ch 1, at n 19.

of personal accusations against him and the adoption of other negative reactions: Montagnini's rooms were searched; he himself was escorted to the border ('sans trop de ménagement', as Salmon puts it).[68]

Incidents arising after the adoption of the VCDR do not assist the restrictive view either. Diplomatic agents have certainly been subjected to personal charges of interference, while the receiving States made clear that the conduct in question had not been a private initiative. An example is the case of the Soviet Ambassador Vsevolod Sofinsky, expelled from New Zealand in January 1980 for giving money to the Socialist Unity Party.[69] On this occasion, the Prime Minister of New Zealand explicitly referred to the duty of diplomatic agents not to 'interfere in the domestic politics' of the receiving State,[70] but he also pointed out that there was 'no doubt the Socialist Unity Party has been financed by the Soviet government for some time'. Indeed, Mr Muldoon stated that it was the personal involvement of the Ambassador which showed 'that this is a matter of official Soviet policy'.[71]

In the majority of instances in which accusations of diplomatic interference have been raised, it is simply not clear whether the underlying conduct had been carried out on instructions or not—nor did it seem to matter much to the receiving State. The Bandini case of 2001 is in fact one of the very few instances in which a State made clear that it was referring to personal conduct only—but even there, the context suggests a different story.[72]

But if States are, by and large, indifferent to the question whether the offensive conduct had been carried out on instructions, why was this matter so important to some commentators on diplomatic affairs?

According to one view, interference on instructions simply did not have a place in a future convention on diplomatic law. ILC member Ago, for instance, accepted the general rule banning 'illicit intervention of a State in the affairs of other States', but thought that it did not belong in an instrument dealing with personal diplomatic duties only.[73]

[68] Salmon 1996, 130; 'Expulsion of a Papal Official' *The Times* (London, 12 December 1906).

[69] 'New Zealand Boots Soviet Ambassador' *Associated Press* (New York, 23 January 1980) and see A.48.

[70] ibid.

[71] 'Soviet Ambassador Expelled' *Facts on File* (New York, 8 February 1980). See also the 1996 case of Marilyn Meyers, the US *chargé d'affaires* in Burma (A.119). In this situation, the State Department clarified that Ms Meyers had indeed carried out her diplomatic tasks 'on instructions from Washington': 'US Rejects Charges of Meddling' *Agence France Presse* (Paris, 2 October 1996).

[72] See above, at nn 50–51.

[73] YILC 1957/I, 149, para 36 [Ago].

It is not a particularly convincing argument, and in the Commission, Ago's opinion was not even shared by all supporters of the narrower view.[74] As a treaty among States, the Convention does of course address the duties of States—it refers to numerous obligations of both the receiving and the sending State, ranging from the granting of inviolability and immunity[75] to the duty to recall unwelcome members of the diplomatic staff.[76] And since the sending State already has conventional obligations relating to the appointment of diplomatic agents,[77] there is no good reason why it should not also have conventional duties regarding their conduct.

Another opinion, which was expressed in the ILC, refers to the subordinate role of diplomatic agents in cases of this kind. In the words of the Chinese member Shuhsi Hsu, a diplomat who was under a duty to engage in conduct which was really an act of State 'could not be blamed' for his behaviour.

That view may have stronger reasons on its side. It does at any rate correspond to a very real concern: The danger that the diplomat has to face the consequences which his master's message provoked. The Bandini incident certainly invites the suspicion that the phenomenon of the diplomatic whipping boy has not disappeared in modern international relations.

But Hsu's opinion is not without difficulties either.

First of all, the limitation of the concept of interference to private conduct does not resolve the underlying problem. Given the fact that the receiving State can still declare any member of the diplomatic staff persona non grata—'at any time and without having to explain its decision',[78] the protection of the diplomatic messenger in these situations remains rather weak.

It may in fact be more tempting for a receiving State to claim that private conduct had triggered the expulsion, instead of the offensive official act. By so doing, the receiving State avoids a direct attack on the adopted policy of the sending State, but the latter will usually understand the real reason for the negative sanction. That was arguably the case in the Bandini incident, but also in various instances of expulsion of diplomats from the territory of Fiji, to which reference has been made above.[79]

Secondly, it is difficult to understand why diplomatic agents should lack personal responsibility for any conduct committed on instructions.

[74] Liang for instance had already made clear that the Convention would 'define the rights and duties of States', YILC 1957/I, 147, para 12 [Liang].

[75] See eg, VCDR art 29 (2) and art 31.

[76] VCDR art 9(1)2.

[77] See VCDR art 10(1).

[78] VCDR art 9(1)1.

[79] When the last of these diplomats was expelled—Sarah Roberts, the Australian acting High Commissioner, in 2010—*Associated Press* pointed out that Australia and New Zealand had been Bainimarama's 'loudest international critics and have pressured the leader to restore democracy', 'Fiji Expels Australia's Top Diplomat', n 2.

That view certainly had supporters in the ILC: Liang for one claimed that a diplomat in such a situation was '… in the same position as a military or naval officer who had to carry out the orders of his superiors and could not use his discretion'.[80] Coming eleven years after the conclusion of the main Nuremberg War Crimes Trial,[81] this was a somewhat surprising remark.

And the analogy fails in several regards. The training received by both professions shows fundamental differences: Instruction in international law may well be expected to be part of diplomatic education,[82] but it cannot be assumed to be present in the training of a soldier and may justify a heavier burden of responsibility on the part of the former. The situational context in which both professions operate differs as well: A soldier's life and that of his comrades may depend on the ability to follow orders in the heat of battle—diplomats on the other hand are typically required to use their own discretion, as only they can fully comprehend all the circumstances of the current position. If, in light of all of this, a soldier is still expected not to react to orders 'like a piece of machinery',[83] then this sentiment must apply *a fortiori* to the diplomatic representative of a sending State.

Thirdly, it is not always easy to distinguish between 'private' and 'official' conduct by diplomatic agents. Some parts of the Vienna Convention call expressly for a distinction along these lines, but even in those cases, it has been difficult to apply this division in practice.[84] In the field of diplomatic interference, the question arises whether such a distinction is ever possible.

One reason for that lies in the fact that the personal conduct of a diplomat can play a role even in cases of alleged State intervention.[85] An agent who is eager to make his involvement in affairs of the receiving State a personal affair, certainly differs from those of his colleagues who, in Fitzmaurice's words, are merely 'mouthpiece[s]' of their governments.[86]

[80] YILC 1957/I, 147, para 12 [Liang]. See also YILC 1957/I, 147, para 22 [Fitzmaurice] and YILC 1957/I, 149, para 38 [Tunkin].

[81] See Nuremberg Charter art 8 on the superior orders defence.

[82] On the need for such instruction see also Conclusion, after n 30.

[83] *Einsatzgruppen Case*, 470.

[84] One may recall incidents which have arisen in relation to members of the service staff who, if not nationals or residents of the receiving State, enjoy immunity 'in respect of acts performed in the course of their duties', VCDR, art 37(3). The distinction between acts 'in the course of their duties' and acts outside them has on occasion be difficult, especially where criminal or criminally negligent behaviour was concerned. See for two very different cases, *Ministère Public and Republic of Mali v Keita*, at 412 (decided against commission in the course of duties) and the decision by the Supreme Court of the Netherlands in *Public Prosecutor v A.d.S.F.* (accepting the possibility of certain offences being committed in performance of duties).

[85] Cf YILC 1957/I, 149, para 38 [Tunkin].

[86] YILC 1957/I, 147, para 22 [Fitzmaurice]. The conduct of the US Ambassador in Argentina in the run-up to presidential elections in that country in 1946 furnishes an example, see ch 6, at n 1.

On the other hand, it is also possible that conduct which is intended to be entirely private in nature, takes on an official character through the subsequent conduct of others. The Bernard incident of 2001 for example,[87] occurred in the course of a private dinner party, and the Ambassador himself insisted on the private nature of the remarks.[88] Had it not made its way to the pages of the *Telegraph*, the conduct might well have been perceived by Bernard's audience as no more than entirely private musings. As it was, it triggered reactions by the office of the Israeli Prime Minister which referred to it as conduct by a 'representative of the French government'[89] as well as an official response by the spokesman of the French embassy.[90] The official nature of diplomatic behaviour, it appears, may depend on factors which lie outside the diplomat's control; and this will inevitably attract doubts even in cases in which the diplomatic agent had gone to great lengths to stress the private nature of his actions.

That is true even in the Sackville case,[91] which supporters of the narrower view in the ILC employed as an example of private interference.[92] Sackville had indeed marked his letter 'Private', and Osgoodby had induced him to believe that their correspondence would remain confidential.[93] But the case raises questions once Sackville's rationale for writing the letter is subjected to scrutiny.

In seeking advice on the forthcoming elections, Osgoodby had been skillful enough to refer to the interests of his 'mother land' (Britain), the sometimes narrow outcome of presidential elections, and the possibility that 'a mere handful of our naturalized countrymen can turn [the election] either way' in California. He also stated that a positive opinion on Cleveland would enable him 'to assure many of our countrymen that they would do England a service by voting for Cleveland'.[94]

Given these circumstances, Sackville's correspondence assumes a somewhat different shape. This was not a private communication a diplomat may have sent to a personal friend on a matter of common interest. Sackville's letter appears to have been an act adopted with a view to protecting the interests of the sending State—a function which the Vienna

[87] See above, at n 15.

[88] Bernard expressed his outrage about the fact 'that a private discussion found its way into the media', *BBC Online*, '"Anti-Semitic" French Envoy under Fire' (London, 20 December 2001).

[89] E MacAskill, 'Israel Seeks Head of French Envoy' *The Guardian* (London, 20 December 2001).

[90] ibid.

[91] See ch 1, at n 1.

[92] YILC 1957/I, 147, para 17 [Hsu]. See also YILC 1957/I, 147, para 15 [Liang], following a contribution in which he stated that the rule on non-interference should refer to private acts only, YILC 1957/I, 147, para 12 [Liang], YILC 1957/I, 147, para 22 [Fitzmaurice].

[93] See ch 1, at n 4.

[94] Hinckley, at 361.

Convention today recognises in Article 3(1)(b). Nor was it necessary for Salisbury or anybody else to give Sackville express orders to that effect. Certain functions are so closely wedded to the diplomatic office that they do not require mention—it would be strange indeed if permanent envoys were sent out without the underlying understanding that it is one of their tasks to look after the interests of the sending State.

In other words: The position of a diplomat involves certain implied instructions (often corresponding to the functions mentioned today in Article 3 VCDR).[95] But if that is the case, the distinction between 'private' and 'official' conduct can become an impossible task. The problem is particularly apparent where the function of representation is concerned—a task which must be presumed to be at the very core of the diplomatic office. But the reach of 'representation' can be so wide that it touches upon aspects of life which diplomats themselves consider quite private.

A case arising in 1895 illustrates the difficulty. In that year, the Hawaiian Minister to the United States, Thurston, was accused of providing information to American newspapers, which reflected negatively on the conduct of the American and British representatives in Hawaii.[96] While Thurston admitted that he had allowed the employee of a press association to copy private letters he had received, he insisted that he had not expressed 'his official or personal views, but … [had shown] the state of feeling in Honolulu'.[97] It was an argument which did not find favour with the receiving State: US Secretary of State Gresham referred back to the general function of representation. 'I asked him', said Gresham, 'if he thought he could with propriety, as the representative of a foreign government at this capital, furnish newspapers with such matter'.[98]

It is, then, difficult to support the view that diplomatic interference must be restricted to private conduct only. Neither is that position well supported by the drafting history, nor does the argument of the 'blameless diplomat' provide a sufficiently good reason for any such limitation. At times, a distinction between private and official conduct might simply not be feasible.

But more important than these considerations is the fact that customary law in no way indicates a restriction along these lines. The instances of State practice which have been reviewed above rather point in the opposite direction.[99] It is the conduct itself that carries significance for receiving

[95] These functions can be said to reflect, at least to a certain degree, customary international law. *cf* Denza, 35, on the recognition of the core functions of the mission in the last 400 years.

[96] The case according to Moore, 503–07, Hyde, 736.

[97] Moore, 506.

[98] ibid. See, for a more recent case in this context, A.180.

[99] See above, at n 69.

States—the question whether it had been adopted on instructions of the sending State or not, does in general not matter for their assessment of diplomatic interference.[100]

4. THE CONCEPT OF INTERFERENCE TODAY

The understanding of interference that emerges from these considerations still embraces a multitude of scenarios and can only be described as extensive.

But if past attempts to limit the scope of interference can, for the reasons outlined above, not be said to have been successful, there is one approach yet which appears altogether more persuasive. It is a view suggested, among others, by Jean Salmon. To him, the distinction between 'non-intervention' and 'non-interference' still carries significance, but it would not run along the lines of official duty versus private act. He rather differentiates between duties owed by the State and duties owed by the diplomat, and he acknowledges the existence of overlaps between the two. If a diplomat became an agent of State intervention (Salmon uses the examples of fostering civil war or giving military or financial support to an armed opposition), he would also violate 'his personal duty as a member of the mission'.[101] It is then the person of the diplomat—not the private capacity in which he performs his act—which triggers the applicability of Article 41; and this personal duty is wider than that of the sending State.[102] In a similar vein, Verdross and Simma express the view that the rule of non-interference as enshrined in Article 41(1) goes 'much further' than the prohibition of intervention contained in the UN Charter.[103]

The advantage of this view is that it weeds out all those incidents in which the diplomatic agent has faced negative sanctions while his own conduct was not even remotely involved—situations, for instance, which are entirely based on critical comments made by the government of the

[100] This position is further supported by those cases in which receiving States acted preventively to ban diplomatic interference, without referring to the question whether such interference would be carried out on instructions. In 2001 for instance, Sri Lanka warned diplomatic agents that statements on the current situation in Sri Lanka would amount to interference and made express reference to art 41 of the Vienna Convention. It did not distinguish between statements made on instructions and statements made as a private initiative. N Silva, 'UN Envoy Wants CJ to Step Aside' *Sunday Times* (Sri Lanka, 19 August 2001). See also Salmon (1976), 41, on the warning issued by Mobutu (President of Zaire) concerning 'any form' ('de quelque manière que ce soit') of interference (paraphrasing by Salmon).

[101] '... il violera aussi son obligation personelle comme membre de la mission', Salmon (1996), 129, para 197.

[102] ibid, 129, para 197.

[103] Verdross and Simma, 567, para 889. They, too, did not make a distinction between official and private acts of the diplomatic agent. Their dividing line between acts by diplomatic agents and State intervention appears to have been determined by the subject matter.

sending State, and in which the receiving State resorted to expulsions to show its displeasure.

It is, moreover, a view which corresponds well to the textual meaning of Article 41(1), which, while addressing the beneficiaries of diplomatic immunities as the bearers of the duty, does not distinguish between official or private conduct. Most of all, it is a view which finds support in State practice. Receiving States, in whose favour the provision exists, require protection from interference by diplomatic agents. The question whether the interfering agent acted on instructions or not, is of secondary importance.

If the various views considered in this chapter are taken into account, it is possible to obtain an understanding of interference which can be employed as the basis for further deliberation. From that perspective, interference under Article 41 is conduct, adopted by a beneficiary of diplomatic privileges and immunities, which introduces an outside element into internal matters of the receiving State, and, by so doing, causes a disturbance.

The boundaries of this definition are still relatively wide; but that does not need to be a disadvantage. A certain flexibility must attach to the concept of interference, if it is to be applied to the wide range of situations in which diplomatic conduct clashes with matters that fall within the jurisdiction of the receiving State. And only if these situations are incorporated, can the protective reach of Article 41(1) be said to be adequately addressed.

At the same time, the fulfilment of the conceptual conditions of Article 41 can be only a first step in the assessment of diplomatic conduct as unlawful interference. The rule against interference, as enshrined in that article, is framed for the benefit of receiving States. An examination which terminates at this stage, would thus ignore the fact that there may be interests which aid the position of the diplomatic agent, and that these interests can sometimes be based on legal foundations which are as strong as those which underlie the rule of Article 41.

These are issues which require more detailed analysis—as does the evaluation of the co-existence of such divergent interests. It is only at the end of a comprehensive analysis of this kind that the question can be answered whether a diplomatic agent has engaged in interference which must be considered in violation of the rules of international law.

> … frankly, if you're a diplomat and you haven't been accused a few times in your career of, you know, interfering in someone else's affairs, you're probably not doing your job very well.
>
> Christopher Hill, US Ambassador to Iraq (2010)[1]

3

Diplomatic Interference and Competing Interests

IN MANY CASES of alleged interference, the sending State does not put up a legal defence. That does not mean that no such defence exists; a State's reluctance to discuss the relevant situation can have its basis in entirely political reasons.[2] And yet there are situations in which sending States insist that their diplomats did not deserve charges of interference, because of certain circumstances which had to be taken into account. There are two scenarios in particular in which States have from time to time defended their diplomats without denying their activities. The first arises when the sending State considers the conduct to fall within ordinary diplomatic functions: The envoy was 'merely doing his job'. The second situation concerns diplomatic engagement in human rights: In these cases, it may be the overly sensitive attitude of the receiving State that is to blame, or the envoy has, once again, only performed tasks which other members of the international community would find entirely acceptable.

1. DIPLOMATIC INTERFERENCE AND DIPLOMATIC FUNCTIONS

In 2009, Iran arrested several employees of the British and the French embassies in Tehran whom she accused of involvement in the unrest that had followed elections in June of that year.[3] A spokesman for the Iranian Foreign Ministry pointed out that the maintenance of diplomatic ties at ambassadorial level 'should mean having good relations and without

[1] 'United States Institute of Peace' *Federal News Service* (Washington DC, 17 February 2010).
[2] See ch 1, at n 27.
[3] J Tapsfield, 'UK Embassy Staff Arrested' *Belfast Telegraph* (Belfast, 29 June 2009).

interference in domestic affairs. But unfortunately in recent events this interference was totally clear'.[4]

In this instance, the sending State did put up a defence of the diplomatic conduct at issue: The British Foreign Office went to some length to outline tasks which in its view were recognised by international law.

> Travel by diplomats, meeting politicians and journalists, encouraging educational links, understanding the economy, showing an interest in what will happen in elections and so on are normal activities in every country, as any experienced diplomat knows. These sorts of activities are recognised as legitimate in the Vienna Convention on Diplomatic Relations, to which both the UK and Iran are parties.[5]

Countering Article 41 with another norm of the Convention seems a powerful way of rebutting a charge of interference; but it presupposes that the conduct falls under the rule in question. Where the tasks of a diplomatic agent are concerned, that rule is Article 3 VCDR, which codifies the functions of the diplomatic mission. It is not an exhaustive list—additional functions may be added through customary international law or through particular agreement between sending and receiving State.

But Article 3 provides the clearest indication of functions on which the international community has been able to reach consensus. The five functions—representation, protection of interests, negotiation, observation and the promotion of friendly relations—are to a significant degree based on pre-existing customary law.[6] Each of them presents a typical example of a permissive norm—a norm which allows the diplomatic agent to take an active role within the receiving State. As such, each also carries the potential of a clash with the restrictive norm of Article 41(1), which may, in the same situation, limit the reach of diplomatic conduct.

1.1. Representation

At the 1961 Conference, Monsignore Casaroli (Holy See) offered an insight into the interplay of the various diplomatic functions: Representation in his view was 'the fundamental [function]; the other four were only adjuncts to it'.[7] Representation—today enshrined in Article 3(1)(a) of the Convention—might indeed be the one task that characterises the entire diplomatic office; but it is at the same time a general concept whose boundaries are difficult to define.

[4] *BBC Monitoring Middle East—Political*, 'Iran TV Airs Discussion' (London, 9 August 2009).

[5] C Woodhouse, '"Velvet Revolution" Plan Denied' *Press Association* (London, 11 August 2009).

[6] See Denza, 35.

[7] Vienna Conference Records Vol 1, 58, para 26.

Its Latin etymon *repraesentare* includes the meanings 'to present in person' and 'to make present to the mind',[8] which to a degree survive in the modern task. Glahn for instance, when discussing the function of representation, points out that diplomats represent 'the policies' of their governments to the receiving state;[9] Sen writes that the diplomat represents the sending State by speaking for his government.[10]

But the function of representation need not involve a verbal message. For the receiving State, it will often be possible to infer the fulfilment of the representative task from conduct: The very presence of a diplomat at a particular event—and even his absence—may serve that purpose. In the history of diplomatic relations, a particularly clear illustration was provided in 1851, after the coup d'état of Louis Napoleon (later Napoleon III) in France. Louis Napoleon had already been President of the French Republic before assuming dictatorial powers, and it had been the custom of his government to hold weekly receptions in the presence of diplomatic agents. After the coup, the American and Swiss representatives decided not to attend; the presence of the others was seen, in the words of the American Minister Rives, as 'adhesion to the patriotic & courageous measures which [have] saved France'.[11]

Presenting the sending State's position can easily lead to conduct which in the eyes of the receiving State constitutes 'meddling' in its own affairs. Such accusations arise in particular when the policy in question is discussed not only behind the closed doors of the Foreign Ministry, but in a public forum. These instances do of course touch upon a particular sensitivity on the part of the host government if the diplomatic remarks imply criticism of the latter.

In February 2006 for instance, Belarus accused Czech diplomats of interference in its internal affairs and of trying to 'subvert the order in the country' by distributing propaganda leaflets.[12] The Czech Foreign Minister denied the charges and stated that the material to which the authorities of the receiving State had referred, had been a report on Belarus by the UN Human Rights Commission.[13] It was not disputed that the diplomats, by so doing, sent out a message which conveyed the position of their masters: The Czech republic had allocated four million crowns to the support of democracy in Belarus, had used part of the money for the printing

[8] Oxford English Dictionary (OED), 'represent, v.1, etymology'.

[9] Glahn (1992), 517.

[10] Sen (1988), 56. Similarly Oppenheim (1967), 785, with regard to the functions of an ambassador. See however Dembinski, 39, 40 for a wider approach to this function.

[11] Shewmaker et al, 182.

[12] *BBC Monitoring Europe—Political*, 'Czech Minister Rejects Belarusia's Allegation' (London, 23 February 2006). Paraphrasing by CTK.

[13] 'Czechs Provide 4 Million Crowns' *CTK National News Wire* (Prague, 23 February 2006).

of a booklet on human rights in that State[14] and had become one of the strongest critics of the Lukashenko regime.[15]

But the function of representation cannot be adequately fulfilled if a diplomat is denied the opportunity of addressing the public. Green states in that regard that a diplomat 'must be permitted to explain publicly the views of his government when opportunity to do so arises'[16] and refers, by way of example, to diplomats who represent a belligerent State in a neutral country or a neutral State in a belligerent country—situations in which the need for the communication of the sending State's stance to the public at large is particularly apparent.

In general, receiving States do not deny the existence of the function of representation or the fact that diplomats are entitled to adopt certain acts to fulfil this task. But they may conclude that the conduct in question did not in fact fall within the function on which the diplomat wished to rely.

One example was provided by an event in Sri Lanka in August 2001. By that time, the political situation in that State had become fraught with difficulties: In addition to the ongoing conflict with the Tamil Tigers, the government had dissolved Parliament to avoid a defeat,[17] and there had been international calls for the Chief Justice to step down from his post until an impeachment motion against him could be decided.[18] In these circumstances, the Foreign Ministry of Sri Lanka issued a note to foreign diplomats, stating that public remarks on the current situation in the receiving State might constitute interference and referring in that regard to Article 41 of the Vienna Convention.

But the note also made clear that diplomats wishing to make representations could do so through the Ministry of Foreign Affairs or with the knowledge of the latter.[19] This implies a general acceptance of the task of representation, but a refusal to consider 'public statements' as falling within acceptable diplomatic conduct. By so doing, Sri Lanka did in fact suggest a way of resolving the meeting between diplomatic functions and the rule of non-interference by limiting the range of permitted diplomatic conduct—a point which will be discussed in more detail later.[20]

1.2. Protection of Interests

The protective function to which the Vienna Convention makes reference in Article 3(1)(b), embraces two aspects: The protection of interests of the

[14] ibid.
[15] 'Czech Embassy in Minsk' *CTK National News Wire* (Prague, 5 February 2008).
[16] Green, 148; see also Sen (1988), 58; Strupp and Schlochauer, 365.
[17] A Jayasinghe, 'US Intervention gets Cold Shoulder' *Agence France Presse* (Paris, 24 August 2001).
[18] N Silva, 'UN Envoy wants CJ to Step Aside' *Sunday Times* (Sri Lanka, 19 August 2001).
[19] ibid.
[20] See ch 4, especially after n 139.

sending State abroad, and the protection of interests of its nationals.[21] For the context of interference, this rule is of particular importance: Cases have arisen in which diplomats expressly referred to this function or in which the circumstances made clear that this task had been at the root of their conduct.

The case of Laurence Silberman, the American ambassador to Yugoslavia in the 1970s, illustrates the emerging conflict between the protection of interests of nationals of the sending State and the duty of non-interference. Silberman had pushed for the release of Laszlo Toth, a naturalised American whom Yugoslavia considered one of her citizens.[22] The ambassador was ultimately successful, but his efforts resulted in a public rebuke by President Tito, who accused him of meddling.[23]

The Silberman case highlights one of the difficulties that can arise where this alternative of the function is concerned—the question of the nationality of the people who are at the centre of the envoy's concern. The issue becomes relevant when diplomats are moved to make comments about the situation of an ethnic group in the receiving State which occupies a significant position in the sending State as well.

Hans-Joachim Vergau for instance, the German Ambassador to Turkey in 1998, was accused by a representative of the Turkish government of interference in that country's internal affairs, after he had stated that the situation relating to the Kurds was of concern not only to Turkey, but to Germany as well.[24] Vergau may well have felt entitled to this statement because of the significant Kurdish population in the sending State; but as the persons in questions lacked German nationality, he could not have raised this alternative of Article 3(1)(b) as a basis for his action.[25]

Matters are even more complicated when the persons whose interests are protected, possess the nationality of both the sending and the receiving State. In these instances, the question arises whether a diplomat can make representations in order to protect the interests of the individuals concerned.

Cases of this kind have to be distinguished from the concept of 'diplomatic protection' in the narrow sense—a concept which refers to situations

[21] The words 'within the limits permitted by international law', which that provision contains, do not constitute a significant addition to the function as such. As Do Nascimento e Silva points out, it is an insertion *ex abundante cautela*, as 'every provision' of the Vienna Convention has to be performed within the limits of international law anyway, Do Nascimento e Silva (1972), 63.

[22] 'Jailed American Freed' *Facts on File* (New York, 31 July 1976).

[23] B Boskovic, '[Yugoslavian relations with the United States]' *The Associated Press* (New York, 11 July 1976); 'Jugoslavia; Neutral on whose Side?' *The Economist* (London, 2 April 1977).

[24] *Süddeutsche Zeitung*, 'Deutscher Diplomat kritisiert', 14 December 1998.

[25] He might have been able to rely on VCDR art 3(1)(b) in the first alternative—ie, protection of the interests of the State itself.

in which a State adopts as its own claim the cause of nationals who have allegedly suffered an international wrong.[26] In both cases however, a determination of the 'nationality' of the person in question has to be made. In the field of diplomatic protection, there appears to be agreement that States can only exercise such protection if the nationality of the sending State is 'predominant'[27]—factors like habitual residence, family ties, language are taken into account for an evaluation of that requirement.[28]

On the other hand, there are still significant differences between the two concepts. There is no doubt that diplomatic protection, which can include bringing the case before an international court or tribunal[29]—is typically a more intrusive method,[30] and it is therefore understandable that the application of that concept is subject to more stringent conditions. The Draft Articles on Diplomatic Protection for instance specify that the injured persons themselves have to exhaust all local remedies[31]—a requirement which does not exist when the State restricts itself to action under Article 3(1)(b).[32] The same difference in intensity allows for the question whether it is necessary to deviate from the ordinary meaning of the term 'nationals' which the VCDR provides. The Convention itself does not distinguish between dual and single nationality; nor was such a distinction discussed during the ILC (International Law Commission) debates on that provision. The diplomatic protection of the interests of individuals with dual nationality remains at any rate, as Salmon concludes from his examination of State practice in this field, a reality.[33]

In addition to the protection of interests of the nationals of the sending State, the Article envisages the protection of interests of the State itself. This task invites a wide range of activities which prima facie cannot be said to fall outside the remit of the diplomatic office. Its reach is particularly

[26] *cf* ILC's Draft Articles on Diplomatic Protection, 26, art 1 and commentary, 27, art 1, paras 3 and 8.

[27] Draft Articles on Diplomatic Protection, 34, art 7. The ILC Commentaries also make reference to *Nottebohm*—a case in which the ICJ discussed the requirement of 'real and effective nationality' in cases of dual nationality. Draft Articles on Diplomatic Protection, 34, art 7, commentary, para 3; *Nottebohm*, 22–23.

[28] Draft Articles on Diplomatic Protection, 35, art 7, commentary, para 5; *Nottebohm*, 22. The traditional view was even stricter—the Hague Convention (1930) did not allow diplomatic protection in cases of double nationality (art 4).

[29] See Draft Articles on Diplomatic Protection, 27, art 1, para 8.

[30] See also YILC (Yearbook of the International Law Commission) 1958/II, 92, para 29 [Verdross].

[31] Draft Articles on Diplomatic Protection, 44, art 14.

[32] A provision calling for the exhaustion of local remedies had been suggested by Chile, but was rejected by the ILC precisely on the basis that such a provision had greater justification in the context of 'diplomatic protection in the narrow sense', YILC 1958/II, 92, para 31 [García Amador] and *cf* para 35 [Padilla Nervo]. On the decision, see YILC 1958/II, 93, at para 59.

[33] Salmon (1996), 107, para 156.

clear when instances are included in which the circumstances reveal the existence of such interests. In 2004 for instance, Sir Edward Clay, the British High Commissioner in Kenya, launched a sharp attack on alleged corruption in the Kenyan government[34]—conduct which has to be considered more than the mere representation of the attitude of the sending State. Britain was the biggest foreign investor in Kenya;[35] corruption in the receiving State therefore would have had a direct effect on her economic interests.

The fulfilment of this function can require a diplomat to adopt acts which the receiving State considers meddling in its internal affairs. Criticism of the policy of the receiving State—as in the Clay incident—is one of them, but a diplomatic agent may also deem it necessary to address the general public to familiarise them with a position taken by the sending State or to clarify a misconception which affects the interests of the latter.

Furthermore, the function of Article 3(1)(b) can lead to the lobbying of individual politicians on matters which affect the interests of the protecting State. An example was provided through the discussions which took place in 1981 between John Ford (the British High Commissioner in Canada) and members of the New Democratic Party, on the British North America Act (which Prime Minister Trudeau intended to replace with a Canadian constitution).[36] This conduct did meet with criticism: The Canadian Foreign Minister MacGuigan stated that Ford's behaviour might have fallen outside 'normal functions'.[37] But Ford's conduct found support in academic debate, where his activities were seen as embraced by ordinary diplomatic functions.[38]

However, Article 3(1)(b) does require that it is the State itself whose protection is sought. An incident in the year 2000, involving Raymond Chrétien, the Canadian Ambassador to the United States, created some difficulties in this regard. In the run-up to the US presidential elections, Chrétien reportedly expressed a preference for Al Gore, whom he called 'a friend of Canada', over George W Bush, about whom he was less complimentary.[39] While 'friend of Canada' may indicate that the ambassador was representing the interests of the sending State, some observers both in the sending and the receiving State appear to have seen this statement by Chrétien, a nephew of the leader of the Canadian Liberals, as protecting

[34] J Vasagar, 'Kenyan President Faces Rebellion' *The Guardian* (London, 24 February 2005).
[35] ibid.
[36] A Hutton, 'Section: Regional News' *United Press International* (Washington DC, 16 February 1981); Richard Doyon, 'Regional News' *United Press International* (Washington DC, 25 February 1981).
[37] Hutton, n 36.
[38] Green, 148. See for a more detailed discussion ch 5, s 2, in particular at n 75.
[39] S Thorne, 'Clark Slams Gore Endorsement' *Timmins Daily Press* (Timmins, 2 June 2000).

the interests of a party rather than a country.[40] Conduct of that kind would fall outside the remit of a diplomatic function which is not concerned with support for a faction, but with the protection of interests of the State as such.

1.3. Negotiation

While negotiation (Article 3(1)(c) of the Vienna Convention) is undoubtedly an essential task of diplomatic agents—Glahn refers to it as the 'original reason for having diplomats'[41]—its role in cases in which interference has been alleged, is rather limited. Advances in direct, inter-governmental exchanges[42] may partially account for its diminished significance in this context.

But a more important reason lies in the very nature of the task and the restricted scope it received in the Convention—which mentions negotiation only with regard to the 'Government' of the receiving State. Attempts to persuade the public of a particular course of action are usually carried out openly.[43] Negotiations with the government are different: No matter how strongly a government may feel that the diplomat has meddled on this occasion, it will be reluctant to discuss this in the press. The subject will often be sensitive, and publicity will put a swift end not only to the meddling, but also to the negotiations.

The existence of cases in which the duty of non-interference encounters the task of negotiation, is therefore theoretically possible; but they receive so little public attention, that it is difficult to tell how the international community evaluates this meeting of divergent norms.

One rare exception was the 1999 case of the US Ambassador to Thailand, Richard Hecklinger. Hecklinger had allegedly, at a meeting with the Thai Minister of the Prime Minister's Office, put pressure on Thailand to go ahead with the construction of the Bor Nok power plant.[44] The United States had a particular interest in that project: Edison Mission Energy, a US based company, partially funded the initiative.[45] Hecklinger had

[40] At the time, the incident was seen by commentators as part of 'Republican-Liberal antagonism'; M Blanchfield, 'Alliance will Americanize Canada' *Welland Tribune* (Welland, 25 October 2000). Joe Clark, leader of the Progressive Conservative Party of Canada, was quoted as saying that any other diplomat but the Prime Minister's nephew would be 'called in for a reprimand' over these statements. Thorne, n 39.

[41] Glahn (1992), 517.

[42] ibid.

[43] See, for a more detailed discussion, ch 7.

[44] K Sukin, 'US Envoy Accused of Meddling' *The Nation* (Thailand, 29 September 1999).

[45] H Mehta, 'Anti-foreign Feeling Resurging' *Business Times* (Singapore, 1 December 1999).

reportedly warned that delays to the construction would negatively affect the business climate in Thailand.[46]

The Ambassador's remarks did result in charges of interference. But it is worth pointing out that the accusations do not seem to have come from the official side; criticism was voiced in particular by an academic observer.[47]

The assessment of Hecklinger's conduct also has to take into account that the Ambassador seems not to have threatened the adoption of any specific sanction by the American government, but to merely have drawn attention to negative consequences that were to be expected if events were allowed to take their natural course. Outlining perceived repercussions, understanding the interests of the other party (and pretending to care about them) is certainly an integral part of negotiation. The limit to this are those lobbying activities which, due to their excessive character, represent a violation of international law.[48] But as long as that ceiling has not been reached, activities of this kind remain an expected aspect of the diplomatic task, and they do not carry the diplomatic conduct outside functions which the Vienna Convention recognises.

1.4. Observation and Reporting

Zimbabwe, like Fiji, is a State which in recent years has shown particular sensitivity to diplomatic conduct she considers meddling. The American Ambassador Christopher Dell has frequently been a target of the Mugabe government in this regard.[49] When, in March 2007, the Zimbabwean Foreign Minister Mumbengegwi summoned a group of Western diplomats and warned them that the Vienna Convention prohibited interference,[50] Dell walked out of the meeting,[51] but voiced his opinion about the charges a few days later in a radio interview. The Zimbabwe government, according to Dell, tended to rely greatly on

> certain Articles of the Vienna Convention on Diplomatic Relations about non-interference in the internal affairs of the receiving State, conveniently ignoring other Articles of the Convention which obligate the receiving State … to allow diplomatic missions to ascertain … the conditions and developments in the receiving State.[52]

The function of observation to which Dell alluded is the first of two aspects which Article 3(1)(d) incorporates (the other refers to the reporting of the

[46] ibid.

[47] Sukin, n 44.

[48] On this point, see ch 5, s 1.2, in particular at n 48.

[49] See A.207 and A.208.

[50] See Introduction at nn 113–15.

[51] A Shaw, 'Zimbabwe Warns Envoys' *Associated Press Online* (New York, 19 March 2007).

[52] V Gonda, Interview with US Ambassador Christopher Dell, *SW Radio Africa*, 20 March 2007.

findings to the sending State). At first sight, it would appear strange that observation could ever give rise to charges of interference—it is a task which seems to involve diplomats in a fairly passive role as recipients of information.[53] But closer inspection reveals a more complex situation. There are, in particular, two facets of this function which need to be taken into account.

First of all, the task of observation may carry a message which the receiving State interprets as interference with its internal affairs. It can in particular create the perception that the sending State had a special interest in the matter in question. An ambassador cannot observe everything with his own eyes; but if he decides to observe certain matters for himself—be it poor housing conditions, court trials with political connotations[54] or the prison cell of an opposition leader[55]—he conveys the message that this object has been worthy of selection. If the object is the opposition of the receiving State, the message will often be seen as one of support.

An illustration for the sensitivity of receiving States in this regard was provided in 1997, when the First Secretary at the US Embassy to Belarus was expelled after he had attended an unauthorised protest against the President of that country.[56] On that occasion, the United States emphasised that their envoy had merely been observing a political demonstration.[57] Support for the reach of this function comes from academic commentators too (the editors of Oppenheim for one point out that it is a diplomatic task to 'watch political events and political parties with a vigilant eye')[58] and indeed from some receiving States themselves. When in 2001 the Pakistani High Commissioner in the United Kingdom, Abdul Jaffer, was accused by a local election agent of campaigning for a Conservative candidate, a spokeswoman for the Foreign Office pointed out that it was 'usual' for diplomatic agents 'to attend and observe political meetings, it's part of their job. The fact that he has been at these meetings is not a problem at all'.[59]

[53] While the function of observation has on several occasions been invoked by diplomats as a defence against criticism by receiving States, it is, in fact, rare that observation activites, on their own, are subject to direct charges of interference. Where diplomatic hosts take exception to them, they tend to refer rather to a conduct of 'espionage' (or, even more commonly, to behaviour 'outside diplomatic functions'). Espionage will often also be considered a violation of the laws of the receiving State (VCDR, first sentence of art 41(1)).

[54] See A.255.

[55] See A.163.

[56] Denza, 466, n 21; *CNN*, 'US Diplomat Leaving Belarus', 23 March 1997; 'US Envoy Expelled' *Facts on File* (New York, 27 March 1997); R Kilborn et al, 'The News in Brief' *Christian Science Monitor* (Boston MA, 28 March 1997).

[57] Kilborn et al, n 56.

[58] Oppenheim (1967), 787.

[59] S Walsh, 'Foreign Office Probes Commissioner's Visit' *This is Bradford* (Bradford, 6 June 2001).

The conduct and impact of election campaigns are certainly significant features of life in the receiving State—as are the views of legitimate opposition parties. Denying diplomatic agents the right of observation in this regard, would considerably curtail the function which the Vienna Convention envisages. Such a limitation is possible if general customary law calls for it—Article 3(1)(d) reiterates the rule that diplomatic functions have to be fulfilled within the limits of international law by stipulating that observation has to be carried out by 'lawful means'. However, given the disagreement that regularly ensues between sending and receiving State when the latter criticises the observation of targets which are publicly accessible, it would be difficult to accept a consistent legal position within the international community on this. The fact that the observation of a particular object is inconvenient to the government of the receiving State offers no sufficient basis for a rule of this kind.

The second aspect of observation which requires consideration in this context relates to the fact that the task may presuppose acts which go beyond the mere reception of information—acts which are preliminary or ancillary in nature. Some sources, for instance, will feel more at ease if the flow of information goes in both directions and may indeed not be prepared to talk if that is not the case.[60] In other instances, the details of some developments are only accessible to diplomatic agents if they participate in the developments themselves.

And conduct of this kind must be embraced by the task of observation. Limiting observation activities to the mere reception of information would reduce the function to a meaningless exercise: Even the purchase of a newspaper could no longer be said to fall within the remit of the task, and diplomats would be compelled to wait for the odd piece of information to reach them in the embassy—not unlike citizens of Cockaigne awaiting the arrival of fried geese. Neither can it be assumed that the drafters of the Vienna Convention envisaged such a narrow remit of observation, nor has the function been limited to that degree in customary law. The rule of Article 26 (freedom of movement) corroborates the view that preliminary and ancillary acts are included in the task: The rationale for the freedom of movement is at least in part to be seen in the fact that it is a necessary aspect of the function of observation.[61]

Supporting conduct of this kind may be as ostensibly harmless as the asking of questions and the discussion of particular events in the receiving State. And yet, this has been considered serious enough to trigger negative sanctions. In 2001, for instance, the British Deputy High Commissioner in Gambia, Bharat Joshi, was expelled, following charges of interference in

[60] John le Carré was not far wrong when he suggested that '[s]ometimes, in order to obtain a confidence, it is necessary to impart one', Le Carré, 99.

[61] Denza, 205.

that country's 'internal and domestic affairs'.[62] The conduct at the root of his expulsion was reportedly described as his 'interacting' with the opposition at a press conference.[63]

At the other end of the range is conduct which involves the diplomatic agent quite intimately in ongoing events.

For instance, in the run-up to the Irish elections in 1981, William Shannon, the US Ambassador to that country, was photographed aboard the campaign bus of the Fine Gael Party.[64] Shannon's conduct drew the criticism of the Irish Prime Minister Haughey, who remarked that his own party would not have considered the Ambassador's involvement in its campaign.[65]

But the incident showed once again the willingness of sending States and their representatives to defend the task of observation. Shannon himself referred to that function and stated that his intention had been to observe the campaigns of each of the three parties.[66]

The characteristic element of the function—the assessment of developments in the receiving State—was certainly still discernible, and that a diplomat in Shannon's position would have had an opportunity to observe events in considerable detail, cannot be denied. Whether the meeting of observation and the duty of non-interference should, even in situations of this kind, be resolved in favour of Article 3, is a different question—a matter which will be explored in more detail later.[67]

The second task—making reports to the Government of the sending State—will typically involve material to which the receiving State has no access.

Typically, but not always: Leaked material, as recent history has shown, constitutes an exception to the rule. The most prominent example was arguably 'cablegate'—an incident which began in November 2010, when the activist website WikiLeaks made more than 250,000 cables, created by US diplomatic missions, available to selected media in Germany, Spain, France and the United States.[68] But even in instances of this kind, governments of receiving States can be reluctant to criticise diplomats for such correspondence, even if the cables revealed the use of quite frank language.

For one, the need for the confidentiality of correspondence between diplomats and their own Foreign Offices is generally understood[69]—the

[62] '"Unacceptable" Overseas Interference' *Agence France Presse* (Paris, 30 August 2001); R Beeston, 'UK Envoy Expelled by The Gambia' *The Times* (London, 24 August 2001).

[63] *West Africa Net*, 'The Joshi case', 24 August 2001.

[64] 'U.S. Ambassador in Controversy' *Associated Press* (New York, 27 May 1981).

[65] ibid.

[66] ibid.

[67] See ch 4.

[68] 'Background: WikiLeaks Documents in Public Interest' *Deutsche Presse-Agentur* (Hamburg, 28 November 2010). For a recent case in which one of the WikiLeaks cables had to be considered by a domestic court, see *Bancoult (No 3)*.

[69] And indeed acknowledged in the Vienna Convention (VCDR art 27).

more so, as it applies to diplomatic agents of the receiving State as well. Criticising diplomats for what they said in these documents might therefore backfire and risks at the very least the appearance that the receiving State approved of the leaks. And if charges of interference were raised, the question may be asked why a cable sent by a diplomat to his masters would constitute meddling in the internal affairs of the receiving State in the first place.

And yet, there were situations in which the leaked cables resulted in negative and very official reactions. When it emerged that Patricia Butenis, the US Ambassador to Sri Lanka, had accused the President of that country and an opposition leader of responsibility for alleged war crimes,[70] the Sri Lankan Foreign Minister expressed the view that 'greater circumspection would be appropriate' in future situations of this kind.[71] The Minister pointed out that he did not condone the leak of the cables, but he made clear that he felt their purpose had been to discredit his country.[72]

The Mexican President Calderón was less guarded when cables by the US Ambassador to that State, Carlos Pascual, were leaked. The cables revealed Pascual's negative views on the Mexican security forces—despite the positive attitude which the United States had displayed when it commented in public on Mexico's fight against drug trafficking.[73] In an interview with the newspaper El Universal, Calderón did mention 'intervention': 'I do not have to tell the U.S. ambassador how many times I meet with my security Cabinet', said the President. 'It is none of his business. I will not accept or tolerate any type of intervention'.[74] Pascual eventually resigned, in a move which was understood to be directly connected to the WikiLeaks revelations.[75]

But even in that case, it was not made clear to what conduct the allegation of intervention actually referred. If the statement was meant to stipulate that an envoy commits interference whenever he expresses himself openly in a cable to his own Foreign Office, it would be a position which does not find general support in the international community.

[70] T Peck, A Buncombe, 'David Miliband Called for Sri Lanka Aid' *The Independent* (London, 2 December 2010).

[71] *Daily the Pak Banker*, 'Sri Lanka Warns US', 22 December 2010.

[72] ibid.

[73] A Olson, 'US Diplomat in Mexico is 1st Casualty' *Associated Press* (New York, 24 March 2011).

[74] 'No acepto ni tolero ningún tipo de intervención'. 'FCH: estados eluden lucha contra crimen' *El Universal* (Mexico, 22 February 2011). See also A Olson, 'US Ambassador to Mexico Quits', *Associated Press* (New York, 20 March 2011).

[75] Olson, n 73.

1.5. Promotion of Friendly Relations

The last of the tasks included in Article 3(1)—the promotion of friendly relations and the development of economic, cultural and scientific relations[76]—suggests a function whose fulfilment appears to be very much in the interest of the receiving State. All the same, its realisation provides particularly fertile ground for charges of interference.

The reason for that must be seen in the fact that the function of Article 3(1)(e) is given a wide remit: The task envisages friendly relations with the receiving State, not only its government. As such, it carries potential for friction. The very concept of friendly relations requires involvement in various fields of life, and may see the diplomat in communication not only with members of the administration, but with the general public and members of the opposition as well.

These are often sensitive areas for the host government; but where claims of interference were made, sending States have sometimes strongly relied on this particular function. When the President of Nauru in 2001 accused a Taiwanese diplomat of meddling, following meetings with opposition politicians,[77] a spokeswoman of the Taiwanese Ministry of Foreign Affairs pointed out that it was a diplomat's 'job to be friends with everyone',[78] and that being friendly with members of the opposition could therefore not be considered interference in that State's internal affairs.

The promotion of friendly relations may be the basis even for critical remarks on the policies of the government. If the sending State harbours views which are opposed to those held by his hosts—for instance, on human rights—a fair representation of the situation may promote mutual understanding (or might at least contain the damage if the public is already aware of the context). A critical evaluation even of differences between the two States may therefore contribute to the fulfilment of the function which Article 3(1)(e) envisages.

Commentators on diplomatic law, in their attempts to capture the concept of the task, tend to stress the significance of one particular aspect—a facet which they sometimes call the 'public relations function'. Glahn points out that a diplomat

> continually tries to create goodwill for his own state and its policies. This propaganda-public relations function means giving and attending parties and dinners; giving lectures and other speeches; attending dedications of monuments, building, and (lately) foreign assistance projects; and so on.[79]

[76] VCDR art 3(1)(e).

[77] See Introduction, n 13.

[78] K Shu-ling, 'Denials' *Taipei Times* (Taipei, 20 August 2002) (paraphrasing a statement by Katharine Chang, spokeswoman of the Taiwanese Ministry of Foreign Affairs).

[79] Glahn (1992), 518.

Richtsteig, in a similar vein, interprets the intentions of the drafters of the VCDR as allowing diplomats also to 'disseminate information about their home country, including that country's views on foreign affairs'.[80] It is a view which, in some situations, has even found express support by the authorities of the receiving State.[81]

On the other hand, if a sending state or a diplomatic agent invokes this aspect of the diplomatic tasks as a defence against accusations of interference, the activities must fit into the framework which the function envisages.

A 2003 incident illustrates the difficulty which this scenario can involve. In that year, in the run-up to Estonia's referendum on joining the European Union, a German diplomat reportedly made a speech from a campaign bus of the European Commission, and called for an affirmative vote.[82] When challenged by a Eurosceptic British MEP (Member of the European Parliament), the diplomat allegedly justified his behaviour by referring to the task of promoting German culture.[83]

Instances of this kind warrant a differentiating assessment. If a diplomatic agent merely yields to the temptation of participating in partisan politics and this conduct is divorced from the relationship between sending and receiving State, he does leave the boundaries of Article 3(1)(e).[84] On the other hand, the views of the sending State and the policies it adopts are not limited to its domestic affairs. Its position on foreign policy, and the way in which certain external events are perceived by the population of that State may carry importance for the nationals of the receiving State, and a speech which mainly concerns this position can generate understanding of these points and thereby serve to fulfil the public relations aspect of the diplomatic function.

The traditional tasks of diplomatic agents therefore open a wide field of diplomatic conduct; and conflicts between their fulfilment and the ban on interference, as the receiving State may understand it, are not uncommon. To diplomats, however, they provide an opportunity to counter accusations of this kind: They are not only accepted in State practice, but expressly recognised by the same Convention that prohibits interference.[85]

[80] Richtsteig, 23 (translation). See also Strupp and Schlochauer, 365.

[81] See ch 1, at n 31.

[82] R Helmer, 'Estonia Faces the EU Propaganda Barrage' *Lincolnshire Echo* (Lincoln, 2 September 2003).

[83] Ibid.

[84] Diplomatic agents may usually find it easier to rely on the function of observation (VCDR art 3(1)(d)), whose fulfilment can cover a broad variety of activities. However, receiving States have on occasion insisted on a clear distinction between this function and other forms of behaviour. See the 1996 case of Myanmar and several Western States; *BBC Summary*, 'Ruling Council Explains Actions' (London, 4 October 1996).

[85] That does not mean that the resolution of the meeting of duties and functions will always favour the latter. See on this point ch 4.

The situation is less clear where diplomatic conduct leaves the remit of Article 3. But cases have arisen in which diplomatic agents have, in defence of their conduct, relied on tasks to which the VCDR does not make express reference—most prominently, on the need to engage in human rights monitoring and the protection of human rights in the receiving State. In these cases it is not only the assessment of a meeting of restrictive and permissive norms which requires consideration, but the very question whether the function which the diplomat and his government invoke, exists in the first place.

2. DIPLOMATIC INTERFERENCE AND DIPLOMATIC INVOLVEMENT IN HUMAN RIGHTS IN THE RECEIVING STATE

Diplomatic involvement in human rights, and in particular human rights monitoring (which is here understood as encompassing observation of the human rights situation, analysing and reporting the findings, but also critical evaluation of the human rights record) has traditionally met with criticism not only by the receiving State, but by commentators on diplomatic law as well. The 1979 edition of Satow still supported this line when it stated that a head of a mission must

> on no account occupy himself with the interests of any but the subjects or ressortissants … of his own sovereign or state, and especially not with those of the subjects of the local sovereign.[86]

Salmon, in his more recent work on diplomatic law, was likewise unable to divorce himself from the traditional view, although he clothed it in somewhat more cautious language. International law, in his opinion, seemed 'well settled' (bien fixé) to the extent that diplomatic agents who demanded respect for human rights risked interference in the internal affairs of the receiving State—at least in the eyes of the latter.[87]

It is a view which relies—with some reason—on the restrictive norms applicable to conduct of this kind. But it tends to do so without asking whether international law might not, at the same time, stipulate grounds on which diplomatic concern for human rights can be based.

Such grounds would certainly exist if diplomatic agents, by monitoring the human rights situation in the receiving State or by protecting human rights, fulfil a recognised function, or if the violation of human rights has a direct impact on the fulfilment of such a function. They also exist if international law recognises norms outside the regime of diplomatic law which

[86] Satow (1979), 450. But see, for a change in direction, Satow (2009), 153, para 9.58 (see ch 4, at n 8).

[87] '[A]u moins aux yeux de ce dernier', Salmon (1996), 129, para 197. Salmon would however have granted this right to the sending States themselves.

allow diplomatic involvement in this area or even call for it. The most prominent example for this may be the principle of self-determination, whose regulatory scope is not limited to the people in whose favour the right exists.

These grounds will be discussed in the following sub-sections. The existence of such reasons does not by itself mean that the diplomatic conduct in a specific situation was lawful, but they indicate that there are permissive rules which, like the restrictive rule on diplomatic interference, have an impact on the legal context of the relevant behaviour.[88]

The human rights discussed in these sections are, primarily, those of persons who do not possess the nationality of the sending State. In cases in which nationals of the sending State are involved, recourse to permissive norms outside traditional diplomatic functions is not necessary: Diplomatic involvement to protect their rights can regularly be based on Article 3(1)(b) of the Convention.

There is one exception to this approach which has been included because of its significance in some situations in this field: From time to time, the claim is advanced that the rights of diplomatic agents themselves require measures which the receiving State may consider interference in its internal affairs. This point is discussed in sub-section 2.3 below.

2.1. Human Rights Involvement within the Framework of Diplomatic Functions

Since Article 3 does not include an exhaustive list of diplomatic tasks,[89] it is possible that general customary law has identified further functions, and that these functions extend to diplomatic involvement in the human rights situation of the receiving State.

But such an assessment cannot be made lightly.[90] There are certainly numerous instances in which diplomatic agents deemed it proper to concern themselves with the general human rights situation in the receiving State or commented on specific rights,[91] and on more than one occasion, the sending State supported their conduct. At the same time, reactions

[88] For the assessment of their co-existence, see ch 4.

[89] See above, after n 5.

[90] A situation arising during the 1975 conference on the CRSIO draft illustrates the problem. Art 6 of the ILC's 1971 Draft Articles on the Representation of States listed the functions of permanent missions to international organisations and, like its equivalent in the VCDR, included the phrase 'inter alia'. But when the conference wanted to add the additional function of the protection of interests of the sending State, it chose to do so by express amendment—a procedure which would have been unnecessary if such a function could easily be assumed to exist as an implied task (as the Indonesian delegate seemed to suggest). Draft Articles on the Representation of States, 289, art 6; 1975 Conference, Records Vol 1,105, para 59 [Joewono]; para 55 [Calle y Calle].

[91] See Behrens (2014b), 197–98.

in the receiving State frequently reveal profound disagreement about the diplomatic role in this context.

The 1996 incident of Robin Meyer offers an illustration. Meyer, a Second Secretary at the US interests section in Havana, who was engaged in monitoring the human rights situation in Cuba, was expelled from the country in August of that year.[92] The Cuban Foreign Ministry accused her of engaging in 'counterrevolution' instead of 'diplomacy'.[93] The United States saw it differently—the State Department expressed the view that Cuba typically took this attitude to human rights work.[94] There was no indication that the State Department considered Meyer's work as falling outside her diplomatic functions: She was allowed to defend her conduct in interviews, and two months after her expulsion, was given the Department's 'Superior Honor Award' and complimented for her 'exceptional performance'.[95]

These and other cases[96] reveal that there is, half a century after the signing of the Vienna Convention, a continued sensitivity among States from different geographical regions and with different political systems, where diplomatic involvement in human rights is concerned. It would therefore be difficult to speak of a generally accepted diplomatic function to this effect. If such a function were to be based on general customary law, the consistency of State practice which custom requires,[97] could hardly be established.

Nothing, of course, prevents individual States from entering into an understanding that, as far as their bilateral relations are concerned, diplomatic involvement in human rights should be recognised as a function. There are in fact numerous instances in which sending States had been able to appoint members of diplomatic missions whose stated purpose it was to deal with human rights affairs, or who were expressly labelled 'human rights attachés'.[98]

[92] DL Marcus, 'Saying No to Fidel' *The Gazette* (Montreal, 12 October 1996).

[93] ibid.

[94] T Lippman, 'Surviving a Nightmare Inside Castro's Cuba' *Washington Post* (Washington, 1 November 1996).

[95] Lippman points out that diplomats of Meyer's rank do not often give interviews, but that she was invited to do so by senior officials at the State Department. Lippman, ibid.

[96] For other incidents which were marked by disagreement between sending and receiving State on the assessment of human rights involvement as falling within diplomatic functions, see the 1997 case of Alexandrov (at n 103 and A.125), the 2007 case of Lawlor (at n 196 and A.223), the 2010 case of Gass (ch 9, at n 48 and A.262) and see Behrens (2014b), 197.

[97] See *Nicaragua*, 98, para 186.

[98] See, for instance, for the Netherlands: Second Secretary, responsible for political affairs and human rights, FIDH (1999), 19; United Kingdom: First Secretary (human rights) in Nepal; ('Money for Rights' *Nepali Times* (5–11 July 2002); United States: Human rights attaché to Cuba (I Varlamov, 'Cuban Minisrty [sic] Scolds US Diplomat' *ITAR-TASS News Agency* (Moscow, 19 September 1998); US human rights attaché to Guatemala (Mahoney and Eguren, 43) and to Ukraine, 'European Diplomats Attending Court Hearings' *Ukraine General Newswire* (Kyiv, 4 August 2011).

If the receiving State has been informed about the appointment of such members and their functions[99] and has not declared the members unacceptable,[100] it conveys the impression that it acquiesces in the sending States' assessment of human rights work as a legitimate function. In those circumstances, it is estopped from claiming at a later stage that such a function did not exist in its relations with the sending State.[101]

Apart from that, it is always possible that diplomatic human rights work constitutes, at least in specific situations, an emanation of one of the 'traditional' diplomatic functions, to which the VCDR refers. The most obvious instance of this kind concerns the intersection between human rights monitoring and the task of observation under Article 3(1)(d).

The reference to 'conditions and developments' in the receiving State is certainly broad enough to cover the assessment of the degree to which the government of that State fulfils its obligations under international human rights law, as long as this is possible by reference to publicly accessible sources. That may include the direct involvement of the diplomatic agent, who will on occasion have been an eyewitness to relevant events.

The wording of the article also takes into account the sometimes dynamic nature of the object of observation ('developments'). This aspect is of some importance where the changing nature of human rights awareness is concerned—in particular in situations in which nationals of the receiving State engage in demonstrations or spontaneous gatherings to protest against human rights abuses by their government.

A diplomat who observes these events can rely on the same legal ground as a diplomat who observes a government function. In that regard, the United States were right in the 1997 case concerning the First Secretary at the US embassy to Belarus,[102] when she evaluated the observation of political demonstrations as 'a normal diplomatic duty'.[103]

But even charges of active participation in the events may sometimes require a more discerning analysis. The function of observation may call for conduct which is indispensable for the collection of information, but which causes the diplomatic agent to move beyond a merely passive presence on the sidelines.[104] The activities of the US diplomat Robin Meyer for

[99] As the VCDR requires in art 10(1)(a).

[100] As is its right under VCDR art 9(1).

[101] An interesting case in this context is that of the diplomat Timothy Brown, assigned to the US Interests Section in Cuba. Brown was described as 'human rights attaché' (Varlamov, n 98). The Cuban government issued harsh criticism of Brown's work, but it can be noted that this was focused on particular aspects of his conduct and that the receiving State expressly referred to 'interference in the internal affairs of our country', instead of claiming that the diplomatic function of human rights observation did not exist in the first place. 'Cuba Accuses US Diplomat of Meddling' *Miami Herald* (Miami, 19 September 1998) and P Fletcher, 'Expulsions Cast Cold War Shadow' *Reuters* (London, 24 December 1998).

[102] See above, at n 56.

[103] Kilborn et al, n 56. See also the US reaction in the case of Hardwood and Hopper (A.79).

[104] See above, at n 60.

instance, in the above mentioned case of 1996, had involved interviews with protesters in Cuba[105]—conduct which is by necessity embraced by the function of observation. It is in fact a classic example of the ancillary and preliminary acts which the task requires.[106]

But the task of observation does not represent the only overlap with diplomatic involvement in human rights. The protection of interests of the sending State and its nationals (Article 3(1)(b)) provides a similar basis for diplomatic conduct in this field and may allow for an extensive range of activities.

At first sight, this function seems to indicate quite a different direction—the human rights situation which diplomatic agents encounter, appears to be an interest of nationals of the receiving and not the sending State. But human rights violations in one State may well have an impact on the interests of another. In this context, Biswanath Sen points out that such violations 'may sow the seeds of a revolution whose repercussions may not be confined within the boundary of the particular state'[107] (a finding which was dramatically confirmed by the wave of revolutions that shook the Arab world in 2011). If a sending State is affected by events of this kind, its diplomats will be able to invoke the protection of interests as a basis for their involvement in the human rights situation in the receiving State.

On other occasions, human rights violations in one State can set in motion a flow of refugees, which becomes a direct concern to its neighbours—and frequently enough, to other States as well. The receiving State might still consider the matter an internal affair and try to dismiss diplomatic representations on this point as interference. But it would find it difficult to claim exclusivity of concern.[108] And there are other situations in which interests of the sending State are directly concerned: Cases where nationals of the receiving State who are working for the sending State are detained; cases where residents in the receiving State working for companies of the sending State are mistreated, and so forth.

Reliance on Article 3(1)(b) however requires a careful assessment of the situation. A diplomat wishing to invoke this ground for human rights work may be challenged to demonstrate in what way the interests of his State are affected. By comparison, it may be easier to rely on the function of observation.

[105] T Lippman, 'Surviving a Nightmare Inside Castro's Cuba' *Washington Post* (Washington DC, 1 November 1996).

[106] See above, at n 60.

[107] Sen, 54.

[108] The situation mirrors a development at the United Nations. A rule of non-intervention is recognised in the UN Charter as well—the United Nations must refrain from intervening 'in matters which are essentially within the domestic jurisdiction of any state' (UN Charter art 2(7)). That does not mean that the UN does not express its concern about grave human rights abuses in member States. As Carey points out, it is the danger that a 'refugee-creating environment' will result in a flow of fugitives to other countries that has in the past given the Security Council a basis for their involvement in situations of this kind. Carey, 246 and see SC Res 812 (1993), preamble, operative para 4.

At the same time, the range of conduct that can be based on the protection of interests is wider than that which the mere observation of events allows. A diplomat engaging in the protective task is, due to its very concept, more than an observer; it is consequently easier to base addresses to the general public, contact with the opposition and even open criticism of the government of the receiving State on this function.

There are, finally, cases, in which a diplomatic agent merely represents views held by the sending State and therefore acts in fulfilment of the function of representation as enshrined in Article (3)(1)(a).

When, for instance, the Canadian ambassador to Ukraine, Andrew Robinson, in 2004 expressed his government's concerns over the possibility that presidential elections in the receiving State would fall below democratic standards,[109] he triggered sharp criticism from official side[110] and was subsequently summoned to the Ukrainian Foreign Ministry.[111] But there can be no doubt that diplomats in situations of this kind can rely on a well-established function which the Convention recognises.

And it is this function in particular which calls for a repositioning of the traditional view on diplomatic involvement in human rights, as expressed by Salmon and others. Salmon would have allowed States themselves to demand respect for human rights, but expressed himself in much more restrictive terms where diplomatic human rights involvement was concerned.[112] But it is of course possible that a sending State uses its diplomat merely as a 'mouthpiece' to voice its concerns in this area, and in those instances, a meaningful distinction between the diplomat and his State is no longer possible.

The significance of the tasks of the diplomatic mission is further underlined by the rule of Article 25, which places a duty upon the receiving State to 'accord full facilities' for the performance of diplomatic functions. This provision primarily addresses the State, but in connection with Article 3, it is possible to derive from it an ancillary right of diplomatic agents who can in this context demand fulfilment of Article 25. As Denza points out, the article is 'usually invoked in order to lend additional weight to a diplomatic claim or protest based on a more specific provision'.[113]

The connection between Article 25 and Article 3 is of particular importance in the field of human rights—especially where nationals of the

[109] *News Bulletin (Interfax-Ukraine)*, 'Canadian Ambassador to Ukraine', 22 September 2004; A Melnichuk, 'Ukrainian Authorities' *Associated Press* (New York, 23 September 2004).

[110] *News Bulletin (Interfax-Ukraine)*, 'Canadian Ambassador to Ukraine', 22 September 2004.

[111] Melnichuk, n 109.

[112] See above, n 87. Salmon does accept the potential overlap between State actions and diplomatic actions when he discusses the general concepts of 'non-immixtion' and 'non-intervention' (ch 2, at n 101) but does not make the point when analysing the right to criticise the human rights record of a State. Ibid, Salmon.

[113] Denza, 202, art 25.

receiving State are concerned who work for a diplomatic mission of the sending State. Receiving States are not always welcoming towards the employment of their nationals and have resorted to intimidation and even arrests and trials of citizens who engaged in work of this kind[114]—as in the above mentioned case of employees of the British and French embassies in Iran in 2009.[115]

In these instances, concerns may arise that the treatment of the staff members does not conform with international human rights standards (in the Iranian case, the British Foreign Office accused Iranian authorities of failing to grant the prisoners their 'basic human rights').[116] If this is the case, the receiving State not only infringes its obligations under human rights law, but also under Article 25 of the Convention. The diplomatic mission is then entitled, on behalf of the sending State, to issue a critical evaluation of the receiving State's conduct and to demand the fulfilment of its obligation. The specific 'functions of the mission' that are affected require assessment on a case-by-case basis—the question which function had been at issue, depends on the task for which the nationals of the receiving State were being employed.

2.2. Human Rights Involvement Based on Other Norms of International Law

In October 1993, several Western diplomats in Sierra Leone called for the release of journalists who had been arrested after they had published an article critical of the country's military leader. The official reaction left no doubt about the government's evaluation of the remarks: The acting Foreign Minister of Sierra Leone referred to them as diplomatic interference 'without justification and contrary to the principles of diplomatic law and practice'.[117]

In situations of this kind, the relevant diplomatic activity may be based on genuine human rights concerns (on this occasion, concerns relating to the freedom of the press). But when no financial or political interests of the sending State are invoked and when diplomats cannot claim to have acted in pursuance of the task of observation or other traditional tasks, the receiving State may find it easy to dismiss the view that their conduct was based on functions which the Vienna Convention recognises.

[114] See Murty, 501.

[115] See above, n 3. *CNN*, 'British, French Embassy Workers', 9 August 2009.

[116] 'British, French Embassy Workers', ibid; A Johnson, 'Miliband's Fury' *The Independent on Sunday* (London, 9 August 2009).

[117] *BBC Summary*, 'Western Diplomats Accused of Interference' (London, 25 October 1993).

At the same time, it may be possible for diplomatic agents in these scenarios to rely on norms of international law which derive from contexts other than diplomatic relations. The addressees of such norms will usually be the States themselves, but where States in international relations make use of diplomatic missions as their organs,[118] diplomats are able to invoke these rules on their behalf. At the same time, they have to observe the limitations which international law imposes on the sending State.

The presence of such permissive rules of international law becomes apparent when a receiving State alleges interference in matters over which it cannot in fact claim exclusive ownership. The most prominent of these situations arises when the matter in question is an obligation which the receiving State owes *erga omnes*—ie, to 'the international community as a whole'.[119] With regard to the rights affected by *erga omnes* obligations, the ICJ emphasised that 'all States can be held to have a legal interest in their protection'.[120]

And reference to *erga omnes* norms is typically made where human rights are involved—particularly where they have been subjected to severe threat. Protection from slavery,[121] racial discrimination,[122] the prohibition of torture[123] and the outlawing of genocide[124] have all been accepted as norms carrying *erga omnes* character. Furthermore, given the connection between international crimes and serious human rights violations,[125] there is good reason to follow those writers on international criminal law who suggest that the suppression of international crimes should be an obligation of *erga omnes* character as well.[126]

This has a direct impact on the assessment of diplomatic involvement in this area: Diplomats who draw attention to the commission of international crimes, can invoke a powerful basis for their conduct.

An incident which occurred in Namibia in 1999 illustrates the situation. In August of that year, a secessionist group launched attacks on government installations in the Caprivi region of that State. The government response was reportedly harsh and indiscriminate—there were allegations of the mistreatment of civilians in the region.[127] In this situation,

[118] See, on the categorisation of diplomatic and consular missions as State organs, Draft Articles on State Responsibility (2001), 44, art 6, commentary, para 4.

[119] *Barcelona Traction*, 32, para 33.

[120] Ibid. See also ILC Study Group on Fragmentation, C. Conclusions, para 37.

[121] *Barcelona Traction* 32, para 34. On the human rights character of the prohibition of slavery, see ICCPR art 8(1) and (2); ECHR art 4(1); ACHR art 6.

[122] *Barcelona Traction*, 32, para 34. See ICCPR art 26; ECHR art 14 and ECHR Protocol 12 art 1; ACHR arts 1(1) and 24.

[123] *cf Furundžija* (Trial Chamber), para 151. See ICCPR art 7; ECHR art 3; ACHR art 5.

[124] *Barcelona Traction*, 32, para 34.

[125] See eg *Blagojević* (Trial Chamber), para 814.

[126] See on this Van den Herik, 1129; see also Laplante, 648.

[127] 'Namibian Government Admits Atrocities' *Agence France Presse* (Paris, 12 August 1999).

the embassy of the United States called on the Namibian government to stop these abuses[128]—conduct which earned it accusations of interference in the country's internal affairs.[129] But mistreatment of the kind which reportedly occurred in the Namibian situation amounts to an international crime,[130] and by calling on Namibia to refrain from the relevant activities, the embassy referred to obligations which the State owed to the international community as a whole.[131]

In the literature, the view has been expressed that, given the importance of the rights affected by *erga omnes* obligations, all States must be able to 'intervene' to defend them.[132] In its 1989 Resolution on Human Rights and Non-Intervention, the Institute of International Law expressed the opinion that the protection of human rights is owed *erga omnes*[133] and that a State is entitled to take 'diplomatic, economic and other measures' against another State which has violated these obligations.[134]

The ILC's Draft Articles on State Responsibility do provide for a right of any State to 'invoke' the responsibility of another State, if the latter has breached an *erga omnes* obligation.[135] While some questions attach to the precise meaning of that term,[136] it is at least clear that the ILC was addressing specific verbal representations: In Article 48(2), the ILC refers to particular 'claims' that the invoking State can make against the responsible State: It can call for cessation of the wrongful act, for assurances and guarantees for non-repetition and can claim performance of the obligation of reparation. Diplomatic statements which reflect critically on the failures of the receiving State with regard to *erga omnes* obligations certainly fall in this category.

The basis for diplomatic involvement in human rights gains additional strength if the sending State not only has the right to claim fulfilment of

[128] 'Namibia; US Expresses Concern' *Panafrican News Agency* (Dakar, 18 August 1999).

[129] C Maletsky, 'US Remarks' *Business Day* (Johannesburg, 20 August 1999).

[130] There had been reports that acts of torture and 'cruel, inhuman treatment and punishment were carried out', 'Namibian Government Admits Atrocities', n 127; the US Embassy itself called on Namibia to fulfil its obligations under the Geneva Conventions, 'Namibia; US Expresses Concern', n 128. On the modern regulation of acts of this nature in international criminal law, see ICTYSt art 2; ICTRSt art 4; ICCSt art 8(2)(c). Since a violation of the Geneva Conventions was alleged, a similar result would be reached by reference to their Common Article 1. See on this below, at n 145.

[131] See also the case of the US Ambassador to Indonesia, Gelbard, who in 2000 called on the receiving State to 'bring to justice' the perpetrators of the violence in East Timor in 1999 (A.145). The fact must be recalled that the events in East Timor were subject of judicial examination by the Special Panels of the Dili District Court and were investigated under various categories of international crimes, including genocide. Dili Court Reg (2000/11), s 10.1(a).

[132] Field, 535.

[133] Institute of International Law (1989) art 1.

[134] Ibid, art 2(2).

[135] Draft Articles on State Responsibility (2001), 126, art 48(1) and see ILC Study Group on Fragmentation, C. Conclusions, n 31.

[136] Focarelli calls the word 'inherently ambiguous', Focarelli (2010), 167.

erga omnes obligations, but a positive duty to do so. But the identification of such duties in international law has proven difficult. Where a suggestion of such an obligation has been made in the literature, both its existence and extent tend to be subject to controversy.

This is even the case where obligations arising from the Genocide Convention are concerned. Not all States are party to the treaty,[137] and the question can therefore be raised if, besides the 'outlawing' of genocide,[138] the duty of prevention and prosecution[139] has also attained the status of an *erga omnes* rule. Focarelli points out that in the past, even contracting States have not felt an obligation to prevent the crime.[140]

The much debated 'responsibility to protect' is even less suitable as a basis for *erga omnes* duties. Apart from the fact that its very character as a norm of international law is subject to controversy,[141] its applicability to *erga omnes* duties owed by individual States is less than clear. The original report of the International Commission on Intervention and State Sovereignty (ICISS) did make reference to actions by individual States,[142] but shied away from allocating specific international obligations to them. Neither did the 2005 World Summit Outcome Document, which in its discussion on the responsibility to protect mentioned the duties of States with regard to their own populations,[143] but otherwise only indicated the responsibility of the 'international community, through the United Nations' to help to protect populations from international crimes.[144] This may indicate an obligation to bring the pending or ongoing commission of international crimes to the attention of the United Nations, but not an obligation of direct action through diplomatic agents in bilateral diplomatic relations.

The strongest case for an obligation to act in the defence of human rights in the receiving State, can arguably be made on the basis of Common Article 1 of the Geneva Conventions of 1949.[145] Under this rule, parties to the conventions 'undertake to respect and ensure respect' for the conventions 'in all circumstances'. Given the universal acceptance of the Geneva regime,[146] there would be good reason to speak in this regard of

[137] At the time of writing, the Genocide Convention has 146 parties. UN Treaty Collection (Online), Genocide Convention (as of 1 January 2015).
[138] *Barcelona Traction*, para 34.
[139] Genocide Convention art I.
[140] Focarelli (2010), 140.
[141] See eg, Focarelli (2008), 193 ff, but also Magnuson, 299.
[142] See ICISS Report, 24, note 3.31 (in the context of universal jurisdiction), 29, note 4.1 and 55, notes 6.39 and 6.30, primarily in the context of military measures.
[143] World Summit Outcome, para 138.
[144] Ibid, para 139.
[145] The four Geneva Conventions are clearly linked to the protection of human rights. Several rules in the treaties attest to that, but see in particular GC-I art 50; GC-II art 51; GC-III art 130; GC-IV art 147, all in conjunction with Common Art 1.
[146] At the time of writing, the Geneva Conventions had 196 parties. ICRC State Parties (as of 29 April 2015).

norms which the international community as a whole accepts as applying to all its members.

The article appears to call for positive action,[147] but it has been pointed out that it is not clear which measures exactly State parties have to adopt to ensure compliance with the relevant rules.[148] At the very least, States can be expected to resort to acts to which they are entitled anyway. In this context, Focarelli mentions in the first place the possibility of 'diplomatic measures',[149] and diplomatic representations may very well define the minimum content of the obligation. Given the *erga omnes* character of the duties, every State—even States not party to the conflict—is entitled to voice diplomatic protests about the violations of the Geneva Conventions and to demand cessation,[150] but it is Common Article 1 which turns this right into a positive duty and allows diplomats to rely on this obligation as a defence against charges of interference.

Outside the regime of the Geneva Conventions however, it is difficult to identify norms which stipulate for all States a duty to act if one State violates *erga omnes* obligations. Such norms would have to arise from general customary law, and it is usually not possible to find the measure of agreement in the international community which is required for that. The reason may well be that States shy away from the consequences of such an assessment,[151] or that their different legal traditions make agreement on such norms less likely.[152]

Where the ICJ did spell out duties incumbent upon all States, they tended to be negative in character—in the *Wall Opinion* for instance, the duty 'not to recognize the illegal situation' arising from the construction of the wall in Palestine, and the duty 'not to render aid or assistance in maintaining the situation created by such construction'.[153]

And negative duties are not without relevance to diplomatic agents. Their fulfilment—for instance, the non-recognition of an illegal situation—may appear easy enough; but it is complicated by the fact that

[147] See Focarelli (2010), 171. It has been interpreted that way by the General Assembly (*cf* GA Res 58/97 (2003), para 3; GA Res 59/122 (2004), para 3; GA Res 62/107 (2007), para 3; GA Res 65/103 (2010), para 3) and by the ICJ, which in the *Wall Opinion* spoke of an 'obligation' upon every State party to ensure that the 'requirements of the instruments in question are complied with', *Wall Opinion*, 199, para 158.

[148] Focarelli (2010), 144.

[149] Ibid, 145.

[150] See above, after n 136; Draft Articles on State Responsibility (2001), 126, art 48(2).

[151] In the context of Common Article 1 of the Geneva Conventions, Focarelli points out that a breach of the Conventions which does not trigger reactions by other States would result in 193 further violations of the Conventions (there were, at that time, 194 parties to the Conventions)—'a very extreme construction which is far from being supported by state practice', Focarelli (2010), 170.

[152] See Brown, who refers to the different treatments which 'bystander responsibility' receives in different States, Brown, at 53, 54.

[153] *Wall Opinion*, 200, para 159.

even the presence of a State representative at a particular function may be perceived as conveying a message. Diplomats have often shown keen awareness of this possibility and have taken care to avoid this appearance.

In 1954 for instance, the American and the British Ambassadors to Moscow (Hayter and Bohlen) were invited to a dinner party which was also attended by the Ambassador of the German Democratic Republic (GDR). At that stage, neither the United States nor the United Kingdom had yet recognised the GDR, and consequently, on realising that the East German Ambassador was present, Hayter and Bohlen decided to leave the event.[154]

And in September 1995, the US Ambassador to Israel, Martin Indyk, decided to stay away from the opening ceremony of 'Jerusalem 3000'—the Israeli commemoration of the declaration, by King David, of Jerusalem as the capital of the Jewish people.[155] Afterwards, there were fences to mend: Warren Christopher, then US Secretary of State, went on record to state that there had been no intention to boycott the events.[156] But given the disputed status of Jerusalem and the fact that the vast majority of invited ambassadors, including those of the European Union, had decided not to attend,[157] Indyk's absence invited a different interpretation. The Israeli Prime Minister was said to have been angry about the decision; Ehud Olmert, then Mayor of Jerusalem, was quoted as saying that the incident showed that Jerusalem was 'like an open wound in the relations between us and the US'.[158]

Even non-attendance can therefore carry a powerful message, and may lead to negative reactions in the receiving State. But in situations where the sending State faced a duty under international law not to act, the diplomatic agent has a basis for his conduct. The receiving State cannot expect diplomats to involve their masters in acts which incur their liability for the breach of norms of international law.

A particular situation of *erga omnes* interests which may form the basis of diplomatic conduct requires special consideration—the case of peoples who are striving for the realisation of self-determination.

Self-determination finds mention in the Charter of the United Nations,[159] but its character as a right was affirmed in Article 1 of the International Covenant on Civil and Political Rights (ICCPR) and of the International

[154] The case according to Satow (1979), 453 (para 44.73).

[155] P Wilson, 'Envoy's Absence Angers Israel' *The Australian* (Surry Hills, 7 September 1995).

[156] H Kuttler, 'Christopher: Indyk didn't Snub Jerusalem 3000' *Jerusalem Post* (Jerusalem, 11 September 1995).

[157] Palestinian leaders had called for a boycott of the event, pointing out that Jerusalem was 'occupied land', 'Jerusalem 3000 Celebrations' *Mideast Mirror* (5 September 1995); Wilson, n 155; 'Indyk's absence' *Jerusalem Post* (Jerusalem, 6 September 1995).

[158] Wilson, n 155.

[159] UN Charter art 1(2).

Covenant on Economic, Social and Cultural Rights (ICESCR).[160] The wording it received in the Covenants makes clear that the rule comprises other, more specific interests: Under the ICCPR and ICESCR, peoples, '[b]y virtue of that right freely determine their political status and freely pursue their economic, social and cultural development'.[161] It is particularly in view of the political aspects of the right, that self-determination has informed the context of diplomatic involvement in human rights.

It has thus become relevant in cases where diplomats sought contact with the political opposition in the receiving State[162] and where they engaged in active criticism of developments in the receiving State which they considered to endanger the realisation of that right.

In 2008 for instance, James McGee, US Ambassador to Zimbabwe, was summoned to the Foreign Ministry of the receiving State,[163] after he had visited the Avenues clinic which treated victims of the political unrest in that State and had then stated that the 'violence in Zimbabwe ha[d] to stop'.[164] The Zimbabwean Minister of Foreign Affairs, Mumbengegwi, branded the remarks 'interference in Zimbabwe's internal affairs' and referred in this context to Article 41 of the Vienna Convention.[165] But there can be little doubt that the diplomatic involvement in this case was directly relevant to the political rights of the people in the receiving State, and in particular to impediments to their ability to freely choose their political status.

That self-determination carries *erga omnes* character, was confirmed in several decisions by the ICJ.[166] And yet, diplomatic involvement in this field will almost unavoidably give the impression of support for a particular faction; and it has therefore proved one of the most fertile fields for charges of meddling. In the ILC debates on the rule against interference, several members referred to this conduct by way of example: Yokota voiced the opinion that it was 'unwarranted interference' for an 'ambassador to encourage or subsidize a political party in the receiving State';[167] Ago thought it an 'improper action' for the head of a mission to give 'moral or financial support to a political party in the receiving State'.[168]

160 ICCPR art 1(1)1 ('All peoples have the right of self-determination'); same wording in ICESCR art 1(1)1.

161 ICCPR art 1(1)2; ICESCR art 1(1)2.

162 See on this the 2008 incident involving the US Ambassador to Bangladesh, Moriarty, who courted criticism when he invited the leaders of several political parties to a 'tea party' at his residence (A.236). It appears that the discussions concerned the state of emergency then in existence in Bangladesh and the viability of 'credible' democratic elections if the situation were to prevail—interests which have a direct impact on the right of the people of the receiving State to freely choose their political status.

163 'Zimbabwe; Govt Summons, Warns U.S. Ambassador' *The Herald* (Harare, 17 May 2008).

164 T McVeigh, 'Tsvangirai Ready to Take on Mugabe' *The Observer* (London, 11 May 2008).

165 'Zimbabwe; Govt Summons, Warns U.S. Ambassador', n 163.

166 *East Timor*, 102, para 29; *Wall Opinion*, 199, paras 155, 156.

167 YILC 1957/I, 146, para 10 [Yokota].

168 YILC 1957/I, 149, para 36 [Ago].

But the view of the international community may have undergone a change in this regard. It is certainly difficult to ignore the many resolutions passed by the General Assembly—some of which arguably reflecting customary law[169]—which call for the rendering of assistance by all States to peoples striving for self-determination,[170] and it is understandable that commentators like Faundez feel that the situation concerning 'intervention' has now been reversed: Where, traditionally, the involvement of third States was allowed only to assist the established government, involvement today appears to be only permitted if it assists a people striving for self-determination.[171]

The need for diplomatic representation in this context becomes particularly clear if the *erga omnes* character of self-determination generates not only a common interest for the international community, but also certain duties incumbent upon the sending State. Negative duties have certainly been accepted in this regard. Reference has already been made in this context to the ICJ's Opinion in the *Wall* case.[172] But the court went further and stated that all States had the obligation to 'see to it' (while respecting international law and the UN Charter) that 'any impediment, resulting from the construction of the wall, to the exercise by the Palestinian people of its right to self-determination' was brought to an end.[173] That wording indicates that self-determination is capable of creating positive duties for third States as well—a view which had earlier been expressed in the Friendly Relations Declaration,[174] in the 1980 Espiell Study[175] and in several General Assembly Resolutions.[176]

The view is not unopposed: Judge Kooijmans, in his Separate Opinion, stated his doubts on the opinion that the violation of *erga omnes* duties by one State must necessarily result in obligations for third States.[177] On the other hand, if self-determination did not trigger duties of this kind,

169 See for instance ICJ in *Nicaragua*, 100, para 188, on the nature of the Friendly Relations Declaration (Annex, 5th Principle).

170 See eg, GA Res 2105 (XX) (1965); GA Res 2160 (XXI) (1966); Friendly Relations Declaration; GA Res 2649 (XXV) (1970); GA Res 3070 (XXVIII) (1973); GA Res 3163 (XXVIII) (1973); GA Res 3328 (XXIX) (1974) and GA Res 31/33 (1976).

171 Faundez, 96. Faundez does however refer to the particular case of self-determination from colonial domination—a perspective which will be discussed in more detail later (see text at n 180).

172 See above, at n 153.

173 *Wall Opinion*, 200, para 159.

174 'Every State has the duty to promote, through joint and separate action, realization of the principle of equal rights and self-determination of peoples, in accordance with the provisions of the Charter ...', *Friendly Relations Declaration*, 5th Principle.

175 A study prepared by the UN Special Rapporteur of the Subcommission on Prevention of Discrimination and Protection of Minorities (Hector Gros Espiell) in 1980.

176 See eg, GA Res 2787 (XXVI) (1971), para 7 and GA Res 36/103 (1981), Annex, Article 2 (III).

177 *Wall Opinion (Separate Opinion Kooijmans)*, para 40.

any statement about the support to be provided to peoples striving for its realisation would be no more than a political promise—hardly the kind of legal right 'to receive support' which the Friendly Relations Declaration envisages.[178] And the support of third countries matters: Peoples faced with severe curtailments of their political rights often have no other way to realise their right to self-determination but through outside assistance.

Such assistance does of course carry its own difficulties. Quite apart from the negative political repercussions that interaction of this kind can generate,[179] the fact remains that the territorial integrity of the State from which the right to self-determination is sought, is likewise recognised in international law—and frequently affirmed by the same instruments which emphasise the principle of self-determination.[180]

In the light of the difficulty caused by these conflicting interests, it is understandable that there have been attempts to limit the remit of self-determination. One approach is the restriction of its applicability to peoples who live under colonial rule[181]—a view that may have appeared particularly convincing at a time when people under colonial rule accounted for more than a third of the world's population.[182] The rationale for this opinion is that in these cases a clash with territorial integrity might in fact be avoided—the colonised land 'already exists as a distinct territorial entity'.[183]

But it is a view which, in light of the wording which the right received in the Human Rights Covenants, is difficult to uphold. There, reference was made simply to a right of '[a]ll peoples'—without the incorporation of any further distinction.[184] When India made a reservation to the

[178] Friendly Relations Declaration, 5th Principle. See also Definition of Aggression art 7(1).

[179] One may recall that Reisman, in a 1987 editorial comment, expressed the view that third States were 'under an obligation' to render help to the Mujahideen who were resisting the Soviet Union and the government in Kabul that was supported by the Soviet Union, Reisman, 909. In 2010, US Secretary of State Hillary Clinton made the following observation: 'We created the Mujahedin force against the Soviet Union. We trained them, we equipped them, we funded them, including somebody named Osama bin Laden', C McFadden, Interview with Secretary of Defense Robert Gates and Secretary of State Hillary Rodham Clinton, *ABC News*, 9 November 2010.

[180] See, on this, Friendly Relations Declaration, Preamble, para 15. UN Charter art 2, dealing with principles, states in its fourth paragraph that members shall refrain from the threat or use of force inter alia 'against the territorial integrity' of any State (UN Charter art 2(4)). GA Res 1514 (XV) (1960), para 6. See also Helsinki Final Act, IV.

[181] See on this Sforza, 496.

[182] Faundez, 88.

[183] Van der Vyver, 23, who distinguishes between secession and a declaration of independence and applies the latter term to colonies breaking free from the colonising State. While some General Assembly Resolutions do consider self-determination in the context of colonial territories or peoples under colonial and foreign domination or subjugation (eg GA Res 2649 (XXV) (1970), para 2; GA Res 3163 (XXVIII) (1973), para 7; GA Res 3328 (XXIX) (1974), para 7), not all of them are restrictive in that regard: The Friendly Relations Declaration for instance speaks of the right of 'all peoples' to self-determination. See also the Helsinki Final Act, VIII, referring to 'all peoples'.

[184] ICCPR art 1; ICESCR art 1. See above, at n 161.

effect that the right should apply 'only to the peoples under foreign domination',[185] she triggered objections from France, Germany, the Netherlands and Pakistan, with Germany and the Netherlands stating expressly that self-determination had to apply to all peoples.[186]

A different approach towards limitation is that of the so-called 'remedial school'. The starting point of this view is a dissection of the principle into two aspects—external and internal self-determination. External self-determination addresses the status of the State itself—it encompasses the declaration of independence for the territory in which the people live, its association with another State or its integration with such a State.[187] Internal self-determination on the other hand is realised within the boundaries of the State in question; it has been described as a people's 'pursuit of its political, economic, social and cultural development' in that State.[188] According to the remedial school, peoples must primarily strive to fulfil their right to self-determination internally; a right to secession exists only as a last resort, if internal self-determination has been denied to them.[189]

For all its conceptual shortcomings,[190] the remedial view is certainly preferable to the wholesale exclusion of certain peoples from the right of self-determination. Its main advantage lies in the fact that it does take into account the competing interest of territorial integrity. The full range of self-determination, including external self-determination, remains available to peoples even outside a colonial context,[191] but a relatively high bar is set for them, based on objective criteria. Peoples who already enjoy internal self-determination will, it is assumed, have the opportunity to implement their political rights and maintain their identity within the framework of their State.

These considerations have a direct impact on the degree to which diplomatic agents as organs of their State can get involved in matters of this kind: They define the contours of the *erga omnes* interests which lift self-determination out of the exclusive domain of the receiving State. From the

[185] UN Treaty Collection (Online), ICESCR.

[186] ibid.

[187] See on these options *Western Sahara*, para 57; GA Res 1541 (XV) (1960), Principle VI.

[188] *Secession of Quebec*, para 126.

[189] See on this ibid, para 138; Dickinson, 553; Sloane, 1306.

[190] One particular difficulty concerns the question of the precise circumstances which could trigger a right to external self-determination. Sloane points out that the Canadian Supreme Court 'did not explain which cases qualify as extreme', Sloane, 1307. The Supreme Court did refer to the denial of 'meaningful access to government to pursue their political, economic, social and cultural development' (*Secession of Quebec*, para 138). Other authors have suggested the violation of fundamental human rights as a trigger (Dickinson, 559) or attacks on the physical existence of a people or violations of their human rights in general, Okoronkwo, 108.

[191] The remedial view also preserves the traditional role of peoples in colonial contexts. In that regard, the Canadian Supreme Court stated that the right of colonial peoples 'to break away from the "imperial" power is now undisputed', *Secession of Quebec*, para 132.

above, it appears that at least the right to internal self-determination can be employed as a basis for relevant diplomatic conduct in this field, when diplomatic assistance towards its realisation is indicated.

This is of particular importance in those cases where diplomatic agents express criticism of the political system of the receiving State. An example was provided by the case of Yves Gaudeul, the French Ambassador to Haiti, who in 2004 commented on the weaknesses of the Haitian system, including perceived human rights violations and the use of taxpayer resources by the Lavalas party to stay in power.[192] These remarks were met with an official reaction: The Haitian Prime Minister met Mr Gaudeul to 'exchange … points of view regarding respect for the Vienna Convention'.[193] But internal self-determination does encompass a people's right to decide its own political development,[194] and assistance in the realisation of that right relates to a duty which the receiving State owes to the international community as a whole.

The same considerations lead to the conclusion that not every situation in which diplomatic agents contact the opposition or even appear to assist a political faction, can be automatically classed as interference.

The case of the Canadian *chargé d'affaires* in Sudan in 2007—Nuala Lawlor—provides an illustration. In August of that year Lawlor was expelled by the Sudanese government for conduct which the latter described as 'interference in the internal affairs of the country'.[195] Lawlor, together with an EU colleague, had called for the release of leaders of the Sudanese opposition who had been detained without charge.[196]

The sending State did not accept the charge of interference: According to the Canadian Foreign Minister, Lawlor had acted 'in the finest traditions of Canadian diplomacy and was standing up for the values of freedom, democracy, human rights and the rule of law in Sudan'.[197] But these are, of course, not only values of significance to one particular State—they are interests which are easily associated with the right to internal self-determination and assistance towards that goal.[198]

However, a diplomat moves on much more difficult ground if he supports the efforts of a people to secede from the State in question. A 1987 case illustrates this point: In May of that year, the Australian Prime Minister Bob Hawke severed diplomatic relations with Libya, ordered the

[192] *BBC Monitoring International Reports*, 'Highlights of Radio Metropole News 1145 GMT 22 APR 02', 24 April 2002. Paraphrasing by Radio Metropole.

[193] *BBC Monitoring International Reports*, 'Foreign Minister on Prime Minister's meeting', 30 April 2002.

[194] See above, at n 188 and ICCPR art 1(1)2; ICESCR art 1(1)2.

[195] 'EU Apologizes' *Xinhua* (China, 25 August 2007).

[196] 'Canada Right to Back Envoy in Sudan Case' *Star Phoenix* (Saskatoon, 29 August 2007).

[197] ibid.

[198] See above, at n 188.

closure of the Libyan people's bureau in Canberra and gave the diplomats staffing it 10 days to leave the country.[199] The circumstances of the case suggest that the demands of a speaker of the aborigines for an autonomous republic was seen in connection with the 'subversive activities' in which the Libyan mission allegedly engaged.[200] Mr Hawke reportedly stated that he would not permit the existence of a Libyan people's bureau which would aid in the spreading of 'dissension within Australia'.[201] It would be difficult to consider the Australia of the 1980s as a State which, through 'subjugation, domination or exploitation' denied the right of internal self-determination to her indigenous peoples. Diplomats who assist a call for secession in these circumstances can therefore not be considered to have helped in the realisation of a right which international law recognises.

The traditional, restrictive, view on diplomatic involvement in human rights of nationals of the receiving State[202] therefore requires repositioning. The existence of *erga omnes* interests and the impact of the right to internal self-determination in particular highlight the weakness of the claim that diplomatic agents are, under any circumstances, prevented from taking an interest in the rights of the nationals of the receiving State.

On the other hand, the question must be asked if diplomatic agents therefore have a basis for their involvement in the protection of *any* human right which international law recognises and any dispute that arises from its interpretation. There seems to be a considerable difference between human rights debates ignited by the ongoing commission of war crimes and those kindled by the question whether headscarves may be worn in institutions of higher education,[203] the charging of tuition fees at universities,[204] or the question whether a State has done enough to provide protection against unemployment.[205] An understanding of diplomatic involvement which extends to all human rights, would unavoidably include diplomatic representations on budgetary decisions of the government of the receiving State[206]—matters which not only affect an area which many States consider a classic example of their exclusive domain,[207] but which also allow the argument that the receiving State is in a much better position to reach an informed decision than diplomats of the sending State.

[199] 'Libya: Australia Involved in Campaign' *United Press International* (Washington DC, 21 May 1987); 'Libyan Diplomats Expelled' *Facts on File* (New York, 22 May 1987).

[200] See Fischer, 568.

[201] T Duboudin, 'Australian Embassies on Terror Alert' *The Times* (London, 20 May 1987).

[202] See above, at n 86.

[203] See on this *Leyla Şahin*, in particular at para 17.

[204] See Tomasevski Report, at paras 65–69.

[205] On this right, see UDHR art 23. See also Sohn, 45 and Harvey, 367.

[206] See on this ICESCR art 2(1) ('to the maximum of [their] available resources').

[207] For an example for the sensitivity of States in matters of budgetary decisions, see the 2001 case of Dan Coats (ch 2, at n 42 and A.171).

Human rights which are at the core of *erga omnes* obligations, are more restricted in number. In light of the examples provided by the ICJ in *Barcelona Traction*, it appears justifiable to limit such rights to certain fundamental norms.[208] Reference has been made above to the prohibition of slavery, racial discrimination and torture and the human rights corresponding to these obligations.[209] If, as has been suggested, duties arising from international criminal law are included in the category of *erga omnes* obligations,[210] the group of corresponding human rights will arguably be extended—but will also be subject to the additional bars which international criminal law imposes. Not every violation of the right to life for instance, constitutes a breach of international criminal law—the taking of life as a war crime or as a crime against humanity requires a particular contextual element; the taking of life as genocide presupposes specific genocidal intent.[211] Not every diplomatic representation which relates to the violation of this right could therefore rely on *erga omnes* interests as its basis.

Similar limitations apply where diplomatic agents act to assist in the realisation of self-determination. Self-determination certainly presupposes the existence of other rights.[212] That includes the 'classical' political rights—chief among them, the right to vote and to stand in elections.[213] It has been suggested that there are additional rights which are affected where self-determination is concerned—in particular, freedom of assembly and association and freedom of expression[214]—and there are good reasons to follow this view. The beneficiaries even of internal self-determination may find it difficult to determine their political status, if they are prevented from forming their own political organisation or if they have to rely on the goodwill of government-controlled media when trying to give publicity to their message.

[208] See on this above, at n 121, n 123 and n 124.

[209] See above, nn 121–23 and corresponding text.

[210] See above, at n 126.

[211] See on this ICTYSt art 4(2)(a), art 5(a), art 2(a); ICTRSt art 2(2)(a), art 3(a) and art 4(a); ICCSt art 6(a), art 7(1)(a) and art 8(2)(a)(i). On the requirement of specific intent for genocide, see Behrens (2012). The 'Elements of Crime' envisage, as an additional bar, a contextual element for genocide (Elements of Crime, art 6, last element of each alternative).

[212] See Musgrave, 98; Shaw, 292.

[213] ICCPR art 25; ACHR art 23, and *cf* ECHR Protocol 1, art 3. ICCPR and ICESCR allude to these rights when they refer to the right of peoples to 'freely determine' their political status, see above, at n 161. *cf* also Charter of Paris (heading 'Human Rights, Democracy and Rule of Law'): 'Democratic government is based on the will of the people, expressed regularly through free and fair elections'; Copenhagen Document, I, para 6. See Wheatley, 237. However, for a critical view, see Thürer, 367. See Asante, 276, 277 and Reiter et al, 640 on the connection between political and other rights, and Skogly, 519.

[214] Shaw, 292; Wheatley, 240, 241; Thornberry, 136. The ICJ in *Western Sahara* noted that 'the application of the right of self-determination requires a free and genuine expression of the will of the peoples concerned', *Western Sahara*, para 55. See also *Socialist Party and Others*, at para 45.

On the other hand, self-determination is a group right, and its beneficiaries are entities which fulfil the criteria of a 'people'.[215] That causes difficulties in those cases in which a diplomat has made representations because the rights only of selected individuals were violated. The general rule here is that this is not an act which assists in the realisation of a right that the receiving State owes *erga omnes*.

There are reasons why group rights and their protection should be prioritised. If the collective right of self-determination is not granted, the people affected by this often have no choice but to rely on the assistance of the international community to ensure the implementation of their rights.[216] If on the other hand the human rights violation concerns only selected members of the group, then these individuals can make themselves heard through the group itself or may even have recourse to the justice system of the receiving State.[217]

But this rule must allow for certain exceptions. It is not uncommon that the receiving State targets selected individuals precisely because of their relevance for the group—the leaders of the group, say, or prominent journalists—and that the restrictions of their rights then affect the exercise of self-determination by the collective. In situations of this kind, diplomatic representations which deal with the human rights of individuals can nevertheless pertain to violations of *erga omnes* obligations.

One example was a 1990 case involving Robert Oakley, then US Ambassador to Pakistan. In a speech in Washington, Oakley had labelled 'discriminatory' the treatment of Benazir Bhutto, the former Prime Minister of the State and leader of the Pakistan Peoples Party, and was subsequently told by the Pakistani Ministry of Foreign Affairs that his comments constituted 'unwarranted interference' in internal affairs.[218] But the considerations outlined above suggest a more discerning assessment. Representations on human rights even of individuals are tasks which diplomatic agents are entitled to fulfil if the rights concerned are necessary for people of the receiving State in their pursuit of the free determination of their political status.

[215] UN Charter art 1(2); ICCPR art 1(1). The Friendly Relations Declaration refers to the duty of every State to 'refrain from any forcible action which deprives peoples … of the principle of … self-determination'. Friendly Relations Declaration, 5th Principle. See also *Secession of Quebec*, paras 123 et seq on the definition of 'people'; and Chadwick, 4 and 5. *cf* also Castellino, in particular, 56, 57 and Christakis, 324 with particular reference to peoples enjoying the right to internal self-determination.

[216] *cf* Cassese (1995), 142 on the limitations pertaining to the lodging of a complaint with the Human Rights Committee, with regard to a violation of ICCPR art 1.

[217] Individuals may in certain circumstances also have the possibility to lodge a complaint with an international human rights body. However, see Dimitrijevic, 55, 57 on the limitations that apply.

[218] 'Pakistan Summons U.S. Charge d'Affaires' *Japan Economic Newswire* (Tokyo, 16 September 1990). See also the 1996 case of Western diplomats in Burma (A.120).

Outside situations in which diplomatic human rights work corresponds to an *erga omnes* interest (or fulfils a recognised function), it may be difficult to identify a basis in international law for involvement in this field. Such a basis can of course be specifically constructed between sending and receiving State,[219] but it can also be derived from the provisions of a multilateral treaty.

The latter scenario is of some importance, as treaties have come into existence which allow State parties to take an interest in the protection of human rights without having to demonstrate that they have been affected by alleged violations. The underlying obligation has been elevated to a level where it is presumed to be of interest to all parties—it has become a duty *erga omnes partes*.[220]

This is certainly the case where the Genocide Convention is concerned. Mention has already been made of the difficulty of classifying the duty to prevent genocide (as opposed to the duty not to commit the crime) as an obligation *erga omnes*.[221] Its status as a duty *erga omnes partes* however, is beyond question.[222] As a consequence, States need not make the case that they would be affected by the commission of genocide in the receiving State, before they can engage in representations on this matter. In fact, State parties have to fulfil their duty of prevention when they 'learn of, or should normally have learned of, the existence of a serious risk that genocide will be committed'.[223] Resorting to diplomatic involvement—for instance, by highlighting the situation and warning of the consequences—is arguably one of the traditional methods in this scenario; it is certainly among the 'means reasonably available' to those State parties that have diplomatic representations in the State at risk.

Of greater practical importance are those situations in which a treaty has elevated the protection of specific human rights to the level of obligations *erga omnes partes*. The most prominent example for that is the European Convention on Human Rights (ECHR), whose Article 33 permits '[a]ny High Contracting Party' to refer alleged violations of the convention and its protocols by another State to the European Court of Human Rights (ECtHR).[224] The character of the duties contained in the ECHR was clarified by the court in *Ireland v The United Kingdom*, when it stated that the treaty created 'objective obligations' and allowed State Parties to require the fulfilment of these obligations without having to 'justify an interest'.[225]

219 See above, at n 98.

220 See ILC Study Group on Fragmentation, 23.

221 Above, at n 139.

222 Genocide Convention Case (2007), para 430.

223 Ibid, para 431.

224 See also Banjul Charter art 47.

225 *Ireland v The United Kingdom*, para 239. See also Tsevelekos, 644.

The Inter-American Court of Human Rights went even further when it applied a similar reasoning to 'modern human rights treaties in general', stating that they—including the American Convention on Human Rights (ACHR)—constituted treaties under which States submitted themselves 'to a legal order within which they, for the common good, assume various obligations, not in relation to other States, but towards all individuals within their jurisdiction'.[226]

It is true that human rights treaties tend to impose restrictions on the option of inter-State complaints. The ICCPR allows the Human Rights Committee to receive claims by one State to the effect that another State has not fulfilled its Covenant obligations only if the latter State has made a declaration recognising the Committee's competence to receive and consider such communications.[227] The ACHR has similar restrictions regarding inter-State complaints to the Inter-American Commission on Human Rights.[228]

However, once a State has accepted this option, it has renounced its right to assert that the human rights situation in its territory is a matter that falls entirely within its internal affairs. And that has direct consequences for diplomatic representations: Diplomatic involvement in human rights which are owed *erga omnes partes*, must, in principle, be possible. A diplomat has a basis for criticism of perceived human rights violations or warnings of possible court action if the violations are allowed to continue, because the sending State itself can claim to have an interest in the matter.

On the other hand, diplomatic agents wishing to avail themselves of this option, also have to observe the limits which the conventions themselves impose or which human rights bodies authorised to interpret the relevant texts have identified. They also have to take into account the discretionary space which individual States may enjoy in their interpretation of specific aspects of individual rights.[229]

Human rights treaties then can considerably enlarge the basis for diplomatic involvement in this area: They incorporate grounds for diplomatic representations—even in the absence of a direct impact of a perceived violation on the sending State. But reliance on this basis requires a keen understanding of the precise interplay between rights and restrictions which emanate from the interpretation of the relevant treaties.

[226] *Effect of ACHR Reservations*, para 29.

[227] ICCPR art 41(1).

[228] ACHR art 45 (1) and (2). See also Torture Convention art 21(1).

[229] Human rights bodies are willing to grant a margin of appreciation to States where limitations of specific human rights are concerned. See for instance *Handyside*, para 57, with regard to the particular context of ECHR art 10(2). But see also para 49 in that judgment.

2.3. The Human Rights of the Diplomatic Agent

On some occasions, diplomatic agents have sought to rely on the exercise of their own human rights as a basis for conduct which the receiving State considered interference. The situation has been of particular relevance where the right to freedom of expression had been concerned.[230] In 2006, for instance, the US Ambassador to Nicaragua, Paul Trivelli, relied on this right when he was accused of interfering in the internal affairs of the receiving State. Trivelli, who had made certain comments on the presidential elections in Nicaragua, was quoted as stating that he was free to express his opinion on any subject.[231]

Some receiving States, too, have defended the right of diplomatic agents to freedom of expression,[232] and commentators on diplomatic law have sometimes expressed themselves in similarly generous terms. As early as 1594 did Gentili state that he did 'not deny ambassadors freedom of speech' and condemned those who had mistreated envoys who had made use of that right.[233] But there is no universal agreement on this point. In more recent days, Salmon has advocated the view that diplomatic agents are subject to certain duties[234] which restrict their ways of expressing themselves.

The thought that members of particular professions must accept restrictions to the freedom of expression, is not new. In this regard, several commentators have drawn an analogy to the situation of State civil servants. When, for instance, the US Secretary of State warned in 1964 against the involvement of Malaysian employees of the US embassy in Malaysia in the forthcoming elections in that State, he referred to the fact that the host government had decided that its own employees would have to resign their posts if they intended to participate in political campaigns.[235] And when the ILC in 1960 discussed the applicability of the duty of non-interference to honorary consuls (who are frequently nationals of the receiving State), ILC Member Edmonds made the analogy to citizens who had accepted public office and found that they, too, had to refrain from involvement in political affairs in some jurisdictions.[236]

The cases of civil servants and soldiers which have been decided by the European Court of Human Rights (ECtHR) shed further light on

[230] For its modern codification see ICCPR art 19(2); ECHR art 10(1); ACHR art 13(1).

[231] F Aleman, 'U.S. Official' *Associated Press* (New York, 27 April 2006). The US government supported this view. *Intelligence Research Ltd*, 'US Takes Active Role in Nicaraguan Elections' (London, 25 April 2006).

[232] See, for France, *AFDI* (1982), 1100; and for the Netherlands: Netherlands, Government Statement 1983, 308.

[233] Gentili, 119.

[234] The 'obligation de réserve', Salmon (1996), 131, para 201.

[235] See A.9 and above, Introduction, at n 73–74.

[236] YILC 1960/I, 217, para 18 [Edmonds].

the nature of the limitations on the freedom of expression applicable in these cases. The Court (and the European Commission of Human Rights) made it clear that members of these professions do not, because of their status, automatically lose their freedom of expression.[237] There were, however, 'duties and responsibilities' which attached to the exercise of this right.[238] Their scope depended on the status of the applicant. In the case of *Haseldine* for instance—a member of the British Foreign Office who was dismissed in 1989 after the publication of a letter which he had written to the Guardian—the Commission thought it relevant that he had been 'responsible for supervising the enforcement of the embargo against South Africa' (his letter had criticised a government decision pertaining to South African diplomats), and found it 'reasonable' that civil servants in sensitive posts should face 'at least some restrictions and conditions' on the freedom of expression, relating to information they gained in their official capacity or relating to their functions, especially when they concerned 'politically sensitive matters'.[239]

A similar view was pronounced by the Court in the 1976 case of *Engel and Others* with regard to military personnel. The ECtHR stated that the functioning of an army necessitated 'legal rules designed to prevent servicemen from undermining military discipline, for example by writings'.[240]

Given the distinction between civil servants 'in sensitive posts', other civil servants[241] and military personnel, the role of a diplomatic agent appears to be closest to the first category. The differences which can be expected to exist between diplomatic agents and soldiers with regard to their training and the discretion they enjoy, have been outlined above.[242] On the other hand, diplomats frequently have to handle sensitive information coming from both the government of the sending State and a variety of sources within the receiving State. To this limited degree, their position in international relations approaches that of civil servants who, on the domestic plane, have been entrusted with sensitive material.

Court and Commission have also elaborated on the kind of limitations which a State can legitimately adopt for its civil servants. In that context, a duty of (political) neutrality has met with the approval of the ECtHR.[243] A duty of discretion was likewise accepted[244]—at least as far as civil

[237] *cf Haseldine (Admissibility)*; *Grigoriades*, para 45.
[238] *Haseldine (Admissibility)*.
[239] ibid.
[240] *Engel and Others*, para 100. See also *Grigoriades (Dissenting Opinion Pettiti, Gölcüklü)*.
[241] See *Glasenapp*, paras 14 and 19.
[242] See ch 2, at n 82.
[243] See *Redfearn*, para 44, for the freedom of association. However, a different situation cannot be assumed for the right to freedom of expression, see *Ahmed*, para 53; Coussirat-Coustere, 414.
[244] Jacobs et al, 283.

servants were concerned who have to handle sensitive matters as part of their employment. Thus, the Commission in *Haseldine* placed particular weight on the question of the accessibility of the information which the applicant had conveyed through his letter: While it did not deny Haseldine's contention that the information was not confidential, it found it 'significant' that he had refused to answer questions about his source and concluded that this information was therefore 'not easily or publicly available'.[245]

In *Kosiek*, the Commission made furthermore reference to a duty of moderation applicable to civil servants;[246] a duty which appears to pertain rather to the methods used in exercising the freedom of expression than to the content of the message.[247]

These are features of the office of a civil servant which appear congruent to certain duties which have been highlighted in the past in cases of diplomatic agents in their relations with receiving States.

A duty of discretion—or 'reserve'—has been accepted for diplomats as well.[248] Salmon notes in this context that 'open' criticism of the government of the receiving State or even of opposition politicians must be avoided to fulfil this obligation.[249] The beneficiary of that duty, however, differs from that in the case of State civil servants: There, the duty exists to safeguard the interests of their government and other affected parties in the State. In diplomatic law, which is not concerned with the relationship between diplomats and their own governments,[250] the duty protects the interests of the receiving State.

And there is evidence that State practice supports the view that discretion is considered part of the position of diplomatic agents. There are certainly numerous cases in which diplomatic agents who engaged in public criticism were told that the appropriate forum would have been the 'diplomatic channels',[251] and while this may at times be a smokescreen behind which the hosts hide their irritation about the criticism itself, it still shows that States feel on safe ground when they attack lack of discretion as a deficiency in the fulfilment of the duties of the diplomatic office.

A civil servant's duty of neutrality also finds its equivalent in diplomatic law, but direction and purpose of the duty are again different in

[245] *Haseldine (Admissibility).*

[246] *Kosiek* 37, para 85.

[247] For instance, the 2005 Charter on Professional Ethics, which is applicable to staff of the Council of Europe, refers to the duty of moderation when it calls on staff members to refrain from acts 'likely to tarnish the Organisation's image or undermine the dignity or integrity of their post' (para 11). See also *Haseldine (Admissibility).*

[248] See *AFDI* (1982), 1100.

[249] Salmon (1996), 131, para 201. See also Glahn (1986), 462 on certain forms of correspondence with the press. See however also below, ch 7, after n 28 and ch 9, at n 82 f.

[250] See on this point Smith, 70.

[251] See ch 4, at n 142, n 143 and corresponding text and *cf* ch 9, n 82.

both cases. In the domestic arena, the duty of neutrality allows the civil service to function with the appearance of a non-biased administration; the parties benefitting from the neutrality of the civil service are the citizens of the State as well as their elected officials.[252]

In diplomatic relations, an unbiased position of diplomatic agents is not expected—they are, after all, representatives of their States and have to defend their positions—but in certain situations a duty of neutrality is nonetheless accepted for the benefit of the receiving State.

That is particularly apparent where diplomatic behaviour at times of political campaigns is concerned. The obligation to refrain from participation in such campaigns was the only example of interference to which the 1958 ILC Commentary made express reference,[253] and State practice supports the existence of this duty. The 1984 incident involving the US Ambassador to El Salvador (Pickering) may be recalled in this context. In May of that year, the Republican Senator Helms demanded, in a letter to President Reagan, Pickering's withdrawal after the Ambassador had allegedly worked for the election victory of the Salvadoran presidential candidate Duarte.[254] Helms referred on this occasion to the duty of neutrality.[255] The American embassy in El Salvador did not deny the existence of such an obligation, but insisted that they had been 'completely neutral' in the elections.[256]

Lastly, the existence of a duty of moderation also appears to be a feature of diplomatic law. The negative State reactions which insulting diplomatic behaviour received in the past, attest to the fact that members of the international community are keen to insist on conduct which observes the boundaries of acceptable diplomatic style.[257]

Reference has already been made to the 'vituperative language' of Catacazy in the nineteenth century;[258] and a more modern example was provided when Libyan representatives in Australia made themselves the subject of criticism in 1983, after they had disseminated copies of a letter in which US President Reagan was called a 'new world Hitler'.[259]

There is evidence, then, that the international community does understand certain limitations as inherent to the diplomatic office. With regard to the affected persons, this restriction of a fundamental human right finds its rationale in the consideration that diplomatic agents, upon accepting

[252] See on this point *Ahmed*, para 53.

[253] B.7, commentary, para 2.

[254] J Frazier, 'Helms, Candidate Charge U.S. Interference' *Associated Press* (New York, 3 May 1984).

[255] ibid.

[256] H Gottlieb, 'Helms Asks Reagan To Fire Ambassador' *Associated Press* (New York, 2 May 1984). See also A.9 and A.10. See also Przetacznik (1975), 309.

[257] See on this in more detail below, ch 9.

[258] See above, ch 1, at n 26.

[259] See A.72; See also A.202.

their particular position, accept an implied waiver of their freedom of expression to the extent of the limits dictated by the office. They are, in that regard, in a position which does not differ much from that of the civil servant Haseldine, in whose case the Commission found that 'by entering the diplomatic service', he had 'accepted certain restrictions on the exercise of his freedom of expression as being inherent in his duties'.[260]

That does not mean that the relevant diplomatic conduct—be it the public expression of controversial opinions, involvement in partisan politics or even engagement in sharp criticism—can never be considered to be in compliance with international law. There may, after all, be legitimate interests of the sending State or *erga omnes* obligations of the receiving State on which such acts might be based.[261] But it means that it will be difficult to base such forms of conduct solely on the enjoyment of a diplomat's own rights: In that regard, their freedom of expression is subject to implied limitations.

With regard to aspects of life which are not affected by the fulfilment of their duties, civil servants continue to enjoy the rights from which each individual in their State benefits.[262] The same consideration applies to diplomatic agents in the receiving State.[263]

Yet the 'diplomatic office' is a broad concept which is capable of leaving its mark on acts whose official character had never been intended.[264] The realm of genuinely private acts will often be limited to a considerable degree; and it would appear that of all the divergent interests which have been discussed in this chapter, the human rights of diplomats offer the least powerful basis for activities which, in the eyes of the receiving State, fulfil the conditions of diplomatic interference.

260 *Haseldine (Admissibility)*.

261 See ch 7 at 29 f; ch 6, at n 31 f and after n 65; ch 9, s 3.

262 See on this *Vogt*, para 53.

263 It is interesting to note in this context that even in the 18th century, *Wolff* stated that ambassadors 'as regards those acts which are required to conduct that business [for which they are sent] … differ from other foreigners … but as regards their own private acts, which have no bearing on that business, they do not differ from other foreigners', Wolff, 534. Civil servants as citizens of the receiving State of course enjoy additional rights outside the freedom of expression—such as certain political rights—which those diplomats who are not nationals of the receiving State do not have.

264 See ch 2, after n 86.

4

Resolving the Meeting of Competing Interests

DIPLOMATS ACCREDITED TO Eastern European countries in 1989 became witnesses to some of the most decisive events of the twentieth century. As the Autumn of Nations embraced Hungary, East Germany, Czechoslovakia, Bulgaria and Romania, diplomatic representatives reported on developments which heralded or directly induced the end of Communist rule in these States. On occasion however, diplomatic observers went further than that.

In December of that year, two British diplomats—Assistant Military Attaché Michael Brown and Second Secretary Susan Laffey—joined students and workers in their march on the national television station in Romania.[1] After the event, the diplomats referred to the function of observation as an explanation of their conduct[2]—a function expressly addressed by the Vienna Convention.[3] The characteristic element of that task—the assessment of developments in the receiving State—was certainly still discernible; nor can it be denied that the diplomats had an opportunity to observe events in considerable detail.

At the same time, Brown and Laffey's activities came under attack even within their own State,[4] and the question may well be asked if the mere availability of a basis for diplomatic actions can be sufficient for a legal assessment of their adoption. If that were the case, conduct with wide-ranging consequences could be lawfully pursued by diplomatic agents—reliance on Article 3(1)(b) for instance could permit the funding (and even establishment) of a party friendly towards the sending State; even a call to arms against a government hostile to its interests.

But the fact that the rule of non-interference faces competing interests which are recognised in international law, does not mean that it has thereby lost all applicability. What it means is that a restrictive norm meets

[1] M White, 'Why We Joined' *Press Association* (London, 26 December 1989); Alan Travis, 'Rebirth of Romania' *The Guardian* (London, 28 December 1989).

[2] R Stacey, 'British Envoys Joined Revolt' *The Times* (London, 27 December 1989).

[3] See ch 3, s 1.4.

[4] British Members of Parliament criticised their actions (Travis, n 1), as did a former British Ambassador, J Graham, 'Undiplomatic Activity' *The Times* (London, 30 December 1989).

permissive rules which have an impact on the same situation. What is required is a mechanism which can resolve the apparent conflict or which allows mediation between the norms before a conflict does arise.

It is somewhat surprising that the Convention itself does not define at least the relationship between diplomatic functions and the rule of non-interference, norms which it both expressly acknowledges. The potential for conflict had, after all, been considered even at the drafting stage. In one of the first comments on the rule on diplomatic duties, the Thai ILC member Khoman referred to the possibility that a diplomatic message on draft legislation in the receiving State might be considered interference, but that it was 'the positive duty of an ambassador to make them', if the intended laws affected interests of the sending State.[5]

The ILC Commentary on the final Draft Article on interference likewise referred to the interplay of the two norms by stating that representations to protect the interests of the sending State or its nationals 'in accordance with international law' did not constitute interference.[6]

The commentary does not refer to the impact of other functions—let alone the impact of the realisation of erga omnes interests or the protection of human rights. Even in the limited scenario which it does envisage, crucial questions remain unanswered. The concept of 'representations' in particular is very wide and could include the use of insulting language or, as no addressee is specified, messages of support to leading opposition parties in the receiving State, as long as that promotes interests of the sending State. It is questionable whether the international community supports such unqualified support of diplomatic representations at the expense of the rule of non-interference.

The ILC is not alone in its employment of sweeping language when assessing the impact of permissive rules. Similar comments have been made where human rights were at the root of diplomatic action. The editors of Satow's *Diplomatic Practice*, who in 1979 still supported the traditional line on non-interference in this matter,[7] have now come out in favour of the opposite extreme and emphasise in the chapter on diplomatic duties that '... international law now requires States to defend and protect human rights abroad'.[8] The editors of Oppenheim, on the other hand, are similarly categorical when it comes to protecting the interests of the receiving State, claiming that diplomatic agents have 'no right whatever to take part in [the] political life [of that State]'.[9]

[5] YILC (Yearbook of the International Law Commission) 1957/I, 145, para 71 [Khoman].
[6] B.8, commentary, para 2.
[7] See ch 3, at n 86.
[8] Satow (2009), 153, para 9.58.
[9] Oppenheim (1967), 787.

But it is questionable whether international law favours solutions which involve the complete suppression of one norm (or one legal regime) by another. Given the proliferation of codified rules of international law and the increasing development of 'specialist systems'[10] within this framework, there has been a rising need to deal with situations in which multiple norms are applicable which ostensibly pull in different directions.

It is true that there are methods in international law which would resolve the meeting of norms in a confrontational manner, by prioritising the applicability of one norm over another. But international law also recognises methods which seek to avoid an open clash and its potential consequences (conciliatory methods). The identification of the appropriate mechanism for dealing with the meeting of norms is therefore an integral part of the assessment of the diplomatic conduct in these situations, and the examination of relevance and feasibility of such methods is part of this process.

1. CONFRONTATIONAL METHODS FOR THE ASSESSMENT OF DIPLOMATIC INTERFERENCE

The use of a confrontational method to resolve the meeting of divergent norms presupposes the existence of a hierarchy in international law. It is this hierarchical structure that allows a determination to the effect that certain norms should, at least in particular situations, be given preferable applicability.

Such a hierarchy can be envisaged by the treaties which incorporate the relevant norms. The classic example is the UN Charter, whose Article 103 makes clear that obligations of Member States under the Charter shall prevail over obligations under other international agreements. However, in treaties whose norms (ostensibly) clash with the prohibition of diplomatic interference—human rights conventions in particular—such provisions are missing. In their absence, it is necessary to have recourse to general international law, and the mechanisms for conflict resolution that it provides.

But the divergent norms which have been discussed that far, reveal an inherent difficulty as far as the application of traditional methods of conflict resolution are concerned. Ben-Asher, who examined conflicts between human rights and diplomatic immunity, states with some justification that hierarchies are useful where they concern 'conflicting rules in the same area, say, continental shelf delimitation, rather than determining priority between distinct areas'.[11] The reason for that is that hierarchies presuppose not only a clash, but also a link between the norms under consideration.

[10] A term used by the ILC in 2006, ILC Study Group on Fragmentation, 3 and 4.

[11] Ben-Asher, at n 226.

The *lex specialis* rule offers an illustration. The stipulation that the more specific norm has to be preferred to the more general one[12] indicates the existence of a particular connection: The respective norms must 'deal with the same subject matter'.[13] That is clearly not the case where rules on diplomatic conduct meet rules on the protection of human rights: Their meeting provides an illustration for the common problem of the existence of special, and separate, intersecting regimes.[14]

Nor is *lex specialis* a helpful mechanism where charges of interference are countered by reference to the fulfilment of diplomatic functions under Article 3 of the Vienna Convention. In this instance, the rules share common ground in as far as they both relate to diplomatic conduct. But speciality presupposes at the very least that the more specific norm contains an element that is additional to the more general rule. A rule which does not incorporate the elements of the more general norm and which might even negate the character of the latter, is not 'more specific'—it is simply a different provision under international law.

Similar problems arise where the *lex posterior* rule is concerned. For situations of that kind, Article 59 of the Vienna Convention on the Law of Treaties (VCLT), which prioritises the treaty that is concluded later in time, specifies that the later treaty must relate to the same subject matter. Accordingly, the ILC makes clear that there is no automatic presumption of precedence of the later norm if the treaties come from different legal regimes.[15]

Even if the hurdle of the subject matter did not exist, it would be difficult to ascertain which norm arose later in time—especially if the adoption of the relevant rules in later instruments is seen as an affirmation of the original provision. The human right to life for instance was enshrined in the European Convention on Human Rights (ECHR) in 1950.[16] The rule on non-interference in its current form was first incorporated in the VCDR in 1961. The right to life was re-affirmed in the International Covenant on Civil and Political Rights (ICCPR) of 1966. The rule of non-interference was re-affirmed in the CSM of 1969[17] and so forth. The applicability of the respective conventions may vary (the Convention on Special Missions does not deal with permanent representatives), but there is no evidence that the drafters of the later documents in the same field did not believe in the continued existence of the respective rules.

[12] See ILC Study Group on Fragmentation, 8 at 2(5). The ILC refers to the *lex specialis* rules as a 'technique of interpretation' (ibid), and see Matheson, 427.

[13] ILC Study Group on Fragmentation, 8 at 2 (5).

[14] See on that Matheson, 428.

[15] ILC Study Group on Fragmentation, 18.

[16] ECHR art 2(1).

[17] CSM art 47(1)2.

The fact must be kept in mind that States are not prevented from entering into treaties that contain contradictory (or seemingly contradictory) messages. If they do so, they may well attract responsibility under both treaties; but the previous treaty does not become invalid merely due to the fact that it was concluded earlier in time,[18] nor does it necessarily lose its applicability.

A different result would be achieved if the international community recognised a hierarchical relationship between the relevant norms, based on the values they incorporate. With regards to human rights, such an elevated value has from time to time been asserted—without necessarily claiming a *jus cogens* character of the rights in question.[19]

Thus, the Sub-Commission on the Promotion and Protection of Human Rights of the UN Economic and Social Council (ECOSOC) spoke in 2000 of the 'primacy of human rights law over all other regimes of international law' and called this a 'basic and fundamental principle that should not be departed from'.[20]

The question whether there are values of higher rank than the rules of diplomatic law, has likewise been discussed on an international level—particularly in cases in which diplomatic immunity and inviolability clashes with the protection of human rights. When the ICJ in the *Tehran Hostages Case* stated that the observance of inviolability of the diplomatic agent and of the mission premises does 'naturally' not mean 'that a diplomatic agent caught in the act of committing an assault or other offence may not, on occasion, be briefly arrested by the police of the receiving State in order to prevent the commission of the particular crime'[21] it went a far way in establishing a hierarchy which gives diplomatic law in this context only second place behind certain other rules of international law. The reference to 'assault' makes it likely that the court paid particular attention to the protection of physical integrity and the right to life.[22]

The British government, in its reply to the House of Commons Foreign Affairs Committee's Review of the Vienna Convention on Diplomatic Relations, was even clearer in the acceptance of such a hierarchy. With regard to the diplomatic bag, it indicated that there may be situations in which the inviolability of the bag may clash (because of its contents) with

[18] See on this Milanović, 76.

[19] The concept of *jus cogens* ('compelling law') refers to rules which, by their very nature, enjoy a superior status over other norms of international law. See below, at n 32 ff.

[20] Oloka-Onyango and Udagama Report, para 63.

[21] *Tehran Hostages Case*, para 86.

[22] The ICJ judgment can be criticised for its rather sweeping nature. Allowing arrest (however briefly) if just about any offence is about to be committed, carries considerable potential for abuse by the receiving State, and it is not evident that such wide powers would enjoy the support of the international community.

'national security or the personal safety of the public or of individuals'.[23] In such cases, the government would 'not hesitate' to adopt actions based on 'the overriding right to self-defence or the duty to protect human life'.[24] These instances point to the possibility that rules of diplomatic law, in particular circumstances, may have to stand back behind other rules of international law, including at least certain human rights.

Such considerations might also apply to the meeting of the rule of non-interference and the protection of human rights. The fact in particular that the guarantee of some human rights corresponds to *erga omnes* obligations incumbent on the receiving State,[25] makes the acceptance of a value-based hierarchy tempting.

But the theory that human rights have to enjoy a place of preference in the framework of international law has also attracted criticism. Shelton points out that the view has (that far) failed to attract support in the international community;[26] Ben-Asher, speaking about the clash of diplomatic immunity and human rights, went so far as to state that '... both will roughly be equal from a hierarchy of sources perspective'.[27]

Indeed, even where the protection of human rights corresponds to *erga omnes* interests, the existence of a value-based hierarchy is not a foregone conclusion. It is true that some authors consider the rationale for the existence of *erga omnes* obligations to lie in the value of the relevant norm;[28] but this view is not free of controversy.

The circle of *erga omnes* norms does embrace certain constitutive norms[29]—such as boundary and territorial issues, which are opposable to all States.[30] To claim that, for example, title to a fishery zone[31] falls within this group because of its special value, would be a somewhat strained interpretation. A common interest is not necessarily the same as a common value, and the character of at least some *erga omnes* norms is arguably accepted rather on grounds of pragmatism and necessity.

That assessment changes if the relevant *erga omnes* norms are at the same time norms which possess *jus cogens* character.[32] *Jus cogens* certainly represents the clearest example of an accepted hierarchy in general international law: By accepting that norms which clash with *jus cogens*

23 UK Government Report (1985), para 48.
24 ibid. *cf* Herdegen, 749.
25 See ch 3, at nn 121–24.
26 Shelton (2006), 294.
27 Ben-Asher, at fn 225.
28 Most prominently the Institute of International Law (2005) art 1.
29 On the distinction between constitutive and regulatory norms, see Linderfalk, 856.
30 ILC Study Group on Fragmentation, 24, at para 38.
31 *cf Jan Mayen Case (Separate Opinion Oda)*, 100, para 40.
32 On the relationship between *jus cogens* norms and *erga omnes* norms, see ILC Study Group on Fragmentation, 24, para 38.

become 'ipso facto void',[33] the international community appreciates the existence of rules which enjoy superior status over all other norms of international law.

But it has always been difficult to identify the members of that particular family. Selected human rights are frequently named among norms which carry *jus cogens* character, and the case has even been advanced that all human rights should belong to this group.[34] Not much evidence has yet been adduced to support that view, and it encounters additional difficulties: If *jus cogens* is considered a norm 'from which no derogation is permitted',[35] then most human rights fail to fulfil exactly this criterion—the leading human rights instruments allow States parties to derogate from most rights, if specific conditions are met.[36]

On the other hand, this line of reasoning also gives room for the view that those rights from which no derogation is possible, must enjoy a better chance of being included in the circle of *jus cogens* norms.[37] The list of 'non-derogables' varies from convention to convention; but the four rights which in the three leading human rights treaties fall in this category, are the right to life,[38] freedom from torture or inhuman or degrading treatment or punishment,[39] freedom from slavery[40] and the *nullum crimen sine lege* principle of criminal law.[41]

To a degree, this perspective is supported by decisions of international courts and human rights bodies. The *jus cogens* character of the prohibition of torture has been claimed by several Trial Chambers of the International Criminal Tribunal for the Former Yugoslavia (ICTY)[42] as well as the European Court of Human Rights (ECtHR).[43] The Inter-American Commission on Human Rights in 1996 expressed the opinion that the right to life likewise belonged to the circle of peremptory norms.[44]

But even the classification of non-derogable rights as *jus cogens* is not undisputed.[45] The right to life might appear as the most likely *jus cogens* candidate among them, if it truly represents (as the ECtHR has argued), the

[33] ILC Study Group on Fragmentation, para 41 and Shelton (2006), 301. Treaties which conflict at the time of their conclusion with existing *jus cogens*, are *ab initio* void: VCLT art 53.

[34] See the discussion at Parker and Neylon, 441 et seq, and in Shelton (2006), 303.

[35] ILC Study Group on Fragmentation, 20, para 32 and fn 26, with reference to VCLT art 53.

[36] ICCPR art 4; ECHR art 15; ACHR art 27.

[37] See Lillich, 118, fn 17 and *Michael Domingues*, para 49.

[38] ICCPR art 6; ECHR art 2; ACHR art 4.

[39] ICCPR art 7; ECHR art 3; ACHR art 5.

[40] ICCPR art 8(1) and (2); ECHR art 4(1); ACHR art 6.

[41] ICCPR art 15; ECHR art 7; ACHR art 9.

[42] See for instance *Delalić* (Trial Chamber), para 454; *Furundžija* (Trial Chamber), paras 153, 154.

[43] *Al-Adsani*, para 61.

[44] *Tugboat Victims*, para 79.

[45] For a discussion, see Caplan, 772 et seq; Herdegen, 755.

'supreme value in the hierarchy of human rights'.[46] But the ECHR, while stating that no derogation shall be made from that right, allows an exception in cases of 'deaths resulting from lawful acts of war' (Article 15(2) ECHR) and even permits limitations of the right (Article 2(2) ECHR). Doubt also attaches to the question whether State practice does in fact support the elevated character of these rights.[47]

The norms whose *jus cogens* character commands the widest support in the international community, certainly include rules which derive from human rights regimes—such as the prohibition of torture,[48] of slavery,[49] of genocide[50]—as well as provisions whose breach will typically result in grave human rights abuses—as is the case where the unlawful use of force is concerned.[51]

But even these rules do not allow an immediate conclusion about a normative hierarchy between diplomatic interference and diplomatic conduct to protect the human rights underlying them. If certain prohibitions carry *jus cogens* character, it does not follow that ancillary rules—such as the prosecution of those who violate the norms, or the making of diplomatic representations in this field—enjoy the same, hierarchically superior, status. States as well as international courts and tribunals have shown themselves hesitant to expand the *jus cogens* concept beyond the core obligations themselves.[52]

[46] *K-H W v Germany*, para 66.

[47] See on this Ben-Asher, at fn 242. See also for a generally critical view D'Amato, 2, with particular reference to Parker and Neylon.

[48] The prohibition of torture featured among the 'most frequently cited examples of jus cogens', to which the International Law Commission in 2006 made reference; ILC Study Group on Fragmentation, 20, para 33. See also Draft Articles on State Responsibility (2001), 85, art 26, commentary, para 5.

[49] ILC Study Group on Fragmentation, 20, para 33; *Michael Domingues*, para 49; Draft Articles on State Responsibility (2001), 85, art 26, commentary, para 5.

[50] *Armed Activities*, 32, para 64; *Michael Domingues*, para 49; ILC Study Group on Fragmentation, 208; Draft Articles on State Responsibility (2001), 85, art 26, commentary, para 5.

[51] See the Draft Articles on the Law of Treaties, 247, art 50, commentary, para 1. In *Nicaragua*, the ICJ referred to these and other materials on the jus cogens nature of the prohibition of the unlawful use of force, without rejecting the view, *Nicaragua*, 100, 101, para 190. See also ILC Study Group on Fragmentation, 20; Shelton (2006), 302. Paradigmatic examples for the unlawful use of force which highlight the link to potential human rights violations (eg the right to life, to physical integrity and to the peaceful enjoyment of one's possessions) can be derived from the list of instances outlined in the General Assembly's 'Definition of Aggression' and the alternatives listed in the 2010 amendment to the ICCSt as agreed by the Assembly of State Parties. Definition of Aggression art 3; ASP Resolution 2010, Annex I, art 8 *bis*.

[52] In relation to torture, for instance, the question may arise whether the *jus cogens* character of the core prohibition of torture would also cover the ancillary right to prosecute offenders and thus elevate that rule to a higher status than conflicting rules of immunity pertaining to State officials. This has been the topic of some debate, see Lord Millet's opinion in the Pinochet case, *Pinochet* (No 3), at 178; against Lord Hope's opinion in the same case, ibid at 146.

The prohibition on genocide is an example: While some authors are happy to state that the 'law of genocide' is a *jus cogens* rule,[53] international courts and tribunals usually express themselves in a more cautious way. The ICJ and the ILC refer to the 'prohibition' of genocide,[54] and the ICTY in the *Blagojević* case drew the distinction between the customary law character of the 'law set out in the [Genocide] Convention' and the *jus cogens* character of the 'norm prohibiting genocide'.[55] It is a distinction of significance: If the entire Genocide Convention enjoyed *jus cogens* status, its Article I (the duty to prevent the crime and punish its perpetrators), would be encompassed by that; and diplomatic representations in this field (as in the Gelbard incident in the year 2000)[56] would therefore be adopted in pursuance of a *jus cogens* mandate.

But there are good reasons to retain the distinction between core prohibitions and ancillary interests. Such differentiation might at first sight appear to favour the State and person of the perpetrator. But often enough, the persons who violated the relevant *jus cogens* norms—torturers, génocidaires and other international criminals—are still in a position of power; frequently in an ongoing armed conflict. If, as a consequence of a wide understanding of *jus cogens*, the rule of non-interference and other ancillary norms were invalidated, there would be little incentive for such perpetrators to enter into negotiations with those seeking a peaceful settlement of the situation.[57]

The greatest difficulty in the application of *jus cogens* is ultimately the prevailing uncertainty about the norms which should enjoy this status.[58] This situation has led to extreme results: Courts are reluctant to assess a meeting of norms on the basis of *jus cogens* alone,[59] whereas academic commentators have all too often yielded to the temptation of assigning *jus cogens* status to rules—frequently, without providing satisfactory substantiation.[60] One of the candidates suggested in this regard is the rule of non-interference itself. In the 1950s for instance, Shurshalov argued that non-interference in the internal affairs of States was a 'basic principle and concept' which rendered invalid those treaties that were in conflict with it.[61]

[53] Ben-Asher, at fn 215.

[54] See above, at n 50.

[55] *Blagojević* (Trial Chamber), para 639.

[56] See ch 3, n 131.

[57] See on this problem, P Behrens, 'Stochern im Wespennest' *Süddeutsche Zeitung* (Munich, 6 March 2009).

[58] The view has been expressed that even the examples of the (prohibition of the) unlawful use of force, genocide, slave trading and piracy are subject to controversy, Shaw, 126. But see Värk (2003), 115, 116.

[59] See on this Milanović, 71 and Shelton (2006), 305 with particular reference to the ICJ.

[60] For further examples, ranging from the duty not to commit transboundary environmental harm to the 'right to life of animals', see the discussion in Shelton (2006), 303.

[61] As referred to in Triska and Slusser, 717 (reference to Shurshalov, 140–44).

Both the difficulty of finding agreement within the international community on the *jus cogens* character of a norm[62] and the destructive effects of *jus cogens* norms[63] have contributed to the prevailing uncertainty of the law. Shurshalov's conclusion on the *jus cogens* character of non-interference was that a whole range of treaties—including the NATO and SEATO pacts—were invalid.[64] It is not surprising that scenarios of this kind help keep alive arguments surrounding the concept and boundaries of *jus cogens*.

While the view is not followed that the rule against diplomatic interference is *jus cogens*, it is undeniable that the rules of diplomatic law are of fundamental character for the international community.[65] The problem that arises here, especially where the ban on interference meets the protection of human rights, is not really the problem of one offensive norm clashing with the most cherished values of the law of nations. It is rather the encounter of two of the most significant strands of modern international law: The rights of the individual meet rules which derive from the sovereign equality of States.

The importance which both systems possess for the international order[66] lends support to the view that the establishment of a hierarchy among them—with the accompanying destructive results—would be ill-suited for the assessment of their meeting.

On the other hand, an approach which acknowledges their respective importance and gives each of them room to exist within the framework of international law, has better hope of finding support in the international community—and indeed in international courts and institutions which largely prefer conciliatory methods to confrontational ones.[67] An understanding of this kind takes up the view suggested by the ILC when it stated that '[c]onflicts between rules of international law should be resolved in accordance with the principle of harmonization …'.[68]

[62] The Chairman of the Drafting Committee at the UN Conference on the Law of Treaties pointed out that the words 'as a whole' (in what is today Art 53 VCLT) were not to be read as requiring unanimous consent, but that support by 'a very large majority' of States would suffice, 1968 Conference, Records, 1st Session, 472. But this support needs to be established, and it appears in keeping with the spirit of VCLT art 53 to demand, as Ben Asher does, agreement of States 'crossing ideological and political divides', Ben-Asher, at fn 242.

[63] Under the VCLT, the clash does not merely result in a reevaluation of the offending articles in the light of *jus cogens*: The clashing treaty itself is void if it collides with an already existing peremptory norm, or becomes void and terminates, if the peremptory norm emerges later. See VCLT arts 53 and 64. See Magalonna, 521, 531. Pavel, 898. See also Linderfalk, 861, considering situations in which *jus cogens* would have a deleterious effect on the UN Charter in its entirety.

[64] Triska and Slusser, 718 (reference to Shurshalov, 148–54).

[65] *cf* on this Danilenko, 131.

[66] *cf* UN Charter art 1(3) on human rights and art 2(1) on the sovereign equality of Member States.

[67] See Milanović, 71.

[68] ILC Study Group on Fragmentation, 25.

Reference to 'conflicts' in this context may in fact not be adequate—harmonisation, after all, is based on the perspective that a conflict in the true sense of the word can be avoided.[69] It is a method which steers clear of the dramatic effects of *jus cogens* and other confrontational approaches: It takes into consideration the diverging norms, but it seeks to preserve them: It acknowledges their respective rights of existence.

2. CONCILIATORY METHODS FOR THE ASSESSMENT OF DIPLOMATIC INTERFERENCE

2.1. The Challenges of Harmonisation

One day after the conclusion of the VCDR in 1961, the Polish Ambassador to the United States became the recipient of a warning note from the American Secretary of State. The background to the letter was constituted by negative remarks which he had made, relating to the government of the Federal Republic of Germany.

In his communication, the Secretary of State stated that he considered representational activities in general 'as falling within the bounds of the Ambassador's diplomatic function', even though the United States might not share the opinions which were expressed in them. But he added that this did not extend to 'public attacks … upon a government with which the United States maintains friendly relations', and that he expected that such activities would not be repeated.[70]

It is one of the few cases in which a receiving State showed an appreciation of the relevant conflicting interests—including the right of the sending State to make its voice heard through its diplomatic representatives. What the Secretary of State suggested was not an evaluation that would remove this interest from the equation—rather, the imposition of certain limitations on diplomatic conduct, which would not affect the existence in principle of either interest. It is an approach which appears to satisfy the requirements of the mechanism of 'harmonisation'.

Harmonisation, in the eyes of the ILC, applies where several norms have an impact on the same subject matter; it is a 'generally accepted principle' that demands that that the resulting assessment gives rise 'to a single set of compatible obligations'.[71] Harmonisation is in fact a technique of interpretation which takes into account the contents of both norms in this situation[72] and thus avoids the assumption of a normative conflict.[73]

[69] *cf* Milanović, 73.
[70] Whiteman (1970), 147.
[71] ILC Study Group on Fragmentation, 8, para 4.
[72] ibid, and see Milanović, 73.
[73] See Milanović, 98 on the presumption against norm conflict in international law.

As such, it derives support from the practice of international courts[74] and from academic writings;[75] but the view that the interpretation of a norm must take into account other rules of international law which have relevance for the instant situation, has also been embraced by Article 31(3)(c) of the VCLT.[76] The underlying rationale appears to be that a conciliatory approach is possible as long as one way can be found for a State and its agents to comply with the conditions that the two rules impose.[77] As a result, one rule may well condition the meaning of the other.[78]

In the past, several ways have been suggested to avoid the emergence of a conflict between norms of international law which send out seemingly divergent messages. The view, for instance, has been advanced that in cases in which an obligation meets a right, a conflict need not arise, because the relevant State can decide not to exercise its right.[79] If that theory were applied, the duty not to interfere would regularly win out against the right to protect the interests of the sending State, to make representations on *erga omnes* interests etc.

But it is a theory that courts controversy. For one, it is not clear why the right should always be the weaker norm—saying that the State does not 'have to' exercise its right if faced with a divergent duty is, after all, merely a more elegant way of stating that the content of the right has been reduced.

The treatment of diplomats during the days of Pol Pot's regime in Cambodia illustrates the problem. In 1977, diplomatic agents in Phnom Penh reportedly lived in conditions best described as a form of house arrest: Diplomatic missions were not allowed to have cars, diplomats were not allowed to walk beyond approximately 200 yards from the compounds, meals were delivered by the Khmer Rouge.[80]

Had the regime been so inclined, it could have invoked obligations enshrined in the Vienna Convention as bases for its actions. It could

[74] See *Al-Adsani*, at para 55, with reference to *Loizidou* (1997), para 43. *Oil Platforms*, 182, para 41. See also Milanović, 128 with further references.

[75] *cf* Jenks, 427, 428 with further references. Sadat-Akhavi had suggested a similar non-confrontational method which he termed the 'reconciliation of norms'. In his view, a differentiation between 'interpretation' (Sadat-Akhavi, 25 et seq) and 'reconciliation' (34 et seq) has to be made. But the method of finding a way which reconciles apparently conflicting rules, is the adoption of an understanding which allows their co-existence—this, however, is an interpretive approach.

[76] See on this Tsevelekos, 624, 631, 644 with further references.

[77] For a similar approach, see Sadat-Akhavi, 34 (reconciliation possible if 'there is at least one way of complying with all [the] requirements' of the two rules).

[78] See the example Sadat-Akhavi provides for a potential clash of ICESCR (International Covenant on Economic, Social and Cultural Rights) art 9 and ICCPR art 26 ICCPR, Sadat-Akhavi, 42.

[79] See Milanović, 72 with further reference.

[80] 'The World: Honorable House Arrest' *Time* (New York, 24 October 1977); and see Glahn (1992), 529.

have declared virtually all of Cambodia a security zone (Article 26),[81] triggering the duty of diplomatic agents not to enter most of the territory. It could have declared that any observation within Cambodia fell within the State's exclusive jurisdiction, so that diplomats going beyond the permitted perimeter would be considered in violation of the duty of non-interference as enshrined in Article 41. Declarations of this kind, of course, would not change the fact that the measures adopted by the Cambodian government clashed with almost all the functions to which Article 3 refers[82] as well as with Article 25. But from the perspective of normative co-existence, these provisions reflect 'merely' rights of the sending State; and in pursuance of the above mentioned view, sending States would be called upon not to exercise these rights in order to avoid a normative conflict. As a consequence, their rights would be stripped of any meaningful content.

It is questionable whether the international community would indeed approve of a solution that would, in the name of harmonisation, invariably prefer duties to rights. It is worth noting that the scenario which the Cambodian restrictions realised had even been envisaged by the ILC, which in its draft commentary stated that the creation of security zones 'must not … be so extensive as to render freedom of movement and travel illusory'.[83]

Another approach to allow a State to comply with both sets of norms would be to consider the concept of interference as being subject to justifications. The concept of justifications applies to situations in which the existence of certain circumstances changes the assessment of a prima facie unlawful form of conduct. The most notable examples in that field are the 'circumstances precluding wrongfulness', to which the ILC's Draft Articles on State Responsibility refer. In situations in which these circumstances—for instance, *force majeure* (Article 23), self-defence (Article 21) and necessity (Article 25)—exist, a State which resorts to action covered by the relevant circumstance is not held to have committed a wrongful act, even though that would have been the assessment if the special situation had not occurred.[84]

[81] See, for an approach along these lines where air travel was concerned, Vienna Conference Records, Vol 1, 151, para 33 [Kahamba (Congo: Léopoldville)]. Cambodia had become party to the VCDR in 1965.

[82] The possible exception being VCDR art 3(1)(c)—the function of negotiation with the government of the receiving State. But the case can be made that this function too relies on other tasks—such as the collection of information about conditions in the country in order to strengthen the negotiating position of the mission.

[83] Draft Articles on Diplomatic Law 1958, 96, art 24, commentary. See also Glahn (1965), 389.

[84] See Draft Articles on State Responsibility (2001), 71, Pt One, Ch V, commentary, paras 1 and 2.

A similar understanding could provide a solution to the meeting of competing interests in the field of diplomatic interference. A diplomatic agent engaged in the protection of human rights might, for instance, still fulfil the material elements of interference, but may be able to invoke conditions which, given the particular situation, justify his conduct.

It is a method which has in fact been suggested in the debate concerning diplomatic asylum. The granting of diplomatic asylum, as mentioned above, had been considered by the ICJ, prima facie, an intervention affecting matters within the exclusive competence of the receiving State.[85] But in her 1975 submission to the Secretary-General, Austria suggested that such conduct might be 'justifiable under special circumstances' including the persecution of a person by the territorial State in a manner incompatible with minimum standards of human rights'.[86]

In most instances, however, it is questionable whether the concept of justifications can appropriately be applied to the meeting of the duty of non-interference and the protection of legitimate interests on the side of the sending State.

Justifications tend to refer to atypical circumstances whose existence, in the special situation they create, leads to an exception from the ordinary applicability of the restrictive rule. The obligation incumbent on the State is not terminated; once the special circumstance ceases to exist, it resumes.[87]

The meeting of the norms outlined above, on the other hand, is a meeting of interests which both claim permanent existence and validity under international law. If a diplomatic agent protects, for example, economic interests of companies of the sending State, this does not mean that he is entitled to do so because of the existence of unusual circumstances which warrant exceptional assessment; nor does it mean that the interests of the receiving State have become inapplicable.

The two methods outlined above—the prioritisation of duties over rights, and the application of the concept of justifications—carry a certain seductive appeal. They appear to be in line with the somewhat idealised 'relationship of interpretation' which the ILC Study on Fragmentation suggests (a relationship in which one norm 'assists in the interpretation of the other')[88] and seem to avoid the 'relationship of conflict', in which a choice between the two norms must be made.[89]

[85] See ch 1, at n 33.

[86] UN Asylum Report, part 1, para 6 (Austria).

[87] Draft Articles on State Responsibility (2001), 71, Pt One, Ch V, commentary paras 2 and 3.

[88] ILC Study Group on Fragmentation, 7–8.

[89] ibid.

It is however questionable whether this choice can be avoided if methods of this kind are applied. The above named examples certainly involve clear choices—in favour of the rule against interference over the exercise of diplomatic functions, or in favour of the protection of 'minimum standards of human rights' over the ban on interference. The reason for the relevant prioritisation has not been made clear in either instance.

This is not harmonisation in the true sense of the term. Harmonisation, it appears, has to move away from the 'either–or' attitude of confrontational methods. It has to recognise that two divergent (permanent) interests exist which both have validity under international law, and it has to provide a solution which allows both interests to survive to the greatest extent possible.

The result is not likely to carry the same rigidity as a hierarchical approach; for the strength of the relevant interests is not predetermined. Depending on the circumstances of a given case, it may be the interests of the receiving State or those of the sending State which prevail.

But that also means that these circumstances, including the underlying diplomatic conduct, have to come under closer scrutiny, and their impact has to be measured carefully.

In the context of interference, the conclusion will inevitably be reached that the impact of diplomatic behaviour on the sovereignty of the receiving State—the interest which the diplomatic duty purports to protect—varies from case to case. There is a world of difference between a diplomat who demands the appointment of certain politicians to governmental positions[90] and a diplomat who merely ventures out of the mission's compound.

A differentiating approach has indeed been embraced by some authorities on diplomatic law. Both Salmon and Blіščenko for instance accept the necessity for certain informative activities by diplomatic agents but call for caution regarding the way in which such information is being disseminated.[91] Some authors go further: Satow, when discussing the 1848 Bulwer case,[92] calls the incident an 'example of the unwisdom of putting in writing language which, if used orally, would have been much less likely to give offence'.[93] Richtsteig stresses that the function of Article 3(1)(b) allows diplomatic agents, in spite of the duty of non-interference, to engage in public criticism of developments in the receiving

[90] See ch 1, at n 19.

[91] Salmon highlights the danger that information bulletins could turn into 'propaganda' and therefore calls for caution in the 'manner' in which diplomats engage in these activities, Salmon (1996), 132. Bliščenko accepts the need to protect the image and the rights of the sending State, but refers in that regard to 'tact and resolve' ('Takt und Festigkeit') that are required on the part of the diplomat. Bliščenko, 181.

[92] See ch 1, at n 19.

[93] Satow (1979), 449.

State if this is 'objectively necessary' in the interest of the sending State.[94] Both writers, it appears, suggest a mechanism which provides for a more exacting assessment of diplomatic conduct by relating it to certain comparators (in particular, other measures which the diplomatic agent could have employed).

These approaches touch upon methods which are well known in other branches of international law. There they are recognised as elements of the principle of proportionality, which embraces a comparative analysis as one of its defining characteristics. And proportionality offers advantages, which are particularly significant in the context of harmonisation: It is a principle which avoids 'either–or' decisions by accepting the values of the competing interests and by employing more sophisticated techniques to identify their relationship. But the consideration of proportionality in the context of diplomatic interference requires the establishment of its basis in diplomatic law, and a general assessment of the consequences which its application induces.

2.2. Diplomatic Interference and the Principle of Proportionality

If the view of some writers on proportionality were followed, establishing its applicability in the law of diplomatic relations would not be an altogether difficult task. Proportionality is understood by them[95] as one of those 'general principles of international law' to which Article 38(1)(c) of the ICJ Statute makes reference. As such, it would 'fill the gaps' in international law[96] and provide a default position which applied in diplomatic law as well, unless States had specifically opted for a deviating regulation.

There are good reasons to follow this approach. It derives its strongest support from the numerous branches of international law in which, in spite of fundamental differences in their nature and their objectives, recourse to the principle of proportionality is regularly made. The origins of its application in international law have been traced by some authors to the *Naulilaa Award*, in which the Arbitral Tribunal established proportionality as a requirement for the lawfulness of countermeasures;[97] a condition which has survived to the present day.[98]

[94] Richtsteig, 98.

[95] See on this Franck, 716; Mazzeschi, 1035 (with reference to Cannizzaro); presumably also Linton and Tiba, 416.

[96] *cf* Andenas and Zleptnig, 404.

[97] Ni, 19; *Naulilaa*, 1028; see Draft Articles on State Responsibility (2001), 134, art 51, commentary, para 2.

[98] Draft Articles on State Responsibility (2001), 134, art 51 and ibid, commentary, paras 2 and 4; *Danube Dam* 56, paras 85, 87.

Today, its applicability is generally accepted in contexts as varied as human rights law,[99] trade law,[100] use of force,[101] the law of armed conflict,[102] international criminal law,[103] restitution and satisfaction for internationally wrongful acts[104] and the law of the sea.[105] In the law of the European Union (and Community Law)—proportionality is recognised as a 'general principle';[106] Xiuli refers to it as a rule which is 'becoming a constitutional principle of Europe'.[107] The Treaty on European Union stipulates that the competences of the Union are 'governed by the principles of subsidiarity and proportionality', and that Union action under this principle 'shall not exceed what is necessary to achieve the objectives of the Treaties'.[108]

Given the manifold uses which so many different fields have found for the principle of proportionality, it takes an adventurous spirit to argue against its essential importance in international law. Its character as a general principle is ultimately based on the fact that it offers a logical solution to a naturally arising need. For problems that stem from the

[99] In particular, in establishing the lawfulness of State interference with specific rights, see *Chassagnou*, 660, para 112; *Olsson*, 285, para 67; *Dudgeon*, 167, para 60; but see also its applicability in situations of derogation, ECHR art 15(1); ICCPR art 4(1); ACHR art 27(1); HRC General Comment No 29, para 4.

[100] eg, in situations where authorisation is granted to a WTO Member to take appropriate countermeasures under the SCM. See SCM art 4.10 and n 9, art 4.11 and n 10. Proportionality also plays a role in the context of GATT art XX, which allows parties to adopt measures in spite of their potentially negative effect on trade, if particular conditions are in place—eg, if they are 'necessary' to public morals or human, animal or plant life or health, GATT art XX (a), (b). Proportionality has been understood as a 'governing principle' in the context of this provision (Andenas and Zleptnig, 415), and see also Franck, 749 with further references. Tests of proportionality have also been read into SPS Agreement art 2.2 and art 5.6, n 3; Andenas and Zleptnig, 418; and into TBT Agreement, art 2.2, Franck, 751.

[101] *Nuclear Weapons*, 245, para 41; *Nicaragua*, para 176; and see Draft Articles on State Responsibility (2001), 135, art 51, commentary, para 5.

[102] *cf* AP1 art 35(2) and art 57(2)(b). Both rules are understood as containing references to proportionality; Kim (2003), 2–8; Franck, 725, 726.

[103] Proportionality plays a role with regard to the substantive law—eg, as an element of the defence of duress, *Erdemovic* (Trial Chamber), para 17, or where the crime of attacks on civilians is charged, *cf Galić* (Trial Chamber), para 58. It also impacts on procedural law: (eg on sentencing considerations), *Erdemovic* (Trial Chamber), para 65.

[104] Regarding restitution, Draft Articles on State Responsibility (2001), 96, art 35 and see ibid, 98, commentary, para 11; regarding satisfaction, Draft Articles on State Responsibility (2001), 105, art 39 and see ibid, 107, commentary para 8. Necessity (Draft Articles on State Responsibility (2001), 80, art 25) probably requires proportionality as well. The commentary clarifies that 'conduct going beyond what is strictly necessary for the purpose will not be covered', ibid, 83, para 15.

[105] Regarding the delimitation of maritime zones, *cf North Sea Continental Shelf* cases 52, paras 98 and 53, para 101; *Case Concerning the Continental Shelf*, 55, para 77. Regarding the rights of States to take measures outside the territorial sea, to protect their coastlines and other interests from pollution, UNCLOS (United Nations Convention on the Law of the Sea) art 221.

[106] *Fedesa*, 4063, para 13.

[107] Han, 637.

[108] TEU art 5(1) and 5(4).

meeting of norms, which, due to the increasing fragmentation of international law and its largely disorganised development, occur in a wide range of different contexts, it provides a mechanism which avoids the often destructive consequences of confrontational approaches while at the same time appreciating the respective values of the affected interests. By according them a specific value, it often provides a way forward which allows the core contents of the competing interests to survive.

The need for a mechanism this kind in situations where the rule against diplomatic interference meets competing interests which are likewise recognised in international law, is beyond doubt; and there is indeed reason for the finding that the international community has embraced the principle of proportionality in this field as well. It derives in particular from the fact that receiving States, in their evaluation of situations in which the rule of non-interference encounters permissive norms, have recourse to tests which indicate the application of proportionality—a point which will be pursued in more detail later.[109]

The very question, however, what tests exactly proportionality involves, is a matter which merits examination in its own right. The tests which international and national courts have suggested that far range from a seemingly simple weighing of the effect of restrictive measures against the aim that is pursued with them[110] to more complex examinations. In *Bartik*, the European Court of Human Rights explained the test of proportionality (in the context of State restrictions on human rights) as demanding that the measure taken by the State 'was in pursuit of [a] legitimate aim, and that the interference with the rights protected was no greater than was necessary to achieve it'.[111] Other approaches (for instance, the dissection of proportionality into suitability, necessity and 'proportionality *stricto sensu*') have been suggested in the literature[112] and in domestic courts.[113]

On the other hand, these tests do allow the identification of certain common traits. On the most basic level, all of them involve a reflection on the measures and interests that have an impact on the particular case; and all tests offer some form of comparison or weighing. On this basis, three stages to the examination of proportionality can be distinguished: The identification of the relevant interests, the identification of the relevant measures and the performance of a comparative analysis.

109 See in particular below, after n 139.

110 *cf R (Q and Others)*, para 32. With reference to measures which employers have to take to protect employees, the Court referred to a test of proportionality which involved 'weighing what is physically involved in taking a precaution against the risk that it will guard against'.

111 *Bartik*, para 46.

112 Andenas and Zleptnig, 388, 382 (with reference to the continental European roots of that understanding of proportionality), Han, 636.

113 See *Alan Robert Matthews*, para 35.

The identification of interests proceeds on the assumption that a situation which requires the mechanism of proportionality is informed by the meeting of two competing interests—that of the decision-maker and that affected by the measure in question. The particular difficulty of the situation lies in the fact that both interests are recognised under international law. If that were not the case—if, say, the decision-maker sought to rely on an unlawful interest—the evaluation of the situation would not need recourse to proportionality to reach a finding in favour of the competing interest.[114]

In situations of alleged diplomatic interference, mention of these interests has already been made when norms were discussed which cause potential conflicts with the ban on interference.[115] For an application of proportionality however, the identification of interests also has to take into account the parameters of the particular situation in which the rights and obligations are claimed.

For instance, aspects such as developments which have not yet occurred, but are foreseeable in the existing situation, can be included in this assessment.[116] The interests of Article 3(1)(b) are therefore not only affected if the current government of the receiving State takes a hostile line to the sending State, but also if an opposition party which left no doubt about its antagonistic stance towards that State is expected to take power after forthcoming elections.

At the same time, the determination of interests has to proceed on an objective basis,[117] and this can pose challenges for a diplomat seeking to invoke an internationally recognised basis for his actions.

A 2006 incident illustrates the problem. In that year, Frente Sandinista de Liberación Nacional (FSLN), a Nicaraguan opposition party, accused the American Ambassador Paul Trivelli of interference with the State's internal affairs, following his political activities in the run-up to elections

[114] It has been suggested that, at least in specific circumstances, lawfulness might not be the only quality that has to attach to an interest. See Andenas and Zleptnig, 398, on 'appropriateness' (in the field of countermeasures).

[115] See ch 3.

[116] The incorporation of foreseeable factors is accepted in several fields where proportionality applies. For instance, where the right to self-defence by States is concerned, the aim pursued is not in fact the achievement of equivalence for a past injury, but protection of the State from the attack for the future. The identified interest is therefore the security of the State in the future; the measures adopted have to be proportionate to that objective. For proportionality in TBT Agreement art 2.2, the identification of the 'legitimate objective' also has to take into account future risks ('the risks non-fulfilment would create').

[117] The need for an objective standard for the assessment of the relevant interests has been highlighted in other contexts where proportionality applies. See SPS Agreement art 2.2 (outlining the need for 'scientific principles' and 'sufficient scientific evidence'). The Panel in *Japan—Measures Affecting the Importation of Apples* interpreted the requirement of evidence based on scientific principles as referring to the interest as well, *Japan (Apples)*, para 8.92.

in that State.[118] Trivelli himself was reported as saying that 'he was merely working to defend Nicaragua's democratic process'.[119]

If that had been the case, the Ambassador might conceivably have been able to rely on an interest which international law acknowledges—the right to vote and stand in elections has been recognised as one of the pillars on which the principle of self-determination rests.[120] But a consideration of the facts of the case allows for a more discerning evaluation: Most of all, there is evidence that Trivelli tried to unite right wing politicians in order to prevent a government of the left.[121]

It is interesting to contrast that case with one occurring 18 years earlier in the same State. Then, in July 1988, Nicaragua expelled US Ambassador Melton amid charges of interference; and on that occasion, it was the Nicaraguan President Ortega who invoked self-determination as one of the affected interests.[122] Melton on the other hand referred to 'normal diplomatic functions' which the US embassy had carried out, including contact with the opposition—it was 'perfectly legitimate to meet with all segments of a given society'.[123] Other sources however pointed out that Melton's contacts had been limited to the opposition of the receiving State.[124]

These incidents highlight the need to move away from an assessment which relies solely on the allegations of a diplomatic agent, where the interest of the decision-maker is concerned and solely on those of the receiving State where the opposing interest is at issue. An objective identification of interests has to take into account how independent observers perceived the case; and an objective assessment of their legal recognition has to ask how States evaluated instances of this kind in comparable circumstances, and what assessment of the interests in question, if any, can be obtained from the opinions of international courts and tribunals.

This evaluation of the competing interests has to be followed by an assessment of the measure which the diplomatic agent adopted in the particular situation—in other words, the conduct that triggered charges of interference. To a certain degree, the conditions that attach to the evaluation of interests apply here as well: The assessment has to proceed on an objective basis, and the measure in question must not be unlawful to begin with.

[118] *Intelligence Research Ltd*, 'US Takes Active Role in Nicaraguan Elections' (London, 25 April 2006).

[119] F Aleman, 'U.S. Ambassador to Nicaragua' *Associated Press* (New York, 21 April 2006).

[120] See ch 3, at n 213.

[121] 'Nicaragua: Montealegre Leads Polls' *Latinnews Daily* (20 April 2006); K Joynes, 'U.S. Holds Talks' *Global Insight* (Lexington, 19 April 2006).

[122] *BBC Summary*, 'Nicaraguan President, Foreign Minister on Expulsion' (London, 13 July 1988).

[123] 'United States: Defends Expulsion' *Inter Press Service* (13 July 1988).

[124] ibid.

The latter requirement in particular illustrates the fact that proportionality cannot in all circumstances be an appropriate mechanism for the evaluation of diplomatic conduct which affects the interests of the receiving State. The classic example is a threat with consequences which the sending State is not entitled to adopt—for instance, threats of an unlawful use of force. There is no evidence that the international community is prepared to consider conduct of this kind acceptable, even if it otherwise meets the requirements of proportionality.[125]

Apart from the lawfulness of the adopted action, there is often a stipulation in case law and literature that the measure in question must show some form of connection to the aim which it is said to pursue.[126] The means employed must at least be capable of achieving the aim—if this is not the case, the diplomatic agent cannot claim that the recognised interest invited measures of this kind. An example which illustrates the difficulty is criticism of the government of the receiving State in which a diplomatic agent engages to stop a humanitarian crisis in a third State. In many cases, this will not be a suitable means to achieve the aim, even if the diplomat acts under the mistaken belief that the government carries responsibility for the crisis.[127] Once a link between the particular government and the crisis is objectively established, the assessment of the suitability of the measure may change.[128]

Of the three stages of the examination of proportionality, the last—the performance of a comparative analysis—is by far the most complex one. Colourful similes have been employed to indicate that some form of comparison has to take place under this principle: With reference to proportionality in the law of armed conflict, the Committee established to review the NATO campaign in Yugoslavia found that 'bombing a refugee camp is obviously prohibited if its only military significance is that people in the camp are knitting socks for soldiers'.[129] In English law, the snappy phrase that a steamhammer may not be employed to crack a nut, has become popular.[130]

[125] See on this ch 10, n 34.

[126] A 'rational connection' to the objective: *Alan Robert Matthews*, para 35; or the measure must be 'appropriate' to fulfil the function, *Bartik*, para 46; and see also *Seco*, para 14; *Rémy Schmit*, para 24. On 'suitability' of the measure for the purpose, see Han, 636; Andenas and Zleptnig, 378. There does not appear to be much of a difference in the practical application of these parameters, Andenas and Zleptnig, 388 with reference to *Seco* and *Rémy Schmit*.

[127] Situations of this kind may generate an *erga omnes* interest on which the diplomatic agent could in principle rely—in particular, if the crisis has involved the commission of international crimes. See ch 3, at n 126.

[128] One may think in this regard of the continuing commercial and military links between China and the leadership of Sudan at a time when allegations of genocide were raised against members of the Sudanese government. See Sudan Divestment Task Force, in particular at 18, 19.

[129] ICTY NATO Report, at para 48.

[130] *Goldstein*, at 155.

In actual practice, a variety of tests have been employed to perform a comparative analysis.[131] What they have in common is that the affected interest plays a greater role at this stage of the examination. Two approaches make frequent appearances in case law and literature: The test of the 'least restrictive means' and 'cost–benefit analysis'.

The test of the least restrictive means inquires whether, in a given situation, alternative measures had been available which would have achieved the same objective, but imposed less of a burden on the affected interest. Is it necessary to use a steamhammer when a nutcracker is available?[132] Two measures then are being compared, and the affected interest has a clear impact on this examination: The question whether the alternative measure could have induced a lesser burden, can only be answered by reference to the impact which that particular interest experienced.

In various branches of international law which accept the principle of proportionality, the question of the 'least restrictive means' is embraced as a prerequisite for the lawfulness of certain measures. It thus makes its appearance in international humanitarian law,[133] in human rights law,[134] trade law[135] and prominently in EU law/Community law.[136]

In the field of diplomatic interference, the applicability of this test is occasionally invited by authors on the topic. Reference has already been made to Satow's comparison between written language and verbal expressions in view of their likelihood to 'give offence'[137]—a comparison which suggests that the latter would be the less intrusive alternative. But the test also plays a role when reference is made to diplomatic conduct which is 'necessary' to pursue recognised interests.[138] The term 'necessary' has been interpreted in various areas of international law as indicating a

[131] *cf* proportionality of countermeasures: These must be 'commensurate with the injury suffered, taking into account the gravity of the internationally wrongful act and the rights in question', Draft Articles on State Responsibility (2001), 341, art 51. Franck understands the European Court of Human Rights as examining whether the objective which the adopted means intends to achieve could have been 'pursued by means that would have derogated less from protected rights', Franck, 762. The test advanced in *Alan Robert Matthews* runs along similar lines by demanding that the means employed to pursue the right must be 'no more than is necessary to accomplish the objective' (para 35).

[132] See Lord Diplock's phrasing of that simile in *Goldstein*, 155.

[133] See on this the rule against weapons and methods of a nature to cause 'superfluous injury or unnecessary suffering' (AP 1, art 35(2)), and on this principle, *Nuclear Weapons*, para 78 ('a harm greater than that unavoidable to achieve legitimate military objectives') and ICRC Commentary, 396, para 1395.

[134] See *C v Australia*, para 8.2; *AD and OD v United Kingdom*, paras 89 and 91.

[135] The 'least restrictive means' test has been read into the word 'necessary' in GATT art XX, see *United States (Section 337)*, 5.26; *Thailand (Cigarettes)*, para 75. See also SPS Agreement art 5.6 and note 3, which refers to alternatives which are 'reasonably available' and which would achieve 'the appropriate level of sanitary or phytosanitary protection and [are] significantly less restrictive to trade'.

[136] See *Fedesa*, para 13; *Stichting*, para 28; *Crispoltoni*, para 40; *Jippes*, para 81.

[137] Above, at n 93.

[138] Richtsteig, 98.

'least restrictive means test':[139] Its use, after all, leads unavoidably to the question whether there would still be a 'need' for the relevant conduct if less intrusive measures are available.

Moreover, there is evidence that States themselves are quite aware of gradations in diplomatic conduct and sensitive towards the fact that in some cases less intrusive alternatives may exist. This is particularly apparent when diplomatic agents issue public statements on matters which require delicate handling—especially where the human rights record of the receiving government is concerned or allegations of corruption are at issue. It is common to encounter on those occasions reactions by officials of the receiving State which highlight the availability of other ways to make one's views heard.

An example is the 2004 case of Edward Clay, the British High Commissioner in Kenya, who had criticised perceived corruption in the government of the receiving State.[140] Clay had made his statements at a meeting of the British Business Association in Kenya and had expressed himself in a particularly forthright manner.[141] His remarks resulted in the summoning of the High Commissioner by the Foreign Office of the receiving State and a statement by the Kenyan Foreign Minister, who criticised him for 'ignoring diplomatic channels in making his views known'[142]—a reference, in other words, to available alternatives to the measure which Clay had adopted. Similar phrases have been used by governments in other cases in which diplomatic agents had chosen a public or semi-public audience for statements which touched on sensitive issues.[143]

Even activities which are expressly regulated in the Vienna Convention, are, when they encounter a competing interest, subject to the requirements of proportionality. Observation activities (Article 3(1)(d)) are prime examples.

The need for a discerning view on diplomatic methods and available alternatives in the fulfilment of this particular function was highlighted in the above mentioned case of the two British diplomats in Romania in

[139] *cf* Franck, 752. See also Han, 636; Andenas and Zleptnig, 378. See also Draft Art 47 Draft Articles on State Responsibility (1996), 67, art 47, commentary, para 4.

[140] See ch 3, at n 34.

[141] See ch 9, at n 95.

[142] L Barasa, 'Criticism That Rubbed Officials The Wrong Way' *The Nation* (Kenya, 3 February 2005) (paraphrasing by Barasa).

[143] Reference to the 'established diplomatic channels' as a preferable alternative was made inter alia in the above named case of the US embassy statement on Namibia (ch 3, at n 127), T Moyo, 'Namibia; Government' *The Namibian* (Windhoek West, 20 August 1999). And when the US Ambassador to Mozambique, Curran, stated in 1998 that forthcoming elections in that State should be democratic and transparent, the General Secretary of the ruling Mozambican party was quoted as saying that 'if he [Curran] really wants to offer his advice or criticism, he can do that through diplomatic channels' *Xinhua* 'US Ambassador Accused of Meddling' (China, 15 September 1998).

1989.[144] Michael Brown, the Assistant Military Attaché, later described how he and his colleague had joined in the cheering of the crowds and shouted '[d]own with Ceaucescus'.[145] He added that the British diplomats 'drove to the TV building and went through the fence and walked through the forbidden zone and stormed the building with [the crowd]', before concluding, somewhat incongruously, that they had gone along as 'fairly passive observers'.[146]

Commentators saw this incident in a different light. In a letter to *The Times*, a former British Ambassador (Sir John Graham), expressed his opinion with these words:

> Whatever the personal feelings of individual diplomats, active participation, as distinct from observation, in the politics of the country to which their ambassador is accredited is inconsistent with their diplomatic status.[147]

But there is common ground among Brown's and Graham's views inasfar as 'fairly passive observation' is seen in a positive light. It is the preferable alternative by comparison to the excessive measure of active participation.[148]

Richtsteig offers a similar evaluation when talking about the diplomatic monitoring of political demonstrations. In his view, a distinction has to be made between 'tacit observation' and behaviour that could be misunderstood as 'ostentatious partisanship' and provocation.[149]

These considerations emphasise that the need to identify less intrusive alternatives exists in this context as well. But it may be challenging to apply such differentiations in practice. Diplomats who 'tacitly' stand at the sidelines, certainly adopt a less intrusive alternative than their colleagues who march with the protesters. But even the former must expect criticism: They did, after all, 'turn up for the event'.

The rationale behind the test of the 'least restrictive means' lies in the fact that it offers a degree of protection to the interest which is affected by the measure in question. At the same time, the argument that a diplomatic agent could have resorted to less intrusive methods is a powerful weapon in the hands of the receiving State. Less invasive alternatives can easily be found: A diplomat could have talked to the government instead of addressing the public, and even in his dealings with the government, differentiations can be made: He could have used oral communication instead of a note verbale,[150] he could have applied less pressure in his

[144] See above, text at n 1.
[145] Stacey, n 2.
[146] ibid.
[147] Graham, n 4.
[148] See also the 1985 case of Hardwood and Hopper (A.79), in which the US embassy pointed out that the diplomats had not participated in events, but had merely fulfilled their function as observers.
[149] Richtsteig, 22, (in the context of art 3(1)(d)).
[150] See on this Behrens (2008).

lobbying activities—he might even have considered not doing anything at all, but letting diplomats of a third State present the case.

The danger of such restrictions is apparent when the fact is taken into account that diplomatic representations may concern issues of importance and urgency—such as the perceived threat of the development of a genocidal campaign in the receiving State. In those situations, envoys who have to comply with limitations of this kind risk becoming the very caricature of their profession—honourable gentlemen who, to borrow Erich Kästner's simile, attempt to solve the 'paralysis of the globe' with camomile tea.[151]

But there is a corrective mechanism which imposes a cap on calls for less intrusive means: Alternative measures must be at least of equal efficiency to achieve the objective which the measure in question pursues. It is a condition which again finds its support in various branches of international law.[152]

And the question of equal efficiency has become relevant in several situations of diplomatic participation in matters in the receiving State. In Michael Brown's case,[153] a spokesman for the British Foreign Office provided an explanation for the diplomat's involvement in the protest march: 'If he had not shown some degree of enthusiasm the crowd might have asked who he was. There were concerns in the crowd about the activities of the security forces'.[154] These considerations indicate that a less intrusive alternative—for example, staying silently on the sidelines—would have endangered the observation activities (and possibly the person of the diplomatic observer as well). The less onerous measure would have been a less efficient measure.[155]

The question of what exactly constitutes an 'efficient' measure, can only be answered by reference to the conditions of the individual situation. One may consider the scenario of a diplomatic representative from a State which enjoys some influence on the UN Security Council, but who is not personally on good terms with the administration of the receiving State. If that diplomat finds it necessary to act to prevent the commission of

[151] Kästner, 31.

[152] See on this Andenas and Zleptnig, 389. For an application of this condition in trade law, see *Australia (Salmon)*, para 194 (with reference to SPS art 5.6); *European Communities (Asbestos)*, paras 172, 174 (with reference to GATT Art XX(b)). In human rights law, *cf C v Australia*, para 8.2 ('less invasive means of achieving the same ends'). The phrasing in EU/Community law tends to be less clear—there, reference is often made to the fact that the choice has to be between several 'appropriate' measures, *Fedesa*, para 13; *Stichting*, para 28; *Crispoltoni*, para 40; *Jippes*, para 81. For an application of the requirement by the European Free Trade Association (EFTA) Court, see *Finmark Family Allowance*, para 61 (concerning residence requirement).

[153] Above, text at n 1.

[154] Travis, n 1; and see Stacey, n 2.

[155] This does not mean that the application of the entire principle of proportionality would therefore favour the diplomatic observer in this case. The article will return to this point (see below, at n 177).

international crimes in the receiving State, a published threat of economic sanctions or even Security Council measures may, given the influence of his State, be heeded. A personal talk with a member of the administration would be a far less intrusive alternative, but not one that promises a similar degree of efficiency.

If, by contrast, the diplomat represents a State which has no such influence, but entertains excellent personal relations with leading members of the receiving State's government, public criticism of the latter may go beyond the desired objective (and might even prove counter-productive). A private conversation might in this situation be not only the less restrictive, but also the more efficient measure. Depending on the circumstances, a cup of camomile tea might yet be the most successful way to solve some of the world's problems.

A final point which deserves consideration where this aspect of proportionality is concerned, is the fact that diplomatic measures, annoying though they may appear to the hosts, will themselves often constitute a less intrusive alternative if compared to other arrows in the quiver of the sending State. Even some of the methods for the peaceful settlement of disputes which the UN Charter envisages (such as conciliation, arbitration and judicial settlement) can carry a greater potential for loss of face on the part of the receiving State.[156] And there are other measures at the disposal of sending States which feel that such action is indicated: They may withdraw aid, resort to other sanctions, suspend cultural ties, even cut diplomatic relations or resort to counter-measures or litigation. In cases falling under universal jurisdiction, the sending State may decide to prosecute nationals of the receiving State, if they are suspected of perpetrating these crimes, in its own courts. In grave cases, the sending State might lobby the Security Council for the adoption of measures involving the use of force. A comprehensive assessment of diplomatic action has to take these options into account. The conclusion may often be that diplomatic representation, even if it involves warnings, harsh criticism, or a threat of negative, but lawful, consequences, is still a measure which has a less disturbing impact on the order of things in the receiving State.[157]

[156] See on the various measures UN Charter art 33; *cf* also GA Res 2734 (XXV) (1970), para 6. There can be overlaps between the measures envisaged by the Charter and those at the disposal of diplomatic agents (in particular, where 'negotiation' as a measure for the peaceful settlement of disputes is concerned).

[157] In some parts of international law, warnings or the making of claims are in fact envisaged before more serious acts are taken. See, for the field of countermeasures, Draft Articles on State Responsibility (2001), 135, art 52(1)(a). In the field of human rights protection, the Institute of International Law suggests that the State which perpetrates human rights violations 'shall be formally requested to desist', before other measures are taken to protect these rights, Institute of International Law (1989), art 4(1). Such representations will typically be made by diplomatic agents as representatives of their States.

The second approach towards the comparative analysis which proportionality requires, is that of the so-called 'cost–benefit analysis'[158] (also called 'proportionality *stricto sensu*' or 'true proportionality').[159] It is a test which calls for a relationship of proportionality between the advantage gained (or expected to be gained) and the negative effects which the measure generates. Is the benefit derived from the opening of a nut worth the damage which the steamhammer will cause?

This form of analysis again relies on a degree of acceptance in international law. It has been adopted in international humanitarian law,[160] human rights law[161] and EU law/Community law,[162] and there is some indication that it may have to play a role in various areas of trade law as well.[163] What is apparent from its application in these fields is that, by establishing a relationship of proportionality between the two sides of the equation, a value has to be assigned to each of them.

However, there is some doubt as to what the sides of the equation actually contain. Case law and the literature sometimes refer to the competing interests themselves.[164] But if cost–benefit analysis were applied in this generalised form, it would presuppose a value that is inherent to the character of the interests. It would, in fact, be based on a discernible hierarchical relationship between the underlying norms and thus re-introduce the challenges which accompany that approach.[165]

[158] *cf* Andenas and Zleptnig, 388.

[159] Han, 637.

[160] See AP 1 arts 57(2)(a)(iii) and 51(5)(b); ICRC Commentary, 477, art 40, para 1598; 648, art 53, para 2079; 672, art 56, para 2169; 804, art 67, para 2764; 995, 996, art 85, para 3478; Parkerson, 47; Gardam, 409.

[161] The phrase frequently employed by the ECtHR is that the 'interference' or the 'restriction' must be 'proportionate to the legitimate aim'. See *Maslov*, para 68; *Stoll*, para 101; *Nilsen and Johnson*, para 43; *Chassagnou*, para 112; *Janowski*, para 30; *Dudgeon*, para 53; *Young, James and Webster*, para 63; *Handyside*, para 49. See also *C v Australia*, para 4.28 (detention not 'disproportionate to the end sought').

[162] *Fedesa*, para 13; *Schräder*, para 21; *Stichting*, para 28; *Crispoltoni*, para 40; *Jippes*, para 81.

[163] The Appellate Body in *Korea (Beef)* found that GATT art XX(d) involved the 'weighing and balancing' of several factors, including the 'contribution made by the compliance measure to the enforcement of the law or regulation at issue, the importance of the common interests or values protected by that law or regulation, and the accompanying impact of the law or regulation on imports or exports' (para 164). It did, however, not specify the 'exchange rate' in force between these interests, which could thus be a higher or a lower standard than proportionality. In the particular field of diplomatic interference, see the reaction of the Swedish Ambassador, Rylander, to Zimbabwe's warnings against diplomatic interference in 2007, implying that a 'balancing act' between diplomatic tasks and interests of the receiving State had to be performed. A Shaw, 'Zimbabwe Threatens to Expel Foreign Diplomats' *Associated Press* (New York, 19 March 2007). On the case, see ch 3, at nn 49–51 and A.217.

[164] See, on this, ICRC Commentary on AP 1, speaking of a 'balance between military necessity, on the one hand, and the requirements of humanity, on the other', ICRC Commentary 392, art 35, para 1389. When analysing proportionality in the context of measures having restrictive results on Community trade, the ECJ weighed the 'national interest in attaining [a legitimate] aim against the Community interest in ensuring the free movement of goods', *Stoke-on-Trent et al*, para 15.

[165] See in particular above, section 1.

All the same, a hierarchical relationship—especially where *jus cogens* norms are concerned—can be of assistance even in the field of conciliatory methods. It has been pointed out that *jus cogens* character usually attaches only to the core duties themselves and not to ancillary rules, such as the obligation on a diplomatic agent to safeguard the relevant norm.[166] But the fact that the international community grants exceptional value to the underlying interest—without which the ancillary norm would, after all, not exist—can still help the determination of cost–benefit analysis. The *jus cogens* concept then does not appear as a destructive force, but as an aid of interpretation.[167]

For instance, since it is only the prohibition of genocide and not the duty to prevent the crime that carries *jus cogens* character, diplomatic representations against the emergence of a genocidal campaign in the receiving State do not invalidate the rule of non-interference. However, the importance of the prohibition of genocide has an impact on the ancillary rule on its prevention—to the extent that the interest which the diplomat in this situation promotes, outweighs (if considered by itself) the competing interest of the receiving State.

The problem is of course that in the overwhelming majority of cases where two recognised interests meet, a clear determination of their place in a normative hierarchy is missing. Considered individually, the relevant interests will often command equal respect under the law, and it will often be possible to advance equally strong reasons for each of their existences.

But there are other factors that help in the performance of the assessment. Cost-benefit analysis is not limited to a simple juxtaposition of abstract interests, for the 'interests' which are subjected to the tests of proportionality appear in the shape given to them by the particular situation.[168] At the stage of cost–benefit analysis, there is an additional feature which has to be taken into account: The relationship between the measure and the relevant interest. What is being compared, is, on the one hand, the negative impact which the measure has on the affected interest and on the other, the benefit which the decision-maker hopes to achieve by adopting the measure.[169]

166 See above, nn 52–57.

167 In its Study on the Fragmentation of International Law, the ILC accepted that hierarchical rules can play a non-destructive role where they meet other norms of international law. In those cases, the latter norm 'should, to the extent possible, be interpreted in a manner consistent with the former', ILC Study Group on Fragmentation, 25, para 42. This consideration relates to a direct encounter between hierarchically superior and hierarchically inferior norms, but it can be argued that the ILC's reflections should a fortiori apply where an obligation which is merely ancillary to the fulfilment of a *jus cogens* norm meets with another recognised interest under international law. In such a case, there is even greater room for the application of harmonisation.

168 See above, after n 115.

169 See on this Han, 637 (comparing the 'effects on the applicant's interest' with the 'interest pursued'); Andenas and Zleptnig, 390 (arguing that the 'effects of a measure' must not be

The result may not be a precise mathematical formula through which the evaluation can be performed,[170] but the introduction of additional parameters, which will often allow for a more exacting assessment than one that relies entirely on abstract interests.

Where the evaluation of the 'benefit' is concerned, questions therefore need to be asked about the shape which the protected interest would have if no diplomatic action were taken. That includes considerations on the gravity of the danger to which the interest is exposed, existing urgency calling for diplomatic measures and the irreversibility of the damage caused if no action were taken.

The interplay of these factors is particularly apparent when the protected interest relates to human rights in the receiving State. The Institute of International Law recognised this point when, in its articles on the Protection of Human Rights and the Principle of Non-Interference, it discussed diplomatic (and other) measures which States under certain conditions are entitled to take against other States which have violated human rights obligations.[171] The Institute found that such measures were 'particularly justified when taken in response to especially grave violations of these rights, notably large-scale or systematic violations'.[172] Such violations would certainly constitute a serious danger to a recognised interest and may often outweigh the negative effect which diplomatic measures have on the competing interests of the receiving State.

To take one example: In the above mentioned case of Western diplomats in Sierra Leone who in 1993 called for the release of journalists,[173] the envoys' involvement in human rights in the receiving State formed the

'disproportionate or excessive in relation to the interests affected'). There is some indication that cost–benefit analysis, where it is adopted in international law, contains a reflection on the impact which the relevant measure had on the affected interests. *cf Fedesa*, para 13, where the ECJ compared the 'disadvantages caused' to the 'aim pursued'. The ECtHR habitually involves the measure concerned in its proportionality analysis when it emphasises that the 'interference' must be 'proportionate to the legitimate aim', see references in n 161.

[170] The question of the exact 'exchange rate', to use Franck's words (Franck, 729), that has to be applied to cost–benefit analysis, is still a matter of some debate. It is, in particular, an open question whether the assessment must be done by application of a strict standard or if an approximation can suffice. See, for the application of a strict standard, the ICRC Commentary, expressing the view that the concept of military necessity 'can never justify a degree of violence which exceeds the level which is *strictly necessary* to ensure the success of a particular operation in a particular case', ICRC Commentary, 396, Art 35, para 1395 (emphasis added). For application of an approximation, see Draft Articles on State Responsibility (2001), 135, art 51, commentary, para 5; *United States (Tax)*, para 5.18. In the field of diplomatic interference, it would certainly be problematic to apply mathematical values to all comparators—it is, for instance, difficult to state what precise (negative) value lobbying activities have when compared to the advantage gained through the promotion of economic interests.

[171] Institute of International Law (1989), art 2(2).

[172] Ibid, art 2(3). The Institute's treatment of diplomatic measures is however not entirely consistent. Its art 3 for instance finds 'diplomatic representations' to be 'lawful in all circumstances', but it subjects diplomatic measures in art 2(2) and (3) to certain criteria.

[173] See ch 3, at n 117.

background to charges of interference. But the application of cost–benefit analysis is likely to lead to the result that the effects of the diplomatic measure were not excessive by comparison to the objective which the diplomats pursued. That objective was an interest which international law recognises—freedom of expression of a people as a prerequisite for their right to determine their own political fate.[174] In the particular case, the right had come under threat, and the threat was immediate and grave—the arrest of dissenting voices is a particularly intrusive means of restricting freedom of expression, and the situation was ongoing.

By comparison, the effect which the diplomatic measure had on the internal workings of the receiving State, cannot be considered as weighing very heavily in the scales. It does not appear to have caused any disturbances in the receiving State—apart from irritation within the government—nor does it seem that any such disturbance had been intended. The impact had also been limited in time; the negative effects, if any, would not have been irreversible.

There are of course cases in which the scales are heavier on the side of the costs. The last named aspect—irreversibility of the damage—plays a significant role in the weighing of the cost; but it is joined by other pertinent factors, such as the extent and the duration of the effects of the diplomatic conduct. Beyond the instant damage, the assessment also has to incorporate foreseeable consequences which arise through the measure in question.[175]

The rendering of material (or even 'just' moral) support to factions within the receiving State for instance, may carry risks which should not be underestimated. While the immediate impact may be low—the direct effects may be confined to the current audience of a diplomatic speaker—the wider consequences can be significant. They may include the creation of unrest within the receiving State—especially when the factions consist of revolutionaries who now act in the belief that they enjoy the support of the State which the diplomat represents.

The assessment of the cost for the affected party in fact underlines the true strength of cost–benefit analysis. The paradigmatic perception of

[174] On the importance of freedom of expression for the realisation of the self-determination of a people, see above (ch 3, at n 214 and after n 217 with particular reference to journalists who have been singled out by the regime of the receiving State). See also *Western Sahara*, 32, para 55; Wheatley, 240, 241; Thornberry, 136.

[175] The need to consider foreseeable consequences was inter alia claimed by several States in their pleadings to the ICJ in the case concerning the legality of nuclear weapons. They noted that a proportionality assessment, as required for the exercise of self-defence, would also have to consider 'the high probability of an escalation of nuclear exchanges', *Nuclear Weapons*, para 43. While the Court did not wish to engage in a 'quantification' of such a danger, it found that the 'profound risks' associated with nuclear weapons had to be borne in mind if States wanted to use them in accordance with the proportionality requirements of self-defence. Ibid.

diplomatic activities is that of conduct which creates only a very limited disturbance within the receiving State.[176] But cases have arisen in which the impact of the diplomatic action had been quite tangible.

The above named incident of the British diplomats in Romania in 1989 serves as an illustration.[177] In ordinary diplomatic intercourse, it is difficult to imagine a diplomatic action with more significant immediate impact than travelling to a television station along with a captured army personnel carrier[178] and storming that building. Nor was the effect, that their presence among the crowd would have, lost on the diplomats. Michael Brown, the Assistant Military Attaché, described the attitude of the protesters as follows: 'They wanted us there because we were British. The British have a tremendous standing with the kids'.[179]

The expected benefit was, however, not described as necessary assistance to human rights in grave danger or in similarly dramatic terms. Brown himself merely referred to the ordinary function of observation.[180]

The events were, of course, also covered by independent observers in Bucharest on the same day.[181] The argument can still be advanced that, if the objective had been to obtain a first-hand account of the events, joining the crowd was a necessary action, and that no alternatives were available which would have been less intrusive, yet equally effective. However, in the light of the considerable impact which Brown's and Laffey's action had, it is difficult to see how a cost–benefit analysis would yield a finding in their favour. It is in fact the classic example of a grossly disproportionate action.[182]

The performance of cost–benefit analysis thus allows for a more detailed assessment of the respective sides of the equation—an examination which goes far beyond the mere allocation of values to the interests concerned and can therefore yield results which the assumption of a normative hierarchy is not able to provide. It also offers an additional test which complements that of the 'least restrictive means' by allowing for the question whether, in cases where the costs outweigh the benefits, the relevant measure had to be adopted in the first place.

And yet, it is noticeable that States, at least in this part of diplomatic law, have much less of an appetite for this kind of examination. Evidence

[176] The reason, presumably, for the Institute of International Law's phrasing of diplomatic representations in Institute of International Law (1989) art 3 (and see above, n 172).

[177] See above, at n 1.

[178] Stacey, n 2.

[179] ibid.

[180] It does not appear that he highlighted a particularly urgent or pressing need for the relevant observation activities. See above, at n 146.

[181] See for instance 'Romania: A Fleeing Dictator' *Inter Press Service* (22 December 1989); M Rosenblum, 'International News' *Associated Press* (New York, 22 December 1989).

[182] The assessment of proportionality can be much more difficult when both cost and benefit weigh heavily on the scales. For an example to this effect, see ch 11, after n 152.

can be adduced for the acceptability of the 'least restrictive means' test.[183] With regards to cost–benefit analysis, this can be a much more difficult task.

A possible reason may be the prevailing difficulty of assigning values to cost and benefit of diplomatic measures—at least in cases in which the lack of proportionality is not manifestly apparent. In most instances, States may also feel that it is enough to point out that a diplomatic agent could have resorted to other, less intrusive, methods.

Another reason is arguably the fact that cost–benefit analysis requires a detailed engagement with the respective interests, the dangers to which they are exposed and the urgency of action. The strength of the test is its curse. It can be embarrassing for States to engage in a precise determination of the interests they are trying to promote, especially if a public airing may raise doubts about their acceptability in international law. It may frequently be more convenient to debate the factual rather than the legal assessment.[184]

Instead of the application of the more exacting test of proportionality, the field is dominated once again by all too familiar phrases—accusations of 'activities incompatible with the diplomatic status'[185] and more of this kind. They are vague expressions, but they have the advantage of conveying disapproval without inviting an intrusive inquiry whose results might backfire on the receiving State. Uncertainty in the legal assessment need not always be an inconvenience.

[183] See above, after n 139.

[184] See for instance the 2008 case of the Zimbabwean opposition leader Tsvangirai who was granted diplomatic asylum by the Netherlands in June of that year amid reports that soldiers had been sent to his house on the same day (see ch 11, at n 68 and 'Troops Hunt for Tsvangirai' *Daily Guide (Ghana)* (Accra, 25 June 2008). The Zimbabwean government does not appear to have engaged in a legal evaluation of the diplomatic measure (which would have involved an assessment of the interests each side had pursued). Instead, Zimbabwean authorities strongly denied the security concerns mentioned by the politician. *BBC Monitoring Africa—Political*, 'Zimbabwe: Police Chief Accuses Tsvangirai of "Stunt"', 24 June 2008.

[185] See on this ch 3, at n 2.

Part II

Fields of Diplomatic Interference

> Examples we decline to give:
> The lawyers, after all, must live.
>
> AP Herbert[1]

Commentators on diplomatic law are not altogether coy when it comes to giving examples. Instances of diplomatic interference are frequently mentioned in academic writings.[2] The problems lie in a different area.

For one, it is not clear whether these examples can always be based on the legal opinion of receiving States that the relevant conduct violates Article 41(1) of the Vienna Convention—appropriate substantiation for this finding is not in all cases provided. Nor are the relevant examples employed to construct a conceptual framework in which each instance of alleged interference could find its place. Even the ICJ, on the few occasions when it had the opportunity to analyse diplomatic interference, limited itself to the cases at hand, instead of developing a framework of rules with general applicability.[3]

But the provision of examples serves a purpose. If they are approached in a systematic manner, and if evidence for their evaluation by the diplomatic hosts is adduced, they allow for the identification of areas which carry sensitivity for receiving States and thus offer guidance for diplomats who may find that their work involves activities in these fields.[4]

However, there is reason to be believe that this method has a significance which reaches beyond that. The formation of examples is far more than the provision of interesting illustrations. It constitutes a particular, and valid, way of defining the conduct of diplomatic interference.

By identifying the rule against interference as a norm on the international plane and by enshrining it in conventional law, the drafters opened it up to traditional methods of treaty interpretation—including the literal interpretation, which takes, as its basis, the 'ordinary meaning' of the term.[5]

An understanding of the 'ordinary meaning' can be reached through the application of the traditional method of categorisation which traces its ancestry to Aristotelian philosophy.[6] It is an approach which involves the identification of categories based on the properties of a particular object. A chair might thus be seen as possessing the properties of four legs, a seat and a back. Each of the properties is a necessary condition for each

[1] AP Herbert's Spring (Arrangements) Bill 1936, s 10(ii), Herbert, 46.

[2] See in particular ch 2, at nn 11–14.

[3] See Introduction, at nn 55–58.

[4] See Salmon (1996), 129 ('une bonne indication des zones sensibles').

[5] For a modern affirmation of this approach (among other methods of interpretation), see VCLT art 31(1).

[6] In particular, his treatise on Κατηγορίαι or categories. See Aristotle, 1a to 15b. See on this also Frank (2001), 672; Taylor, 643, 644.

member of the category,[7] and each member of the category carries equal weight.[8]

There exists a certain propensity among lawyers to approach the understanding of concepts from this perspective. It appears to offer certain advantages. It promises a framework based on objective features, which is exhaustive in nature: As long as objects possess all the necessary parameters, the name of the concept can be applied to them. Both a modern kitchen chair and an eighteenth century Chippendale chair easily fit the understanding of 'chair' that has been offered above, as both fulfil all the criteria of the concept.

On the basis of this approach, the concept of 'diplomatic interference' can be defined through its constituent definitional elements; and it is in line with this perspective that an understanding of the term has been provided above.[9]

At the same time, the traditional method is not entirely free from criticism: The question can in particular be raised whether it can ever offer a sufficient understanding of the concepts at hand. Its seemingly exhaustive nature must be subject to particular doubt: At the borders of the formula, challenges are unavoidable. Is a defective chair—one that is missing a leg, say, or one that is missing its back—still a 'chair'?

Similar questions arise where the objectiveness of the approach is concerned. The choice of features which are necessary for a member of a particular category can be subjective in nature, as the above mentioned concept of 'chair' demonstrates: There are, after all, chairs which have a more extravagant design and whose number of legs therefore varies (or which dispense with legs altogether), the egg chair may make a distinction between 'back' and 'seat' difficult, and so on.[10]

In linguistics, a theory which, to a degree, addresses these criticisms, has gained a steady following since the 1970s. It is commonly referred to as 'prototype theory'—a theory with whose development the American psychologist Eleanor Rosch is credited, and which has received particular discussion in the field of cognitive linguistics.[11]

Prototype theory is based on the view that users of words understand categories by reference to their most representative member

[7] Taylor, 643.

[8] *cf* Fuhrmann, 319.

[9] See ch 2, after n 103.

[10] See also Taylor, 645 on the debate whether Pluto fulfils the 'classical definition' of a planet. Labov's study on 'receptacles' is similarly instructive. On presenting subjects with drawings of receptacles (cups, bowls, vases etc) and asking them to imagine the relevant containers filled with mashed potatoes, coffee, or flowers, it was noted that different names were accorded to the receptacles according to their contents, Labov, 355–65. These findings suggest that the 'ordinary concept' of a particular object may change according to its context—an observation which holds value for the concept of 'diplomatic interference' as well—especially if competing interests are taken into account. See ch 3.

[11] See Giannakopoulou, in particular at s 2; Fuhrmann, 319, Johnson, 22.

(the 'prototype').[12] The other members of the category belong to it by reason of their similarity to the prototype.[13] Unlike members of a category under the traditional approach, members of categories which are defined by their 'prototypes' therefore do not carry equal weight.[14] In the category 'chair', for instance, a 'kitchen chair' may serve as a typical example; a dentist's chair or a ducking stool would be less representative members. A similar method has been employed in various examples in which the validity of prototype theory had been tested, and which yielded an amount of agreement among the participants in the relevant studies on objects which were 'good examples' of a particular category.[15]

Prototype theory thus avoids some of the rigidity of the traditional approach and offers a better reflection of the mindset of users of words, who do not appear to think in abstract terms when identifying the concept of things, but undergo a psychological process based on instances encountered in everyday life.[16] It is a theory which has thus found its supporters not only in linguistics, but also in anthropology and psychology.[17]

Its usefulness for international law is based on a similar rationale. States, as the creators of the concept of 'interference' under customary international law, do not tend to consider the relevant conduct in abstract terms, but tend to take issue with very specific cases. When they take exception, for instance, to certain forms of diplomatic partisanship,[18] the funding of political candidates[19] or incitement to particular acts,[20] they are approaching the 'category' of interference by relating to some of its most representative members, without excluding the possibility that it embraces other, less typical members, as well.

It is an approach which has been adopted even by the drafters of the rule against diplomatic interference. The ILC, in its commentary to the final set of draft articles, did not provide a lexical definition of the concept of interference, but referred to an example which must have appeared in the eyes of the members as one of the most typical representatives of the category, that is, diplomatic participation 'in political campaigns'.[21] 'Prototypes' of interference were also employed during the ILC debates: In

[12] Taylor, 643, 649, 652; Giannakopoulou, s 2.2.
[13] Taylor, 643, 652; Giannakopoulou, s 2; Fuhrmann, 320.
[14] Taylor, 645. *cf* Fuhrmann, 320.
[15] Rosch, 197–99 and 229–33; Giannakopoulou, s 2.
[16] *cf* however Taylor on the 'exemplar view', in particular Taylor, 654.
[17] Palmer, 264.
[18] See on this ch 6.
[19] See, for example, ch 8, at n 14.
[20] See ch 7, s 3.
[21] Annex B.8, commentary, para 2.

that regard, reference was made to the posing of diplomatic ultimata,[22] the encouraging or subsidising of political parties,[23] participation in electoral campaigns,[24] and even the fomenting of civil war.[25] On occasion, members referred to historical instances as prototypes—the Sackville case, for example, was described as a 'classical instance' of 'meddling in the affairs of the receiving State by over-zealous diplomatic agents'.[26]

One criticism regarding prototype theory relates to the fact that the formation of 'representative examples' for a category may be strongly dependent on cultural conditions: Sub-Saharan users of words may have quite different ideas of the 'prototypical bird' than, for instance, Northern Europeans.[27]

That holds true in relation to diplomatic interference as well. Every receiving State is primarily concerned with the particular forms of diplomatic interference which it believes to have seen in its own diplomatic relations, and it must be assumed that the political culture, the prevailing ideology and the internal structure of the State will have shaped the sensitivity with which it meets this phenomenon.

By itself, however, this is not an impediment to the validity of prototype theory. It is, rather, a challenge which attaches to the identification of the group of subjects whose opinion as 'users of the term' matters. If this group is composed by all independent States—across political and ideological divides—and if certain forms of conduct are regularly seen by members of that group as emanations of 'diplomatic interference', then it is possible to speak of diplomatic behaviour which the international community has accepted as prototypes for this category.[28] Such instances are not mere reminders of an underlying concept: They have become part of the very definition of the term and indicate the direction in which customary international law on the rule of non-interference has developed.

And there is evidence that instances which carry representative character for the concept of 'diplomatic interference', exist. To name one example: Any sovereign State, regardless of political structure or prevailing ideology, is likely to view diplomatic attempts to overthrow its government as a prototype of diplomatic interference. The concerns which the case of Don Bernardino de Mendoza in the 1580s triggered,[29] were therefore not symptomatic for the sensitivities of one particular political system,

[22] See YILC 1957/I, 145, para 80 [Bartos]. See also ch 10, at n 12.

[23] YILC 1957/I, 146, para 10 [Yokota]. See also ch 6 at n 43.

[24] YILC 1957/I, 149, para 34 [Sandström]. See also ch 6, at n 53.

[25] YILC 1958/I, 250, para 27 [Liang]. See also ch 7, ss 2 and 3.

[26] YILC 1957/I, 147, para 17 [Hsu]. See also YILC 1957/I, 147, para 15 [Liang]. On the Sackville case, see ch 1, at nn 1 f.

[27] See also Taylor, 650 regarding the 'cultural embeddedness' of categories.

[28] See also Introduction, nn 123–25.

[29] See ch 1, at n 13.

but had relevance for every member of the international community and therefore gave the underlying conduct the character of a good representative of the relevant concept.

In many situations, prototypes for interference will not be quite as dramatic as that. In the subsequent chapters, seven areas are explored in which accusations of diplomatic interference tend to arise from receiving States which represent a variety of political, historical and geographical backgrounds. They are lobbying activities (chapter 5), partisan behaviour (chapter 6), propaganda activities (chapter 7), the employment of money and other material means (chapter 8), criticism and insults (chapter 9), threats and intimidating behaviour (chapter 10) and the granting of diplomatic asylum (chapter 11).

Overlaps between the fields have occasionally come into existence—where that is the case, they will be resolved in favour of the particular aspect of the diplomatic conduct to which the main thrust of the negative assessment by the receiving State referred. If a case therefore involves, for example, allegations of both partisan and propaganda activities, but the main criticism of the host government concerns diplomatic support of a particular faction, the incident will primarily be discussed in the chapter on partisan conduct.

On the other hand, the fact that accusations by the receiving State are taken as a principal defining factor for the identification of fields of interference, also imposes certain limitations. Reference has been made at a previous stage to the views of some commentators on diplomatic relations who tend to allow the concept of diplomatic interference to embrace a wide variety of conduct, ranging from the kidnapping of dissidents to espionage and the assassination of opponents.[30] But receiving States, while clearly taking a position on instances of this kind, rarely refer to them in the conceptual context of 'interference'. It rather appears that the diplomatic conduct in these cases is seen as a wrongful act in its own right, or as embraced by other prohibitive norms—not least the law of the receiving State itself, which diplomatic agents, under the provisions of the Vienna Convention, are under an obligation to respect.[31] These forms of conduct are therefore not at the centre of the subsequent discussions.

The identification of areas in which accusations of interference typically arise does not mean that the legal assessment of the relevant conduct has to go against the diplomatic agent. In that regard, the considerations outlined in chapters 3 and 4 have to be taken into account; but the legal assessment may also depend on certain factors germane to the field in which the alleged interference occurred. It will be seen that in some subject areas

[30] See on this ch 2, at nn 11–14.

[31] VCDR, first sentence of art 41(1).

additional norms of international law have arisen, which may serve to strengthen—or weaken—the position of the individual diplomatic agent. International instruments on corruption are examples for additional restrictive norms in cases in which diplomatic agents employed money or other material means,[32] the jurisdictional provisions of human rights treaties are examples for additional permissive norms in situations in which diplomatic asylum has been provided on mission premises.[33] These are aspects which will be explored in more detail in the following chapters.

[32] See ch 8, after n 17.
[33] See ch 11, after n 101.

5

Lobbying Activities

IN FEBRUARY 1995, Aurelia Brazeal, the US Ambassador to Kenya, found herself at the centre of controversy. In a meeting with Johnstone Macau, the Kenyan Minister for Information, Mrs Brazeal reportedly noted that the government of the United States 'would like to see Kenya legalise private radio and television stations before the end of June'.[1]

Within days, no less than three of Makau's ministerial colleagues registered their objections to these comments. The Education Minister spoke of 'external interference in the licensing of radio and television'; the Minister for Agriculture found it 'particularly annoying when an ambassador arrogantly decides to issue an ultimatum to a government minister';[2] and the Minister for Land Reclamation, Regional and Water Development referred to Kenya's sovereignty and her right to vet, in the interests of 'national unity and security', those who wished to establish private stations.[3]

The US embassy defended Brazeal's conduct,[4] and the Ambassador herself denied that she had mentioned a specific date in her meeting with the Information Minister.[5] Her remarks however led eventually to a meeting with the Kenyan Minister of Foreign Affairs 'to discuss the confusion' that had arisen over the incident.[6]

The Brazeal case stands as an illustration of many instances in which diplomatic agents had to face criticism over conduct which is best considered in the context of lobbying. Activities of this kind can meet with particular sensitivity on the side of the receiving State and have in the past resulted in stern reactions, including expulsions[7] and passionate

[1] 'US Ambassador Accused of Meddling' *Agence France Presse* (Paris, 16 February 1995).
[2] ibid.
[3] *BBC Summary*, 'Kenya; Minister Criticizes US Ambassador's Reported Remarks', (London, 20 February 1995). Paraphrasing by source.
[4] 'US Ambassador Accused of Meddling', n 1.
[5] *BBC Summary*, 'Kenya; US Ambassador Denies Giving Deadline' (London, 20 February 1995).
[6] ibid. Paraphrasing by source.
[7] See for instance the 2007 case of Nuala Lawlor (A.223 and ch 3 at n 195) and the 1992 case of the Australian Acting High Commissioner in Vanuatu, James Pearson, 'Roundup: Australia-Vanuatu Ties Strained' *Xinhua* (China, 6 July 1992).

rebukes which, at least on one occasion, led to the complete suspension of diplomatic relations.[8] At the same time, lobbying relates to a crucial aspect of the diplomatic office—a fact which has been appreciated in writings on diplomatic law for a long time.[9]

An examination of lobbying activities therefore has to raise questions about the particular feature of the conduct which triggered the negative reaction. With regard to its addressees, it is at least possible to distinguish two major aspects of this form of behaviour: Lobbying of the government and lobbying of other bearers of public office, in particular members of parliament. As the legal context shows certain differences which accompany this distinction, it appears appropriate to consider these addressees in separate sections.

For the purposes of this study, lobbying is understood as the attempt to persuade persons (or factions) in public positions of a particular course of conduct.[10] It therefore excludes cases in which diplomatic agents sought to influence public opinion,[11] but lobbying can also be distinguished from situations in which the expression of a critical opinion, rather than the attempt to sway the addressee's mind, took centre stage.[12] Lobbying of non-governmental addressees also differs from situations in which diplomatic contact with the opposition was barred as such, or in which the discussion of a particular subject with opposition politicians, or the encouragement of certain parties, was the focus of the accusations.[13] Overlaps between these scenarios do exist and will be addressed, where this is indicated.

[8] In 1975, the Ugandan President Idi Amin accused the Soviet ambassador Zakharov of trying to 'force' the receiving State to recognise the Angolan Popular Liberation Movement and suggested that Zakharov may have been drunk when handing him a note, 'Amin Shifts on Break With Russia' *Milwaukee Journal* (Milwaukee, 12 November 1975). In the course of the dispute, the Soviet Union suspended relations with Uganda, 'U.S.S.R. Severs Diplomatic Relations' *Facts on File* (New York, 15 November 1975). In a case in 2003, a lawsuit was reportedly filed by a lawyer against the US Ambassador to Cairo (Welch), after the latter had called for changes to the political and economic strategies of the receiving State. The claimant intended to effect the ambassadors expulsion. 'Lawyer Sues Welch' *Al-Ahram Weekly* (Cairo, 12–18 June 2003).

[9] *cf* Szilassy, 141.

[10] This understanding is somewhat more wider than that advanced by the OED (Oxford English Dictionary), which, for the relevant meaning of the term, refers to the exertion of influence on 'members of a house of legislature' only, OED, 'lobby, v.' at 1. *cf* however Merriam Webster, 'lobby *verb*', http://www.merriam-webster.com/dictionary/lobby.

[11] On situations of this kind, see ch 7.

[12] On situations involving diplomatic criticism, see ch 9.

[13] On situations of this kind, see ch 6.

1. LOBBYING THE GOVERNMENT

1.1. Approaching the Government: The Sensitivities of the Receiving State

Cases of diplomatic lobbying of government officials account for a sizeable percentage of all instances of diplomatic interference. At the same time, the host government is of course one of the principal points of contact for diplomatic agents—in fact, diplomats have been accused of turning too often to 'establishment sources', which clearly encompass the authorities of the host State.[14]

The VCDR expressly envisages a particular branch of government—the Foreign Ministry of the receiving State—as the designated channel for business the sending State entrusts to its diplomats.[15] That raises the question whether other governmental institutions are outside the circle of persons whom diplomats can legitimately approach on official matters. Some incidents in diplomatic relations may suggest such a restrictive interpretation: After the Canadian *chargé d'affaires* to Sudan in 2007 had reportedly written to the Sudanese National Intelligence and Security Service to call for the release of opposition politicians, the direct approach to this authority was one of the bases for charges of interference which were raised in that case.[16]

Nothing, of course, prevents sending and receiving State to come to an agreement to the effect that in their diplomatic relations official business can also be conducted with other branches of the receiving State's government. Article 41(2) makes express reference to that option by stating that another 'ministry' may be designated as a channel, and such arrangements are common.[17]

But even in the absence of such agreements, there is reason to accord a restrictive interpretation to this aspect of Article 41. The words 'all official business' may indicate an extensive scope, perhaps even one which

[14] See Clark, 74. US critics 'have accused ambassadors of relying too heavily on local government sources for information, thus rendering themselves inadequately informed as to the actual conditions within the country', Miller, 17 (referring to the examples of Iran and Vietnam).

[15] VCDR art 41(2). See also Havana Convention on Diplomatic Officers (1928) art 13; Green, 148; Sen, 58.

[16] S McCarthy, 'Ottawa Recalls Envoy to Sudan' *Globe and Mail* (Toronto, 27 August 2007). On the case, see A.223 and ch 3 at n 195.

[17] *cf* Richtsteig, 99; Hardy, 17; Satow (1979), 134, para 15.33. In the older literature, see Strupp and Schlochauer, 'Gesandtschaftsrecht', 670. See also B.7, commentary, para 3; B.8, commentary, para 3. Salmon refers to 'pratique international' (rather than, it seems, a rule of international law) which would allow specialised attachés to deal directly with the ministries of their subject areas, *cf* Salmon (1976), 45.

encompasses all functions to which Article 3 makes reference, but it is testament of poor drafting rather than of a deliberately wide remit.

Concerns about the scope of the norm—and indeed the wisdom of its conclusion—had been raised even in the ILC debates,[18] but the reference to 'official business' was retained in the draft articles (and, later, in the Vienna Convention). It is, on the other hand, interesting to note that the co-sponsor of the article, Padilla Nervo, himself had given the provision a restrictive scope when his colleague Scelle (France) pointed out that there were instances in which diplomatic missions may want to discuss matters with a 'leading recognized authority, perhaps ecclesiastic, perhaps scientific, or perhaps even political', and asked him whether such missions really had to first receive permission of the Foreign Ministry to do so.[19] Padilla Nervo replied that this was 'naturally' not what he had intended:

> Paragraph 2 referred only to official business, in other words to negotiations with government departments designed to lead up to an agreement or arrangement between the two States concerned.[20]

There arose no opposition to this construction of the rule in the ILC—although Scelle noted that contacts of the kind to which he had referred might still lead to charges of improper attempts to influence the receiving State, unless they were seen as 'official business'.[21]

Padilla Nervo's view certainly amounts to a narrow understanding of the norm[22]—it is an interpretation on whose basis it would not even be possible to claim all forms of negotiation as the exclusive domain of the Foreign Ministry. And yet, it is an understanding is which arguably more compatible with prevailing State practice.

Where, however, activities are involved which receiving States deem to fall within the remit of the Foreign Ministry, there is a tendency among diplomatic hosts to jealously guard the domain of that branch of government. This sentiment is often expressed by reference to the proper 'diplomatic channels' which would have been at the disposal of the relevant agent[23] and becomes particularly clear when diplomats contact persons other than the foreign ministry on these matters (or indeed present their

[18] YILC 1957/I, 50, para 73 [Sandström]; YILC 1957/I, 50, para 74 [Spiropoulos]. The contributions of some members even cast doubt on the consistency of State practice as a necessary precondition for the existence of the relevant rule under customary international law, *cf* YILC 1957/I, 50, para 76 [Tunkin] and YILC 1957/I, 50, para 81 [Fitzmaurice].

[19] YILC 1957/I, 150, para 45 [Scelle].

[20] YILC 1957/I, 150, para 46 [Padilla Nervo].

[21] YILC 1957/I, 150, para 47 [Scelle].

[22] See also on the narrow interpretation adopted by the co-sponsor of the norm, García Amador, YILC 1957/I, 219, para 58 [García Amador].

[23] See on this also ch 4, n 143 and corresponding text.

case to the public at large, seemingly bypassing the Foreign Ministry altogether).[24]

Outside situations in which tasks of specific negotiation have been entrusted to diplomatic agents, direct approach to other branches of the government must still be an option.

That, however, does not mean that all forms of lobbying activities will be acceptable to the receiving State. Where lobbying assumes a particular shape—critical remarks, say, or the use of threats or the employment of money—diplomatic agents may well touch on particular sensitivities of their hosts. These are aspects of diplomatic conduct which deserve consideration in their own right and will thus be discussed at a later stage.[25]

But the reason for negative reactions may also lie in the fact that a topic has been broached which carries particular sensitivity for the receiving State—especially if the link between the subject of negotiation and the interests of the sending State or the international community is not immediately apparent.

A classic case from pre-Convention days which has relevance in this context, is that of Henry Bulwer, the British Minister to Spain in 1848, to which reference was made above.[26] That the appointment of government officials would be seen by the receiving State as one of those sensitive issues which should fall within its exclusive jurisdiction, is not an unexpected development. And yet, Bulwer found his successors in the more recent past: In July 1997, the American Ambassador to Israel, Martin Indyk, was accused of urging Prime Minister Netanyahu not to appoint Ariel Sharon as Finance Minister of that State.[27]

And in the autumn of 2000, the Indonesian Minister of Defence accused the US Ambassador to that State, Robert Gelbard, of putting pressure on the receiving State to appoint Lieutenant General Agus Wirahadikusumah as chief of the army (a charge denied by the American embassy).[28]

[24] In situations of this kind, the real addressee of the diplomatic message may still be the government of the State: Delivering the message to a public audience often serves to impose particular pressure on the government. See the 2000 case of Craig Murray, British Deputy High Commissioner in Ghana, who faced criticism by the Ghanaian government after he had, during a conference on business accountability, launched an attack on corruption in the receiving State. Members of the government formed part of his audience. *Dispatch*, 'Ghana; Government To Deport Diplomat?' 5 September 2000, and see A.148. In diplomatic relations, the term 'megaphone diplomacy' has on occasion been used to describe conduct of this kind. OED, 'megaphone, n. … Compounds … C.2, megaphone diplomacy, n.'

[25] See chs 9, 10 and 8 respectively.

[26] See ch 1, at n 19.

[27] Indyk denied the charge, but Sharon himself did not appear to have accepted the Ambassador's version. U Dan and D Eisenberg, 'An American Vassal?' *Jerusalem Post* (Jerusalem, 10 July 1997).

[28] 'Indonesia Probes Foreign Involvement' *Agence France Presse* (Paris, 17 October 2000).

On other occasions, States have taken exception to suggestions which related to budgetary decisions made by the hosts. Reference has in this regard already been made to the designated US Ambassador to Germany, who in 2001 triggered criticism when he suggested that Germany should allocate more resources to NATO; statements which his future hosts perceived to touch upon a purely 'internal' issue.[29]

On other occasions again, diplomatic lobbying activities met with disapproval when they related to relations between the receiving State and third States or entities. In 1985 for instance, the Israeli Ambassador to Argentina reportedly expressed himself against the establishment of an office by the Palestinian Liberation Organisation in Buenos Aires and met subsequently with negative reactions in the receiving State.[30] Critics included the Argentinian congressman Paleari, who called the Ambassador 'insolent' and accused him of 'meddling in matters of national concern'.[31]

But instances of this kind also show that the identification of interfering conduct on the basis of the chosen topic of lobbying can be a difficult task, and one which is ill-suited for subjective assessment. There may be a wide range of matters which receiving States consider to fall within their exclusive domain while sending States feel that the relevant fields are of mutual concern or, at least, not to be considered subjects of merely internal importance. Nor can it be said that the international community will always side with the hosts in this area: The considerations made above on the determination of 'internal affairs' have to be taken into account in any given case.[32]

What is more: A consideration of the sensitivities of the receiving State in this field, even if they serve to demonstrate the underlying rationale behind the rules of Article 41(1) and Article 41(2) VCDR, does not provide a comprehensive evaluation of the relevant diplomatic conduct.

The fact remains that lobbying activities are among the principal areas in which sending States are likely to invoke interests of their own on which the persuasive efforts of their agents are based; and it cannot always be said that these interests have no foundation in international law. For a legal understanding of diplomatic activities in this field, it is thus indispensable to explore the reasons which diplomatic agents and their masters have advanced when charges of interference have arisen from lobbying activities, and to reach an understanding of the way in which international law envisages the co-existence of the competing interests.

[29] See ch 2, at n 42.

[30] *BBC Summary*, 'Peronist Deputy to Seek Expulsion of Israeli Ambassador' (London, 11 March 1985).

[31] ibid.

[32] See ch 2, s 2.

1.2. Lobbying the Government: An Evaluation

One of the most important reasons that lead to diplomatic lobbying of the host government, lies in the fact that diplomatic agents often perceive a need to engage in such action to protect interests of the sending States and its nationals. In situations of this kind, it is therefore not difficult to establish the link to Article 3(1)(b) of the Vienna Convention.

The case of Patrick Duddy, the US Ambassador to Venezuela, may be recalled in that context. In 2008, the Venezuelan President Hugo Chávez accused Duddy of interference, after the diplomat had made comments on the rise of drug smuggling in the receiving State.[33] Duddy was expelled in September of that year.[34]

But Duddy's remarks touched upon an issue which was of significant importance to the sending State as well. Chávez had, in 2005, stopped Venezuelan cooperation with the American Drug Enforcement Administration, and the Ambassador's statements referred to the impact which that decision had generated: 'drug traffickers,' according to him, were 'taking advantage of the gap that exists between the two governments'.[35]

The protection of interests is not the only function which is of relevance in cases of lobbying activities, although it is of prominence in this field. It is, of course, possible that the interests of sending and receiving State are not entirely congruent—a fact which will often be the starting position when diplomats embark on the task of negotiation (Article 3(1)(c)), whose very character makes it a basis for diplomatic lobbying, and whose restrictions have been outlined above.[36] But there are also other functions which have been invoked when conduct of this kind had been adopted.

In the 1995 case of Aurelia Brazeal, the 'public relations function', as an aspect of the general task of promoting friendly relations (Article 3(1)(e)),[37] played a certain role. According to a spokesman of the American embassy, Brazeal had merely expressed 'US government policy on civil liberties'[38]—an activity which would certainly be encompassed by the task of disseminating information about the sending State, as Richtsteig understood it.[39]

[33] 'Venezuelan President Chavez' *Xinhua* (China, 31 August 2008).

[34] 'Venezuela; Chavez Expels U.S. Ambassador' *Facts on File* (New York, 18 September 2008).

[35] I James, 'US, Venezuela Increasingly at Odds' *Associated Press* (New York, 2 September 2008).

[36] See above, at n 23 and 205. See also the 1999 case of Hecklinger, A.138.

[37] See ch 3, s 1.5.

[38] 'US Ambassador Accused of Meddling' *Agence France Presse* (Paris, 16 February 1995). Paraphrasing by source.

[39] See ch 3, at n 80.

On other occasions again, diplomatic agents may have acted on the basis of obligations of the receiving State which carry *erga omnes* character.[40] The case of Marilyn Meyers, the US *chargé d'affaires* in Burma in 1996, serves as an illustration.[41] Meyers had stated that the party of Aung San Suu Kyi should be allowed to hold a forthcoming meeting without any disturbance, and had addressed these remarks to the Director-General of the Political Department of the Burmese Foreign Ministry.[42] There was therefore little reason for the Burmese side to find fault with the statement on the basis that an inappropriate channel had been selected. All the same, the Burmese government did take offence and referred to the conduct as 'interference' in Burmese internal affairs.[43] Yet there can be little doubt that a call for free elections amounts to support of one of the foremost political human rights, and one which is of crucial importance to a people seeking the realisation of its self-determination.[44]

On the other hand, this incident also stands as a testament for the acknowledgment of gradations in the relevant diplomatic conduct by the receiving State. It is comparably rare that the host government would criticise diplomats over the conduct of lobbying the administration on its own: In general, it appears well understood that diplomats are sent abroad with particular objectives which involve an effort at persuasion. Difficulties arise when they appear to dictate a particular policy.

In the case of Meyers, the Director-General of the Political Department (Khin Maung Win) stated that it went beyond 'norms of diplomacy' for a sending State to 'come to responsible officials of the Foreign Ministry and to say officially what should or should not be done'.[45] On a previous occasion, he had reportedly stated that Meyers had presented him with an ultimatum and threatened negative consequences if the National League for Democracy were not allowed to hold its congress[46]—a claim denied by the State Department.[47] It is a subject which has relevance in various contexts, and which will be discussed in more detail at a later stage.[48]

But States have also objected to certain forms of lobbying below the level of actual threats. There are instances when a particularly vigorous effort at lobbying had sufficed for a negative reaction. When the US Ambassador to Yugoslavia, Laurence Silberman, attempted to achieve the release of an

[40] See ch 3, at n 119.

[41] A.119.

[42] *BBC Summary*, 'Ruling Council Explains Actions' (London, 4 October 1996); 'U.S. Denies Burma Interference Charges' *Reuters* (London, 2 October 1996).

[43] 'U.S. Denies Burma Interference Charges', n 42.

[44] See above, ch 3, at n 213.

[45] 'Ruling Council Explains Actions', n 42.

[46] 'US Rejects Burmese Charges' *Associated Press* (New York, 2 October 1996).

[47] ibid.

[48] See on this ch 10.

arrested American citizen, he met with criticism by President Tito,[49] but it appears that the particularly forthright manner of his activities played a role in this matter. Silberman himself noted that the State Department had described his efforts as 'too zealous',[50] and Tito himself was quoted as stating that the US Ambassador was 'saying that it pays to exert pressure on Yugoslavia'.[51]

A crucial point in the case of Aurelia Brazeal appeared to be the question whether she had mentioned a date for the liberalisation of the relevant media. It may seem a trifling issue; but the application of the principle of proportionality to this situation[52] reveals the importance of the matter. There is a considerable difference between a diplomatic agent who explains the sending State's own view on liberalisation and a diplomat who insists on its implementation by a specific date. Even in the absence of threats, the latter form of conduct can easily be construed as the imposition of pressure on the receiving State; and it is difficult to see why behaviour of this kind would be objectively necessary to fulfil the diplomatic task of conveying information about the sending State. Less intrusive means would have been available.

On occasion, diplomatic agents had to face criticism even when their activity consisted 'merely' of the offer of advice which the receiving State had not solicited. A case in this context arose in 2001, when the US Ambassador to Bangladesh, Mary Ann Peters, suggested a 'five-point action economic agenda' which the next government of the receiving State should adopt for the improvement of the local economy, and which extended to areas such as power, telephones and natural gas.[53] Unwanted advice may well be perceived as a nuisance, but it must be said that State reactions in this field are not frequently reported: Even in Peters' case, criticism arose apparently mainly from smaller parties 'and left-leaning organisations'; the Prime Minister confined herself to stating that every political party had its manifesto on whose basis it would operate.[54]

At the same time, the cases of Mary Ann Peters and Aurealia Brazeal, of Laurence Silberman and Marilyn Meyers, assist in the identification of those areas of diplomatic lobbying which meet with particular sensitivity in the receiving State, and they underline the need for awareness of conduct which may be perceived as the imposition of a policy. The resulting concept of acceptable behaviour may involve diplomatic agents in the drawing of fine distinctions. But it is this ability to apply the necessary

[49] See ch 3, at n 23.
[50] 'Jailed American Freed' *Facts on File* (New York, 31 July 1976).
[51] 'Tito Attacks US Envoy' *Facts on File* (New York, 14 August 1976).
[52] See ch 4, s 2.2.
[53] H Habib, 'U.S. Envoy's Remarks Raise Hackles' *The Hindu* (Chennai, 16 June 2001).
[54] ibid.

tact and reserve to the pursuit of legitimate interests which has contributed to the fact that the positive connotations associated with the terms 'diplomacy' and 'diplomatic style' transcend their original and more technical use.[55]

That is not to say that there are no situations in which an objective assessment requires strong representations, even if the receiving State may perceive them as pushing or imposing a particular view. If, for instance, the application of pressure is the only viable means of safeguarding a vital and legitimate interest of the sending State or its nationals, diplomats who resort to this form of conduct will regularly have a good defence against claims that they had engaged in unlawful interference.

Similar situations can arise where *erga omnes* interests are at issue. The 2008 incident involving James McGee has been mentioned before[56]—the case of the American Ambassador to Zimbabwe who had called for the violence in the receiving State to end, and had thus, given the context of the situation, assisted a people striving for the realisation of its self-determination. But the Ambassador's lobbying for this particular goal, while made in a public forum, also satisfied the principle of proportionality. McGee had resorted to a method which carried the promise of greater efficiency than direct and more discreet negotiations with a government which had contributed to the volatile situation in the first place. The violence to which the Ambassador referred was ongoing and grave in nature; and a comparison of the affected interests is therefore likely to support the position of the diplomatic agent.

Vigorous representations therefore, and even instances of 'megaphone diplomacy',[57] serve a purpose in diplomatic relations, and their assessment will not always disadvantage the diplomatic agent. But the legitimate interest in whose defence the diplomat engages in lobbying activities of this kind, needs to be firmly established—not every violation of human rights, for instance, is a violation of *erga omnes* interests—and an evaluation which favours more intrusive methods of lobbying is possible only if more lenient alternatives had to be dismissed.

The 2004 case of Edward Clay, the British High Commissioner in Kenya, may be recalled in that context.[58] Clay too had been referred to diplomatic channels which he could have approached instead of presenting his case before the British Business Association in Kenya.[59] But Clay had a strong defence at his disposal: He had reportedly raised that issue with the

[55] *cf* OED, 'diplomacy, n' at 3 and 'diplomatic, a' at 4.
[56] See ch 3, at n 163.
[57] See above, n 24.
[58] See ch 3, at n 34; ch 4, at n 140.
[59] L Barasa, 'Criticism That Rubbed Officials The Wrong Way' *The Nation* (Kenya, 3 February 2005).

government of President Kibaki before;[60] and he could thus have been held to have exhausted the less intrusive venues which international law provides to diplomatic agents in these circumstances. At the same time, even in situations of this kind, doubts about the efficiency of particularly forceful representations cannot always be dispelled.[61]

2. LOBBYING FACTIONS AND INDIVIDUAL POLITICIANS

At the end of March 2006, the Office of the President of Malawi issued an unusual press release. While the administration did not want to prevent diplomats from meeting people, it noted that they had at all times to notify the host government if they wanted to hold meetings with individual contacts or institutions within Malawi.[62]

In this absolute form, the position taken by Malawi would certainly exceed the mandate of Article 41(2) of the Vienna Convention, which does not demand that 'any' contact with persons outside the government has to be maintained through the government of the State.[63] Numerous diplomatic functions—chief among them, the tasks of observation and the promotion of friendly relations—call for direct interaction with private persons, but also with politicians outside the administration. Subjecting such contacts to the goodwill of the government would run counter to the effective fulfilment of these tasks and would have no basis in State practice.

Lobbying, of course, exceeds the boundaries of the 'mere' maintenance of contact; but there are good reasons to argue that even activities of this kind, directed at persons and institutions outside the government, must be an option. Where persuasive activities are directed at the population at large, reference will be made to it at a later stage of this study.[64] Communication with political parties and individual politicians, however, is certainly part of the diplomatic office, and this behaviour must include the possibility that the recipients will become more favourable to the sending State than they had hitherto been.[65] Nor are lobbying activities in these fields—both by their own nationals and by foreign agents—an

[60] ibid.

[61] Especially since Clay had expressed his concerns in a particularly blunt manner. See ch 9, at n 95.

[62] *BBC Monitoring Africa—Political*, 'Malawi Cautions Diplomats', 29 March 2006. Paraphrasing by source.

[63] See above after n 18.

[64] See on this ch 7.

[65] See ch 3, s 1.5. On the dangers of having to wait with such activities until, for instance, an opposition party is able to form the new government of the receiving State, see ch 6, after n 32.

entirely unexpected phenomenon; persons who engage in the political life of their country will have to expect this form of conduct as part of their daily work.[66]

And yet, there are instances in which diplomatic lobbying was resented, even when the recipients held political mandates.[67] The US Ambassador to Israel, Martin Indyk, for instance, faced criticism when in 1995 he allegedly attempted to persuade members of the Knesset to oppose a Bill which would have made it more difficult for Israel to return the Golan Heights to Syria.[68] The accusations levelled at Indyk referred to 'US interference in internal Israeli affairs'.[69]

Some areas of activity reveal a greater sensitivity on the part of the receiving State than others. There is, for instance, a tendency for the emergence of negative State reactions when the persuasive conduct shows a close connection to electoral campaigns. The case of Mason Hendrickson appears in that context: Hendrickson, First Secretary at the US Embassy in Singapore, was expelled in 1988 amid allegations of meddling in the country's internal affairs.[70] According to the government of the receiving State, the diplomat had encouraged a local lawyer to run as an opposition candidate in the forthcoming general election and had suggested the organisation of a 'more effective opposition'.[71]

On other occasions, diplomats were accused over the forceful manner of their representations towards factions or politicians in the receiving State. In the classical case of Monsignore Montagnini for instance,[72] the accusations made against the Vatican diplomat related not only to the fact that he had maintained contact with the French bishops; there was also an allegation that he had exerted pressure on them; and it appears that this part of his behaviour was instrumental for the decision to expel him from French territory.[73]

However, outside of situations in which diplomats were entrusted with a specific task of negotiation—and in which therefore Article 41(2) of the Vienna Convention would be applicable[74]—it is not possible to derive a

[66] On the significance of lobbying as part of diplomatic tasks, see Berridge, 124.

[67] See the 1981 case of Ford (A.58); the 1984 case of Bergold (A.77); the 2001 case of Miller (A.161).

[68] *Zionist Organization of America*, 'Ambassador Indyk Reportedly Interfered' (9 July 1997).

[69] 'US Envoy Intervenes' *Agence France Presse* (Paris, 26 July 1995). See also the 1984 case of Harry Bergold, 'Nicaragua: U.S. Ambassador Accused of Interfering' *Inter Press Service* (25 October 1984).

[70] R Matthews, 'Singapore Slaps The Hand That Feeds It' *Financial Times* (London, 23 May 1988).

[71] N Cumming-Bruce, 'Expelled Envoy in New Row' *The Guardian* (London, 21 May 1988). See also ch 6, after n 47.

[72] See also above, ch 2, at n 68.

[73] Salmon (1996), 129, para 199.

[74] See above after n 19.

clear rule against the lobbying of parties and politicians from the text of the Convention itself.

On the contrary, diplomatic agents who endeavour to change the minds of these contacts, will often be able to invoke the fulfilment of recognised tasks as a basis for their conduct.

The need in particular to protect the interests of the sending State may be of significance even if the recipient of the message does not form part of the government of the receiving State. If, for instance, a political party in the receiving State is fundamentally opposed to that State's membership in an international organisation to which the sending State belongs as well, then the interests of the sending State require that diplomats do not have to wait until the party forms the new government before they can attempt to persuade it of a different position. It is precisely in the period between elections, when the policy of the party is still at its formative stage, that such an attempt may yield the most promising results. Barring diplomatic agents from this activity would deprive them of the most efficient way of fulfilling their function of protection in this regard.

In a similar vein, the maintenance of friendly relations allows for a range of activities which may result in the changing of attitudes and opinions of factions in the receiving State. The 1981 case of the British High Commissioner in Canada, John Ford, illustrates the situation.[75] Ford was accused of trying to influence the votes of two members of the Canadian Parliament on changes to the constitutional relationship between Canada and the United Kingdom.[76] According to the High Commissioner himself, he had merely referred to the difficulties which changes to the British North America Act could encounter in the Westminster Parliament;[77] conduct which, in his opinion, was part of his job of conveying the British perspective.[78]

Leslie Green for one appeared to accept that understanding of Ford's conduct and noted that the High Commissioner had only fulfilled his functions by explaining 'his understanding of the views of the British government or members of parliament'.[79] He was scathing about Ford's critics: Charges of interference 'merely indicated that the complainants, regardless of their official position, knew little of the true function of the diplomat'.[80] It is a view that is not much removed from that which Richtsteig would later hold when he found that the expression of the

[75] See above, ch 3, at n 36 and A.58.

[76] C Hanley, 'An AP News Special' *Associated Press* (New York, 15 February 1981).

[77] A Hutton, 'Section: Regional News' *United Press International* (Washington DC, 16 February 1981).

[78] A Gavshon, 'Ambassador Retired' *Associated Press* (New York, 10 February 1981).

[79] Green, 148.

[80] ibid.

opinion of the sending State was part of the public relations function incumbent on diplomatic agents under Article 3(1)(e).[81]

But it is worth noting that even the Foreign Minister of the receiving State (MacGuigan) shared the assessment of this part of the diplomatic conduct. As far as the 'mere' explanation of potential problems in Westminster was concerned, MacGuigan noted that Ford had engaged in an 'entirely appropriate type of diplomatic activity', but pointed out that his conduct had also strayed into the realm of intervention (without providing details on this allegation).[82]

Negative reactions by receiving States, relating to the lobbying of politicians or parties by itself, are in fact not altogether frequent, and do at any rate not reveal the necessary degree of generality and consistency to allow for the assumption of a rule of customary international law outlawing this form of behaviour. Montagnini and Hendrickson were indeed expelled by their hosts. But in the 1995 case of Martin Indyk, the charges of interference were made by political parties, rather than the government of the receiving State,[83] and even in Ford's case, MacGuigan stated that he would not lodge a complaint with the sending State.[84]

It appears that reciprocity plays again a role in these considerations—the awareness in particular that restrictions on foreign diplomats may easily be used against the agents of the receiving State. In 2011 for instance, when the WikiLeaks revelations had cast some light on past lobbying by US diplomats, including envoys posted to India, the former Indian diplomat Parthasarathy called for calm, pointing out that lobbying was not restricted to the American side. India's own diplomats, said Parthasarathy, did, after all, not 'hesitate to mobilise the Indian community and the pro-Indian Jewish community in the US … to lobby and influence American policies'.[85]

That is not to say that every form of lobbying (be it direct or indirect in nature) is consistent with international law, as long as interests of the sending State form the basis of the diplomatic activity. Not all activities are, after all, necessary to fulfil the underlying aims, and not all interests of the sending State enjoy, under international law, the same value as the competing interests of the receiving State.

The 1984 case of Harry Bergold illustrates the problem. In October of that year, Bergold, the US Ambassador to Nicaragua, faced accusations of interference after a team of the US embassy had allegedly asked

[81] Richtsteig, 23.
[82] Hutton, n 77.
[83] Likud and the Tsomet party; 'US Envoy Intervenes', n 69.
[84] Hutton, n 77.
[85] G Parthasarathy, 'Our Leaders' *The New Indian Express* (Chennai, 3 April 2011).

political parties in the receiving State to stay away from the forthcoming general election.[86] While these activities would certainly have been in keeping with the Nicaraguan policy pursued by the American administration at that time—the Reagan government had declared its opposition to the election[87]—it would be difficult to reach an evaluation of the case which would prefer Bergold's conduct to the realisation of the Nicaraguan people's right to self-determination. The interests of the sending State stood in no proportion to the potential damage inflicted on rights of the receiving State and its nationals.

The Shmagin case on the other hand, which took place in the preceding year, exemplifies a situation in which the relevant assessment under international law would have reached quite a different conclusion. The recall of Yevgeny Shmagin, Second Secretary at the Soviet Embassy to West Germany, and that of three of his colleagues, was reportedly requested by the government of that State in May 1983.[88] Shmagin himself was accused of presenting Soviet arguments for Western disarmament to peace movements in West Germany, at whose meetings he had been present.[89]

But the explanation of the sending State's own position corresponds to a core task of the diplomatic office, and even the portrayal of that position in a positive light and the generation of goodwill for these views must be considered to fall within the reach of that function.[90] In the absence of additional elements to diplomatic conduct of this kind,[91] the receiving State would find it difficult to support the claim that the underlying conduct constituted a disproportionate intrusion in its own interests. The very establishment and maintenance of diplomatic relations implies the possibility that nationals of the receiving State, and most certainly its politicians and political parties, will be exposed to views held by the sending State, and there is little evidence in State practice that the right to territorial sovereignty includes a monopoly on the relevant information which is allowed to reach its citizens.[92]

[86] 'Nicaragua: U.S. Ambassador Accused of Interfering', n 69.

[87] ibid.

[88] T Paterson, 'Four Soviets Exposed as Spies' *United Press International* (18 May 1983).

[89] ibid.

[90] See on this ch 3, in particular at n 79.

[91] In the case of Shmagin, the existence of such additional elements cannot be positively excluded. The charges against the four Soviet diplomats also extended to the field of espionage, and according to at least one news report, Shmagin himself had allegedly 'tried to recruit an agent to work for him'. Paterson, n 88.

[92] On this point, see also ch 7, in particular at n 24.

6

Partisan Behaviour

FOR MANY RECEIVING States, it is difficult to accept that diplomatic functions might extend to involvement with the opposition or to the adoption of a position which the government of the receiving State may consider as favouring one political faction over another.

The 1946 incident involving Spruille Braden has in that regard attained the level of a textbook case. Braden, US Ambassador to Argentina, participated so enthusiastically in the elections in that year,[1] that the *Times* of London claimed his name had been better known to many voters than that of Colonel Juan Perón's main contender.[2] But the incident is not only an illustration of diplomatic partisanship; it also casts doubt on the wisdom of such conduct. Braden's involvement not only soured bilateral relations, it was counterproductive. Perón turned the Ambassador's activities to his own advantage, adopting the slogan 'Perón "si" Braden "no"'.[3] He won the election by a handsome margin.[4]

Yet a receiving State which expected the other extreme—a diplomatic agent who is invariably in agreement with the policies of his hosts—would hardly represent a realistic attitude, or one which is shared by the international community as a whole. Diplomats who are sent abroad with the task of protecting the interests of their masters are, by that very fact, partisan. That stance may bring them into close proximity with opposing voices on the political scene of the receiving State; but if a position of this kind is adopted in pursuit of their functions, they are able to rely on legitimate grounds for their conduct.

The significance of diplomatic partisanship did not escape commentators on diplomatic law even prior to the conclusion of the Vienna Convention. Fiore's draft code banned the use of mission premises 'as an asylum

[1] *cf* KE Meyer, 'The Diplomat's Tightrope' *New York Times* (New York, 26 July 1988); 'U.S. "Interference" in Argentina' *The Times* (London, 14 February 1946).

[2] 'Col Perón's Victory Certain' *The Times* (London, 30 March 1946).

[3] J Fenzi, Interview with Elizabeth Lewis Cabot, *Association for Diplomatic Studies and Training*, 28 April 1987.

[4] *cf* 'Col Perón's Victory Certain', n 2, noting that the publication of anti-Perón material by the US side 'was a windfall for Colonel Perón, because it was interpreted as foreign intervention'.

for plotting against the government of a friendly state'[5] and stated that diplomatic agents must also 'refrain from fomenting any conflict between political parties and abstain from any intrigue to approve or disapprove the acts of the government'.[6] Lord Phillimore's draft code specified that diplomats and the members of their suite had an obligation not to 'engage in conspiracies or actions against the Government and well-being of the State …'.[7]

In the ILC debates, it was likewise clear that partisan behaviour was considered as strongly associated with the conduct of interference[8]—and the only example which the ILC commentary on the rule against interference provided, did refer to a case of partisan conduct (diplomatic agents were not to 'take part in political campaigns').[9]

That the governments of receiving States show sensitivity about diplomatic involvement with the opposition cannot be surprising. It is, after all, one of the principal aims of the opposition to replace the current government, and the conduct of foreign diplomats can be instrumental in this endeavour—be it through the provision of information on important political matters, be it through the rendering of moral and material assistance or in other ways.

State practice after the entry into force of the Vienna Convention confirms that receiving States continued to feel unease about diplomatic conduct which could be considered partisan in nature. At the same time, few States go as far as to ban contact with the opposition altogether—and there is some evidence that such a position would not find the approval of the international community.

The case of the Nationalist Party in Malta may be recalled in that context. On 10 January 1983, the Maltese Foreign Ministry sent identical notes to all diplomatic missions, in which it told ambassadors to make sure that diplomats refrained from 'contacts of any kind with members of the Nationalist Party'[10]—a party which had won more than 50 per cent of the popular vote in the 1981 election on the island, but had, due to the prevailing electoral system, not been able to form the government and had refused to take their seats in the legislature.[11]

[5] Fiore, 155, para 370.

[6] ibid 161, para 483.

[7] Phillimore, 180, art 34.

[8] *cf* YILC 1957/I, 146, para 10 [Yokota]; 1957/I, 149, para 34 [Sandström].

[9] B.7, commentary, para 2; B.8, commentary, para 2. ILC Secretary Liang criticised the prominent place which partisanship carried in the commentary, noting that diplomats might interfere 'in much more serious ways as, for example, in fomenting civil war'. YILC 1958/I, 250, para 27 [Liang].

[10] 'Parliamentary Boycott Ended' *Facts on File* (New York, 8 April 1983); H Kamm, 'Malta Takes on the World' *New York Times* (New York, 20 February 1983).

[11] Kamm, n 10.

Reactions by sending States were unusually strong. The United States doubted the validity of the ban; and several diplomatic missions were said to have ignored it.[12] The European Parliament condemned it and called for the cancelling of EC aid to Malta.[13] A joint note of protest was issued by the representatives of Libya, Kuwait, Tunisia and the PLO—a significant step, as Malta had endeavoured to be on friendly terms with Arab States.[14] In the end, the Maltese government gave in to the barrage of negative reactions and allowed contacts under certain conditions.[15]

What the Maltese case illustrates is that an absolute prohibition on diplomatic contact with the opposition does not command a wide degree of acceptance in the world. It would in fact be a measure which rendered the fulfilment of certain core tasks of the diplomatic office—including the function of observation—impossible.[16] Nor is it true that receiving States regularly go to that extent to express their sensitivities in the field. It is far more common that they refer to a particular facet of diplomatic behaviour which allegedly justifies a negative reaction.

There are two areas of diplomatic conduct in this context in which negative reactions are frequently provided. The first concerns situations in which a particular subject was made the topic of debate between the diplomatic agent and factions in the receiving State; the second relates to instances in which diplomatic agents were considered to have 'taken sides' in a particular political situation.

1. DIPLOMATIC DISCUSSIONS OF SPECIFIC TOPICS WITH FACTIONS IN THE RECEIVING STATE

The identification of specific topics at the centre of the relevant diplomatic conduct carries a certain attraction for hosts who claim that interference had taken place. A more general accusation—such as objection to contact with a particular channel—risks (as the Maltese case has shown) the collective protests of a multitude of missions. By singling out a particular topic which diplomats have allegedly discussed with a particular faction, the receiving State individualises the charge and thus increases the possibility that other members of the international community consider the incident a matter between sending and receiving State which does not warrant their involvement.

[12] A MacLeod, 'Malta's Democracy' *Christian Science Monitor* (Boston MA, 1 March 1983).

[13] 'Parliamentary Boycott Ended', n 10.

[14] Kamm, n 10.

[15] '[C]ontacts designed to give an image of the Nationalists as the alternative government' were still banned, ibid.

[16] See, in the Maltese case, the reaction by the US Ambassador to Malta, James Rentschler, ibid and MacLeod, n 12.

A prominent topic which, in this context, has met with negative reactions by diplomatic hosts, is the party itself, its existence and its manifesto. In 2009 for instance, the US Ambassador to Afghanistan, Karl Eikenberry, was accused by the Afghan President Karzai of 'interference', after he had attended a press meeting hosted by one of Karzai's competitors in the forthcoming presidential elections.[17] In this situation, Karzai made clear that he did not, in principle, take exception to the presence of diplomatic observers at meetings of political candidates. What he found objectionable was the discussion of the candidates' platforms on those occasions.[18]

Eleven years earlier, the new British Consul-General in Hong Kong, Andrew Burns, faced criticism when his office invited candidates in the forthcoming legislative election to an 'informal meeting'.[19] The topic of the gathering appears to have been, once again, the political platforms of the various parties. Burns encountered negative reactions from the Chinese foreign ministry, which referred to the conduct as 'direct interference' in the affairs of Hong Kong,[20] but criticism came also from some of the candidates themselves: Lau Kong-wah, member of a pro-Chinese party, expressed his surprise at the consulate's interest in his election programme, and was reported as stating that he considered this a form of interference.[21]

On other occasions, receiving States took exception when diplomats engaged in conversations on matters which allegedly touched upon the security of the State. In that context stands the case of Glenn Warren, a US political officer, who was expelled from Sudan in 2000 after he had, according to the Sudanese Foreign Minister Ismail, discussed 'issues related to Sudanese security and stability' with 'non-registered political organizations'.[22] The United States offered a somewhat different account of events: The meeting, which had taken place between Warren and members of the 'Democratic National Alliance', served to discuss the 'general political situation' of the receiving State.[23]

The argument that diplomatic discussions on these topics fall within the scope of interference cannot be lightly dismissed. If the basis for the rule against interference is seen as rooted in the sovereignty of independent

[17] 'Karzai Protests US Diplomat's Presence' *Indo-Asian News Service* (Noida, 29 June 2009).

[18] ibid.

[19] J Pringle, 'Invitation by British' *The Times* (London, 8 May 1998); D Gittings, 'Beijing Offers a Blast from the Past' *South China Morning Post* (Hong Kong, 10 May 1998).

[20] Pringle, n 19.

[21] 'China Lashes out at Britain for "interfering" in Hong Kong' *Associated Press* (New York, 7 May 1998).

[22] *CBS*, 'U.S. Diplomat Kicked Out Of Sudan', 7 December 2000.

[23] *CNN*, 'U.S. Diplomat Expelled from Sudan', 7 December 2000. See also the 2008 case of the US Ambassador to Bangladesh (James Moriarty) who was criticised after he had allegedly discussed the state of emergency in that country with leaders of political parties, A.236.

States,[24] the concerns of receiving States are, to a certain degree, understandable.

Talks with oppositional factions both about their own manifestos and strategies and about issues relating to the security of the State can easily be construed as initiatives which affect sovereign rights. In the first case, a claim can be advanced that the relevant diplomatic conduct touches upon the political independence of the State; in the second, discussions of this kind might even affect that State's territorial integrity—aspects of sovereignty whose recognition under international law is beyond doubt.[25] In the ILC debates, it was the principle of political independence in particular to which reference was made: El-Erian emphasised that it was a duty incumbent on diplomatic agents, both in their official and personal capacity, to respect this right of their hosts.[26]

At the same time, the fact must be taken into account that sending States and their agents did not always accept the view that they had to refrain from involvement in the matters under debate—and that they sometimes had good reasons for their position.

In the 1998 case of Andrew Burns,[27] the Consul-General himself explained that it was part of his job to follow the forthcoming elections,[28] and a spokesman for his office made direct reference to the function of observation, when he stated that Burns was 'merely informing' himself about the election and that the intention had been only to 'listen to what they [the candidates] have to say'.[29]

On the other hand, if observation is the function on which the diplomatic agent seeks to rely, the argument may be advanced that this task can be fulfilled without active political participation, so that it would extend to the reception of information, but not, for example, to taking part in the relevant discussions.

Malaysia expressed herself along similar lines in 2001, when she criticised several foreign diplomats after they had attended a meeting by the National Justice Party (Parti Keadilan Nasional, an opposition party).[30] On this occasion, Rais Yatim, Minister in the Prime Minister's Department, made clear that the distinction mattered to him: 'I wish to stress here', said the minister, 'that it is not wrong for a diplomat to accept an invitation by a political party to listen to speeches but they should not take an active part in the function or be partisan'.[31]

[24] *cf* for this understanding of the foundations of interference in general, GA Res 36/103 (1981), preamble, para 5. See ch 1, after n 35.

[25] *cf* Friendly Relations Declaration, Annex, preamble, para 15; UN Charter art 2(4); Helsinki Final Act, IV; ch 3, n 180.

[26] YILC 1957/I, 148, paras 23 and 24 [El-Erian].

[27] See above at n 19.

[28] Gittings, n 19.

[29] Pringle, n 19.

[30] 'Meddling Diplomats can be ordered to leave' *Malaysia General News* (6 April 2001).

[31] ibid.

It is a view which, in light of a literal reading of Article 3(1)(d), may appear seductive. It is, however, also a view which very much removes the understanding of the diplomatic office from the real demands it faces on a daily basis. Diplomatic observation, it appears, relies on a host of other activities, and participation in debates is a prime example for the necessary preliminary and ancillary activities which this task involves.[32]

The discussion of political issues with the opposition—even matters relating to State security—finds further grounds in other functions, including the protection of the interests of the sending State and its nationals (Article 3(1)(b)) and the function of representation (Article 3(1)(a)). Today's opposition may be tomorrow's government, and diplomatic agents who have to wait with the debate of salient political issues until a certain faction has attained this position, face considerable and possibly irreversible disadvantages. They may in particular not have been able to correct prejudices which the opposition harbours regarding the external policies of the receiving State; and the sending State might be deprived of an opportunity to adjust its own policies in order to reach a compromise with the potential future government of the receiving State.

The friendly relations function (Article 3(1)(e)) is of similar significance in this context. The fact must be kept in mind that 'friendly relations', as envisaged in the Vienna Convention, are not limited to the government of the receiving State,[33] and there is evidence that sending States are keen to base contact with the opposition on this particular task.[34] It is also a function which allows for informative activities,[35] and there is, prima facie, no reason why the 'public relations' aspect of this function should not extend to political discussions with the opposition, especially when this is required to rectify an image of the sending State which the government of the receiving State may have promoted.[36]

The fulfilment of diplomatic functions therefore extends to a wide range of activities and can thus form a basis even for diplomatic conduct which the receiving State may consider partisan in nature. However, even if the remit of these functions were not affected, the possibility could not be discounted that a sending State has grounds, arising from other norms of international law, on which the adoption of such conduct can be based. Diplomatic agents, for instance, who discuss 'sensitive' matters with the

[32] See ch 3, at n 60–65.
[33] See ch 3, after n 76.
[34] See K Shu-ling, 'Paraguay Reaffirms Relations with Taiwan' *Taipei Times* (Taipei, 20 August 2002).
[35] See ch 3, at nn 79, 80.
[36] This aspect of diplomatic activity might fall within the scope of more than one function. *cf* Richtsteig, on the right to *Gegendarstellung* (from the German perspective and in the context of Art 3(1)(b)), Richtsteig, 21.

opposition, can invoke a powerful basis for their conduct, if they did so in an attempt to assist in the realisation of *erga omnes* obligations of the receiving State.

But the invocation of such grounds in situations in which the government of the receiving State is reluctant to fulfil its obligations, will almost unavoidably convey the impression that diplomatic agents have 'taken sides' on a particular topic (a scenario which will be discussed in more detail in section 2).

The assessment of the meeting of interests of sending and receiving State often shows that the diplomatic hosts are quite aware of gradations in the agents' conduct and frequently insist on the adoption of less intrusive means. The Malaysian criticism in 2001 of diplomats who participated in a meeting of the National Justice Party[37] is an example in this field. While the diplomatic aim in this case may be understood as the gathering of information, the distinction offered by Minister Rais Yatim does emphasise the existence of various options to achieve that goal: Listening to speeches, for one, as an alternative to 'active participation', and as a method which would appear less intrusive to the government of the receiving State.

But it is questionable whether methods of this kind can be seen as carrying an efficiency which is equal to that of conduct adopted by the diplomatic agents.[38] If the aim is the promotion of friendly relations or the protection of interests of the sending State, a good case can be made for the need to actively discuss even sensitive issues; less intrusive, but equally effective alternatives may simply not exist. Participation in party meetings certainly gives diplomatic agents an opportunity to further the task of observation as well: By asking questions, by confronting points of view, even by challenging the positions of party members. And yet, the fact must be taken into account that involvement in party debates may also change the way in which the opposition responds to particular matters and can thus prove counterproductive, if the real aim is the identification of that faction's position unaffected by external influence. In situations of this kind, a more passive role may be not only a less intrusive, but also a more effective way to pursue the stated aim. The assessment under the least restrictive means test therefore depends strongly on the circumstances of the individual case, but also on the specific goal which the diplomatic agent pursues.

Where the discussion of 'sensitive matters' is concerned, the second test of proportionality—cost–benefit analysis—plays a particularly significant role. If a diplomat acts to protect the interests of the sending State, the

[37] See above at n 30.

[38] See ch 4, at n 152.

need to talk about sensitive issues with an opposition which, for instance, is likely to win forthcoming elections, may be very real—especially if such action can correct a misleading impression which the opposition has of the sending State. Given the fact that elections are pending, the matter may be of great urgency as well; forcing a diplomat to refrain from these debates may cause irreparable damage to the sending State.

But it would be wrong to conclude that the evaluation of debates with the opposition will therefore inevitably favour the diplomatic agent. The ghost of Don Bernardino de Mendoza still walks the corridors of foreign offices, and the fear of diplomats who are plotting the overthrow of the government is all too present. It arose in August 2000, when the US diplomats Burgess and Moran were expelled from the Democratic Republic of the Congo after they had allegedly suggested to opposition leaders the toppling of President Kabila;[39] it also played a crucial role in the 2008 expulsion of the US Ambassador to Venezuela, whom President Chávez had accused of assisting a plot against his life.[40] In both cases, the allegations were strongly rejected by the sending State, but these situations emphasise the concerns which receiving States harbour in this regard—or at least, their view that negative reactions would, given allegations of this nature, meet with approval by the international community.

It would indeed be difficult to find an independent State which would disagree with the assessment that activities of this kind would amount to unacceptable diplomatic conduct. In the framework of cost–benefit analysis, that means that the disturbance which diplomatic activities of this kind causes to the internal workings of the receiving State would be so severe that the expected benefit, even if it consisted in the promotion of interests of the sending State, stands in no acceptable relation to it.

What the variety of cases in which diplomats discussed political topics with members of the opposition illustrates, is that both the ban on such debates when they touch subjects which the receiving government considers sensitive, and an unbridled freedom to engage in these activities, can lead to abuse and trigger grave consequences. If the Mendoza case constitutes one extreme in this discussion, the Eikenberry case stands at the other end of the scale: If diplomatic agents really had to excuse themselves whenever a party platform is being discussed, their task of observing political developments in the receiving State would be limited to an intolerable degree.[41]

What is required, is an assessment which, on the basis of objective and verifiable information, engages in a comparison of the expected benefits

[39] S Walters, 'Kinshasa Expels US Diplomats' *BBC Online* (London, 19 August 2000).
[40] C Toothaker, '2 Arrested' *Associated Press* (New York, 25 September 2008).
[41] See above, at n 18.

and the damage of the diplomatic measure in the specific case. Results however, which, as in both of these instances, lead to a complete suppression of the legitimate rights of one of the States involved, are not likely to satisfy the requirements of proportionality: They lead away from an interpretation on the basis of true harmonisation and re-introduce the difficulties of hierarchical solutions, to which reference has been made above.[42]

2. TAKING SIDES IN THE POLITICAL AFFAIRS OF THE RECEIVING STATE

The possibility that diplomatic agents may favour a particular party in the receiving State, had been a topic of discussion even at the drafting stage of the rule against interference and served as one of the examples for the violation of that norm. ILC member Yokota noted in that context that the provision by an ambassador of encouragement or funding to a political party in the host State would constitute 'unwarranted interference'.[43]

Charges of partisan support continued to play a role in diplomatic relations after the conclusion of the VCDR. In 1984 for instance, the US Ambassador to El Salvador, Thomas Pickering, was accused of favouring the Christian Democrat candidate in the presidential elections in that country over his right-wing rival.[44] The case gained particular significance due to the fact that criticism of Pickering arose both within the receiving and the sending State. In El Salvador, the vice presidential candidate Hugo Barrera called for his immediate replacement;[45] in the United States, Senator Jesse Helms demanded Pickering's withdrawal,[46] reportedly stating that '[t]he U.S. is supposed to be neutral down there and should cling to that'.[47]

At times, the host government went further and accused diplomats not only of favouring particular parties, but of creating opposition where none had existed or of taking a proactive role in its organisation.

[42] See above, ch 4, at nn 11 ff.

[43] YILC 1957/I, 146, 147, para 10 [Yokota]. On the funding of political parties, see ch 8, at nn 13 ff.

[44] H Gottlieb, 'Helms Asks Reagan To Fire Ambassador' *Associated Press* (New York, 2 May 1984).

[45] J Frazier, 'Helms, Candidate Charge U.S. Interference' *Associated Press* (New York, 3 May 1984).

[46] 'Moderate, Rightist, Both Claim Salvador Election Victory' *Facts on File* (New York, 11 May 1984).

[47] Frazier, n 45. Helms' reaction was the more remarkable as the Senator did not, as a general rule, object to activities by US organs affecting developments in other States. *cf* Helms (2000). For other cases in which diplomatic agents met with negative reactions following alleged support for factions, see the 1988 case of Hendrickson (A.90); the 1996 case of Indyk (A. 117); the 2008 case of Goldberg (A.238).

In March 2013, Venezuela expelled two American air attachés over such conduct: The diplomats had allegedly met with Venezuelan military officials,[48] and had, according to the Venezuelan Foreign Minister, encouraged them to engage in 'destabilizing projects'.[49] On this occasion, the Minister made direct reference to the duty of non-interference.[50] Other incidents indicate that the 'fostering of dissent' and the 'organisation of opposition' count among the most prominent accusations which are levelled at diplomatic agents in this context.[51]

On the other hand, there are also cases in which meetings between diplomatic agents and members of the opposition had been enough to trigger suspicions of partisanship, and sometimes negative reactions by the receiving State. The extreme position adopted by Malta in 1983[52] is certainly not shared by many receiving States, at least if the opposition operated lawfully in their territories. A particular context however, may change the assessment dramatically.

If, for instance, a diplomatic agent seeks contact with members of the opposition in the middle of an electoral campaign, even seemingly innocuous talks can send out a powerful message. The participation in electoral campaigns is, in fact, a classic example of conduct which prima facie falls within the concept of interference. Its prominent place in the ILC work on interference has already been mentioned.[53] Commentators on diplomatic law have lent further support to this position: Sen for one refers to the principle of interference as encompassing the '[r]endering of aid or active assistance … in favour of a party in the national elections'.[54]

And there is evidence that 'mere' discussions, and even the very presence of a diplomat at party events will in this context often be seen as amounting to 'participation'. In the 1998 case of Andrew Burns,[55] the politician Lau Kong-wah pointed out that there was a 'difference between normal contacts and contacts before an election', before adding that he considered the activity 'some kind of interference'.[56]

It is a sensitivity which is shared by receiving States—around the world and across political and ideological divides. In 1977, the French President

[48] J Lopez and C Shoichet, 'U.S. Expels 2 Venezuelan Diplomats' *CNN* (11 March 2013).
[49] ibid.
[50] ibid.
[51] *cf* the 1981 case of Polyakov (A.60); the 1987 case of the Iranian embassy in Tunisia (A.83); the 2006 case of Trivelli (A.213).
[52] See above at n 10.
[53] See above at n 9, but also YILC 1957/I, 149, para 34 [Sandström].
[54] Sen, 90.
[55] See above, at n 19.
[56] 'China Lashes out at Britain for "Interfering" in Hong Kong' *Associated Press* (New York, 7 May 1998).

Valery Giscard d'Estaing took exception to the fact that members of the American embassy in France had met with Jean Kanapa, a member of the political bureau of the French Communist Party—a meeting which the President appeared to have seen in the context of the municipal elections which took place in France that year.[57] On that occasion, Giscard d'Estaing emphasised the fact that he himself had refused to see leaders of the US Democratic Party during an election campaign in America.[58] And in 1981, the fact that William Shannon, the American Ambassador to Ireland, was seen on the campaign bus of an opposition party in the run-up to that country's elections was enough to trigger a negative reaction from the host government. Charles Haughey, the Irish Prime Minister, stated that the ambassador had 'put his foot in', and that his own party would not have 'contemplate[d] having him take part in our campaign or being associated with us in any way'.[59]

The fact that cases of this kind frequently meet with criticism from receiving States[60] with varying political systems might suggest that modern customary law contains an outright ban on diplomatic participation in elections abroad. Evidence for the relevant State practice in the field can certainly be adduced.[61]

But the question may justifiably be asked whether such reactions are truly based on a legal opinion, or whether they may have been influenced by considerations of political convenience. After all, not all involvement in elections irks the host government. A case has yet to be reported in which the government of a receiving State objected to participation on the side of the governing party—or to diplomatic criticism of the opposition.

A more convincing case for the existence of customary law could be made on the basis of negative reactions which the sending State gave to its own diplomats, or of measures which it adopted to prevent its diplomats from participating in the elections of the receiving State. A State which resorts to these actions stands to gain little from it, and the underlying considerations might well point to a legal evaluation.

And cases like this have come into existence. In this context, the 1964 case of the US Ambassador to Lebanon, Meyer, may be recalled, who warned embassy employees not to take any action suggesting that the government of the US took sides in the forthcoming general elections in that State.

[57] C Hargrove, 'French Leftist Views put Across to US Diplomats' *The Times* (London, 6 April 1977); 'Giscard Scores U.S. Talks with Left' *Facts on File* (New York, 9 April 1977).

[58] Hargrove, ibid.

[59] 'U.S. Ambassador in Controversy' *Associated Press* (New York, 27 May 1981).

[60] Frequently, but not always. See below at n 71.

[61] See also the 1984 case of Bergold (A.77); the 1989 case of several Western diplomats in Poland (A.96); the 2002 case of a Taiwanese diplomat in Nauru (A.184).

'In other words', wrote Meyer, 'a strict attitude of non-involvement by this Embassy must be maintained throughout the election period'.[62]

But sending States and their agents do not always show this degree of circumspection where diplomatic activities in the context of elections are concerned, and there certainly are situations—as will be seen—in which defences to conduct of this kind are advanced.[63]

It is not only in the context of electoral campaigns that the message which the 'mere' presence of diplomatic agents at certain events carries, can attain a level of significance. In more than one case, the government of a receiving State took exception to diplomatic participation in demonstrations: In 1997 for instance, Serzh Alexandrov, First Secretary at the US embassy in Belarus, was expelled after he had been detained at an anti-government protest;[64] and when the UK diplomats Brown and Laffey joined a demonstration in Romania in 1989, critical reactions came even from commentators within the sending State.[65]

On the other hand, the fact must be taken into account that the sending State and its agents, even in situations in which the message of support for the opposition appeared quite clear, may be able to invoke legitimate grounds on which the relevant conduct could be based.

The diplomatic function of observation occupies a prominent place in this regard, and the task, if it is to be properly fulfilled, must indeed embrace the opportunity to observe the relevant actors on the political plane. Sending States have shown awareness of this need: When, for instance, Poland in 1985 expelled an American diplomat and an American consul on charges of taking an active part in a May day demonstration, the US embassy put up a staunch defence of their conduct and stated that the agents had performed 'normal diplomatic functions as observers repeat observers of events'.[66] Similar arguments were advanced in the 1989 case of the British diplomats in Romania[67] and by the United States in the 1998 case of Serzh Alexandrov.[68]

But the task of observation has also made its appearance when sending States and their diplomats sought to defend behaviour which was considered to amount to involvement in electoral campaigns. In the Shannon case of 1981 for instance, the American ambassador pointed out that his intention had not been to take sides, but to observe the campaigns of each of the major parties in Ireland.[69]

[62] See A.10 and Whiteman (1970), 143. See also A.9.

[63] See, for instance, below, n 69 and corresponding text.

[64] See A.125.

[65] See ch 4, at n 147.

[66] M Vita, 'International News' *Associated Press* (New York, 3 May 1985).

[67] See ch 4, at n 146.

[68] See R Kilborn et al, 'The News in Brief' *Christian Science Monitor* (Boston MA, 28 March 1997).

[69] 'U.S. Ambassador in Controversy', n 59. See also the defence put forward in the case of the British Consul-General to Hong Kong, Andrew Burns. Above, at n 28.

On occasion, even the receiving State emphasises the significance of the observation function in this context. In the run-up to the British general elections in 2001, the British Foreign Office took this position, when an election agent in Bradford had complained about the conduct of the Pakistani High Commissioner, who had allegedly 'asked people to support … the Conservative candidate'.[70] The Foreign Office promised to investigate the issue, but noted also that '[i]t is usual for foreign diplomats to attend and observe political meetings, it's part of their job. The fact that he has been at these meetings is not a problem at all'.[71]

Diplomatic conduct in this field, could, in theory, be based on any of the other recognised functions as well. In practice, however, it is much rarer that reference to any of these tasks is made. The invocation of the protection of interests in particular is a double-edged sword: It is difficult for a sending State to claim that this task allows involvement on the side of the opposition, while avoiding the stigma of selfishness and maintaining the pretence of neutrality. Especially at election time, reliance on this function may appear a blunt tool, when more subtle arguments (such as the view that a candidate's commitment to particular democratic or economic values deserved support), are often available.

The maintenance of friendly relations, too, is not regularly invoked as a basis for diplomatic conduct in this field. But when, in 2002, a Taiwanese diplomat was criticised for meeting members of the opposition in Nauru,[72] Katharine Chang, a spokeswoman for the Taiwanese Ministry of Foreign Affairs, stated that it was the task of a diplomat to 'make friends with everyone', and that being friendly to members of the opposition could thus not amount to interference in the internal affairs of the receiving State.[73]

Among *erga omnes* interests which sending States may be able to invoke, the right to self-determination occupies a prominent place where partisan conduct is concerned—here perhaps more than in any other field of alleged diplomatic interference. The link between aim and action in this context appears obvious, yet the fact remains that the traditional view in the literature has been restrictive where diplomatic measures of this kind were concerned,[74] and some members of the ILC, too, voiced the opinion that diplomatic endorsement of factions would be an 'improper action'.[75]

[70] S Walsh, 'Foreign Office probes Commissioner's visit' *This is Bradford* (Bradford, 6 June 2001).

[71] ibid.

[72] See ch 3, at n 77.

[73] K Shu-ling, 'Paraguay Reaffirms Relations with Taiwan' *Taipei Times* (Taipei, 20 August 2002).

[74] See ch 3, at n 86.

[75] YILC 1957/I, 149, para 36 [Ago] and *cf* Yokota, ch 3, at n 167.

The rationale for the concerns of receiving States in this regard becomes particularly clear when the supported faction is not a lawful party, but is composed of underground activists, dissidents or revolutionaries.

And yet, the endorsement of parties may be the very conduct which is indicated by the need to support a people in the realisation of the right to determine their own political fate—a need which was underlined by numerous General Assembly Resolutions calling for the rendering of 'moral and material assistance' by all States to peoples striving for self-determination[76] and for the provision of 'all necessary measures' to facilitate its implementation.[77]

Even support of unlawful factions cannot automatically be perceived as falling outside the scope of diplomatic assistance towards this aim. The criminalisation of inconvenient movements is a popular instrument in the hands of an authoritarian government, and it often enough affects an oppressed people seeking self-determination. Not only will measures of this kind regularly be themselves in violation of international law, but sending States have in the past demonstrated that they did not feel obliged to refrain from the promotion of factions of this kind. The case of the African National Congress [ANC] in South Africa is an example—a group which was for a long time banned by the ruling government and which during that period depended not only on moral, but also material, assistance from the outside to continue its endeavours to achieve self-determination for the black majority.[78] In light of this, it would be difficult to speak of a customary rule excluding assistance towards unlawful factions from the remit of support of a people in its struggle to realise this right.[79]

At the same time, the interests of the receiving State have not disappeared. The need to preserve its internal peace and order, and even its territorial integrity, is arguably even more apparent where moral and material support by diplomats is at issue, than in cases in which diplomats

[76] *cf* GA Res 2105 (XX) (1965); GA Res 2649 (XXV) (1970); GA Res 3070 (XXVIII) (1973); GA Res 3163 (XXVIII) (1973) and GA Res 3328 (XXIX) (1974).

[77] GA Res 2160 (XXI) (1966), para 2(b). *cf* also GA Res 31/33 (1976), GA Res 2649 (XXV) (1970).

[78] See OK Dingake, 'Botswana', *Mmegi/The Reporter* (Gaborone, 15 December 2006). For the traditional, critical view on the provision of moral and financial means to a political party, see Ago, ch 3, at n 168.

[79] That does not mean that receiving States could not declare contact with such factions unlawful. If a situation of this kind were to arise, diplomatic conduct of this kind might still violate the first sentence of Art 41(1) of the Vienna Convention in, ie, the obligation to 'respect the laws' of their hosts. The question whether this duty covers cases in which local law is incompatible with the receiving State's obligations under international law can be expected to be of increased relevance in the future (and see also YILC 1957/I, 146, para 5 [Tunkin]), but it falls outside the limits of this study.

'merely' discussed certain matters with members of the opposition. Where the assessment of this meeting of interests is concerned, the question will often arise whether less intrusive alternatives may not have been available. It is a point which receiving States have on occasion emphasised,[80] but which sometimes even features in the assessment of expert commentators within the sending State.[81] It is at that point, too, that Richtsteig's distinction between 'tacit observation' and 'ostentatious partisanship' (in the context of the monitoring of political demonstrations)[82] carries significance: The former appears as the less burdensome alternative by comparison to the latter.

However, the question whether silent observation constitutes an equally efficient measure to fulfil the (legitimate) goals of the sending State, will to a significant degree depend on the parameters of the situation. The nature of the particular interest which the diplomatic agent seeks to protect plays a role in this assessment,[83] as does the gravity of the threat which that interest encounters. Of equal importance are the mechanisms which the receiving State itself provides for addressing the underlying right. If that right consists of self-determination, and the people concerned have recourse to an independent judiciary which is authorised to rule on their claim, or have other venues which provide effective representation, it may be difficult for a diplomatic agent to assert that 'ostentatious partisanship' was objectively required.

Similar considerations apply when it is the diplomatic agent himself who could have resorted to means which, while causing less of an intrusion, carried the promise of equal or even greater efficiency. Alternative measures of this kind can include talks with the government of the receiving State, or the soliciting of the help of third States whose relations with the government of the receiving State may be stronger than those which the sending State enjoys. And the search for the 'least intrusive means' may require clear distinctions which take into account the interest which the diplomatic agent pursues. If the relevant interests consist merely in the fulfilment of the diplomatic task of observation, attendance at political rallies may well be indicated and there may be no less restrictive, but equally efficient, measure to fulfil that task. The wearing of garments of a political party at such an event, is more difficult to explain.[84]

It is at the stage of cost–benefit analysis that a more precise assessment of the interests of the receiving State, in the particular shape they received

[80] It is at that stage that the references to 'diplomatic channels' which should have been used, is again of relevance. See on this above, ch 3, n 251, ch 4, n 142.

[81] See ch 4, n 147.

[82] See ch 4, n 149.

[83] *cf* above after n 26 and after n 65.

[84] See the 2013 case of the Chinese Ambassador to Tanzania, 'Ministry Cautions Envoys' *Tanzania Daily News* (Dar es Salaam, 18 September 2013) and A.296.

through the diplomatic measure, becomes possible—as do the advantages which the measure promises to the sending State or the international community.

These benefits can be significant. A case involving Western diplomats in South Africa in 1987 may be recalled in that context. In the summer of that year, PW Botha, President of that country at a time when apartheid was still the prevailing system, launched a sharp attack on diplomats from Western countries. He noted that several envoys had gone to some length to express their sympathy with the black population[85] and talked about the possibility of travel restrictions on diplomats engaging in 'extra-parliamentary politics'—a phrase which was understood as referring to meetings with the ANC.[86]

But the international interests pursued by diplomats who engaged in conduct of this kind carried considerable weight. In that regard, the fact must be taken into account that freedom from racial discrimination has been accepted as a right with *erga omnes* character,[87] and that apartheid itself has been understood in international law as constituting a crime against humanity.[88] The value which the international community attached to its removal can hardly be in doubt;[89] and there is no evidence that the diplomatic measure had any grave or lasting negative impact on interests which the hosts could have claimed with some measure of legitimacy.

In situations in which diplomatic agents act in the defence of a strong interest on the side of the sending State or the international community, the assessment of their action may further be tilted in favour of the diplomatic measure if the cost arising to the receiving State appears low by comparison to other actions which the sending State could have adopted. In some situations, the impact of such alternative measures could have been significant: They may include international complaint mechanisms, the adoption of economic sanctions and even, where the legal conditions for that are in place, participation in an international military intervention.

It is, however, true that not all situations are marked by a danger to a fundamental interest of the sending State or an *erga omnes* interest, and

[85] J Jones, 'Botha Threat To Curb Diplomats' *Financial Times* (London, 14 August 1987); J Lehrer et al, 'Raging Bull', *The MacNeil/Lehrer NewsHour*, 13 August 1987.

[86] P Goodspeed, 'South Africa Stages Propaganda Attack against Clark's Visit' *The Toronto Star* (Toronto, 14 August 1987). On the travel restrictions, see also Lehrer et al, n 85.

[87] See ch 3, at n 122.

[88] See Sec Res 556 (1984), 1st operative paragraph; GA Res 2671 (XXV) (1970), F, 1st operative para; *Convention on the Non-Applicability of Statutory Limitations* art I(b); Apartheid Convention art I. For its qualification as a crime against humanity in international criminal law, the relevant elements have to be proven in each situation, including the contextual element. See, for today's regulation, ICCSt art 7(1)(j) and Elements of Crime art 7(1)(j).

[89] See also ch 11, at n 83.

there are scenarios in which both cost and benefit weigh heavily on the scales. An accurate analysis therefore requires a meticulous application of the criteria which have been identified above. Reference has already been made to the consequences which the rendering of material or moral support can create for the hosts[90]—consequences which can be irreversible and indeed harmful to the order of the receiving State.

From a legal perspective, cost–benefit analysis shows its greatest significance precisely in situations where both the dangers of a diplomatic measure and the dangers of diplomatic inaction are so pronounced, that an exacting mechanism is required. If applied with precision and in a dispassionate manner, it assists not only in the evaluation of behaviour which has triggered objections by the receiving State in a given case, but it identifies the clear limits of diplomatic partisanship and thus establishes invaluable guidance for future conduct in this field.

[90] See ch 4, after n 175.

7

Propaganda

1. A BLANKET BAN ON PROPAGANDA?

BEFORE DAYBREAK ON 28 June 2009, the Honduran President Manuel Zelaya was awoken by gunshots. Armed forces entered his home; half an hour later he was dragged outside, then—still in his pyjamas—put on a plane to Costa Rica.[1] In Honduras, the speaker of the National Congress was sworn in as the country's interim president.[2]

But ousting the President proved more difficult than expected. Shortly after the coup d'état, Zelaya attended a meeting of Latin American leaders in Nicaragua,[3] a special session of the Organization of American States[4] and the UN General Assembly which he addressed only two days after his departure from Honduras.[5]

Then, in September 2009, Zelaya managed to return to his home State, where he found refuge in the Brazilian embassy in Tegucigalpa.[6] Hundreds of his supporters turned up at the embassy, where the former President addressed them with slogans such as 'Restitution, Fatherland or Death!'[7] The government of Honduras expressed the fear that Zelaya's conduct threatened the 'peace and internal public order of Honduras'.[8] It considered the situation serious enough to declare a curfew;[9] scuffles broke out between protesters and security forces; tear gas was fired by police forces at the demonstrators.[10]

[1] W Weissert and F Cuevas, 'Honduran Military Ousts President' *Associated Press* (New York, 29 June 2009); 'Lula Urges African Union to Denounce Honduras Coup' *Agence France Presse* (Paris, 1 July 2009).

[2] 'Newly Appointed Honduras Leader' *Agence France Press—English* (29 June 2009).

[3] *RTÉ News*, 'Curfew Imposed in Honduras', 30 June 2009.

[4] G Thompson and M Lacey, 'Honduras gets an Ultimatum' *International Herald Tribune* (2 July 2009).

[5] H Parr, 'Politics: Deposed Honduran President' *Inter Press Service* (30 June 2009).

[6] R Carroll, 'Manuel Zelaya Refuses to Leave Honduras' *The Guardian* (London, 10 December 2009).

[7] J De Cordoba, 'Crisis in Honduras' *Inside Costa Rica* (San José, 10 October 2009).

[8] Honduras Application, para 5.

[9] De Cordoba, n 7.

[10] G Palencia, 'Honduras Police Break Up Pro-Zelaya Protest' *Reuters* (London, 22 September 2009).

The toppling of a democratically elected head of government can, by itself, be a matter of concern for international law.[11] But in the specific circumstances of the case, the events also warranted assessment under diplomatic law—in view in particular of the fact that the embassy of Brazil had allowed Zelaya to use mission premises to address his supporters.

On 28 October 2009, the Honduran Ambassador in The Hague filed a case against Brazil with the ICJ.[12] In her application, Honduras stated that Zelaya had, since his arrival, used the embassy of Brazil 'as a platform for political propaganda and thereby threaten[ed] the peace and internal order' of the State.[13] It furthermore accused the Brazilian diplomats of allowing Mr Zelaya the use of embassy facilities 'in order to evade justice in Honduras, and to conduct illegal activities against the lawful and legitimate Government of Honduras by calling for insurrection of Honduran nationals against the constitutionally established authority'.[14]

In the event, the ICJ never had the opportunity to express its opinion on the Honduran case. Following elections in Honduras in November 2009 and the assumption of office of a new president, the State decided to withdraw its application, and the case was therefore removed from the court's list.[15]

But the incident highlights the contentious nature of conduct which the receiving State considers propaganda, and for which it holds agents of the sending State responsible.

'Propaganda' in this context is understood in the way Ioannou suggested and which seems to best reflect its use in international relations: 'a method of communication which attempts, in a systematic way, to influence and manipulate the behaviour of people, so as to produce a predetermined effect'.[16] As in the case of lobbying activities, diplomatic agents involved in propaganda thus engage in an effort of persuasion—but the recipient in this case is the general public. This differentiation may matter for the assessment of this form of conduct. Unlike the government of the receiving State, the public is not designated as the official channel for diplomatic communication, and unlike politicians and political factions, it does not have to expect lobbying efforts by foreign agents.

Historically, the public had not occupied a high rank among the available channels of diplomatic conduct—Akzin speaks in this regard of an

[11] In particular, because of its impact on a people's right to realise their self-determination. In the Zelaya case, both the UN General Assembly and the OAS condemned the coup d'état. See United Nations News Centre, 'General Assembly Condemns Coup in Honduras', 30 June 2009; Organization of American States, 'OAS Permanent Council Condemns Coup d'État in Honduras', 28 June 2009.

[12] See Introduction, at n 59.

[13] Honduras Application, para 5.

[14] ibid, para 6.

[15] *Diplomatic Relations*, 304.

[16] Ioannou, 1135. See also OED 'propaganda, *n*'; (no 3). *cf* for the somewhat wider term of 'public diplomacy', Alam, 52.

'attitude of indifference or diffidence'[17] on the part of diplomatic agents, which probably changed only after the First World War. Today, there is no doubt that Foreign Ministries around the world consider relations with the public an essential part of the tasks of their diplomats abroad.[18]

At the same time, receiving States have on occasion shown some concern when diplomatic agents addressed the public or expressed opinions in situations in which they had to be aware that the message would reach the public in due course.[19]

But it is clear that several diplomatic tasks do require contact with the general public—including the functions of representation and the protection of interests of the sending State and its nationals,[20] as well as—perhaps even more prominently—engagement in public relations as part of the promotion of friendly relations.[21]

It would be difficult to derive a rule from general customary international law to the effect that contact with the public is altogether removed from the remit of diplomatic activity. The days are gone when the American Attorney-General stated that a diplomat had 'no authority to communicate his sentiments to the people of the United States'.[22] State practice today furnishes many cases in which diplomatic agents did give public talks (let alone express themselves on generally accessible embassy websites) without encountering negative sanctions, and on occasion, diplomats have even met with consternation if they stayed away from public events.[23] If concerns arose in cases in which the public was approached, the focus of the accusations usually rested on an additional element to the diplomatic conduct.[24]

It is questionable whether propaganda on its own can furnish this additional element to such a degree that there would be reason to speak of a rule in customary international law preventing its conduct by diplomatic agents. Propaganda has certainly met with suspicion in the past: Berridge for one notes that propaganda activities are 'not diplomacy. [They are]

[17] Akzin, 2.

[18] *cf* Blankenhorn, 430.

[19] One example are situations in which remarks were made in the presence of journalists (see the 1975 case of William Porter, A.29), or to a select group of individuals in circumstances in which the message is likely to reach the general public in due course (see the 1982 case of Deane Hinton, the US Ambassador to El Salvador, in which the relevant comments had been made to American Chamber of Commerce, 'US Backs Off' *Facts on File* (New York, 19 November 1982).

[20] See on this ch 3, at n 16.

[21] See ch 3, at n 79.

[22] Correspondence of the Attorneys General, separate entry of 27 July 1797 (Charles Lee), quoted in Hoffman, 352.

[23] See the 1995 case of Indyk (A.114).

[24] In the 1975 case of Porter, for instance (above, n 19), the Canadian Prime Minister referred to the substance and form of the remarks, rather than the fact that a particular channel had been approached. *RGDIP*, 'Chronique des faits internationaux' (1976), 898.

a form of political advertising'.[25] Nicolson adds to that sentiment that, '[i]n the days of the old diplomacy, it would have been an act of unthinkable vulgarity to appeal to the common people any issue of international policy'.[26]

Propaganda activities have also been at the centre of negative assessments by receiving States. But it is often not the conduct of propaganda on its own that characterises the relevant diplomatic behaviour. When Pakistan, for instance, in 1994 ordered India to close her consulate general in Karachi, the Pakistani Foreign Minister did raise accusations of 'propagation of disaffection and propaganda against the unity, territorial integrity and sovereignty of Pakistan', which had allegedly been committed by the Indian side.[27] But the consulate general was also allegedly involved in the stirring up of unrest in Karachi—conduct which goes beyond the mere performance of propaganda.[28]

The fulfilment of diplomatic functions does require engagement in activities which carry a persuasive element. The very fact that the population of the receiving State may harbour a misconception about certain aspects of the sending State and its nationals, may call for attempts to effect an adjustment of this opinion. Richtsteig thus states with some justification that the mission must have the right to engage in public criticism or in the correction of a perception ('*Richtigstellung*') if that is objectively necessary.[29] Bliščenko likewise highlights the need to protect the image and the rights of the sending State.[30] The protective function is involved in activities of this kind: The appropriate fulfilment of Article 3(1)(b) of the Convention will often require no less than an effort at persuasion.

The promotion of friendly relations and the development of economic, cultural and scientific relations can likewise necessitate activities which carry a persuasive aspect. Blum emphasises the danger that informative activities in the fields of economics, culture etc may be perceived as 'intervention' by the receiving State.[31] On the other hand, if the public relations function imposes the task on diplomatic agents to explain the policies of the sending State to the public, the possibility cannot be discounted that diplomats will succeed in changing preconceived views held by the general population.

[25] Berridge, 128.

[26] Harold Nicolson, quoted in Regala, 43.

[27] S Zubeiri, 'Pakistan Accuses India of Terrorism' *Agence France Presse* (Paris, 26 December 1994).

[28] A Iqbal, 'Pakistan Closes Indian Consulate' *United Press International* (26 December 1994). See also the 2006 case of Czech diplomats in Belarus (A.210), in which the fact that they had distributed leaflets referring to the human rights situation in Belarus, may have contributed to the sensitivity on the part of the latter.

[29] Richtsteig, 98. *cf* also Bliščenko, 181.

[30] '[D]as Prestige und die Rechte des eigenen Staates', Bliščenko, 181.

[31] Blum, 1038.

What is more: There is evidence that receiving States are aware of the fact that the need to fulfil diplomatic functions can lead to persuasive activities affecting the general public. Reference has already been made to the 1949 incident in which the US Assistant Secretary of State, Gross, defended the function of influencing public opinion in favour of the sending State.[32] More than 20 years later, a similar situation arose when the Belgian Foreign Minister found himself defending the Chilean ambassador, after the latter had tried to justify the coup d'état of General Pinochet. According to the Minister, it was 'normal' for a diplomat to explain the prevailing situation in his own country and the position of his government.[33]

That is not to say that efforts at persuasion will always meet with approval in the international community and be considered in agreement with international law. As with lobbying activities directed at government and politicians of the receiving State, the particular way in which diplomats tried to achieve their aims plays a role in the evaluation of their conduct.

And commentators on diplomatic law have indeed tried to identify the dividing line between acceptable and excessive conduct in this field. Salmon probably goes too far when focusing exclusively on the informative nature of diplomatic interaction with the public. In his view, diplomats need to devote particular care to the manner in which they inform; he thus points out that the publication of information bulletins by the embassy carries the risk of leaning towards propaganda activities.[34] That however points in the direction of an absolute rejection of persuasive conduct which, in this form, is difficult to derive from State practice.

The approaches suggested by Richtsteig (a general acceptance of public criticism or activities to clarify a perception among the population of the receiving State, if that is 'objectively necessary')[35] and by Bliščenko, who argues in favour of the application of 'tact and resolve' where the image and interests of the sending State are to be protected,[36] appear to be more in line with the position taken by the international community.

What this indicates, is, that in this field too, the question arises whether alternatives to the adopted measure had been available, which would have caused less of an intrusion in the affairs of the receiving State.[37] A recent case involving Canada and Iran exemplifies the situation. In July 2012, the Canadian Ministry of Foreign Affairs warned Iranian diplomats of interference, after Hamid Mohammadi, a cultural counsellor at the Iranian embassy, had called on ethnic Iranians living in Canada to

[32] See ch 1, at n 31.
[33] Salmon (1996), 132.
[34] Salmon, (1996), 132, 133, para 202. See also Do Nascimento e Silva (1992a), 1028.
[35] See above, at n 29.
[36] 'Takt und Festigkeit', Bliščenko, 181.
[37] See ch 4, at n 132.

'resist being melted into the dominant Canadian culture' and to 'occupy high-level key positions'.[38] In the media, a human rights activist of Iranian origin was quoted as stating that the Iranian embassy in Canada 'sometimes uses cultural events as an excuse to spread their own propaganda'.[39]

That embassies engage in cultural activities is of course not an unknown phenomenon—neither is the promotion of the culture of the sending State and the maintenance of links with people who share the ethnicity of that State. Putting pressure on them and engaging in negative value judgements about the culture of the receiving State is a different matter, and it is difficult to see how these forms of conduct can be said to be necessary, or even efficient, tools for the fulfilment of the diplomatic function of the promotion of friendly relations.[40]

That does not mean that propaganda per se is to be perceived as an unlawful task. The restrictive view which is sometimes expressed in this context will often take, as its basis, the negative connotation which the term 'propaganda' has acquired in ordinary use over the years.[41] But it is more than questionable whether this is the understanding which prevails in international law even today.[42] The fact has to be recalled that the General Assembly has on occasion expressly called on Member States to promote friendly relations 'by all means of publicity and propaganda available to them'.[43]

Where a clear negative line has been taken on propaganda in general international law, additional elements of the underlying conduct invariably played a role in the establishment of the negative sanction.[44] A similar understanding has emerged in the practice of States relating to forms of diplomatic propaganda. There are three types of propaganda in particular which, in view of the assessment given to them by members of the international community, merit particular observation: Persuasive activities which relate to a purpose that is condemned by the international community; instigation to certain forms of conduct; and propaganda which relies on false or distorted information.

[38] 'Ottawa Eyes Iranian Embassy' *Jerusalem Post* (Jerusalem, 15 July 2012); KB Carlson, 'Close the Iranian Embassy: Afshin-jam' *National Post* (Toronto, 12 July 2012).

[39] Carlson, ibid.

[40] In the Mohammadi case, Byers thus drew a distinction between 'cultural outreach' activities and the recruitment of Canadian citizens—with the latter form of conduct, in his view, constituting interference in the internal affairs of the receiving State, KB Carlson, 'Embassy "Needs to be Kept in Check" [Interview with Prof Michael Byers]' *National Post* (Toronto, 13 July 2012).

[41] *cf* OED, 'propaganda, n.', at 3 ('esp in a biased or misleading way').

[42] For alternative concepts, see Ioannou, 1135, but also De Brabandere (2012), para 1.

[43] GA Res 110(II) (1947), para 2.

[44] See on this in more detail, De Brabandere, para 10 et seq.

2. PROPAGANDA FOR ILLEGITIMATE PURPOSES

In 1980, Musa Kusa—later to be Gaddafi's Minister of Foreign Affairs—already occupied a significant position in the Libyan diplomatic service as Secretary of that State's 'People's Bureau' in London, a position which has been equated to an ambassadorial post.[45]

Once in place, he was soon at the centre of controversy. Only hours after the Foreign Office had recognised him as head of the Libyan diplomatic mission, Kusa answered questions by the *Times* about threats to assassinate dissidents of the Gaddafi regime. Speaking from the steps of the mission, Kusa explained that revolutionary committees had 'decided last night to kill two more people in the United Kingdom. I approve of this'.[46] Kusa added that the Libyan side was now 'seriously thinking of cooperating with the IRA if the British Government continues to support those Libyans who are hiding here'.[47] In reaction to his remarks, the Foreign Office summoned Kusa and told him that his continued presence in Britain was 'no longer in the interests of Anglo-Libyan relations.'[48]

That Musa Kusa's words would affect particular sensitivities of the receiving State was to be expected. But the United Kingdom is not alone in trying to withdraw certain topics from the remit of lawful propaganda: Such attempts have been made on the international level as well, especially on the initiative of organs of the United Nations.

Prominent fields in this regard are propaganda on behalf of violence[49] and terrorism,[50] as well as propaganda for international crimes (in particular, apartheid),[51] racial discrimination, other forms of discrimination and 'hatred among nations'[52] and war.[53]

[45] *cf* 'Profile: Libya's Moussa Koussa' *BBC Online* (London, 31 March 2011). Various transliterations of his name exist; the form which is preferred in this chapter is the one which was employed by *The Times* at the time of the 1980 incident.

[46] M Horsnell, 'Gaddafi Men Sentence to Death' *The Times* (London, 13 June 1980); and *cf* S Tendler et al, 'Head of Libyan Mission is Expelled' *The Times* (London, 14 June 1980).

[47] Horsnell, n 46.

[48] N Finke, 'British Expel Libyan Diplomat' *Associated Press* (New York, 13 June 1980).

[49] *cf* GA Res 33/73 (1978), para II(a)(ii).

[50] SC Res 1624 (2005), preamble, operative paras 4 and 8; para 1.

[51] Mass Media Declaration, preamble, para 5.

[52] UNESCO Res 4.301 (1970), preamble, operative para 6; para 1; Mass Media Declaration, preamble, operative paras 4 and 16; CERD, art 4; GA Res 33/73 (1978), para II.(a)(ii). For the prohibition of propaganda pertaining to national, religious or racial hatred in the field of human rights, *cf* ICCPR art 20(2); ACHR art 13(5).

[53] Prominently GA Res 33/73 (1978), preamble, 13th operative para; para I.3; GA Res 34/88 (1979), para II (f); UNESCO Res 4.301, para 1; and see, with differing phrasings of the ban, Friendly Relations Declaration, 1st principle, para 3; GA Res 42/22 (1987), Annex 1.I.9.; GA Res 381(V) (1950), para 2(1); Convention on the International Right of Correction, Preamble, operative para 3; GA Res 110(II) (1947), para 1; UNESCO Res IV.1.5.021 (1954); UNESCO Res 4.301 (1970), preamble, para 5. Mass Media Declaration, preamble, paras 4, 16 and 13. For the prohibition of propaganda for war in the context of human rights, see ICCPR art 20(1); ACHR art 13(5).

But it is not always clear whether a rule of general international law exists which bars 'merely' persuasive efforts in this field (such as attempts to create understanding for the various subject areas) as opposed to more involved forms of conduct (such as incitement to particular actions[54] or conduct involving threats and intimidation).[55]

The extension of the restriction to persuasive activities would have far-reaching consequences for diplomats. Envoys of authoritarian governments would thus be able to justify the existence of the relevant regimes,[56] but they would be barred from offering an explanation for those policies of their masters which fall in the above named categories—even if such policies have come under attack in the sending State.

This might well be the case, if the international community were in agreement on the establishment of such an extensive limitation. And yet, evidence for the necessary elements of a rule of customary law to this effect is not always easy to adduce.

The strongest case for the existence of such a rule can arguably be made where propaganda on behalf of war is concerned.[57] 'Propaganda for war' was expressly addressed in Article 20(1) ICCPR and Article 13(5) ACHR whose parties undertake to outlaw this form of conduct (and, by implication, not to commit it in the first place).[58]

The extent of the term 'propaganda' had become the topic of discussion even during the codification of the relevant norm in the ICCPR. In the Third Committee, it was the Brazilian delegate Mello who made clear that the concept would extend beyond direct incitement to war, but would incorporate also certain expressions of opinion 'for the purpose of creating a climate of hatred and lack of understanding between the peoples of two or more countries, in order to bring them eventually to armed conflict'.[59]

However, it is difficult to speak of uniform acceptance of the relevant restriction. Several States appended reservations or declarations to Article 20, with some expressing a clear rejection of the provision,[60] and

[54] On this, see below, s 3.

[55] On this, see ch 10.

[56] See, on this, the 1978 case of the Chilean ambassador in Belgium, above, at n 33.

[57] The rule is more appropriately understood as a ban of propaganda on behalf of unlawful recourse to armed force—otherwise, even diplomats of States engaged in lawful self-defence would be barred from justifying the policy of their States abroad. See HRC General Comment No 11 (1983), para 2; but also reservations and declarations by France (Declarations and Reservations 1980, para 7) and Thailand (Interpretative Declarations 1996, para 4) on ICCPR art 20. UN Treaty Collection (Online), ICCPR.

[58] For the link between the duty to prevent a crime and the duty not to commit it in the first place, see *Genocide Convention Case* (2007), para 166.

[59] GA Third Committee, 1079th Meeting, 97, para 2 [Mello]; and see Kearney (2007), 125.

[60] See Denmark (2014), para 3; Iceland (1979), para 5; The Netherlands (2010) on ICCPR art 20(1); Sweden (1971) on ICCPR art 20(1); Finland (1975), para 3, UN Treaty Collection (Online), ICCPR.

others voicing the view that they did not have to adopt any domestic legislation to comply with Article 20[61] or reserving the right not to do so.[62]

Propaganda on behalf of racism or racial hatred invites similar considerations. The language of Article 4 of the Convention on the Elimination of All Forms of Racial Discrimination (CERD) appears quite clear: State parties condemn 'all propaganda ... based on ideas or theories of superiority of one race or group of persons of one colour or ethnic origin, or which attempt to justify or promote racial hatred and discrimination in any form'.[63] They also agree to declare the dissemination of ideas 'based on racial superiority or hatred' punishable by law, and declare propaganda which promotes racial discrimination, illegal.[64]

But few articles were to prove as controversial as this provision of CERD. No less than 20 States deemed it necessary to make reservations or declarations with reference to this rule[65]—many of them out of concern for the impact which that article might have on the right to freedom of expression.

Where propaganda relating to violence and terrorism is concerned, the situation is even less settled. General Assembly Resolution 33/73 does refer to 'advocacy of violence', and Security Council Resolution 1624 mentions 'justification or glorification (apologie) of terrorist acts', and both measures were passed with impressive majorities.[66] But they shy away from a clear outlawing of the relevant propaganda: The General Assembly Resolution calls on States to 'discourage and eliminate' advocacy for violence,[67] and the Security Council Resolution merely 'repudiat[es]' attempts at justification or glorification.[68]

And the question whether glorification of terrorism could qualify for a ban on the international level is cause for controversy,[69] with the

[61] Belgium (Declarations 1983, para 6); Luxembourg (2004, para (d)); United States (Reservations 1992, para 1). UN Treaty Collection (Online), ICCPR.

[62] Australia (Reservations 1980, on ICCPR art 20); Ireland (1989, on ICCPR art 20(1)); Malta (Reservations 1990, para 5); New Zealand (Reservations 1978)—but referring to the fact that it had already adopted certain legislation in the field, similarly United Kingdom (1976). UN Treaty Collection (Online), ICCPR. The United States and Israel also abstained from General Assembly Resolution 33/73 which affirmed the duty of States to 'refrain from propaganda for wars of aggression', citing concerns over its impact on freedom of expression. Kearney (2007), 68.

[63] CERD art 4.

[64] CERD art 4(a) and (b).

[65] Antigua and Barbuda (1988), Australia (1975), Austria (1972), Bahamas (1975), Barbados (1972), Belgium (1975), France (1971), Grenada (2013), Ireland (2000), Italy (1968), Japan (1995), Malta (1968), Monaco (1995), Nepal (1971), Papua New Guinea (1982), Switzerland (1994), Thailand (2003), Tonga (1972), United Kingdom (1969), United States (1994), See UN Treaty Collection (Online), CERD.

[66] GA Res 33/73 (1978) was carried by 138 votes to none, but with two abstentions (USA, Israel). Kearney (2007), 68; Ioannou, 1136. SC Res 1624 (2005) was passed unanimously. SC Resolutions and Decisions (2006), 146.

[67] GA Res 33/73 (1978), para II(a)(ii).

[68] SC Res 1624 (2005), preamble, 4th operative para.

[69] See De Brabandere, para 28.

UN Secretary-General speaking about a 'troubling trend' to proscribe glorification, 'involving statements which may not go so far as to incite or promote the commission of terrorist acts, but nevertheless applaud past acts' and finding that glorification, unlike incitement, 'may not' be legally prohibited.[70]

To a degree, this uncertainty is reflected in the practice of States relating to diplomatic propaganda for terrorism and violence. In Musa Kusa's case, the reaction of the United Kingdom was unambiguous.[71] Twenty years later, the British position in the face of diplomatic comments which were understood as offering justification for violence and terrorism, was not quite as clear. The relevant case involved the Saudi Ambassador to the United Kingdom, Dr Ghazi Algosaibi. Algosaibi, who had also gained a reputation as a poet in Arab countries, had written a poem, entitled 'The Martyrs', which was published in April 2002 in a London-based newspaper.[72] The poem referred to a young Palestinian suicide bomber,[73] for whom Algosaibi found complimentary words: 'You died to honour God's word', it said, and: 'She embraced death … Doors of heaven are opened for her'.[74]

The reaction of the British Foreign Office was somewhat reserved. Its spokesman was quoted as saying that Britain regarded 'suicide bombings as a form of terrorism, and we would like to make our views known to the Saudi ambassador'.[75] But to that, he added: 'We're not saying reprimand or rebuke. We don't intend to take the matter any further.'[76]

Algosaibi left Britain five months after his poem had been published. Even then, a Saudi official denied that the withdrawal had been connected to the poem[77]—the official explanation was that Algosaibi had been given a new appointment as Water Minister.[78]

Instances, then, in which diplomatic agents resort to glorification of violence, do not unavoidably result in a censure of the author of the statements. The assessment of the British position on the Algosaibi case is certainly not without its challenges. On the one hand, the generally friendly state of affairs between sending and receiving State is likely to have contributed to the absence of stronger sanctions. On the other hand, the same consideration gives room to a different understanding: The fact that Britain, despite

[70] UN Terrorism Report, para 61. But see also COE Explanatory Report (with regard to incitement to 'violent terrorist offences'), para 91, and De Brabandere, paras 28, 29.
[71] S Tendler et al, 'Head of Libyan Mission is Expelled' *The Times* (London, 14 June 1980).
[72] P Harris, 'Saudi Envoy Praises Bombers' *The Observer* (London, 14 April 2002).
[73] 'Diplomat Censured over Bomb Poem' *BBC Online* (London, 18 April 2002).
[74] Harris, n 72.
[75] 'Diplomat Censured over Bomb Poem', n 73.
[76] ibid.
[77] 'Saudi Official' *Agence France Presse* (Paris, 19 September 2002).
[78] A La Guardia, 'Saudi Arabia Recalls Renegade Ambassador' *Daily Telegraph* (London, 19 September 2002).

her political friendship with Saudi Arabia, saw it necessary to 'make [her] views known to the Saudi ambassador', may well indicate the severity of the underlying conduct.[79] In the world of diplomacy, an invitation to an exchange of opinions among friends may carry similar weight as an expulsion order among States whose relationship is less amicable.

Any evaluation of propaganda on behalf of the subjects outlined above faces the difficulty that not many instances exist in which diplomats engaged in such conduct without an additional element—such as incitement—being present. Nor is it apparent that in the few cases of 'pure' propaganda in these fields, the relevant diplomats engaged in attempts to justify their conduct by reference to diplomatic functions, let alone *erga omnes* interests.

At the same time, the case of Algosaibi raises a point which merits further consideration. The diplomat reportedly stated that he was a poet as well as an ambassador: It had been the poet Algosaibi who had written 'The Martyrs'.[80]

That invites the question whether texts of this kind might not be based on the right of freedom of expression from which diplomats, like other individuals under the jurisdiction of the receiving State, could benefit. But quite apart from the particular conditions of the diplomatic office which constitute implied limitations on that right,[81] there are also general limitations which apply under all major human rights instruments, regardless of the claimant's office. ICCPR, ECHR and ACHR all contain lists of grounds which allow the relevant State to interfere with the exercise of the right—including the protection of rights and reputation of others.[82] Where propaganda for war is concerned, parties to the ICCPR and the ACHR have to accept a limitation to freedom of expression directly under these instruments,[83] as long as they have not made valid reservations from this restriction. The same reasoning applies to State parties of CERD.[84]

It is true that it would be difficult to derive a similar restriction for other forms of propaganda which have been discussed, including propaganda on behalf of violence and terrorism.[85] In these fields however, receiving States are within their rights to impose such restrictions on the basis of the protected grounds which the relevant human rights instruments provide. If a State has adopted legislation to this effect which meets the conditions

[79] See also Introduction, n 112 and corresponding text.

[80] S Henderson, 'The West Must Stop' *Daily Telegraph* (London, 11 July 2002).

[81] See ch 3, s 2.3.

[82] ICCPR art 19(3); ECHR art 10(2); ACHR art 13(2).

[83] See on this Human Rights Committee, General Comment No 11 (1983), para 2. *cf* also Kearney's understanding of GA Res 819 (IX) (1954); Kearney (2007), 60.

[84] See above, at n 63.

[85] See above, at nn 67–70. But see De Brabandere, para 9.

which the treaties impose, the diplomatic freedom of expression is, like that of any other individual, limited to the extent of these measures.[86]

3. INCITEMENT

In December 1995, the town of Petra, a historic landmark in the south of Jordan, witnessed an unusual form of diplomatic activity. Saeid Bateni, Deputy Head of the Iranian mission to Jordan, arrived at Petra by taxi and reportedly engaged in enquiries about the travel itineraries of Israeli tourists.[87] According to some sources, he went further than that: Bateni allegedly called on Jordanians to launch attacks on them.[88] Bateni's taxi driver made a report to the police,[89] and the diplomat found himself expelled from the country for 'activities … not in line with diplomatic norms'.[90]

Incitement is a form of propaganda which goes beyond basic efforts at persuasion.[91] A person engaging in incitement does so to bring about a particular action as a direct result of this conduct.[92] The propagandist introduces his audience to a potentially new line of reasoning, but there is every possibility that, in a cool moment of reflection, his recipients may reject his arguments. The inciter deprives his audience of this moment of detachment, and the receiving State will often not have a chance to correct the impression thus conveyed. It is a point which carries particular significance in situations in which the audience already has an emotional stake in the matter broached by the speaker, but still possesses certain psychological hurdles which prevent it from acting upon its feelings.

The international community has, for a long time, been concerned with the problem of incitement to acts unlawful under international law; and numerous international instruments address this matter. The topics of incitement that appear in this field are similar to the subjects identified in the debate on propaganda.

[86] The relevant restriction derives in cases like these not only from the rule against interference, but also from the first sentence of Art 41(1) of the Vienna Convention, which imposes on beneficiaries of diplomatic privileges and immunities an obligation to respect the laws and regulations of the receiving State.

[87] 'Section: International News' *Associated Press* (New York, 9 December 1995); 'Jordan Expels Iranian Diplomat' *Xinhua* (China, 10 December 1995).

[88] Bunce and Offer, 18; 'Jordan Expels Iranian Diplomat', n 87.

[89] 'Section: International News', n 87.

[90] ibid.

[91] On the element of persuasion that characterises the basic concept of propaganda, see above, at n 16.

[92] *cf*, for the particular case of genocide, *Akayesu* (Trial Chamber), para 560.

Thus, reference is made to incitement to war,[93] racial discrimination[94] and violence[95] as well as incitement to subversive activities[96] and terrorism.[97] And it is clear that there is, in this context, stronger evidence for a ban under customary international law on inciting activities than for a prohibition of 'mere' propaganda.

For one, the States which took the clearest position against Article 20 ICCPR[98] limited their reservations to its first paragraph (which contains the obligation to prohibit 'propaganda' for war) and did not extend it to its second paragraph, which makes reference to incitement to discrimination, hostility and violence. Several of those States which found that Article 20 did not require them to adopt any (further) legislation (or reserved the right not to do so),[99] likewise referred in particular to the first paragraph of the norm.[100]

Where propaganda for terrorism is concerned, reference has already been made to the distinction which the UN Secretary-General drew between glorification on the one hand and incitement on the other.[101] Security Council Resolution 1624, in a similar way, 'repudiat[ed]' attempts at glorification,[102] but found stronger words for incitement: Incitement was 'condemn[ed] … in the strongest terms', and all States were called upon to prohibit 'by law incitement to commit a terrorist act or acts'.[103]

In some situations, incitement can rise to the level of an international crime. The most prominent example exists in the field of genocide, where

[93] For an early example, see Broadcasting Convention (1936) art 2. See also Mass Media Declaration, preamble, 4th para GA Res 381 (V) (1950) condemns propaganda constituting incitement to 'conflicts or acts of aggression' (para 2 (1)). Related terms were used in GA Res 42/22 (1987), Annex, para 1.I.4 and in GA Res 110(II) (1947), para 1.

[94] GA Res 33/73 (1978), para II(a)(ii). In the field of human rights, see ICCPR art 20(2) and see also CERD art 4. The duty contained in AHRC art 13(5) envisages more specific conduct: advocacy of 'national, racial, or religious hatred that constitute[s] incitement … to lawless violence' is to be considered a punishable offence.

[95] ICCPR art 20(2); ACHR art 13(5); CERD art 4(a). See also SC Res 1161 (1998), para 5, with regard to the situation in Rwanda.

[96] See Friendly Relations Declaration, 3rd principle, para 2; GA Res 2131 (1965), para 2. Similarly GA Res 42/22 (1987), Annex, para 1.I.6; Broadcasting Convention art 1; GA Res 36/103 (1981), para 2(II)(f); GA Res 290(IV) (1949), para 3.

[97] SC Res 1624 (2005), Preamble, operative paras 4 and 8 and para 5; SC Res 1373 (2001), para 5; GA Res 2131 (XX) (1965), para 2; Friendly Relations Declaration, 3rd principle, para 2. Similarly GA 42/22 (1987), Annex, para 1.I.6.

[98] Denmark (2014), Iceland (1979),The Netherlands (2010), Sweden (1971), Finland (1975), see above, n 60.

[99] Above n 61 and n 62.

[100] See Belgium (1983), Ireland (1989), Luxembourg (2004). UN Treaty Collection (Online), ICCPR.

[101] Above, at n 70.

[102] Above, at n 68.

[103] SC Res 1624 (2005), preamble, operative para 4; and para 1(a) of the text. See also SC Res 1373 (2001), para 5.

'direct and public incitement' is declared a punishable act by the Genocide Convention and subsequent instruments on international criminal law.[104]

And yet, it would be difficult to speak of a general rule which banned incitement wherever an internationally wrongful act was concerned. As the ILC work has shown, such a rule could not even be assumed where the addressee of incitement is another State,[105] and similar difficulties arise when the inciter addresses the population of the receiving State. The treatment of incitement under international criminal law is a case in point: Outside the crime category of genocide, incitement does not find express mention in any of the statutes of the international criminal courts and tribunals.[106] Incitement to crimes against humanity and war crimes might be seen as a particular form of perpetration (for example instigation or soliciting) and charged as such,[107] or it might, in the case of crimes against humanity, fall under the crime of persecution.[108] But the incorporation of incitement in these categories is only possible if specific additional conditions which they impose are fulfilled.[109]

Similar difficulties emerge outside the field of international criminal law in situations in which the State whose agents engage in incitement, is not party to a treaty which expressly addresses the relevant conduct.[110]

Where alleged incitement by diplomats is concerned, the particular topic to which the diplomatic comments referred is thus of considerable significance. Negative State reactions have not arisen in all areas, and the question therefore becomes indispensable whether a rule against incitement can be derived from customary international law in the field which the diplomatic activity addressed.

The most prominent area in which negative reactions have come into existence concerns conduct which could best be described as encouragement of 'subversive activities'—civil strife, revolution or other acts against the established order of the receiving State.

[104] Genocide Convention art III(c); ICTYSt art 4(3)(c); ICTRSt art 2(3)(c); ICCSt arts 6 and 25(e); Dili Court Reg (2000/15), s 14.3(e).

[105] See on this Draft Articles on State Responsibility (2001), 65, before art 16, commentary, para 9. However, where incitement causes the wrongful act, there must be a strong assumption that the conduct of the inciting State attracts at least responsibility under Art 16 of the Draft Articles on State Responsibility (2001), 65 (as an 'assisting State').

[106] See for instance, for the case of incitement to war crimes, Gordon (2012), 282.

[107] *cf* Ibid, 283.

[108] See *Ruggiu* (Trial Chamber), para 22.

[109] 'Soliciting' and 'inducing', for instance, require the commission or attempt of the relevant international crime by the principal perpetrator, *cf* Gordon (2012), 301. As does instigating, *Galić* (Trial Chamber), para 168. Persecution as a crime against humanity presupposes the existence of a contextual element, ICCSt art 7.

[110] Incitement to war is an example. For the parties to the Broadcasting Convention, an obligation not to engage in incitement to war, can be read into art 2 (see on this Kearney (2009), para 7). Outside that Convention, the foundations for such a ban are less certain and would, to a considerable degree, have to rely on General Assembly resolutions (see above, n 93) which, in view of their often far-reaching language, are not likely to reflect general and consistent State practice.

Reactions in this field can be severe. In March 1987, Tunisia cut diplomatic relations with Iran amid accusations that the Iranian embassy had sowed 'religious discord' in the country.[111] The embassy had allegedly assisted extremists in their efforts of establishing connections with certain Iranian groups to create disturbances in the receiving State.[112] In other cases, diplomats were expelled for inciting strife or creating unrest in the receiving State.[113] In some instances, the alleged disturbance related to labour disputes: In 1983 for instance, two US diplomats were expelled from Suriname, after the government had accused them of 'instigating labor unrest' in the receiving State.[114]

Receiving States have also shown particular sensitivity when diplomatic agents exhorted their addressees to violence. A few months before the Musa Kusa case, two Libyan diplomats in the United States had been involved in an incident which highlighted the distinction between propaganda and incitement: The diplomats, who had distributed literature which called for the assassination of dissidents to the Gaddafi regime,[115] had certainly crossed the line between approval and encouragement to direct action. Both were expelled in April 1980.[116]

State reactions are similarly strong in cases in which diplomatic agents have been accused of incitement to terrorism.

In the 1994 incident between India and Pakistan, for instance,[117] the Pakistani Foreign Minister claimed that the Indian side had instigated terrorism and violence in Karachi,[118] and it was clear that he assigned personal responsibility to the consulate in that city.[119] Pakistan ordered the closure of the consulate in December of that year.[120]

It is true that allegations of incitement to terrorist acts are not a particularly common feature in diplomatic relations, and when they arise, questions sometimes attach to their veracity.[121] But there can be little doubt that

[111] 'Tunisia Breaks Diplomatic Relations' *Xinhua* (China, 26 March 1987).

[112] 'Tunisia Asks Iran to Withdraw Diplomats' *Xinhua* (China, 26 March 1987). See also the 1987 case of the Libyan mission to Australia (A.84).

[113] See the 1987 case of four Soviet and one East German diplomat in Ghana (A.39); the 1981 case of Polyakov (A.60); the 1988 case of Melton, (A.91).

[114] See A.67. See also the 1979 case of three Soviet diplomats in Costa Rica, (A. 47).

[115] 'Another Libyan Exile Assassinated in London' *Washington Post* (Washington DC, 26 April 1980).

[116] ibid. See also the 1995 case of Saeid Bateni, above, at n 87.

[117] See above, at n 27.

[118] G Bourke, 'Pakistan Shuts Indian Mission' *The Guardian* (London, 27 December 1994).

[119] A Iqbal, 'Pakistan Closes Indian Consulate' *United Press International* (26 December 1994).

[120] ibid.

[121] See on this, the 1988 case of the US Ambassador to Nicaragua, Richard Melton, who also had to face claims of involvement in terrorism. See *BBC Summary*, 'Nicaraguan President, Foreign Minister on Expulsion' (London, 13 July 1988). On the case, see Introduction at n 96. But the accusations by the Nicaraguan Foreign Minister were neither clear on the precise involvement of Melton (the question in particular whether he had incited 'terrorism', remained unsettled) nor does it appear that the concept of 'terrorism' which d'Escoto employed ('state terrorism which the USA has been promoting') would necessarily have met with consensus in the international community.

receiving States consider this a form of conduct on which strong negative reactions could reasonably be based, which are likely to meet with understanding in the international community. The evaluation of diplomatic behaviour in this field therefore does not vary from the considerations outlined above: The ban on incitement to terrorism appears to be accepted as a rule of contemporary international law.[122]

In cases like these, the invocation of freedom of expression does not provide a valid basis for diplomatic action which defies this prohibition. Here, too, international law recognises a limitation to the relevant human right; and the increased proximity between diplomatic statements and the unlawful act, which regularly exists in situations of incitement, adds strength to this view. It is a limitation which was expressly accepted by the Human Rights Committee where the second alternative of Article 20 ICCPR was concerned ('advocacy of national, racial or religious hatred that constitutes incitement to discrimination, hostility or violence');[123] and with regard to the ban on 'direct incitement to commit terrorist acts', De Brabandere noted that this rule can 'easily be seen as a legally valid exception to freedom of expression'.[124]

In areas in which international law has not been able to positively settle the question whether the existence of an unlawful act also means that incitement to such an act is internationally unlawful, it is of course still within the discretion of the receiving State to adopt the prohibition of such conduct through its own criminal code. The validity of such measures will have to be determined under international human rights law. But if the relevant State observes the conditions under which a limitation of this kind can be made, diplomatic agents accredited to its government will, like any other person under the jurisdiction of the receiving State, be addressed by the measures in question.[125]

The history of diplomatic relations, however, provides no evidence that sending States and their agents have tried to construct a basis for incitement to terrorism, to violence, murder or any of the other acts discussed above, by reference to freedom of expression—or indeed other grounds recognised under international law. Outright denial of the charges is the typical reaction in situations of this kind.[126] In light of this, it appears fair to say that the international community does not recognise the validity of competing interests where a clear prohibition on a particular form of incitement exists.

[122] See above, at nn 101–03.

[123] HRC General Comment No 11 (1983), para 2.

[124] De Brabandere, para 30.

[125] See also above, after n 85.

[126] *cf* for the 1994 incident between Pakistan and India, A Iqbal, 'Pakistan Closes Indian Consulate' *United Press International* (26 December 1994); on the reaction by the US State Department in the 1988 Melton case, 'Nicaragua, US Trade Diplomatic Expulsions' *Facts on File* (New York, 15 July 1988).

Incitement to acts which are lawful under international law follows a different pattern. It may, at first sight, appear quite clear that incitement of this kind is quite removed from the examples which have been discussed above. But the extensive meaning which inhabits the term 'interference'[127] does at least allow for the possibility that such incitement is covered by its scope. And some States have indeed shown sensitivity where this form of conduct had been at issue. Even activities which could be understood as 'incitement to peace', have encountered objections by receiving States who felt that the diplomatic agent had taken an interest in matters which fell within the exclusive concern of that State. The case of James McGee may in this context be recalled—the American ambassador to Zimbabwe who in 2008 issued a call for an end to the political violence in that country, and had to face accusations of interference as a result.[128]

It has been pointed out above that McGee's statements found a strong basis in the assistance which they afforded to a people striving for self-determination.[129] The same grounds apply where diplomatic agents call on the people of the receiving State to participate in (legitimate) elections—as the US Ambassador to Macedonia, Lawrence Butler, did in 2004.[130] If De Brabandere is to be followed, advocacy for 'peaceful change in a regime' would at least not be 'covered by the prohibition of subversive propaganda under current international law';[131] and calling for participation in elections would appear to be a prime example for incitement in keeping with the *erga omnes* obligations of the receiving State.

But the Butler incident also demonstrated that the dividing line between incitement to the realisation of self-determination and incitement as an expression of partisanship may sometimes be difficult to determine. Butler, too, faced accusations of interference—but in his case, they came from the former Macedonian Minister of the Interior, Boskovski, who had been excluded from the presidential race and had called for a boycott of the elections.[132] Whether incitement to lawful acts constitutes unlawful interference, will ultimately turn on the application of the conciliatory mechanisms which have been identified above;[133] and at least in situations in which a diplomatic call for participation in elections did not specify particular candidates, an assessment under the principle of proportionality is, in view of the significance of the right involved, likely to favour the diplomatic agent.[134]

[127] See on this ch 2, especially s 4.

[128] See ch 3, at n 163.

[129] ch 3, after n 165.

[130] *Radio Free Europe/Radio Liberty*, 'Macedonian Presidential Candidate rejects US, EU calls', 26 April 2004.

[131] De Brabandere, para 14.

[132] See above, n 130.

[133] See above, ch 4, s 2.

[134] For the assessment which cases of genuine partisanship require, see ch 6, s 2.

4. FALSE OR DISTORTED INFORMATION

For Bangladesh, sovereignty came at a terrible price. The 1971 War of Liberation, which preceded her independence from Pakistan, left scars that are felt even today, and it remains at the root of ongoing tension between the two States. Bangladesh speaks of 'genocide' which had been committed in the conflict.[135] The number of Bangladeshi victims is difficult to assess, but even conservative estimates put the number of deaths at 300,000,[136] while the government of Bangladesh claims that no less than three million people had lost their lives.[137]

When therefore the Pakistani Deputy High Commissioner in Bangladesh, Irfanur Raja, in November 2000 stated that it had been the Awami League—the ruling party in Bangladesh in 1971—and not the Pakistani side which had begun the atrocities,[138] it was foreseeable that his statements would create controversy. Raja did not stop there: He put the number of people killed in the conflict at 26,000,[139] and asked, reportedly, why it should be his country that had to apologise 'when we lost half of Pakistan'.[140] Raja's remarks triggered protests outside the High Commission in Dhaka; Pakistan eventually decided to recall her diplomat.[141]

The Bangladeshi reaction was reflective of a concern within the international community about statements which are perceived as misleading or as a distortion of the truth. Efforts have indeed been undertaken at the international level to prevent conduct of this kind.

Several international instruments expressly mention defamatory conduct: The 1981 Declaration on the Inadmissibility of Intervention and Interference in the Internal Affairs of States in particular refers to the duty of States, as part of the 'principle of non-intervention and non-interference', to 'abstain from any defamatory campaign ... for the purpose of intervening or interfering in the internal affairs of other States'.[142]

Other instruments refer to misinformation in a more general sense. In General Assembly Resolution 127(II), States were invited to study measures which might be adopted 'to combat ... the diffusion of false or distorted reports likely to injure friendly relations between States'.[143]

[135] M Hossain and S Price, 'Dhaka Expels Pakistani Diplomat' *BBC Online* (London, 15 December 2000). See also 'Bangladesh War Crimes Trial' *BBC Online* (London, 17 July 2013).

[136] M Dummett, 'Bangladesh War' *BBC Online* (London, 16 December 2011); see also Rummel, 155.

[137] Dummett, n 136.

[138] 'Pakistan Recalls Dhaka Diplomat' *BBC Online* (London, 30 November 2000).

[139] Hossain and Price, n 135.

[140] 'Pakistan Recalls Dhaka Diplomat', n 138.

[141] ibid.

[142] GA Res 36/103 (1981), Annex, para 2.II.(j).

[143] GA Res 127(II) (1947), para 1.

Similar language was used in General Assembly Resolution 634(VII) (entitled 'Question of false or distorted information'),[144] the Broadcasting Convention,[145] the Convention on the International Right of Correction[146] and the Mass Media Declaration.[147]

Surprisingly, and in spite of Sir Henry Wotton's famous bonmot,[148] accusations of deliberate falsehoods are not a very common feature of modern diplomatic relations. Exceptions exist—in 2005, for instance, the British High Commissioner in Kenya was called a 'congenital liar' by the Kenyan Minister of Foreign Affairs, after he had publicly spoken about corruption in the government of the receiving State.[149] On the whole, however, receiving States shy away from such strong allegations which do, after all, carry the potential of further aggravating the situation; and diplomatic agents often find ways to be selective with the truth instead of misstating the facts altogether.

Once claims of misinformation have been advanced, sending States tend not to invoke diplomatic functions or the promotion of *erga omnes* interests as a basis for the diplomatic activity. They are more likely to insist on the truth of the relevant statements—or to deny that any statements had been made in the first place. This, for instance, was the case when Commodore Bainimarama, the ruler of Fiji, accused Larry Dinger, the US Ambassador to that country, of misinformation.[150] The background to this incident was formed by the findings of an American congressional delegation to Fiji, which had called the recent coup d'état in Fiji 'disastrous',[151] leading Bainimarama to state that the delegation had not received the 'real story' from Mr Dinger.[152] The US embassy on the other hand denied that they had attempted to influence the findings of the delegation; according to Dinger, the congressmen had come 'to their own conclusions'.[153]

At the same time, not every form of misinformation—even if such conduct can be positively established[154]—falls within the scope of a

[144] GA Res 634(VII) (1952), preamble, operative para 1.

[145] Broadcasting Convention art 3.

[146] Convention on the International Right of Correction, preamble, operative paras 4 and 5.

[147] Mass Media Declaration, preamble, operative para 11.

[148] 'An Ambassador is an honest man, sent to lie abroad for the good of his country', Berridge and James, 279.

[149] *BBC Monitoring International Reports*, 'British Envoy Congenital Liar—Kenyan Foreign Minister', 4 February 2005; 'Kenya: Kibaki's Men Furious Over "Clay's Insults"' *The Nation* (Kenya, 4 February 2005).

[150] P Ligaiula, 'US Envoy Criticized by Fiji Military Ruler' *Associated Press State & Local Wire* (New York, 11 July 2007).

[151] ibid.

[152] 'US Getting Wrong Information about Fiji' *New Zealand Herald* (Auckland, 11 July 2007). See also ch 2, n 4 and corresponding text.

[153] Ligaiula, n 150.

[154] On the value of situations in which the veracity of allegations by the receiving State is in doubt, see Introduction, after n 104.

prohibition under international law. The instruments which address this question are more restrictive than that and tend to qualify their assessment by referring to behaviour which is 'likely to injure friendly relations'[155] or which leads to damage to 'international harmony'[156] or damage to 'international understanding'.[157] There may be good reason to ask whether the truth, especially if offered in an uncharitable form, will always be conducive to 'international harmony'.[158] But the fact remains that none of the instruments which have been discussed above, focuses on the making of false statements as such—such conduct is addressed only in the context of a risk of specific harm. That is even the case where those instruments are concerned which make reference to 'defamatory campaigns'.[159] Defamation is more than the production of false information: It targets the dignity of its victims and thus involves harm to a protected interest.[160]

Even in situations in which a clear risk of a particular form of harm inhabits the relevant statements, the evaluation of such conduct cannot escape the difficulties outlined above.[161] Where States are parties to a treaty in this field, they are bound by its restrictions. Beyond that, it is difficult to identify a rule of general customary international law prohibiting behaviour of this kind. The very limited number of States which have ratified conventions in this area[162] casts doubt on the existence of widespread acceptance of the relevant norms.[163]

The reason for the prevailing attitude in this field must be seen in the fact that widely different concepts of the limits of freedom of expression have been embraced by members of the international community, and in most

155 GA Res 127(II) (1947), para 1; Mass Media Declaration, preamble, para 11; Convention on the International Right of Correction, preamble, operative paras 4 and 5.

156 GA Res 634(VII) (1952), operative para 1.

157 GA Res 634(VII) (1952), operative para 3; Broadcasting Convention (1936) art 3 (with regard to transmissions on the respective State's own territory).

158 In this context, Wilhelm Busch's poem 'Wer möchte diesen Erdenball', is illuminating. Busch, 506. The making of statement which reach the level of insults, is discussed in more detail in ch 9.

159 See in particular GA Res 36/103 (1981), Annex, para 2.II.j.

160 See also OED, 'defame (v)', 1. to 2. (to 'bring ill fame, infamy or dishonour upon …', to 'attack the good fame or reputation of (a person)' etc. The only meanings which could not be considered to convey an attack on the dignity of the victim, are obsolete (3. and 4.)

161 See above, at n 110, for the particular field of incitement.

162 For the Broadcasting Convention, see UN Treaty Collection (Online), Broadcasting Convention. The Convention on the International Right of Correction has 17 parties. UN Treaty Collection (Online), Convention on the International Right of Correction.

163 It is true that GA Res 36/103 (1981), which refers to the duty of States to 'abstain from any defamatory campaign', was passed with a significant majority, see Zemanek (1997), 57. But six States abstained and there were 22 votes against the resolution—mainly from Western States—which led Zemanek to comment that it would be difficult to see in this the foundation of general *opinio iuris* (ibid). Resolutions of this kind, it appears, are expressions of aspirations rather than reflections of customary law.

cases it is not possible to speak of a rule which finds general acceptance across political and ideological divides.

This has a direct impact on the evaluation of false diplomatic statements (or distorting statements) as interference. Given the reluctance of sending and receiving States to offer a legal opinion on this kind of conduct, it does not seem possible to derive an understanding of such activities as an intrusion into internal affairs either from conventional or customary law. There do not appear to be any instances in which diplomatic hosts have taken exception to the making of false statements as such—in the few instances in which negative sanctions were advanced, the statements in question did involve the risk of a certain form of harm, including harm to the dignity of the target of the relevant comment (a point which will be discussed in more detail below).[164] By itself, however, the diplomatic lie is not a good exemplar for the concept of diplomatic interference.

[164] See ch 9, at 106, and at nn 107–11.

8

Employment of Money and Other Material Means

1. AREAS OF DIPLOMATIC FUNDING AND INTERNATIONAL RESTRICTIONS

THE USE OF material goods in the pursuit of diplomatic aims is not a new phenomenon in international relations. One of the most remarkable cases in the field occurred in the early history of the United States of America: The affair of 'Citizen Genêt'—that is, Edmond-Charles Genêt, the French Minister Plenipotentiary to the young republic.[1]

Genêt arrived in 1793, but even before he had presented his credentials, he had begun to fit out armed privateers to attack British merchant ships and to enlist US citizens in the French fight against Britain—even though the United States were neutral in the ongoing conflict. Genêt also initiated an attack on Louisiana, which was then in Spanish hands,[2] and thus territory of a British ally. These projects cost money—Genêt's expenses were estimated at at least 400,000 livres.[3] In an unusual twist, the funds would have at least partially come from the receiving State: The French Minister intended to use the money from a US debt settlement which he had been authorised to collect.[4] The United States eventually requested Genêt's recall, which the French government granted.[5]

International law, at least in its codified form, has been slow to react to funding by foreign agents. Abbott goes so far as to state that, prior to the 1990s, corruption had been considered 'a fact of life and a taboo subject in international fora' and that 'many development advocates viewed it as an essential lubricant for economic activity'.[6] As late as 1964 did the editor of

[1] See Satow (1979), 180, para 21.17. *cf* also Lowitt, 252, 253.

[2] Campbell (2008), 779.

[3] Campbell (2010), 543. It is not clear whether Campbell is referring to the costs of the offensive against Louisiana only. See also Lowitt, 256.

[4] Campbell (2010), 543 and 527, at n 60.

[5] Satow (1979), 180.

[6] Abbott, para 5.

Satow maintain that '[i]t may be that the Law of Nations is not concerned with bribery. It seems rather a question of morality'.[7]

Other authors however, were quite clear in their condemnation of the use of money to achieve the aims of diplomacy. Yakembe for instance stated that the diplomatic mission must at all costs avoid having recourse to 'corruption',[8] and several scholars considered this form of behaviour one of the principal examples of interference.[9]

A third opinion called for a closer examination of the relevant behaviour. Sen, too, notes that bribery in general 'overstep[s] the boundaries of propriety'.[10] But he also draws attention to the difference between bribery and the customary exchange of presents: In some countries, there was, after all, a tradition to give 'small presents and flowers on certain occasions such as Christmas or the New Year Day'.[11]

The ILC itself focused in its 1957 debates on a particular form of funding: Financial support rendered to parties in the receiving State—which, in the eyes of some of its members, would constitute interference[12] or improper conduct.[13]

It is a view consistent with the prevailing sensitivity among members of the international community: In the vast majority of cases in which diplomatic funding triggered charges of interference, the beneficiary of the underlying conduct was a political party or faction in the receiving State.

In 1999, for instance, Malaysia claimed that Canadian and other diplomats were providing funds to the opposition ahead of elections in the country.[14] In this context, the Deputy Prime Minister of that State declared that diplomats found to interfere in Malaysian politics would not be allowed to serve there.[15]

The official reaction by governments of sending States might question the factual basis of the allegations, but they do not usually deny that the giving of money to a party constitutes interference. In the Malaysian case, a Canadian Minister was quoted as saying that the sending State did not use its money '... for political funding ... If it were, we would take action, but I'm sure it is not. We're pretty careful with how our money is spent'.[16]

[7] Satow (1964), 103. He did however concede that 'the employment of bribes to obtain secret information' was generally condemned. Ibid.

[8] Yakembe, 67.

[9] Salmon (1996), 129, para 197; and see Oppenheim (1967), 787 with particular reference to the case of the French Ambassador to Britain, 1677–1681.

[10] Sen (1965), 59, see also Mukharji, 23.

[11] Sen (1965), 60. See also Satow (1964), 103.

[12] See YILC 1957/I, 146, 147, para 10 [Yokota]. See also ch 3, at n 167.

[13] Ago noted that the 'head of mission' could not with propriety give 'financial support' to a political party in the receiving State. YILC 1957/I, 149, para 36 [Ago]. See also ch 3, at n 168.

[14] 'Malaysia tells West to Butt Out' *Toronto Star* (Toronto, 26 November 1999).

[15] ibid. See also the 1972 case of Soviet diplomats in Bolivia (A.22); the 1980 case of Sofinsky (A.48); the 2006 case of Kazécki (A.212); the 2007 case of Goldberg (A.226).

[16] M Trickey, 'Ottawa Denies Funding' *Calgary Herald* (Calgary, 25 November 1999). Australia and Britain likewise denied that donations had been made; B Pereira, 'Diplomats

It is true that the international regulation of situations in which material goods were provided by foreign agents, did not proceed at a quick pace. But in 1975, the General Assembly did condemn 'all corrupt practices, including bribery' (albeit with particular reference to 'transnational and other corporations, their intermediaries and others involved').[17] Today, a panoply of instruments exists which have relevance in this regard: Among them, the Inter-American Convention against Corruption of 1996 (IACAC),[18] the EU Protocol of the same year[19] and the EU Convention on the Fight against Corruption Involving Officials of the European Communities or Officials of Member States of 1997,[20] the Council of Europe (CoE) Criminal Law and Civil Law Conventions on Corruption,[21] the Organisation for Economic Co-operation and Development (OECD) Convention on Combating Bribery of Foreign Officials,[22] the African Union (AU) Convention on Preventing and Combating Corruption,[23] the UN Convention against Transnational Organized Crime of 2000[24] and the UN Convention against Corruption of 2003 (UNCAC).[25]

These instruments provide guidance on the forms of conduct which the international community considers an illicit provision of material means. The understanding of 'corruption' or 'bribery' is remarkably similar in all of them:[26] There is agreement that the act involves, on the one hand, the offering (or promising, giving etc) of a monetary or other benefit to

"Giving Money to Opposition"' *Straits Times* (Singapore, 25 November 1999). The United States also denied the accusations, 'Malaysia Accuses Diplomats' *BBC Online* (London, 24 November 1999).

[17] GA Res 3514 (XXX) (1975), para 1.

[18] IACAC (1996).

[19] EU Financial Interests Protocol (1996).

[20] EU Corruption Convention (1997).

[21] CoE Criminal Law Convention (1999); CoE Civil Law Convention (1999).

[22] OECD Bribery Convention (1997).

[23] AU Corruption Convention (2003).

[24] UN Transnational Crime Convention (2000).

[25] UNCAC (2003). UNCAC has 174 parties. UN Treaty Collection (Online), UNCAC (as of 1 March 2015).

[26] The terminology differs. GA Res 3514 (XXX) (1975) appeared to consider 'corruption' the wider term and 'bribery' only a sub-set. That distinction was retained in UNCAC, which refers to 'bribery' as only one of several forms of financial misbehaviour (arts 15, 16 and 21 and see arts 17–20 and arts 22–23). 'Corruption' is used as an umbrella term. But what UNCAC describes as 'bribery' is the equivalent to conduct which the UN Transnational Crime Convention calls 'corruption' (art 8); see also IACAC art VI; EU Financial Interests Protocol arts 2 and 3; EU Corruption Convention arts 2 and 3; CoE Civil Law Convention on Corruption art 2; SADC Protocol art 3. For rules preferring the word 'bribery', see also OECD Bribery Convention art 1; CoE Criminal Law Convention arts 2–11. The AU Corruption Convention uses the phrase 'acts of corruption and related offences' (art 4(1)).

the recipient[27] and, on the other hand, the intended provision of a service (which can be an act or an omission)[28] or at least a change in the conduct of the recipient.[29] In almost all instruments, a reciprocal relationship is at the centre of the activity; expressed through the phrase 'in exchange for'[30] or 'in order to',[31] or simply 'for him (or her) to act'.[32] The advantage offered might thus be direct or indirect in nature, but a return service is expected—the act of bribery is goal-oriented.

UNCAC, in line with most of the instruments, also refers to the character of the means provided to the recipient: They must constitute an 'undue advantage'.[33] It is an important distinction which rules out incidents in which, for instance, legitimate fees attached to administrative work or to the use of particular facilities are owed to the recipient or his organisation.

The application of this concept to the provision of material goods to political parties in the receiving State, carries certain difficulties. If a diplomat offers funds to a party, the result which he expects in return will regularly not be a specific service, but the strengthening of a faction deemed to be favourable to the policies of the sending State—or the weakening of a faction deemed to be dangerous to its interests.[34]

Difficulties may also arise where the distinction between 'due' and 'undue' advantages is concerned. If a diplomatic agent subscribes to a party newsletter or attends events for which the party charges admission, it will be understood that due payment has to be provided in return. There is no reported case where a receiving State would have taken exception

[27] IACAC arts VI and VIII; EU Financial Interests Protocol art 3; EU Corruption Convention art 3; CoE Criminal Law Convention arts 2 and 5; CoE Civil Law Convention art 2; OECD Bribery Convention art 1; AU Corruption Convention art 4(1)(b); UN Transnational Crime Convention art 8; UNCAC arts 15, 16 and 21.

[28] IACAC arts VI and VIII; EU Financial Interests Protocol, art 3; EU Corruption Convention art 3; CoE Criminal Law Convention art 2; OECD Bribery Convention art 1; AU Corruption Convention art 4(1)(b); UN Transnational Crime Convention art 8; UNCAC arts 15, 16, 21.

[29] *cf* the phrasing in CoE Civil Law Convention art 2.

[30] IACAC arts VI and VIII; AU Corruption Convention art 4(1)(b); see also SADC Protocol art 3(1)(b) and APEC Conduct Principles for Public Officials, principle 3.

[31] OECD Bribery Convention art 1(1). UN Transnational Crime Convention art 8 has 'in order that', as do UNCAC arts 15, 16 and 21.

[32] EU Financial Interests Protocol art 3; EU Corruption Convention art 3; CoE Criminal Law Convention art 2. Similarly, GA Res 51/191 (1996), Annex, para 3.

[33] UNCAC art 15(a); UN Transnational Crime Convention art 8(a); CoE Criminal Law Convention art 2; and see also OECD Bribery Convention art 1(1); CoE Civil Law Convention art 2; AU Corruption Convention art 4; GA Res 51/191 (1996), Annex, para 3; APEC Conduct Principles for Public Officials, principle 2.

[34] It may be recalled that, when Salvador Allende had come to power in Chile, the recipients of US financial contributions included not only the conservative Christian Democratic Party, but also the Radical Party of the Left, in an effort to weaken the Socialist government of the elected President. 'Report: CIA Funded Chilean Parties' *Associated Press* (New York, 13 November 2000).

to the provision of material advantages in these situations;[35] but it is true that the dividing line between due and undue advantages may be thin.[36]

Most of all, however, a direct application of the instruments mentioned above remains problematic, as most of them envisage, as the recipient of the advantage, a national[37] or foreign official,[38] or, on occasion, an elected representative or member of a public assembly.[39] The African Union Convention is the only one which imposes an obligation upon State parties to 'proscribe the use of funds acquired through illegal and corrupt practices' to finance political parties.[40] UNCAC merely obliges States to 'enhance transparency in the funding of candidatures for elected public office and, where applicable, the funding of political parties'.[41]

It would thus be difficult to derive, on the basis of these instruments alone, evidence for the existence of customary international law banning the provision of material funds to parties. That may seem surprising, since a good number of the relevant treaties and resolutions realise that the fight against corruption is, at least in part, based on the need to combat a danger to the values of democracy[42] and to political stability.[43]

A more persuasive argument for the existence of such a rule may be derived from evidence that members of the international community consider the funding of parties a damaging intrusion in their own affairs.

A great number of States, covering a wide spectrum of different political systems and beliefs, have indeed adopted legislation which deals with the particular issue of party financing through foreign funding. In 2006, the Agency for Legislative Initiatives concluded that, out of a sample of 111 countries, 64 per cent had adopted legal regulations on the foreign funding of political parties.[44] The International Institute for Democracy

[35] As opposed to attendance of party meetings as such. On this see ch 6, at n 10.

[36] On this aspect of diplomatic conduct, see also below, at n 82.

[37] IACAC art VI.1.b; EU Financial Interests Protocol art 3 and EU Corruption Convention art 3; CoE Criminal Law Convention art 2; GA Res 51/191 (1996), para 3(a); UN Transnational Crime Convention art 8(1)(a) and UNCAC art 15(a). The AU Corruption Convention has one of the widest ranging provisions in this regard by referring to any person who performs 'public functions' (art 4(1)(b)).

[38] IACAC art VIII; OECD Bribery Convention art 1(1); CoE Criminal Law Convention art 5; UN Transnational Crime Convention art 8(2); UNCAC art 16(1).

[39] CoE Criminal Law Convention arts 4 and 6; GA Res 51/191 (1996), para 3(a).

[40] AU Corruption Convention art 10.

[41] UNCAC art 7(3); see also AU Corruption Convention art 10(b).

[42] See UNCAC preamble, 1st and 7th operative paras; GA Res 55/188 (2000), preamble, 2nd operative para; CoE Criminal Law Convention preamble, 4th operative para; CoE Civil Law Convention preamble, 3rd operative para; IACAC preamble, 1st and 2nd operative paras.

[43] AU Corruption Convention preamble, 6th operative para; see also SADC Protocol preamble, 2nd operative para.

[44] Agency for Legislative Initiatives (Ukraine), slide 15. See also Wall, 515–17, for the practice of the United Kingdom and the United States.

and Electoral Assistance found in 2012, on a data basis of 180 countries,[45] that 68 per cent of them banned foreign donations to political parties and 51 per cent banned foreign donations to candidates.[46] The ban on foreign donations to parties was therefore the second most popular ban on political donations (out of a total of 12 options).[47]

One of the reasons for the underlying concern is the fact that the exercise of influence on the electoral process by foreign powers impacts on the political rights of the nationals of the receiving State. The right to free elections has been recognised by the leading human rights instruments;[48] and this freedom is endangered if, during the electoral campaign, funding received by a foreign power allows one party to gain significant advantages over its competitors.

The intrusive aspect of foreign funding becomes particularly apparent where the provision of material assistance is made by a wealthy State for the benefit of parties in a less affluent country. This was the situation when, in 1964, the United States engaged in large scale funding of the presidential campaign of Eduardo Frei in Chile, who then emerged as the successful candidate.[49]

Where funding activities involve a diplomatic agent as the provider of the material means and a party or political candidates as their recipient, it would be difficult to deny the existence of far-reaching consensus in the international community to the effect that conduct of this kind constitutes, prima facie, an intrusion in internal affairs.[50]

That does not mean that the prohibition on the funding of political parties is the only restriction which diplomatic agents encounter if they provide material means to a recipient. When France in 1975 expelled Raul Sainz Rodriguez, First Secretary at the Cuban Embassy in Paris, along with two other Cuban diplomats,[51] a more sinister aspect of international relations was affected:[52] The diplomats had allegedly supplied money and instructions to the Venezuelan terrorist 'Carlos the Jackal'.[53]

Financial support to terrorists and terrorist organisations is an ongoing concern of the international community. However, as in the case of corruption, international law has been slow to react: An international treaty

[45] Not all countries responded, but the response rate on the inquiry into bans on donations was, at an average of 84%, very high, Ohman, 12.

[46] ibid, 13.

[47] ibid, 16. OK Dingake, 'Botswana' *Mmegi/The Reporter* (Gabarone, 15 December 2006).

[48] ICCPR art 25; ECHR Protocol 1 art 3; ACHR art 23(1).

[49] 'Report: CIA Funded Chilean Parties' *Associated Press* (New York, 13 November 2000). Kornbluh (2004).

[50] See above, n 15; also n 16 and corresponding text.

[51] R Wigg, 'Expulsion of Cubans in Paris "Jackal" Case' *The Times* (London, 11 July 1975).

[52] R Carroll et al, 'All Roads Lead to Paris' *Newsweek* (New York, 21 July 1975); 'Latin America; Goodbye Che' *The Economist* (London, 26 July 1975).

[53] Carroll et al, n 52.

banning the financing of terrorism was not concluded until 1999.[54] But its speedy ratification (two years after it had opened for signature), and the extremely large number of State parties which have joined it in the years of its existence[55] provides good reason for the assumption that its text, at least in its substantive provisions, reflects general customary law.[56]

After the 2001 attacks on the Pentagon and the World Trade Center, the Security Council adopted Resolution 1373, whose first paragraph addressed the matter of funding of terrorism,[57] and which incorporated the declaration that 'knowingly financing … terrorist acts' was 'contrary to the purposes and principles of the United Nations'.[58] However, few cases have arisen in which accusations of diplomatic financing of terrorists have been made, and on those rare occasions, the sending States have not claimed the existence of permissive norms allowing the conduct. In the Sainz Rodriguez incident, the Cuban embassy denied any involvement in the matter and stressed that the Cuban government rejected the methods of terrorists[59]—a statement which rather serves to underline the generally accepted ban on the financing of terrorists.

Salmon makes reference to another area of funding which raises concerns: In his view, a diplomatic agent commits interference if he engages in military or financial support to an armed opposition.[60] Here, too, instances of conduct of this kind by permanent diplomats are not all too common.

One of the cases in which these accusations did emerge, was that of the Pakistani *chargé d'affaires* in India, Jalil Abbas Jeelani. In February 2003, Mr Jeelani and three of his colleagues at the Pakistani embassy were given 48 hours to leave India,[61] amid charges that they had funded militants in the Himalaya province.[62] Jeelani himself had allegedly handed over $6,250 to a Kashmiri recipient, money which was meant for anti-Indian separatists.[63]

The paucity of instances of this kind makes it difficult to reach an evaluation of such conduct in the face of the possible existence of permissive

[54] Terrorism Financing Convention (1999).

[55] 186 States have become party to the treaty. UN Treaty Collection (Online), Terrorism Financing Convention (as of 1 March 2015).

[56] Note however the limits of the scope of its applicability (Terrorism Financing Convention art 2). On the ongoing debate about the definition of terrorism, see Saul, in particular 129–42, 168–90, 247–48, 250–53 and 270.

[57] SC Res 1373 (2001), para 1(a)–(d). See also ibid, paras 2(d), (e) and 3(d).

[58] ibid, para 5.

[59] Wigg, n 51.

[60] Salmon (1996), 129.

[61] 'Pakistan Daily Outlines "Bitter" Diplomatic Relations' *Financial Times* (London, 10 February 2003).

[62] P Kumar, 'AFP: India, Pakistan Ties Sink Further' *World News Connection* (8 February 2003).

[63] ibid.

norms. The fact, however, must be taken into account that Salmon's concept of giving financial assistance to an armed opposition covers a wide range of scenarios, depending both on the way in which aid is provided and the nature of the recipient. Such assistance can easily include the funding of an opposition in the knowledge of the existence of a military wing, but without any intent to support a military action, the sponsoring of a party when individual members, without the party's consent, commit violent acts, and even instances of humanitarian assistance to an armed group.[64]

It is likely that at least the intentional financing of *direct* armed action, organised by an opposition against the government, will in all receiving States be considered interference, and that the margin for arguing in favour of the existence of permissive norms in such situations will be very small. Such conduct does not differ much from incitement to violence:[65] In both cases, the absence of significant intervening steps between action and effect, and the very direct involvement of the diplomatic agent in the resulting harm, militate in favour of an absolute prohibition.

In 1986, the ICJ had opportunity to discuss (in the wider context of State intervention) the funding of an armed opposition group by another State, when it rendered its judgment in the *Nicaragua* case—a case in which Nicaragua claimed, inter alia, that the United States (which had provided financial and other support to the contras) had intervened in her internal affairs.[66] It was the opinion of the ICJ that a case of intervention existed when a State, 'with a view to the coercion of another State, supports and assists armed bands' in the latter State, if it was the purpose of such bands to overthrow the government.

But the concept of intervention which emerges from this finding is too broad in nature. It fails to take into account the possibility that there may be legitimate divergent interests which may have an impact on the legal evaluation of the relevant conduct on the part of the State. The Court did raise the question whether certain justifications might have been at the disposal of the respondent[67]—but that (as has been stated at an earlier stage)[68] is a different matter; for the investigation of justifications presupposes that the conduct of intervention had been committed in the first place. The existence of divergent interests, however, cannot easily be dismissed, and where the funding of insurgents is concerned, they may often

[64] The fact may be recalled that the ICJ had observed that assistance of this kind would not qualify as 'unlawful intervention, or, as in any other way contrary to international law', *Nicaragua*, 124, para 242.

[65] See ch 7, after n 125.

[66] *Nicaragua*, 22, para 23.

[67] *Nicaragua*, 126–28, paras 246–49.

[68] See ch 4, at nn 84 f.

take the shape of interests which are recognised under international law—prominently, the interest of States to assist a people in the realisation of self-determination.

The history of international relations provides examples for situations of this kind. If assistance to the African National Congress (ANC) was considered an illustration for the fact that support even for factions outlawed under domestic law can find its basis in international law,[69] then the fact must be taken into account that the ANC too, had a military wing[70] and engaged in acts against military installations and sabotage.[71]

That does not mean that diplomatic funding in these situations will always be outside the scope of interference. What it does mean, is that in most cases of diplomatic funding—even in those where the recipient had been an armed opposition—a consideration of diverging legitimate interests has to become part of the evaluation and that a correct assessment of the interests can only be achieved through the application of the conciliatory methods outlined above.[72] There remain few actions which do not allow room even for this consideration—in fact, where the provision of material means is concerned, only the funding of terrorists and of direct armed actions have been identified as exceptions to the rule—either because of an overwhelming international reaction which does not permit for a limitation of the scope of interference in this context, or because of the existence of such considerable proximity to the employment of force that the diplomatic conduct eliminates any significant intervening steps between cause and result. Other cases in which material means had been provided still allow room for a possible impact by permissive norms in this field and for the application of proportionality as the principle mediating between the relevant interests.

2. THE IMPACT OF LEGITIMATE INTERESTS ON DIPLOMATIC FUNDING

When 'Plan of Attack'—Bob Woodward's book on the background of the 2003 war in Iraq—was published, its revelations on certain Saudi activities in the run-up to the 2004 US presidential elections caused consternation. Woodward reported that, according to the Saudi Ambassador, Prince Bandar, 'the Saudis [had] hoped to fine-tune oil prices to prime the economy in 2004. What was key, Bandar understood, were the economic conditions before a presidential election, not at the moment of the election'.[73]

[69] See ch 6, at n 78.
[70] Pfister, 54; Seidmann, 164.
[71] Seidmann,165.
[72] See ch 4, section 2.2.
[73] Woodward, 324.

That conduct of this kind would raise criticism cannot be surprising. Jamie Rubin, spokesman for the State Department under Clinton, was clear in his condemnation and declared that the attempt by the Saudi side 'to pick America's president [was] an interference of the highest order'.[74] Bandar's reported conduct differs from cases of straightforward funding of political parties: There was no allegation that money or other material means had been given to the Republican party or its candidate by the Saudi Ambassador. However, if the parameters identified in the context of corruption of officials are applied here, the alleged behaviour bears all the hallmarks of the provision of an advantage to a faction which was the sending State's party of choice in the forthcoming elections.

At the same time, the question may be asked whether an attempt to steer the politics of the receiving State into a direction which is advantageous to the sending State is not one of the most basic tasks of the diplomatic office. The protective task of Article 3(1)(b) of the Vienna Convention certainly allows for that interpretation. The problem that presents itself in the case of Prince Bandar thus appears to be more of a question of the extent to which a sending State and its agents can go to achieve an outcome which is conducive to its own purposes.

Similar considerations apply where the task of promoting friendly relations (Article 3(1)(e)) is concerned. It is a function which almost unavoidably involves a diplomatic agent in contact with individual factions in the receiving State,[75] but the maintenance of such contacts can easily lead to the provision of material means. The incident involving James Moriarty, the US Ambassador to Bangladesh who in 2008 invited political leaders to a 'tea party' at his residence,[76] may serve as an illustration for innumerable cases in which diplomatic agents have provided material goods in the shape of sustenance to invited guests—entertainment allowances are indeed allocated to missions for exactly these purposes. What is more: Article 3(1)(e) may positively require such conduct. If it is the custom in a receiving State—as in the example to which Sen refers—to give flowers or small presents on specific holidays, ignoring such traditions could defeat the very objective of the diplomatic task.

In other situations again, the function of observation (Article 3(1)(d)) opens the door to the diplomatic provision of material means—including means which may not cause much criticism in the receiving State. Clark for instance mentions the case of a Japanese embassy which paid a journalist $2,500 per year for a weekly report on the political scene,[77] and it

[74] R Insana et al, 'The News on CNBC (20:00)' *CNBC* (19 April 2004).
[75] See on this also ch 6, at nn 33–36.
[76] ch 3, n 162, and A.236.
[77] Clark, 73.

cannot be expected that conduct of this kind would encounter criticism in the majority of receiving States.

But diplomatic funding, even if performed in the pursuit of legitimate functions, will not always be perceived in a positive light. There is a difference between a diplomat who treats party members to tea or dinner and his colleague who funds a party website.[78] There is also a difference between paying a journalist for writing a political analysis and paying an official in the intelligence service of the receiving State for the provision of military secrets. In the latter scenarios, the divergent nature of the relevant interests becomes particularly clear, and an evaluation of these situations requires the application of the conciliatory principles outlined above.[79] Questions thus have to be raised about the availability of alternatives to the relevant form of diplomatic funding[80] and about the establishment of a proportionate relationship between the benefit which diplomatic funding brings to interests pursued by the sending State and the impact which the diplomatic measure has on interests which the receiving State seeks to protect.

The very nature of an impact of this kind can be open to debate. In this regard, the various aspects of funding which have been identified where the international concept of 'corruption' or 'bribery' was concerned, play a significant role.[81] It is, for instance, possible that the funding activity could not be seen as conferring an 'undue' advantage on the recipient. If diplomats subscribe to a party newsletter,[82] it will be understood that they, like any other recipient, have to provide due payment in return. Similar questions arise where the 'goal oriented nature' of the conduct is concerned. Diplomatic agents who invite members of political parties to a roundtable discussion during which the embassy provides catering, may well seek to fulfil the tasks of the promotion of friendly relations and of observation, but it would be more difficult to conclude that the offer of food and drink came with the expectation of a specific 'return service'.

Where these elements are missing, the argument can be advanced that the impact of the funding activity on the interests of the receiving State never did reach a particular level of significance. It is true that a party might, for instance, use the proceeds of party publications for the next electoral campaign. But this effect will usually require intervening steps by the party organisers, and the involvement of considerations to which the provider of such funds will not be privy. What is more: The charging of

[78] See the 2001 case of Michael Kozak, the US Ambassador to Belarus (A.175), I Traynor, 'Belarussian Foils Dictator-buster' *The Guardian* (London, 14 September 2001).

[79] Such evaluation is without prejudice to the applicability of more specific instruments on corruptions to which the relevant States may be party (see above, at n 18–n 25). On methods of conciliation, see ch 4, section 2.2.

[80] See below, at nn 98 ff.

[81] See above, after n 25.

[82] See above, at n 35.

a price of this kind applies regardless of the existence of diplomatic funding; and the fact that some of the recipients of party literature and other goods may have been diplomats, does therefore not generate a significant change to the pre-existing situation.

In other situations—instances for example in which diplomatic agents provide direct material support to an electoral campaign—the (intended) impact on the internal order of the receiving State is undeniable, and a precise assessment of the weight of the competing interests is unavoidable. Where diplomatic functions are to be considered as a basis for funding activities, it becomes particularly clear that international law will not accord the same level of support to the fulfilment of all the tasks enshrined in the Vienna Convention. The reason for that does not lie in the greater validity of certain functions, but rather in the fact that some functions provide a greater potential for conflict with legitimate competing interests and therefore require a more restrictive application where funding activities are concerned.

The protection of interests of the sending State and its nationals provides the leading example. It would not be difficult for any sending State to base a wide range of activities, including the funding of an entire presidential campaign, on that particular function. An interpretation which gives Article 3(1)(b) such wide scope would, however, deprive both the right to self-determination and the sovereign rights of the receiving State of all meaningful content and would form a clear contradiction of the principle that the receiving State still retains jurisdiction over its territory and the persons inhabiting it.[83]

In that regard, reactions provided by sending States and their agents in cases in which allegations of funding had been raised are of interest: It does, at any rate, not appear that the function of protection has been a popular defence in past situations of this kind. There are again instances in which diplomatic agents simply denied the factual basis of the allegations. When Sofinsky, the Soviet Ambassador to New Zealand, was expelled in 1980 amid accusations of giving money to a political party,[84] he referred to the charges as 'lies' and 'slander'.[85]

Prince Bandar's explanation was somewhat more interesting.

Bandar did not deny that it had been the Saudi intention to keep the oil price at a low level ahead of the election.[86] He also stated that he was always in favour of the re-election of an incumbent president.[87] But the Ambassador

[83] See on his point ch 11, after n 36.

[84] See ch 2, at n 69.

[85] 'Soviet Ambassador Expelled' *Facts on File* (New York, 8 February 1980).

[86] D Froomkin, 'No Saudi Oil "Deal"' *Washington Post* (Washington DC, 20 April 2004).

[87] ibid, and W Blitzer et al, 'CNN Late Edition [Interview with Prince Bandar]', 25 April 2004.

stressed that he had entertained good relations both with Democratic and Republican presidents[88] and vehemently denied that the intended adjustment of the oil price had been designed to facilitate the reelection of George W Bush.[89] Saudi Arabia, according to Bandar, had 'hoped' that oil prices would stay low, 'because that's good for America's economy … good for our economy and the international economy'.[90]

These statements suggest a shift of the basis of the diplomatic activity—but one with potentially far-reaching consequences. If the adjustment of the oil price had been performed for the benefit of both States, the promotion of interests of the sending State would be displaced by the promotion of friendly relations—a task to which international law undoubtedly accords eminent weight.[91] It is a different question whether such a claim can be backed up by the circumstances of the case: The fact in particular that the adjustment had been promised in close temporal proximity to a presidential election, casts doubt on its portrayal as an impartial gesture.[92]

Reference has already been made to the fact that self-determination can constitute the basis for assistance by another State, including the diplomatic provision of material means.[93] In some situations, the General Assembly has contributed to the interpretation of this rule: In the case of apartheid for instance, it spoke of the 'duty of every State' to contribute to the implementation of the rule of self-determination[94] and appealed to all governments 'to provide every assistance', including direct assistance, 'to the national movement of the oppressed people of South Africa in their legitimate struggle'.[95] In other situations, it called upon all States to provide 'moral and material assistance' to peoples striving for self-determination.[96]

But the provision of material means in these situations will often mean that the sending State empowers a party whose very purpose is the disruption of the prevailing order of the receiving State. This in turn carries potential for a clash with rights on the side of that State, which are likewise recognised under international law. The problem gains particular clarity when diplomatic agents finance a party whose declared aim is the

[88] Blitzer et al, n 87.

[89] ibid.

[90] Froomkin, n 86.

[91] *cf* UN Charter art 1(2); Friendly Relations Declaration preamble, 1st and 5th operative para and 5th principle, para 2.

[92] On that occasion, Rubin observed that Bush's opponent Kerry had called for a change in the Saudi Arabian oil policy 'at the last OPEC meeting', but that the Saudi side had 'refused to increase production to lower prices.' J Gibson and D McDowell, 'Government Cracking Down on Indecency [Interview with Jamie Rubin]', *Fox News Network* (19 April 2004).

[93] See above, after n 68.

[94] GA Res 2787 (XXVI) (1971), para 7.

[95] GA Res 2775 (XXVI) (1971), para 6.

[96] ch 6, at n 76.

breaking away of a particular region from the receiving State and thus support potential acts against its territorial integrity.

But even in situations in which a faction seeks to realise its right to self-determination internally,[97] not every form of funding can expect to be considered in compliance with the principles of international law. Not every provision of material means is objectively needed to achieve the aim of self-determination; and funding of groups which pursue that objective is not always the least restrictive means to assist in the realisation of that right.

The Canadian position adopted after Malaysia had accused her and other States in 1999 of funding the opposition, offers an illustration.[98] Lloyd Axworthy, the Canadian Foreign Minister, stated that there had been 'no interference'.[99] But he did refer to a form of funding which Canada had adopted, and which, it appears, constituted in his eyes an alternative that fell outside the remit of interference. 'The only support we have been offering', he said, 'is to a couple of non-governmental organizations … to provide monitoring of the election itself'.[100]

Assistance given to an NGO which works outside the partisan political context would thus appear as a viable, but less restrictive alternative to the funding of a party which stands in direct opposition to the ruling government.

But even here, difficulties may arise. There is, for instance, reason to believe that cases in which substantial financial support to NGOs results in a strong dependency on the State donor, will raise concerns about the exercise of undue influence.

An incident which arose in Russia in 2006 exemplifies the problem. In January of that year, the FSB (the Russian Federal Security Service) stated that a group of British diplomats had provided funds to NGOs, including groups concerning themselves with human rights in the receiving State. The chief spokesman of the FSB claimed that the service had 'obtained evidence' that the diplomats were 'financing a number of non-governmental organizations … We are investigating what the money was being spent on.'[101] Anthony Brenton, the British ambassador to Russia, defended the funding of NGOs and reportedly stated that there was 'nothing unlawful or improper about it'.[102] The position taken by the Russian President Putin on the other hand, was more discerning: He noted that NGOs were

[97] See ch 3, at n 188 and n 189.

[98] See above, at n 14.

[99] MR Cohn, 'Dirty Tricks Accusation' *Toronto Star* (Toronto, 27 November 1999).

[100] Above, n 14.

[101] P Finn, 'Russia Says British Used Rock' *Washington Post* (Washington DC, 24 January 2006).

[102] V Isachenkov, 'Report: Russia's Spymaster' *Associated Press* (New York, 21 February 2006). Paraphrasing by source.

'needed by society as controls over the activities of the state itself and its structures of authority', but he objected to NGOs being 'led by puppet masters from abroad' and asserted that 'states cannot use NGOs as an instrument of foreign policy on the territory of other states'.[103]

As the expression of a general concern, this statement should not be lightly dismissed. There may indeed be situations in which diplomatic funding of NGOs assumes such dimensions that the impartiality of the organisation is imperilled. In scenarios of this kind, the provision of material means may have even more troublesome consequences than in situations in which a political party is the recipient of the funds. A partisan recipient does not aspire to standards of objectivity; but an NGO will often enjoy a continuing reputation as an impartial and objective observer.

Whether the 'infiltration' of an NGO had indeed been at the root of the Russian reaction in 2006, is a question of factual rather than legal assessment. Certain aspects of the case cast doubt on such a reading: Not least the fact that the 'Moscow Helsinki Group' had been among the beneficiaries of the diplomatic conduct—an organisation described as a 'frequent critic of President Vladimir Putin'.[104]

Where legitimate concerns about a sending State's influence on an NGO arise, it may be necessary to identify less restrictive alternatives to funding activities of this kind. The provision of material means to support local educational or informative initiatives or the rendering of assistance to development projects—which benefit all parties in the receiving State on an equal basis—can constitute alternative ways of assisting the population of that State in the realisation of their rights. Miller refers to 'little pockets of aid money' which may be available, and mentions by way of example, 'women's projects, village self-help, and similar projects'[105] which, depending on the relevant situation, may be viable means at the disposal of the diplomatic agent.

But the situational parameters are key to the correct assessment of the conduct of diplomatic funding in any given case; and the application of proportionality will vary accordingly. When opposition parties can operate without hindrance and free and fair elections exist, the very need for diplomatic action attracts doubt, and the question unavoidably arises whether the people in question cannot realise its right to self-determination through means which are already at its disposal. In a State in which the fairness of elections is in doubt, but in which the work of

[103] *BBC Monitoring Former Soviet Union—Political*, 'Putin says Spy Scandal will not Harm Relations', 31 January 2006. *cf* also *Official Kremlin Int'l News Broadcast*, 'Press Conference with President of the Russian Federation', 31 January 2006.

[104] M Mainville, 'Between a Rock and a Spy Case' *Toronto Star* (Toronto, 24 January 2006).

[105] Miller, 29.

political parties is otherwise unimpeded, the funding of NGOs which monitor the elections may be indicated and necessary. In a State in which not even political factions representing the people can carry out their work without hindrance, there may be no viable way of rendering assistance to self-determination but the provision of material means to the relevant political parties; and in extreme cases, this may even include factions operating outside domestic law.[106]

The fact remains that the government of the receiving State will often find it easy to point to alternatives to diplomatic funding which should have been adopted, and it is not uncommon for such governments to try and limit the available alternatives through legislative measures. But not all alternatives reach the same level of efficiency as the provision of material means; and in some instances, the adoption of other, less intrusive alternatives, will put interests which enjoy legitimate status under international law in considerable peril or bar their realisation altogether.

[106] Reference may again be made to the situation of the African National Congress when apartheid was still in place. Few commentators today would claim that the transition in South Africa owed nothing to the influence of the ANC; yet it was a group which was for a long time banned by the ruling government and which, during that period, depended on material assistance from the outside to continue its struggle for self-determination for the black majority. *cf* T Leon, 'Attitude for Gifts' *Business Day* (South Africa, 10 October 2005); Dingake, n 47.

9

Insults and Criticism

1. INSULTS

IN 1980, ROBIN Berrington, press officer at the US embassy to Ireland, put on paper his reflections on the receiving State.[1] He did not mince his words. Ireland was 'small potatoes compared to the rest of Europe. The weather and the food are well matched to each other, they're dull'.[2] Berrington referred to the 'high cost of goods', the 'long, dark and damp winters'[3] and noted that the hottest item there was the question 'whether Ronald Reagan's ancestors really came from Tipperary'.[4]

That diplomats write candid reports is to be expected.[5] What is more unusual is that such letters find their way into the press. In Berrington's case, they were, for some unfathomable reason, included in publicity material on President Reagan which was distributed to journalists. The *Irish Times* subsequently decided to print excerpts.[6]

The reaction of the receiving State was not entirely clear—according to some reports, the Irish Prime Minister had been 'disappointed and concerned';[7] but that allegation was denied by other sources.[8] The incident however provided sufficient grounds for the sending State to take steps: After the publication of the letter, US Ambassador Shannon apologised to the Irish members of his staff, and Berrington was recalled to Washington.[9]

The use of insulting language has, for a long time, presented diplomatic relations with difficulties. In the early eighteenth century, Callières called on diplomatic agents to communicate 'without too much heat' and 'without always wanting to have the last word';[10] but his warning has not

1 AG Flynn, 'Irish Laud Diplomat' *New York Times* (New York, 8 February 1981).
2 P Jennings, 'World News Tonight' *ABC News Transcripts* (29 January 1981).
3 Flynn, n 1.
4 Jennings, n 2.
5 For an interesting collection of diplomatic letters of this kind (in the tradition of 'valedictory despatches'), see Parris and Bryson (2011).
6 Flynn, n 1.
7 'Diplomat Has Irish Stewing' *West Palm Beach Post* (Palm Beach FL, 29 January 1981).
8 Flynn, n 1.
9 ibid, and see C O'Clery, 'WikiLeaks' *Global Post* (Boston MA, 29 November 2010).
10 Callières (1716).

always been heeded. In 1871, the Russian Minister Catacazy's conduct[11] even found mention in the State of the Union Address of the US President. According to the US Secretary of State, Catacazy had '[i]mportun[ed] Senators and Members of Congress', shown himself in personal conversation 'severe and unrestrained' and made use of 'abusive and vituperative language toward very many persons'.[12] President Grant found that it was 'impossible, with self-respect or with a just regard to the dignity of the country, to permit Mr Catacazy to continue to hold intercourse with this Government after his personal abuse of Government officials…'.[13]

In 1898, a letter written by the Spanish Minister to the US, Dupuy de Lôme, had even more severe consequences. Dupuy de Lôme offered a damning account of the incumbent US President McKinley, describing him as 'weak and a bidder for the admiration of the crowd, besides being a would-be politician (politicastro), who tries to leave a door open behind himself while keeping on good terms with the jingoes of his party'.[14] The letter was intercepted[15] and found its way into William Hearst's *New York Journal*.[16] It is today considered one of the contributory factors to the outbreak of the Spanish–American war of 1898.[17]

Conduct which is perceived as insulting need not involve offensive words. Among the more modern instances, the 1995 case of Martin Indyk, the US Ambassador to Israel, may be recalled, in which officials of the receiving State took exception to the envoy's absence at a specific event (the opening ceremony of 'Jerusalem 3000').[18]

But it is true that many incidents of alleged insults involve a verbal message—frequently one which betrays the personal views of the diplomatic agent rather than a policy adopted by the sending State.[19]

Commentators on diplomatic law tend to adopt the view that insulting remarks are incompatible with the position of a diplomat and represent interference in the internal affairs of the receiving State.[20] Even in pre-Convention days did US regulations provide that officers of her Foreign Service had to 'refrain from expressing harsh or disagreeable opinions upon local political questions or other controversial subjects',[21] and after the conclusion of the VCDR, Bliščenko expressed the view that an

[11] See ch 1, at n 23.
[12] 'The Catacazy Letters' *New York Times* (New York, 8 December 1871).
[13] Grant (1871), 271.
[14] Moore, 507–08. On Canelejas, see García Barrón, 43, at n 9.
[15] Satow (1979), 181.
[16] García Barrón, 51.
[17] ibid, 43, and *cf* Offner, 21.
[18] See ch 3, at n 158.
[19] See the 1964 case of Randle Reid-Adam (A.8); the 2002 case of Algosaibi (A.180).
[20] See Przetacznik (1976), 58, at no 2; Bliščenko, 181; Richtsteig, 23; Salmon (1996), 131, para 201.
[21] Foreign Service Regulations of the United States, ch 1, s 15.

insulting speech would regularly lead to demands for the recall 'of this tactless person'.[22]

Agents who engage in conduct of this kind certainly create an obstacle to the fulfilment of the functions of their missions, as they significantly reduce the basis of trust which these tasks presuppose. It is a consideration which was well illustrated in the Catacazy case. In that case, the US Secretary of State remarked that the Minister's behaviour, 'both official and personal, has been for some time past such as to impair his usefulness to his own Government and to render intercourse with him, either for business or for social purposes, highly disagreeable.'[23]

But another reason for negative reactions in this context is formed by the fact that insulting conduct, from the perspective of the receiving State, presents itself as an attack (verbal or otherwise) on persons or institutions in that State—or in third States. Where targets in a third State are concerned,[24] the adoption of a negative reaction constitutes a protective mechanism: If no reaction were provided at all, the receiving State would invite the charge that it approved of the message which the diplomatic conduct carries.[25]

On the other hand, the question whether any target—including institutions—qualifies as a victim of insults, has been the subject of some controversy. The European Court of Human Rights had to deal with this aspect of offensive conduct in *Grigoriades*, a case involving a Greek officer against whom criminal proceedings had been initiated after he had written a letter expressing strong opinions on conditions and objectives of the Greek army. The proceedings were based on the Greek Military Criminal Code which outlawed insults of the armed forces, when committed by one of its members.[26]

The majority of the court found that a violation of Article 10 ECHR (which guarantees freedom of expression) had taken place.[27] The particular target of Grigoriades' letter mattered for the assessment. The majority admitted that the letter contained 'strong and intemperate remarks', but stressed that they had been made 'in the context of a general and lengthy discourse critical of army life and the army as an institution' and did not contain 'any insults directed against either the recipient of the letter or any other person'.[28] The implication is that institutions are incapable of being insulted; insults are targeted at the *personal* dignity of the victim.

It is a view which is open to criticism. Judge Jambrek, in a concurring opinion, suggested a wider understanding of the concept of insults. While

[22] Bliščenko, 181. See also Plischke, 313 with reference to the US position.
[23] 'The Catacazy Case' *New York Times* (New York, 21 March 1895).
[24] See ch 2, s 2 and see the 2002 case of Algosaibi (A.180). *cf* also Richtsteig, 23.
[25] See ch 2, at n 39.
[26] *Grigoriades*, in particular paras 14, 16, 24 and 26.
[27] ibid, para 33; see also paras 41 and 48.
[28] ibid, para 47.

he agreed that institutions did not possess 'personal honour', he noted that the applicant's remarks had approached 'the concept of a collective insult' and found that the army too should, in principle, enjoy protection against insults.[29]

In the field of diplomatic relations, there certainly have been incidents when derogatory remarks about institutions (the State, the government and its policies) met with negative reactions. Reference has already been made to the derogatory remarks which the French Ambassador to Britain in 2001 had allegedly made about a third State,[30] and in the Berrington case it is likewise possible to support the view that the target had been the State as such.[31]

The 2000 incident involving the Pakistani Deputy High Commissioner in Bangladesh, Irfanur Raja, is illuminating in that regard. Raja was withdrawn following a controversy over his remarks about the Bangladeshi War of Liberation (in particular, comments which had cast doubt on the official death toll of that conflict).[32]

The case demonstrates the difficulty of identifying the dividing line between insults affecting individuals and insults affecting the collective. It would be difficult to deny that Raja's statements related to the State of Bangladesh itself, which owed its existence to the war of independence. At the same time, they certainly caused offence to those who were affected by the atrocities committed in the war.

Similar difficulties arise when the target is a person who cannot easily be separated from the institution he represents (such as the Head of the receiving State). In 1967, for instance, Ecuador accused the US Ambassador, Wymberley Coerr, of engaging in 'open criticism of the Constitutional President of the Republic of Ecuador, Dr. Otto Arosemena Gómez'.[33] The Ambassador was withdrawn shortly thereafter.[34]

In the light of the existing instances of negative State reactions given to collective insults, it does not appear possible to reach the conclusion that the international community withdraws this form of conduct from the scope of diplomatic interference. As in the case of personal insults, the offending behaviour clashes with feelings and attitudes in the receiving State, and State practice indicates that diplomatic attacks on institutions will be considered no less serious than attacks *ad hominem*.

[29] ibid, *(Concurring Opinion Jambrek)*, paras 3–5.

[30] See ch 3, at n 15. On insults regarding third States, see also Wagner et al, 367.

[31] See above, at n 1–n 9.

[32] See above, ch 7, at n 135–n 141.

[33] Whiteman (1970), 145.

[34] ibid and *RGDIP*, 'Chronique des faits internationaux' (1968), 431. See also the 1983 case of the Libyan People's Bureau in Australia (ch 2, at n 37 and below, at n 105). On the entitlement of a Head of State to protection of his honour and dignity under customary international law, see *Assistance in Criminal Matters*, 238, para 174.

But there is also some indication that sending States too do, in principle, acknowledge the severity of insulting conduct. There does not appear to be a single case in which the sending State or its agents have sought to rely on permissive grounds while accepting that diplomatic insults had taken place.

The case of Wymberley Coerr offers an illustration for a more typical response. The State Department made clear that it did not agree with the negative evaluation which the behaviour of its diplomat had received[35]—a consideration which is of significance where the necessity of the diplomatic measure is concerned, and to which this examination will return.[36] But the measure itself is in these instances not seen as an example of insulting conduct. From the perspective of the sending State it appears, at most, as a form of criticism—and critical remarks do allow for the possibility of the existence of permissive grounds.

2. CRITICISM

The sensitivity of receiving States relating to diplomatic criticism—even in the absence of accusations of insulting behaviour—has a long history. One may recall in this context the incident of the Russian Ambassador to Great Britain, Mikhail Bestuzhev-Ryumin, who in 1720, made official representations about alleged injustices which had been done to Tsar Peter the Great by the British government.[37] Satow recounts that this form of conduct 'naturally' caused deep irritation; Bestuzhev-Ryumin was expelled, and it took more than 10 years before diplomatic relations with Russia were restored.[38]

Diplomats in post-Convention days have likewise encountered negative reactions when engaging in criticism of the receiving State or its policies. That was certainly the case when diplomats offered critical remarks on the prevailing human rights situation in that State[39] and when criticism appeared as diplomatic partisanship.[40]

But this sensitivity also emerged when other policies of the receiving State were affected. The 1982 case of the US Ambassador to Canada, Paul Robinson, appears in that context. Robinson had noted that Canadian expenditure on social services had been too large; he encouraged the government to spend more money on warships, to increase the defence

[35] Whiteman (1970), 146.

[36] See below, nn 51–58 and after n 89.

[37] Satow (1979), 187, para 22.4 and Hill, 256, fn 22.

[38] Satow (1979), 187, para 22.4.

[39] See for instance, the 1999 case of the US embassy in Namibia (A.137 and ch 3, at n 127) and see Behrens 2014(b), 197.

[40] *cf* the 1997 case of the First Secretary at the US embassy in Belarus (A.125) and in general ch 6.

budget and to dispatch another brigade to Europe.[41] Robinson's remarks triggered stern reactions in the receiving State, including a call for his expulsion, expressed by a member of Parliament.[42]

In other cases, diplomatic comments related to the composition of the host government. In 1984, for instance, the US Ambassador to France, Evan Galbraith, was moved to voice his opinion after members of the Communist party had joined the French government. Galbraith stated that a French Communist was a 'poor Frenchman gone wrong',[43] and that '[e]verybody knows very well that the Soviet foreign policy is followed by the French Communist Party'.[44] Galbraith's comments earned him a summons by the French Prime Minister, Pierre Mauroy, who told him that such remarks were 'unacceptable'.[45]

In the literature, the opinion has sometimes been expressed that there exists a blanket ban even on certain forms of criticism. Bliščenko, for instance, includes in his consideration of interfering conduct speeches which 'sharply criticise the ruling order in that country'.[46] Taulbee, similarly, states that 'diplomats may not … endorse or criticize the host government, political parties, or party platforms'.[47]

But it is questionable whether such an extensive understanding of interference finds its basis in customary law. The fact must be taken into account that, where critical remarks are concerned (as opposed to insults), there are numerous examples of diplomats and sending States claiming a right to express their views on the relevant topics.

The Simon Gass case of 2010 exemplifies the situation. In December of that year, Gass, the UK Ambassador to Iran, noted that people 'who stand up for the rights of others', were nowhere 'under greater threat than in Iran' and that '[s]ince last year human rights defenders [had] been harassed and imprisoned'.[48] Gass was summoned by the Iranian Foreign Ministry, which issued a protest and declared that his statement was 'contrary to diplomatic principles'.[49]

The British government however expressed support for its Ambassador. The Foreign Office Minister for the Middle East was quoted as stating that it was 'only through open and frank dialogue that we can solve the

41 A Cohen, 'Regional News' *United Press International* (13 May 1982); Salmon (1996), 132.

42 Cohen, n 41.

43 'An Envoy's Faux Pas' *Newsweek* (New York, 13 February 1984).

44 M Santini, 'Shultz tells Envoy' *Gainesville Sun* (Gainesville, 14 February 1985). The fact that Galbraith's remarks were directed not only at Communists in general, but at the composition of the government (see also Salmon (1996), 132), was further clarified in a later interview, 'Ex-ambassador' *The Bulletin* (18 July 1985).

45 Above n 43.

46 Bliščenko, 181 (translation).

47 Glahn and Taulbee, 416.

48 S Gass, 'International Human Rights Day' *UK Embassy in Iran* (9 December 2010).

49 'Britain Backs Envoy' *Agence France Presse* (Paris, 13 December 2010).

problems we face'.[50] Neither was the factual assessment of the situation denied, nor did it even seem that the Foreign Office failed to appreciate the sensitivity of the receiving State in this matter—but the expressed position was that criticism on this occasion had been an appropriate measure.

The Gass case is only one of several instances in which sending States felt that critical comments by their agents were based on acceptable grounds.[51] In the light of this, a distinction between diplomatic criticism and diplomatic insults appears appropriate. A differentiation along these lines was also apparent in the views of several judges in *Grigoriades*.[52] Jambrek, for one, found that, while the army was in theory capable of being insulted, it 'should not be shielded from criticism'[53]—a distinction which had been of particular importance to the applicant,[54] but which also carried some significance for the law of the respondent State.[55] Judge Casadevall likewise differentiated between 'criticism' and 'insults', noting that criticism would in principle be embraced by the freedom of expression.[56]

It is a differentiation which carries value in the field of diplomatic interference as well.

Where criticism is concerned, legitimate interests will often form the basis of remarks which stand in opposition to policies or institutions of the receiving State, and sending States have not been shy in invoking these bases. A reading which deprived diplomatic agents of the possibility of criticism would be unjustifiably restrictive and could hardly be seen as complying with the receiving State's obligations to allow the mission the necessary facilities for the performance of its functions.[57]

The difficulty lies in finding the dividing line between criticism and insults. An attempt to differentiate between the two can hardly escape the danger of a subjective assessment, but it is possible to identify certain parameters which allow at least an approach towards a feasible distinction. This is a matter which carries particular significance for the question whether diplomatic criticism had been 'necessary' by comparison to available alternatives, and it will therefore be explored in more detail at that stage.[58]

[50] ibid.

[51] See for instance the reaction by the State Department in the 2013 case of Ricciardone (A.269). See also the 1963 case of Coerr (A.15) and above, at n 35.

[52] See above, at n 36.

[53] *Grigoriades (Concurring Opinion Jambrek)*, para 5.

[54] *Grigoriades*, paras 18, 22, 42.

[55] Ibid, para 27 (reference to Art 181 of the Greek Criminal Code).

[56] '... provided that the criticism is couched in terms that are not excessive and strike a fair balance with regard to the rights of others, order and morals ...', *Grigoriades (Dissenting Opinion Casadevall)*, para 3.

[57] VCDR art 25.

[58] See below, in particular after n 101.

3. BETWEEN CRITICISM AND INSULTS: MEASURING DIPLOMATIC CONDUCT

In November 2005, the American ambassador to Zimbabwe, Christopher Dell,[59] found himself at the centre of controversy after he had delivered a lecture at Africa University in eastern Zimbabwe. Dell had referred to the economic situation in the receiving State and stated that 'neither drought nor sanctions' were the root cause for the current problems, but that '[t]he Zimbabwe government's own gross mismanagement of the economy and its corrupt rule has brought on the crisis'.[60]

The Zimbabwean Foreign Minister Mumbengegwi reacted by stating that Dell had 'falsely portray[ed] the government as a villain' and had incited the people against their government 'in flagrant violation of the provisions of the Vienna Convention'.[61]

In this instance, the sending State defended the conduct of its diplomatic agent, with the State Department noting that Dell had 'effectively refuted regime propaganda that blames Zimbabwe's economic problems on American and European sanctions'.[62] In other words, Dell had corrected the impression of the sending State which the government of the receiving State had sought to convey.

That however is an essential aspect of the exercise of diplomatic functions. It is this form of conduct to which Richtsteig refers when he states that the protection of interests of the sending State entitles a diplomatic agent to a corrective reply (*'Gegendarstellung'*) in circumstances of this kind.[63] It is one of many examples which illustrate the fact that the fulfilment of diplomatic functions can require statements which will be seen as criticism of the receiving State. The protection of interests does indeed feature prominently in that context: States around the world expect their agents to speak out when their rights have been put in danger, and there are situations in which the failure of a sending State to lodge a protest may result in the loss of a decisive position under international law.[64]

In other cases, diplomatic agents acted in fulfilment of the second alternative of Article 3(1)(b)—the protection of the interests of nationals of the sending State. In June 2012 for instance, the Chinese Minister of Environmental Protection protested after US diplomatic and consular missions in China had monitored the presence of harmful particles in the air and had

[59] See also ch 3 at n 49.
[60] 'Mugabe Tells US Envoy' *Mail & Guardian* (Johannesburg, 8 November 2005).
[61] *BBC Monitoring Africa—Political*, 'Zimbabwe Media', 18 November 2005.
[62] 'U.S. Government' *Deutsche Presse Agentur* (Hamburg, 8 November 2005).
[63] Richtsteig, 21 ('Interessenwahrnehmung im Gastland'). See ch 6, n 36.
[64] See for instance *Preah Vihear*, 30, 31; Concluding Thoughts, after n 43.

made the data available on Twitter and on websites.[65] In this instance, the Minister made express reference to the duty of non-interference.[66] That the perception of diplomatic (and consular) criticism was at least one of the reasons for the government's reaction, was clear from the context of the case. The publication of air quality data had raised public debate in particular because the American data and those released by Beijing often showed differences, with the US embassy 'generally report[ing] worse conditions'.[67]

But in this case, too, the sending State stood its ground. The State Department noted that the United States had provided 'the American community [in China] … information it can use to make better daily decisions regarding the safety of outdoor activities'.[68] It is a statement which leaves no doubt that the sending State on this occasion acted to protect the interests of its nationals located in the receiving State.

On other occasions, diplomatic agents engaged in criticism of the receiving State and its government to act in pursuit of their function of reporting on conditions and developments in that State to their own Foreign Offices (Article 3(1)(d)). The rendering even of candid accounts and analyses of conditions in the receiving State is integral to the diplomatic task; the entitlement to freedom of communication, which Article 27 recognises, is at least in part based on the need to carry out the function of reporting in an unrestricted manner.[69]

It is sometimes even the first alternative of Article 3(1)(d)—the 'mere' observation of conditions, which leads to the suspicion that criticism had been intended. When, in 1998, the former Deputy Prime Minister of Malaysia, Anwar Ibrahim, stood trial in his own country on charges of corruption, diplomatic agents from various States, including Canada and the USA, were prevented from attending the trial.[70] The Presiding Judge, Augustine Paul, referred to the possibility that the presence of diplomats may send out a critical message: Paul stated that allowing observers would be an 'insult to the court' and would convey the impression that 'it may not be dispensing justice'.[71] The attendance of 'these people,' he noted, 'would amount to interference in the powers and functions conferred on me by the constitution'.[72]

There is no indication that this assessment was shared by the diplomats or their States. James Rubin, then spokesman for the US State Department, was quoted as saying that the United States believed that Anwar Ibrahim

[65] Crook, 851.
[66] ibid.
[67] ibid.
[68] A Ramzy, 'Conflict in the Air' *Time* (New York, 6 June 2012).
[69] See Denza, 211.
[70] J Beltrame, 'Malaysian Politician's Trial' *Vancouver Sun* (Vancouver, 3 November 1998).
[71] M Frei et al, 'Anwar Upbeat as Trial Opens' *BBC Online* (London, 2 November 1998).
[72] ibid.

'should have the opportunity to defend himself in fair and open trials, and we will continue to monitor these proceedings',[73] and a spokesman for the Canadian Foreign Ministry declared that the Canadian High Commission would be watching the events 'very closely'.[74]

Even the promotion of friendly relations (Article 3(1)(e) of the Convention) can serve as a basis for criticism of the receiving State. The public relations aspect of this function requires a diplomatic agent to explain the position of the sending State,[75] and this may include the clarification of points on which the views of sending and receiving State differ considerably. This can be the case, for instance, if the sending State is a member of a supranational organisation which has decided on a political course critical to that adopted by the receiving State. A fair representation of the situation aids in the promotion of mutual understanding, and a frank evaluation even of the differences between sending and receiving State therefore contributes to the fulfilment of this task.

Critical remarks made to assist a people in its right to self-determination[76] can likewise provide fertile ground for controversy, but may be indispensable for the fulfilment of that task.

Reference has in this regard already been made to several relevant incidents, including that of the Canadian *chargé d'affaires* in Sudan, Nuala Lawlor, who in 2007 had called for the release of leading members of the opposition of the receiving State—a message which clearly implied criticism of the government which had detained them without charge.[77] In this instance, too, the diplomatic agent received the support of her Foreign Office, whose Minister found that Ms Lawlor had stood up for the 'values of freedom, democracy, human rights and the rule of law in Sudan'.[78]

Critical remarks by diplomatic agents can therefore often rely on norms under international law which permit this course of action. But criticism also offers a clear illustration for the fact that the mere presence of such norms cannot be enough to reach a conclusive assessment of the relevant conduct.

In this regard, reference may be made to the case of Edward Clay, the British High Commissioner in Kenya in 2004, which has been mentioned before.[79] Clay's attack on corruption in the Kenyan government had been noted as the example of a diplomat who engaged in the protection of interests of the sending State—Britain, as Kenya's largest foreign investor,

[73] Beltrame, n 70.
[74] ibid.
[75] See ch 3, at n 79.
[76] See ch 3, at nn 159 ff.
[77] See ch 3, at n 195. See also the 2008 case of James McGee, the US Ambassador to Zimbabwe (A.233).
[78] See ch 3, at n 197.
[79] See ch 3, at n 34; also ch 4, at n 140 and ch 6, at n 58.

would have been able to claim a legitimate interest in reducing corruption in that country.[80]

But Clay's statements also showed features which set them apart from other instances in which the protective task was involved. They were made to the British Business Association in Kenya, and thus before a semi-public forum; and the manner in which Clay expressed himself had been particularly forceful. There is evidence that both aspects of his conduct contributed to the negative reaction by the receiving State.[81] But they also stand for elements of critical behaviour which require consideration if an accurate evaluation of diplomatic conduct in this field is to be obtained.

The first aspect—the forum chosen for the diplomatic message—is a factor which had been of significance even in some of the historical examples of diplomatic criticism.[82] But some modern commentators on diplomatic law and diplomatic relations likewise take a restrictive view on the discussion of certain matters in a public forum.[83] Plischke for one points out that diplomatic agents may 'not publicly criticize the actions of the legislative or executive branches of the governments' of the receiving States.[84]

Contemporary State practice affirms the sensitivity of the receiving State when critical remarks have been made in public: Not only where such criticism relates to corruption,[85] but also where its targets were government personalities or the structure of the government,[86] the State itself and its boundaries or disputed territories,[87] or specific policies—on the justice system for instance,[88] and, prominently, on human rights.[89]

The rationale for this concern must be seen in the impact which critical remarks on the government and its policies can generate in the receiving State. The outcome of criticism uttered behind closed doors can be controlled. But public criticism may foster in the people of the receiving State sentiments which are antagonistic to the policy of the government and may influence their political choice.

[80] See ch 3, at n 35.

[81] See on the reaction by the Kenyan Foreign Minister, L Barasa, 'Criticism That Rubbed Officials The Wrong Way' *The Nation* (Kenya, 3 February 2005).

[82] Bestuzhev-Ryumin in 1720 (above, at n 37) could certainly have invoked the protective task when complaining about alleged insults to his head of State. The fact that his grievances were 'published simultaneously with their delivery' (Satow (1979), 187, para 22.4) would however help to explain the subsequent negative reactions.

[83] Glahn (1986), 462 and see Do Nascimento E Silva, who points out that '[n]o negotiations, be they of a diplomatic nature or not, can be conducted openly'. Do Nascimento e Silva (1992b) 1034.

[84] Plischke, 313.

[85] See also the 2000 case of Murray (A.148).

[86] See the 1967 case of Coerr (A.15).

[87] See the 2000 case of Martin Indyk (A.151).

[88] See the 2000 case of Yves Gaudeul (A.181).

[89] See the 2008 case of McGee (A.233), the 2002 case of Murray (A.186), the 1999 comments by Curran (A.131) etc.

Within the structure of the legal assessment of this form of conduct, these considerations carry significance for the comparative tests required under the principle of proportionality. The question in particular arises whether public criticism had been the only effective way of safeguarding the interests in whose defence the diplomatic agent had acted, or whether there had been alternatives which would have minimised the detrimental impact in the receiving State.

In Clay's case,[90] the fact may be recalled that the High Commissioner had already conveyed his concerns to President Kibaki before making his remarks to the British Business Association.[91] A negative sanction was reported only when the latter situation materialised.[92]

At the same time, the fact must be taken into account that to many governments the possibility of escaping the consequences of effective criticism is the very reason why they are keen to avoid public criticism. Addressing the public may not always lead to a change of attitude in the host government,[93] but it may at least draw the attention of the international community to a situation which, in some cases, constitutes a serious violation of interests recognised under international law. Diplomatic conduct of this kind may often be the only effective method to safeguard a legitimate interest, and, if that is the case, the choice of a public forum will fulfil the conditions of 'objective necessity', to which reference had been made above.[94]

The second aspect which marked the statements of Edward Clay in Kenya was the manner of his criticism. Clay did not shy away from strong language when talking about corruption in the administration: 'They may expect we shall not see, or notice, or will forgive them a bit of gluttony because they profess to like Oxfam lunches', said the High Commissioner. 'But they can hardly expect us not to care when their gluttony causes them to vomit all over our shoes'.[95]

The reaction triggered by Clay's remarks made clear that the forceful manner of his representations had contributed to the negative assessment his conduct received. The Kenyan Foreign Minister stated on that occasion that Clay's job was not 'like that of a comedian. He has abused us and we are telling him to explain the facts of the case or else he should shut up'.[96]

[90] Above, at n 79.

[91] See ch 6, at n 60.

[92] See also the 1999 case of the US embassy in Namibia (A.137), in which the receiving State found that heads of mission should use 'established diplomatic channels', 'Namibia; US Expresses Concern' *Panafrican News Agency* (Dakar, 18 August 1999), and see ch 3, at n 127. T Moyo, 'Namibia; Government' *The Namibian* (Windhoek West, 20 August 1999), and see ch 4, n 143.

[93] For a situation giving rise to similar considerations, see ch 11, at n 156.

[94] See ch 4, at n 94. See also Wagner et al, 367.

[95] Barasa, n 81.

[96] J Vasagar, 'Kenyan President Faces Rebellion' *The Guardian* (London, 24 February 2005).

For the legal evaluation of diplomatic criticism, the employment of strong language carries considerable significance. Like the choice of a public forum,[97] the use of harsh words can indicate the adoption of a measure which goes beyond the necessary, and thus fails to fulfil the 'least restrictive means' test. Where the statements are so strong that they veer into the realm of insults, this will invariably be the case—as has been found above, insults do not even allow for the invocation of permissive norms:[98] They are, by their very nature, excessive measures. What is more: There is good reason to argue that insults are not even an 'effective' option to safeguard legitimate interests to begin with,[99] so that insulting behaviour might not even possess the necessary preconditions to enter into a comparison with other available measures.

On the other hand, the determination of the border line between harsh, but potentially legitimate, criticism and insults causes considerable difficulties. Clay himself, when reflecting on the 2004 incident a few months later, did not appear to consider the nature of his statements excessive: 'I regret three things', said the British High Commissioner, 'not speaking out much earlier; underestimating the scale of the looting afoot; and the moderation of the language I used then: that was clearly inexcusably polite in relation to what we see going on'.[100]

Evaluations like these raise the question whether the categorisation of conduct as 'insulting' might not always be hampered by subjective considerations and thus constitute an exercise whose outcome is strongly dependent on the personal views of the observer.

And yet, the distinction between criticism and insults is seen as important in several areas of international law[101] in which it has been considered necessary to differentiate these concepts.

The derivation of a precise and immutable formula for this endeavour under customary law may be difficult. State practice, however, does allow for the identification of certain parameters which make an objective assessment of conduct as 'insulting' a more likely occurrence.

The fact that an 'attack' on certain interests in the receiving State had taken place, is arguably not enough for that: Attacks can, after all, be the very essence of sharp criticism,[102] which may still be advanced on the basis of legitimate interests.

[97] Above, after n 81.

[98] Above, after n 34.

[99] The fact must be recalled that States have at times considered it pointless to have further dealings with diplomats in situations of this kind. See above, at n 13.

[100] Vasagar, n 96.

[101] For the field of human rights (limitations to freedom of expression), see above, after n 27.

[102] It may be recalled that the remarks of the US Ambassador to Canada in 1982, Paul Robinson, on various aspects of Canadian policy, had likewise been qualified as 'attacks' by one of his critics (Pauline Jewett, MP for the New Democratic Party). Cohen, n 41.

But certain commonalities can be found among cases which members of the international community will usually consider to involve an insulting element. In the Catacazy case, it was the 'abusive and vituperative language' and Catacazy's 'abuse of Government officials' which formed one of the core accusations against the Russian Minister.[103] In de Lôme's case, the diplomat's negative remarks about the personality of President McKinley were at the centre of the evaluation.[104]

And in an incident in the latter part of the twentieth century, the Libyan representative in Australia received a sharp rebuke after Libyan diplomats had made available copies of a letter which called the American President Reagan a 'new world Hitler' and described his leadership as a return to 'incredibly savagery'.[105]

What these and other incidents in this context have in common, is the fact that the dignity (and often the self-respect) of the victim had been affected by the offending conduct—regardless of the question whether that victim had been a natural person or an institution.[106]

This is an aspect which also carried considerable significance when attempts were made by individual States and their organs to approach the meaning of 'insults'.

When the *Grigoriades* case was still before the national courts,[107] the Greek Court of Cassation found that the concept of insults included 'every show of contempt damaging the esteem, and respect for, and the reputation of, the protected value'.[108] Insulting expressions had to convey 'contempt, taunt and denigration; it [was] not sufficient merely to call into question the protected value'.[109]

German criminal law moves in a similar direction when it understands 'insulting' conduct (a crime under section 185 of the German penal code) as the 'unjustified attack on the honour of another through intentional manifestation of disregard or disrespect'.[110] where 'honour' is interpreted as the 'inner value or the dignity' of the victim.[111]

As the above mentioned incidents have shown, these approaches retain their validity in the field of diplomatic relations and in situations in which such conduct forms the basis of allegations of interference.

[103] See above, at n 13.
[104] See above, at n 14.
[105] 'Diplomatic and Consular Relations' (1981–1983) *Aust YBIL*, 505, 506. See ch 2, at n 37.
[106] For an example of remarks relating to institutions, see the 1976 case of Joseph John-Jova (A.30).
[107] Above, at n 26.
[108] *Grigoriades*, para 24.
[109] *Grigoriades*, para 24.
[110] Tröndle, 987 at marginal 1 (translation).
[111] ibid, at marginal 2.

A strong indication for the existence of an attack on the dignity of the victim is the use of negative emotional, rather than objective, language: A diplomatic agent who intends to claim that his statements merely constituted legitimate criticism, would certainly have a stronger basis if the remarks had been informative in nature.

An illustration was provided in April 2000, when, at the time of the presidential election in Peru, the British Ambassador to that country (Roger Hart) stated that the British side did not have 'a lot of confidence in the voting process' and referred in that regard to 'a lot of irregularities during the campaign and during the day of the vote'.[112] Hart's comments did attract negative reactions, but it could hardly be doubted that they constituted the objective assessment of a factual situation: According to news media, thousands of reports of voting irregularities had been made, and election monitors had investigated claims of fraud in Peru.[113] The rebuke which Hart received was made by one of the vice-presidential candidates;[114] the receiving State itself does not seem to have provided a reaction.[115]

The use of emotional language, on the other hand, is an indication, but not a necessary requirement, for the existence of insulting conduct. There have been several incidents in diplomatic relations in which remarks which ostensibly stayed clear of emotional terms had caused great, and understandable, offence. The expression of revisionist accounts on war and atrocities are an example.[116] On occasion, however, even the omission of certain terms can cause offence. In 1847, the US *chargé d'affaires* in Peru, Albert Jewett, found himself reproached by the US Secretary of State (Buchanan), after he had left out the titles of 'Excellency' or 'Honourable' in correspondence with the Peruvian Foreign Minister.[117] Buchanan noted that Jewett might have considered this a 'small matter in itself', but he emphasised that 'such breaches of established etiquette often give greater offence than real injuries'.[118]

Both revisionist remarks and disregard for the rules of diplomatic courtesy can certainly be perceived as attacking the dignity of persons in the receiving State.

112 M Hayes, 'Peru's Presidential Race' *Associated Press* (New York, 13 April 2000).

113 'Fujimori Faces Runoff' *Toronto Star* (Toronto, 13 April 2000).

114 'Peruanischer Praesident Fujimori' *Associated Press—German* (13 April 2000).

115 See also the 1967 case of Coerr (above, at n 35), in which the US defended her Ambassador's remarks by noting that he had engaged in a 'reasoned, non-polemical discussion', Whiteman (1970), 146.

116 See, eg, the 2000 case of Irfanur Raja (A.159) and the 2002 case of Ghazi Algosaibi (A.183).

117 Moore, 493, and see Satow (1979), 180, para 21.17.

118 Moore, 493.

The ultimate determination of the dividing line between insults and sharp criticism is still dependent on the context of the diplomatic conduct, and it remains one of the challenges of the diplomatic office that its bearers are expected to have an awareness of the ingrained cultural and political conditions in the country in which they are posted.

But what the existing incidents and the attempts by individual States to approach the concept of insults have shown is that the identification of objective parameters in this field is possible. They provide guidance to representatives who are faced with situations of this kind, but they remain general in character: The precise point at which permissible sharp criticism turns into insulting conduct, can only be evaluated with a clear awareness of the conditions of each individual case.

Insults go beyond the questioning of particular values and even beyond strong disagreement with positions held by the receiving State. Nor will any form of attack suffice to carry diplomatic conduct outside the realm of mere criticism. Insults presuppose an attack on the dignity of the target, be it a person or an institution, and they constitute conduct which is often (though not invariably) marked by emotional language rather than informative statements.

These features, together with a good understanding of the cultural and historical framework of the receiving State, allow for the emergence of a borderline between conduct which can still be based on interests of the sending State and the international community and behaviour which is excessive in nature and does not permit the invocation of competing interests and the application of mediating mechanisms.

10

Threats and Intimidation

1. IDENTIFYING THE RATIONALE OF THE BAN

FROM 1977 ONWARDS, civil war raged in the Republic of Mozambique. Two factions stood on opposing sides: The Front for the Liberation of Mozambique (FRELIMO) and the Mozambique Resistance Movement (RENAMO), but it was FRELIMO which held the reins of the country throughout that period.[1] The conflict only came to an end in October 1992, when the parties signed a peace accord.[2] By that time, it was estimated that 600,000 people had lost their lives; millions more had been displaced.[3]

The first multi-party elections in the history of independent Mozambique were arranged for October 1994.[4] It was not to be the end of discord in the country. Even before voting had come to a close, the leader of RENAMO claimed that the government had committed electoral fraud.[5] More than three years later, RENAMO, along with 15 other opposition parties, decided to boycott local elections in the country, referring again to alleged electoral fraud.[6] In this situation, Brian Curran, the US Ambassador to Mozambique, emphasised that the forthcoming presidential elections had to be democratic and transparent and had to involve all opposition parties.[7] Curran added that his government would, if the opposition were to boycott the elections, withdraw its financial support for the event.[8]

Curran's statement met with unease: The Secretary General of FRELIMO considered it interference in the internal affairs of Mozambique and reportedly stated that 'political and financial blackmails are outdated,

[1] See A Roberts, 'Mozambique Pique' *American Spectator* (Arlington, March 1992).

[2] Harrison, 20.

[3] 'Skeptical and Confused' *New York Times* (New York, 27 September 1994).

[4] Harrison, 20.

[5] B Keller, 'Mozambican Elections Thrown in Doubt', *New York Times* (New York, 28 October 1994). The United Nations, however, doubted the basis of the allegations, ibid. For further details on the elections and their outcome, see 'Mozambique Leader Wins Multiparty Vote' *New York Times* (New York, 20 November 1994).

[6] 'International News' *Associated Press* (New York, 16 September 1998).

[7] 'US Ambassador Accused of Meddling' *Xinhua* (China, 15 September 1998).

[8] ibid.

particularly in an era of economic globalization when all nations should respect each other'.[9]

Historically, threats and ultimata played a significant role in diplomatic relations. The most prominent illustration may well have been the ultimatum preceding Britain's entry into the Second World War: It was handed to the German government by the British Ambassador Henderson on 3 September 1939 and envisaged a state of war if German troops were not withdrawn from Poland by 11am on that day.[10]

But examples of this kind also demonstrate that generalisations are not helpful in an evaluation of diplomatic conduct of this kind: Legitimate interests may be involved even in situations of grave threats.

The literature, too, has not always advocated a clear negative line on threatening behaviour. As late as 1974 did Mookerjee state that the concept of diplomacy referred to an 'intelligently devised method of implementing the foreign policy of a government or of a monarch ... by means of negotiation, persuasion, threat and pressure'.[11]

It was, however, at least at that stage, an increasingly isolated opinion. In the ILC debates, the negative opinion on threats was quite clear, and was given voice by the Yugoslav Member Milan Bartos who noted that the rule of 'non-intervention' would preclude 'anything constituting a "diplomatic" ultimatum to the receiving State to change its policy'.[12] Padilla Nervo, when discussing the meaning of 'intervention', referred to the concept of 'dictatorial interference', which he understood as implying a 'peremptory demand for positive conduct or abstention—a demand which, if not complied with, involved threat to or recourse to compulsion, though not necessarily physical compulsion, in some form'.[13]

The concept of intimidation, however, is wider than that of threats made with the intention to change the opinions of their targets. The warning of negative consequences may suffice to render the recipient fearful, even if the diplomatic agent did not anticipate a direct advantage from this measure.[14]

Yet it is clear from the practice of receiving States that this conduct on its own can be sufficient to affect sensitivities of the receiving State. An illustration is a 1982 incident involving an Iraqi diplomat who reportedly adopted 'threatening behaviour' during a demonstration by the Islamic Union of Iraqi Students in the United Kingdom—conduct which

[9] ibid.

[10] 143 *State Papers* (1939), 176, 177.

[11] Mookerjee, 100.

[12] YILC 1957/I, 145, para 80 [Bartos].

[13] YILC 1957/I, 145, para 83 [Padilla Nervo]. See also Q Wright, 5: 'In general, persuasion is legitimate, coercion illegitimate'.

[14] *cf* the definition provided by the OED on the verb 'intimidate': 'To render timid, inspire with fear; to overawe, cow; in modern use *esp.* to force to or deter from some action by threats or violence', OED, intimidate (v).

prompted 'strong representations' by the Foreign Office, but also a statement by the Iraqi embassy noting that the incident 'was regretted and would not be repeated'.[15]

Diplomats on the other hand who merely voice a desire that a certain form of conduct be adopted, cannot usually be said to engage in behaviour which carries properties of intimidation. The case of Aurelia Brazeal, which has been mentioned before, offers an illustration. When Brazeal, the US Ambassador to Kenya in 1995, urged the government of the receiving State to enact a law that would liberalise electronic media,[16] she did trigger negative reactions, with the Kenyan Minister of Agriculture declaring his objection to ambassadors who 'arrogantly' issued ultimata to government ministers.[17] But cases like this invite closer scrutiny.

It is certainly true that the classification of remarks as 'intimidation' depends on the context of the situation. The possibility of implied threats cannot always be discounted: In situations, for instance, in which the sending State is already amassing troops at the border to the receiving State, an envoy can afford to speak softly in the knowledge that the other side is aware of the big stick in the background.

However, as a bare minimum, intimidation (and also 'threats' in the way in which Padilla Nervo understood them) require at least the indication, expressly or implied, of negative consequences.[18] Statements which, as in the Brazeal incident, simply call for the adoption of a course of action, fall below that standard.[19] They may meet with restrictions for different reasons: For instance, if they constitute insults or lobbying activities which exceed the bounds of the necessary.[20]

The sensitivities of the receiving State can be affected through intimidation relating to various targets, but the rationale for a negative State reaction will not always be the same. In cases in which the object of intimidation is the receiving State itself or its policies,[21] the negative evaluations given by receiving States appear to be shared in the literature[22] and in the views of other expert commentators.[23] The rationale in these instances is quite clear: The sovereignty of the receiving State is directly affected, as is its right to decide its own political fate.

[15] National Union of Students in House of Commons Report (1984), 55, para 17.

[16] See ch 5, at n 1, n 37 and n 52.

[17] 'US Ambassador Under Fire' *Xinhua* (China, 16 February 1995).

[18] See in this context also the definition provided by the OED: 'A denunciation to a person of ill to befall him [...] *fig.* an indication of impending evil', OED 'threat (n)'.

[19] That is even the case if the diplomatic agent envisages the adoption of the relevant action by a particular date. The question whether Brazeal had stipulated a certain date, was in fact a matter of some dispute. See ch 5, at n 5.

[20] See on these possibilities, ch 5 and ch 9.

[21] See the 1998 case of Curran, above, at n 7. See also the 1982 case of Hinton, below at n 53.

[22] See for instance Oppenheim, with regard to the particular case of intimidation of political parties, Oppenheim (1967), 787.

[23] See Institute of International Law (1989) art 5.

On occasion, however, intimidating conduct had been directed at individuals living under the jurisdiction of the receiving State.

In 1979 for instance, Ho Xuan Dich, a Second Secretary at the Vietnamese embassy in Ottawa, was expelled amid accusations of intimidation: According to a government statement, Ho had made threats against Vietnamese immigrants and warned them of reprisals against their relatives in Vietnam.[24]

The sensitivity of receiving States in this area is underlined by the fact that negative reactions have been issued in the past even when a diplomatic threat had not taken an explicit form. In 1980, for instance, the Libyan People's Bureau in the United States requested State Department cooperation in a plan to obtain a list of all Libyan citizens in the US—'the list to show in each instance the individual's full name, passport number, address in the United States, purpose of residence, and date of entry into the United States'.[25] It was enough to make the State Deaprtment summon the head of the mission (El Houderi) and to issue a warning to him. The context of the case revealed a potentially more sinister background to what may have otherwise appeared as a mere administrative request. At the time of the Libyan suggestion, reports had already reached the State Department about an 'imminent campaign of threats and intimidation against Libyan opponents … living in the United States', and Colonel Gaddafi had apparently made a public announcement to the effect that opponents to his regime would be 'liquidated'.[26]

On other occasions, intimidation was used to effect the repatriation of nationals of the sending State. These instances, too, have met with negative reactions by the diplomatic hosts.[27] But the rationale for the sensitivity of the receiving State in that regard—and indeed, the interests which are involved on its side—are more difficult to define. In the literature, Green has expressed the view that attempts at persuading nationals of the sending State to return to that country were not by themselves interference in 'local matters', but that it went 'beyond [diplomatic] functions to apply pressure or to detain them for this purpose'.[28]

In the context of contacts between diplomatic missions and nationals of the sending State, Dembinski speaks of a 'right' of the receiving State

[24] 'Vietnamese Diplomat Expelled' *Facts on File* (New York, 13 April 1979). See also the 1980 case of Musa Kusa, ch 7, at n 46.

[25] The case according to Nash, 327.

[26] Nash, 326, 327. See in this context also the expulsions of Libyan diplomats from the US later in that year (A.49 and A.50).

[27] See the warning against attempts at forcible repatriation of nationals, which was given to the Polish Ambassador to the United States in 1956, Whiteman (1970), 138.

[28] Green, 149.

'to make sure that no coercion is exercised to force any of the nationals of the sending State to come to the mission against their will'.[29]

But there is also evidence that receiving States consider these incidents as directly related to questions of sovereignty. When for instance in 1967 South Korean agents abducted several South Korean nationals from the territory of the Federal Republic of Germany, Germany demanded the recall of three members of the embassy who had participated in the abduction, and protested in a note verbale against South Korea's violation of German territorial sovereignty.[30] And threatening conduct against individuals need not have reached this level of gravity before sovereign rights of the receiving State are involved. In that context, Salmon points out that 'foreigners living on the soil of the receiving State' (and this could, of course, be extended to the receiving State's own nationals), are, after all 'under the protection of its laws'.[31] The exertion of pressure on individuals in the receiving State therefore constitutes at least prima facie an intrusion in matters which fall within its jurisdiction; and the receiving State can claim with good cause that diplomatic conduct of this kind touches not only upon the concerns of private citizens, but affects also the internal affairs of the State itself.

The existence of legitimate interests on the side of the receiving State, however, does not preclude the possibility that the sending State may rely on grounds which are likewise recognised in international law. The reasons underlying the British ultimatum to Germany in 1939, for instance, have not lost their validity in modern international law: If a State is entitled to resort to collective self-defence, it must at the very least be entitled to give fair warning of its intention to do so, and to provide an aggressor with the opportunity to adapt its conduct accordingly.

Even where individuals are the targets of diplomatic threats, the existence of permissive norms on the side of the diplomatic agents cannot be ruled out. Situations for instance in which terrorists operating from the territory of the receiving State have targeted objects in the sending State, involve legitimate interests of the latter. A diplomat who warns of the possible freezing of their bank accounts if such actions continue, may thus be held to have acted to protect objectives, including the sovereignty of his own State, which are recognised under international law.

These are questions of evaluation, which require consideration in their own right. What they demonstrate is the fact that binary statements on the nature of the relevant diplomatic conduct cannot offer a satisfactory conclusion. Here, as in other instances of alleged interference, it is only the

[29] Dembinski, 244. The coercive element certainly contributes to the sensitivity of the receiving State in that regard. See above, at n 27 and National Union of Students in House of Commons Report, 54, para 13.

[30] ZaöRV, 'Berichte und Urkunden' (1970), 665, 666.

[31] Salmon (1996), 134.

consideration of the wider context which allows for an appropriate assessment of the relevant diplomatic behaviour in the receiving State.

2. THE EVALUATION OF DIPLOMATIC THREATS AND INTIMIDATION

Not every situation of diplomatic intimidation allows for an evaluation of the grounds on which the relevant conduct had been based. If the consequences to which the threat refers were themselves prohibited under international law, this stage of the analysis will not even be reached. The clearest example for that is provided by cases in which diplomatic agents resorted to threats with an unlawful use of force.[32] In modern diplomatic relations, instances of this kind are, thankfully, rare. But they have happened in the past: In August 1914, for instance, the German Minister to Belgium presented a note to the Belgian Foreign Minister, announcing the German intention to enter Belgian territory to fend off an anticipated French attack and stating that, if there should be any opposition by Belgium, Germany would 'to her regret' have to consider Belgium an enemy power.[33]

In modern international law, a threat of military force against a State which had not engaged in an armed attack faces the prohibition of Article 2(4) of the UN Charter. In the absence of circumstances justifying the use of force, such conduct constitutes a threat with means which the international community does not consider to be within the discretion of the sending State,[34] and it leaves no room for the application of the various tests which the principle of proportionality envisages.

There are, on the other hand, situations in which legitimate and strong interests on the side of the sending State do exist. International law may itself have placed the means to which the diplomatic threat refers at the disposal of the sending State—a situation which is particularly clear in instances in which a threat represents little more than an attempt by the sending State to defend its sovereignty or its own resources.

If a State, for instance, warns that it would resort to military action in self-defence if it were to be the target of an armed attack, the diplomat

[32] A threat with a declaration of war was historically one of the principal meanings of the term 'ultimatum' in the realm of diplomatic relations See OED, 'ultimatum (n)' (no 1).

[33] Note by Below-Saleske (2 August 1914).

[34] The position of Art 2 (4) of the UN Charter is reinforced by VCLT art 52 which denies legal value to concessions made because of a threat or use of force. See also various resolutions of General Assembly and Security Council on the inadmissibility of the acquisition of territory through force: GA Res 2936 (XXVII), preamble, 6th operative para; GA Res 34/30 (1979), preamble, 3rd operative para; SC Res 242, preamble, 2nd operative para. See also the Friendly Relations Declaration which seeks to outlaw threats against 'political, economic and cultural elements' of a State (3rd principle, para 1).

advancing the threat would merely refer to an option available under Article 51 of the UN Charter (and corresponding customary law).

A more frequent scenario is posed by situations in which sending States warn of the discontinuation of financial aid, if the purpose of such assistance has been put in danger. Cases of this kind occur if receiving States show themselves unwilling to take the necessary steps in the fight against corruption and allow financial support to disappear into channels which were not the intended recipients of the aid (and might even be opposed to the sending State as such).

But a diversion of the purpose of financial aid has also come into existence if the very objective which gave rise to its grant has undergone a fundamental change. If, for instance, the sending State is prepared to render aid for the holding of free elections, then the purpose of the support is no longer guaranteed if the main opposition parties decide to boycott the event—a situation which formed the framework of the 1998 Curran incident, to which reference has been made above.[35]

In these cases, manifest interests of the sending State exist; and a diplomatic agent who resorts to threats in order to defend their existence, can invoke the task of the protection of interests (Article 3(1)(b)) as a ground for his actions.

In other instances, it is the second alternative of that provision—the protection of interests of nationals—which will be at the root of intimidation or threats by diplomatic agents.

The 1999 incident involving the US Ambassador to Thailand, Richard Hecklinger, may be recalled in this context.[36] Hecklinger faced accusations of interference after he lobbied for speedy progress in the construction of the Bor Nok power plant. The perceived threat consisted in the fact that Hecklinger had allegedly warned that delays in the construction process could endanger future investments by the United States.[37] In that instance, the circumstances of the case left no doubt that the interests of private parties in the United States were involved, and had been put at risk through the delays: The American company Edison Mission Energy had partially funded the project,[38] and it is thus clear that Article 3(1)(b) formed the basis for diplomatic conduct in this case as well.[39]

Conduct which is perceived as threatening or intimidating can also have its foundations in the representation of the sending State's policies (Article 3(1)(a))—a function which will regularly be involved if a diplomatic agent advances an official warning of the adoption of military

[35] See above, at nn 6–9.

[36] On the case, see ch 3, at n 44, and A.138.

[37] *Greenpeace*, 'Edison Out', 2002.

[38] H Mehta, 'Anti-foreign Feeling Resurging' *Business Times* (Singapore, 1 December 1999).

[39] See also the 1804 incident of the US Ambassador to Spain, Charles Pinckney; Satow (1917), 371.

or other sanctions against the receiving State. But even the maintenance of friendly relations (Article 3(1)(e)) may form the basis for conduct perceived as threatening. This may seem a counterintuitive suggestion. But cases have come into existence where sending States have, in this context, referred to this particular function. Maxwell Taylor, for instance, the US Ambassador to Vietnam in 1964, had to face accusations of interference after he had stated that US aid to that country was dependent on the stability of its government and 'orderly political evolution'.[40] The United States however denied that 'improper' conduct had taken place, and emphasised that 'all' of Taylor's 'activities were designed to serve the best interests of both Vietnam and the United States'.[41]

The maintenance of friendly relations as a ground for diplomatic conduct of this kind gains even greater clarity in instances in which the sending State cannot claim to have any influence, or has only partial influence, on the negative consequences which the diplomatic agent outlines to the receiving State.

An incident in the year 2000 involving the US Ambassador to Indonesia, Robert Gelbard, illustrates the situation. In September of that year, Gelbard criticised the perceived failure of the Indonesian government to disband militias in West Timor and to prosecute the killers of three UN refugee workers.[42] Gelbard also stated that Indonesia risked 'losing moral support if this issue [were] not addressed'.[43]

These statements certainly touched upon sensitivities in the receiving State, and it was reported that even the expulsion of the Ambassador had been discussed.[44] But this case was not an incident which involved a warning with consequences dependent on the discretion of the sending State. In the light of growing international sensitivity towards the commission of international crimes, the negative results of Indonesian inaction would have occurred in the ordinary course of events even without contributory activity by the United States.[45] As such, a note of caution sounded by a State which normally maintains friendly relations with the receiving State can certainly be helpful to the latter and is therefore

[40] 'Embassy Denial of Interference' *The Times* (London, 24 December 1964). Paraphrasing by source.

[41] ibid.

[42] 'UN Security Council Delegation' *Agence France Presse* (Paris, 25 September 2000).

[43] J Morrison, 'Ivry Discovers America' *Washington Times* (Washington DC, 27 September 2000).

[44] Simon (2000).

[45] *cf* Stowell, who stated that a 'foreign representative must be allowed to communicate … the consequences which he believes will result from the adoption of the proposed measure', Stowell, 325. On the international repercussions which the killing of the three aid workers had, see n 42.

compatible with the spirit of the diplomatic function of the promotion of friendly relations.

In other situations again, the right to self-determination may offer grounds for threatening action. When Curran in the above mentioned case[46] threatened the withdrawal of financial aid for forthcoming elections if they were not democratic and transparent, he could have relied not only on the protection of interests (including economic interests), but also on the need to assist the Mozambican people in the realisation of their right to self-determination. Whether a particular threat which purports to promote this right will be able to outweigh the competing interests of the sending State is a different question, and one which requires assessment under the established tests of proportionality.[47]

In some situations, international law not only provides grounds for conduct perceived as threatening, but establishes a positive duty on States to adopt this course of action. The concept of countermeasures illustrates this point. The use of countermeasures is an option at the disposal of injured States, if certain requirements are met.[48] The ILC's Draft Articles on State Responsibility do however clarify that an injured State must, before it resorts to countermeasures, '[n]otify the responsible State of any decision' to take them and 'offer to negotiate with that State'.[49] The temporal relationship between the notification and the adoption of the relevant measure is not immediately clear from a literal reading of that article, but the ILC appears to interpret the relevant rule as meaning that even the *intention* to take countermeasures requires notification,[50] and the Commission clarified in its commentary that, since countermeasures can have 'serious consequences for the target State', the latter 'should have the opportunity to reconsider its position'.[51] A receiving State faced with a diplomatic warning of that kind is likely to understand this as a threat with consequences which are dependent on a decision by the sending State; and yet such action corresponds to a mandate under international law, and establishes one of the circumstances required for the lawful exercise of this option.

However, even threats and intimidation based on interests recognised under international law have to comply with the conditions of proportionality which have been outlined above.[52] Given the powerful nature of this kind of conduct, the 'least restrictive means' test retains particular

[46] See above, at n 8.
[47] See on this point below, at nn 52 ff.
[48] See ch 4, at n 97, 98.
[49] Draft Articles on State Responsibility (2001), 135, art 52(1)(b).
[50] Draft Articles on State Responsibility (2001), 135, art 52, commentary, para 1.
[51] ibid, 136, para 5.
[52] See ch 4, s 2.2.

significance in that context. Its importance is underlined by the fact that even sending States are aware of the gravity of the relevant behaviour. The 1982 case of the US Ambassador to El Salvador, Deane Hinton, may be recalled at this stage. In remarks to the American Chamber of Commerce, Hinton had warned that US aid to El Salvador was in danger unless 'substantial progress' had been made on the human rights situation in the receiving State.[53]

Hinton's statements triggered criticism in El Salvador.[54] He did however receive a measure of support from the White House which affirmed the general principle of 'quiet diplomacy', which the United States pursued, but added that 'from time to time we will speak out'.[55]

It is a statement which highlights one of the main characteristics of threatening conduct: The message, even when it is expressed in a private setting, is loud and unambiguous. In comparison to 'ordinary' lobbying activities, criticism and even critical remarks in front of a public audience, it can easily be considered the more intrusive measure—it leaves little discretion on the side of the receiving State and often involves significant loss of face. The negative consequences of threats and intimidation tend to be direct, and the danger they conjure up, is often real: There is little point in warning of certain consequences, if there is not a good probability that they will materialise.

On the other hand, the detailed scrutiny which the test of the 'least restrictive means' necessitates, may at times cast doubt on the evaluation supported by receiving States in this context.

Allegations of intimidating conduct were, for instance, raised against diplomatic agents in Slovakia who in 2010 attended the disciplinary hearing of Jozef Kandera, a Justice of the Supreme Court. The proceedings against Kandera were one of several cases which Štefan Harabin, President of the Slovakian Supreme Court, had initiated,[56] and which gained notoriety as some of the judges who had to submit themselves to them—including Kandera—counted among Harabin's critics.[57] Kandera's hearing was attended by the British Ambassador and diplomatic representatives from Austria, Canada, Norway and the United States.[58]

[53] 'U.S. Backs Off' *Facts on File* (New York, 19 November 1982). See also M Simons, 'Salvador Aid' *New York Times* (New York, 22 November 1982).

[54] See A.64.

[55] 'U.S. Backs Off', n 53. In the 1998 Curran case, it was a faction in the receiving State which referred to less intrusive alternatives: The Secretary-General of FRELIMO mentioned 'advice or criticism' which the US could have offered, 'US Ambassador Accused of Meddling', n 7.

[56] For other cases, see K Javorčíková and M Gavalec, '13 Disciplinary Actions' *Za Otvorenú Justíciu* (Bratislava, 4 May 2010).

[57] *cf* 'Diplomats Observe Disciplinary Case' *Slovak Spectator* (Bratislava, 22 March 2010).

[58] Ibid.

In that instance, it was Harabin himself who accused diplomatic agents of attempted intimidation of the members of the disciplinary commission.[59]

The very question whether observation could be understood as intimidation is open to doubt—some of the diplomats in this case certainly denied that assessment.[60] But even if the diplomatic conduct were seen as carrying a threat,[61] its assessment as unlawful would also mean that it failed the requirements of proportionality.

That raises questions where the 'least restrictive means' test is concerned. If diplomatic agents have already limited themselves to silent observation, it may in fact be difficult to identify methods which would have had a lesser impact, but would have been of equal or greater efficiency. Private talks with government officials may have been available, but it is not apparent that they would have sufficiently addressed concerns about the judiciary in the receiving State. Diplomatic presence at the hearings at least conveyed a clear message, which appears to have reached its intended recipients.

At the same time, the efficiency of diplomatic threats and warnings will regularly depend on situational factors, including the position of influence which the sending State enjoys, the status of relations between sending and receiving State, and so forth.[62] Threats can on occasion guide a receiving State in the intended direction, but they will often, especially if uttered in a public setting, force a decision from its government; and as many administrations may feel that they cannot be seen to give in to pressure, they may ultimately yield counter-productive results.

Cost-benefit analysis plays arguably a greater role where threats and intimidation are concerned than in many other aspects of diplomatic conduct which attract allegations of interference. One of the reasons for that is to be seen in the fact that the respective interests on whose basis the comparison is carried out are often well defined where this kind of conduct emerges.

If, for instance, a sending State threatens the discontinuation of economic aid, there will be a strong presumption that its interests, from a legal perspective, carry greater weight than those of the receiving State. If the possibility of financial support has not assumed the shape of a contractual obligation, the allocation of a State's own resources will, in

59 *BBC Monitoring Europe—Political*, 'Outgoing UK Envoy' (26 December 2010).

60 ibid.

61 That is how one observer, writing in the Slovak Spectator, understood it: 'The presence of diplomats is a serious warning', 'The Diplomats' Day in Court', *Slovak Spectator* (Bratislava, 22 March 2010).

62 Doubts were cast even on the efficiency of the remarks made in the Deane Hinton case, Simons, n 53.

principle, fall within its own discretion: It is no less than an emanation of its sovereign rights.[63]

That consideration certainly applies when the warning of discontinuation is based on the fact that the receiving State has put the purpose of the aid in danger or if the objective of financial aid has disappeared or has undergone a fundamental change.[64] The need to protect the economic interests of that State in situations of this kind is undeniable. The withdrawal of aid may still have a considerable effect on the affairs of the receiving State, but it is outweighed by the right of the sending State to protect its resources.

By the same token, a different assessment must be given to situations in which the receiving State had been able to form a legitimate expectation that financial aid would be advanced if certain conditions were met, and has met the conditions. If the sending State then threatens withdrawal of aid, but bases this on extraneous considerations, the weighing of interests may yield a different result. There is still a negative impact on interests of the receiving State, but the benefits for the sending State show a much weaker link to the protection of the original objectives, and thus diminish the weight of its own interests considerably.

An illustration was provided by the so-called 'Article 98 agreements' which the United States had concluded with a number of States from 2002: Agreements which seek to ensure that members of US forces will not be surrendered by the relevant State to the International Criminal Court.[65] Refusal to sign agreements of this kind could result in the cut-off of economic assistance, including military aid.[66] Diplomatic agents were

[63] See for instance GA Res 1515 (XV) (1960), para 5; GA Res 1803 (XVII) (1962), preamble, 4th operative para; Charter of Economic Rights and Duties of States, ch II, art 2 (1); Declaration on the Establishment of a New International Economic Order, para 4(e). The relevant discretion enjoyed by States in that regard, has in some of the resolutions been considered an 'inalienable right' of that State. See GA Res 1803 (XVII), preamble, 4th operative para; Declaration on the Establishment of a New International Economic Order, para 4(e).

[64] See above, at n 35.

[65] These agreements take their name from ICCSt art 98(2), which imposes a bar on requests for surrender of a person to the court, if such request would require the relevant State to act 'inconsistently with its obligations under international agreements pursuant to which the consent of a sending State is required to surrender a person of that State to the Court'.

[66] The Coalition for the International Criminal Court noted that, in the fiscal year of 2005, 24 out of 56 State Parties to the ICC (International Criminal Court) who refused to sign a bilateral agreement, had lost US aid. Coalition for the International Criminal Court, 'Status of US Bilateral Immunity Agremeents (BIAs)'. For a more recent status of Art 98 agreements, see AMICC, 'Countries Concluding Bilateral Immunities Agreements'. At the time of writing, such Art 98(2) agreements were still in force, but it was no longer US policy to pursue agreements of this kind (Andersen, 314), and US Congress had repealed s 2007 of the American Servicemembers' Protection Act. S 2007 had contained a general prohibition on military assistance to ICC Member States (with certain exceptions, including Presidential waiver in cases in which the recipient State had entered into a bilateral agreement with the USA). On the details, see Barbour and Weed, 26.

certainly involved in efforts to obtain agreement by States to such initiatives. In 2003, for instance, it was reported that the US Ambassador to the Bahamas, Richard Blankenship, had threatened the discontinuation of US funding, including support for the lighting and paving of an airport runway, if the receiving State reacted 'unfavourably' in that matter.[67]

In situations of this kind, the disruption on the side of the receiving State is undisputable,[68] and the fact that the discontinuation was based on reasons extraneous to the grant in its original form allows for an assessment which differs from instances in which the purpose of the grant has been endangered. In the former scenario, there is good reason to conclude that, in a weighing of cost and benefits, the advantages for the interests of the sending State carry lesser weight than the damage which the action causes in the receiving State.

Threats and intimidation constitute an area in which the instinctive reaction of receiving States, regardless of their political systems, is likely to be a clear rejection of such conduct as unlawful interference—so powerful is the nature of the diplomatic measure, and so great is the loss of face which it is likely to incur. But the fact remains that in these situations, too, legitimate interests can exist on the side of the sending State and that international law at times even calls for the adoption of warnings, which may regularly be perceived by the receiving State as carrying a threatening character. The fact, too, bears observation that threats, however serious their impact, are regularly less intrusive than their realisation. In situations in which the law places the causation of damaging consequences into the hands of a sending State, there is little room to argue that warning of such results lay outside the discretion of the diplomatic agent.

[67] Kielsgard, 30; 'Gambia; As US Ultimatum Over Immunity Pact Expires' *The Independent* (London, 4 July 2003); 'US Penalises States' *Irish Times* (Dublin, 2 July 2003). See also the 2005 case of the US Ambassador in Kenya, 'Kenya: How Nation Rejected America's ICC Plot' *The Nation* (Kenya, 7 March 2011).

[68] See, for instance, for the case of Jordan, Harkavy, 943.

11

Diplomatic Asylum

ON 19 JUNE 2012, the Ecuadorian embassy to London welcomed an unusual guest: The activist Julian Assange sought and was granted asylum on mission premises.[1]

Assange had risen to notoriety as the founder of WikiLeaks, the website which had published thousands of classified US diplomatic cables[2] and documents relating to the armed conflicts in Iraq and Afghanistan.[3] But he was also wanted for questioning by the authorities in Sweden after two women accused him of sexual assault when he had visited the country.[4]

Assange himself claimed that he had been secretly indicted in the United States and was at risk of eventually being extradited to that State.[5]

The event soon bore all the hallmarks of a major international incident. The British Foreign Office resorted to strong language, stating that Britain was allowed 'to take actions in order to arrest Mr Assange in the current premises of the Embassy'.[6] Ecuador, on the other hand, received support from the Organization of American States[7] as well as from the Union of South American Nations, which referred to the 'sovereign right of States to grant asylum'.[8]

It is its potential for interference in the internal affairs of the receiving State which has given diplomatic asylum particular significance in the field of diplomatic relations—to that degree that it provided the ICJ with one of very few opportunities to discuss interference by diplomatic missions (in the *Asylum Case* of 1950).[9] The background to this case was formed by the grant of refuge by the Colombian embassy in Lima to the Peruvian

[1] S Hui and G Solano, 'Ecuador says WikiLeaks Founder …' *Associated Press Online* (New York, 19 June 2012).

[2] 'WikiLeaks says Published … ' *Agence France Presse* (Paris, 2 September 2011).

[3] *CNN*, 'Ecuador says WikiLeaks Founder … ', 19 June 2012.

[4] Hui and Solano, n 1; *CNN*, n 3.

[5] J Lawless, 'UK: Assange is Beyond …' *Associated Press Online* (New York, 20 June 2012).

[6] R Alleyne, 'WikiLeaks' *Daily Telegraph* (London, 17 August 2012). In this regard, Britain made reference to domestic law (the Diplomatic and Consular Premises Act 1987).

[7] *India Blooms*, 'Julian Assange', (Kolkata, 25 August 2012).

[8] UNASUR, *Statement of Guayaquil* (2012).

[9] See also Introduction, at n 56; ch 1, at nn 32–37.

politician Víctor Raúl Haya de la Torre in January 1949.[10] While the court was primarily concerned with specific asylum rules recognised in Latin America,[11] it also had the opportunity to refer to the grant of diplomatic asylum in general and held it to be 'an intervention in matters which are exclusively within the competence of that State'.[12]

The grant of diplomatic asylum certainly occupies a special position among the fields of interference. Unlike, for instance, lobbying activities, its impact is direct—especially if the receiving State intended to exercise jurisdiction over the relevant person who has now been withdrawn from its reach. The diplomatic measure will usually generate strong publicity and force a reaction by the receiving State. But it is not a new phenomenon in diplomatic history: Some commentators trace its roots to the beginnings of permanent diplomacy more than 500 years ago.[13] Among those to whom asylum was granted are illustrious names—in 1961, the former Cuban President Manuel Urrutia sought asylum in the Venezuelan embassy (in the disguise of a milkman),[14] and in 1992, the former Peruvian President García found refuge in a building of the Colombian embassy in that country.[15] In 1956, one of the most celebrated cases of diplomatic asylum occurred when the US embassy in Budapest granted asylum to the Hungarian Cardinal Mindszenty. The Cardinal was to stay in the embassy for nearly 15 years.[16]

Given the prominence of diplomatic asylum in international affairs, it cannot surprise that an attempt was made in the Sixth Committee to extend the work of the ILC on diplomatic relations to this concept.[17] But the suggestion was not successful[18]—most Committee members found

[10] The terms 'refuge' and 'refugee' in the context of this chapter are employed with reference to persons seeking diplomatic asylum. They are thus used without prejudice to the question whether that person meets the relevant definitions which exist under refugee law. See Refugee Convention art 1; UNHCR Handbook 1992.

[11] See below, s 2.1.

[12] *Asylum Case* 275.

[13] Riveles, 144. See also UN Asylum Report (Pt 2), para 3 and Den Heijer, 401–05.

[14] Cuzán, 185.

[15] 'Peruvian President Sets October Election' *Washington Post* (Washington DC, 2 June 1992); *NPR*, 'Show: All Things Considered', 1 June 1992.

[16] D Balz, 'A Lengthy Stay' *Washington Post* (Washington DC, 13 June 1989); Green, 144 and see A Last, 'Fifteen Years Holed Up' *BBC Online* (London, 6 September 2012).

[17] GA Sixth Committee, 315th Meeting, 63–64, paras 26–28 [Henao y Henao]. In his introduction of the amendment on behalf of Colombia, Henao y Henao expressed the view that the topic of 'asylum' was 'manifestly connected with diplomatic immunities' (para 26) and made in that context reference to the *Asylum Case* (para 27). In later contributions, he clarified the fact that the focus of the amendment was indeed on diplomatic asylum proper (see 65, para 45, and 316th Meeting, 72, para 61).

[18] GA Sixth Committee, 316th Meeting, 73.

that this was a separate topic[19] which should more appropriately be considered under the 'general question of asylum'.[20]

For a topic they were not supposed to discuss, the ILC spent a surprising amount of time on it,[21] with the British member Fitzmaurice going so far as to suggest the inclusion of an article to prohibit the granting of shelter on mission premises to persons charged with offences under local law.[22] It was not a successful initiative, but it is clear that the members of the Commission were aware that omitting such an important issue would create a gap in their work.[23] A little defiant mention of asylum made its way into the commentary to the draft articles, but it did not contain significant elaboration on its concept or its implications for diplomatic interference.[24]

The United Nations revisited the topic of diplomatic asylum in 1974, when the General Assembly invited Member States to submit their opinions on the issue and requested the Secretary-General to prepare a report before its thirtieth session.[25] The report was published in 1975.[26] Covering two parts and running into nearly 100,000 words, it provided a detailed reflection on the development and the concept of diplomatic asylum. But it was as far as the United Nations was ever able to go in an effort to offer elaboration on the subject.[27] To this date, neither a universal convention on diplomatic asylum, nor even a set of draft articles on this matter have come into existence. The views which members of the United Nations expressed in the 1970s certainly attested to a significant degree of divergence of opinion in this area; and some authors suspect that States in general felt that the time had not been 'ripe' for codification.[28]

Diplomatic asylum thus remains an ill-defined concept whose boundaries are anything but certain. Its legal assessment and its potential evaluation as a form of interference is left to customary international law, whose determination is, in this context, fraught with doubt.

[19] GA Sixth Committee, 315th Meeting, 64, para 29 [Chairman], para 31 [Maurtua], para 33 [El-Tanamli], 65, para 36 [Guerreiro], para 37 [Mendez], para 38 [Pathak], GA Sixth Committee, 316th Meeting, 68, para 15 [Molino], 69, para 20 [Suarez], 71, para 44 [Tarazi], 72, para 64 [Mendez].

[20] YILC 1957/I, 2, para 7 (paraphrasing by Sandström).

[21] YILC 1957/I, 54–58 and 220–21.

[22] Fitzmaurice's article envisaged certain exceptions: In cases in which shelter was necessary to 'save life or prevent grave physical injury in the face of an immediate threat or emergency,' or where such shelter was recognised 'by any established local usage' and where the offences were political in nature. Ibid, 54, para 33 [Fitzmaurice], and see also the alternative text ibid. See also Värk (2012), 251.

[23] See YILC 1957/I, 55, paras 45 [Fitzmaurice], 50 [Tunkin] and 56, paras 59 [Ago], 62 [Pal].

[24] See below, at n 29.

[25] GA Res 3321 (XXIX) (1974), paras 1 and 2.

[26] UN Asylum Report (Pt 1) and UN Asylum Report (Pt 2).

[27] *cf* GA Res 3497 (XXX) (1975).

[28] Jeffery, 16.

1. RESTRICTIONS ON DIPLOMATIC ASYLUM UNDER INTERNATIONAL LAW

While the VCDR does not directly address the matter, the grant of diplomatic asylum nonetheless constitutes a case in which diplomatic conduct is subject to restrictions which derive not only from the rule against interference. Article 41(3) VCDR establishes a prohibition against the use of mission premises 'in any manner incompatible with the functions of the mission as laid down in the present Convention or by other rules of general international law or by any special agreements in force between the sending and the receiving State'. It was this article which provided the ILC with an opportunity to mention asylum: In its commentary, the Commission noted that 'among the agreements referred to in paragraph 3 there are certain treaties governing the right to grant asylum in mission premises'.[29] Treaties of this kind have come into existence on a regional level—most prominently, in the Latin American region.[30]

But the commentary itself does not provide clarification on the stance of general international law where the granting of diplomatic asylum is concerned. The very question whether such an act would be encompassed by the 'functions of the mission' has proved a challenging issue.

If it were to be considered a function which exists in addition to those named in Article 3, its establishment would need to fulfil all the requirements of a rule of general customary law, including consistency and generality of State practice as well as the existence of *opinio iuris*.[31] Such evidence is difficult to adduce; opinions on this matter have traditionally shown a wide degree of variation.

The US State Department emphasised as early as 1930 that the 'affording of asylum is not within the purposes of a diplomatic mission'.[32] ILC Member Scelle on the other hand referred during the 1957 round of the Commission's debates to the granting of asylum as 'an essential, traditional, and, in his opinion, praiseworthy, function of missions'.[33] Where State practice is concerned, the fact remains that several States have consistently voiced opposition to the institution of diplomatic asylum.[34]

It is this prevailing disagreement that has led some authors to conclude that it is simply not possible to derive a positive assessment from the rules

[29] YILC 1958/II, art 40, commentary, para 4.

[30] See below, at nn 45–53.

[31] See Introduction, at nn 69–70.

[32] State Department Instructions (1930).

[33] YILC 1957/I, 221, para 90 [Scelle]. Scelle did not differentiate between the general practice of granting asylum and the practice prevailing in Latin America.

[34] On the views of the Soviet Union in that regard, see Riveles, 157. For other States, see also Jeffery, 16 and fn 49.

of international law on that issue. Jeffery speaks of a 'grey area' of international law and states that there is neither a 'recognized right' of asylum, nor an 'express prohibition against it'.[35]

That however, is an undue simplification, based on the premise that the absence of precise rules suggests the existence of a vacuum. What it fails to take into account is that there might be more general norms and principles which may have an impact on the granting of asylum, without having been specifically designed to address the relevant situation. Reference to the most pertinent of these principles was made in the *Asylum Case*,[36] when the ICJ highlighted the 'territorial sovereignty' of the receiving State, from which the grant of diplomatic asylum would derogate. Both Article 41(1) and 41(3) appear in this context as norms which serve this principle and uphold the jurisdiction of the receiving State as one of the emanations of its rights as a sovereign member of the international community. That must be the default position: The failure of the international community to reach universal agreement on the evaluation of diplomatic asylum[37] rather suggests that it would be difficult to speak of a norm of general customary law accepting an unqualified right to resort to this kind of conduct.

The question whether a grant of asylum under more particular circumstances (for instance, when humanitarian concerns are at issue) is embraced by customary law, is a different one. But it is also possible that international law recognises norms which, while not specifically constructed to deal with the issue of asylum, have an impact on situations in which refuge has been provided on diplomatic premises. Both aspects deserve consideration in their own right.[38] However, the basic premise which emerges from the considerations at this stage, is the fact that the receiving State's right to territorial jurisdiction retains its place in general international law, and that diplomatic asylum constitutes prima facie a breach of that right.

2. DIPLOMATIC ASYLUM AND THE EXISTENCE OF PERMISSIVE NORMS UNDER INTERNATIONAL LAW

The protection which territorial jurisdiction enjoys under general customary law does, of course, not prevent individual States from choosing a more restrictive concept of jurisdiction in their mutual relations. Evidence

[35] Jeffery, 28.
[36] See above, 2.2 and 3.
[37] See above, at n 28 and at nn 32–33.
[38] See below, ss 2.2 and 3.

for a decision of this kind can derive from particular treaties, but also from customary law if, in specific situations, it accords diplomatic asylum treatment which allows for a derogation from the sovereignty of the receiving State.

Neither of these options leads to a general exception to the jurisdiction of the territorial State. They rather constitute concepts which reduce the remit of the sovereign rights of the receiving State only if specific parameters apply. Two situations require closer analysis: The practice on asylum as adopted in Latin America and the possibility of the existence of a limited right to diplomatic asylum under customary law.

2.1. The Prevailing Practice in Latin America

The practice of Latin American States has traditionally allocated to diplomatic asylum a more significant position than that existing in other regions of the world. However, even in this area, the existence of a rule of customary law allowing for shelter on mission premises, has been doubted:[39] Jeffery for instance expressed the view that *opinio iuris* as a required element of customary law is missing, and bases this view on the ICJ judgment in the *Asylum Case*.[40]

That, however, appears to be a misreading of the court's opinion. The main concern of the ICJ was not the existence of the principle of diplomatic asylum in local customary law, but the much narrower question whether the State granting asylum can, unilaterally, determine the nature of the offence of which the person seeking asylum is accused.[41]

And the nature of the offence matters: It does not appear that Latin American practice allows for the granting of asylum in cases where the refugee seeks to escape territorial jurisdiction for 'common' (as opposed to political) offences.[42] If however the alleged offence is political in nature, the prevailing evidence suggests that Latin American States do accept a right to grant asylum on embassy premises. The basis for this is not only constituted by numerous examples of State practice (in the 1974 debates of the Sixth Committee, Colombia pointed out that three of her presidents owed their lives to the grant of diplomatic asylum)[43] and corroborated by

[39] *cf* Sinha, 238.

[40] Jeffery, 14.

[41] See *Asylum Case*, 273.

[42] See below, n 49 and corresponding text.

[43] GA Sixth Committee, 1505th Meeting, 243, para 20 [Escobar]. To name but a few examples from past State practice: See the 1961 case of Manuel Urrutia, above, at n 14; the 1974 case of Rodolfo Puiggros, a university rector and member of the Peronist Left, granted asylum in the Mexican Embassy in Argentina, J Kandell, 'Argentines Given Embassy Refuge' *New York Times* (New York, 25 September 1974); the 1981 case of Hugo Cespedes, former Defence

the views of expert commentators on this subject;[44] it also derives support from the text of subsequent treaties which codified the relevant norm of customary law.

While these treaties took the general principle of asylum in Latin America as their starting point, they were also able to address questions on which customary law had not been able to provide a satisfactory degree of clarity (including the very question of the determination of the nature of the offence).[45] Today, they constitute the most sophisticated instruments on diplomatic asylum which have yet emerged with applicability to a multitude of members of the international community.

Treaties of this kind go back to the nineteenth century—the 1889 Montevideo Treaty on International Penal Law already addressed the right to grant asylum on premises of the diplomatic mission.[46] The following 50 years saw the conclusion of three treaties which gained particular importance for the regulation of diplomatic asylum in the Latin American region: The Havana Convention on Asylum of 1928; the Montevideo Convention on Political Asylum of 1933 and the Montevideo Treaty on Political Asylum and Refuge of 1939.

In the wake of the *Asylum Case*, another initiative for the codification of diplomatic asylum was launched,[47] which resulted in the signing, in March 1954, of the Convention on Diplomatic Asylum (the 'Caracas Convention'), to which 14 American States have become party.

Recurring themes in these conventions are the limitation of the right to asylum to persons charged with political offences,[48] the express exclusion

Minister of Bolivia, granted asylum in the Brazilian embassy in Bolivia, J Enders, 'Official Accused Of Drug Trafficking' *Associated Press* (New York, 30 March 1981); the 1990 case of Gomez Perez, a former Panamanian legislator, granted asylum in the Cuban embassy in Panama, 'Former Noriega Associates' *United Press International* (11 May 1991); and the 2005 case of Lucio Gutierrez, former president of Ecuador, granted asylum in the Brazilian embassy in Quito, *BBC Monitoring Latin America—Political*, 'Ecuador's Gutierrez' (23 April 2005).

[44] *cf* UN Asylum Report (Pt 2), paras 15 and 35. See also the contributions by various members of the ILC who, arguably with the Latin American context in mind, emphasised that a right to grant asylum was not necessarily dependent on the existence of a treaty to that effect. YILC 1957/I, 220, para 82 [François], 221, para 83 [Fitzmaurice], 221, para 87 [García Amador], 221, para 93 [Hsu].

[45] *Asylum Case*, 277; see for the regulation in contemporary law, Caracas Convention art IV.

[46] Montevideo Treaty on International Penal Law art 17.

[47] UN Asylum Report (Pt 2), paras 74–79.

[48] See on this Montevideo Treaty on International Penal Law art 17; Art 2 Havana Convention on Asylum art 2; Montevideo Convention on Political Asylum arts 2 and 3. The Montevideo Treaty on Political Asylum and Refuge and the Caracas Convention on Diplomatic Asylum contained somewhat more liberal rules and allowed asylum for 'persons pursued for political reasons or offenses, or under circumstances involving concurrent political offenses, which do not legally permit of extradition' (Montevideo Treaty on Political Asylum and Refuge art 2) and for 'persons being sought for political reasons or for political offenses' (Caracas Convention art 1) as well.

from the remit of asylum of persons accused of 'common offences',[49] the duty to notify the territorial State of the grant of asylum[50] and the right to require safe exit for the refugee.[51] Some of the conventions recognise that a danger of interference may also be created by allowing the asylum seeker to carry out certain acts on mission premises[52]—and therefore contain rules limiting conduct which the refugee is allowed to adopt.[53]

However, once the conditions for diplomatic asylum under these conventions are fulfilled, the territorial State, if it is party to them, is obliged to recognise it and is bound by the commitments which the treaties impose. In that regard, State parties have agreed to a deviation from general customary law: They recognise an exception to the principle of territorial jurisdiction under circumstances which they themselves specified.

2.2. A Right to Grant Diplomatic Asylum in Certain Circumstances Under General Customary Law?

From time to time, the claim has been raised that there are other specific forms of diplomatic asylum which may have attained the status of customary law. Reference is occasionally made to the granting of asylum in cases in which 'humanitarian concerns' for the refugee exist and in which the affording of shelter might be limited to the period in which these concerns are in existence.[54]

A prime example for scenarios of this kind are cases of 'mob violence'—situations in which the refugee finds himself pursued by parts of the

[49] Havana Convention on Political Asylum art 1; Montevideo Convention on Political Asylum art 1; Caracas Convention art 3 and *cf* Montevideo Treaty on Political Asylum and Refuge arts 2 and 3. The Montevideo Treaty on International Penal Law states that refugees charged with 'non-political' offences shall be surrendered to the local authorities (art 17).

[50] Montevideo Treaty on International Penal Law art 17; Havana Convention on Political Asylum art 2; Montevideo Treaty on Political Asylum and Refuge art 4; Caracas Convention art 8. The Montevideo Convention on Political Asylum does not contain a provision on notification. However, that treaty cannot be considered in isolation: Its declared purpose was to provide a definition of 'the terms of the one signed at Havana' (Montevideo Convention on Political Asylum, preamble, operative para 1), and it therefore did not seek to deviate from art 2 of that convention.

[51] Montevideo Treaty on International Penal Law art 17; Havana Convention on Political Asylum art 2; Montevideo Treaty on Political Asylum and Refuge art 6; Caracas Convention arts 5 and 11–13. The Montevideo Convention on Political Asylum does not contain an express reference to this right, but the considerations outlined above, in n 50, are applicable here as well.

[52] See on this issue, the Zelaya case, below, at n 153.

[53] Havana Convention on Political Asylum art 2; Montevideo Treaty on Political Asylum and Refuge art 5; Caracas Convention art 18.

[54] *cf* for instance Riveles, 158 (with reference to persons 'under threat of life and limb'), Fruchterman, 170 (with reference to 'temporary refuge' in cases in which the lives of persons are endangered 'because of unlawful action such as mob violence'). See also Denza, 142.

population before he reaches the haven of the embassy.[55] But even in these limited situations, it is difficult to adduce evidence for a customary right to grant asylum. On the objective side, the practice of asylum in these circumstances is hardly generally and consistently applied—there are of course, numerous cases of mob violence which did not induce diplomatic missions to act.

Doubts also attach to the existence of *opinio iuris* relating to the acceptance of such a right. Some States appear to allow for this exception where their own diplomatic missions are concerned: The United States, for one, while generally opposed to a right to asylum, has in the past expressed a more generous attitude towards 'uninvited fugitives whose lives are in imminent danger from mob violence', as long as the danger was still ongoing.[56]

General Assembly Resolution 3321, which invited members of the United Nations to express their views on diplomatic asylum,[57] had also mentioned the 'humanitarian' aspects of that matter,[58] and several States referred to this facet of asylum in their replies.[59] But not all of them were happy to base a customary right to grant asylum on humanitarian concerns.

Czechoslovakia, for instance, pointed out that she was 'fully aware of the humanitarian aspects of the institution of asylum', but still asserted her view that, in the absence of special agreements, diplomatic asylum was not recognised in international law.[60]

Acceptance of a customary right to grant asylum on humanitarian considerations would thus be fraught with difficulties—beginning with the very question whether 'humanitarian concerns' are capable of an interpretation which yields a sufficient degree of precision to allow the assumption of a rule with normative character. The replies to the General Assembly Resolution certainly suggest that States harboured widely varying ideas of what the 'humanitarian aspects' of asylum should encompass.[61]

The fact bears observing that even within the Latin American institution of diplomatic asylum, reasons of humanity are, by themselves, not sufficient to establish a right to give refuge on mission premises. The significant

[55] *cf* the 1986 case of Jener Cotin—a former official of the Duvalier regime in Haiti, who had been attacked by a mob and found refuge in the Brazilian embassy. 'Ex-Duvalier Police Chief' *Associated Press* (New York, 24 February 1986); S Beaulieu, 'Former Duvalier Supporters' *United Press International* (24 February 1986).

[56] State Department Instructions (1930).

[57] See above, at n 25.

[58] GA Res 3321 (XXIX) (1974), preamble, 2nd operative para.

[59] *cf* in particular Argentina, Australia, Belgium, Denmark, Jamaica, Uruguay, in UN Asylum Report (Part 1), para 6.

[60] ibid. *cf* also the submissions by Bahrain and Poland, ibid.

[61] See, eg, Denmark ('imminent physical threat'), Liberia ('imminent personal danger of persecution on account of race, religion, nationality, membership of a particular social group and political opinion'), Pakistan ('imminent danger to life', but not 'danger to liberty'), Uruguay (a 'duty' to grant asylum 'for reasons based on human rights'). Ibid.

feature of diplomatic asylum, as it appears in the relevant treaties, is the fact that persons seeking asylum are accused of political offences or pursued for political reasons.[62] If humanitarian reasons had been the decisive factor, diplomatic asylum would have been opened to those accused of 'common offences' as well[63]—even the common criminal might, after all, be threatened with mob violence.

Humanitarian considerations, it appears, do not easily induce consensus on their suitability as a basis for diplomatic asylum. The most that can be said, based on the positive statements issued by some States on this matter,[64] is that this is an area of international law which is in development.[65] There might even be evidence for a nascent norm of customary law, but, at present, international law does not appear to recognise a right to diplomatic asylum based on these considerations alone.

3. THE IMPACT OF *ERGA OMNES* NORMS AND HUMAN RIGHTS OBLIGATIONS

In several cases of diplomatic asylum, the background of the situation indicates that considerations of self-determination may have played a role in the decision made by agents of the sending State.

It is true that self-determination is a group right,[66] and if diplomatic asylum is therefore granted because the rights of select individuals (and not a 'people') have come under threat, self-determination could not easily be invoked as a basis for that action. At the same time, reference has already been made to the fact that some receiving States target certain individuals precisely because of their relevance for the group, and that restrictions of their rights then affect the exercise of self-determination by the collective.[67] In situations of this kind, diplomatic action whose immediate benefits are felt by individuals, can still relate to the (threatened) breach of an *erga omnes* obligation.

An example is the 2008 case of the Zimbabwean opposition leader Morgan Tsvangirai, who in June of that year sought refuge in the embassy of the Netherlands in Harare.[68] Tsvangirai himself stated that threats to his security existed, and these claims were confirmed by third parties.[69]

[62] See above, at n 48.
[63] See on this point above, at n 49.
[64] See above, at n 59.
[65] See also Pakistan's reply to GA Res 3321 (XXIX) (1974), noting that the matter was 'essentially de lege ferenda', UN Asylum Report (Pt 1), para 6.
[66] See ch 3, at nn 215–17.
[67] See ch 3, after n 217.
[68] 'Mugabe Rival' *Los Angeles Times* (Los Angeles, 24 June 2008).
[69] 'Troops Hunt for Tsvangirai' *Daily Guide (Ghana)* (25 June 2008).

But his request for shelter followed a campaign of widespread political violence against the opposition;[70] and there could have been little doubt that a threat to the Zimbabwean people's right to 'freely determine their political status' existed. The decision by the embassy therefore went beyond the protection of the rights of one individual: It benefitted the people in whose interest the right had been established.

In some situations, the character of the underlying interests raises the possibility that the sending State may not only have a right, but a positive duty to act. The 1984 case of the 'Durban Six' has been discussed in that context.

In September 1984, six refugees turned up at the British consulate in Durban, South Africa and asked the British Consul, Simon Davey, for refuge.[71] They included activists of the United Democratic Front (UDF) and the Natal Indian Congress (NIC)—organisations which had called for a boycott of recent parliamentary elections in South Africa.[72]

The South African system of apartheid formed the background to this case—the new South African Parliament was envisaged as a body containing racially segregated chambers, and the boycott movement was intended to cast doubt on the credibility of the elections.[73] By the time they requested shelter in the consulate, the activists were sought by the security police of the receiving State.[74]

There were several reasons for the grant of asylum which the consulate could have invoked and which enjoyed recognition under international law. The non-white population of South Africa was, during the existence of apartheid, certainly prevented from exercising its right to internal self-determination (a right which was expressly recognised by the General Assembly for the 'peoples of southern Africa').[75] The prohibition of racial discrimination has likewise been recognised as an obligation *erga omnes*;[76] and the General Assembly had emphasised that the system of apartheid was 'necessarily' based on theories of racial discrimination.[77] Apartheid also constitutes a crime against humanity, if the elements are in place which international criminal law requires,[78] and its commission therefore gives rise to *erga omnes* obligations on this basis as well.[79]

Given this confluence of competing interests, it is perhaps not surprising that some authors have argued strongly in favour of a right of the

[70] See above n 68.
[71] M Hornsby and R Kennedy, 'Fugitives Shelter' *The Times* (London, 14 September 1984).
[72] ibid.
[73] J Smith, 'International News' *Associated Press* (New York, 13 September 1984).
[74] Hornsby and Kennedy, n 71.
[75] GA Res 2649 (XXV) (1970), para 5.
[76] See ch 3, at n 122.
[77] GA Res 395 (V) (2 1950), Preamble, 4th operative para.
[78] See on this ch 6, at n 88.
[79] See ch 3, at n 126.

United Kingdom to provide refuge to the Durban Six—and even for an 'obligation to grant diplomatic asylum'.[80]

The ICJ's Advisory Opinion in the *Wall* case certainly opened the door to the possibility of positive duties of third States in the field of self-determination.[81] In the case of South Africa, it was the General Assembly which appealed to governments to 'provide every assistance ... to the national movement of the oppressed people of South Africa in their legitimate struggle'[82] and requested all States to take 'more effective action' towards the elimination of apartheid.[83]

On the basis of this understanding of *erga omnes* interests, the view appears justified that the grant of diplomatic asylum can, in some situations, be based on a duty incumbent on the sending State.

It is true that the grant of asylum on diplomatic premises goes far beyond, for example, verbal representations to alert the receiving State or the international community to the breach of *erga omnes* obligations.[84] That however is a question about the degree of action necessary to fulfil the sending State's obligations, rather than a matter relating to the prima facie existence of a need to act. It is, after all, possible that the granting of asylum was the only available means which rendered effective assistance to the protected interest—just as it is possible that, under certain circumstances, less intrusive means would have been at the disposal of that State.[85]

Another—and potentially more common—basis for the existence of interests on the side of the sending State in this context is formed by provisions contained in human rights treaties to which it is party.

It may seem an unusual suggestion that sending States should not only be entitled to take an interest in the state of human rights in the host country,[86] but be direct addressees of human rights obligations in that State. It is, traditionally, the territorial State which is seen as the guarantor of the rights of its inhabitants. But there are cases in which the question arose whether human rights regimes might not impose obligations on sending States in this context as well.

A case which reached the English courts in 2003, provides an illustration.

In the morning of 18 July 2002, two little boys—the brothers Alamdar and Muntazer Bakhtiari—turned up at the British consulate in Melbourne

[80] Riveles, 158.
[81] See ch 3, at n 173.
[82] *cf* GA Res 2775(XXVI) (1971) F, para 6.
[83] ibid, para 8.
[84] On the right to make verbal representations if *erga omnes* obligations have been violated, see Draft Arts on State Responsibility (2001), 126, art 48(2), in conjunction with 126, art 48(1)(b).
[85] See below, at nn 136 ff.
[86] On this, see ch 3, section 2.

and requested asylum.[87] They had arrived in Australia as asylum seekers in 2001 and had, under the Migration Act 1958, been put in the Woomera Detention Centre.[88] Woomera was a camp which the Commonwealth Ombudsman had described as a 'stark place, lacking warmth or a sense of community'.[89] Others found more graphic words for it.[90] Facilities in the centre were in a poor state, provisions for medical care were inadequate.[91] According to former Woomera guards, violence was an ever-present phenomenon;[92] riots occurred and were put down with tear gas and water cannons.[93] There were reports of sexual violence.[94] Instances in which detainees had harmed themselves were common.[95] The two brothers themselves had reportedly been exposed to tear gas and water cannons, been hit and pushed into razor wire by staff at Woomera and had on several occasions engaged in acts of self-harm.[96] They escaped the camp with 33 other detainees around 29 June 2002.[97]

After the boys had reached the British consulate, a decision was made to bring them into the office area of the premises, while the Vice-Consul and the Deputy High Commissioner tried to obtain instructions from their superiors.[98] The advice eventually received from the Foreign and Commonwealth Office was that grounds to consider a request for asylum existed only in the country of 'first asylum'.[99] The Deputy High Commissioner explained to the boys that they would not be allowed to remain in the consulate, and the brothers then left on their own accord.[100]

Following these events, the brothers, through representatives, sought judicial review of the decision to deny them asylum and expel them from the consulate. When the case reached the Court of Appeal of England and

[87] See *B and Others*, in particular at para 7. In 2003, the Bakhtiari family's treatment by Australian authorities was considered by the Human Rights Committee from a different perspective (the question of violations of the ICCPR by Australia), *Bakhtiari 2003*, para 9.3. The transcription of the names varies; for current purposes, the spelling employed by the Court of Appeal will be preferred.

[88] *B and Others*, paras 5 and 7.

[89] *B and Others*, para 90.

[90] The leader of the Australian Democrats, Natasha Stott Despoja, having visited Woomera camp in early 2002, called it a 'hell-hole'. P Barkham, 'PM Calls Asylum Protest Blackmail' *The Guardian* (London, 26 January 2002).

[91] *Australian Broadcasting Corporation*, '"... About Woomera"', 19 May 2003.

[92] *Australian Broadcasting Corporation*, '"The Guard's Story"', 15 September 2008.

[93] *B and Others*, paras 11 and 12.

[94] See n 91 above.

[95] Barkham, n 90 and see *B and Others*, para 91. It appears that some of the guards too, attempted suicide, see n 92 above.

[96] *B and Others*, paras 11 and 12.

[97] ibid, para 7.

[98] ibid, paras 14–16.

[99] 'Law Report' *The Independent* (London, 10 November 2004).

[100] *B and Others*, para 17.

Wales, part of the Court's considerations turned on issues of human rights law—it was the contention of the claimants that there had been a threat to their rights under Articles 3 and 5 of the ECHR (freedom from inhuman or degrading treatment and the right to liberty and security, respectively).[101]

The fact that diplomatic and consular premises are located in the territory of the receiving State is not by itself a bar to the applicability of human rights instruments. Article 1 ECHR contains the general obligation of every contracting State to 'secure to everyone within their jurisdiction' the rights and freedoms of that convention—it does not, therefore, expressly limit its applicability to the territory of the relevant State. The equivalent phrase in the ICCPR refers to 'all individuals within' the State's 'territory and subject to its jurisdiction';[102] whereas the ACHR refers only to the 'jurisdiction' of the relevant State.[103]

The European Court of Human Rights (ECtHR) has on several occasions accepted the extraterritorial reach of a contracting State's jurisdiction,[104] and similar findings have been made by the Human Rights Committee (HRC) and the Inter-American Commission on Human Rights with regard to the ICCPR[105] and the ACHR[106] respectively.[107]

It has always been much more difficult to state precisely which grounds trigger extraterritorial jurisdiction, but it is remarkable that even chambers which otherwise adopt a restrictive line in this field agree that acts of diplomatic and consular agents are at any rate capable of engaging the jurisdiction of the contracting State.[108]

In principle, therefore, a ground for extraterritorial jurisdiction might exist if the consular officers of a State—as in the case of the Bakhtiari brothers—decide to hand over refugees to the authorities of the receiving State.[109]

[101] Ibid, para 22.

[102] ICCPR art 2(1).

[103] ACHR art 1(1).

[104] *cf Loizidou* (1995), para 62 ('not restricted to the national territory'); *Medvedyev*, para 64 and *Jamaa*, para 72 (limiting such jurisdiction to 'exceptional cases'). See also, for specific grounds, *Al-Skeini*, para 135; *Jamaa*, paras 73, 75; *Medvedyev*, para 67; *Loizidou* (1995), para 62.

[105] HRC General Comment No 31 (2004), para 10.

[106] *Saldaño*, para 17; *Alejandre*, para 23.

[107] The opinion of the HRC is of particular interest, as a literal reading of the ICCPR would allow the conclusion that the terms 'territory' and 'jurisdiction' in art 2 are cumulative requirements. The HRC adopted a more generous construction, see *Burgos*, paras 12.1 ff. See also *Wall Opinion*, para 111. But *cf Burgos* (*Separate Opinion Tomuschat*).

[108] See *Banković*, para 73. See also *Medvedyev*, para 65; *Al-Skeini*, para 134; *Jamaa*, para 75. For the ACHR system, see *Saldaño*, para 20.

[109] According to newspaper reports, the boys were taken to a detention facility by Australian federal police officers on 18 July 2002, M Brace, 'British Diplomats Turn Away Boys' *The Times* (London, 19 July 2002). The fact that the potential violations of ECHR rights would have been performed by agents of the receiving State, does not change the material assessment of this situation. In this regard, an analogy to the evaluation of extradition proceedings has been accepted in the past. In situations of that kind, the ECtHR had stated

In another case concerning extraterritorial asylum, the European Commission of Human Rights was quite explicit on the question of jurisdiction. In September 1988, a group of 18 citizens of the German Democratic Republic (GDR) turned up at the Danish embassy in (East) Berlin and requested that negotiations be conducted to allow them to leave East Germany.[110] The Danish ambassador eventually called in the GDR police, who led the refugees away. The subsequent treatment of the refugees included periods of detention, the temporary removal of their children and, reportedly, long periods of interrogation.[111] Before the European Commission of Human Rights (in the case of *WM v Denmark*), the applicant claimed, inter alia, that his right to liberty and security of the person (Article 5 ECHR) had been violated when he was transferred to police custody. The Commission agreed that the relevant acts of the Danish Ambassador 'affected persons within the jurisdiction of the Danish authorities within the meaning of Article 1 (Art 1) of the Convention'.[112]

In the *Bakhtiari* case, the Court of Appeal took a similar view and found that, 'while in the consulate, the applicants were sufficiently within the authority of the consular staff to be subject to the jurisdiction of the United Kingdom for the purpose of article 1'.[113]

Mere presence in the consulate, however, did not seem to be a sufficient basis for this finding. There had to be more than that—what was required was at least some act of assumption of jurisdiction on the part of the officials. The court referred to the fact that the applicants were assured of their safety while they were on the premises and that they were brought from the reception area into the 'office' area of the consulate.[114] The decision in *WM v Denmark* can be read in a similar light: Acts of the officials were involved when they initially allowed the refugees to stay in the embassy while they were carrying out negotiations with authorities of the receiving State.[115]

This, indeed, must be the right approach towards establishment of jurisdiction. It is consistent with the foundations on which extraterritorial exercise of jurisdiction has been accepted in other circumstances: Whatever the nature of the ground—be it authority over occupied territory, control over a vessel or the running of a prison on foreign soil—it appears

that the 'liability' of the extraditing state is incurred 'by reason of its having taken action which has as a direct consequence the exposure of an individual to proscribed ill-treatment', *Soering*, para 91. See also General Comment No 31 (2004), para 12; *WM v Denmark* with reference to *Soering* and, for a more detailed discussion, Behrens (2014b), 345, 346.

[110] *WM v Denmark.*

[111] ibid.

[112] ibid.

[113] *B and Others*, para 66.

[114] ibid.

[115] See *WM v Denmark*. This is the way in which the Court of Appeal understood that decision, *B and Others*, para 64.

that a voluntary act on the side of the relevant State had always contributed to the establishment of jurisdiction.[116] It would be difficult to adduce evidence to the effect that in the absence of any conduct by the State—for instance, in scenarios in which a diplomatic mission is overrun by refugees—customary international law allocates jurisdiction to an unwilling State.

At the same time, the question arises whether the (threatened) violation of just about any human right can trigger jurisdiction of this kind. In other situations in which a State exercised control over individuals through agents operating abroad, the ECtHR has indeed confirmed that only rights 'that are relevant to the situation' need to be secured, and that the rights enshrined in the ECHR therefore can be 'divided and tailored'.[117]

Apart from more fundamental concerns attaching to a pick and mix approach to human rights, this statement fails to provide guidance on the rights which are fortunate enough to survive when a State exercises jurisdiction abroad. Human rights bodies have struggled with this problem.

There appears to be some agreement that genuine threats to the right to life and freedom from torture would involve the jurisdiction of the contracting State.[118] In the *Bakhtiari* case, the Court of Appeal, similarly, accepted that the granting of diplomatic asylum was possible if the fugitive faced the 'risk of death or injury as the result of lawless disorder'.[119]

Outside situations of this kind, the controversy is more pronounced. In *WM v Denmark*, the European Commission of Human Rights did not, in the end, find that Denmark had deprived the applicant of his right to liberty or security of the person: It considered the treatment which the applicant received by the GDR authorities as being not 'so exceptional as to engage the responsibility of Denmark'—but provided no authority for this secondary status of the relevant rights.[120]

In the *Bakhtiari* case, the Court of Appeal likewise rejected the view that there was a requirement under human rights law to grant diplomatic asylum to persons outside situations in which they faced serious injury,[121] and specifically stated that a 'threat of indefinite detention' was not enough to 'justify … or require' such a grant.[122] It too, did not provide any authority for this exclusion.[123]

116 For the acceptance of extraterritorial jurisdiction in these circumstances, see *Loizidou* (1995), para 62; *Banković*, para 73; *Al-Skeini*, para 136.

117 *Jamaa*, para 74.

118 *cf* HRC General Comment No 31; *Soering*, para 88 (with reference to ECHR art 3).

119 *B and Others*, para 88.

120 *WM v Denmark*.

121 *B and Others*, para 89.

122 ibid, para 95.

123 The court would, however, have accepted the granting of asylum as permissible, if the receiving State had intended to subject the refugee to 'treatment so harsh as to constitute a

The fact remains that none of the relevant provisions of the leading human rights instruments—neither Article 1 ECHR nor Article 2 ICCPR nor Article 1 ACHR— differentiates between various forms of jurisdiction or allows for the wholesale exclusion of certain human rights if particular forms of jurisdiction are involved. The basic premise remains that, once jurisdiction has been established, the whole range of human rights under these instruments becomes applicable and imposes obligations on the contracting State.

Restrictions do exist. But the reason for their existence is that the obligation of the contracting State under human rights law is not the only interest in this field: The interests of the receiving State yet survive. If an assessment of the meeting of the divergent norms leads to the result that interests of the receiving State weigh heavier in the scales, the rights which the mission seeks to protect may experience a limitation, and the evaluation may even lead to the result that, given the circumstances of the situation, a right to grant diplomatic asylum did not exist.

4. RECONCILING DIVERGING INTERESTS IN THE FIELD OF DIPLOMATIC ASYLUM

The impact which divergent norms exercise on the grant of diplomatic asylum appears to have been recognised by courts and commentators only in the relatively recent past. But when the case of *Al-Saadoon and Mufdhi* reached the European Court of Human Rights, the Court reflected, in an obiter dictum, on this aspect of diplomatic asylum. It reached the conclusion that there are certain obligations which the sending State owed to the receiving State—including the duty of non-interference—and that these obligations applied in cases in which refugees sought asylum in embassies.[124] The Court did continue to say that there may, however, 'be conflicting obligations, for example under the Convention [the European Convention on Human Rights]'.[125]

Where solutions to the meeting of norms have been suggested, they sometimes move in the direction of confrontational approaches.[126] Riveles for example, speaking about instances in which threats emanating from a system of apartheid meet with the interest of the receiving State in its

crime against humanity'. *B and Others*, para 88. For a discussion of this, see Behrens 2014(a), 347; Den Heijer, 423. With regard to situations which involved a 'lesser level of threatened harm', the court contented itself with stating that the law was ill defined. *B and Others*, para 89.

[124] *Al-Saadoon and Mufdhi*, para 140.

[125] ibid.

[126] See ch 4, at nn 7–9 and s 1.

ability to exercise territorial jurisdiction, advocates a solution in favour of the obligation to grant asylum.[127] The result is a subordination of restrictive to permissive norms, but without inquiring whether the conditions of certain situations may allow for variations in the application of this rule.

The Court of Appeal in the *Bakhtiari* case went in the opposite direction. The court held that the European Convention on Human Rights could not call on States to grant consular asylum 'if to do so would violate international law',[128] and referred in that regard in particular to Article 55 VCCR.[129] Granting asylum would have constituted an 'abuse of the privileged inviolability accorded to diplomatic premises': It would have 'infringed the obligations of the United Kingdom under public international law'.[130] Here too, then, one legal system is subordinated to the other; but the reasons for this are far from clear. It is, after all, easy enough (and equally unsatisfactory) to reverse the reasoning and to demand that the VCCR must not be allowed to infringe Britain's obligations under the ECHR.

The fact remains that both the ban on diplomatic interference (and of the misuse of mission premises) and the divergent norms they encounter—including the human rights obligations of the sending State—represent important strands of international law. Given their significance for the international community,[131] there is no apparent reason why they should not demand equal validity.

The approach adopted by the ICJ in the *Asylum Case* follows a more discerning line. The court appreciated that there may be situations in which the 'derogation from territorial sovereignty' which diplomatic asylum constituted might be permissible—but it demanded that the legal basis for this be established in each instance.[132] A differentiating approach is also chosen by those States which refer to the shape which the protected interest received through the conditions of a particular scenario. Austria for instance, in her response to General Assembly Resolution 3321 (XXIX) of 1974, found that the granting of diplomatic asylum, while constituting a 'grave interference with the sovereignty of the receiving country' was permissible if a person was in 'immediate, serious danger',[133] and the Canadian Department of External Affairs similarly accepted a right to asylum if the individual faced 'a serious and imminent risk of violence'.[134] From this perspective, it is not the relevant human right on its own, but

[127] Riveles, 158.
[128] *B and Others*, para 84.
[129] ibid, para 88.
[130] ibid, para 96.
[131] See ch 4, at n 65–66.
[132] *Asylum Case*, 275.
[133] UN Asylum Report (Pt 1), para 6 (Austria).
[134] Green, 143.

its particular form in a specific situation, that triggers a right to resort to diplomatic decisions of this kind.

These are perspectives which are more in line with the conciliatory approach as a preferable method for the resolution of the meeting of divergent norms.[135] A decision to grant asylum might, after all, not be the most appropriate method to pursue the legitimate aims of the receiving State, even if the situation involves an immediate risk to a legally recognised right. Other measures might exist, and might even possess a greater degree of efficiency. Proportionality—and the least restrictive means test as one of its elements—plays a significant role in this context as well.

In her submission pursuant to General Assembly Resolution 3321 (XXIX), Australia went so far as to state that diplomatic asylum had to be the 'only resort open to the fugitive'.[136] In a similar vein, the Court of Appeal in the *Bakhtiari* case explored available alternatives to the grant of asylum that existed in the specific case. It referred to the fact that a hearing on the Bakhtiaris' refugee status was pending in the courts of Australia at the same time at which they requested asylum in the consulate;[137] and pointed out that the receiving State was a country which 'observe[d] the rule of law'.[138] The judges also found it 'significant' that the High Court of Australia had commented on Australian criminal, civil and administrative law as providing 'avenues of redress to aliens who alleged that they had suffered mistreatment while in detention'.[139]

But even in circumstances of this kind, the question has to be asked whether the available alternatives promised equal efficiency for the protection of the relevant interests. In the *Bakhtiari* case, for instance, the observations by the Court of Appeal would have been more persuasive if the Court had not also found that Australian law did not 'include a right to challenge a failure to secure the enjoyment of human rights', and if it had not pointed out that neither the ICCPR, nor the ICESCR nor the Convention on the Rights of the Child nor the Convention Relative to the Status of Refugees and its amending Protocol had been transformed into Australian domestic law.[140]

The availability of equally effective alternatives will inevitably be shaped by the internal structure of the receiving State and both its willingness and ability to secure the rights in question. It is the nature of the relevant interest which allows conclusions on the efficiency of the available options in this context: If the right to self-determination is at issue, a State which

135 See ch 4, s 2.
136 UN Asylum Report (Pt 1), para 6 (Australia), para 23.
137 *B and Others*, para 94.
138 ibid, para 95.
139 ibid, para 95.
140 ibid, para 90.

possesses strong mechanisms for the protection of minority rights will find it easier to support the claim that appropriate alternatives to asylum exist than a State which does not. If the interest is based on conventional obligations to secure human rights, the receiving State would have to possess means of fulfilling such obligations through its own authorities, if it wishes to claim that 'effective alternatives' had been in place.

That does not mean that only a very specific form of government is capable of securing the interests which diplomatic asylum seeks to protect. A more decisive factor is the question whether past experiences suggest that the receiving State is able and willing to work towards their protection.

When in 1956 Cardinal Mindszenty sought asylum in the US embassy in Budapest, he did so a few days after the Hungarian uprising of that year and at a time when Soviet troops were about to crush the revolution. Shortly before his appearance at the embassy, Mindszenty had, in a radio speech, underlined the concepts of 'national independence and democracy';[141] and it would be fair to say that the Cardinal had come to be considered one of the representatives of those Hungarian movements which desired a change from communist rule and thus embodied the people's struggle to determine its own political fate.

If assistance towards self-determination was thus the reason for the granting of diplomatic asylum, the opinion that there had been alternatives, and that Mindszenty could have been referred to the authorities of the receiving State or the occupying power, would appear quixotic from the outset. But there was more to the case: Experiences made in comparable incidents underlined the fact that effective alternatives to the granting of asylum were difficult to find.

Imre Nagy, the reformist Prime Minister who had been in office during the uprising, had likewise taken refuge in diplomatic premises—together with colleagues of his administration, he had sought asylum in the Yugoslav embassy in Budapest.[142] The new Hungarian government promised Nagy safe conduct if he wished to leave the country; yet when he did emerge from the embassy, he was arrested (and later executed).[143] At least at that stage, it must have been clear that recourse to the authorities of the receiving State offered a viable alternative neither to an asylum seeker nor to the people whose right to self-determination was affected.

The grant of diplomatic asylum can also be the only effective alternative if the receiving State is unable to protect the legitimate interest in the specific circumstances of the relevant situation. It is at that stage that the scenario of a threat of 'mob violence', which has been invoked by several

[141] Government of Hungary, Mindszenty Conference (2012).

[142] BA Akinterinwa, 'Nigeria, Cote d'Ivoire' *This Day* (Lagos, 8 October 2000).

[143] ibid; Riveles, 157.

commentators on diplomatic asylum,[144] gains significance—not in the shape of an automatic right to asylum that would apply in any situation of this kind,[145] but as a factor which has an impact on the evaluation of the diplomatic measure. If general disorder has engulfed the area around mission premises, it is possible that diplomatic agents are able to offer a faster, and thus more effective, defence of the affected rights than agents of the receiving State. Situations of this kind underline the fact that the granting of asylum may sometimes be the best available method of securing rights which are recognised under international law.[146]

Emphasis has on occasion been placed on the allegedly low level of involvement of the sending State in situations in which diplomatic asylum has been granted. According to Porcino, asylum represents only a 'passive infringement';[147] the sending State 'does not enter the territory of the sovereign state uninvited … there is no application of force or aggression against the territorial state'.[148] These are considerations which matter for the evaluation of the diplomatic measure, but also for cost–benefit analysis.

And yet, the understanding of the grant of asylum as a 'passive infringement' constitutes a generalisation. For one—as the law of State responsibility demonstrates—the international community attaches as much significance to positive acts as to omissions.[149] But a positive act does in fact exist—in the shape of the decision to afford shelter in the first place.[150] Porcino does not deny that, yet he stresses that this decision is made 'only' upon the initiative of the refugee.[151] In most cases, that will be a valid observation.[152] But it should not lead to the conclusion that the grant of asylum therefore cannot carry considerable weight. When Manuel Zelaya, for instance, was granted asylum in the Brazilian embassy in Tegucigalpa in 2009, the demonstrations of Zelaya's supporters outside the mission were considered so serious by the government of the receiving State, that

[144] See on this *B and Others*, para 88; State Department Instructions (1930); and see the 1986 case of Jener Cotin, above, n 55.

[145] On this point, see above, at n 55.

[146] *cf* also Jeffery, 22.

[147] Porcino, 446.

[148] ibid.

[149] Draft Articles on State Responsibility (2001), 34, art 2. See also ibid, 35, art 2, commentary, para 4 ('no difference in principle exists between the two').

[150] See above, at n 114.

[151] Porcino, 446.

[152] There was however some discussion in the 2008 case of Anwar Ibrahim as to whether diplomatic asylum in this instance had been based on a request by the refugee or an invitation by the Turkish Ambassador. See on that J Eyal, 'Pushing the Limits' *Straits Times* (Singapore, 5 July 2008).

it resorted to the use of the police force and the military to disband the crowd.[153]

Incidents of this kind emphasise the far-reaching consequences which can emanate from the diplomatic decision to allow private individuals the use of embassy premises—consequences which, in volatile situations, may include public disorder and even armed strife within the receiving State. Such impact is likely to be grave and may well be irreversible. And yet, if Porcino's considerations are applied, the conduct of the embassy itself, throughout the entire development of the situation, could only be described as a 'merely passive' infringement of the sovereignty of the receiving State.

That does not mean that, even in situations of this kind, a comparison of available measures and a weighing up of cost and benefit cannot lead to a result favourable to the sending State. In the Zelaya incident, the fact bears observing that the ouster of the President was the removal of a democratically elected head of State—an act which raised questions about its impact on the Honduran people's right to determine their own political fate and which subsequently met with condemnation by the United Nations and the Organization of American States.[154] The fact remains that a granting of diplomatic asylum which constitutes a significant contribution to the protection of a right whose exercise is seriously imperilled, may pass the test of cost-benefit analysis even if it generates a powerful impact on the order in the receiving State.

In many cases of diplomatic asylum, it is likely that the benefits of the measure may indeed outweigh its negative impact. The reason for that is not the 'passive role' which the sending State plays in granting asylum, but the fact that asylum is often adopted as a temporary measure only and is usually extended to a very limited circle of persons. On the other hand, the interests which the diplomatic mission seeks to protect, often constitute recognised rights that have come under considerable threat.

An illustration is provided by an incident in June 2008 involving the former Malaysian Deputy Prime Minister, Anwar Ibrahim, who sought asylum in the Turkish embassy in Kuala Lumpur. Mr Ibrahim had been accused by the Malaysian authorities of homosexual conduct (which Malaysia criminalised), but there were reasons to suspect a political background to the case: Ibrahim was the leader of the Pakatan Rakyat opposition at a time when the government had on several occasions attempted to stifle opposition movements and rallies.[155] Granting diplomatic asylum

[153] W Booth and J Forero, 'New Honduran Leadership' *Washington Post* (Washington, 30 June 2009) and see ch 7, at nn 8–10.

[154] See for the United Nations, GA Res A/63/L.74 (2009) as orally revised; and for the Organization of American States, Resolution on the Political Crisis in Honduras (2009).

[155] See on this Human Rights Watch, 'Malaysia' (2009).

therefore aided not only the individual refugee, but assisted the interests which he represented: The right of a people striving for the realisation of self-determination. The provision of refuge was temporary in nature, and it does not appear that it occasioned irreversible or even sustained damage to the criminal justice system of the receiving State.

It is true that there may be a tendency to overstate the beneficial influence of the granting of diplomatic asylum—it appears, in particular, naïve to claim that diplomatic asylum may (by itself) have the potential of persuading the territorial State to 'mend its ways'.[156] A more tangible benefit lies in the fact that it draws the attention of the international community to a particular situation and can thus, in the long term, create sufficient pressure to effect a change of the relevant conditions.

In cases in which the protected interest is based on the sending State's obligations under human rights law, cost–benefit analysis can lead to a distinction between the human rights that are affected. But this is not a distinction along the hierarchical lines which judicial authorities have sometimes suggested.[157] The important issue is not whether the protected interests belonged to an exclusive circle of rights—any right to which the conventional obligation refers can be relevant. The decisive question is whether the damage which such a right would experience in the absence of the diplomatic measure would be serious and irreversible.

That may indeed often lead to the conclusion that the rights to life and to freedom from torture enjoy a privileged position: Their violation furnishes an obvious case for grave and irreparable damage. But that does not mean that the protection of other rights can never lead to an assessment in which the benefit of their protection outweighs the costs of the measure.

It is, for instance, too simple to state, as the Court of Appeal did in the *Bakhtiari* case, that the threat of indefinite detention could not be the basis for the grant of asylum under human rights conventions.[158] What is required is a more detailed investigation of the harm threatened to the asylum seeker, and its comparison to the impact of the diplomatic measure. In the particular instance of the Bakhtiaris it would be difficult to ignore medical evidence relating to the grave effects which indefinite detention has on detainees in general,[159] and on children in particular.[160] It is clearly not possible to consider the restrictions on the asylum seeker's right to liberty and security as divorced from the impact these restrictions have on

[156] For a different view, see Jeffery, 21.

[157] See above, at nn 120–23.

[158] *B and Others*, para 95.

[159] See on this Cheyette, 2.

[160] See on this International Detention Coalition, 48 ff. In the *Bahktiari* case, the HRC did reach the conclusion that a violation of ICCPR art 9(1) (the right to liberty and security of person) had come into existence, *Bakhtiari 2003*, para 9.3.

other rights. That includes the right to a family life,[161] but also the right to physical and moral integrity.[162] In the *Bakhtiari* case, a youth worker dealing with the situation noted in early 2002 that she had seen, over the period of one year, a 'continual decline in the children's well-being, particularly related to their socialisation and psychological state'.[163] When the Human Rights Committee dealt with the case in 2003, it referred to the 'traumatic experiences' of the Bakhtiari family in 'long-term immigration detention' (which, in its view, violated the right to liberty and security of person).[164]

Diplomatic agents might not always have full knowledge of all features of the situation in which the asylum seekers would find themselves in the absence of diplomatic action. But in the *Bakhtiari* case, the relevant aspects were known at the time.[165] Under these circumstances, the consular officers had the opportunity, and, given the human rights obligations of the sending State, the duty, to perform an appropriate assessment of the threat facing the children. Aspects which should have played a role in an evaluation of this kind were the conditions at the detention facility, the particularly vulnerable position of the asylum seekers (based in part on their age and their past traumatic experiences) and the length of their stay at Woomera—which, by the time of their escape, had been close to one year and a half.

In situations in which the potential negative impact on the refugee is as well defined as that, it is difficult to see how the benefit of securing their human rights could be outweighed by the costs of withdrawing them from a system that showed little inclination of welcoming them in the first place. An assessment under the principle of proportionality cannot reach

[161] On this right, see ECHR art 8(1); ICCPR art 17(1) and art 23; ACHR art 11(2) and art 17. The Human Rights and Equal Opportunities Commission of Australia noted that 'the longer … families are in detention, the further the capacity of parents to care for their children is compromised', Human Rights and Equal Opportunities Commission (Australia), 376. See also International Detention Coalition, 49.

[162] For the right to physical integrity, see *expressis verbis* ACHR art 5. The ECtHR has read this right into the right to a 'private life' (ECHR art 8). See *X and Y*, para 22; *Glass*, para 70. See also ICCPR art 17. Where children are concerned, the fact must be taken into account that indefinite detention prevents them from pursuing their natural development in the formative years of their lives. *cf* Lorek et al, 582; International Detention Coalition, 51.

[163] Quoted in International Detention Coalition, 52.

[164] *Bahktiari 2003*, para 9.6. The fact must also be taken into account that, under certain circumstances, detention of children can amount to inhuman treatment (ECHR art 3). See *Mayeka and Mitunga*, paras 58, 59. The case concerned a five year old detained in a Belgian Transit Centre as an illegal immigrant. While the young age of the applicant played a role in the court's considerations, conditions at the centre were described in significantly friendlier terms than those at Woomera. Ibid, paras 37, 52. The detention had lasted for two months, ibid, para 50. On the long-term effects of detention in general, see Cheyette, 17; Coffey et al, 2076.

[165] *B and Others*, para 6 and paras 11–12.

any other result but that the diplomatic (or consular) officials were entitled to grant asylum and, in the circumstances of the case, required to protect the human rights which had come under threat.

Among the fields of potential diplomatic interference, the granting of asylum constitutes one of the clearest illustrations for situations in which the need for precise cost–benefit analysis is beyond doubt. The rights of the hosts have not disappeared, and the fact must be taken into account that mission premises are still part of the sovereign territory of the receiving State.[166] At the same time, diplomatic asylum is hardly ever afforded for frivolous reasons, and in some situations, the diplomatic mission may even face an obligation to safeguard the rights of asylum seekers. Adequate mechanisms for the defence of these interests within the receiving State do not always exist, and effective protection may rely on the assistance of other States. An accurate assessment of these situations cannot be performed without appreciation of the intrusive, and invariably direct, impact which the granting of asylum exercises as well as of the danger which looms for the interests of the primary beneficiaries and the international community alike.

[166] Any other interpretation would hark back to the days in which the doctrine of extraterritoriality had still been given validity. See Young, in particular 147, 151, and for today's basis of diplomatic immunities VCDR preamble, 4th operative para.

Concluding Thoughts

1. BETWEEN SENSITIVE AREAS AND LEGITIMATE INTERESTS: CONSTRUCTING A SYSTEM OF DIPLOMATIC INTERFERENCE

FEW RULES OF international law live without neighbours. International norms today must expect to share the streets on which they reside—often with rules which were constructed with quite different purposes in mind, but which exert an impact on the same situation.

Diplomatic law is no exception, and the rule against diplomatic interference is a paradigmatic example for this situation. Its neighbours come from many regions: Some from the field of human rights, others from international criminal law, others again from the VCDR itself; some help diplomatic agents, some restrict their work, and all of them claim applicability at the same time as Article 41. In this case, codification has not helped: The phrasing of the rule in today's Convention is reflective of a minimum consensus on an exceedingly complex issue, and the few, embryonic, attempts by the ILC to address the co-existence of norms in this field[1] have done little to resolve the situation.

In light of this, the view of those observers who feel that it may not be possible to develop guidelines on the rule against interference,[2] appears understandable. And yet, the situation is not as desperate (or as simple) as that. The development of objective parameters for the concept of diplomatic interference can be achieved, and part of this study has been dedicated to this endeavour. But the result does not necessarily remove the complexity of the issue, and the legal assessment may often deviate from that which observers of diplomatic conduct may have expected.

An analysis of this kind may, however, carry advantages to the holders of diplomatic office around the world. As a very minimum, it is possible to identify key areas in which diplomatic activity must be allowed, even though they may appear basic in character. Contact with the government of the receiving State (and not 'merely' its Foreign Ministry) falls

[1] See, on the hierarchical solution which the ILC suggested for the meeting of the rule of non-interference and the protection of interests of the sending State or its nationals, ch 4, at n 6; Annex B.8, commentary, para 2. In 1971, the ILC suggested a similar hierarchical solution in the context of what would later be the CRSIO—in situations in which the duty to recall a diplomat in cases of 'grave and manifest interference' met with the performance of 'functions of the mission or the tasks of the delegation', YILC 1971 II/2, 326, art 75(2).

[2] See, for the position of the Government of the Netherlands, Introduction, at n 39.

in this category, as does contact with factions and individual politicians (including members of a lawful opposition) and with the general public—regardless of the concerns which the host government may voice.

But an examination of diplomatic interference also benefits States which may have to deal with diplomats whose conduct they consider to exceed the reserve becoming a guest. Such conduct can go far beyond the making of inconvenient statements: As shown in this study, it can extend to instances in which diplomatic agents resorted to threats against the lives of persons, incited the population to violence and unrest and to situations in which public disturbances were caused through the granting of asylum on mission premises. In other fields, the impact of the relevant activity may be less intrusive, but the conduct will still mark a sensitive area for the receiving State—as is the case where diplomatic lobbying on budgetary decisions is concerned or where talks with opposition parties have been carried out in the context of political campaigns. In some of these fields, domestic laws may strengthen the position taken by the receiving State (as in many instances where the funding of parties is at issue). In other fields again, the risk of a loss of face constitutes one of the principal concerns of the government of the State—as is the case when the human rights record of the State is subjected to scrutiny and when diplomatic observers attend the trials of public figures.

At the same time, a comprehensive analysis also offers sending States a way to make their interests heard. And such interests can be based on powerful and legitimate reasons. The pursuit of concerns of the sending State may require a very intimate involvement with areas which the hosts may wish to reserve to themselves—such as active engagement with the opposition of that State.

The protection of interests of nationals of the sending State can involve activities which may be considered criticism of the diplomatic hosts (as in the air quality case involving American diplomatic missions in China).[3] The function of observation may see diplomats turn up at political demonstrations (as in the case of diplomats who visited the Red Shirts protests in Thailand in 2010)[4] and at events which the receiving State might consider part of political campaigns. The creation and maintenance of friendly relations can extend to propaganda activities (a point which, as the exchange between US Assistant Secretary of State Gross and Congressman Klein made clear, had been appreciated even in the 1940s).[5] All of these forms of conduct correspond to diplomatic tasks which represent legitimate interests of the sending State and are indeed recognised in the same instrument that outlaws diplomatic interference.

[3] See ch 9, at nn 65–67.
[4] See Introduction, after n 4.
[5] See ch 1, at n 31.

The circle of legitimate bases on the side of the sending State becomes even wider if obligations are considered which the receiving State owes to the international community as a whole (*erga omnes* obligations). That includes, prominently, the grant of self-determination to peoples striving for the realisation of this right. The relevance of this interest has become particularly clear in certain situations in which the receiving State objected to diplomatic conduct which it perceived as partisan in nature—the increased space for diplomatic action in this field must indeed be considered one of the major changes in the assessment of the charge of interference since the entry into force of the Vienna Convention. But it is not the only area affected by self-determination: Even threats (such as that of the termination of financial aid if certain aspects of a people's right to self-determination are not guaranteed) can find their basis in this interest of the international community. Other *erga omnes* obligations include the prevention, suppression and punishment of international crimes; diplomats who criticise the receiving State for failing to comply with the corresponding duties can therefore invoke a powerful basis under international law.

In some situations, the group of legitimate interests is further increased through the existence of obligations which a receiving State has accepted under a human rights treaty to which the sending State is party as well. These situations have been discussed within the category of '*erga omnes partes* interests'—obligations in whose fulfilment every party to a treaty, under specific circumstances, can claim a legitimate interest. It is a point which has achieved particular significance where the granting of diplomatic asylum is concerned—a situation in which the relevant treaties can form a strong basis for the underlying diplomatic decision. Once such asylum has been provided, the protection of the asylum seeker may indeed obtain the status of an obligation incumbent on the sending State under the relevant human rights regime (although the extent of such obligations is still subject to controversy).

The study of the existing literature on diplomatic interference may often convey the impression that international law is chiefly concerned with the protection of the interests of the receiving State,[6] and that diplomats have little choice but to subject themselves to the assessment given by their hosts.

In light of this, it is surprising that there is, in the vast majority of cases in which charges of interference had been advanced, not only room for a consideration of interests on the side of the sending State and its agents, but also for the application of mechanisms (in particular, the principle of proportionality) which mediate between the divergent values. There are, in fact, very few forms of behaviour in which an evaluation of this kind has to be excluded from the outset.

[6] See on this Introduction, nn 44–46.

On the other hand, the tests of proportionality require an exact consideration of the circumstances of the individual case in light of their parameters. The 'least restrictive means' test in particular can involve the making of fine distinctions, depending on the specific aspects of the relevant situation. The funding of non-governmental organisations may appear at first blush a less intrusive alternative to the funding of parties. But even this form of conduct has triggered criticism which is not always easy to dismiss. Financial support to an NGO may create a dependancy of the latter on the will of foreign paymasters and may thus change its internal direction while its appearance as an impartial and reliable institution remains intact.

The granting of diplomatic asylum may seem a very understandable choice, if the rights of the asylum seeker are in danger; but it also involves an exacting assessment of the options already available to that person under the system of the receiving State. And questions of this kind cannot be answered by merely considering the political system of the State: Even democratic States may still fail in their duty to protect a specific right which, in the circumstances of a particular situation, had come under threat.

Criticism is certainly a 'less intrusive alternative' by comparison to insults of persons or institutions, but here, too, finer distinctions may be indispensable. A host who complains about excessive conduct may have a point, if a diplomatic agent chose a public (or semi-public) forum over a private conversation with the relevant government department. Similar questions attach to matters of style. Was it necessary to resort to emotive language? Did the speaker take into account the cultural specificities of his hosts? Did he use the right form of address and the correct titles?

And yet, the 'least restrictive means' test does not always favour the position of the receiving State. The fact must be taken into account that there is a corrective mechanism which limits the alternative options which qualify as suitable comparators: Such options must have an efficiency that is at least equal to that of the measure which the diplomatic agent had adopted.

The efficiency of a measure is to a significant degree dependent on the interest which the diplomatic agent seeks to pursue. If that interest consists in the exercise of an (ordinarily) simple diplomatic function, such as the task of observation, an efficient fulfilment of that interest may not require activities which generate a great impact on the internal order of the receiving State. The more complex the protected interest, the greater is the possibility that a diplomatic agent may indeed have to adopt actions which his hosts will consider meddling: Assistance towards a people's right to self-determination, for instance, might at times make resort to such conduct inescapable, as less intrusive, but equally effective alternatives simply do not exist. At the same time, diplomatic agents who pursue such interests must be aware that their conduct will often encounter a much stricter level of scrutiny than that applied to their colleagues who merely behave as 'diplomatic observers'.

The efficiency of a measure also depends on the factual parameters of the situation. The personal relations which a diplomatic agent enjoys with influential figures in the receiving State may play a role in this,[7] as does the general perception of the sending State in the receiving State and culturally conditioned responses to certain forms of conduct. A diplomat who is in the habit of airing his thoughts in the newspapers before speaking to the government of the receiving State and a diplomat who phrases the views of the sending State as imperative demands rather than suggestions, must not be surprised if his activities turn out to be counterproductive. The louder diplomat is not always the more efficient one.

At least in certain situations, the need for the second test of proportionality—that of cost–benefit analysis—has gained particular clarity. In the field of diplomatic asylum, for instance, it would be difficult to reach a conclusive evaluation of the underlying diplomatic conduct without taking into account the immediate impact which the withdrawal of a person from the justice system of the receiving State generates, as well as the further consequences which emanate from that decision which—as has been seen in the past—can reach the level of public disturbances and disorder.[8] The sending State, on the other hand, will at times be able to refer to the threats to which legitimate interests, including a people's right to self-determination, would have been exposed without the diplomatic measure. If the grant of asylum is—as is usually the case—only temporary in nature, and if its negative effects are limited and not irreversible, an assessment may well favour the sending State and its agents.

A reflection of diplomatic interference which limits itself to complaints raised by receiving States is thus bound to lead to unduly restrictive results. A precise application of the above named parameters does offer considerable room for diplomatic action and allows for the very real possibility that diplomats may, even in controversial areas, have pursued legitimate interests in a proportionate manner and thus followed an entirely lawful course of conduct.

There are, in fact, only very few instances in which diplomatic action in this field has to be considered unlawful from the outset, and in which the application of the tests of proportionality thus is not even a permissible mechanism.

Threats with consequences which are unlawful under international law fall in this category; as does incitement to genocide and terrorism (and possibly also to racial discrimination, hostility and violence). The funding of terrorists and of direct armed activities must be seen in the same light (whereas the funding of an 'armed opposition' is not enough to

[7] See ch 4, after n 155.

[8] See ch 11, at n 153.

withdraw the diplomatic conduct from the application of proportionality). Diplomatic insults, too, constitute by themselves a form of interference—they are by definition an excessive form of conduct if compared to sharp criticism which does not reach that level.

This makes for a rather small circle of activities; but its identification carries significance. Not only do they delineate areas in which no receiving State, regardless of its political or cultural system, is likely to permit diplomatic conduct—the fact remains that a differentiation between various forms of diplomatic interference has at times attained a meaning of its own. Within the framework of the Vienna Convention on the Representation of States in their Relations with International Organizations of a Universal Character (CRSIO), specific duties are incumbent on the sending State if its diplomatic agents have committed 'grave and manifest interference in the internal affairs of the host State'.[9] All of these forms of conduct are likely to fall within this category, with the possible exception of insults. Insults constitute attacks on the dignity of their targets and are thus likely to qualify as obvious, and thus manifest interference with prevailing matters in the host State, but the question whether such interference is considered 'grave' in nature, will strongly depend on the individual circumstances of the particular case.

2. DEALING WITH THE SPECTRE OF INTERFERENCE: TOWARDS AN IDENTIFICATION OF GUIDELINES

The demands of the legal framework which emerges from the considerations outlined above do not pose insurmountable challenges to Foreign Ministries, who can rely on the knowledge of the resident experts in their legal departments. They do, however, place a burden on diplomats around the world, who may not have the luxury of leisurely contemplation. If, for instance, a citizen of the receiving State turns up at the doorstep of an embassy, requesting asylum on mission premises, diplomats are put in a situation which brooks little delay.[10]

[9] See on this, Introduction, at n 36 and CRSIO art 77(2)2.

[10] The challenge faced by diplomatic agents in this regard is not dissimilar to that encountered in other areas of international and domestic law, where a complex legal framework causes difficulties to its application in the field. With regard to international humanitarian law, Alexander's reference in 1999 to rules relating to flights over Bosnia offers an illustration: Such rules had become 'so complicated that jokes were made in NATO suggesting adding a third seat in each aircraft so that a lawyer could fly as an additional crew member', Alexander, 190. For an example in domestic law, see the UK handbook 'The Judge Over Your Shoulder', which instructs civil servants on the basic mandates of administrative law, and whose first edition had been described as being, in tone, 'implicitly critical of the courts for making things so difficult for the administrators, and also of those individuals and pressure groups who have used judicial review for their own ends', Bradley, 487; Treasury Solicitor's Department (2006).

Yet the need to engage in a detailed assessment of the underlying conduct may be the price which States and their agents have to pay for their resolve to grant the rule against diplomatic interference the status of law rather than protocol. Nor does there seem to be much appetite in the international community for turning back the wheel of time. On the contrary, it appears that diplomatic agents and foreign offices make more, rather than less, reference to the Vienna Convention in the context of conduct which allegedly interferes with the internal affairs of the receiving State.[11] What is more: Failure to consider the legal implications of diplomatic conduct can lead to detrimental results for the States which the relevant agents are representing, and even to the loss of an important position under international law.[12]

At the same time, the law can be an effective tool—to foreign ministries as well as to diplomats whose measures are at the centre of the relevant debate. That may require not only knowledge of its correct application but also of the need to resort to measures of this kind and an awareness of the place of the law among the options at the disposal of the relevant actors. On the basis of this understanding and on the basis of past incidents in this field, it is possible to identify certain points which offer guidance to affected parties in cases in which conduct of diplomatic interference may be at issue.

For receiving States in situations of this kind, the following considerations carry significance.

- A first step must be the examination of the need for the adoption of any action against the relevant diplomatic agent. An honest exploration of the motives behind such sanction is indispensable: The fact that the receiving State feels it may have lost face through a diplomatic action does not mean that the international community will side with the hosts. And in a surprising number of cases, it is only the revelation of the hosts' irritation which gives the situation the necessary publicity to create an international incident. Ignoring the diplomatic agent can be a sanction, too, and perhaps not the least efficient one.
- If it is felt that more express measures are indicated, the question still arises whether an evaluation of the relevant conduct is required. Reciprocity enters into the consideration here: The condemnation of certain forms of conduct sets a precedent for the receiving State's

[11] For diplomatic agents, see the above mentioned case of Christopher Dell in Zimbabwe, ch 3, at n 52. For a recent reference by the Foreign Ministry of the receiving State to VCDR art 41, see the Tanzanian reaction in the 2013 case of Lu Youqing (A.296); for a recent reference by the Foreign Ministry of the sending State to that Convention in the context of allegations of interference, see the Singaporean defence in the 2012 case of Ong Keng Yong, *Channel NewsAsia*, 'Singapore Dismisses', 22 June 2012, and A.284.

[12] See on this, below, at nn 44–49.

own agents abroad. And there are numerous sanctions which can be adopted without the need for (public) evaluation, including warnings, expressions of surprise and the summoning of the diplomatic agent. Even a declaration persona non grata can be advanced without the need to provide reasons for the expulsion.

— If the adoption of a legal evaluation is considered inevitable, the language employed by the receiving State carries significance. The use of political or emotive terms—the description of a diplomat as a 'congenital liar', say[13]—risks being considered by the international community as the expression of irritation rather than the making of a protest with legal meaning.
— The expression of a legal opinion also requires a measure of consistency. Adopting harsh measures against agents from antagonistic States and no sanction at all when diplomats from friendly nations are concerned, may make sense on the political plane, but is counterproductive if a legal evaluation is intended.
— Finally, the overstepping of boundaries by a diplomatic agent does not relieve his host of its duties under the Vienna Convention. The obligations to protect the person of a diplomat[14] and to refrain from subjecting him to criminal jurisdiction[15] therefore remain in place. Immunities are not conditional on good conduct; and even grave breaches of the rule against interference cannot justify the violation by the receiving State of the duties it has assumed in this regard.

Where diplomats themselves are concerned, the following considerations are of relevance:

— Accurate knowledge of the factual situation is indispensable in situations which may lend themselves to charges of interference. That may seem obvious; yet this level of awareness, extending to cultural, historical and social preconditions in the country of his hosts, remains one of the chief justifications for the continued importance of the diplomatic office even in the age of videoconferencing. It is the diplomat, rather than his Foreign Minister, who can be expected to know at what stage criticism in the receiving State will be perceived as insult and warnings as threats. Such knowledge also includes awareness of the likely long-term impact of diplomatic action. The granting of diplomatic asylum for instance can lead to a lasting impasse, in which the diplomatic mission may have to endure all the difficulties which incidents of this kind involve—which may include

[13] See on this A.205.
[14] VCDR art 29.
[15] VCDR art 31(1).

surveillance by authorities of the receiving State,[16] and other impediments to the proper fulfilment of its functions.[17]

— At the same time, diplomatic agents must attain adequate familiarity with the legal framework in which the relevant measure is embedded—the more so, as the rule against interference may not be the only norm which applies to their actions. Treaties may be in force which exercise a restrictive impact (for instance, in situations of diplomatic funding) or influence the situation in a permissive way (for instance, where the granting of diplomatic asylum is concerned). A good understanding of the law can give support to the position of the diplomatic agent—at least to the degree that the law recognises certain interests on which diplomatic measures can often validly be based.[18] Yet the law also contains pitfalls which only diplomats who are aware of the legal implications of their conduct, can hope to avoid. Seemingly innocuous acts—such as that of taking an asylum seeker from the reception area to the 'office area' of a diplomatic mission, can have wide ranging consequences,[19] and even the absence of any action may carry particular risks.[20]

— Diplomatic agents also enjoy a certain influence on the shaping of customary international law in this field, but awareness of the conditions which apply to the exercise of such power is indispensable. As their situation in that regard is similar to that of their hosts, it is, for instance, not advisable to resort to emotive language[21] if a diplomatic statement is intended to offer a legal evaluation; and a diplomat who intends to claim the right to resort to certain forms of activities must be aware that diplomats assigned to the sending State may, on that basis, be tempted to claim the same right.

— Accurate knowledge of existing alternatives to the intended diplomatic measure is of crucial importance. Controversial measures are likely to come under close scrutiny, and the question will often be raised whether less intrusive options had been available. A staggered

[16] Both in the cases of Mindszenty and Assange, the receiving State made clear that it had not forgotten about the 'guests in the embassy'. In the case of Mindszenty, security police reportedly continued to take pictures of the cardinal on his walks through the courtyard even 14 years after his asylum had begun, A Last, 'Fifteen Years Holed Up' *BBC Online* (London, 6 September 2012). In the case of Assange, police guards remained outside the Ecuadorian embassy years after his asylum had begun. 'Julian Assange Security' *BBC Online* (London, 10 February 2015).

[17] That is not to say that such methods, as far as the receiving State has responsibility for them, should invariably be considered lawful. The receiving State is under a continuing duty to 'accord full facilities for the performance of the functions of the mission' (VCDR art 25).

[18] For an effective invocation of such interests by a diplomatic agent, see ch 3, at n 52.

[19] See ch 11, at n 114.

[20] See above, at n 12 and below, at nn 44–49.

[21] See for instance the statement by the Syrian embassy in January 2014 (A.303).

approach is often advisable, starting with measures whose disruptive impact is comparably low. That often means that the government of the receiving State has to be the first point of contact. Even if such talks seem pointless from the outset, receiving States are in a strong position if they can claim that the diplomat never used 'diplomatic channels' and had not given their governments an opportunity to respond to grievances.

— A staggered approach may involve the making of very fine distinctions. Warnings may not be necessary if criticism is sufficient; criticism may not be necessary if suggestions are efficient enough, and even refraining from any action may be an option, if the case can be more effectively made by a diplomatic colleague who entertains better relations with the host government. It may seem cumbersome that the law calls for such minute differentiations. At the same time, there is reason to believe—especially in the field of diplomatic communication—that this degree of discernment is often already part of diplomatic practice.[22] Proportionality may be little more than the younger sister of diplomatic discretion.

— Cooperation with other diplomatic missions is a particularly powerful way of strengthening the case which the diplomatic agent pursues. Examples of joint action had come into existence even before the conclusion of the Vienna Convention,[23] and for members of certain regional organisations, specific mechanisms of collective action have developed over the years.[24] Joint action is particularly suitable when diplomats seek to achieve an objective which is shared by several States and can therefore be appropriate when the underlying concerns relate to human rights.[25] The advantages of collective action are obvious: In the eyes of his hosts, the lone critical diplomat is an embarrassment; a group of embassies is a force which is

[22] See, for instance, the examples provided by Barder: Sending States which intend to convey a grievance to a receiving State without exacerbating the situation, might decide to do so not through the ambassador himself, but through a diplomat of lower rank; the language used in such representations might be that of a 'complaint' rather than a 'protest', the representation might be made orally rather than through a note verbale, and so forth. Barder, 51.

[23] See Satow (1979), 46–47 for examples of collective notes issued by the British, French and Italian representatives to Hungary in 1921.

[24] One of the most prominent examples is arguably the issuing of joint démarches by representatives of missions of Member States of the European Union. See on this King, 317, and for a specific example, Murray, 131. It is interesting to note that, even in this context, awareness of the impact of the relevant forms of joint statements (public statements, public *démarches*, confidential *démarches*) exists, and that the relevant actors in this field appear to appreciate the need for a staggered approach (King, 317; but see also King, 318 for the view ascribed to the European Parliament).

[25] See for instance the joint letter published by ambassadors and *chargés d'affaires* in Slovakia in 2010 and in 2011 in support of Lesbian, Gay, Bisexual and Transgender (LGBT) marches in that country (A.257 and A.275).

less easy to dismiss. Collective action can also have legal significance: If, say, 20 ambassadors, representing their States, support a particular initiative,[26] it may be difficult for the diplomatic hosts to assert that the relevant conduct is still unlawful interference. There may not yet be new customary law, but the collective measure may represent a nascent norm; and receiving States will find it challenging to claim that their interpretation of the law must be the only acceptable one.

The considerations which apply to sending States will often mirror those relating to their agents. There are, however, certain points which are of particular significance to Foreign Ministries due to the position which they occupy.

— As in the case of receiving States, the legal evaluation of diplomatic conduct is not always a necessary course of action and carries certain risks. However, if it is felt that legal assessment is required, certain conditions apply. The relevant statement has to reflect a legal, rather than political, opinion, and it must be an assessment which has relevance to international law: Stating that the diplomat has acted in compliance with his instructions, with the views of his Foreign Ministry or his President, is not likely to carry weight in the law of nations.[27]

— The most effective way of avoiding situations in which charges of interference are likely to appear, is the adoption of measures at the preventative level. It is therefore a matter of prudence to raise awareness among the holders of diplomatic office of the implications which their actions carry and indeed, as some Foreign Ministries have done, to issue specific warnings about sensitive areas of diplomatic conduct.[28] Beyond that, the fact must be borne in mind that diplomats have the potential of shaping the position of their States under international law[29]—sometimes, even through their failure to take action in the first place.[30] That means that appropriate training of members of

[26] See on this A.275.

[27] Nevertheless, sending States do at times employ such considerations in the debate about the relevant diplomatic conduct. See the 1996 case of the US *Chargé d'affaires* in Burma (A.119) and the case of the Spanish Ambassador in Cuba in the same year (A.121). It is, of course, not an entirely original attitude. In 1793, the Qianlong Emperor of China told the British special envoy, Lord Macartney: '[m]y capital is the hub and centre around which all quarters of the globe revolve', Gentzler, 26.

[28] Cf the communication by the State Department to the US Ambassador in Malaysia in 1964 (A.9), and the warning issued by the US Ambassador in Lebanon in the same year (A.10).

[29] The fact may be recalled that heads of diplomatic missions are, 'in virtue of their functions and without having to produce full powers' considered to represent the sending State for the purpose of adopting the text of a treaty or expressing that State's consent to be bound by the treaty. VCLT art 7(2)(b).

[30] See on this below, at nn 44–49.

the diplomatic service before they are sent abroad is indispensable. International law must play a key role in this—a State which fails to provide such training or contents itself with a few token lessons on the subject, must not be surprised if its representatives later involve it in obligations with far reaching consequences or commit acts which lead to claims for reparations.

— Due care must also be taken in the selection of candidates for diplomatic office. Given the complexity of the tasks and the risks attaching to the diplomatic position, governments of sending States are well advised to reject the temptation of using ambassadorships as rewards for political benefactors and to appoint career diplomats to such offices instead. That is not to say that political appointments are always a mistake—the history of diplomatic relations has seen political appointees who have acquitted themselves masterfully. But such appointments carry risks. The expertise which professional diplomats acquire by countering challenges which attach to their postings in a wide range of different societies is difficult to achieve through other career paths. That is particularly true where communicatory skills are involved, which play such an important role in diplomatic engagement with fields which carry sensitivity for the receiving government. Career diplomats tend to have an advantage in that regard—the master of the political sabre is not necessarily master of the diplomatic épée.

3. OF EXPECTATIONS AND OPPORTUNITIES: DOES THE WORLD NEED THE MEDDLING DIPLOMAT?

That diplomatic interference is a concept whose legal assessment is a matter of some complexity, is beyond doubt. To diplomats around the world it is, however, also a phenomenon which is subject to public expectations—some of which may have undergone considerable change in the course of diplomatic history.

Two cases, two generations apart, illustrate the difficulty. In August 1915, Henry Morgenthau, US Ambassador to the Ottoman Empire (and father of the later US Secretary of the Treasury, Henry Morgenthau Jr), was an early observer of what would become known as the Armenian genocide.[31] But Morgenthau felt the fetters of diplomatic office: In a communication to the State Department he noted that it was 'difficult' for him to restrain himself 'from doing something to stop this attempt to

[31] On the prevailing debate on the classification of the crimes against the Armenians, see Sarkissian, 3–15 and Cayci, 17–27.

exterminate a race, but I realize that I am here as Ambassador and must abide [by] the principles of noninterference'.[32]

The other case occurred in November 1991. In that month, the Kenyan Foreign Ministry summoned the American and the German Ambassador as well as their colleagues from five other countries and accused them of interference in internal affairs.[33] The decision came after charges of human rights violations had been made against the Kenyan government and after US Ambassador Hempstone and the German Ambassador had tried to attend a pro-democracy rally.[34]

But on that occasion, the diplomats and their masters showed themselves unrepentant. Ambassador Hempstone, whose conduct had been fiercely attacked, put up an equally passionate defence.[35] The State Department strongly defended its Ambassador;[36] the German Foreign Ministry even summoned the Kenyan Ambassador and expressed its concerns about human rights violations in the receiving State.[37]

Diplomatic involvement in the human rights situation of the receiving State may indeed be one of the more obvious examples in which the diplomatic attitude towards sensitive areas in the receiving State has changed over the years.[38] The same can be said about public expectations of the diplomatic office: Observers in many States today would side rather with a Hempstone than a Morgenthau, and there is evidence that contemporary diplomatic action is at times seen as not going far enough in the defence of certain interests abroad.[39] What is more: There is reason to believe that the international community today will often support diplomatic agents who have resorted to representations to protect certain interests, even if the receiving State considers them to fall within its domestic sphere.[40]

[32] Letter from US Ambassador in Turkey to US Secretary of State (11 August 1915), quoted in Bazyler, 593.

[33] N Henry, 'Kenya Levels Broadside' *Washington Post* (Washington DC, 19 November 1991) and 'Undiplomatic Relations' *Washington Post* (Washington DC, 24 November 1991).

[34] Henry, n 33.

[35] At a news conference, the Kenyan Foreign Minister had described Hempstone's attitude as 'that of a slave owner who wants to guide Africans to wherever he wants them to go'. Hempstone, who had encouraged political pluralism in Kenya, countered charges of racism by posing the rhetorical question 'Who is the racist? The one who suggests Kenyans are mature enough to handle multi-party democracy or those who suggest they are too primitive to handle it?', ibid.

[36] *Washington Post*, 'Undiplomatic Relations', 24 November 1991.

[37] Henry, n 33.

[38] See Behrens (2014b), 194, 195.

[39] See King, 318, on views ascribed to the European Parliament.

[40] This change in the evaluation of diplomatic conduct of this kind is made particularly clear through the acceptance of *erga omnes* obligations which may arise on the side of the receiving State, and in whose fulfilment all members of the international community can claim to have a legitimate interest. See ch 3, at nn 119–20. Situations in which diplomats, as in the case of Henry Morgenthau Sr, are faced with the suspected commission of international crimes in the receiving State, would most likely trigger such *erga omnes* obligations on behalf of the diplomatic hosts. See ch 3, at 126.

It is, on the other hand, not difficult to understand that some diplomatic agents, even in the 21st century, may shy away from involvement in these fields. The reasons are often pragmatic in nature: Diplomats still have to live in the country to which they are assigned; they have to deal with the governments whose policies may be the target of such conduct, and they will often be in a weaker position than a host who has numerous sanctions at its disposal when it comes to dealing with wayward agents.

At the same time, the fact remains that involvement in sensitive matters may correspond not only to a right of the sending State and its agents, but to a positive duty under international law.

Recent developments have seen an increasing identification of such obligations under general customary law, such as the duty, in certain situations, to remove impediments to the realisation of the right to self-determination,[41] and (less controversially) the general duty of an injured State to give notification to the responsible State of a decision to take countermeasures against it.[42] And duties to act may arise with even greater frequency under special treaty regimes which impose obligations on those States that are parties to them.[43]

Beyond that, however, there are situations in which inaction by diplomatic agents will result in the loss of a significant position which the sending State may hitherto have claimed. A case which was decided by the ICJ one year after the conclusion of the Vienna Convention is illuminating. The matter concerned the Temple of Preah Vihear—a territorial area disputed between Cambodia and Thailand (formerly the Kingdom of Siam).[44] The Court found, by a majority, that the temple was in territory which fell into Cambodia's sovereignty,[45] and it based its decision on various considerations, including acts which allegedly showed that Thailand had accepted such sovereignty.[46] They included (as 'much the most significant episode')[47] a visit to the temple in 1930 by the Siamese Prince Damrong, President of the Royal Institute of Siam, as part of an archaeological initiative. Upon arrival, the Prince was received by the French resident (Cambodia being then part of French Indo-China), 'with the French flag flying'.[48] The lack of a protest by the Prince was

[41] See ch 3, at n 173.

[42] See ch 10, at n 49, with reference to Draft Arts on State Responsibility (2001), 135, art 52(1)(b).

[43] See, for instance, for the duty to prevent genocide as enshrined in the Genocide Convention, ch 3, at n 222, and for duties in the context of human rights protection when sending States have assumed jurisdiction over persons outside their territories, ch 11, at nn 102 ff.

[44] *Preah Vihear*, 6 ff.

[45] ibid, 34.

[46] ibid, 30.

[47] ibid.

[48] ibid.

of particular significance in the eyes of the Court, which found that the incident appeared 'to have amounted to a tacit recognition by Siam of the sovereignty of Cambodia … over Preah Vihear'.[49] But if the 'quasi-official character' of the delegation sufficed in this case for the view that Damrong's conduct bound the government of Thailand, there can be little doubt that such a conclusion would stand on even firmer ground if the relevant person had been the holder of diplomatic office.

There are therefore situations in which the range of options for diplomatic agents is considerably reduced—and which leave diplomats with no choice but to take action, no matter how controversial that may appear to their hosts.

But the reasons why the diplomatic voice must be heard, even in areas of great sensitivity, transcends the interests of individual sending States.

The Murrays, Donnellys and Gaudeuls of this world[50] are at the forefront of international relations, and they have knowledge of circumstances of which their masters, back at home, may not be aware (or choose not to be aware). There is a responsibility which attaches to such knowledge.

In situations in which human rights abuses take place on a large scale, in which the commission of international crimes is imminent, in which peoples are deprived of their right to determine their own political fate, diplomatic agents find themselves in a unique position.

They, more than most other individuals in the receiving State, are able to issue an authoritative protest, and to draw the attention of other States to the significance and urgency of the situation in the host country. But there is more to it than that. In a situation of oppression, when all legitimate venues of relief within the territorial State have been barred, diplomatic missions are, often enough, the only remnants of the voice of the international community. It is a voice which gives hope where hope is dearly required.

The masters of the land may well consider such conduct interference in their own affairs. It would be surprising if they did not. But if that be the measure of assessment, the conclusion on diplomatic conduct in this area has to be clear: A world in which States advance their own discretion above the mandates of international law, has unabated need for the meddling diplomat.

[49] ibid, 30 and 31.

[50] See A.186; A.182; A.181.

Annex A—Timeline of Diplomatic Interference

The subsequent timeline is a compilation of incidents of reported diplomatic interference, dating from April 1961 (the month in which the Vienna Convention was signed) to April 2014 (the fiftieth anniversary of its entry into force). It does not claim to be an exhaustive list.

The cases which have been included relate to interference by diplomatic agents. Reference has also been made to incidents concerning agents whose offices show sufficient proximity to that of traditional diplomats (such as members of Libyan People's Bureaux and members of interests sections in cases in which sending and receiving State do not entertain official diplomatic relations). On rare occasions, cases have been included in which diplomats had not yet been appointed to their prospective posts (especially if charges of interference led to rejection by their potential receiving States). Incidents of consular interference and interference by agents of international organisations, on the other hand, are not included—neither are cases in which the alleged interference had been committed not by diplomats, but by other State organs (such as the Government of the sending State), even if the consequences of the receiving State's displeasure were then felt by a diplomat 'on the ground'.

In principle, preference has been given to those cases in which organs of the receiving State have issued a reaction, but on some occasions, incidents are included in which influential observers (such as Members of Parliament etc) have responded to conduct which they considered interference in internal affairs. On rare occasions, it is the sending State which warned its diplomats against interference—these cases, too, have been incorporated (see eg, A.9 and A.10).

As a general rule, cases of diplomatic asylum have not been included. They often arise in the Latin American context, where specific rules outside the regime of the Vienna Convention on Diplomatic Relations governs their assessment (see on this, chapter 11, section 2.1).

1. 1961, April

After the Polish Ambassador to the US had, in public addresses, attacked the Federal Republic of Germany, the US Secretary of State issues a warning letter to him on 19 April 1961, stating that 'representational activities' did not extend to making public attacks 'upon a government with which the United States maintains friendly relations'.

— Whiteman (1970), 147, 148

2. 1961, August

The US Embassy to Brazil announces the departure of John Moors Cabot, the US Ambassador to that country. Cabot's departure follows a statement by the Ambassador on the possibility of Brazil's attendance of a meeting of 'uncommitted nations'. The Ambassador noted that Brazil was not an uncommitted country, as it was in an alliance with the United States and other American States. At the time, Brazilian president Quadros stated that Brazil would 'not tolerate meddling from anyone'.

— *St Petersburg Times*, 'U.S. Envoy Will Leave Brazil Post', 1 August 1961
— *Ottawa Citizen*, 'U.S. Replaces Brazil Envoy', 2 August 1961

3. 1962, May

Wilhelm Grewe, West German Ambassador to the United States, is recalled, following several incidents which revealed differences in attitude between him and his hosts. In autumn 1961, Grewe had in an interview recalled the treaty obligations of the four powers with regard to Berlin and warned against the making of concessions to Russia on that question. It is reported that President Kennedy had referred to Grewe as 'incompatible'.

— *The Times*, 'Summoned Home for Consultation', 8 May 1962

4. 1962, November

Petros Moliviatis, Second Secretary at the Greek Embassy in Moscow, is expelled amid accusations of espionage activities. Greece denies the accusations and states that the expulsion showed the Soviet intention to impede contacts between the Greek Embassy and ethnic Greeks in the Soviet Union. An estimated population of 51,000 Greeks lives at that time in parts of the Soviet Union; Moliviatis had visited Soviet Greeks in July 1962.

— *RGDIP*, 'Chronique des faits internationaux' (1963), 179–80
— Salmon (1996), 133

5. 1963, June

Three Chinese diplomats are expelled from the Soviet Union after they had allegedly distributed a 'party letter' which dealt with 25 points which the Chinese side wanted to discuss at Sino-Soviet talks in Russia. The letter allegedly contains accusations targeted at Khrushchev's personal policy of peaceful coexistence.

China, while complying with a Soviet demand for immediate withdrawal of the diplomats, calls the Soviet measure an 'unreasonable demand'.

— *The Times*, 'China Condemns Russia for Expulsions', 1 July 1963
— Salmon (1976), 42

6. 1963, August

An official note of protest is sent by the Bolivian Ministry of Foreign Affairs to Robert LaSalle, the Cuban *chargé d'affaires* in that country. Bolivia complains about interference by members of the Cuban mission in strikes which, in July 1963, had been started by trade unions in the Catavi region and which affected the mining industry.

In the following year, Bolivia severs diplomatic relations with Cuba altogether.

— *RGDIP*, 'Chronique des faits internationaux' (1964), 164
— *St Petersburg Times*, 'Bolivia Breaks Ties With Cuba', 22 August 1964

7. 1963, November

Boris Voronin, Counsellor at the Soviet Embassy to Congo-Léopoldville (today Democratic Republic of Congo), is expelled amid allegations of subversive activities.

Voronin had allegedly provided active support to a plot against the Congolese Government. Voronin is arrested together with Yuri Myakotnykh, the Soviet Press Attaché and is put on an airplane to Brussels. Voronin also claims to have been beaten by Congolese security forces.

— *The Times*, 'Russian Official Leaves Congo', 23 November 1963

8. 1964, March

The British Ambassador to Panama, Randle Reid-Adam, faces criticism in the local press, after he had reportedly stated, at a cocktail party, that every Panamanian could be bought for £100. On 27 March, a molotov cocktail is thrown from a passing car and explodes near the terrace of the Embassy, in the proximity of the Ambassador.

Toward the end of March, Reid-Adam returns to London, where during a medical check-up, it is found that he is not fit for service in Central America. The Ambassador is replaced in May.

— *The Times*, 'Envoys Return from Panama', 2 April 1964
— Rousseau, 167
— *RGDIP*, 'Chronique des faits internationaux' (1964), 956

9. 1964, March

The US Department of State sends a communication to the US Ambassador in Malaysia (James Bell), warning against partisan political activities by Embassy employees.

Parliamentary elections were due to take place in Malaysia in April 1964. US Secretary of State Rusk's letter notes that Malaysian employees of the American Embassy would be required to resign their position if they participated in partisan political activities. The Malaysian Government had adopted a similar policy with regard to its own employees. It is Rusk's view that a foreign State should use even more caution.

— *The Times*, 'The Tunku Wins A Sweeping Victory', 27 April 1964
— Whiteman (1970), 144

10. 1964, March

The US Ambassador to Lebanon, Armin Meyer, warns US diplomats against involvement in the electoral campaign in Lebanon in that year (Parliamentary elections were due to take place in April and May 1964). Meyer cautions Embassy 'employees and their dependents … against taking any actions or making any statements which could in any way suggest that [the US] favors any candidate or candidates in the forthcoming general elections …. In any discussions on local political matters it should be made clear that the American Embassy supports no candidate and has no role in the elections.'

— Whiteman (1970), 143

11. 1964, December

General Maxwell Taylor, US Ambassador to South Vietnam, is accused of interference in internal affairs. The accusations were apparently made by General Nguyễn Khánh, one of the military leaders of South Vietnam. In a talk with members of the Government, Taylor had pointed out that US aid to Vietnam depended on the 'promise of Government stability and orderly political evolution' (Times).

The US Embassy states that Taylor's conduct had not been 'improper', and that his activities had been 'designed to serve the best interests of both Vietnam and the United States'.

— *The Times*, 'Embassy Denial of Interference', 24 December 1964

12. 1965, June

David Bartov, First Secretary at the Israeli Embassy in Moscow, is accused of propaganda.

In the course of a journey to Georgia, Bartov had allegedly distributed cigarettes as well as Israeli books and journals and had urged Soviet citizens to leave the Soviet Union and to settle in Israel.

According to a Georgian newspaper, Bartov had engaged in 'zionist propaganda'. His conduct had, according to the newspaper, been rejected by the population of Georgia 'with indignation'.

— *RGDIP*, 'Chronique des faits internationaux' (1965), 833
— *The Miami News*, 'Soviets Rap Israel Envoy', 1 June 1965
— Salmon (1996), 133

13. 1965

The Chargé d'affaires of the People's Republic of China is accused by the Government of the Netherlands of anti-American propaganda. The 'propaganda material' had been exhibited in the Chargé d'affaires' office.

— Salmon (1996), 135
— Panhuys et al, vol 3, 250

14. 1966

The Soviet Union accuses Israeli diplomats of 'zionist propaganda'; conduct which, it is alleged, is incompatible with their functions.

— Salmon (1996), 133

15. 1967, October

The recall of Wymberley Coerr, US Ambassador to Ecuador, is requested. The measure follows a speech Coerr gave in Quito, in which he had dealt with remarks made by the Ecuadorian President.

Ecuador complains that Coerr's statements revealed an 'attitude of public, open criticism' of the President and states that this would make it difficult for the Ambassador to contribute to the strengthening of friendly relations between the two countries.

Coerr is recalled, but the US notes that his speech was a 'reasoned, non-polemical discussion …', that the relevant issues were of 'transcendental importance to all members of the Alliance for Progress' and that no 'member's opinion should be immune from respectful and friendly examination by others'.

— Whiteman (1970), 145
— *RGDIP*, 'Chronique des faits internationaux' (1968), 431

16. 1968, May

Semyon Tsarapkin, Soviet Ambassador to West Germany, is accused of interference after his participation in a demonstration by the Extraparliamentary Opposition (*Außerparlamentarische Opposition*, APO).

Tsarapkin had joined a demonstration by students of the extreme left, who formed part of the APO. Tsarapkin is criticised for this conduct by two Conservative Members of Parliament, who accuse the Ambassador of 'interference with the internal affairs of Germany which was difficult to tolerate'.

German authorities however point out that the demonstration had been officially authorised and provide no further comment.

— Przetacznik (1975), 309
— *RGDIP*, 'Chronique de faits internationaux' (1969), 155

17. 1969, August

At the time of the trial in Kinshasa (Democratic Republic of Congo) of students who had participated in anti-government demonstrations, General Mobutu asks the doyen of the diplomatic corps (the apostolic nuncio) to forbid the diplomatic corps accredited in Kinshasa to interfere in any way in the internal affairs of the State.

— Salmon (1996), 134

18. 1970, April

The Embassy of the Soviet Union to the Netherlands faces criticism after it distributes publications attacking Israeli leaders. In the States-General, it is suggested to the Government that, while embassies had the right to make the views of their governments public, a campaign which drew 'parallels between Israeli leaders and Nazi criminals', was outside the boundaries of the permissible.

The Minister of Foreign Affairs replies that he had stated 'in the proper quarters that distribution of publications directed against third countries should be outside the scope of activities of embassies' in the Netherlands.

— Sik, 167

19. 1970, April

The Greek Ambassador to Belgium is criticised over a conference, supported by the Greek Embassy, which coincided with the anniversary of the coup d'état in Greece. The Belgian Government had asked him to use his influence to postpone the conference; the event did, however, take place, resulting in serious clashes between protesting students and Belgian security.

The Ambassador is afterwards summoned by the Belgian Foreign Minister and told that the role of diplomats envisaged the facilitating of relations between States. The Ambassador subsequently effects the cancellation of some further events and celebrations.

— *RBDI*, 'La pratique belge' (1972), 316–19
— Salmon (1996), 134

20. 1971, July

Several diplomats from the Soviet Union, Yugoslavia, Romania, Poland and Czechoslovakia are expelled from the (DR) Congo amid allegations of involvement in anti-Government student demonstrations.

President Mobutu, who considers the demonstrations as part of a plot against the Government and a plan to kill him, is quoted as stating that 'a foreign hand had sought to use the students of Lovanium to achieve its aims'. In an interview, he also warns of a 'cascade of diplomatic breaks' [sic].

— *New York Times*, 'Congo Expels Soviet Aides', 29 July 1971
— *The Times*, 'Congo Expels Communist Block Diplomats', 30 July 1971

21. 1971, October

The US Ambassador (Tasca) and the West German Ambassador (Limbourg) to Greece, are criticised by the Greek regime for maintaining contacts to certain politicians. Limbourg had visited the former conservative Prime Minister Kanellopoulos and a leading politician of the Greek Centre Union (Mavros). Tasca had visited former Prime Minister Karamanlis. The Greek military junta expresses the opinion that foreign ambassadors should not keep contact with former politicians who 'had placed themselves outside the country's political system by refusing to recognize the constitution'.

— Salmon (1996), 131
— *The Times*, 'Greek Cabinet Minister Attacks German Envoy', 14 October 1971

22. 1972, March

119 Soviet diplomats, Embassy employees and dependants are expelled from Bolivia.

The expulsion comes amid charges that the diplomats had maintained contact to a Communist guerilla organisation. The Government also accuses the Embassy of financing leftist rebel movements, and there are allegations that those expelled were involved in a Cuban-organised plot to invade Bolivia. The Soviet Ambassador denies the charges.

— *New York Times*, 'Bolivia Is Ousting 112 Soviet Aides', 30 March 1972
— R Wigg, 'Soviet Poet "Expelled" After Visit to Bolivia', *The Times*, 1 April 1972
— J De Onis, 'Russians Ask 69 Exit Visas', *The New York Times*, 8 April 1972
— Francis (1985)

23. 1972, August

The Soviet Ambassador to France (Abrassimov), is criticised for a letter which he had allowed to be published. The letter replied to concerns raised by Mitterrand on the situation of the Jews in the Soviet Union and on obstacles put in the way of their emigration to Israel. Abrassimov wrote that he was forced to communicate his reply through the press, as Mitterrand, too, had made his statements publicly. He strongly defended Soviet measures on emigration. The Secretary-General of the *Ligue des droits de l'homme* reportedly states that an ambassador had rarely used such insolence, and such an authoritarian tone.

— *RGDIP*, 'Chronique des faits internationaux' (1973), 1214
— Rousseau, 167

24. 1973, July

The recall of Vincent de Roulet, the US Ambassador to Jamaica, is requested after de Roulet had stated before the US Senate that he had struck a deal with the Jamaican Prime Minister Manley ahead of elections in 1972. According to de Roulet, he had agreed that the United States would not interfere in the elections, whereas Manley had promised not to raise the issue of the nationalisation of the bauxite industry (which was owned by the United States) in the campaign.

— *Press Courier, The*, 'Jamaica Demands Envoy Recall', 22 July 1973

25. 1973, August

Both houses of the Argentinian Parliament pass resolutions calling on the Government to consider declaring Max Krebs, the US *chargé d'affaires*, persona non grata. Mr Krebs met the displeasure of Parliament after he had issued a letter and several memoranda in which he criticised governmental plans to nationalise foreign banks and to issue certain laws on foreign enterprises. Krebs felt that these bills would have a negative effect on foreign investment in Argentina.

— *The Age*, 'Argentina May Expel U.S. Envoy', 3 August 1973
— *Calgary Herald*, 'Expulsion of Diplomat Demanded', 4 August 1973

26. 1974, May

The Chilean Ambassador to Belgium (Nuño) is criticised after he made a statement to a news agency, in which he tried to justify the role of the Chilean armed forces during the overthrow of the Allende Government.

In May 1974, Senator Calewaert states that the Ambassador's attitude was contrary to diplomatic usage and rules of courtesy.

The Minister of Foreign Affairs replies that Nuño's remarks may have been unusual, but that it was part of the tasks of a diplomat to explain the prevailing situation in his country and the position of his Government.

— *RBDI*, 'La pratique belge' (1976), 186–88

27. 1975, July

Three Cuban diplomats working in the cultural section of the Cuban Embassy to France are expelled. The diplomats had allegedly maintained contact with the Venezuelan terrorist Ilich Ramirez Sanchez ('Carlos the Jackal'). It is reported that they had transferred money and instructions to Ramirez Sanchez.

The Cuban Chargé d'affaires is summoned by the French Foreign Ministry and told about the decision to expel the three diplomats.

The Cuban Embassy denies allegations of involvement with Carlos and states that the Cuban Government rejects terrorist methods.

— R Wigg, 'Expulsion of Cubans in Paris "Jackal" Case', *The Times*, 11 July 1975
— R Carroll et al, 'All Roads Lead to Paris', *Newsweek*, 21 July 1975

28. 1975, November

The Ugandan President Idi Amin accuses the Soviet Ambassador Andrei Zakharov of interference. Zakharov had allegedly exerted pressure on Uganda to recognise the Popular Liberation Movement in Angola. Amin calls for Zakharov's withdrawal; the Soviet Union on the other hand decides to suspend diplomatic relations with Uganda.

— *Milwaukee Journal*, 'Amin Shifts on Break With Russia', 12 November 1975
— *Milwaukee Sentinel*, 'Russ Break Ties With Uganda', 12 November 1975

29. 1975, December

William Porter, US Ambassador to Canada, is criticised for remarks made to journalists. Porter had criticised certain Canadian economic policies, including increases in oil and gas prices, efforts of the Province Saskatchewan to buy or nationalise potassium deposits, the ban on American advertisements on cable television in Canada and controls on foreign investment.

The Canadian Prime Minister Pierre Trudeau accuses Porter in a speech to Parliament of having exceeded the limits of diplomatic propriety. Porter's opinions reportedly surprised him with regard to their substance and their form. On 18 December, a communiqué, issued after a meeting of Kissinger and MacEachen (his Canadian counterpart) implied a rejection of Porter's opinions.

— *Newsweek*, 'Canada: The Bitter Truth', 29 December 1975
— *RGDIP*, 'Chronique des faits internationaux' (1976), 897, 898

30. 1976, March

The US Ambassador to Mexico, Joseph-John Jova is criticised for comments made at the University of Washington. Jova had stated that the political system in Mexico was one of 'monarchical succession, no matter how democratic' where the current practice of presidential succession was concerned.

Lopez Portillo, candidate in the July presidential elections of Mexico, speaks of Jova's comments as 'apparent efforts to destabilise through mocking criticism'.

Following the reactions, Jova publishes a statement in which he described Mexico as 'a model of democracy and authentic freedom' and her President as 'one of the century's great leaders'.

— *Intelligence Research Ltd, Latin America*, 'News in Brief: Mexico', 2 April 1976
— *RGDIP*, 'Chronique des faits internationaux' (1976), 1218, 1219
— Rousseau, 166

31. 1976, April

Malcolm Toon, US Ambassador to Israel, is criticised for comments made about aspects of Israeli policy. At a news conference, Toon had accused Israel of trying to pressure the US Congress into providing more aid.

The Israeli Government reportedly considers the comments a violation of the rules of diplomacy; Israeli Foreign Minister Yigal Allon states that he would ask Toon to explain his behaviour.

The US State Department disassociates itself from Toon's remarks.

— *New York Times*, 'Israelis Rebuke U.S. Ambassador', 10 April 1976
— *Facts on File*, 'U.S., Israel dispute aid', 17 April 1976

32. 1976, June

François Puaux, the French Ambassador to Italy, is criticised for attending the meeting of Democrazia Cristiana, an Italian party. In Rome, a French Parliamentarian expresses his surprise about Puaux' conduct.

French Prime Minister Jacques Chirac however accuses the Parliamentarian of a 'surprising ignorance of diplomatic usages. A diplomat would in fact always attend, as an observer, political meetings to which he is invited. That is true in all the countries of the world'.

— AFDI, 'Pratique française' (1976), 1000

33. 1976, June

Milod El-Sedik Ramadan, the Libyan Ambassador to Egypt, is expelled after he had, according to Egyptian officials, handed out pamphlets which were hostile to the Government of President Sadat. He was detained and questioned by security authorities and later declared persona non grata by the Egyptian Government.

— Satow (1979), 186, para 21.24
— *The Times*, 'Libyan Envoy is Expelled from Egypt', 1 July 1976

34. 1976, July

The American Ambassador to Yugoslavia, Laurence Silberman, is criticised for his attempts to help effect the release of Laszlo Toth, a US citizen, who had been imprisoned for espionage.

In an interview with Tanyug (the official Yugoslav news agency), the President of Yugoslavia, Tito, sharply accuses Silberman of interference in the affairs in the receiving State. But Silberman also faces criticism from within the receiving State. The Eastern European Section of the State Department allegedly finds the Ambassador 'too zealous'.

— *Facts on File*, 'Tito Attacks U.S. Envoy', 14 August 1976
— *Facts on File*, 'Jailed American Freed', 31 July 1976

35. 1976, July

The Yugoslav President Tito accuses Silberman, US Ambassador to Yugoslavia, of initiating 'a campaign against us in the U.S.... He is saying that it pays to exert pressure on Yugoslavia ... He is giving lessons about our internal and foreign policy and interfering in our affairs'. Tito's concerns are seen in the context of potential American attempts to 'compromise' Yugoslavia ahead of the summit of the Non-Aligned Movement.

The State Department notes that Silberman had the full confidence of President Ford and that it was 'against US policy to interfere in internal affairs of Yugoslavia'.

— *Facts on File*, 'Tito Attacks U.S. Envoy', 14 August 1976
— *New York Times*, 'Washington Denies "Campaign"', 1 August 1976

36. 1977, April

After two US diplomats visit an official of the French Communist Party in Paris (at the time of municipal elections in France), French President Giscard d'Éstaing expresses his concern and says that US contacts of this kind amounted to interference. The US Embassy states that the two diplomats had merely talked about foreign policy with the politicians, that the US would not interfere in the 'electoral affairs' of other countries and that there was 'nothing new' about talks of this kind.

— C Hargrove, 'French Leftist Views Put Across to US Diplomats', *The Times*, 6 April 1977
— *Facts on File*, 'Giscard Scores U.S. Talks with Left', 9 April 1977

37. 1977, June

The Chilean Ambassador to France (Irarrázaval) is criticised for remarks made about the reception by the President of France of Mrs Allende, widow of Salvador Allende (the deposed Chilean President).

Irarrázaval had reportedly complained about the reception, but had also added that the President had perhaps welcomed Mrs Allende out of politeness. The French Foreign Minister considers the remarks of the Chilean Ambassador as not conforming to the customs and the duty of reserve that are incumbent upon ambassadors.

— Salmon (1996), 132
— *AFDI*, 'Pratique française' (1977), 1071

38. 1977, July

The Greek Government declares the designated US Ambassador to Greece, Schaufele, undesirable. Schaufele had reportedly, during his Senate hearing, stated that boundaries which had been set in the past in a thoughtless manner were the reasons for certain tensions between Greece and Turkey.

The Greek Ambassador to the United States, states that the comments by Schaufele appeared to question Greece's right to the territory.

In December 1977, President Carter declares that instead of Schaufele, McCloskey would become Ambassador to Greece.

— *RGDIP*, 'Chronique des faits internationaux' (1977), 827
— *RGDIP*, 'Chronique des faits internationaux' (1978), 276
— *Facts on File*, 'Schaufele Rejected as U.S. Envoy', 6 August 1977

39. 1978, September

Several Soviet and East German diplomats are expelled from Ghana. According to reports from Ghana, the diplomats were accused of fomenting unrest. They had carried out activities in trade unions, universities and the press of Ghana which were deemed undiplomatic and hostile. Ghana charges the diplomats with interference in internal affairs.

According to other reports, an alleged engagement in espionage activities may have contributed to the decision by the Ghanaian Government.

— *Xinhua*, 'Four Soviet Diplomats Expelled from Ghana', 11 September 1978
— *Xinhua*, 'Kenyan Paper Exposes Soviet Spying Activities', 4 October 1978
— *Facts on File*, 'Ghana', 3 November 1978

40. 1979

The Ambassador of Zaire (now Democratic Republic of the Congo) to Belgium is criticised for remarks on party politics which were published in a Belgian newspaper.

The Ambassador had issued a critical opinion on the President of one of the major political parties in Belgium. The Belgian Minister for Foreign Affairs expresses his regret over these statements which in his view could have been interpreted as polemic.

— Salmon (1996), 132

41. 1979

The French military attaché in Argentina is criticised after he expressed his 'public support and admiration for the conduct of the Argentine military forces in defending freedom against subversion'. At that time, cases of disappearance and breaches of human rights had become widely known in Argentina (and denounced by human rights organisations and the Organization of American States). The French Minister for Foreign

Affairs distances himself from the attaché's statements and declares that the attaché has been removed from the Embassy post.

— Denza, 467

42. 1979, January

According to a Turkish Parliamentarian, the UK Ambassador to Turkey, Dodson, had congratulated the leader of an opposition party, after a vote on the declaration of martial law in 13 provinces.

Turkish Prime Minister Ecevit notes that a diplomat may converse with people in Parliament and that he could not imagine that any ambassador who knew Turkey 'would indulge in talk [calculated] to influence Turkey's internal affairs'.

Dodson denies the allegations.

— *BBC Summary*, 'British Ambassador Accused of Interfering', 5 January 1979
— *BBC Summary*, 'British Ambassador Accused of Interfering', 6 January 1979

43. 1979, January

Following the publication of letters he had written to US newspapers, the Taiwanese diplomat Loh I Cheng is withdrawn from the United States. In the context of the intention of the Carter administration to pursue full diplomatic relations with PR China, Cheng had written letters critical of the policy and inter alia accused the United States of 'shabby treatment' of the population of Taiwan. It is reported that the US Government considered Cheng's conduct to violate 'general diplomatic practices'.

— D Morgan, 'Taiwan Recalls Diplomat Who Scored U.S. Policy', *The Washington Post*, 30 January 1979
— Gedda, G, 'Washington. The Carter Administration has Expelled', *Associated Press*, 30 January 1979

44. 1979, March

Ho Xuan Dich, Second Secretary at the Vietnamese Embassy to Canada, is expelled. Ho was accused of intimidating members of the Vietnamese community in Canada. According to an investigation carried out by the

Royal Canadian Mounted Police, he had threatened reprisals against relatives of the Vietnamese exiles who still lived in Vietnam.

The Vietnamese Embassy states that the decision to expel Ho had been based on 'false reasons'.

— *Facts on File*, 'Vietnamese Diplomat Expelled', 13 April 1979

45. 1979, May

The Vietnamese Ambassador to Sweden, Nguyen Viet, is summoned to the Swedish Foreign Ministry over his conduct during the visit of Geng Biao, the Vice Prime Minister of China, to Sweden. At the time, the Ambassador had hosted a press conference during which he had reportedly made personal attacks on the Chinese leader and accused China's frontier forces of the commission of crimes. According to the Swedish side, this constituted a 'contravention of international practice'.

— *Xinhua*, 'Vietnamese Ambassador to Sweden Rebuked', 20 May 1979

46. 1979, June

Iran rejects designated US Ambassador Walter Cutler. The Iranian Foreign Minister refers to the alleged US intervention in Zaire (today Democratic Republic of the Congo), while Cutler was US Ambassador there.

The US State Department declares that there were no plans to withdraw Cutler's name or to reassign him and that President Carter and Secretary of State Cyrus Vance maintained 'full confidence' in Mr Cutler.

— *Facts on File*, 'U.S. Ambassador Barred', 8 June 1979
— J Hoagland, 'U.S. Rebuffs Iran', *The Washington Post*, 5 June 1979

47. 1979, August

Three Soviet diplomats are expelled from Costa Rica. The expulsion comes at a time of labour strikes and incidents of violence, with the Costa Rican President stating that 'international agitators' were behind these events. The diplomats had reportedly 'violated the principle of non-interference in the internal affairs' of Costa Rica.

The Soviet Embassy denies charges of interference in Costa Rica's internal affairs.

— *Associated Press*, 'International News. San Jose, Costa Rica', 20 August 1979

— *Facts on File*, '3 Soviet Envoys Expelled', 7 September 1979
— *Xinhua*, 'Costa Rica Not to Allow Moscow', 10 September 1979

48. 1980, January

The Soviet Ambassador to New Zealand, Vsevolod Sofinsky, is expelled. According to the Prime Minister of New Zealand (Muldoon), Sofinsky had been involved in the transfer of money from the Soviet Government to the Socialist Unity Party of New Zealand. Muldoon notes that the 'personal involvement of the Ambassador shows that this is a matter of official Soviet policy'. He also states that it was an 'established international convention that a diplomatic representative does not interfere in the domestic politics' of the receiving State. Sofinsky and the Socialist Unity Party deny the allegations.

— *Associated Press*, 'New Zealand Boots Soviet Ambassador', 23 January 1980
— *Facts on File*, 'Soviet Ambassador Expelled', 8 February 1980

49. 1980, April

Two diplomats of the Libyan people's bureau in the United States (Tarhuni and Ibrahim) are expelled after allegedly distributing documents which called for the 'liquidation' of opponents of Gaddafi, who were living in the United States. Colonel Gaddafi had, from February 1980 on, warned that his enemies would be 'eliminated physically'.

— *Washington Post*, 'Another Libyan Exile Assassinated in London', 26 April 1980
— C Hartman, 'Expelled Libyans Refusing to Leave U.S.', *Associated Press*, 7 May 1980

50. 1980, May

The US State Department announces the expulsion of four members of the Libyan diplomatic mission, accusing them of engagement 'in intimidation activities' toward Libyan dissidents in this country. The State Department refers to their conduct as involvement 'in activities that we consider unacceptable'.

— J Ritchie, 'U.S. Expels 4 More Libyan Diplomats', *Washington Post*, 4 May 1980
— *Associated Press*, 'U.S. Expels Libyan Diplomats', 5 May 1980

51. 1980, May

Four people connected to the Libyan People's Bureau in the United Kingdom are expelled. The four had allegedly threatened Libyan exiles in London with death if they did not return to Libya.

Douglas Hurd, then Minister of State at the Foreign Office, announces the expulsion of the four for 'activities incompatible with their functions'.

— *The Times*, 'Libya Agrees to Withdraw', 13 May 1980
— *Washington Post*, 'Libya Recalls 4 Envoys', 13 May 1980
— HC Deb 12 May 1980, vol 984, c 846

52. 1980, June

The commander of a powerful Bolivian military corps declares a 'state of emergency' in East Bolivia, which is to remain in effect until the US Ambassador to that country, Marvin Weissman, would have left the State. Weissman is accused of interfering in the internal affairs of Bolivia by taking a position in favour of general elections. (Bolivian military commanders had called for a postponement of elections.)

— *Xinhua*, 'Bolivia's Armed Forces Call for Delaying of General Elections', 11 June 1980
— *New York Times*, 'Bolivia Military Chiefs Call for Postponement', 10 June 1980

53. 1980, June

Musa Kusa, Secretary of the Libyan diplomatic mission to London is expelled. Following recent executions of Libyan dissidents in Europe, Kusa had reportedly stated to a journalist: 'The revolutionary committees have decided last night to kill two more people in the United Kingdom. I approve of this. They [the targets] are resident in Britain …'. Kusa also noted: 'We are now seriously thinking of cooperating with the IRA if the British Government continues to support those Libyans who are hiding here'.

His remarks prompt an investigation by Scotland Yard's anti-terrorist squad. On the day after his statement, Kusa is summoned by the Foreign Office and informed about his expulsion.

— M Horsnell, 'Gaddafi Men Sentence to Death', *The Times*, 13 June 1980
— S Tendler et al, 'Head of Libyan Mission is Expelled', *The Times*, 14 June 1980

54. 1980, August

The US Ambassador to Bolivia (Weissman), is criticised for allegedly allowing a journalist (Bonner) to send a story through diplomatic channels. Bonner's story had referred to the events relating to the recent coup d'état, to attempts by the armed forces 'to tighten their grip on Bolivia's major cities …', and to instances of disappearances.

The Bolivian Information Minister states that the use of Embassy channels for the transmission of such 'false and libelous' material was a 'direct foreign intervention in Bolivia's internal affairs'.

— Tom Fenton, 'U.S. Ambassador Accused', *Associated Press*, 4 August 1980

55. 1980, November

The Cuban Ambassador to Jamaica, Ulises Estrada, is expelled from the country, following accusations of interference in internal affairs. In 1979, Estrada had accused a Jamaican newspaper of lying about the Government of Cuba and about himself. Calls for his expulsion had been refused by the then Prime Minister of Jamaica; but when Edward Seaga of the Labor Party became Prime Minister in 1980, he requested Estrada's removal shortly after taking office.

— *Associated Press*, 'Envoy Goes Home to Havana', 3 November 1980
— J Thomas, 'Jamaican Campaign Going On', *New York Times*, 12 July 1980

56. 1980, November

The Soviet Ambassador to Australia (Soudarikov) is criticised after he attacks, at a State luncheon, the Australian Government for 'slandering' the Soviet Union, for discriminating against the sending State and for misunderstanding its 'noble policies' towards Australia. Both the independent Senator Harradine and a spokesman for the Premier of Tasmania voice their criticism of this conduct. Margaret Guilfoyle however, representing the Minister for Foreign Affairs, states in the Australian Senate that the reported remarks did not 'technically … constitute a departure from customary diplomatic behaviour'.

— *Aust YBIL*, 'Diplomatic and Consular Relations' (1978–1980), 403
— *Xinhua*, 'Soviet Ambassador Attacks Australian Government', 22 November 1980

57. 1981, January

The US Press Officer in Ireland, Berrington, is recalled, after a letter he had written accidentally reaches the press. In it, Berrington had stated that Ireland was 'small potatoes compared to the rest of Europe', had referred to strikes and goods shortages and to the 'high cost of goods'.

US newspapers report that Irish Prime Minister Haughey was upset about Berrington's comments, but this is denied by an official of the Irish Foreign Ministry, who also emphasises that Haughey had not sought Berrington's removal.

— AG Flynn, 'Irish Laud Diplomat', *New York Times*, 8 February 1981
— P Jennings, 'World News Tonight ', *ABC News Transcripts*, 29 January 1981

58. 1981, January

The British High Commissioner in Canada (Ford) is criticised after he talked to two MPs about initiatives to amend the British North America Act. Ford reportedly stated that the legislation would not be passed by the British Parliament. The New Democratic Party accuses Ford of interference.

The Canadian External Affairs Minister notes that Ford had probably gone 'beyond … normal functions into internal political matters'. Ford points out that he had carried out his professional duties by attempting to relay British views.

— A Gavshon, 'Ambassador Retired', *Associated Press*, 10 February 1981
— C Hanley, 'An AP News Special', *Associated Press*, 15 February 1981
— A Hutton, 'Section: Regional News', *UPI*, 16 February 1981

59. 1981, May

The American Ambassador to Ireland (Shannon) is photographed sitting with the leader of the Fine Gael party in the party's electoral campaign bus.

Shannon explains that he intended to spend a day observing each of their campaigns. The Embassy's public affairs officer confirms that Shannon had 'no intention of taking part in the campaign' and was not 'taking a partisan position'.

The Irish Prime Minister (Haughey, Fianna Fáil Party) notes that the Ambassador had 'put his foot in', adding that his party would not contemplate his participation in its campaign.

— *Associated Press*, 'U.S. Ambassador in Controversy', 27 May 1981
— *Washington Post*, 'U.S. Envoy to Ireland Criticized', 28 May 1981

60. 1981, September

The Soviet Ambassador to Egypt (Polyakov) is expelled for 'meddling in Egypt's internal affairs'. Six other Embassy employees are also expelled. Polyakov was allegedly involved in the conflict between Muslims and Coptic Christians in Egypt and was reportedly accused of plotting against Sadat and of fomenting civil and religious unrest. The Egyptian Government accuses the Soviet Union of 'recruiting agents in Egypt … exploiting religious strife, and influencing the spread and escalation of the sectarian conflict'. Polyakov is told by the Foreign Ministry that the conduct of the diplomats was 'tantamount to intervention in Egypt's internal affairs.'

— L Balouny, 'Section: International News', *Associated Press*, 16 September 1981
— M Guindi, 'Egypt-Soviet Relations Close to Total Break', *UPI*, 16 September 1981

61. 1982

In the context of discussions about the Israeli invasion of Lebanon, the Israeli Ambassador to Belgium refers to Belgian journalists as liars and insinuates that it could not be proved that they were (not) paid by the PLO. The Belgian Minister for Foreign Affairs (Tindemans), expresses his regret over the tone of the diplomatic message and the lack of moderation, but states that, in this case, there had been no interference with the affairs of Belgium.

— Salmon (1996), 132

62. 1982, May

The US Ambassador to Canada (Robinson) is criticised after he had made public statements on aspects of Canadian policies—including a call on Canada to increase her defence budget, to place missiles on F-18 fighter planes and to send another brigade of troops to Europe. An MP of the New Democratic Party notes that Robinson 'interferes too much in Canadian affairs' and was 'insulting and patronizing to this country and its people'. A Conservative MP agrees that Robinson's conduct had been 'unwise and

[an] unwarranted intervention', but did not think the Ambassador should be recalled.

— Salmon (1996), 132
— A Cohen, 'Regional News', *UPI,* 13 May 1982

63. 1982, May

The President of Uruguay states that a US diplomat (later identified as James Cason) has been expelled for 'attempting to interfere in internal affairs' of Uruguay.

Cason had reportedly had 'improper discussions' with an official of the Foreign Ministry and a naval chief. According to other sources, Cason had had contacts with political dissidents. Others report that Cason had repeated the criticism expressed by some US generals on the Government of Uruguay.

The US Ambassador denies any wrongdoing by Cason.

— *Associated Press*, 'US Envoy Recalled', 30 May 1982
— D Martin, 'Move by Uruguay', *New York Times*, 3 June 1982
— *Facts on File*, 'Uruguay', 23 July 1982

64. 1982, November

The US Ambassador to El Salvador (Hinton) faces criticism after he states that the US might withdraw aid if El Salvador did not make 'substantial progress' on human rights and on bringing the murderers of US citizens to justice. Hinton also said that the rightist 'mafia'—parts of the armed forces that had carried out murder and kidnapping—had to be stopped.

The El Salvadorian Chamber of Commerce voices concerns over Hinton's comments, as does the White House; but a White House spokesman declares that Hinton's comments were 'in keeping with the major outlines of [US] policy with El Salvador'.

— *Facts on File*, 'U.S. Backs Off', 19 November 1982

65. 1982, December

Two officials at the Australian Embassy to Iran (Dunn and McDonald) are expelled after they allegedly insisted that two women (who had applied for visas) be photographed without their headdress. The Iranian *Chargé d'affaires* in Australia (Jeddi) states that the Australian Government had shown 'contempt for Islamic principles' and notes that under 'diplomatic practices and convention and usage, no Embassy has the power or authority to impose rules and regulations contravening the Constitution of the ruling State'. Iran expels Dunn and McDonald. Sources in the Australian Foreign Ministry deny the accusations; Australia retaliates by expelling two Iranian diplomats.

— *Aust YBIL*, 'Diplomatic and Consular Relations' (1981–1983), 506–09

66. 1983, January

Malta instructs heads of foreign missions to ensure that diplomats refrain from 'contacts of any kind with members of the [oppositional] Nationalist Party'. The stated reason was that diplomats should not give the impression that the Nationalists were an 'alternative government'.

Several embassies protest against the ban. The US Ambassador to Malta refers to the diplomatic task of observation as permitted under the Vienna Convention. Opposition comes also from embassies of countries with which Malta sought to maintain good relations, including many Arab States. The European Parliament sharply criticises the ban.

— H Kamm, 'Malta Takes on the World', *New York Times*, 20 February 1983
— *Facts on File*, 'Parliamentary Boycott Ended', 8 April 1983

67. 1983, January

Two US diplomats (LaRoche and Donovan) are expelled from Suriname amid allegations that they had instigated labour unrest in the State. Suriname accuses the diplomats of meddling in internal affairs. The US State department denies the charges and retaliates by expelling a Surinamese diplomat.

The charges against LaRoche and Donovan had been made several months ago; the expulsion order however was made only after the US had suspended a $1.5m aid programme and had criticised the execution of opponents to the Surinamese Government.

— G Gedda, 'US Sees Sharp Leftward Drift', *Associated Press*, 5 January 1983

68. 1983, March

In a speech, the South African Ambassador to Australia (Worrall) reportedly describes the Australian policy towards South Africa as 'confrontational, prescriptive and intrusive'. The Australian Foreign Minister Hayden notes that diplomats are entitled to present their governments' views, but that it was not appropriate to publicly criticise policies of the Australian Government.

The South African Foreign Minister declares his agreement with these principles, but notes that Worrall had only referred to foreign policy in general and had only provided a factual description of South African perception of Australian policy.

— *Aust YBIL*, 'Diplomatic and Consular Relations' (1981–1983), 505
— *BBC Summary*, 'Pik Botha's Response', 30 March 1983

69. 1983, May

Iran expels 18 Soviet diplomatic and consular officials amid accusations of 'interfering with the internal affairs ... through establishing contacts and taking advantage of treacherous and mercenary agents'. The allegations reportedly referred to contacts the Soviet officials had kept with members of Tudeh (a Communist party).

— *New York Times*, 'Iranians Dissolve Communist Party', 5 May 1983
— *BBC Summary*, 'Expulsion of Iranian Diplomats from the USSR', 27 May 1983

70. 1983, May

Yevgeny Shmagin, Second Secretary at the Soviet Embassy in Bonn, is expelled after he had reportedly tried to influence the West German peace movement by attending their meetings and putting forward Soviet arguments for disarmament by the Western States.

However, Shmagin is also accused of having tried to recruit an agent. He is expelled together with three other high-ranking Soviet diplomats who were charged with espionage—an allegation which the Soviet Union denies.

— T Paterson, 'Four Soviets Exposed as Spies', *UPI*, 18 May 1983
— T Paterson, 'West German Magazine Tabs Four Soviets', *UPI*, 19 May 1983

71. 1983, June

The US Ambassador to Brazil, Langhorne Motley, sends a letter to 209 Brazilian Parliamentarians who had condemned the policy of the United States in Central America. Motley's reply, which contained a defence of that policy, was described by its addressees as 'flippant'. Airton Soarès, head of the Parliamentary opposition, calls the Ambassador's remarks 'offensive from a protocolary point of view'. Motley is accused by other Parliamentarians of interference in the internal affairs of Brazil.

— Salmon (1996), 132
— *RGDIP*, 'Chronique des faits internationaux' (1984), 212, 213

72. 1983, November

Suleiman Oreibi, the Libyan representative in Australia, is criticised after the Libyan People's Bureau had distributed copies of a letter by Colonel Gaddafi. The letter, which was a reaction to the invasion of Grenada, called US President Reagan a 'new world Hitler' and his presidency a 'setback for humanity' and a return to 'incredible savagery'. The letter was also sent to the Australian Prime Minister Hawke (and returned as 'undelivered').

The Australian Department of Foreign Affairs calls the letter 'unacceptable'—a move which is interpreted as a reproach of the Libyan representative himself.

— *Aust YBIL*, 'Diplomatic and Consular Relations' (1981–1983), 505, 506

73. 1984, February

The US Ambassador to France, Evan Galbraith, states in an interview that a French communist was 'a poor Frenchman gone wrong'.

One of the Communist Ministers in Mitterrand's Government calls the remarks 'crude and stupid'. It is reported that even the Gaullist party describes the Ambassador's conduct as interference in internal affairs. The French Prime Minister Mauroy summons Galbraith and tells him that his statement had been 'unacceptable'.

The US maintains that the incident had been a 'misunderstanding', arising from an erroneous version of the interview.

— P Webster, 'US Envoy Makes French See Red', *Manchester Guardian Weekly*, 12 February 1984
— *Newsweek*, 'An Enovy's Faux Pas', 13 February 1984

74. 1984, March

The US Ambassador to Mexico (Gavin) denies that transnational companies are responsible for the economic plight of developing countries and states that the companies have in fact assisted development. Gavin also states that introducing foreign capital would be 'the most feasible' route for Mexico's development.

Gavin faces criticism for these remarks: A Parliamentarian of the Democratic Party asks the Ambassador not to interfere in Mexico's internal affairs; and the Workers Party asks the Government to expel Gavin.

— *Xinhua*, 'Mexican Public Blasts U.S. Ambassador', 16 March 1984

75. 1984, May

US Senator Helms requests the dismissal of the US Ambassador to Ecuador, allegedly accusing Ambassador Pickering of taking 'actions which support only one candidate' and of 'manipulat[ing] the electoral results'. The letter reportedly also states that the US was 'supposed to be neutral ... and should cling to that'.

The US Embassy denies the charges and states that diplomats had been 'completely neutral in these elections. Our own interest ... is that they be free, open and honest and we support any procedures to arrive at that'.

— H Gottlieb, 'Helms Asks Reagan To Fire Ambassador', *Associated Press*, 2 May 1984
— J Frazier, 'Helms, Candidate Charge U.S. Interference', *Associated Press*, 3 May 1984

76. 1984, August

The US Ambassador to Mexico (Gavin) meets members of the conservative National Action Party and Catholic clergymen in Hermosillo. The Mexican press subsequently accuses Gavin of plotting with the opposition; the President of the ruling Institutional Revolutionary Party states that his party rejected 'any intervention in our country's politics' by foreign ambassadors, and the Popular Socialist Party calls for Gavin's dismissal. Similar accusations of interference are made in October, after Gavin had made further visits to the National Action Party.

— F Kiel, 'U.S. Ambassador to Mexico Embroiled in Dispute', *UPI*, 24 September 1984
— *UPI*, 'Leftist Parties want Gavin Expelled', 26 October 1984

77. 1984, October

The vice-presidential candidate of the ruling Sandinistas (Bayardo Arce), accuses the US Ambassador to Nicaragua (Bergold) and a US Embassy team of 'going [from] house to house in the political parties, getting them to abstain' from participation in elections, and accuses the Ambassador of interference in Nicaragua's internal affairs.

Similar allegations had been raised by a member of the Democratic Conservative Party who stated that diplomats were putting pressure on their candidates to withdraw from the elections.

— *IPS*, 'Nicaragua: U.S. Ambassador accused of Interfering', 25 October 1984

78. 1985, March

Antonio Paleari (a Peronist congressman) calls the Israeli Ambassador to Argentina (Schmorack) 'insolent' and accuses him of 'meddling in matters of national concern'. He also expresses his intent to call for Schmorack's expulsion. Schmorack had allegedly stated that Argentina should not permit the establishment of a PLO office in Buenos Aires.

— *BBC Summary*, 'Peronist Deputy to Seek Expulsion of Israeli Ambassador', 11 March 1985

79. 1985, May

The Polish Government expels a US diplomat (Hardwood) and a US consul (Hopper), after they had allegedly participated in an illegal parade whose leaders shouted anti-state slogans. According to the Polish Foreign Ministry, this conduct constituted 'unacceptable interference in Poland's internal affairs'.

The State Department denies the charges and retaliates by expelling four Polish diplomats. The US Embassy states that Hardwood and Hopper had performed 'normal diplomatic functions as observers repeat observers of events ... They were not in any way participating in these events'.

— M Vita, 'International News', *Associated Press*, 3 May 1985
— C Bobinski, 'Poland warns U.S.', *Financial Times*, 8 May 1985

80. 1985, December

In a speech, the Chilean President Pinochet states that it was not the function of ambassadors to take sides with certain political groups in Chile. Pinochet's speech follows a reception which ambassadors of the European Communities had given to representatives of eleven parties committed to the Chilean transition to democracy.

— Salmon (1996), 131
— *BBC Summary*, 'Pinochet on US Relations', 5 December 1985

81. 1986, July

The US Embassy to France expresses its 'surprise' about a four year sentence given to a Lebanese terrorist by a court in Lyon, stating that it was a lighter sentence by comparison to those seen in similar cases in other European countries. The French Foreign Minister refers to this statement as 'unacceptable', notes that it betrays 'a serious lack of knowledge of the principle of the independence of justice' and summons the US chargé d'affaires to the Foreign Ministry.

— C Page, 'Paris Raps US', *The Guardian*, 14 July 1986
— P Treuthardt, 'New Row Between Paris and Washington', *Associated Press*, 12 July 1986

82. 1987, January

The Dutch Ambassador to Suriname (Van Houten) is expelled amid accusations of interference. The decision is considered to be connected to a cable by the Dutch Embassy in which reference was made to 15 people who had allegedly died in the Surinamese capital during military counterinsurgency actions. Suriname accuses the Netherlands of supporting anti-government rebels, but the sending State denies the accusations.

— B Graham, 'Suriname's Military Rulers Firm Up Libyan Ties', *Washington Post*, 24 February 1987
— *New York Times*, 'Suriname Asks Dutch To Withdraw Envoy', 12 January 1987

83. 1987, March

According to the Tunisian Foreign Ministry, the Iranian Embassy in Tunisia had helped extremists in the country to get in touch with certain Iranian organisations to create disturbances in the receiving State. Tunisia accuses Iranian diplomats of creating 'religious discord in Tunisia', of propagating anarchy and religious sedition, and of recruiting Tunisian extremists abroad for subversive activities. Tunisia subsequently breaks off diplomatic relations with Iran.

— *Xinhua*, 'Tunisia Asks Iran to Withdraw Diplomats', 26 March 1987
— *Associated Press*, 'Tunisia Breaks Relations With Iran', 26 March 1987

84. 1987, May

The Australian Government severs diplomatic ties with Libya. The Australian Prime Minister Hawke accuses Libya of causing unrest in the Pacific region and states that Libyan representatives were arranging 'training in the techniques of propaganda, agitation and guerilla work …'. The decision follows calls by a speaker of the Australian Aborigines for an autonomous republic, after he had visited Libya.

The Libyan Foreign Ministry reportedly states that it aimed at 'cooperation on the basis of mutual respect and non-interference in internal affairs in accordance with international principles and conventions'.

— T Duboudin, 'Australian Embassies on Terror Alert', *The Times*, 20 May 1987
— *UPI*, 'Libya: Australia Involved in Campaign', 21 May 1987
— *Aust YBIL*, 'Diplomatic and Consular Relations' (1984–1987), 463
— Ipsen, 568

85. 1987, August

South African President Botha criticises Western embassies and states that some diplomats abused their posts. Botha says that several diplomats had gone to some lengths to express solidarity with the black population and names as examples attendance at funerals in black townships. Botha accuses the diplomats of meddling in the country's affairs (according to other sources, of meddling in opposition politics).

— J Lehrer et al, 'Raging Bull', *The MacNeil/Lehrer NewsHour*, 13 August 1987

— J Jones, 'Botha Threat To Curb Diplomats', *Financial Times*, 14 August 1987
— *Facts on File*, 'Mbeki Restricted', 31 December 1987

86. 1987, August

During an attempted coup d'état against Philippine President Aquino, US military attaché Raphael reportedly tries to persuade an assault team not to attack rebels at Camp Aguinaldo. Following that, a military official is quoted as stating that Raphael should be dismissed because of his links with the leader of the attempted coup.

The US Ambassador to the Philippines denies that diplomats had supported the rebels and says that Raphael had merely monitored events.

— Japan Economic Newswire, 'Asian News—Philippines; U.S. Diplomat Accused of Interfering', 22 October 1987
— D Jones, 'Security Increased for Aquino's Davao Visit', *UPI*, 22 October 1987

87. 1987, December

The Ugandan High Commissioner in Kenya (Katungi) is expelled. The Kenyan Foreign Ministry reportedly states that Katungi had accused the Kenyan President Moi of lying, when Moi had given his account on recent incidents of fighting across the Kenyan-Ugandan border. The Kenyan Foreign Ministry refers to Katungi's remarks as 'an incredible insult on the person of President Moi'.

Katungi denies the allegations. According to him, he had only distributed copies of a speech by the Ugandan President Museveni, who had mentioned 'false allegations', but not 'lies'.

— P Vallely, 'Moi Expels Uganda Envoy and Closes Gadaffi's Embassy', *The Times*, 19 December 1987

88. 1987, December

Kenya orders the closure of the Libyan Embassy. According to a statement handed by the Kenyan Foreign Minister to the Libyan *chargé d'affaires*, the public was aware that the Libyan mission had 'been used consistently for gross interference in the internal affairs of Kenya'. Libyan diplomats have in the past been accused by Kenya of the creation of dissent. According to Kenyan media, Libya had been involved in riots which took place at the

University of Nairobi and in border incidents between Kenya and Uganda (see above, A.87).

— P Vallely, 'Moi Expels Uganda Envoy and Closes Gadaffi's Embassy', *The Times*, 19 December 1987
— *Xinhua*, 'Libyan Embassy In Kenya Closed', 18 December 1987

89. 1988, April

The Iranian Ambassador to Turkey, Mottaki, reportedly participates in a meeting for the Palestinian people, hosted in Konye. The Turkish Foreign Ministry later states that Mottaki had also taken part in the function 'by appearing on the rostrum', and had received a warning by the Foreign Minister about conduct which was 'contrary to diplomatic practices and the relevant provisions of the Vienna Convention relat[ing] to the functions of diplomats'.

— *BBC Summary*, 'Iran Links Diplomatic Row', 5 April 1989
— *BBC Worldwide Monitoring*, 'Turkey Says Iranian Foreign Minister-designate Not Persona Non Grata in 1989', 16 August 2005

90. 1988, May

A US diplomat (Hendrickson) is expelled from Singapore amid Government allegations that he interfered in internal affairs by encouraging Singaporean lawyers to run as candidates in elections. Singapore also accuses Hendrickson of promoting the formation of a 'group of young professionals to contest the next general election and become a more effective opposition'.

The US Government denies that there had been a plan to interfere in internal affairs and states that Hendrickson had only fulfilled his diplomatic duties.

— R Matthews, 'Singapore Slaps The Hand That Feeds It', *Financial Times*, 23 May 1988
— N Cumming-Bruce, 'Expelled Envoy in New Row', *The Guardian*, 21 May 1988

91. 1988, July

Several US diplomats to Nicaragua, including Ambassador Melton, are expelled.

The Nicaraguan Foreign Minister states that Melton had encouraged 'illegal activities by provocative extreme right-wing groups'. He also accuses him of 'attempting to set up an internal front to overthrow the government' and of violating the Vienna Convention 'which expressly prohibits any interference in the internal affairs of other states'.

The American Government denies the allegations and retaliates by expelling several Nicaraguan diplomats.

— *BBC Summary*, 'Nicaraguan President, Foreign Minister on Expulsion', 13 July 1988
— L Barber and T Coone, 'Washington Expels Nicaraguan Ambassador', *Financial Times*, 13 July 1988

92. 1988, November

The US diplomat Rankin is expelled from Iraq, apparently over his contacts with the Kurdish population. Rankin had reportedly made an unauthorised journey to north Iraq, where 3.5 million Kurds lived.

The State Department notes that it was the job of diplomats to 'know the countries in which they live and work' and that they therefore had to deal with 'parties in power [and] parties in opposition'. The US retaliates by expelling an Iraqi diplomat.

— *Xinhua*, 'U.S. Expels Iraqi Diplomat ', 17 November 1988
— D Ottaway, 'Iraq Said to Have Expelled High-Level U.S. Diplomat', *Washington Post*, 17 November 1988
— *Federal News Service*, 'State Department Regular Briefing', 17 November 1988

93. 1988, November

A Hungarian diplomat (Gyoerfi) in Romania is detained and later expelled. According to the Romanian Foreign Minister, Gyoerfi had distributed 'inciting, hostile leaflets'; Romania accuses him of 'anti-Romanian, anti-socialist and provocative actions'.

The Secretary General of the Hungarian Communist Party denies the allegations against Gyoerfi. Hungary retaliates by expelling a Romanian diplomat.

— *Associated Press*, 'Romania, Hungary Feud', 18 November 1988
— J Blitz, 'Old Nationalist Tensions', *Financial Times*, 26 November 1988
— *BBC Summary*, 'Hungarian Romanian Relations; Hungarian Expulsion of Romanian Diplomat', 28 November 1988

94. 1989, April

The South African Ambassador to Australia (Tothill) faces criticism after he made remarks which appeared to implicitly condone an attack on the house of a representative of the African National Congress in Australia.

The Australian Foreign Minister notes the Government's rejection of Tothill's comments and adds that his department had stressed to the Embassy the need for diplomatic statements to 'observe normal proprieties', and that material should not be phrased in offensive terms.

— *Aust YBIL*, 'Diplomatic and Consular Relations' (1988–1989), 451
— *Hobart Mercury*, 'Mr Eddie Funde', 31 January 1989
— *BBC Summary*, 'South and Southern Africa in Brief', 1 February 1989

95. 1989, May

Several US diplomats are expelled from Nicaragua for (according to a spokesman of the ruling Sandinistas) 'interfering in the internal affairs of the country'. They are accused of 'distributing money and exhorting teachers to strike'. The diplomats had reportedly met with members of the Social Christian Party and the Labor Unification Union at two private schools.

The State Department denies the accusations and states that the diplomats had engaged in normal activities compatible with their positions.

— D Pilarte, 'Nicaragua Expels Two U.S. Diplomats', *Associated Press*, 25 May 1989

96. 1989, May

Poland accuses US Embassy officials of active participation in Solidarność's campaign ahead of national elections. A Government statement also notes that Western diplomats had not 'limit[ed] themselves to expressing their political sympathies, this being a private affair', but had 'actively participate[d] in various meetings and events staged by the Opposition, and sometimes even fulfil[led] instructive functions'. The US Embassy denies any improper activities or active support of one candidate or group over another.

— J Tagliabue, 'US Diplomats Accused of Meddling in Campaign', *Sydney Morning Herald*, 1 June 1989

97. 1989, November

The Indian High Commissioner in Fiji (Sreenivasan) is expelled amid official allegations of interference. Sreenivasan had reportedly protested against the firebombing of Indian temples in Fiji and had linked these incidents to an initiative to adopt a constitution which would have given a preferential position to the political rights of indigenous Fijians over those of other groups.

— *Fiji Times* (Australia), 'Voice of the People', 24 May 2008
— G Spencer, 'Diplomat Denies Claims', *Sydney Morning Herald*, 3 November 1989

98. 1989, December

After the fall of Ceauşescu, two British diplomats in Romania join students and workers, who storm a television station.

Several British MPs claim that this conduct had put the concept of diplomatic immunity at risk. A former British Ambassador notes that 'active participation', as opposed to observation, in politics of the receiving State was incompatible with the diplomatic status.

One of the diplomats states that they had been 'fairly passive observers'.

— R Stacey, 'British Envoys Joined Revolt', *The Times*, 27 December 1989
— A Travis, 'Rebirth of Romania', *The Guardian*, 28 December 1989
— J Graham, 'Undiplomatic Activity', *The Times*, 30 December 1989

99. 1990, May

It is reported that the Kenyan President Moi, in a speech, referred to sanctions that might be adopted against interfering diplomats and in particular to restrictions of movement. This statement is seen in the context of recent remarks by the US Ambassador to Kenya (Hempstone), who had advocated a move to a multi-party system in Kenya. Moi's party, with specific reference to Hempstone, declares that 'national interest must never be dictated by external forces'; Kenya was 'a sovereign state, a fact that is not negotiable and which cannot be compromised at any cost'.

— *Associated Press*, 'U.S. Envoy Irks Kenya's President', 5 May 1990
— C Mbitiru, 'Opposition Leader Ordered Released', *Associated Press*, 9 June 1991

100. 1990, May

Fiji orders the closure of the Indian Embassy, declaring that the 'continued interference by the Embassy of the Republic of India' is considered 'unfriendly and in contravention of international law and practice'.

The background to the decision is apparently formed by India's position towards a planned new Constitution in Fiji which would have given ethnic Fijians a preferred position by comparison to other groups, including ethnic Indians.

The Indian Embassy 'categorically repudiates' allegations of interference', states that it has voiced policies of the Indian Government which was 'opposed to racism in Fiji' and that 'India will stand by its commitment to … multiracialism in Fiji'.

— *Advertiser*, 'Fiji Tells Indian Envoys to Leave', 24 May 1990
— *UPI*, 'Indian Diplomats Ordered Out of Fiji', 23 May 1990

101. 1990, July

The Kenyan Foreign Minister Ayah takes exception to statements made by the US Ambassador to the country (Smith Hempstone). Hempstone had voiced the State Department's concerns about the arrest of persons opposed to Moi's Government.

Ayah declares himself 'very unhappy' about Hempstone's conduct and states that Hempstone had 'acted in a very unorthodox manner and contrary to the normal international behavior of an accredited diplomat'. He adds that Americans were 'very ignorant about Africa and Kenya'.

— N Fleming, 'Police Shoot Two Amid Fresh Unrest', *UPI*, 11 July 1990

102. 1990, September

While in Washington, the US *chargé d'affaires* in Pakistan (Oakley) criticises the treatment of Pakistani politician Benazir Bhutto as discriminatory. He objects to politically selective prosecutions on account of corruption (such charges had been raised against Bhutto) and allegedly states that members of the Islamic Democratic Alliance should be brought to account.

According to the Pakistani Government these remarks amount to interference in internal affairs.

The State Department notes that Oakley had spoken 'for the US government'.

— *Japan Economic Newswire*, 'Pakistan Summons U.S. Charge d'Affaires', 16 September 1990
— *New York Times*, 'Straight Talk on Pakistan', 24 September 1990
— *Federal News Service*, 'State Department Regular Briefing', 25 September 1990

103. 1991, May

The UK High Commissioner in Sri Lanka (Gladstone) is expelled on charges of interfering in local council elections. Gladstone had reportedly referred a situation of electoral malpractice in the Dikwella constituency to the police. The Sri Lankan Foreign Ministry notes that Gladstone's conduct had been in excess of normal diplomatic functions and constituted a violation of norms of diplomatic practice.

— *Agence France Presse*, 'Expelled British Envoy to Leave within 10 Days', 31 May 1991

104. 1991, November

The ambassadors of seven Western States, including Germany and the USA, are summoned to the Kenyan Foreign Ministry where they are criticised for alleged interference. This follows attempts by embassies to observe a pro-democracy demonstration and concerns they expressed over human rights violations. The Kenyan Foreign Minister accuses the US Ambassador Hempstone of arrogance and of involvement in the organisation of 'events', stating that his attitude was 'that of a slave owner'.

The US State Department defends Hempstone; the German Foreign Ministry expresses its concerns about human rights violations in Kenya and recalls the German Ambassador to Kenya for consultations.

— N Henry, 'Kenya Levels Broadside', *Washington Post*, 19 November 1991
— *Washington Post*, 'Undiplomatic Relations', 24 November 1991

105. 1992, July

The Australian Acting High Commissioner in Vanuatu (Pearson) is expelled after he voiced concerns about an Act which gave the Government authority to revoke business licences without explanation or possibility of appeal. In Australia's view, this put Australian investment in Vanuatu at risk.

Vanuatu's Foreign Minister declares that Vanuatu would not tolerate interference in its internal affairs. Australia maintains that the expulsion was unjustified and cancels goodwill visits of two Australian ships to Vanuatu.

— P Atkinson, 'Vanuatu Dumps Aussie', *Sunday Mail (Australia)*, 5 July 1992
— *Xinhua*, 'Roundup: Australia-Vanuatu Ties Strained', 6 July 1992
— *Aust YBIL*, 'Diplomatic and Consular Relations' (1992), 575

106. 1992, August

The Polish Ambassador to Lithuania (Widacki), is criticised after he reportedly says that Poles living in Lithuania never had left Poland. (Poland and Lithuania had historically formed a union.)

The Chairman of the Lithuanian Parliamentary Foreign Affairs Committee says that the remarks reflected a wish to disrupt relations between Lithuania and Poland; they formed part of a propaganda campaign which aimed at exerting pressure on Lithuania and could be qualified as interference in the internal affairs of another State.

— *BBC Summary*, 'Other Reports', 25 August 1992

107. 1993, October

Several Western diplomats to Sierra Leone are criticised for urging the release of journalists arrested for critical remarks on the military ruler of Sierra Leone, Strasser (and, reportedly, for publishing stories of corruption concerning high-ranking military officials). The German Ambassador Prinz had also gone to a Freetown police station and met with the journalists.

The acting Foreign Minister states that the diplomats had interfered 'without justification and contrary to the principles of diplomatic law and practice'.

— *BBC Summary*, 'Western Diplomats Accused of Interference', 25 October 1993
— L Fofana, 'Sierra Leone—Politics: German Diplomat Ordered to Leave', *IPS*, 9 April 1994

108. 1994, February

The US Ambassador to Trinidad and Tobago (Cowal) comments on the 'seeming paralysis' of the Government to deal with crime in the country and notes that 'better courts and better pay for policemen' were needed. The leader of the Bank and General Workers Union reacts to this by stating that the remarks constituted 'grave interference in the internal affairs of Trinidad and Tobago'.

According to the Trinidadian Minister of Information, the Government was, however, 'not offended' by Cowal's comments.

— Beard, D, 'In Land Of Calypso', *Associated Press*, 1 March 1994

109. 1994, April

The German Ambassador to Sierra Leone (Prinz), is expelled after he had visited Charles Taylor, the Liberian guerilla leader—later President of Liberia, and a supporter of a militia who fought against the Sierra Leonean Government.

The Foreign Minister of Sierra Leone refers to the 'undiplomatic and unfriendly behaviour' displayed by Prinz and to three formal protests which the Government of the receiving State had made to Germany.

— L Fofana, 'Sierra Leone—Politics: German Diplomat Ordered to Leave', *IPS*, 9 April 1994
— *Süddeutsche Zeitung*, 'Sierra Leone weist deutschen Botschafter aus', 11 April 1994

110. 1994, September

After Haiti issues a ban on demonstrations 'to avoid the chaos and the bloodbath so evidently desired by some', a spokesman of the US Embassy (Schrager) reportedly remarks that, if the United States were to support democracy, they could not 'support a ban that prohibits demonstrations'.

Charles David, Foreign Minister of the de facto Government of Haiti, accuses Schrager of making 'incendiary declarations', of interference in Haitian affairs and of 'deliberately inciting the population to violence'.

— A Snow, 'U.S. Forces Begin Dismantling', *Associated Press*, 22 September 1994
— D Beard, 'Haitians Explode With Joy', *Associated Press*, 24 September 1994

111. 1995, February

The US Ambassador to Kenya (Brazeal) allegedly states that the US would like to see the enactment of a law which would allow private radio and television stations in Kenya before the end of June.

In response, the Education Minister states that external involvement with these licensing matters was 'tantamount to interference'. The Minister for Foreign Affairs meets Brazeal to discuss the situation.

The US Embassy states that Brazeal had followed US policy; Brazeal denies that she had given the Government a deadline.

— *Agence France Presse*, 'US Ambassador Accused of Meddling', 16 February 1995
— *BBC Summary*, 'Kenya; US Ambassador Denies Giving Deadline', 20 February 1995

112. 1995, July

The US Ambassador to Israel (Indyk) reportedly lobbies politicians against the passing of a bill which would have reduced the likelihood of Israel ceding the Golan Heights to Syria. According to one of the politicians, Indyk had stated that the bill could be used to slow down the peace process and that Israel would be blamed for halting negotiations.

Several parties speak of US interference in Israeli affairs; the US Embassy admits the meetings, but denies lobbying activities.

— *Agence France Presse*, 'US Envoy Intervenes', 26 July 1995
— J Morrison, 'Indyk on the Spot', *Washington Times*, 27 July 1995

113. 1995, July

After the German Ambassador to Kenya (Mützelburg) condemns the continued violence in Kenya and suggests that conflicts be resolved through dialogue, the Kenyan President (Moi) accuses him of interference in Kenya's internal affairs and of using non-governmental organisations as tools for the incitement of Kenyans. In this context, Moi threatens the expulsion of diplomats, if they assumed the role of a mouthpiece of the opposition ['Sprachrohr der Opposition', paraphrasing by *Süddeutsche Zeitung*].

— *Xinhua*, 'German Ambassador Accused of Interfering', 13 July 1995
— *Süddeutsche Zeitung*, 'Moi erneuert Angriffe auf deutschen Botschafter', 18 July 1995

114. 1995, September

The US Ambassador to Israel, Indyk, misses a ceremony opening celebrations for the 3000th anniversary of Jerusalem (a controversial event because of Jerusalem's disputed international status). Indyk's absence triggers talks between the Israeli Ambassador in Washington and the US administration. Both the Israeli Prime Minister and the Mayor of Jerusalem are reportedly unhappy about Indyk's decision.

Indyk and the US Secretary of State deny that the US boycotted the event; Indyk cites prior engagements.

— *BBC Summary*, 'Issue of Jerusalem 3000', 7 September 1995
— P Wilson, 'Envoy's Absence Angers Israel', *The Australian*, 7 September 1995
— H Kuttler, 'Christopher: Indyk didn't Snub Jerusalem 3000', *Jerusalem Post*, 11 September 1995

115. 1995 September

An Iranian diplomat to Jordan (Bateni) is expelled for 'activities that are not in line with diplomatic norms'. Bateni had allegedly visited the city of Petra to inquire about tourist itineraries. It is reported that Bateni had implicitly urged Jordanians to attack Israeli tourists.

Iran retaliates by expelling a Jordanian diplomat for conduct 'inconsistent with the nature of his diplomatic activity'.

— *Associated Press*, 'Section: International News', 9 December 1995
— *Payk.Net*, 'Jordan Expels Diplomat', 13 December 1995
— *Xinhua*, 'Jordan Expels Iranian Diplomat', 10 December 1995

116. 1995, February

Bahrain expels an Iranian diplomat (Dokoohki), reportedly for 'activities incompatible with his diplomatic status'. Neither Bahrain nor Iran provide details, but according to *United Press*, Dokoohki had been seen contacting members of the Shi'ite opposition. Bahrain had accused Iran of instigating violent Shi'ite protests in the country.

— T Hussain, 'Bahrain Orders Iranian Diplomat Out', *UPI*, 1 February 1996
— *Payk Net*, 'Bahrein Expels Iranian Diplomat', 1 February 1996
— R Allen, 'More Detained in Bahrain Unrest', *Financial Times*, 5 February 1996
— *Iran Brief*, 'Bahrain and Iran Expel Diplomats', 5 February 1996

117. 1996, May

Officials of the Israeli Likud Party accuse US Ambassador Indyk of 'crafting Clinton's strategy of openly backing … Shimon Peres [the candidate of the Labor Party]' (Samber). There is some speculation in the media that this situation marred relations between Clinton and Netanyahu, who emerged as winner of the elections, and may have explained Indyk's replacement as Ambassador in 1997. (Indyk does return for a second stint in 2000).

— S Samber, 'Roller Coaster Diplomat Career of Ambassador Martin Indyk', *Jewish Telegraphic Agency*, c 29 September 1996
— M Arnold, 'U.S. Envoy Hit Over Remarks On Jerusalem', *Forward*, c 22 September 2000

118. 1996, August

Cuba expels a US diplomat (Meyer), who had monitored human rights, interviewed participants at demonstrations, met dissidents and distributed materials, including the booklet 'How to Organize a Trade Union Meeting'. The Cuban Foreign Ministry states that she had supported and organised 'small counterrevolutionary groups'.

The US Government retaliates by expelling a Cuban diplomat (Ponce) who states that, while Meyer had 'interven[ed] in Cuban affairs', his own role had been to 'try to open lines of communication and lessen tensions'.

— J Morrison, 'Mr Ponce Packs Up', *Washington Times*, 26 August 1996
— T Lippman, 'Surviving a Nightmare Inside Castro's Cuba', *Washington Post*, 1 November 1996

119. 1996, September

The US *chargé d'affaires* in Burma (Meyers) reportedly warns a senior official of the Burmese Foreign Ministry of negative consequences if action were taken against a meeting of the National League for Democracy (NLD). According to the official, this went 'beyond the accepted norms of diplomacy' and must be considered 'interference in our internal affairs'.

The State Department states that Meyers had 'been carrying out her diplomatic role on instructions from Washington'.

— *United States Information Agency*, 'State Department Report', 2 October 1996
— *Associated Press*, 'US Rejects Burmese Charges', 2 October 1996
— *BBC Summary*, 'Ruling Council Explains Actions', 4 October 1996

120. 1996, October

Burmese officials express their dismay about frequent diplomatic visits to Aung San Suu Kyi. A Foreign Ministry official highlights the need of diplomats to adhere to Article 41 of the Vienna Convention; a Ministry of Defence official states that, while meetings with politicians to learn more about the country were 'acceptable', it was outside 'routine diplomatic [study] visits' to see a politician more than a hundred times (as allegedly had happened in the case of Aung San Suu Kyi).

— *BBC Summary*, 'Ruling Council Explains Actions', 4 October 1996
— *Japan Economic Newswire*, 'U.S. Diplomat Breaches Norms of Diplomacy, Myanmar Says', 1 October 1996

121. 1996, November

After the designated Spanish Ambassador to Cuba (Cordech Planas) states that he would keep his doors open to members of the anti-Castro opposition, Cuba withdraws his approval. The Cuban Foreign Ministry reportedly notes that his comments constituted open and unacceptable interference and a breach of the Vienna Convention.

The Spanish Foreign Minister reportedly states that Cordech Planas' remarks were 'extremely prudent and open to dialogue' and in line with Government policy.

— *Xinhua*, 'Cuba to Revoke Approval to Spanish Ambassador', 26 November 1996
— *Agence France Presse*, 'Spanish Embassy, Under Siege', 27 November 1996

122. 1997, January

The Swiss Ambassador to the USA (Jagmetti), resigns his post. This follows the leak of a message by Jagmetti to Switzerland, dealing with the 'Nazi gold crisis' (a situation triggered by reports that Switzerland had hidden Nazi gold and refused to give it to families of Holocaust survivors). Jagmetti had referred to a 'campaign against Switzerland', to Switzerland's 'adversaries' and expressed the view that the situation was 'a war' which Switzerland had to win.

The State Department states that Jagmetti's quotes, if accurate, were 'very troubling' and that any diplomat advocating 'a PR campaign against US Jewish organizations is just wrong-headed'.

— *UPI*, 'U.S. Troubled by Ambassador's Memo', 27 January 1997
— *Stoll v Switzerland*, para 16
— *Agence France Presse*, 'State Department and D'Amato', 27 January 1997

123. 1997, February

The Iranian Ambassador to Turkey (Baqeri) states that it was the main goal of Iranians, as Muslims, to support 'the rule of Islam' and reportedly also calls for the liberation of Jerusalem.

Turkish media and politicians accuse Baqeri of interference in internal affairs; the Government expels him.

Baqeri claims that he had kept to facts concerning Israel and that he had not referred to Turkey.

Iran retaliates by expelling the Turkish Ambassador and the Consul General to Oroumiyeh.

— Karmon (2000)
— H Mottalebi, 'Tehran-Ankara Ties Revived', *Echo of Islam*, April 1998

124. 1997, March

The Chairman of the Knesset Foreign Affairs and Defense Committee, Landau, accuses the US Ambassador to Israel (Indyk) of 'pressuring members of government' and 'interfering in Israel's internal political affairs', after it is reported that Israeli ministers interrupted a Government meeting on withdrawal from the occupied territories several times to seek Indyk's approval. Former Israeli Prime Minister Shamir is quoted as saying that no Israeli Government had tolerated as much interference as the current one.

— Y Harel, 'Like a Viceroy', *Jerusalem Post*, 21 March 1997
— *Zionist Organization of America*, 'Ambassador Indyk Reportedly Interfered', 9 July 1997

125. 1997, March

A US diplomat (Alexandrov) is expelled from Belarus after he attended an unauthorised protest against Belarusian President Lukashenko.

Belarusian authorities accuse Alexandrov of provocative actions, of fomenting anti-government sentiment and of working for the CIA.

The US states that Alexandrov had been observing a political demonstration; a behaviour to which it referred as a normal diplomatic duty.

In apparent retaliation, a Belarusian diplomat is expelled from the US.

— *CNN*, 'US Diplomat Leaving Belarus', 23 March 1997
— *Facts on File*, 'U.S. Envoy Expelled', 27 March 1997
— R Kilborn et al, 'The News in Brief', *Christian Science Monitor*, 28 March 1997

126. 1997, June

The US Ambassador to Peru (Jett) criticises the Peruvian decision to buy MiG-29 combat planes and notes that the money 'should be used to build new schools'. He encourages a debate about the country's priorities.

According to the President of the Peruvian Congress, Jett's remarks were '[against] what the Vienna Convention says about non-interference in internal affairs'. The Peruvian Foreign Minister asks Jett for an explanation; Jett states that he would continue to express his opinions 'since it is not unfriendly to defend Peruvian democracy'.

— J Morrison, 'Making a Name', *Washington Times*, 27 June 1997
— A Lama, 'Peru—Politics: U.S. Ambassador Sparks political uproar', *IPS*, 4 July 1997

127. 1997, July

It is reported that the US Ambassador to Israel (Indyk) put pressure on the Israeli Government to prevent the appointment of Ariel Sharon to the office of Finance Minister. According to the *Yediot Ahronot* newspaper, Indyk had held secret conversations with the Israeli Minister of Defence (Mordechai) on that matter.

This alleged lobbying by Indyk leads to accusations in the media and by Jewish organisations in America of interference in the internal affairs of Israel.

— Zionist Organization of America, 'Ambassador Indyk Reportedly Interfered', 9 July 1997,
— U Dan / D Eisenberg, 'An American Vassal?', *Jerusalem Post*, 10 July 1997

128. 1997, October

The Canadian Ambassador to Mexico (Perron) states in an interview that the corruption in Mexico 'makes you want to cry …'. He also describes Mexican efforts to deal with drug trafficking as 'a joke'.

It is reported that the Mexican Foreign Minister subsequently complains to his Canadian counterpart (Axworthy) about the comments. Perron resigns his post; Axworthy is quoted as saying that Perron's remarks, as the Ambassador 'recognizes, were inappropriate for a diplomatic representative'.

— *Ottawa Citizen*, 'I Thought I Knew Everything About Corruption…', 7 October 1997
— A Lindgren, 'Diplomat Resigns Post', *Ottawa Citizen*, 7 October 1997

129. 1998, January

The designated US Ambassador to Egypt (Kurtzer) criticises Egypt for boycotting an economic conference in Doha, allegedly saying that the boycotting States had sent out a 'wrong message' and that the Doha conference was meant to benefit all Middle East States.

The Chief Editor of *Al Akhbar*, an Egyptian Government-owned newspaper, states that Kurtzer had to take care not to infringe the sovereignty of Egypt and had to refrain from criticism 'if he want[ed] to serve the interests of his country'.

— *Associated Press*, 'Egyptian Paper Says', 16 January 1998
— J Morrison, 'Blaming Egypt', *The Washington Times*, 16 January 1998

130. 1998, September

Following the killing of Iranian diplomats, the Taleban leadership accuses the dead of having been military advisors who had aided the Afghan opposition. They call on Iran to apologise for interference in Afghanistan's internal affairs.

Taleban leader Mullah Omar claims that Iran condemned the killings only 'to hide Iranian interference in Afghanistan during which thousands of people were killed' and urges the United Nations to condemn Iran for the interference in Afghanistan.

— *BBC Online*, 'Taleban Accuse Iran', 13 September 1998

- M Theodoulou, 'Tehran Puts Military on War Alert', *The Times*, 16 September 1998
- C Thomas, 'Iran Reinforces Border', *The Times*, 18 September 1998

131. 1998, September

The US Ambassador to Mozambique (Curran) allegedly says that the Mozambican elections of 1999 require the participation of opposition parties in order to be 'fair, democratic, transparent and serious' and warns of US withdrawal of financial support for the elections, if there were a boycott.

The General Secretary of the ruling Mozambican party (Tomé) reportedly states that Curran should not pass messages 'through the press' and that he could offer advice or criticism through diplomatic channels. He also notes that 'political and financial blackmails' were 'outdated'.

- *Xinhua*, 'US Ambassador Accused of Meddling', 15 September 1998
- *Associated Press*, 'International News', 16 September 1998

132. 1998, September

The US *Chargé d'affaires* in Burma (Wiedemann) reportedly states in an interview that Aung San Suu Kyi would not be deported from the country and that the measures which Burma adopted to prevent the convening of Parliament were detention measures.

A commentator of the Burmese newspaper *Myanmar Alin* subsequently criticises this conduct as interference in the internal affairs of Myanmar, refers to Article 41 of the Vienna Convention and points out that the question of Aung Suu Kyi's deportation and measures taken by the Burmese Government were 'internal affairs of Myanmar'.

- *BBC Worldwide Monitoring (Myanmar Alin, Myanmar)*, 'Paper Attacks Foreign Media, Diplomats', 19 September 1998

133. 1998, September

A US diplomat (Brown) in Cuba is accused of inciting Castro opponents to stage a public anti-government demonstration, after he had been outside a Havana courtroom when the trial of a dissident took place. The Cuban Foreign Ministry claims Brown had conducted activities falling 'within the definition of interference in the internal affairs of our country and promotion of counterrevolutionary activities', and that his behaviour had 'absolutely nothing to do with his status as a diplomat'.

— *Miami Herald*, 'Cuba Accuses U.S. Diplomat of Meddling', 19 September 1998
— P Fletcher, 'Expulsions Cast Cold War Shadow', *Reuters*, 24 December 1998

134. 1998, November

A US diplomat is denied access to the court at the trial of the politician Ibrahim in Malaysia. The presiding Judge notes that allowing official observers would be an 'insult to the court' and give the impression that 'it may not be dispensing justice'. Their presence would amount to 'interference' with his functions.

The State Department states that it saw no reason for denying access to diplomats who complied 'with the court-stated procedures for entering the courtroom'.

— M Frei et al, 'Anwar Upbeat as Trial Opens', *BBC Online*, 2 November 1998
— *CNN*, 'Malaysia's Anwar Returns to Court', 3 November 1998

135. 1998, December

The German Ambassador to Turkey (Vergau) is criticised after he states that the situation of the Kurds was not only a matter for Turkey, but for Germany as well. Vergau had referred to the considerable number of Kurds in Germany.

A representative of the Turkish Government reportedly calls the statement 'insolent' ('eine Frechheit') and notes that the remarks constituted interference in internal affairs.

— *Süddeutsche Zeitung*, 'Deutscher Diplomat kritisiert', 14 December 1998

136. 1999, February

The Sri Lankan Foreign Ministry sends a note to all foreign missions in which it states that premature comments on the election controversy in Wayamba could constitute interference. This follows concerns which the US Embassy had raised about violence, intimidation and vote rigging at provincial polls in Wayamba.

The US Embassy declines to withdraw its statement, noting that it was 'concerned about news reports of violence surrounding the election and about the allegations of voting day irregularities …' and that it believed that 'fair and free elections are essential for democracy'.

— F Jansz, 'Diplomatic Row over Wayamba', *The Sunday Times (Sri Lanka)*, 7 February 1999

137. 1999, August

The US Embassy in Namibia expresses its concern about reports of mistreatment of civilians in the Caprivi region. It urges Government forces to refrain from human rights abuses.

The next day, the Namibian Government calls on diplomatic missions and international organisations to 'stop interfering in the country's internal affairs'. It draws attention to Article 41 of the Vienna Convention and states that heads of missions should 'use the established diplomatic channels to raise their concerns'.

— *Panafrican News Agency*, 'Namibia; US Expresses Concern', 18 August 1999
— *Xinhua News Agency*, 'Namibia Unhappy with U.S. Comments on Caprivi', 20 August 1999

138. 1999, September

At a meeting with a Government official, the US Ambassador to Thailand (Hecklinger) reportedly expresses concerns about delays in the construction of a power plant (partially funded by Edison Mission Energy) and warns of risks to further investments.

An academic observer (Limpadanai) refers to this as 'pressure' and 'internal interference'. The US Embassy, however, emphasises its '… duty to advocate U.S. business in the same way Thai embassies do in other countries'.

— K Sukin, 'US Envoy Accused of Meddling', *The Nation*, 29 September 1999
— *Greenpeace*, 'Edison Out', 2002

139. 1999, October

Zimbabwe expels the Malawian diplomat Kaluluma Phiri for 'unpalatable utterances'. Phiri had allegedly called Zimbabwean President Mugabe an 'old man who had run the country into economic despair'.

Phiri is later also dismissed from the Malawian diplomatic service, but then reinstated by a court which notes that he had not been given a proper explanation for this decision and that the Government procedure had been 'fraught with irrationality and procedural impropriety'.

— D Langeveldt, 'Zimbabwe Expels Foul-mouthed Malawian Diplomat', *African Eye News Service*, 19 October 1999
— *Agence France Presse*, 'Malawi Court Re-instates Diplomat', 25 May 2001

140. 1999, October

The speaker of the Indonesian People's Consultative Assembly (Rais) accuses the US Ambassador to that country (Gelbard) of 'direct, concrete intervention with an element of insult'. This follows reports that Gelbard had suggested that Glenn Yusuf, Chairman of the Indonesian Bank Restructuring Agency, should not be replaced.

Gelbard later states that his remarks had not aimed at interference in Indonesia's internal affairs.

— *Agence France Presse*, 'Chief Legislator Accuses Washington of Meddling in Indonesian Politics', 29 October 1999
— *Straits Times*, 'Pals Again', 6 November 1999

141. 1999, November

Malaysia alleges that diplomats from Australia, Canada, the UK and the US have provided funds to the opposition with a view to toppling the Government, stating that this amounts to interference in internal affairs.

Canada replies that her diplomats were, as part of their routine tasks, in touch with the opposition; but support was given only to non-governmental organisations. The US Embassy declares it did not interfere in elections; press events by parties were attended in the exercise of 'normal diplomatic function[s]'.

— *BBC Online*, 'Malaysia Accuses Diplomats', 24 November 1999
— M Trickey, 'Ottawa Denies Funding', *Calgary Herald*, 25 November 1999
— *Toronto Star*, 'Malaysia Tells West to Butt Out', 26 November 1999

142. 2000, April

The UK Ambassador to Peru (Hart) states that Britain did not 'have a lot of confidence' in the voting process in that country, referring to irregularities during the campaign (for presidential elections).

A candidate for the office of Vice President (Tudela) calls these remarks an interference in the internal affairs of Peru. In his view, foreign governments were making judgements about elections even before the results had been announced.

— *Associated Press—German*, 'Peruanischer Praesident Fujimori', 13 April 2000
— M Hayes, 'Peru's Presidential Race', *Associated Press*, 13 April 2000

143. 2000, May

The Canadian Ambassador to the US (Chrétien) comments on two presidential candidates: He remarks that, while Gore was 'a friend of Canada', Bush did not know Canada 'as much' and Canada would have 'to work on him quite a lot'; but she would 'deal with whomever is elected'.

The Bush camp reportedly feels offended by the comments. According to the Canadian Foreign Ministry, Chrétien had not expressed a political preference.

— S Thorne, 'Clark Slams Gore Endorsement', *Timmins Daily Press*, 2 June 2000
— M Blanchfield, 'Alliance will Americanize Canada', *Welland Tribune*, 25 October 2000
— M Solberg, 'Time to Stop Shooting from the Hip', *Hill Times*, 12 February 2001

144. 2000, June

The US Ambassador to Tanzania (Stith) reportedly refers to Salmin Amour, the outgoing President of Zanzibar (a semi-autonomous region of Tanzania) as a 'lame duck'.

The Tanzanian Foreign Ministry subsequently releases a statement criticising Stith for 'attack[ing] a leader of a country in the media' and noting that there were 'diplomatic ways' for him to express his opinion.

Zanzibar states that it was 'unbecoming and contrary to diplomatic practice to make remarks in local and foreign media that are likely to divide people and foster hatred'.

Stith denies having made derogatory comments.

— *Agence France Presse*, 'Tanzania Government Issues Formal Protest to US Envoy', 9 June 2000

145. 2000, July

The US Ambassador to Indonesia (Gelbard) 'encourage[s]' Indonesia to bring to justice those responsible for the violence in East Timor in 1999. He also calls on Indonesia to keep her promise to introduce economic reforms.

Gelbard is subsequently accused by legislators of applying pressure to the Government; military leaders claim that he interfered in Indonesia's internal affairs. President Wahid however rejects calls for Gelbard's expulsion.

— Gelbard (2000)
— G Spencer, 'US Support for Indonesia Declines Amid Anti-Americanism', *Joyo Indonesian News*, 30 October 2000

146. 2000, August

Two US diplomats (Burgess and Moran) are expelled from the Democratic Republic of Congo. According to the Congolese Ambassador to the US, they had urged guests at a dinner party, who were members of the opposition, to overthrow President Kabila.

The US Embassy does not comment, but a spokesman for the US State Department refers to the claims as 'utterly false and outrageous'. Two Congolese diplomats are expelled from the US in retaliation.

— J Morrison, 'Diplomats Expelled', *Washington Times*, 23 August 2000

147. 2000, August

The US Ambassador to Indonesia (Gelbard) states US concerns about existing opportunities in Indonesia for foreign terrorist groups to 'burrow in and implant themselves' in the country. Gelbard also criticises the membership of certain persons in the cabinet who had shown a critical attitude to US companies.

It is subsequently reported that the Foreign Ministry had asked Gelbard for clarification, as his remarks were considered interference in Indonesia's internal affairs.

— *Jakarta Post,* 'U.S. Ambassador in Jakarta Ruffles Feathers Again', 4 September 2000
— *Antara,* 'Indonesia: Foreign Ministry asks US Envoy to Clarify his Statements', 8 September 2000

148. 2000, August

The UK Deputy High Commissioner in Ghana (Murray) states at a workshop that '[t]here is corruption in Ghana. The perception is that it is rising'.

Following this, Government officials are quoted as saying that they would ask the (Ghanaian) Foreign Minister to summon Murray, and that Murray had to either provide examples or apologise. A Government minister states that Murray's comments took many people 'by surprise because the Forum was not the right one'.

— *Dispatch,* 'Ghana; Government To Deport Diplomat?', 5 September 2000
— *Financial Times,* 'Observer: Speak low. Observer Column', 3 October 2000

149. 2000, September

The UK Ambassador to Burma (Jenkins) tries to reach the house of Tin Oo, a National League for Democracy politician who has been under house arrest since 1 September. He is reportedly stopped by a plainclothes security officer.

The Burmese Government accuses Jenkins of overstepping 'universal diplomatic norms' and states that it was 'difficult to understand why a foreign ambassador was so adamant to intrude into the internal affairs of an independent and sovereign nation'.

— *Associated Press Online,* 'Myanmar Accuses West of Instigating', 5 September 2000

150. 2000, September

The Chinese Ambassador to South Korea (Wu) is summoned to a meeting with the Vice Foreign Affairs-Trade Minister Ban Ki-Moon, after he had made comments about a possible visit to South Korea by the Dalai Lama. Wu had said that, in spite of the visit, Sino-Korean relations would probably not 'deteriorate to the extent that we should sever diplomatic ties', but that 'hurting the sentiment of the Chinese people' would affect relations in some way.

— *Korea Times*, 'Dalai Lama's Future Trip', 9 September 2000

151. 2000, September

The US Ambassador to Israel (Indyk) states that '[t]here is no other solution [on Jerusalem] but to share the holy city'. Following this, a Likud Member of the Knesset calls on Prime Minister Barak to expel Indyk.

The US Embassy states that US policy on Jerusalem had not changed, and that Indyk had made the 'obvious point that tolerance and coexistence will be required by all for there to be a genuine and lasting peace'.

— *People's Daily*, 'Barak Urged to Declare U.S. Ambassador "Persona Non Grata"', 18 September 2000
— M Arnold, 'U.S. Envoy Hit Over Remarks On Jerusalem', *Forward*, c 22 September 2000

152. 2000, September

The US Ambassador to Indonesia (Gelbard) states that the Indonesian General Syahnakri had created 'rumours' and that he 'should concentrate on his daily duties'. This follows Syahnakri's allegations (denied by Gelbard) that US marines were deployed in West Timor.

Following that, the Chairman of Commission I of the Indonesian House of Representatives states that Gelbard had committed undue interference in Indonesia's internal affairs. Commission I urges the Indonesian Foreign Ministry to summon the Ambassador to clarify his statements.

— *Joyo Indonesian News*, 'Syahnakri Plays Down Spat with US Ambassador Gelbard', 28 September 2000
— *Antara*, 'House Commission Urges Foreign Ministry to Summon US Envoy', 28 September 2000

153. 2000, September

The US Ambassador to Indonesia (Gelbard) accuses Indonesia of failing to bring the military under greater civilian control and of failing to disarm militias accused of killing three UN refugee workers in West Timor.

The Ambassador's comments result in charges of US interference in Indonesian affairs. Defence Minister Mahfud threatens Gelbard's expulsion; President Wahid however rejects this option.

— Simon (2000)

154. 2000, September

The Government of Burma, with apparent reference to diplomatic support for the opposition politician Suu Kyi and her National League for Democracy, expresses its disappointment about 'foreign government representatives' who acted to assist and encourage 'one political party or … one individual of their choice in order to be able to destabilize and overthrow the government of the host country'. It notes that '[t]heir blatant interference in the host country's internal affairs under the pretext of human rights and democracy is quite something'.

— *BBC Monitoring Asia Pacific*, 'Burmese Ruling Council Uses British PM's Words', 26 September 2000

155. 2000, October

According to the Indonesian Minister of Defence (Mahfud), the US Ambassador to Indonesia (Gelbard) had pressured the Government to pick Lieutenant General Agus Wirahadikusumah as the new head of the army. Mahfud threatens Gelbard's expulsion.

The US Embassy states that it is 'deeply concerned' about these statements which it calls irresponsible. Gelbard denies the charge of trying to influence appointments.

— *BBC Online*, 'US Denies Interfering in Indonesia', 16 October 2000
— R Galpin, 'Wahid Urged to Remove US Ambassador', *BBC Online*, 2 November 2000
— Simon (2000)

156. 2000, October

The Indonesian Minister of Defence (Mahfud) claims that the US Ambassador to Indonesia (Gelbard) had prevented the deportation of a US citizen (Aaron Maness), whom Indonesia had arrested on 21 October (reportedly amid accusations of espionage).

In a press release, the Embassy states that reports 'that US ambassador Robert Gelbard intervened in the case to demand the transfer of the detained American' were 'untrue' and emphasises that the Embassy did not interfere with the handling of Maness' case.

— *Antara*, 'Indonesia: US Embassy Denies American Arrested in Irian Jaya was Spy', 23 October 2000
— *Agence France Presse*, 'Minister Says Indonesia Caught US "Inflitrator"', 23 October 2000

157. 2000, November

The Chinese Ambassador to South Korea (Wu Dawei) states that Korea should have consulted with China over the possible reopening of direct air flights between Seoul and Taipei.

The Korean Foreign Affairs-Trade Minister subsequently notes that the Ambassador had, with these remarks, 'crossed the line of acceptable speech for a diplomat serving in Seoul …' and that the Government had conveyed a message to him 'through an appropriate channel'.

— *Korea Times*, 'Seoul Protesteds [sic] China Envoy's Inappropriate' Remarks', 23 November 2000
— S Key-young, 'China Envoy Angers Koreans Again', *Korea Times*, 17 November 2000

158. 2000, November

The Foreign Minister of Ghana (Gbeho) refers to comments made by the UK Deputy High Commissioner in that country (Murray) as bordering on interference. Murray had called on the electoral commission to let only people with new identity cards vote.

UK High Commissioner Pullen notes that the remarks had been made without malice and that the UK had provided funds for the identity card replacement exercise.

Later in the month, Gbeho warns foreign governments against interference, noting that 'donor assistance confers no licence' to interfere in matters 'that fall within the domestic jurisdiction of Ghana'.

— *Agence France Presse*, 'Ghana Warns Against Foreign Interference', 28 November 2000

159. 2000, November

The Pakistani Deputy High Commissioner in Bangladesh (Raja) denies Bangladeshi estimates about the number of people killed in the 1971 war between East Pakistan (now the People's Republic of Bangladesh) and West Pakistan (now the Islamic Republic of Pakistan) and states that atrocities committed during the war were triggered by 'miscreants' of Bangladesh's ruling party rather than the Pakistani army.

In December, Bangladesh expels Raja with the explanation that his conduct had been incompatible with his diplomatic status. Pakistan rejects this assessment, stating that the expulsion had not been in keeping with the spirit of friendly relations between the States.

— M Hossain and S Price, 'Dhaka Expels Pakistani Diplomat', *BBC Online*, 15 December 2000
— *E-mela*, 'Pakistan Regrets Over Controversial Remark', c December 2000

160. 2000, December

A US diplomat in Sudan (Warren) meets leading opposition politicians. According to the Sudanese Foreign Minister, Warren had discussed issues relating to Sudanese security and stability. According to the official *Al-Anbaa* newspaper, participants at the meeting had plotted 'an armed act with American support'.

Sudan expels Warren. The State Department notes that the meeting had involved discussions about Sudan's general political situation and that the US had never been told that they could not meet with the relevant group.

— *CNN*, 'U.S. Diplomat Expelled from Sudan', 7 December 2000
— *CBS*, 'U.S. Diplomat Kicked Out Of Sudan', 7 December 2000

161. 2001, February

The Serbian member of the Bosnian presidency (Radišić) accuses foreign diplomats of putting pressure on politicians ahead of elections in the country. He mentions 'secret meetings' and blackmail and refers to 'security concerns'. Radisic notes that he had already given a warning to US Ambassador Miller and mentions the possibility of expelling diplomats who overstepped their boundaries.

The US Embassy states that Miller's activities were compatible with the responsibilities of US Ambassadors and notes that diplomats in Bosnia regularly met with politicians 'across the spectrum'.

— *Deutsche Presse-Agentur*, 'U.S. Defends Envoy', 6 February 2001
— A Cerkez-Robinson, 'Bosnian Presidency Considers Expelling US Ambassador', *Associated Press*, 6 February 2001

162. 2001, March

Boris Smirnov, Counsellor at the Russian Embassy to Bulgaria, is expelled. It is alleged that Smirnov had 'lobbied' for the success of pro-Russian candidates in the Parliamentary elections. Smirnov is accused of interference in the domestic affairs of Bulgaria.

— *RIA Novosti*, 'Bulgaria Identifies Expelled Russian Diplomats', 19 March 2001

163. 2001, March

The Chairwoman of the Bangladesh Nationalist Party (Zia) claims that an Indian and a Palestinian diplomat (according to other sources, a diplomat and an intelligence officer) have met former Bangladeshi President Ershad in prison to persuade him to dissociate himself from the opposition alliance. Zia refers to this as 'conspiracy' and interference in internal affairs.

The Indian High Commission denies the charges.

— *New Nation*, 'Khaleda Blasts Diplomats Visit to Central Jail', 20 March 2001.
— A Rahman, 'RAW Hand' [sic] in Bid to Break Up Alliance', *Tribune News Service*, 21 March 2001
— H Habib, 'Bangla Opposition Alliance Faces Split', *The Hindu*, 28 March 2001

164. 2001, April

After diplomats attend a briefing (given by the Malaysian National Justice Party) on the medical condition of the opposition politician Anwar Ibrahim, a Minister in the Malaysian Prime Minister's department (Rais) states that diplomats who interfered in internal affairs could be asked to leave. He notes that it was not wrong for diplomats 'to accept an invitation by a political party to listen to speeches but they should not take an active part in the function or be partisan'. However, he also states that diplomats should be asked why they had been so keen to attend the National Justice Party meeting.

— *Malaysia General News*, 'Meddling Diplomats Can be Ordered to Leave', 6 April 2001

165. 2001, April

The UK Deputy High Commissioner in Ghana (Murray) is criticised after he suggests that the Ghana Commercial Bank and the Ghana Civil Aviation Authority be privatised and declares agreement with the Government's decision to put some public officials on leave while investigating their record.

The National Democratic Party considers legal action against Murray, in spite of his immunity, 'for his interference in the internal affairs of Ghana'.

— O Yanquoi, 'NDC Accuses British Diplomat Of Political Interference', *Expo Times*, 11–24 April 2001
— *Accra Mail*, 'Ghana; Government Asked to Privatise GCB And GCAA', 16 April 2001

166. 2001, April

The Deputy National Chairman of the National Democratic Party (NDC) of Ghana accuses the British Deputy High Commissioner in Ghana (Murray) of having 'forced his presence' (Yanquoi) into the operation room of the electoral commission building during the elections in December 2000. He notes that this conduct infringed Ghana's sovereignty as an independent State and states that Murray's behaviour was 'beyond his diplomatic mission, and totally unacceptable to the NDC and the entire Ghanaian citizenry' (Yanquoi).

— O Yanquoi, 'NDC Accuses British Diplomat Of Political Interference', *Expo Times*, 11–24 April 2001

167. 2001, April

The Kenyan President (Moi) warns UK High Commissioner Jeffrey James to cease meddling in the Kenyan constitutional review process, stating that it was not a British project and fell not within James's domain.

James had apparently met members of the constitutional review commission; reportedly triggering concerns by the Kenyan Government that he might have attempted to influence the process.

— *Agence France Presse*, 'Kenya's Moi Tells British Envoy to "Keep Off" Reform Process', 15 April 2001
— *BBC Monitoring Africa—Political*, 'Kenya: Paper Analyses Why British Envoy was Rebuked', 2 December 2001

168. 2001, April

The Chinese Chargé d'affaires in Australia is summoned to the Australian Foreign Ministry. This follows criticism by the Chinese Embassy of Australian Prime Minister Howard's support for the US promise to help defend Taiwan and his statement that he did not want to see aggression by China against Taiwan. The Embassy objects to the word 'aggression' in particular.

Howard in turn states that he found the Embassy's reaction neither appropriate nor necessary.

— *Taipei Times*, 'China Rebukes Australian PM over Taiwan', 28 April 2001.
— A Crabb, 'Howard Carpets Chinese Envoy', *The Age*, 28 April 2001.

169. 2001, June

The election agent (North) of a candidate in general elections in the United Kingdom criticises the conduct of the Pakistani High Commissioner Jaffer. According to North, Jaffer had visited mosques and asked people to support the conservative candidate Riaz; conduct which North considered interference in British elections.

The British Foreign Office notes that it was investigating the allegations, but that it was 'usual for foreign diplomats to attend and observe political meetings …' and that such attendance by Jaffer was 'not a problem at all'.

— *Telegraph & Argus*, 'Foreign Office Probes Commissioner's Visit', 5 June 2001
— S Walsh, 'Foreign Office Probes Commissioner's Visit', *This is Bradford*, 6 June 2001

170. 2001, June

US Ambassador to Bangladesh Peters outlines problems which the Government of Bangladesh should solve as a priority, including streamlining power and telecommunication sectors and preparing 'for garment exports in a quote-free world' (*Agence France Presse*).

While the Bangladeshi Communist party considers these statements direct interference in domestic affairs; the Bangladeshi Prime Minister points out that every party had its own election manifesto on which it would run the Government.

— *Agence France Presse*, 'US Envoy Sets Economic Targets', 16 May 2001
— *Xinhua*, 'Bangladeshi Leftist Party Blasts U.S. Ambassador', 17 May 2001
— H Habib, 'U.S. Envoy's Remarks Raise Hackles', *The Hindu*, 16 June 2001

171. 2001, July

At his confirmation hearing for the post of US Ambassador to Germany, Dan Coats states that, if Germany were to maintain 'a central partnership in NATO', this policy had to be 'accompanied by resources'. Coats notes that there would be a 'great danger' that the European rapid-response force would be a 'hollow force', if Germany did not increase her military spending.

German officials are reportedly 'astonished' at the remarks on a matter which they consider an internal issue.

— D Lindsey, 'US Ambassador Starts off on Stern Foot', *Christian Science Monitor*, 6 August 2001

172. 2001, August

Three diplomatic and consular officials from the United States, Australia and Germany are expelled from Afghanistan, after they had tried to visit Western aid workers detained on charges of preaching Christianity.

The Taleban explanation is that their presence had hampered an investigation into a conspiracy to spread Christianity. The expelled officials are told that foreign interference would be 'counter-productive'.

David Donahue, the US Consul-General in Pakistan who was involved in the diplomatic efforts in Afghanistan, emphasises the detainees' right to consular access.

— Z Hussein and R Boyes, 'Taleban Tell Diplomats to Leave Country', *The Times*, 17 August 2001
— K Gannon, 'Disappointed Diplomats to Leave Afghanistan', *Associated Press*, 20 August 2001

173. 2001, August

In the context of an ongoing political crisis in Sri Lanka, foreign diplomats are warned by the Foreign Ministry that their comments on the current situation might amount to interference in internal affairs. Such public statements would run counter to norms on diplomatic conduct. The Ministry draws the diplomats' attention to Article 41 of the Vienna Convention and notes that diplomats wishing to make representations could do so through the Ministry of Foreign Affairs or with its knowledge.

— N Silva, 'UN Envoy Wants CJ to Step Aside', *Sunday Times (Sri Lanka)*, 19 August 2001

174. 2001, August

A British diplomat in Gambia (Joshi) is expelled after he attended an opposition press conference. The Ministry of Justice reportedly states that the decision had come as a result of diplomatic interference in internal affairs.

The Foreign Office notes that 'no satisfactory reason' had been given, and that reporting on political events was standard diplomatic work. The UK retaliates by expelling a Gambian diplomat.

— R Beeston, 'UK Envoy Expelled by The Gambia', *The Times*, 24 August 2001
— *Agence France Presse*, '"Unacceptable" Overseas Interference', 30 August 2001
— UK High Commission in New Delhi, 'Britain's Measures', 1 October 2001

175. 2001, September

The Belarusian President Lukashenko states his intention to expel US Ambassador Kozak, who is accused of being behind the alleged 'White Stork' conspiracy to overthrow the President.

Kozak had previously stated that the US pursued the same objective as in Nicaragua in 1989/1990 and aimed to establish some 'press access for the opposition and a transparent vote-counting process'. It is reported that the US Embassy has funded websites, newspapers and opinion polls and supported a student resistance movement.

— M Kozak, 'Letter', The Guardian, 25 August 2001
— S Peterson, 'US Spends Millions to Bolster Belarus Opposition', *Christian Science Monitor*, 10 September 2001

176. 2001, September

The Italian Ambassador to Eritrea (Bandini) is expelled after he had delivered an EU *démarche* to Eritrea, which denounced human rights violations in the country, following the arrest of dissidents, detention of journalists and the closure of the private press.

Eritrea states that Bandini had been interfering in internal politics. According to Italy, he was singled out as he was also Dean of the EU diplomatic corps. Italy in turn expels the Eritrean ambassador.

— A Last, 'Eritrea Plays Down Diplomatic Row', *BBC Online*, 2 October 2001
— *BBC Online*, 'Eritrea Expels Italian Ambassador', 1 October 2001
— *BBC Online*, 'Italy Expels Eritrea's Ambassador', 2 October 2001

177. 2001, October

In the case of the Italian Ambassador Bandini (see above, A.176), speculation arises that he had been expelled from Eritrea because he maintained contact with dissidents while they were still in office and had held a meeting with them after their dismissal from office.

The Director of European Affairs at the Eritrean Foreign Ministry states that Bandini's 'expulsion was a personal matter', not linked to the *démarche* and that Eritrea had two or three weeks ago asked Italy to withdraw the Ambassador.

— A Last, 'Eritrea Plays Down Diplomatic Row', *BBC Online*, 2 October 2001
— *Integrated Regional Information Network*, 'Eritrea: Italian Community Worried', 9 October 2001

178. 2001, December

The French Ambassador to the UK (Bernard) allegedly refers to Israel as a 'shitty little country' which was putting the world in danger of a third world war.

A spokesman for the Israeli Prime Minister states that these remarks, if true, were anti-semitic and required 'strong condemnation'.

Bernard asserts that his comments had been distorted. His spokesman denies that Bernard had used these words, but says he had referred to Israel as 'little' in terms of geographical size.

— E MacAskill, 'Israel Seeks Head of French Envoy', *The Guardian*, 20 December 2001
— B Amiel, 'Islamists Overplay their Hand', *Daily Telegraph*, 17 December 2001

179. 2002, January

The US Ambassador to Israel, Kurtzer, states that Israel should allocate money to the disabled, rather than to Jewish settlements, and that the US, as a major investor, should have a say in the budget allocation.

A member of the Knesset (Hendel) subsequently states that how Israel spent her money was none of Kurtzer's business and that he had meddled in an 'internal Israeli dispute'.

— D Bloomfield, 'No Different Standards for Jewish Envoys', *Washington Jewish Week*, 17 January 2002
— *Jewish Bulletin News of Northern Carolina*, 'Drama Erupts in the Knesset', 11 January 2002
— *Focus on Israel*, 'Disabled Protesters Making Most Noise …', 10 January 2002

180. 2002, April

The Saudi Ambassador to the UK (Algosaibi) publishes his poem 'The Martyrs' which praises a young Palestinian suicide bomber.

The UK Foreign Office states that it regards suicide bombing 'as a form of terrorism', and that it wishes to make its views known to Algosaibi.

Algosaibi later notes that he was both a poet and an ambassador; the text had been written in his role as a poet.

— P Harris, 'Saudi Envoy Praises Bombers', *The Observer*, 14 April 2002
— *BBC Online*, 'Diplomat Censured over Bomb Poem', 18 April 2002
— S Henderson, 'The West Must Stop', *Daily Telegraph*, 11 July 2002

181. 2002, April

The French Ambassador to Haiti (Gaudeul) criticises Haiti, referring inter alia to human rights violations in the country, corruption of the public administration, degradation of the educational system and a 'confusion of the roles of the police and the justice department'.

The Haitian Government speaks of 'inappropriate statements' and refers to 'racist connotations'. It further states that it considers the remarks interference in internal affairs. At a meeting between the Haitian Prime Minister and Gaudeul, Gaudeul's attention is drawn 'to the role of accredited diplomats' in Haiti.

— *BBC Monitoring International Reports*, 'Haitian Minister to Question French Ambassador', 22 April 2002
— *BBC Monitoring International Reports*, 'Highlights of Radio Metropole News 1145 GMT 22 APR 02', 24 April 2002
— *BBC Monitoring International Reports*, 'Foreign Minister on Prime Minister's Meeting', 30 April 2002

182. 2002, June

The UK High Commissioner in Zimbabwe (Donnelly) is reportedly placed under 24 hour surveillance. The measure is adopted after two lawyers had allegedly contacted him to thank him for supporting a campaign to restore civil rights in the country. The State-run *Herald* subsequently accuses Donnelly of 'meddling in Zimbabwean politics' and of undermining the Government.

The UK Foreign Office denies the allegations.

— *BBC Online*, 'Zimbabwe "Tracking" British Diplomat', 15 June 2002
— *Hindustan Times*, 'British Ambassador to Harare Placed Under Surveillance', 15 June 2002

183. 2002, July

The Saudi Ambassador to the United Kingdom (Algosaibi) states, with regard to the Israeli occupation of Palestinian territory, that the 'war of occupation' was more severe 'than anything the Germans did when they occupied Europe in World War Two'.

The UK Foreign Office calls the remarks 'wrong and insensitive'; the Israeli Embassy notes that the statements were 'outrageous and irresponsible'.

— R Beeston, 'Occupation "Worse than Nazis"', *The Times*, 10 July 2002
— S Sadeh, 'Saying as he Pleases, Wishing to do More', *Ha'aretz*, 14 July 2002

184. 2002, August

Nauru severs diplomatic relations with Taiwan, after a Taiwanese diplomat had been accused by the President of Nauru of trying to interfere in national elections and wanting to be 'seen talking with the opposition'. A spokeswoman for the Taiwanese Foreign Ministry admits diplomatic contacts with the opposition but states that this was appropriate conduct—it was the task of diplomats to make friends with everyone, and it could not be considered interference if they were friendly to members of the opposition.

— K Shu-ling, 'Paraguay Reaffirms Relations with Taiwan', *Taipei Times*, 20 August 2002
— *China Post*, 'MOFA Dismisses Interference Charge by Nauru President', 20 August 2002

185. 2002, September

The UK High Commissioner in Kenya (Clay) states that the UK was 'not concerned with who wins the election, but how he wins it, because our main interest is in the electoral process and how the competing parties conduct their campaigns ....' He reportedly also states that the elections were of 'great concern both to Kenyans and foreigners'.

The Kenyan President Moi reportedly accuses Clay of interference and states that the UK High Commissioner had 'no right to interfere with our affairs, because we do not interfere with the political affairs of Britain'.

— *Agence France Presse*, 'Kenyan President Accuses Britain of Interference', 4 October 2002

186. 2002, October

The UK Ambassador to Uzbekistan (Murray) states in a speech that 'Uzbekistan is not a functioning democracy'. He also refers to mistreatment of political prisoners and the committing of dissidents to institutions for the mentally ill.

Murray is subsequently summoned to the Uzbekistan Foreign Ministry which expresses its misgivings about the speech. However, it is also reported that Murray's superiors in London advise him against upsetting Uzbekistan in the future.

— Murray, 109, 110, 122
— J Ungoed-Thomas and M Franchetti, 'The British Ambassador Says his Hosts are Boiling People to Death…' *Sunday Times*, 26 October 2003

187. 2002, October

The German Ambassador to Kenya (Weerth) calls on the Government to guarantee free, peaceful and fair elections.

The Kenyan President Moi subsequently accuses the German Government of 'getting deeply involved in the internal affairs of Kenya to a level which can no longer be tolerated'. He points out that, while Western countries talk about 'free and fair elections', he would 'request them not to interfere in the internal affairs of Kenya and not to take sides'.

— *Agence France Presse*, 'Kenya's Moi Accuses Germany of Interference in Domestic Affairs', 26 October 2002

188. 2003, January

The US Ambassador to Pakistan (Powell) states that Pakistan must implement its promise to stop infiltrations of militants across a ceasefire line in Kashmir and calls on Pakistan not to use the country as a platform for terrorism.

Powell is subsequently summoned to the Pakistani Foreign Ministry; Pakistani Prime Minister Jamali states that serious notice would be taken if comments were seen to be interference in internal affairs.

— *Press Trust of India*, 'Nancy Powell Asks Pak to End Infiltration', 23 January 2003
— *Pakistan Newswire*, 'Nancy Visits FO', 24 January 2003
— *BBC Worldwide Monitoring*, 'Pakistani Premier Says Interference in Pakistani Affairs Not to be Allowed', 26 January 2003

189. 2003, February

Five Pakistani diplomats are expelled from India, including the *Chargé d'affaires* (Jeelani). India accuses Jeelani of having personally provided monetary funds to separatists in the Indian zone of Kashmir.

The Pakistani mission in New Delhi refers to the accusations as 'ridiculous and baseless'.

- P Kumar, 'AFP: India, Pakistan Ties Sink Further', *World News Connection*, 8 February 2003
- *Sunday Mail (Queensland, Australia)*, 'Diplomat Expelled', 9 February 2003
- *Independent on Sunday*, 'Diplomats Expelled', 9 February 2003

190. 2003, February

A second secretary at the Iraqi Embassy to the Philippines is expelled. This reportedly occurs after one of his telephone calls was traced back to Abu Sayyaf, a terrorist organisation.

The Iraqi Foreign Ministry debates the facts of the allegations and states that an unsuccessful attempt had been made by the US Embassy to persuade the diplomat to betray national secrets.

- L Harris et al, 'Chief Weapons Inspectors Give Another Update on Iraq', *CNN*, 13 February 2003
- *Xinhua*, 'Expelled Iraqi Diplomat Leaves Philippines', 14 February 2003
- *Post and Courier*, 'Terrorism Advances and Warnings', 5 March 2003

191. 2003, February

The Saudi Ambassador to the US (Prince Bandar) reportedly tells President Bush that his country 'hope[s] to fine-tune oil prices over 10 months to prime the economy for 2004' (a year of US presidential elections). When this is reported, a former State Department spokesman (Rubin) accuses Saudi Arabia of interference.

Prince Bandar states that Saudi Arabia had hoped that oil prices would stay low in the interests of the American, Saudi and world economy.

- R Insana et al, 'The News on CNBC (20:00)', *CNBC*, 19 April 2004
- D Froomkin, 'No Saudi Oil "Deal"', *Washington Post*, 20 April 2004
- R Novak, 'Critics are Distorting', *Augusta Chronicle*, 29 April 2004

192. 2003, June

Legal proceedings are initiated against the US Ambassador to Egypt (Welch) following a speech made in June 2003.

In his speech, Welch sharply criticised the performance of the Egyptian Government and called for changes to the currently existing political and economic strategies.

As a consequence, an Egyptian lawyer (El-Wahsh) files a lawsuit against Welch, on the grounds that the Ambassador had interfered with the internal policies of Egypt.

— *Al-Ahram Weekly*, 'Lawyer Sues Welch', 12–18 June 2003

193. 2003, September

In the run-up to the Estonian referendum on joining the European Union, a German diplomat reportedly makes a speech from the campaign bus of the European Commission, calling for an affirmative vote. A Eurosceptic British Member of European Parliament (Helmer) who reported the incident, expresses the view that the diplomat had committed a 'direct interference in an internal Estonian political debate' and thus violated Article 41 of the Vienna Convention. According to Helmer, the diplomat invoked the promotion of German culture by way of justification.

— R Helmer, 'Estonia Faces the EU Propaganda Barrage', *Lincolnshire Echo*, 2 September 2003

194. 2003, September

The Ambassador of the Solomon Islands to Taiwan (Gukuna) is replaced after his criticism of a Taiwanese politician. Gukuna had expressed his disappointment after Parris Chang, who represents the Democratic Progressive Party in the Taiwanese legislature, had criticised the 'dollar diplomacy' in which the State of Nauru allegedly engaged. (The Solomon Islands were, to a degree, beneficiaries of Nauru's support.)

Chang calls Gukuna's remarks 'inappropriate' and damaging to ties between the two countries. Chang also calls for an apology by Gukuna.

— M Chen, 'Taiwan: AIT Denies Director Leaving for White House', *World News Connection*, 9 September 2003

195. 2003, December

After the Zimbabwean High Commissioner in Australia (Chitauro) accuses Australian Prime Minister Howard of acting like a dictator (as member of the Commonwealth troika on Zimbabwe), she is summoned to the Australian Foreign Ministry.

Afterwards, Chitauro reports that she had said she was there 'to protect the head of state I represent and the country … The President of Zimbabwe has been called all sorts of names, and I am here to make sure that I take a position'.

— *Agence France Presse*, 'Zimbabwe's Australia Ambassador Unrepentant', 11 December 2003
— *Deutsche Presse-Agentur*, 'Australia Reprimands Zimbabwe Diplomat Over "Dictator" Jibe', 11 December 2003

196. 2003, December

The US Ambassador to the Bahamas (Richard Blankenship) calls for reform of the Bahamian police department. The Foreign Minister of the Bahamas, Frank Mitchell, takes issue with the remarks and calls them an 'unexpected attack' (*Associated Press*).

— *Associated Press*, 'Outgoing U.S. Ambassador in Bahamas Urges Island Chain to Sign Treaty', 10 June 2003

197. 2003, December

A diplomat at the Cuban Interests Section in Washington is expelled. It is reported that he had regularly visited imprisoned Cuban spies, and had reportedly associated with 'criminal elements'.

The Cuban Foreign Ministry declares that he had undertaken no activities violating his diplomatic status and had always abided by 'the 1961 Geneva Convention on Diplomatic Relations [sic]'.

— G Gedda, 'U.S. Expels Cuban Diplomat', *Associated Press*, 3 January 2004
— A Snow, 'Cuba Defends Diplomat Expelled from US', *Associated Press*, 8 January 2004
— *Xinhua*, 'Cuba Refutes US Accusation Against its Diplomat', 9 January 2004
— *Miami Herald*, 'Claims of Drug Ties', 9 January 2004

198. 2004, January

The Israeli Ambassador to Sweden (Mazel) physically attacks an art installation which incorporates the photograph of a suicide bomber. Mazel is expelled from the museum; the Swedish Foreign Ministry describes his conduct as 'unacceptable' and states that it would summon Mazel.

Mazel reportedly refers to the artwork as a glorification of suicide bombers and incitement to genocide against Israelis. The Israeli Prime Minister supports Mazel's conduct.

— *ONASA News Agency*, 'Israeli Ambassador Kicked Out Of Swedish Museum', 17 January 2004
— *Channel News Asia*, 'Sweden and Israel in Furious Diplomatic Row', 18 January 2004
— G Rosenberg, 'Das Meer der Wölfe', *Süddeutsche Zeitung*, 24 January 2004

199. 2004, March

The German Ambassador to Iran (Maltzahn) is accused of interference after he had met with Grand Ayatollah Montazeri. The United States, Israel, Judaism, Iraq, and elections in Iran were allegedly topics of discussion.

Right-wing newspapers in Iran speak of interference in internal affairs; the pro-Khamenei newspaper *Kayhan* calls the meeting 'wilful and illegal' and reports that Maltzahn is to be withdrawn. The Iranian Vice President Abtahi however denies this.

— *BBC Monitoring International Reports*, 'BBC Monitoring Quotes from the Iranian Press', 7 March 2004
— *Die Welt*, 'Iran; Gerüchte um Ausweisung des deutschen Botschafters', 8 March 2004
— B Nirumand, 'Rüffel aus Teheran', *taz (Die Tageszeitung)*, 9 March 2004

200. 2004, April

The US Ambassador to Macedonia (Butler) is criticised after he called on voters to participate in presidential elections. The former Macedonian Minister of the Interior (Boskovski) calls Butler's remarks a 'gross interference in the internal affairs of Macedonia'. Boskovski himself had called for a boycott of the elections.

— *Radio Free Europe/Radio Liberty*, 'Macedonian Presidential Candidate rejects U.S., EU calls', 26 April 2004

201. 2004, June

The US Ambassador to Ukraine (Herbst) states, with regard to Ukrainian Members of Parliament: 'The Soviet Union was one of the most primitive and twisted experiments of the last century. People who began their careers in the communist period absorbed a very great deal of those political methods. And so it is not surprising that people brought up in that system can express themselves in precisely that primitive way'. Following these statements, a pro-government weekly notes that Herbst had made 'undiplomatic and ill-mannered' remarks (BBC).

— *BBC Monitoring International Reports*, 'Ukrainian Weekly Dubs US Ambassador Undiplomatic', 12 June 2004

202. 2004, July

The UK High Commissioner in Kenya (Clay) criticises corruption in that State and notes that members of the Kenyan Government 'can hardly expect us not to care when their gluttony causes them to vomit all over our shoes'.

The Kenyan Foreign Minister (Mwakwere), is quoted as stating that Clay's job was not that of a comedian; that he had 'abused us and we are telling him to explain the facts ... or else ... shut up.'

— L Barasa, 'Criticism That Rubbed Officials The Wrong Way', *The Nation*, 3 February 2005

203. 2004, September

The Canadian Ambassador to Ukraine (Robinson) expresses his country's concerns that forthcoming presidential elections may 'fail to meet democratic standards'.

Robinson is subsequently summoned to the Ukrainian Foreign Ministry. A Ministry spokesman refers to Robinson's statement as a 'preconceived personal opinion', but also takes issue with its timing, coming at a time when the electoral campaign was ongoing.

— A Melnichuk, 'Ukrainian Authorities', *Associated Press*, 23 September 2004

204. 2004, November

A Rwandan diplomat (Wizeye) is expelled from Uganda amid claims that he had links with the People's Redemption Army (PRA), a group fighting the Ugandan Government. The Ugandan Information Minister accuses him of involvement in activities 'meant to destabilise our country' and notes that he had been named by eight members of the PRA who had been arrested in northwest Uganda.

— *Agence France Presse*, 'Uganda, Rwanda Expel Low-ranking Diplomats', 26 November 2004

205. 2005, February

The UK High Commissioner in Kenya (Clay) says that he has given a dossier to the Kenyan Government, apparently implicating four cabinet ministers in corruption.

The Kenyan Foreign Minister (Mwakwere) states that Clay was 'talking nonsense. I think he had taken one too many'. He also calls Clay 'a congenital liar'.

The Kenyan Vice-President (Awori), is quoted as saying that Kenyans 'would not allow themselves to be dictated by foreigners' (*Xinhua*).

— *BBC Monitoring International Reports*, 'British Envoy Congenital Liar—Kenyan Foreign Minister', 4 February 2005
— *Xinhua General News Service*, 'Roundup: Kenyan Officials Angered', 4 February 2005

206. 2005, May

A Polish diplomat (Bucko) is expelled from Belarus because of 'his attempts to destabilize the Belarusian society'.

It is reported that the Belarusian Government takes exception to Bucko's contacts with Poles in Belarus and with the Belarusian opposition. The Belarusian President had accused Western States of using the Polish minority to incite revolution and Polish diplomats of interference in internal affairs.

— M Scislowska, 'Poland Says it will Expel Belarusian Diplomat', *Associated Press*, 18 May 2005
— *Interfax News Agency*, 'Polish Diplomat Expelled', 19 May 2005
— *BBC Worldwide Monitoring*, 'Polish Consul Expelled', 15 July 2005

207. 2005, October

The US Ambassador to Zimbabwe (Dell) is detained for half an hour after he allegedly tried to enter a restricted area near the residence of Robert Mugabe.

According to the Zimbabwean Foreign Ministry, Dell's conduct 'was clearly intended to provoke an unwarranted diplomatic incident'. Government sources state that the occurrence had been part of an American attempt to effect 'regime change' in Zimbabwe.

— A Penketh, 'US Ambassador Is Held At Gunpoint', *Independent*, 15 October 2005
— *Bahrain News Agency*, 'US Ambassador to Harare Seized by Security Forces', 14 October 2005

208. 2005, November

The US Ambassador to Zimbabwe (Dell) is criticised after he accuses the Zimbabwean Government of corruption and draws attention to the demolition of thousands of homes which, in his view, resulted in a humanitarian crisis.

Zimbabwean President Mugabe reportedly tells Dell to explain why he was 'meddling in the internal affairs of Zimbabwe'. A Zimbabwean academic (Kurebwa) is quoted as stating that Dell had 'a mission to … foment trouble in Zimbabwe against the government'.

— A Shaw, 'Report: Mugabe to Summon U.S. Ambassador', *Associated Press*, 6 November 2005
— *BBC Worldwide Monitoring*, 'Zimbabwean Dons Say US Envoy "Main Agent for Political Upheaval"', 10 November 2005

209. 2006, January

A British diplomat in Russia (Doe) is accused of funding NGOs. Russian President Putin acknowledges the importance of NGOs, but reportedly states that Russia wanted NGOs not 'to be led by puppet masters from abroad'.

UK Ambassador Brenton insists that the funding had been done 'transparently', was partly aimed at helping rape and torture victims, and that there was nothing improper about it.

— *BBC Worldwide Monitoring*, 'Putin Comments on Spy Allegations', 31 January 2006

— N Walsh, 'Ambassador Defends Diplomat in Spying Row', *The Guardian*, 1 February 2006
— V Isachenkov, 'Report: Russia's Spymaster', *Associated Press*, 21 February 2006

210. 2006, February

Belarus claims that Czech diplomats have distributed propaganda leaflets ahead of the presidential elections in the country, in an attempt to breach the peace. The Belarusian authorities speak of interference in internal affairs.

The Czech Foreign Minister denies activities of interference and states that the material in question had been a UN Human Rights Commission report on Belarus.

— *CTK National News Wire*, 'Czechs Provide 4 Million Crowns', 23 February 2006
— *CTK National News Wire*, 'Czech Embassy in Minsk', 5 February 2008

211. 2006, March

The Government of Malawi responds to certain remarks by foreign diplomats, including comments on alleged (State) interference with the judiciary and harassment of the legislature by the executive. In a press release, the Government outlines the duty of the Dean of the diplomatic corps to raise diplomatic concerns with the Foreign Ministry and not have them disseminated through the local press—the latter conduct would be considered interference in internal affairs. It also calls on diplomats to notify the Foreign Ministry if they wished to hold meetings with persons or institutions.

— *BBC Monitoring Africa—Political*, 'Malawi Cautions Diplomats', 29 March 2006

212. 2006, April

A Czech diplomat in Cuba (Kazécky) is expelled. The Foreign Ministry refers to 'subversive tasks' carried out by Kazécky and accuses him, inter alia, of giving money and material goods to opposition groups. Kazécky claims that his expulsion was connected to his having met leaders of the opposition.

— Rodriguez, 'Cuba Says Expelled Czech Diplomat is Spy', *Associated Press*, 14 April 2006
— *The Australian*, 'Cubans Expel Czech "for Spying"', 17 April 2006

213. 2006, April

The Frente Sandinista de Liberación Nacional (FSLN) in Nicaragua accuses US Ambassador Trivelli of interference, after he met right wing parties, allegedly urging them to support the Allianza Libera presidential candidate. Trivelli also stated that Nicaragua was threatened by a 'creeping coup'.

Trivelli insists that he was free to express his views and was merely trying to defend Nicaragua's democratic progress.

— *Miami Herald*, 'Rebel Ambush Kills 16 from Military Convoy', 22 April 2006
— I James, 'Nicaragua's Ortega Accuses U.S.', *Associated Press*, 23 April 2006
— *Intelligence Research Ltd*, 'US Takes Active Role in Nicaraguan Elections', 25 April 2006
— J Russow, 'US Intervention in Nicaragua Election', *PEJ News*, 4 November 2006.

214. 2006, July

Two US diplomats are expelled from Kyrgyzstan amid allegations of interference. According to a US Embassy statement, they were accused of maintaining inappropriate contacts with leaders of Kyrgyz NGOs.

The Embassy denies allegations of inappropriate conduct and notes that the measure could be considered an 'attempt to intimidate embassies and silence the voice of civil society'. It also notes that the US would 'continue to maintain contact with all sectors of Kyrgyz society'.

— *Times of Central Asia*, 'Kyrgyzstan Expels Two US Diplomats', 13 July 2006
— *Facts on File*, 'Kyrgyzstan; U.S. Air Base Agreement Signed', 24 August 2006

215. 2006, September

The Australian High Commissioner in the Solomon Islands (Cole) is expelled for alleged meddling in internal affairs. This reportedly follows talks between Cole and the opposition and his criticism of the establishment of a commission to investigate recent riots (Australia was concerned that the commission would blame the police, including Australian police officers serving in the country).

The Australian Foreign Minister calls the expulsion 'outrageous', a personal attack on Cole and an 'extremely unprofessional thing'.

— *Australian Associated Press*, 'Fed: Govt Must Quickly Investigate', 13 September 2006
— *Australian Associated Press*, 'Fed: Aust Diplomat Expelled from Solomons', 13 September 2006
— *Daily Telegraph (Australia)*, 'Diplomat Expelled', 13 September 2006

216. 2006, October

A Russian diplomat (Riabchikov) is expelled from Lithuania—allegedly after he had attempted to influence Lithuania's position in the ongoing conflict between Russia and Georgia. Lithuania, Poland and Ukraine had offered to mediate in this conflict, but Lithuania had also shown herself supportive of Georgia.

— *Ottawa Sun*, 'World Sunflashes Column', 9 October 2006
— *Agence France Presse*, 'Lithuania Expels Russian Diplomat', 11 October 2006

217. 2007, March

The Foreign Minister of Zimbabwe summons diplomats from Australia, Canada, the EU, Germany, Sweden, the UK and the US and criticises them for their alleged support of the opposition. According to one diplomat, the diplomats were 'basically told to stop meddling in Zimbabwe's internal affairs or get kicked out'.

The US Ambassador Dell walks out of the meeting; the UK Embassy states that '[s]uch threats' would not prevent the UK from speaking out against 'misgovernance and human rights abuses in Zimbabwe'.

— B Peta, 'Zimbabwe Threatens Diplomats', *The Independent*, 20 March 2007
— *BBC Monitoring Africa—Political*, 'Foreign Diplomats in Zimbabwe', 22 March 2007

218. 2007, April

The Sri Lankan Government warns foreign diplomats against meddling in internal affairs and states that diplomats found interfering could be expelled. It also indicates that one particular diplomat—who remains unnamed—is being investigated.

The warning is seen by some commentators (Vestergaard) in the context of increasing criticism within the international community of Sri Lanka's human rights record.

— *Agence France Presse*, 'Sri Lanka Threatens to Expel Diplomats', 18 April 2007
— T Vestergaard, 'Sri Lankan Government Threatens to Expel Diplomats', *Global Insight*, 19 April 2007

219. 2007, April

The UK High Commissioner in Sri Lanka (Chilcott) visits the office of Champika Liyanaarachchi, a newspaper editor who had allegedly received a death threat from the Sri Lankan Defence Secretary. Chilcott's visit comes a day after Sri Lanka had warned diplomats against interference (see above, A.218). The visit is seen as a gesture of support.

Following his visit, Chilcott is summoned to the office of the Sri Lankan Secretary of Defence, Gotabhaya Rajapakse.

— *Agence France Presse*, 'Sri Lanka Editor Faces Death Threat', 18 April 2007
— *Agence France Presse*, 'British Envoy Embroiled in Sri Lanka Media Crisis', 19 April 2007

220. 2007, April

Following reports that members of the Russian Embassy have given instructions to Russian extremists in Estonia, Russian Ambassador Uspensky has a meeting with a member of the Estonian Foreign Ministry. In a later statement, the Russian Embassy states that regular meetings with representatives of Russian groups do take place, but that they are done to protect their legal rights and interests. It emphasises that this is 'normal practice, in line with the practice of all democratic countries', including Estonia herself and that Russian diplomats act in compliance with the Vienna Convention.

— *Baltic News Service*, 'Russian Embassy in Tallinn Denies Giving Instructions', 18 May 2007

221. 2007, June

The High Commissioner of New Zealand (Green) is expelled from Fiji amid charges of interference. The Acting Foreign Minister refuses to give precise reasons for the expulsion, but there are reports that Fiji's ruler (Bainimarama) was irritated when Green had been guest of honour at a rugby match between New Zealand and Fiji. According to other reports, Green had met members of the deposed Government.

- — *BBC Online*, 'Fiji Expels New Zealand Diplomat', 14 June 2007
- — D Brooks, 'Fiji Expels New Zealand Ambassador', *Agence France Presse*, 14 June 2007
- — *Fiji Times*, 'NZ Unfair, Cries Voreqe', 16 June 2007

222. 2007, July

The ruler of Fiji (Bainimarama) says that the US Ambassador to the country (Dinger) has disseminated misleading information about the recent coup d'état in Fiji. Bainimarama's comments are made after a US Congressional delegation, which had visited Fiji, had stated that coups of this kind were 'disastrous'.

Bainimarama claims that they were 'getting the same story from their ambassador … as Helen Clark [the Prime Minister of New Zealand] was getting from hers, Michael Green' (see above, A.221). He asserts that they were not 'getting the real story of what's happening in Fiji'.

- — P Ligaiula, 'US Envoy Criticized by Fiji Military Ruler', *Associated Press State & Local Wire*, 11 July 2007

223. 2007, August

Sudan expels the Canadian *Chargé d'affaires* (Lawlor) and the EU diplomat Degerfeld for involvement in conduct constituting 'intervention into the internal affairs of Sudan'. The diplomats had written a letter to the National Intelligence and Security Service in which they requested the release of certain opposition politicians.

According to the Canadian Foreign Minister, Lawlor had acted 'in the finest traditions of Canadian diplomacy' and had defended 'the values of freedom, democracy, human rights and the rule of law in Sudan'.

- — *Star Phoenix*, 'Canada Right to Back Envoy in Sudan Case', 29 August 2007
- — S McCarthy, 'Ottawa Recalls Envoy to Sudan', *Globe and Mail*, 27 August 2007

224. 2007, September

The UK High Commissioner in Kenya (Wood) reportedly states that his country would abide by diplomatic principles which prohibit interference in internal affairs. Britain would therefore 'play an impartial role in the elections that are scheduled to be held at the end of the year'. Wood added, however, that the United Kingdom would keenly observe the political situation in Kenya.

— *BBC Monitoring Africa—Political,* 'Britain to Remain Impartial in Kenya's General Elections', 5 September 2007

225. 2007, October

A Bolivian Minister (Quintana) threatens the expulsion of US Ambassador Goldberg, if Goldberg did not apologise for certain remarks. After Bolivian President Morales had suggested that UN headquarters should be moved, Goldberg had stated that he would not be surprised if Bolivia wanted to move Disney headquarters, too.

The Bolivian Foreign Minister Choquehuanca reportedly calls these comments 'racist'. An apology is eventually extended by Goldberg and accepted by the Bolivian Government.

— *BBC Monitoring Latin America—Political,* 'Bolivian Presidency Minister Considers Making US Envoy "Persona Non Grata"', 18 October 2007
— *Xinhua,* 'Bolivia Accepts U.S. Ambassador's Apologies', 23 October 2007

226. 2007, November

Bolivia threatens the expulsion of the US Ambassador to the country, Philip Goldberg. The Government of the Bolivian President (Morales) accuses Goldberg of providing funds to the opposition. At the Ibero-American summit in Chile, Morales claims that Goldberg is leading an 'international right-wing network'.

— M Arostegui, 'Morales Puts U.S. Diplomat in Sights', *Washington Times*, 28 November 2007

227. 2007, November

On State television, the Venezuelan Foreign Minister (Maduro) presents a document which had allegedly been written by a US Embassy official and which referred to a plan to prevent the Chávez Government from winning a constitutional referendum. Maduro states that, if this were true, the official would be declared 'persona non grata and eject[ed] … from the country', noting that this would amount to interference in Venezuela's internal affairs.

— E Lopez, 'Venezuela Threatens To Expel US Embassy Official', *Associated Press*, 29 November 2007
— *Xinhua*, 'Venezuela Threatens to Expel U.S. Diplomat', 29 November 2007

228. 2007, December

It is reported that two Romanian diplomats, including the Embassy's cultural adviser, have been expelled from Moldova. According to a Moldovan politician (Stepaniuc), this follows their involvement 'in political activities aimed against Moldovan sovereignty and independence'. Regarding the dismissal of the 'envoy for culture issues', Stepaniuc notes that 'Romania should not support newspapers which are mouthpieces of some Moldovan opposition parties'.

Romania refers to the decision as an 'unfriendly, totally unjustified act'.

— *BBC Monitoring International Reports*, 'Moldova Says Romanian Diplomats Banned', 14 December 2007
— *BBC Monitoring Europe—Political*, 'Romania Expresses Regret', 15 December 2007

229. 2008, March

The US Embassy to Libya informs the Libyan Foreign Ministry of its intention to visit the Berber community in the country for talks with local officials.

As a result, US diplomats are summoned by the Libyan Foreign Ministry. During the meeting, a Foreign Ministry official (Ayad) states that there was no (distinct) Berber community; the Berber language was 'merely a dialect or accent'. He accuses the Embassy of 'unacceptable interference' and urges it 'not to try to find obstacles' to the improvement of relations between the two States.

— *Daily Telegraph*, 'Libya's Berber Minority Still Out in the Cold', 31 January 2011

230. 2008, February

The US Ambassador to Algeria (Ford) and a political and economic adviser at the Embassy (Shapiro) meet with representatives of political parties to discuss the current political situation in Algeria.

In March, the Head of the Algerian Government (Belkhadem) states with reference to that meeting that the Algerian Government did 'not accept this type of interference' and that the Government asked political parties 'not to go through the embassies to express their concerns'.

— *BBC Monitoring Middle East—Political*, 'Algerian Premier Criticizes US Ambassador's Interference', 4 March 2008

231. 2008, March

After some Bangladeshi media referred to certain diplomatic remarks as interference, the Bangladeshi Government calls on diplomats to respect Bangladeshi sovereignty.

This statement follows meetings which the US diplomat Geeta Pasi had had with leaders of political parties. Pasi reportedly expressed herself in favour of a dialogue between political parties and the Government to create an atmosphere that would allow the holding of general elections. Pasi denies claims of interference.

— *BBC Monitoring South Asia—Political*, 'Bangladesh Urges Diplomats to Stop "Interference"', 21 March 2008
— *BBC Monitoring South Asia—Political*, 'US Envoy Refutes "Claims of Interference"', 24 March 2008

232. 2008, March

The food adviser of the Bangladeshi Government, Shawkat Ali, accuses the Indian High Commissioner Pinak Chakravarty of going beyond 'diplomatic norms' and urges the Foreign Ministry to take steps in the matter.

This follows comments by Chakravarty to the effect that Bangladesh was responsible for delays in the import of rice from India

— *BBC Monitoring South Asia—Political*, 'US Envoy Refutes "Claims of Interference"', 24 March 2008

233. 2008, May

The US Ambassador to Zimbabwe (McGee) visits, together with other diplomats, the Avenues Clinic in Harare, which treats victims of the political unrest in the country. McGee states afterwards that the 'violence in Zimbabwe has to stop'.

McGee is subsequently summoned to the Foreign Ministry. The Zimbabwean Foreign Minister Mumbengegwi claims that McGee had made 'politically charged and inflammatory remarks', constituting 'interference in Zimbabwe's internal affairs', in violation of Article 41 of the Vienna Convention.

— T McVeigh, 'Tsvangirai Ready to Take on Mugabe', *The Observer*, 11 May 2008
— *The Herald*, 'Zimbabwe; Govt Summons, Warns U.S. Ambassador', 17 May 2008

234. 2008, May

Cuba claims that a US diplomat in the country (Parmly) has provided funds, on a monthly basis, to a political activist. The Cuban Foreign Minister (Perez Roque) states that the payments violated international law and cites in particular the Vienna Convention, referring apparently to the rule against interference.

— R Carroll, 'Cuban Sting Shows US Diplomat Handing Over Cash', *The Guardian*, 24 May 2008
— W Weissert, 'Cuba Demands U.S. Answer Charges', *Associated Press*, 22 May 2008

235. 2008, June

The Bangladeshi Foreign Ministry releases a statement which refers to reports in the Bangladeshi media on remarks by diplomatic missions which might be considered interference in internal affairs. It expresses the hope that 'any such statements that may give rise to such interpretations will be avoided'.

The Ministry statement comes after the US Embassy had requested clarification from the Bangladeshi Government on the reasons for the arrest of leaders of political parties.

— *BBC Monitoring South Asia—Political,* 'Bangladesh Asks Foreign Envoys to Refrain from "Interference"', 3 June 2008

236. 2008, July

The US Ambassador to Bangladesh (Moriarty) holds a 'tea party' at his residence, at which the leaders of several political parties express the view that the state of emergency must be lifted before parliamentary elections can take place.

The Secretary General of the Communist Party of Bangladesh (Selim) voices his criticism of the event, reportedly stating that the 'US ambassador should be declared persona non grata for interfering in internal political affairs'.

— *BBC Monitoring South Asia—Political,* 'US Envoy Discusses Emergency with Bangladesh Leaders', 16 July 2008
— *New Age (Bangladesh),* 'Foreign Interference in Local Politics Condemned', 17 July 2008

237. 2008, August

The Venezuelan President Chávez threatens the expulsion of US Ambassador Patrick Duddy. Duddy had stated that drug traffickers were taking advantage of the rift between Venezuela and the US (Venezuela had suspended cooperation with the US Drug Enforcement Administration in 2005).

Chávez states that his Government was 'not going to accept interference in our internal affairs'. (Duddy is eventually expelled on 11 September 2008, see below A.239.)

— I James, 'US, Venezuela Increasingly at Odds', *Associated Press,* 2 September 2008
— *Thomson Financial,* 'Venezuela's Chavez Threatens to Expel US Ambassador', 1 September 2008
— *Facts on File,* 'Venezuela; Chavez Expels U.S. Ambassador', 18 September 2008

238. 2008, September

The Bolivian President Morales expels US Ambassador Goldberg. Morales is quoted as saying that Bolivia did '... not want people here who conspire against democracy'. Goldberg is reportedly accused of supporting oppositional groups in the Tarija department.

Goldberg denies allegations of supporting the opposition and warns of 'serious consequences' which would follow the incident.

— P Zygel, 'US Ambassador Warns of "Serious Consequences"', *Agence France Presse*, 14 September 2008
— *States News Service*, 'U.S.-Bolivian Relations: Halting An Avalanche', 15 June 2009

239. 2008, September

The US Ambassador to Venezuela (Duddy) is expelled. The Venezuelan President Chávez accuses him of aiding a plot to assassinate him. According to the Venezuelan Justice Minister, a plan had been uncovered to kill the President and to sow 'violence in our country'. The expulsion was, however, also seen as a gesture of solidarity with the President of Bolivia who had just expelled US Ambassador Goldberg from his country (see above, A.238).

— *The Frontrunner*, 'Diplomatic Row Escalates In South America', 12 September 2008.
— C Toothaker, '2 Arrested', *Associated Press*, 25 September 2008

240. 2008, December

New Zealand's Acting High Commissioner in Fiji (Caroline McDonald) is expelled amid accusations of meddling.

The expulsion comes after the Fijian ruler (Bainimarama) had threatened her expulsion if a visa was not granted to the son of a senior official so that he could resume studies in New Zealand.

McDonald calls the Fijian decision 'arbitrary and unwarranted'. New Zealand reacts by expelling a Fijian diplomat.

— *New Zealand Herald*, 'Acting High Commissioner Home from Fiji today', 28 December 2008
— *New Zealand Press Association*, 'Fiji Denies Backdown Over McDonald Expulsion', 23 December 2008
— *Daily News*, 'Expulsion is Revenge, says Commissioner', 29 December 2008

241. 2008, December

The Nepalese Foreign Minister (Yadav) criticises the Indian Ambassador to Nepal (Sood) over a meeting with the country's former head of State. Yadav reportedly states that the Ambassador had met the former King Gyanendra without informing the Foreign Ministry beforehand and had thus been in breach of diplomatic norms.

— *United News of India*, 'Indian Ambassador has Broken Diplomatic Norms: Nepal Foreign Min', 22 December 2008

242. 2009, January

The German Ambassador to Sri Lanka (Weerth) is summoned to the Sri Lankan Foreign Ministry. This follows a speech he had delivered at the burial of Wickrematunga. Wickrematunga—the editor of a newspaper who had been critical of the Sri Lankan Government—had been shot on his way to work.

In his eulogy, Weerth suggested that diplomats should have spoken out earlier; '[t]oday it is too late. Today is a day when humanity has lost a major voice of truth.'

The Sri Lankan Foreign Minister reportedly expresses his displeasure about these remarks.

— A Buncombe, 'Sri Lankan Army "Victory" is Marred', *The Independent*, 15 January 2009
— A Jayasinghe, 'Sri Lankan Govt Under Intense Fire', *Agence France Presse*, 12 January 2009

243. 2009, February

Ecuador expels a US diplomat (Sullivan) for 'unacceptable meddling'. According to Ecuadorian Foreign Minister Fander Falconí, Sullivan had been critical about a police appointment (the transfer of the head of the Unit of Special Investigations to lead the judicial police in a province of Ecuador). Sullivan had allegedly threatened the stopping of US assistance to the unit, whose tasks include the investigation of cases of drug trafficking.

The US Embassy rejects 'any suggestion of wrongdoing by Embassy staff'.

— J Valdivieso, 'Ecuador Expels US Embassy official', *Associated Press*, 18 February 2009
— C Volkel, 'Ecuador Expels Another U.S. Diplomat', *Global Insight*, 19 February 2009

244. 2009, June

The US Ambassador to Afghanistan (Eikenberry) attends a press conference at which a presidential candidate talks about his plans to decentralise the Government.

The incumbent Afghan President Karzai states that the election was an internal Afghan issue in which foreigners should not interfere. Karzai notes that he did not object to diplomats meeting candidates as long as candidate platforms were not discussed.

The Obama administration states that contacts with presidential contenders were in line with US policy in Afghanistan.

— *Indo-Asian News Service*, 'Karzai Protests US Diplomat's Presence', 29 June 2009
— *Pajhwork Afghan News*, 'Meet Poll Contenders Thru Govt', 23 June 2009

245. 2009, June

A member of the UK Embassy staff in Iran (Rassam) is put on trial, along with other persons, including a staff member of the French Embassy. According to the Islamic Republic News Agency, Rassam told the court that, ahead of elections in the country, £300,000 had been earmarked to establish contacts with political groups.

The UK protests against the trial, noting that it was part of diplomatic tasks to understand the receiving State and that meeting politicians and journalists were 'normal activities in every country' and 'recognised as legitimate in the Vienna Convention'.

— C Woodhouse, '"Velvet Revolution" Plan Denied', *Press Association*, 11 August 2009

246. 2009, July

The Indian High Commissioner in Bangladesh (Chakravarty) comments on persons protesting against the Tipaimukh dam (a project involving the building of a dam in India which would affect a river flowing through

Bangladesh). Chakravarty states that 'so-called water experts' attempted to poison the minds of the people of Bangladesh and speaks of 'criticism of India and India-phobia' which had 'become an instrument for deriving political mileage for a particular section'.

The Bangladeshi Foreign Minister (Moni) reportedly states that Chakravarty may have deviated from diplomatic norms.

— *Dhaka Courier*, 'Pinak Overstepping the Bounds of Diplomatic Norms', 26 June 2009
— *BBC Monitoring South Asia—Political*, 'Indian Envoy Perhaps Breached Norms', 2 July 2009

247. 2009, July

A Russian diplomat (Lysenko) and a Russian consul (Grachev) are expelled from Ukraine, amid accusations that they had 'repeatedly [made] statements in public that cast doubt on Ukraine's territorial integrity' and had assisted 'radical anti-Ukrainian organizations'.

The Russian Foreign Minister (Lavrov) states that the situation was 'seen in Russia as another step in a series of unfriendly moves on the part of Kiev in relation to Russia. It will not remain without consequences'.

— *BBC Monitoring Former Soviet Union—Political*, 'Russian Newspaper Examines Escalating Diplomatic Row', 3 August 2009
— *RIA Novosti*, 'An In-depth Look at the Russian Press', 27 July 2009

248. 2009, September

The ousted Honduran President Zelaya addresses supporters from the Brazilian Embassy where he had taken refuge, and allegedly encourages them to hold demonstrations. Honduran security clashes with the supporters; Honduras cuts water, electricity and telephone lines to the Embassy. In October, the Honduran Government lodges an application with the ICJ, invoking inter alia the rule against diplomatic interference.

— R Carroll, 'Security Forces Clash with Protestors in Honduras', *The Guardian*, 23 September 2009
— *Thai News Service*, 'Honduras/Brazil', 30 September 2009
— *Honduras Application*

249. 2009, November

The Australian High Commissioner in Fiji (Batley) and a New Zealand diplomat (Cleaver) are expelled from Fiji amid accusations of interference in internal affairs. The ruler of Fiji (Bainimarama) reportedly accuses the diplomats of involvement in a negative campaign against the Government. There are, however, also reports that the expulsion came as a reaction of both country's efforts to, in Bainimarama's view, 'undermine' Fiji's judiciary, her institutions and economy.

— C Merritt and P Walters, 'Fiji Expels High Commissioner', *The Australian*, 4 November
— *Hindustan Times*, 'Pacific Tit-for-Tat on Cards', 4 November 2009

250. 2009, December

Diplomats from Australia, Canada, Germany, the UK and the US try to attend the trial in China of the activist Liu Xiaobo. The US Embassy calls on China to release Xiaobo, stating that '[p]ersecution of individuals for the peaceful expression of political views is inconsistent with internationally recognised norms of human rights'.

The Chinese Foreign Ministry refers to diplomatic statements criticising Xiaobo's detention as 'gross interference [in] China's internal affairs'.

— G Wong, 'China Blasts Diplomats', *Associated Press*, 24 December 2009
— M Barriaux, 'China Dissident Jailed', *Agence France Presse*, 25 December 2009

251. 2010, January

The Iranian Deputy Minister of Intelligence reportedly states that two German diplomats, operating under the names 'Yogi' and 'Ingo' were arrested following their participation in riots during the Ashura festival in Tehran.

The German Foreign Ministry denies the allegations, but the German Government withdraws two police officers stationed at the German Embassy in Iran, for 'security reasons'.

— M Gehlen, 'Yogi und Ingo', *Stuttgarter Zeitung*, 28 January 2010
— *Agence France Presse*, '"Spiegel": Zwei Bundespolizisten zur Sicherheit aus Iran abgezogen', 31 January 2010
— *Iranian Students News Agency*, 'Iran's Deputy Minister: German Diplomats have Interfered', 27 January 2010

252. 2010, February

The Iraqi Prime Minister reportedly accuses US Ambassador Hill of interference, after Hill had criticised the decision to ban candidates from elections who had previously been members of the Baath Party and stated that it would 'bring about tension and create problems'.

Hill is quoted as stating that it was his 'job … to make sure everybody in that country understands the U.S. government position.'

— *Federal News Service*, 'United States Institute of Peace', 17 February 2010
— *Associated Press Online*, 'Iraqi PM Says he Won't Allow US to Meddle', 5 February 2010
— *Kurdish Globe*, 'Barred Candidates Allowed to Stand March Polls', 7 February 2010

253. 2010, February

The Law Minister of Bangladesh (Shafique Ahmed) accuses the Pakistani High Commissioner (Qureshi) of violating diplomatic norms by interfering with Bangladesh's internal affairs.

Qureshi had stated that the matter of war criminals (perpetrators of crimes in the 1971 war) had been resolved through a 1974 agreement between Bangladesh, India and Pakistan. Bangladesh supports the opinion that the agreement does not bar the trial of those who had committed international crimes.

— *United News of Bangladesh*, 'Bangladesh-India-Pakistan Simla Treaty', 27 February 2010
— *Indo-Asian News Service*, 'War Crimes Trial Not Closed', 28 February 2010

254. 2010, March

In Bahrain, 240 community leaders (owners of *majlises*) call for the expulsion of UK Ambassador Bowden, after he had met with politicians who advocate a Bahraini cabinet chosen by the elected Parliament.

According to the community leaders, Bowden had committed 'interference … in our domestic affairs', had 'not respected international and diplomatic laws and traditions' and had violated 'the 1961 Vienna Convention on Diplomatic Relations, especially Article 41'. The UK Embassy denies any interference.

— *BBC Monitoring Middle East—Political*, 'Bahraini Petition Reiterates Call for Expulsion', 16 March 2010
— C Johnston, 'Activists Condemn UK Interference', *The Scotsman*, 18 March 2010

255. 2010, March

Diplomats from Austria, Canada, Norway, the UK and the US attend the hearing of Jozef Kandera in Slovakia. Kandera is a judge at the Slovakian Supreme Court who faces disciplinary charges about his handling of criminal cases; but he is also known as a critic of Štefan Harabin, the President of the Supreme Court.

Harabin reportedly states that the diplomats were trying to intimidate members of the disciplinary commission. The UK Ambassador Roberts disagrees with that assessment.

— *BBC Monitoring Europe—Political*, 'Outgoing UK Envoy', 26 December 2010
— *Slovak Spectator*, 'Diplomats Observe Disciplinary Case', 22 March 2010

256. 2010, April

Several diplomats in Thailand reportedly take up an offer by the 'Red Shirts' movement to visit the ongoing protests in the country. The Thai Foreign Minister subsequently tells diplomats not to intervene in internal affairs, stating that Thailand had a 'functioning government'.

An African diplomat points out afterwards that contacting all parties should be 'the right thing to do' (*The Nation*).

— *Agence France Presse*, 'Thai FM Draws Fence', 29 April 2010
— *Thai News Service*, 'Pime [sic] Minister Tells Foreign Countries Not to Meddle', 14 May 2010
— *The Nation*, 'Diplomats Chafe at Rebukes', 13 May 2010

257. 2010, May

Seven ambassadors and three *Chargés d'affaires* in Slovakia publish an open letter in which they express their support for the LGBT (lesbian, gay, bisexual, transgender) Pride Parade in Bratislava.

Conservative media accuse the diplomats of interference in internal affairs. In an interview, the UK Ambassador Roberts expresses 'a little bit' of surprise at the reactions, and declares that his Government and he himself agreed 'with the values expressed by the march'.

- — *Slovak Spectator*, 'Pride—An Open Letter', 24 May 2010
- — *BBC Monitoring Europe—Political*, 'Outgoing UK Envoy', 26 December 2010

258. 2010, July

Australia's Acting High Commissioner in Fiji (Roberts) is expelled. According to the Fijian Foreign Minister, Roberts had 'interfer[ed] with the internal affairs of Fiji' and conducted 'unfriendly acts'. The ruler of Fiji (Bainimarama) declares that even the establishment of guidelines for diplomats would not prevent interference, stating that 'they will not work under any guidelines we set for them'.

The Australian Prime Minister calls the expulsion 'unreasonable and uncalled-for'.

- — C Alexander, 'FED: Gillard Protests Fiji Envoy's Expulsion', *AAP Newsfeed*, 13 July 2010
- — N Park, 'PAC: Fiji Not Keen to Replace Aust Diplomat', *AAP Newsfeed*, 16 July 2010
- — A Caldwell, 'Expelled Australian Diplomat Leaves Fiji', *ABC Premium News*, 14 July 2010

259. 2010, August

The ambassadors of several Western States leave the funeral of Mugabe's sister in Zimbabwe, after Mugabe, during the funeral, reportedly stated (with reference to Europeans and Americans): 'We say to hell, hell, hell with them … They will not decide who is going to lead the people of Zimbabwe'.

The Zimbabwean Foreign Minister summons several Western ambassadors, telling them that this behaviour was 'unacceptable and will not be tolerated'. Both the US and the German ambassador reportedly defend their conduct.

- — *BBC Monitoring Africa—Political*, 'Zimbabwe Ruling Party Threatens to Expel "Interfering" Western Diplomats', 21 December 2010
- — *Deutsche Presse-Agentur*, 'Western Ambassadors Rebuked', 3 August 2010

260. 2010, August

Following the acquittal on corruption charges of an ally of the incumbent Zambian President, several diplomats raise questions on that matter, and donor States express doubts about Zambia's willingness to fight corruption. Zambia's President Banda accuses diplomats of trying to effect regime change, reportedly stating that they were 'sticking their noses into our business to try and influence the election; that is colonialism.'

— E Mbao, 'Banda Tells Off Diplomats', *The Nation*, 27 August 2010
— *Times of Zambia*, 'Banda Right On Donors', 28 August 2010

261. 2010, August

In a statement, the Indian Embassy in Nepal refers to 'unethical practices' by the Nepalese media. This follows media reports on a Government investigation into the quality of products of the Indian-headquartered Dabur Nepal company.

The (Nepalese) Parliamentary Committee on International Relations and Human Rights considers the statement a 'direct attack' on freedom of the press and 'directs' the Government to take action against the Embassy. Members of the committee speak of intervention by the Indian Embassy in internal affairs.

— *BBC Monitoring South Asia*, 'Nepal Parliament Body Asks Indian Envoy to Explain', 31 August 2010
— *EKantipur.com*, 'Embassy Statement Row', 30 August 2010

262. 2010, December

On his Embassy's website, the UK Ambassador to Iran (Gass) refers to 'lawyers, journalists and NGO workers who place themselves at risk to defend their countrymen' and states that they are '[n]owhere … under greater threat than in Iran.' He mentions harassment and imprisonment to which 'human rights defenders' are subjected.

Gass is subsequently summoned by the Iranian Foreign Ministry. The UK Foreign Office supports him, stating that it was 'only through open and frank dialogue' that problems could be solved.

— *Thai Press Reports*, 'Iran/United Kingdom', 21 December 2010
— *Agence France Presse*, 'Britain Backs Envoy', 13 December 2010

263. 2010, December

The President of Côte d'Ivoire (Gbagbo) accuses western diplomats of interference by trying to persuade military officers and senior media officials to change their allegiance to his opponent Ouattara. Gbagbo's Interior Minister warns the Government 'will no longer tolerate meddling by any diplomat' in internal affairs.

The French Cooperation Minister (de Raincourt), states that '[t]here is no interference, there will never be interference, this does not correspond with France's policy on this continent'.

— *BBC Monitoring Africa—Political*, 'French Minister Denies Interference', 13 December 2010
— *Agence France Presse*, 'EU Set to Punish Ivory Coast', 13 December 2010

264. 2010, December

The party of Zimbabwean President Mugabe (Zimbabwe African National Union—Patriotic Front, or ZANU-PF) releases a communiqué stating that 'foreign envoys who promote the West's regime change agenda and interfere in the internal affairs of Zimbabwe [will] be expelled'. Mugabe himself is quoted as stating that, in 2008, the US Ambassador had supported the (opposition party) Movement for Democratic Change (MDC) and that that 'will not happen' at the forthcoming elections. 'Any ambassador who does will kick him out [sic]. We have been too good'.

— *BBC Monitoring Africa—Political*, 'Zimbabwe Ruling Party Threatens to Expel "Interfering" Western Diplomats', 21 December 2010
— *CNN*, 'Zimbabwe's President Threatens "Revenge"', 17 December 2010

265. 2010, December

The Pakistani Minister of the Interior (Malik) criticises diplomats for meeting politicians without informing the Foreign Ministry and suggests the formation of a committee to establish guidelines on that matter. According to Malik, politicians allowed diplomats to interfere in internal affairs. Malik is quoted as stating: 'Let's decide today that nobody will meet any diplomat. We will force them to follow the laws'.

This follows comments allegedly made by US Ambassador Cameron Munter to politicians on matters of draft legislation, corruption and the dismissal of ministers.

— M Tirimizi, 'Nisar Blasts US Pressure', *The Nation*, 20 December 2010
— *Right Vision News*, 'Govt-opposition Warming in NA', 22 December 2010

266. 2010, December

WikiLeaks publishes a cable by the US Ambassador to Sri Lanka (Butenis), which notes that the prosecution of war crimes in the country was 'complicated by the fact 'that responsibility for many alleged crimes rests with the … leadership, including President Rajapaksa … and opposition candidate General Fonseka'.

The Sri Lankan Foreign Minister (Peiris) subsequently states that 'at least where future instances may be concerned, greater circumspection … would be appropriate'.

— *Agence France Presse*, 'Sri Lanka Warns US', 21 December 2010
— M Lee, 'On Sri Lanka', *InnerCityPress*, 11 December 2010

267. 2011, January

Following the collapse of the Hariri Government in Lebanon, US Ambassador Connelly meets a Christian MP (Fattoush) who had fallen out with the Government.

Acting Lebanese Foreign Minister Shami refers to the visit as interference in internal affairs; the speaker of the Lebanese Parliament calls the meeting interference in parliamentary deliberations and the 'scandal of [all] scandals'.

During a subsequent meeting with Shami, Connelly states that the US 'has regular contact with personalities from across Lebanon's political spectrum as part of its diplomatic mission'.

— *Agence France Presse*, 'US Envoy to Lebanon Summoned', 17 January 2011
— *BBC Monitoring Middle East—Political*, 'Lebanese Minister Summons US Envoy', 18 January 2011

268. 2011, January

The Afghan President Karzai states at the opening of the Afghan Parliament that foreigners had interfered with recent elections in the country. This is understood as a reference to Western diplomats who had called on Karzai to proceed with the inauguration of Parliament. Karzai himself had wanted to delay the opening of Parliament for a month, in the light of fraud allegations by losing candidates.

— *Agence France Presse*, 'Foreigners Behind Afghan Parliament Crisis: Karzai', 25 January 2011
— J Boak, 'Karzai Opens Afghan Parliament', *Washington Post*, 27 January 2011

269. 2011, February

US Ambassador to Turkey Ricciardone declares that the US is 'trying to make sense' of the fact that Turkey supports freedom of the press, but also detains journalists.

As a result, Turkish officials refer to interference by the US Ambassador. The Turkish Prime Minister states that Ricciardone showed a lack of knowledge about the legal situation and advises him to 'wait, … learn what the judiciary will do on this'.

The State Department supports Ricciardone and notes that, in Turkey, freedom of expression remains a concern.

— J Morrison, 'Diplomatic Flap', *Washington Times*, 18 February 2011
— *Thai News Service*, 'Press Freedom in Turkey Criticized Again', 21 February 2011

270. 2011, February

It is revealed that the US Ambassador to Swaziland, Parker, sent a cable to Washington in 2009 in which he commented on a UK refusal to allow the sale of weapons to Swaziland. Parker notes that the reason had been 'end-use concerns', including the fear that the Government may have wanted to deploy the arms domestically or was 'acting as an intermediary for a third party'.

After the cable becomes public, the Ministry of Defence accuses Parker of interfering in internal affairs.

— J Ball, 'UK Blocked $60m Arms Deal', *The Guardian*, 24 February 2011
— *Swazi Media Commentary*, 'Govt and Secret Arms Deal', 4 March 2013

271. 2011, March

The US Ambassador to Zambia (Storella) declares his Government's support for the parallel vote tabulation system (a system for the observation of elections which facilitates the work of election monitors, but was rejected by the Zambian Government).

The Zambian Foreign Minister subsequently considers making an official protest to the US Government; while the Zambian Information Minister points out that Storella was 'accredited to work in Zambia and should do so in accordance with the laws of the land'.

— A Simuchoba, 'Diplomatic Row Brewing', *Sunday Times (South Africa)*, 20 March 2011
— *Times of Zambia*, 'Zambia: Govt to Complain Over Meddling US Envoy', 10 March 2011

272. 2011, March

US Ambassador to Mexico Pascual resigns his post. This follows the revelation, through WikiLeaks, of a cable in which he had referred to infighting in the Mexican military and their alleged inefficiency in the fight against drug lords.

The Mexican President Calderon reacts with irritation to the cable. Calderon reportedly states that he did not have to tell Pascual how many times he met with his security cabinet. 'It is none of his business. I will not accept or tolerate any type of intervention'.

— *Associated Press*, 'US Ambassador to Mexico Quits', 20 March 2011
— *New Zealand Herald*, 'Calderon Ejects US Diplomat', 22 March 2011

273. 2011, March

Bahrain expels an Iranian diplomat (Fadli), reportedly over his contacts with opposition groups. According to other sources, Fadli had carried out 'dubious activities' (BBC) and contacted a terrorist group. An official of the Bahraini Foreign Ministry is quoted as stating that 'the Iranian diplomat has abused his authority as a diplomat'.

The expulsion comes only a day after Bahrain had complained to the United Nations about perceived interference in internal affairs by Iran.

— *BBC Monitoring Middle East—Political*, 'Pan-Arab Daily Reports on Downturn', 29 March 2011
— *Press Trust of India*, 'Foreign Plot Against Gulf Foiled', 21 March 2011

274. 2011, April

The British High Commissioner in Malawi (Cochrane-Dyet) is expelled after the leak and publication of one of his cables to London. In the communication, he described the Malawian President as 'ever more autocratic and intolerant of criticism' and stated that the 'governance situation continues to deteriorate in terms of media freedom, freedom of speech and minority rights'. A spokesman for the Malawian Government notes that the 'tone in the leaked cable was not diplomatic' and that the Government had 'lost confidence' in Cochrane-Dyet.

In October, the presidency of Malawi 'reverses' the expulsion.

— G Mapondera and D Smith, 'Malawi Declares Envoy "Persona Non Grata"', *The Guardian*, 20 April 2011
— *DefenceWeb*, 'UK, Malawi Expel Each Other's Diplomats', 28 April 2011
— *Agence France Presse*, 'Malawi Agrees to Allow British Envoy to Return', 14 October 2011

275. 2011, June

In Slovakia, the ambassadors of 20 countries sign a statement in support of an LGBT march (see also above, A.257). The statement affirms that '[e]veryone, including LGBT people, should be free to enjoy the rights and freedoms laid out in the Universal Declaration of Human Rights'.

After the march, a statement is signed by several public figures who consider the diplomatic statement unfortunate and an interference in internal affairs.

— *Slovak Spectator*, 'LGBT Police Readied For March', 6 June 2011
— *Slovak Spectator*, 'Pride Diplomats React', 13 June 2011

276. 2011, July

Candidates in Afghanistan's parliamentary elections complain about intervention by foreign diplomatic missions. The background to this are allegations of fraud which had arisen in elections in the previous year and the subsequent setting up of an election tribunal which then disqualified 62 members of Parliament on charges of fraud. It is claimed that foreign diplomats have expressed themselves in favour of incumbent members of Parliament.

The Afghan Attorney General's office is quoted as stating that foreign diplomats should not interfere in the matter, which it considered a 'legal issue' (Afghan Islamic Press).

— *Afghan Islamic Press*, 'Poll Candidates Warn Against "Political Deal"', 2 August 2011

277. 2011, July

The US Ambassador and the French Ambassador to Syria visit the city of Hama, while large protests against the Government of President Assad take place.

The Syrian Foreign Ministry subsequently summons the diplomats. Syria calls the visit a 'clear interference in Syria's internal affairs' and refers to it as evidence for US attempts to 'incite an escalation'. The State Department denies this and states that the intent had been to 'stand in solidarity' with the Syrians' right 'to demonstrate peacefully'.

— *AlArabiya.net*, 'US Rejects Syrian Allegation', 8 July 2011
— *Xinhua*, 'Syria Summons U.S., France Ambassadors', 10 July 2011

278. 2011, August

It is reported that a Canadian diplomat in Jordan has stated that reforms (in Jordan) will happen soon.

The Jordanian Foreign Minister subsequently summons the Canadian Ambassador and protests against the comments, stating that Jordan rejects interference in her internal affairs.

— *BBC Monitoring Middle East—Political*, 'Jordanian Paper Slams Act', 16 August 2011

279. 2011, November

According to news reports, the US Ambassador to Nigeria (McCulley) had a telephone conversation with the Nigerian President, in which he expressed his concerns about the volatile situation in the Nigerian State of Bayelsa, citing business interests of the United States. The Ambassador reportedly highlighted the need to maintain stability and to allow democratic development.

A presidential spokesman however denies knowledge of this and states that this would have been 'highly improbably'—it was 'not standard diplomatic practice for a diplomat to interfere in the internal affairs of a country'.

— *The Moment*, 'Nigeria; U.S. Wades Into Bayelsa Governorship Battle', 5 November 2011

280. 2012, January

It is reported that the US Ambassador to Slovenia (Mussomeli) has expressed himself in favour of the formation of a coalition government with the participation of the leading political parties, Positive Slovenia and the Slovenian Democrats. Mussomeli has reportedly also met all leaders of parliamentary parties.

The Slovenian President Tuerk accuses Mussomeli's of engaging in inappropriate interference in internal affairs. The US denies Mussomeli's involvement in coalition talks and notes that he was carrying out his 'regular duties'.

— *Xinhua*, 'American Ambassador Criticized', 5 January 2012
— *Xinhua*, 'Slovenia-U.S. Disputes Over Alleged Interference', 10 January 2012

281. 2012, May

Zambian President Sata expresses his concern about the involvement of diplomats with the Zambian opposition and reportedly asks his Foreign Minister to investigate the matter. Sata states that his Government 'will not take kindly to diplomats interfering in local affairs'.

The comments are seen in the context of attempts of the Barotse National Council, which strives for independence from Zambia, to arrange meetings with a number of embassies.

— *BBC Monitoring Africa—Political*, 'Sata Asks Foreign Diplomats to "Re-evaluate" Ties', 12 May 2012
— *BBC Monitoring Africa—Political*, 'Zambian Leader Raps Diplomats' "Interference"', 11 May 2012

282. 2012, May

The British High Commissioner in Sri Lanka (Rankin) is summoned by the Sri Lankan Foreign Minister (Peiris). This follows the publication of a video on the High Commission's website, in which Rankin commented on the need for a reduced military presence in the north of the country.

According to Rankin, these views had already been voiced by the British Parliament. Peiris on the other hand states that such comments should not be made by a diplomat and refers to the need to take into account the timing of such remarks.

- — *The Hindu*, 'Sri Lanka Sends a Signal', 28 May 2012
- — *BBC Monitoring South Asia—Political*, 'Sri Lankan Minister Criticises UK Envoy', 29 May 2012

283. 2012, June

The Chinese Vice Minister of Environmental Protection (Wu Xiaoqing) takes exception to the monitoring of air quality in China by US diplomatic and consular missions and the publication of the results on the internet. Wu refers to the diplomatic duty of non-interference.

According to the State Department, the air quality information is offered as a service to the American community in China, including Embassy employees.

- — Crook, 851
- — A Ramzy, 'Conflict in the Air', *Time*, 6 June 2012

284. 2012, June

The Malaysian Foreign Minister (Aman) summons the Singaporean High Commissioner (Ong Keng Yong) to protest against the attendance of three Singaporean diplomats at the 'Bersih 3.0' rally in April (a demonstration for fair elections). Aman states that the conduct was 'inappropriate' and that the Foreign Ministry may have to resort to 'stronger diplomatic actions'.

Singapore denies the allegations, with her Foreign Ministry stating that Singaporean officials did not interfere, but had been 'impartial observers' carrying out their professional tasks.

- — *Channel News Asia*, 'Singapore Dismisses Malaysian Media Allegations', 22 June 2012
- — T Wee, 'Other Foreign Envoys at Bersih Rally Too', *Straits Times*, 27 June 2012

285. 2012, July

The Canadian Foreign Ministry warns the Iranian Embassy against interfering with Iranian Canadians who had chosen to reject 'the oppressive Iranian regime and … to come to Canada to build better lives'. The warning comes after an Iranian diplomat (Mohammadi) had reportedly advised Iranian Canadians to 'occupy high-level key positions' and resist 'being melted into the dominant Canadian culture'.

The Iranian *chargé d'affaires* denies allegations of recruitment and states that the Vienna Convention allows the Embassy to engage in 'outreach activities' (Thai News Service).

— *Agence France Presse*, 'Canada Warns Iran Diplomats', 11 July 2012
— *Thai News Service*, 'Embassy Dismisses Report', 12 July 2012

286. 2012, July

The Bahraini Foreign Minister (Khalid bin Ahmed) complains about interference by Iranian diplomats in internal affairs, stating that such conduct was in violation of international law. He calls on political groups not to allow diplomats to deal with internal affairs during their meetings with them.

— *Bahrain News Agency*, 'Foreign Minister Holds Meeting', 19 July 2012

287. 2012, September

The Zambian President Sata warns that he would expel diplomats interfering in internal affairs. Sata reportedly admonishes diplomats to 'leave our internal politics to us'. He also says that some embassies were already interfering in Zambian affairs.

It is not immediately clear to what kind of conduct Sata is referring. The President does however take exception to diplomats who go to State House (the presidential office) to see him without appointment instead of contacting the Foreign Ministry first.

— *Times of Zambia*, 'Zambia; Don't Meddle in Internal Politics', 8 September 2012
— *Xinhua*, 'Zambian Leader Threatens to Expel "Nosy" Diplomats', 7 September 2012

288. 2012, October

In a motion, the Bahraini Parliament calls on the Government to stop interference by US Ambassador Krajeski. This comes amid accusations that Krajeski had maintained contacts 'of a suspicious nature' (BBC Monitoring), had met with the opposition and commented on the political crisis in Bahrain.

Krajeski denies claims of interference, stating that he had sought the strengthening of bilateral relations. He also maintains that his positions reflected the foreign policy of his country, and were not personal views.

— *BBC Monitoring Middle East—Political*, 'Bahraini MPs Urge Government to End "Interference"', 21 October 2012
— *Daily Tribune*, 'Envoy Denies Interference', 4 December 2012

289. 2012, December

Afghan senators take exception to the comments of an Iranian diplomat who had referred to Afghanistan as an 'occupied country'. The senators decide to summon the Afghan Foreign Minister, whose 'calmness' (BBC Monitoring) about the diplomat's remarks they criticise. They also note that the comments constituted direct interference in the affairs of the country.

The Afghan Foreign Minister rejects the Iranian assessment, stating that Afghanistan had, in spite of problems, preserved her national sovereignty.

— *BBC Monitoring South Asia—Political*, 'Afghan Senators Call Paris Conference Against Diplomatic Principles', 19 December 2012
— *BBC Monitoring South Asia—Political*, 'Afghan Minister Rejects "Occupied Country" Remark', 26 December 2012

290. 2013, February

The US Ambassador to Turkey (Ricciardone) criticises aspects of the Turkish justice system, including the fact that Members of Parliament, professors and students were put behind bars. He claims that the system 'confuses people like that for terrorists'.

The Turkish Foreign Ministry states that Ricciardone's conduct is considered interference in internal affairs.

The US Ambassador emphasises the fact that Turkey's progress is of importance to her allies and urges 'a careful reading of the full text' of his remarks.

— *Agence France Presse*, 'Turkey Tells US Envoy to Stop Meddling', 7 February 2013
— *Today's Zaman*, 'Turkey Warns US Ambassador', 12 February 2013

291. 2013, March

Venezuela announces the expulsion of two US air attachés. The diplomats are accused of conducting meetings with members of the armed forces in an attempt to persuade them to carry out 'destabilizing projects'. The Venezuelan Foreign Minister (Jaua) is quoted as saying that Venezuela 'will not allow any foreign interference'.

A spokesman for the State Department denies the allegations, noting that '[t]his fallacious assertion of inappropriate U.S. action leads us to conclude that, unfortunately, the current Venezuelan government is not interested an improved relationship'.

— J Lopez and C Shoichet, 'U.S. Expels 2 Venezuelan Diplomats', *CNN*, 11 March 2013

292. 2013, March

Kenyan officials accuse foreign diplomats of interference in connection with the tallying of the vote in the Kenyan presidential elections. They criticise the UK High Commissioner in Kenya (Turner) in particular for his 'shadowy, suspicious and rather animated involvement' in the matter and allege that the UK had lobbied for the inclusion of invalidated votes.

The UK Foreign Office refers to claims of British interference as 'entirely false and misleading'. Turner too rejects the allegations.

— *Deutsche Welle World*, 'Kenyans in Suspense', 6 March 2013
— *Deutsche Presse-Agentur*, '2ND LEAD: Problems Hit Kenyan Vote-counting', 6 March 2013

293. 2013, March

The Sri Lankan High Commissioner in India, Kariyawasam, reportedly observes that the Sinhalese were descended from Odiyas and Bengalis (ethnic groups originating from the Indian sub-continent) and were therefore deserving of Indian support.

As a result, the publisher Lena Kumar calls on the Indian Foreign Minister and the Indian Prime Minister to expel Kariyawasam. Kumar claims that Kariyawasam exceeded the limits of his diplomatic office and had made 'seditious, inflammatory and provocative' remarks. When his suggestions remain unsuccessful, Kumar brings a public interest claim in the Madras High Court, to effect the diplomat's expulsion.

— *Colombo Gazette*, 'Case Filed', 20 November 2013

294. 2013, May

The lower chamber of the Bahraini Parliament accuses US Ambassador Krajeski (see also above, A.288) of meeting with 'instigators of sedition'—a phrase understood to mean Shiite protesters. The Bahraini cabinet approves a proposal passed by Parliament to take action to stop Krajeski's 'interference' in internal affairs. It is however reported that such measures would not include Krajeski's expulsion.

— *Agence France Presse*, 'Bahrain Seeks to End US Envoy "Interference"', 5 May 2013
— *BBC Monitoring Middle East—Political*, 'Bahrain Denies Reports', 8 May 2013

295. 2013, June

The Jordanian Foreign Minister Judeh criticises the Syrian Ambassador Suleiman, noting that Suleiman had 'violated all diplomatic norms', 'obviously lacks the minimum requirements of diplomacy' and had been warned to stop making remarks 'that insult Jordan's civil and military institutions'. He threatens Suleiman's expulsion if the Ambassador's conduct did not change.

Suleiman had reportedly, on Facebook, called Jordanians 'ignorant' (with regard to certain aspects of Syrian military equipment) and had called the Jordanian politician Manasir a 'servant of the enemies of Syria and Jordan'.

— K Neimat, 'Syrian Envoy's Remarks to Dominate', *Jordan Times*, 9 June 2013
— *Agence France Presse*, 'Stop the Insults', 6 June 2013

296. 2013, September

The Tanzanian Ministry of Foreign Affairs states that the Chinese Ambassador to the country (Lu Youqing) has violated rules of diplomatic law through his involvement in internal affairs of the State, and refers to Article 41 of the Vienna Convention in particular. This follows media reports (and protests by an opposition party) about Lu's participation in a political demonstration, where he was seen wearing a cap with colours and symbols of the Chama Cha Mapinduzi party.

— *BBC Monitoring Africa—Political*, 'Tanzania's Opposition Raps Chinese Envoy', 17 September 2013
— *Tanzania Daily News*, 'Ministry Cautions Envoys', 18 September 2013

297. 2013, September

The US Embassy to Cambodia publishes a statement saying that the attendance of US Ambassador Todd at the opening of the National Assembly did not indicate endorsement of the election outcome (allegations of fraud had been made following the general elections in Cambodia).

The Cambodian Ministry of Foreign Affairs subsequently warns foreign diplomats against interference in internal affairs and states that Cambodia did not need the endorsement of election outcomes by foreign envoys.

— *Phnom Penh Post*, 'Foreign Envoys Turn Out in Force', 24 September 2013
— *Azeri Press Agency*, 'Cambodian Gov't Warns Foreign Diplomats', 25 September 2013

298. 2013, October

The French and EU Ambassadors and the UK High Commissioner in Papua New Guinea release a statement criticising the suggestion to resume implementation of the death penalty, which they call 'an inhuman and archaic way of punishment'.

Acting Foreign Minister Kua expresses his surprise, noting that he had explained to the diplomats that capital punishment was 'legislated by Parliament'. According to Kua, it was not the diplomats' 'place' to make such statements; he urges them 'not to implicitly threaten … this country' on its social development agenda.

— *PNG Post-Courier*, 'Kua Blasts EU Envoys', 15 October 2013
— *PACNEWS*, 'Keep Out of Our Affairs', 15 October 2013

299. 2013, December

The Chinese Foreign Ministry criticises a Japanese diplomat (Horinouchi). Reacting to Chinese claims that the passing of a Japanese 'secrecy law' would lead to militarism, Horinouchi had reportedly stated that, in that case, China was already a militarist nation. He had also criticised the 'Air Defense Identification Zone' (which China had established), claiming that it had unilaterally altered the status of the East China Sea.

The Chinese Foreign Ministry declares that it was 'wrong and ridiculous' that Horinouchi had 'confused right and wrong' and had attacked China.

— *China Business News*, 'China Strongly Dissatisfied', 10 December 2013
— *Xinhua*, 'China Upset', 9 December 2013

300. 2013, December

The Ukrainian President Yanukovych reportedly criticises Western diplomats over their alleged attempts to interfere in the internal politics of the receiving State.

The statement follows the visits by several politicians and diplomats from Western countries to the anti-government rallies in Kiev. It is reported that the US Ambassador to Ukraine (Geoffrey Pyatt) was among diplomats visiting Independence Square, as were several diplomatic agents from EU member States.

— *Deutsche Welle Europe*, 'Yanukovych Criticizes West', 19 December 2013
— Z Hong, 'West Still Pushing Democracy', *Global Times (China)*, 17 December 2013

301. 2014, January

India expels a US diplomat (Wayne May) amid allegations of involvement in the Khobragade case. (Devyani Khobragade was an Indian consul in the US, who had been accused of exploiting her Indian born housekeeper, Sangeeta Richard.) Wayne had reportedly granted visas to the Richard family. Wayne faces accusations of interfering with the work of legal authorities in India.

— *The Capital*, 'AP News in Brief at 5:58 p.m. EST', 11 January 2014
— C Kasturi, 'Tit-for-Tat Kick', *The Telegraph (India)*, 1 January 2014
— *Hindustan Times*, 'Devyani Home', 11 January 2014

302. 2014, January

India expels the community liaison officer of the US Embassy (Alicia May, wife of Wayne May—see above, A.301). The expulsion is seen as retaliation for the treatment of Devyani Khobragade in the United States.

However, it is also reported that Ms May had, on her Facebook page, given the picture of a cow the caption 'stupid cow' and had stated that she would like to see an article 'on how many vegetarians rape women here every day'.

— C Rajghatta, 'Wayne's World', *Times of India*, 13 January 2014
— *Asian News International*, '"Racist" US Diplomat Expelled from India', 16 January 2014

303. 2014, January

After the Jordanian MP Obeidat called the Syrian President Assad 'damned by God', the Syrian Embassy releases a statement, reportedly calling Obeidat a 'nobody' and an 'idiot' and claiming that he had insulted 'the symbol of the Syrian people'.

The Jordanian Parliament calls the remarks 'an infringement on diplomatic boundaries … by a sister state'; the Jordanian Government, however, does not confirm reports about the pending expulsion of the Syrian Ambassador.

— K Neimat, 'House Speaker wants Gov't to Look into "Syrian Insults"', *Jordan Times*, 16 January 2014
— *Anadolu Agency*, 'Jordan to Expel Syrian Ambassador', 16 January 2014

304. 2014, January

The US Ambassador to Slovenia (Mussomeli) reportedly states that Slovenia may have won her independence 'too easily'. Mussomeli is quoted as saying that '[t]en people died in the war [the Slovenian war of independence]'. 'I think that when you bleed together … you have more of a sense of national identity'.

Mussomeli's remarks trigger criticism from veterans' associations and from the Slovenian Foreign Minister (Zbogar), who refers to them as 'unnecessary and inappropriate'.

— *Xinhua*, 'U.S. Ambassador Under Fire', 17 January 2014
— *Philippines News Agency*, 'U.S. Ambassador Under Fire', 18 January 2014

305. 2014, January

Before the East African Legislative Assembly, the Ugandan President Museveni criticises diplomats in South Sudan, apparently over their contacts with members of various 'tribes' who were warring in that country. Museveni says he had told the diplomats that they were the 'ones who invite these people to [their] embassies and give them tea', and that they 'encourage[d] them'. In the media, these comments are understood as criticism of diplomats who committed interference through partisan conduct.

— East African Community (2014) 13, 14
— *Independent* (Kampala, Uganda), 'South Sudan Conflicts', 22 January 2014

306. 2014, January

The Burmese Foreign Ministry warns diplomats and journalists against 'releasing unverified information', which it asserts is tantamount to interfering in the internal affairs of the State.

This follows claims by the United Nations that at least 48 Muslims had apparently been killed when a village had been attacked by Buddhist mobs. According to the Foreign Ministry, reports of the event were 'based on unjustified conclusions drawing on unverified information' and would contribute to misunderstanding among ethnic groups in that particular area.

— *St Louis Post-Dispatch*, 'World Briefs', 25 January 2014
— R McDowell, 'UN: Myanmar Buddhists Killed More than 40 Muslims', *Associated Press*, 24 January 2014

307. 2014, February

A Russian diplomat in Ukraine (Vorobyev) states that Ukraine had seen an informal development towards a federation and has already lived for three months as a federation.

Vorobyev is subsequently summoned to the Ukrainian Foreign Ministry, told to refrain from interference in Ukraine's domestic affairs and to comply with the provisions of the Vienna Convention.

The Russian Foreign Ministry declares its 'bewilderment' about the reaction and denies that Vorobyev's conduct had been 'subversive'.

— *BBC Monitoring Kiev Unit*, 'Ukrainian Foreign Ministry Calls in Russian Diplomat', 13 February 2014
— *Ukraine General News Service*, 'Russia Sees Nothing Subversive About its Diplomat's Statements', 14 February 2014

308. 2014, February

An MP (Fazlul Karim Selim) of the Awami League (the ruling party in Bangladesh) states that diplomats should not interfere in internal affairs. Selim also warns that the Government would take steps if they continued to interfere. Selim urges US diplomats in particular to follow diplomatic norms. The MP appears to take particular exception to the fact that a diplomat had met Khaleda Zia (leader of the Bangladesh Nationalist Party) four times since the national elections.

— *BBC Monitoring South Asia—Political*, 'MP Asks Foreign Diplomats not to Interfere', 17 February 2014
— *United News of Bangladesh*, 'Selim Asks US Diplomats to Follow Norms', 16 February 2014

309. 2014, February

The President of Suriname (Bouterse) threatens the expulsion of the US Ambassador (Anania), if he could not provide a reason for conduct which Bouterse considers interference in internal Surinamese affairs. Bouterse is quoted as stating that '[t]his bold civil servant is trying to obstruct the elections' (referring to general elections in 2015).

Anania had paid a visit to the Independent Elections Bureau and to the Minister of Home Affairs to inquire about the progress of the preparations for the elections.

— *Daily Herald (Chicago, USA)*, 'Bouterse Threatens to Boot US Ambassador', 25 February 2014
— *CANA News*, 'Suriname-Politics-President Bouterse Threatens to Expel US Ambassador', 27 February 2014

310. 2014, March

The President of the Zimbabwean Movement for Democratic Change—Tsvangirai (MDC-T) criticises diplomats who are allegedly supporting calls for a renewal of the party leadership. Tsvangirai poses the rhetorical question whether this '[i]s … the work of diplomats'.

This follows reports that diplomats in Zimbabwe have met with MDC rebels, and that Western diplomats (including UK Ambassador Bronnert) met Tsvangirai to express their concern about instances of violence within the party.

— A Bell, 'More Calls', *SW Radio Africa*, 24 February 2014
— T Sibanda, 'Attempts to Oust Tsvangirai', *SW Radio Africa*, 5 March 2014

311. 2014, April

After diplomats from 10 Western countries (including Germany, UK, US) and the EU mission to South Sudan condemn the 'continued obstruction of UNMISS operations by government and oppositions forces', the Deputy Foreign Minister of South Sudan (Gbandi) calls the statement a 'serious interference' in internal affairs, and refers specifically to Article 41(1) of the Vienna Convention.

The head of the EU delegation states that it was the 'sovereign right of diplomatic missions to issue a press statement'.

— *Sudan Tribune*, 'S. Sudan Accuses Western Diplomats', 4 April 2014
— M Rwakaringi, 'Govt Demands Apology', *Voice of America*, 3 April 2014

Annex B—Draft Codes and Travaux Préparatoires

The following materials are excerpts from four draft codes on diplomatic law (Bluntschli (1868), Fiore (1890), the Project of the American Institute of International Law (1925) and the Project of the International Commission of American Jurists (1927)), followed by material emanating produced by the International Law Commission (ILC) and its members (Sandström Draft Article 27 (1950), the Padilla Nervo and García Amador amendment (1957), ILC Draft article 33 (1957) and commentary; ILC Draft article 40 and commentary (1958)).

Materials B.1 to B.4 (Draft codes on diplomatic law) are reprinted with permission of the American Society of International Law. Materials B.5 to B.7 (Preparatory material by the International Law Commission) are reprinted with permission of the United Nations.

B.1 BLUNTSCHLI'S DRAFT CODE (1868)

225

L'envoyé est tenu de respecter avec soin l'indépendance et l'honneur de l'état auprès duquel il est accrédité. Il ne doit pas se mêler sans motif des affaires du pays, et s'abstiendra de tout acte qui constituerait un empiétement sur les droits de l'état auprès duquel il est accrédité. Il doit éviter toutes les provocations, toutes les menaces, toutes les promesses attentatoires à la liberté du peuple, à l'autorité du gouvernement et à l'honorabilité politique des citoyens.

J Bluntschli (1932) 26 *American Journal of International Law Supplement* 151

B.2 FIORE'S DRAFT CODE (1890)

455. It is incumbent upon the diplomatic agent to make use of his privileges with dignity and in good faith and not to avail himself of the immunities that are granted to him either to favor third parties or to procure for himself certain commercial advantages.

481. It is incumbent on a diplomatic agent to protect srupulously the interest of the state he represents; to carefully look to the maintenance of good relations between the respective governments; to remove any cause which might disturb harmony between the two governments.

It is incumbent on him, also, to safeguard the interests of his fellow nationals and to defend them against any abuse of power on the part of the state to which he is accredited.

482. The diplomatic agent is bound to fulfill his mission with prudence and moderation. He must abstain from any direct interference with the local administrative or judicial authorities with a view to defending the interests of his countrymen; he must be content to take diplomatic action with proper reserve before the Ministry of Foreign Affairs. He must scrupulously avoid every form of pressure, provocation, and threat, and content himself with giving his assistance to the just claims of his fellow nationals, by facilitating them in pursuing the regular channels to obtain justice from the local authorities.

483. It devolves upon the diplomatic agent to respect the institutions and national customs of the country. He must abstain from every act calculated to give affront to the convictions of the people; he must also respect popular prejudices, of which the masses, less cultured, are especially jealous.

He must refrain from fomenting any conflict between political parties and abstain from any intrigue to approve or disapprove the acts of the government.

484. Any direct or indirect interference of diplomatic agents in the internal affairs of the state to which they are accredited must be considered as directly contrary to their mission, and may justify the government in preventing or repressing such an illegitimate interference.

485. A diplomatic agent must not avail himself of the privilege of extraterritoriality which the legation enjoys, to make it available to conspirators who might wish to assemble with impunity in order to prepare or uphold a revolution or to organize an attack against the security of the state or the authority of the government. The non-observance of such duty would justify all the measures taken by the government to prevent an attack against the safety of the state, even by withdrawing the privilege of exterritoriality from the legation building.

P Fiore (1932) 26 *American Journal of International Law Supplement* 158–61

B.3 PROJECT OF THE AMERICAN INSTITUTE OF INTERNATIONAL LAW (1925)

SECTION IV.—DUTIES OF DIPLOMATIC AGENTS

Article 16. Foreign diplomatic agents may not interfere in the internal or external political life of the nation here they discharge their functions.

Pan American Union (1932) 26 *American Journal of International Law Supplement* 169

B.4 PROJECT OF THE INTERNATIONAL COMMISSION OF AMERICAN JURISTS (1927)

SECTION IV.—DUTIES OF DIPLOMATIC AGENTS

Article 16. Foreign diplomatic oficials may not interfere in the domestic or foreign political life of the state in which they exercise their functions.

Comisión Internacional de Jurisconsultos Americanos (1932) 26 *American Journal of International Law Supplement* 173

B.5 THE SANDSTRÖM DRAFT (1950)

[Note: The original Draft Articles prepared by Special Rapporteur Sandström's draft made no reference to the duty of non-interference.]

Draft Article 27

Nonobstant les privilèges et immunités diplomatiques le bénéficiaire a le devoir de se comporter d'une manière compatible avec l'ordre intérieur de l'État accréditaire et notamment de se conformer aux lois et règlements dont il n'est pas exempté par le présent règlement et pourvu qu'ils ne fassent pas obstacle à l'exercice de ses fonctions.

Sandström Report, YILC1955/II, 12

B.6 THE PADILLA NERVO/GARCIA AMADOR AMENDMENT (1957)

[Excerpt from the debates of the International Law Commission 1957]

ARTICLE 27

54. The CHAIRMAN invited Mr. Padilla Nervo to introduce the joint amendment submitted by him and Mr. García Amador to article 27 of the Special Rapporteur's draft.

55. Mr. PADILLA NERVO introduced the following text to replace the existing text of article 27:

"1. It is the duty of diplomatic agents to conduct themselves in a manner consistent with the internal order of the receiving State, to comply with those of its laws and regulations from whose application they are not exempted by the present provisions, and, in particular, not to interfere in the domestic or foreign politics of that State.

2. All official business entrusted to a diplomatic mission by its Government shall be conducted with or through the ministry of foreign affairs.

3. The premises of the mission shall be used solely for the performance of the functions recognized as normal and legitimate under the provisions herein laid down or other rules of general international law and any special agreements in force between the sending and the receiving States."

YILC 1957/I, 143 [Padilla Nervo]

B.7 ILC DRAFT ARTICLE 33 AND COMMENTARY (1957)

Article 33

1. Without prejudice to their diplomatic privileges and immunities, it is the duty of all persons enjoying such privileges and immunities to respect the laws and regulations of the receiving State. They also have a duty not to interfere in the internal affairs of that State.

2. Unless otherwise agreed, all official business with the receiving State, entrusted to a diplomatic mission by its government, shall be conducted with or through the Ministry for Foreign Affairs of the receiving State.

[…]

Commentary

(1) The first sentence of paragraph 1 states the rule already mentioned, that in general it is the duty of the diplomatic agent, and of all persons enjoying diplomatic privileges and immunities, to respect the laws and regulations of the receiving State. Immunity from jurisdiction implies merely that the agent may not be brought before the court if he fails to fulfil his obligation. The duty

[p. 143] naturally does not apply where the agent's privileges and immunities exempt him from it. Failure by a diplomatic agent to fulfil his obligations does not absolve the receiving State from its duty to respect the agent's immunity.

(2) The second sentence of paragraph 1 states the rule that persons enjoying diplomatic privileges and immunities must not interfere in the internal affairs of the receiving State. In particular, they must not take part in political campaigns.

(3) Paragraph 2 lays down that the Ministry for Foreign Affairs of the receiving State is the normal channel through which the diplomatic mission shall conduct all official business entrusted to it by its Government; in the event, however, of agreement (whether express or tacit) between the two States, the mission may deal directly with other authorities of the receiving State.

[…]

Draft Articles on Diplomatic Law (1957), YILC 1957/II, 142, art 33

B.8 ILC DRAFT ARTICLE 40 AND COMMENTARY (1958)

Article 40

1. Without prejudice to their diplomatic privileges and immunities, it is the duty of all persons enjoying such privileges and immunities to respect the laws and regulations of the receiving State. They also have a duty not to interfere in the internal affairs of that State.

2. Unless otherwise agreed, all official business with the receiving State entrusted to a diplomatic mission by its Government, shall be conducted with or through the Ministry for Foreign Affairs of the receiving State.

[...]

Commentary

(1) Paragraph 1, which remains unchanged, states in its first sentence the rule already mentioned, that in general it is the duty of the diplomatic agent, and of all persons enjoying diplomatic privileges and immunities, to respect the laws and regulations of the receiving State. Immunity from jurisdiction implies merely that the agent may not be brought before the courts if he fails to fulfil his obligations. The duty naturally does not apply where the agent's privileges and immunities exempt him from it. Failure by a diplomatic agent to fulfil his obligations does not absolve the receiving State from its duty to respect the agent's immunity.

(2) The second sentence of paragraph 1 states the rule that persons enjoying diplomatic privileges and immunities must not interfere in the internal affairs of the receiving State; for example, they must not take part in political campaigns. The making of representations for the purpose of protecting the interests of the diplomatic agent's country or of its nationals in accordance with international law does not constitute interference in the internal affairs of the receiving State within the meaning of this provision.

(3) Paragraph 2 states that the Ministry for Foreign Affairs of the receiving State is the normal channel through which the diplomatic mission should conduct all official business entrusted to it by its Government: nevertheless, by agreement (whether express or implied) between the two States, the mission may deal directly with other authorities of the receiving State, as specialist attachés, in particular, frequently do.

[...]

Draft Articles on Diplomatic Law 1958, YILC 1958/II, 104, art 40

Annex C—Selected Instruments on Diplomatic Law (excerpts)

The following texts are excerpts of the Havana Convention on Diplomatic Officers (1928), the Havana Convention on Consular Agents (1928), the Vienna Convention on Diplomatic Relations (1961), the Vienna Convention on Consular Relations (1963), the Convention on Special Missions (1969) and the Convention on the Representation of States in their Relations with International Organizations of a Universal Character (1975). They are reprinted with permission of the United Nations.

C.1 HAVANA CONVENTION ON DIPLOMATIC OFFICERS (1928)[1]

[…]

SECTION I. Chiefs of mission

[…]

Article 6

Diplomatic officers, duly authorized by their governments, may, with the consent of the local government, and upon the request of a State not represented by an ordinary officer before the latter Government, undertake the temporary or accidental protection of the interests of the said State.

[…]

SECTION III. Duties of diplomatic officers

Article 12

Foreign diplomatic officers may not participate in the domestic or foreign politics of the State in which they exercise their functions.

Article 13

Diplomatic officers shall, in their official communications, address themselves to the Minister of Foreign Relations or Secretary of State of the country to which they are accredited. Communications to other authorities shall also be made through the said Minister or Secretary.

SECTION IV. Immunities and prerogatives of diplomatic officers

[…]

Article 15

States should extend to diplomatic officers every facility for the exercise of their functions and especially to the end that they may freely communicate with their governments.

[1] Havana Convention on Diplomatic Officers (1928), 155 LNTS 259.

C.2 HAVANA CONVENTION ON CONSULAR AGENTS (1928)[2]

[…]

SECTION I. Appointments and functions

[…]

Article 10

Consuls shall exercise the functions that the law of their State confers upon them, without prejudice to the legislation of the country where they are serving.

Article 11

In the exercise of their functions, consuls shall deal directly with the authorities of their district. Should their representations not be heeded, they may then pursue them before the Government of the State through the intermediary of their diplomatic representative, but should not communicate directly with the Government except in the absence or non-existence of a diplomatic representative.

[…]

SECTION II. Prerogatives of Consuls

Article 14

In the absence of a special agreement between two nations, the consular agents who are nationals of the State appointing them, shall neither be arrested nor prosecuted except in the cases when they are accused of committing an act classed as a crime by local legislation.

[…]

Article 16

Consuls are not subject to local jurisdiction for acts done in their official character and within the scope of their authority. In case a private individual deems himself injured by the consul's action, he must submit his complaint to the Government, which, if it considers the claim to be relevant, shall make it valid through diplomatic channels.

[2] Havana Convention on Consular Agents (1928), 155 LNTS 289.

Article 17

In respect to unofficial acts, consuls are subject, in civil as well as in criminal matters, to the jurisdiction of the State where they exercise their functions.

Article 18

The official residence of the consuls and places used for the consulate's offices and archives are inviolable and in no case may the local authorities enter them without the permission of the consular agents; neither shall they examine nor seize, under any pretext whatsoever, documents or other objects found in a consular office. No consular officer shall be required to present his official files before the courts or to make declaration with respect to their contents.

[…]

Article 19

Consuls are obliged to deliver, upon the simple request of the local authorities, persons accused or condemned for crimes who may have sought refuge in the consulate.

[…]

C.3 VIENNA CONVENTION ON DIPLOMATIC RELATIONS (1961)[3]

The States Parties to the present Convention

Recalling that peoples of all nations from ancient times have recognized the status of diplomatic agents,

Having in mind the purposes and principles of the Charter of the United Nations concerning the sovereign equality of States, the maintenance of international peace and security, and the promotion of friendly relations among nations,

Believing that an international convention on diplomatic intercourse, privileges and immunities would contribute to the development of friendly relations among nations, irrespective of their differing constitutional and social systems,

Realizing that the purpose of such privileges and immunities is not to benefit individuals but to ensure the efficient performance of the functions of diplomatic missions as representing States,

Affirming that the rules of customary international law should continue to govern questions not expressly regulated by the provisions of the present Convention,

Have agreed as follows:

[...]

Article 3

1. The functions of a diplomatic mission consist inter alia in:
   (a) representing the sending State in the receiving State;
   (b) protecting in the receiving State the interests of the sending State and of its nationals, within the limits permitted by international law;
   (c) negotiating with the Government of the receiving State;
   (d) ascertaining by all lawful means conditions and developments in the receiving State, and reporting thereon to the Government of the sending State;
   (e) promoting friendly relations between the sending State and the receiving State, and developing their economic, cultural and scientific relations.

[3] Vienna Convention on Diplomatic Relations (1961), 500 UNTS 95.

2. Nothing in the present Convention shall be construed as preventing the performance of consular functions by a diplomatic mission.

[…]

Article 9

1. The receiving State may at any time and without having to explain its decision, notify the sending State that the head of the mission or any member of the diplomatic staff of the mission is persona non grata or that any other member of the staff of the mission is not acceptable. In any such case, the sending State shall, as appropriate, either recall the person concerned or terminate his functions with the mission. A person may be declared non grata or not acceptable before arriving in the territory of the receiving State.
2. If the sending State refuses or fails within a reasonable period to carry out its obligations under paragraph 1 of this Article, the receiving State may refuse to recognize the person concerned as a member of the mission.

[…]

Article 11

1. In the absence of specific agreement as to the size of the mission, the receiving State may require that the size of a mission be kept within limits considered by it to be reasonable and normal, having regard to circumstances and conditions in the receiving State and to the needs of the particular mission.
2. The receiving State may equally, within similar bounds and on a non-discriminatory basis, refuse to accept officials of a particular category.

[…]

Article 22

1. The premises of the mission shall be inviolable. The agents of the receiving State may not enter them, except with the consent of the head of the mission.
2. The receiving State is under a special duty to take all appropriate steps to protect the premises of the mission against any intrusion or damage and to prevent any disturbance of the peace of the mission or impairment of its dignity.

[…]

Article 25

The receiving State shall accord full facilities for the performance of the functions of the mission.

Article 26

Subject to its laws and regulations concerning zones entry into which is prohibited or regulated for reasons of national security, the receiving State shall ensure to all members of the mission freedom of movement and travel in its territory.

Article 27

1. The receiving State shall permit and protect free communication on the part of the mission for all official purposes. [...]

[...]

Article 29

The person of a diplomatic agent shall be inviolable. He shall not be liable to any form of arrest or detention. The receiving State shall treat him with due respect and shall take all appropriate steps to prevent any attack on his person, freedom or dignity.

[...]

Article 31

1. A diplomatic agent shall enjoy immunity from the criminal jurisdiction of the receiving State. He shall also enjoy immunity from its civil and administrative jurisdiction, except in the case of:

    (a) a real action relating to private immovable property situated in the territory of the receiving State, unless he holds it on behalf of the sending State for the purposes of the mission;

    (b) an action relating to succession in which the diplomatic agent is involved as executor, administrator, heir or legatee as a private person and not on behalf of the sending State;

    (c) an action relating to any professional or commercial activity exercised by the diplomatic agent in the receiving State outside his official functions.

[...]

Article 37

1. The members of the family of a diplomatic agent forming part of his household shall, if they are not nationals of the receiving State, enjoy the privileges and immunities specified in Articles 29 to 36.

2. Members of the administrative and technical staff of the mission, together with members of their families forming part of their respective households, shall, if they are not nationals of or permanently resident in the receiving State, enjoy the privileges and immunities specified in Articles 29 to 35, except that the immunity from civil and administrative jurisdiction of the receiving State specified in paragraph 1 of Article 31 shall not extend to acts performed outside the course of their duties. They shall also enjoy the privileges specified in Article 36, paragraph 1, in respect of articles imported at the time of first installation.

3. Members of the service staff of the mission who are not nationals of or permanently resident in the receiving State shall enjoy immunity in respect of acts performed in the course of their duties, exemption from dues and taxes on the emoluments they receive by reason of their employment and the exemption contained in Article 33.

4. Private servants of members of the mission shall, if they are not nationals of or permanently resident in the receiving State, be exempt from dues and taxes on the emoluments they receive by reason of their employment. In other respects, they may enjoy privileges and immunities only to the extent admitted by the receiving State. However, the receiving State must exercise its jurisdiction over those persons in such a manner as not to interfere unduly with the performance of the functions of the mission.

[…]

Article 41

1. Without prejudice to their privileges and immunities, it is the duty of all persons enjoying such privileges and immunities to respect the laws and regulations of the receiving State. They also have a duty not to interfere in the internal affairs of that State.

2. All official business with the receiving State entrusted to the mission by the sending State shall be conducted with or through the Ministry for Foreign Affairs of the receiving State or such other ministry as may be agreed.

3. The premises of the mission must not be used in any manner incompatible with the functions of the mission as laid down in the present Convention or by other rules of general international law or by any special agreements in force between the sending and the receiving State.

[…]

C.4 VIENNA CONVENTION ON CONSULAR RELATIONS (1963)[4]

CHAPTER I. CONSULAR RELATIONS IN GENERAL

Section I. ESTABLISHMENT AND CONDUCT OF CONSULAR RELATIONS

[…]

Article 5

Consular functions

Consular functions consist in:

(a) protecting in the receiving State the interests of the sending State and of its nationals, both individuals and bodies corporate, within the limits permitted by international law;

(b) furthering the development of commercial, economic, cultural and scientific relations between the sending State and the receiving State and otherwise promoting friendly relations between them in accordance with the provisions of the present Convention;

(c) ascertaining by all lawful means conditions and developments in the commercial, economic, cultural and scientific life of the receiving State, reporting thereon to the Government of the sending State and giving information to persons interested;

(d) issuing passports and travel documents to nationals of the sending State, and visas or appropriate documents to persons wishing to travel to the sending State;

(e) helping and assisting nationals, both individuals and bodies corporate, of the sending State;

(f) acting as notary and civil registrar and in capacities of a similar kind, and performing certain functions of an administrative nature, provided that there is nothing contrary thereto in the laws and regulations of the receiving State;

(g) safeguarding the interests of nationals, both individuals and bodies corporate, of the sending State in cases of succession mortis causa in the territory of the receiving State, in accordance with the laws and regulations of the receiving State;

[4] Vienna Convention on Consular Relations (1963), 596 UNTS 261.

(h) safeguarding, within the limits imposed by the laws and regulations of the receiving State, the interests of minors and other persons lacking full capacity who are nationals of the sending State, particularly where any guardianship or trusteeship is required with respect to such persons;

(i) subject to the practices and procedures obtaining in the receiving State, representing or arranging appropriate representation for nationals of the sending State before the tribunals and other authorities of the receiving State, for the purpose of obtaining, in accordance with the laws and regulations of the receiving State, provisional measures for the preservation of the rights and interests of these nationals, where, because of absence or any other reason, such nationals are unable at the proper time to assume the defence of their rights and interests;

(j) transmitting judicial and extrajudicial documents or executing letters rogatory or commissions to take evidence for the courts of the sending State in accordance with international agreements in force or, in the absence of such international agreements, in any other manner compatible with the laws and regulations of the receiving State;

(k) exercising rights of supervision and inspection provided for in the laws and regulations of the sending State in respect of vessels having the nationality of the sending State, and of aircraft registered in that State, and in respect of their crews;

(l) extending assistance to vessels and aircraft mentioned in sub-paragraph (k) of this Article and to their crews, taking statements regarding the voyage of a vessel, examining and stamping the ship's papers, and, without prejudice to the powers of the authorities of the receiving State, conducting investigations into any incidents which occurred during the voyage, and settling disputes of any kind between the master, the officers and the seamen in so far as this may be authorized by the laws and regulations of the sending State;

(m) performing any other functions entrusted to a consular post by the sending State which are not prohibited by the laws and regulations of the receiving State or to which no objection is taken by the receiving State or which are referred to in the international agreements in force between the sending State and the receiving State.

[…]

Article 17

Performance of diplomatic acts by consular officers

1. In a State where the sending State has no diplomatic mission and is not represented by a diplomatic mission of a third State, a consular officer may, with the consent of the receiving State, and without affecting his consular status, be authorized to perform diplomatic acts. The performance of such acts by a consular officer shall not confer upon him any right to claim diplomatic privileges and immunities.

[...]

Article 23

Persons declared non grata

1. The receiving State may at any time notify the sending State that a consular officer is *persona non grata* or that any other member of the consular staff is not acceptable. In that event, the sending State shall, as the case may be, either recall the person concerned or terminate his functions with the consular post.

[...]

3. A person appointed as a member of a consular post may be declared unacceptable before arriving in the territory of the receiving State or, if already in the receiving State, before entering on his duties with the consular post. In any such case, the sending State shall withdraw his appointment.
4. In the cases mentioned in paragraphs 1 and 3 of this Article, the receiving State is not obliged to give to the sending State reasons for its decision.

[...]

CHAPTER II. FACILITIES, PRIVILEGES AND IMMUNITIES RELATING TO CONSULAR POSTS, CAREER CONSULAR OFFICERS AND OTHER MEMBERS OF A CONSULAR POST

Section I. FACILITIES, PRIVILEGES AND IMMUNITIES RELATING TO A CONSULAR POST

Article 28

Facilities for the work of the consular post

The receiving State shall accord full facilities for the performance of the functions of the consular post.

[…]

Article 31

Inviolability of the consular premises

1. Consular premises shall be inviolable to the extent provided in this Article.
2. The authorities of the receiving State shall not enter that part of the consular premises which is used exclusively for the purpose of the work of the consular post except with the consent of the head of the consular post or of his designee or of the head of the diplomatic mission of the sending State. The consent of the head of the consular post may, however, be assumed in case of fire or other disaster requiring prompt protective action.
3. Subject to the provisions of paragraph 2 of this Article, the receiving State is under a special duty to take all appropriate steps to protect the consular premises against any intrusion or damage and to prevent any disturbance of the peace of the consular post or impairment of its dignity.

[…]

Article 34

Freedom of movement

Subject to its laws and regulations concerning zones entry into which is prohibited or regulated for reasons of national security, the receiving State shall ensure freedom of movement and travel in its territory to all members of the consular post.

Article 35

Freedom of communication

1. The receiving State shall permit and protect freedom of communication on the part of the consular post for all official purposes. [...]

[...]

Section II. FACILITIES, PRIVILEGES AND IMMUNITIES RELATING TO CAREER CONSULAR OFFICERS AND OTHER MEMBERS OF A CONSULAR POST

Article 40

Protection of consular officers

The receiving State shall treat consular officers with due respect and shall take all appropriate steps to prevent any attack on their person, freedom or dignity.

Article 41

Personal inviolability of consular officers

1. Consular officers shall not be liable to arrest or detention pending trial, except in the case of a grave crime and pursuant to a decision by the competent judicial authority.
2. Except in the case specified in paragraph 1 of this Article, consular officers shall not be committed to prison or liable to any other form of restriction on their personal freedom save in execution of a judicial decision of final effect.
3. If criminal proceedings are instituted against a consular officer, he must appear before the competent authorities. Nevertheless, the proceedings shall be conducted with the respect due to him by reason of his official position and, except in the case specified in paragraph 1 of this Article, in a manner which will hamper the exercise of consular functions as little as possible. When, in the circumstances mentioned in paragraph 1 of this Article, it has become necessary to detain a consular officer, the proceedings against him shall be instituted with the minimum of delay.

[...]

Article 43

Immunity from jurisdiction

1. Consular officers and consular employees shall not be amenable to the jurisdiction of the judicial or administrative authorities of the receiving State in respect of acts performed in the exercise of consular functions.
2. The provisions of paragraph 1 of this Article shall not, however, apply in respect of a civil action either:
   (a) arising out of a contract concluded by a consular officer or a consular employee in which he did not contract expressly or impliedly as an agent of the sending State; or
   (b) by a third party for damage arising from an accident in the receiving State caused by a vehicle, vessel or aircraft.

[...]

Article 55

Respect for the laws and regulations of the receiving State

1. Without prejudice to their privileges and immunities, it is the duty of all persons enjoying such privileges and immunities to respect the laws and regulations of the receiving State. They also have a duty not to interfere in the internal affairs of that State.
2. The consular premises shall not be used in any manner incompatible with the exercise of consular functions.

[...]

CHAPTER III. REGIME RELATING TO HONORARY CONSULAR OFFICERS AND CONSULAR POSTS HEADED BY SUCH OFFICERS

Article 58

General provisions relating to facilities, privileges and immunities

1. Articles 28, 29, 30, 34, 35, 36, 37, 38 and 39, paragraph 3 of Article 54 and paragraphs 2 and 3 of Article 55 shall apply to consular posts headed by an honorary consular officer. In addition, the facilities, privileges and immunities of such consular posts shall be governed by Articles 59, 60, 61 and 62.

2. Articles 42 and 43, paragraph 3 of Article 44, Articles 45 and 53 and paragraph 1 of Article 55 shall apply to honorary consular officers. In addition, the facilities, privileges and immunities of such consular officers shall be governed by Articles 63, 64, 65, 66 and 67.
3. Privileges and immunities provided in the present Convention shall not be accorded to members of the family of an honorary consular officer or of a consular employee employed at a consular post headed by an honorary consular officer.
4. The exchange of consular bags between two consular posts headed by honorary consular officers in different States shall not be allowed without the consent of the two receiving States concerned.

Article 59

Protection of the consular premises

The receiving State shall take such steps as may be necessary to protect the consular premises of a consular post headed by an honorary consular officer against any intrusion or damage and to prevent any disturbance of the peace of the consular post or impairment of its dignity.

[...]

Article 63

Criminal proceedings

If criminal proceedings are instituted against an honorary consular officer, he must appear before the competent authorities. Nevertheless, the proceedings shall be conducted with the respect due to him by reason of his official position and, except when he is under arrest or detention, in a manner which will hamper the exercise of consular functions as little as possible. When it has become necessary to detain an honorary consular officer, the proceedings against him shall be instituted with the minimum of delay.

Article 64

Protection of honorary consular officers

The receiving State is under a duty to accord to an honorary consular officer such protection as may be required by reason of his official position.

[...]

C.5 CONVENTION ON SPECIAL MISSIONS (1969)[5]

[...]

Article 3

Functions of a special mission

The functions of a special mission shall be determined by the mutual consent of the sending and the receiving State.

[...]

Article 12

Persons declared 'non grata' or not acceptable

1. The receiving State may, at any time and without having to explain its decision, notify the sending State that any representative of the sending State in the special mission or any member of its diplomatic staff is persona non grata or that any other member of the staff of the mission is not acceptable. In any such case, the sending State shall, as appropriate, either recall the person concerned or terminate his functions with the mission. A person may be declared non grata or not acceptable before arriving in the territory of the receiving State.
2. If the sending State refuses, or fails within a reasonable period, to carry out its obligations under paragraph 1 of this article, the receiving State may refuse to recognize the person concerned as a member of the special mission.

[...]

Article 15

Organ of the receiving State with which official business is conducted

All official business with the receiving State entrusted to the special mission by the sending State shall be conducted with or through the Ministry of Foreign Affairs or with such other organ of the receiving State as may be agreed.

[...]

[5] Convention on Special Missions (1969), 1400 UNTS 231.

Article 22

General facilities

The receiving State shall accord to the special mission the facilities required for the performance of its functions, having regard to the nature and task of the special mission.

[...]

Article 25

Inviolability of the premises

1. The premises where the special mission is established in accordance with the present Convention shall be inviolable. The agents of the receiving State may not enter the said premises, except with the consent of the head of the special mission or, if appropriate, of the head of the permanent diplomatic mission of the sending State accredited to the receiving State. Such consent may be assumed in case of fire or other disaster that seriously endangers public safety, and only in the event that it has not been possible to obtain the express consent of the head of the special mission or, where appropriate, of the head of the permanent mission.
2. The receiving State is under a special duty to take all appropriate steps to protect the premises of the special mission against any intrusion or damage and to prevent any disturbance of the peace of the mission or impairment of its dignity.

[...]

Article 27

Freedom of movement

Subject to its laws and regulations concerning zones entry into which is prohibited or regulated for reasons of national security, the receiving State shall ensure to all members of the special mission such freedom of movement and travel in its territory as is necessary for the performance of the functions of the special mission.

Article 28

Freedom of communication

1. The receiving State shall permit and protect free communication on the part of the special mission for all official purposes [...]

Article 29

Personal inviolability

The persons of the representatives of the sending State in the special mission and of the members of its diplomatic staff shall be inviolable. They shall not be liable to any form of arrest or detention. The receiving State shall treat them with due respect and shall take all appropriate steps to prevent any attack on their persons, freedom or dignity.

[...]

Article 31

Immunity from jurisdiction

1. The representatives of the sending State in the special mission and the members of its diplomatic staff shall enjoy immunity from the criminal jurisdiction of the receiving State.
2. They shall also enjoy immunity from the civil and administrative jurisdiction of the receiving State, except in the case of:
   (a) a real action relating to private immovable property situated in the territory of the receiving State, unless the person concerned holds it on behalf of the sending State for the purposes of the mission;
   (b) an action relating to succession in which the person concerned is involved as executor, administrator, heir or legatee as a private person and not on behalf of the sending State;
   (c) an action relating to any professional or commercial activity exercised by the person concerned in the receiving State outside his official functions;
   (d) an action for damages arising out of an accident caused by a vehicle used outside the official functions of the person concerned.

[...]

Article 36

Administrative and technical staff

Members of the administrative and technical staff of the special mission shall enjoy the privileges and immunities specified in articles 29 to 34, except that the immunity from civil and administrative jurisdiction of the receiving State specified in paragraph 2 of article 31 shall not extend to acts performed outside the course of their duties. They shall also enjoy the privileges mentioned in paragraph 1 of article 35 in respect of articles imported at the time of their first entry into the territory of the receiving State.

Article 37

Service staff

Members of the service staff of the special mission shall enjoy immunity from the jurisdiction of the receiving State in respect of acts performed in the course of their duties, exemption from dues and taxes on the emoluments they receive by reason of their employment, and exemption from social security legislation as provided in article 32.

Article 38

Private staff

Private staff of the members of the special mission shall be exempt from dues and taxes on the emoluments they receive by reason of their employment. In all other respects, they may enjoy privileges and immunities only to the extent permitted by the receiving State. However, the receiving State must exercise its jurisdiction over these persons in such a manner as to interfere unduly with the performance of the functions of the special mission.

Article 39

Members of the family

1. Members of the families of representatives of the sending State in the special mission and of members of its diplomatic staff shall, if they accompany such members of the special mission, enjoy the privileges and immunities specified in articles 29 to 35 provided that they are not nationals of or permanently resident in the receiving State.
2. Members of the families of members of the administrative and technical staff of the special mission shall, if they accompany such members of the special mission, enjoy the privileges and immunities specified in article 36 provided that they are not nationals of or permanently resident in the receiving State.

[…]

Article 47

Respect for the laws and regulations of the receiving State and use of the premises of the special mission

1. Without prejudice to their privileges and immunities, it is the duty of all persons enjoying these privileges and immunities under the present Convention to respect the laws and regulations of the receiving State. They also have a duty not to interfere in the internal affairs of that State.

2. The premises of the special mission must not be used in any manner incompatible with the functions of the special mission as envisaged in the present Convention, in other rules of general international law or in any special agreements in force between the sending and the receiving State.

[…]

C.6 VIENNA CONVENTION ON THE REPRESENTATION OF STATES IN THEIR RELATIONS WITH INTERNATIONAL ORGANIZATIONS OF A UNIVERSAL CHARACTER (1975)[6]

[Note: At the time of writing, this convention had not yet entered into force]

[…]

Part II. Missions to International Organizations

[…]

Article 6

Functions of the permanent mission

The functions of the permanent mission consist, inter alia, in:

(a) ensuring the representation of the sending State to the Organization;

(b) maintaining liaison between the sending State and the Organization;

(c) negotiating with and within the Organization;

(d) ascertaining activities in the Organization and reporting thereon to the Government of the sending State;

(e) ensuring the participation of the sending State in the activities of the Organization;

(f) protecting the interests of the sending State in relation to the Organization;

(g) promoting the realization of the purposes and principles of the Organization by cooperating with and within the Organization.

Article 7

Functions of the permanent observer mission

The functions of the permanent observer mission consist, inter alia, in:

(a) ensuring the representation of the sending State and safeguarding its interests in relation to the Organization and maintaining liaison with it;

[6] Vienna Convention on the Representation of States in their Relations with International Organizations of a Universal Character (1975) <http://legal.un.org/ilc/texts/instruments/english/conventions/5_1_1975.pdf> (visited 18 March 2015).

(b) ascertaining activities in the Organization and reporting thereon to the Government of the sending State;

(c) promoting cooperation with the Organization and negotiating with it.

[...]

Article 20

General facilities

1. The host State shall accord to the mission all necessary facilities for the performance of its functions.
2. The Organization shall assist the mission in obtaining those facilities and shall accord to the mission such facilities as lie within its own competence.

[...]

Article 23

Inviolability of premises

1. The premises of the mission shall be inviolable. The agents of the host State may not enter them, except with the consent of the head of mission.
2. (a) The host State is under a special duty to take all appropriate steps to protect the premises of the mission against any intrusion or damage and to prevent any disturbance of the peace of the mission or impairment of its dignity.

   (b) In case of an attack on the premises of the mission, the host State shall take all appropriate steps to prosecute and punish persons who have committed the attack.

[...]

Article 26

Freedom of movement

Subject to its laws and regulations concerning zones entry into which is prohibited or regulated for reasons of national security, the host State shall ensure freedom of movement and travel in its territory to all members of the mission and members of their families forming part of their households.

Article 27

Freedom of communication

1. The host State shall permit and protect free communication on the part of the mission for all official purposes. […]

Article 28

Personal inviolability

The persons of the head of mission and of the members of the diplomatic staff of the mission shall be inviolable. They shall not be liable to any form of arrest or detention. The host State shall treat them with due respect and shall take all appropriate steps to prevent any attack on their persons, freedom or dignity and to prosecute and punish persons who have committed such attacks.

[…]

Article 30

Immunity from jurisdiction

1. The head of mission and the members of the diplomatic staff of the mission shall enjoy immunity from the criminal jurisdiction of the host State. They shall also enjoy immunity from its civil and administrative jurisdiction, except in the case of:

   (a) a real action relating to private immovable property situated in the territory of the host State, unless the person in question holds it on behalf of the sending State for the purposes of the mission;

   (b) an action relating to succession in which the person in question is involved as executor, administrator, heir or legatee as a private person and not on behalf of the sending State;

   (c) an action relating to any professional or commercial activity exercised by the person in question in the host State outside his official functions.

[…]

Article 36

Privileges and immunities of other persons

1. The members of the family of the head of mission forming part of his household and the members of the family of a member of the diplomatic staff of the mission forming part of his household shall, if they

are not nationals of or permanently resident in the host State, enjoy the privileges and immunities specified in articles 28, 29, 30, 32, 33, 34 and in paragraphs 1(b) and 2 of article 35.

2. Members of the administrative and technical staff of the mission, together with members of their families forming part of their respective households who are not nationals of or permanently resident in the host State, shall enjoy the privileges and immunities specified in articles 28, 29, 30, 32, 33 and 34, except that the immunity from civil and administrative jurisdiction of the host State specified in paragraph 1 of article 30 shall not extend to acts performed outside the course of their duties. They shall also enjoy the privileges specified in paragraph 1 (b) of article 35 in respect of articles imported at the time of final installation.

3. Members of the service staff of the mission who are not nationals of or permanently resident in the host State shall enjoy immunity in respect of acts performed in the course of their duties, exemption from dues and taxes on the emoluments they receive by reason of their employment and the exemption specified in article 32.

4. Private staff of members of the mission shall, if they are not nationals of or permanently resident in the host State, be exempt from dues and taxes on the emoluments they receive by reason of their employment. In other respects, they may enjoy privileges and immunities only to the extent admitted by the host State. However, the host State must exercise its jurisdiction over those persons in such a manner as not to interfere unduly with the performance of the functions of the mission.

[…]

Article 41

Protection of premises, property and archives

1. When the mission is temporarily or finally recalled, the host State must respect and protect the premises, property and archives of the mission. The sending State must take all appropriate measures to terminate this special duty of the host State as soon as possible. It may entrust custody of the premises, property and archives of the mission to the Organization if it so agrees, or to a third State acceptable to the host State.

[…]

Part III. Delegations to Organs and to Conferences

[…]

Article 51

General facilities

1. The host State shall accord to the delegation all necessary facilities for the performance of its tasks.
2. The Organization or, as the case may be, the conference shall assist the delegation in obtaining those facilities and shall accord to the delegation such facilities as lie within its own competence.

[…]

Article 56

Freedom of movement

Subject to its laws and regulations concerning zones entry into which is prohibited or regulated for reasons of national security, the host State shall ensure to all members of the delegation such freedom of movement and travel in its territory as is necessary for the performance of the tasks of the delegation.

Article 57

Freedom of communication

1. The host State shall permit and protect free communication on the part of the delegation for all official purposes. […]

Article 58

Personal inviolability

The persons of the head of delegation and of other delegates and members of the diplomatic staff of the delegation shall be inviolable. They shall not be liable, inter alia, to any form of arrest or detention. The host State shall treat them with due respect and shall take all appropriate steps to prevent any attack on their persons, freedom or dignity and to prosecute and punish persons who have committed such attacks.

[…]

Article 60

Immunity from jurisdiction

1. The head of delegation and other delegates and members of the diplomatic staff of the delegation shall enjoy immunity from the criminal jurisdiction of the host State, and immunity from its civil and administrative jurisdiction in respect of all acts performed in the exercise of their official functions.

[…]

4. Nothing in this article shall exempt such persons from the civil and administrative jurisdiction of the host State in relation to an action for damages arising from an accident caused by a vehicle, vessel or aircraft, used or owned by the persons in question, where those damages are not recoverable from insurance.

[…]

Article 66

Privileges and immunities of other persons

1. The members of the family of the head of delegation who accompany him and the members of the family of any other delegate or member of the diplomatic staff of the delegation who accompany him shall, if they are not nationals of or permanently resident in the host State, enjoy the privileges and immunities specified in articles 58, 60 and 64 and in paragraphs 1 (b) and 2 of article 65 and exemption from aliens' registration obligations.
2. Members of the administrative and technical staff of the delegation shall, if they are not nationals of or permanently resident in the host State, enjoy the privileges and immunities specified in articles 58, 59, 60, 62, 63 and 64. They shall also enjoy the privileges specified in paragraph 1 (b) of article 65 in respect of articles imported in their personal baggage at the time of their first entry into the territory of the host State for the purpose of attending the meeting of the organ or conference. Members of the family of a member of the administrative and technical staff who accompany him shall, if they are not nationals of or permanently resident in the host State, enjoy the privileges and immunities specified in articles 58, 60 and 64 and in paragraph 1 (b) of article 65 to the extent accorded to such a member of the staff.
3. Members of the service staff of the delegation who are not nationals of or permanently resident in the host State shall enjoy the same immunity in respect of acts performed in the course of their duties as is

accorded to members of the administrative and technical staff of the delegation, exemption from dues and taxes on the emoluments they receive by reason of their employment and the exemption specified in article 62.

4. Private staff of members of the delegation shall, if they are nationals of or permanently resident in the host State, be exempt from dues and taxes on the emoluments they receive by reason of their employment. In other respects, they may enjoy privileges and immunities only to the extent admitted by the host State. However, the host State must exercise its jurisdiction over those persons in such a manner as not to interfere unduly with the performance of the tasks of the delegation.

[…]

Article 70

Protection of premises, property and archives

1. When the meeting of an organ or a conference comes to an end, the host State must respect and protect the premises of the delegation so long as they are used by it, as well as the property and archives of the delegation. The sending State must take all appropriate measures to terminate this special duty of the host State as soon as possible.

[…]

Part IV. Observer Delegations to Organs and to Conferences

[…]

Article 72

General provision concerning observer delegations

All the provisions of articles 43 to 70 of the present Convention shall apply to observer delegations.

Part V. General Provisions

[…]

Article 77

Respect for the laws and regulations of the host State

1. Without prejudice to their privileges and immunities, it is the duty of all persons enjoying such privileges and immunities to respect the

laws and regulations of the host State. They also have a duty not to interfere in the internal affairs of that State.

2. In case of grave and manifest violation of the criminal law of the host State by a person enjoying immunity from jurisdiction, the sending State shall, unless it waives the immunity of the person concerned, recall him, terminate his functions with the mission, the delegation or the observer delegation or secure his departure, as appropriate. The sending State shall take the same action in case of grave and manifest interference in the internal affairs of the host State. The provisions of this paragraph shall not apply in the case of any act that the person concerned performed in carrying out the functions of the mission or the tasks of the delegation or of the observer delegation.

3. The premises of the mission and the premises of the delegation shall not be used in any manner incompatible with the exercise of the functions of the mission or the performance of the tasks of the delegation.

4. Nothing in this article shall be construed as prohibiting the host State from taking such measures as are necessary for its own protection. In that event the host State shall, without prejudice to articles 84 and 85, consult the sending State in an appropriate manner in order to ensure that such measures do not interfere with the normal functioning of the mission, the delegation or the observer delegation.

[…]

Bibliography

LITERATURE

Abbott, Kenneth W, 'Corruption, Fight Against' in Rüdiger Wolfrum (ed), *Max Planck Encyclopedia of Public International Law* (September 2009), http://opil.ouplaw.com.ezproxy.is.ed.ac.uk/view/10.1093/law:epil/9780199231690/law-9780199231690-e918?rskey=8hv2iT&result=1&prd=EPIL, accessed 28 April 2015

Agency for Legislative Initiatives (Ukraine), 'Efficiency of Political Parties in Ukraine: Problems and Prospects' (Donetsk, 8–10 December 2006), http://www.authorstream.com/Presentation/Ulisse-54553-Analitics-eng-Efficiency-Political-Parties-Ukraine-Problems-Prospects-1-Election-System-Responsibility-a-Education-ppt-powerpoint/, accessed 1 March 2015

Akzin, Benjamin, 'Propaganda by Diplomats' (1936) 5(7) *International Law and Relations* 1

Alam, Shahidul, 'Stretching the Parameters of Diplomatic Protocol: Incursions into Public Diplomacy' (2001) 2(1) *Exchange* 49, http://surface.syr.edu/exchange/vol2/iss1/5, accessed 28 April 2015

Alexander, John B, *Future War: Non-Lethal Weapons in Modern Warfare* (New York, St Martin's Press, 1999)

American Non-Governmental Organizations Coalition for the International Criminal Court (AMICC), 'Countries Concluding Bilateral Immunities Agreements' c (2011), http://www.amicc.org/usicc/bialist, accessed 9 March 2015

American Society of International Law, 'Fourth Annual Meeting of the American Society of International Law' (1910) 4 *American Society of International Law Proceedings* 12 [Clarke]

Andenas, Mads and Zleptnig, Stefan, 'Proportionality: WTO Law: In Comparative Perspective' (2007) 42 *Texas International Law Journal* 371

Andersen, Elizabeth (moderator), 'Presentation and Discussion of the ASIL Task Force Report on U.S. Policy towards the International Criminal Court' (2009) 103 *American Society of International Law Proceedings* 311

Annuaire Française de Droit International, 'Pratique française du droit international' (1976), (1977), (1982) [AFDI, 'Pratique française']

Aristotle, 'Categoriae and de Interpretatione' in WD Ross (ed), *The Works of Aristotle. Volume I* (Ella Mary Edghill tr, Oxford, Clarendon Press, 1928)

Asante, Kofi Darko, 'Election Monitoring's Impact on the Law: Can it be Reconciled with Sovereignty and Nonintervention?' (1993–1994) 26 *New York University Journal of International Law and Politics* 235–84

Australian Yearbook of International Law, 'Diplomatic and Consular Relations' (1978–1980) (1981–1983) (1984–1987) (1988–1989) (1992) [Aust YBIL]

Barbour, Emily and Weed, Matthew, *The International Criminal Court (ICC): Jurisdiction, Extradition and U.S. Policy* (Congressional Research Service, March 2010), http://fas.org/sgp/crs/row/R41116.pdf, accessed 27 May 2015

Barder, Brian, *What Diplomats Do: The Life and Work of Diplomats* (Lanham, Rowman & Littlefield, 2014)

Bassiouni, M Cherif, 'A Functional Approach to "General Principles of International Law"' (1990) 11 *Michigan Journal of International Law* 776

Bazyler, Michael J, 'Re-examining the Doctrine of Humanitarian Intervention in Light of the Atrocities in Kampuchea and Ethiopia' (1987) 23 *Stanford Journal of International Law* 547

Behrens, Paul, 'Diplomatic Communications, Forms of' in Rüdiger Wolfrum (ed), *Max Planck Encyclopedia of Public International Law*, (August 2009), http://opil.ouplaw.com.ezproxy.is.ed.ac.uk/view/10.1093/law:epil/9780199231690/law-9780199231690-e1770?rskey=btQ4wZ&result=1&prd=EPIL, accessed 29 April 2015

——, 'The *Mens Rea* of Genocide' in Ralph Henham and Paul Behrens (eds), *Elements of Genocide* (Abingdon, Routledge, 2012) 70–96 [Behrens (2012)]

——, 'The Law of Diplomatic Asylum—A Contextual Approach' (2014) 35(2) *Michigan Journal of International Law* 319 [Behrens (2014a)]

——, '"None Of Their Business?" Diplomatic Involvement In Human Rights' (2014) 15 *Melbourne Journal of International Law* 190 [Behrens (2014b)]

Ben-Asher, Dror, *Human Rights meet Diplomatic Immunities: Problems and Possible Solutions* (Cambridge, Harvard Law School, November 2000)

Berridge, Geoff R, *Diplomacy. Theory and Practice* (Basingstoke, Palgrave Macmillan, 2005)

—— and James, Alan, *A Dictionary of Diplomacy* (Basingstoke, Palgrave Macmillan, 2003)

Bindschedler, Rudolf L, 'Die Wiener Konvention über die diplomatischen Beziehungen' (1961) 18 *Schweizerisches Jahrbuch für Internationales Recht* 29

Bland, Nevile (ed), *Satow's Guide to Diplomatic Practice* (London, Longmans, 1957, new impression with corrections 1964) [Satow (1964)]

Blankenhorn, Herbert, 'Diplomatie (La)', in A-F Frangulis (ed), *Dictionnaire diplomatique* (Paris, Académie diplomatique internationale, c 1932–1973)

Bliščenko [Blischtschenko], Igor Pavlovič, Durdenevskij [Durdenewski], Vsevolod Nikolaevich, *Das Diplomaten- und Konsularrecht* (Berlin, Staatsverlag der Deutschen Demokratischen Republik, 1966)

Blum, Yehuda Z, 'Diplomatic Agents and Missions' in Rudolf Bernhardt (ed), *Encyclopedia of Public International Law, Volume 1* (Amsterdam, London, New York, Tokyo, Max-Planck-Institut für ausländisches öffentliches Recht und Völkerrecht, 1992) 1034

Bluntschli, Johann Kaspar, 'Le droit international codifié [extract]' (1932) 26 *American Journal of International Law Supplement* 144

Bradley, Anthony W, 'The Judge Over Your Shoulder' [1987] *Public Law* 485

Brown, Bartram S, 'Intervention, Self-Determination, Democracy and the Residual Responsibilities of the Occupying Power in Iraq' (2004) 11 *UC Davies Journal of International Law and Policy* 23

Bruns, Kai, *A Cornerstone of Modern Diplomacy. Britain and the Negotiation of the 1961 Vienna Convention on Diplomatic Relations* (New York; London; New Delhi; Sydney, Bloomsbury, 2014)

Bunce, Peter J and Offer, Derek F, 'Dual Containment and Iran. Understanding and Assessing US Policy' (US Air Force Academy, 1997), http://www.dtic.mil/cgi-bin/GetTRDoc?AD=ADA367885, accessed 29 April 2015

Busch, Wilhelm, 'Wer möchte diesen Erdenball' in Friedrich Bohne, *Historisch-kritisiche Gesamtausgabe in vier Baenden, Band 2* (Wiesbaden und Berlin, Vollmer, 1960), 506

Callières, François de, *De la manière de négocier avec les souverains* (Paris and Amsterdam 1716) quoted in Satow (1979), 445, para 44.29

Camden, William, *Annales Rerum Anglicarum et Hibernicarum, regnante Elizabetha* (R N Gent tr, 3rd edn, 1635), quoted in Satow (1979), 179, para 21.16

Campbell, Wesley J, 'The French Intrigue of James Cole Mountflorence' (2008) 65(4) *The William and Mary Quarterly* 779–96 [Campbell (2008)]

——, 'The Origin of Citizen Genet's Projected Attack on Spanish Louisiana: A Case Study in Girondin Politics' (2010) 33(4) *French Historical Studies* 515–44 [Campbell (2010)]

Cannizzaro, Enzo, *Il principio della proporzionalità nell'ordinamento internazionale* (Milan, Giuffrè, 2000)

Caplan, Lee M, 'State Immunity, Human Rights and *Jus Cogens*: A Critique of the Normative Hierarchy Theory' (2003) 97 *American Journal of International Law* 741

Carey, Carlyn M, 'Internal Displacement: Is Prevention Through Accountability Possible? A Kosovo Case Study' (1999) 49 *American University Law Review* 243

Cassese, Antonio, *Self-determination of Peoples* (Cambridge, Cambridge University Press, 1995)

Castellino, Joshua, *International Law and Self-Determination* (The Hague, Boston, London, Martinus Nijhoff, 2000)

Cayci, Sadi, 'Armenian Genocide Claims: A Contextual Version of the 1915 Incidents' in Ralph Henham and Paul Behrens (eds), *The Criminal Law of Genocide*, (Aldershot, Ashgate, 2007) 17

Chadwick, Elizabeth, *Self-Determination, Terrorism and the International Humanitarian Law of Armed Conflict* (The Hague; Boston; London, Martinus Nijhoff, 1996)

Cheyette, Cara M, *Punishment Before Justice: Indefinite Detention in the US* (Scott Allen ed, 2011), http://physiciansforhumanrights.org/library/reports/indefinte-detention-june2011.html, accessed 29 April 2015

Christakis, Théodore, *Le Droit à l'auto-determination en dehors des situations de décolonisation*, (Paris, Centre d'études et de recherches internationales et communautaires, Université d'Aix-Marseilles III, 1999)

Clark, Eric, *Corps Diplomatique* (London, Allen Lane, 1973)

Clarke: See American Society of International Law

Coalition for the International Criminal Court, 'Status of US Bilateral Immunity Agremeents (BIAs)' (c 2006), http://www.iccnow.org/documents/CICCFS_BIAstatus_current.pdf#page=1&zoom=auto,0,800, accessed 29 April 2015

Coffey, Guy J; Kaplan, Ida; Sampson, Robyn C and Tucci, Maria Montagna, 'The Meaning and Mental Health Consequences of Long-Term Immigration Detention for People Seeking Asylum' (2010) 70 *Social Science and Medicine* 2070

Coquillette, Daniel R, 'The English Civilian Writers: 1523–1607' (1981) 61 *Boston University Law Review* 1

Comisión Internacional de Jurisconsultos Americanos, Reunión de 1927, '[Project of the International Commission of American Jurists]' (1932) 26 *American Journal of International Law Supplement* 171

Coussirat-Coustere, Vincent, 'Article 10 § 2' in Pettiti, Louis (ed), *La Convention européenne des droits de l'homme: commentaire article par article* (Paris, Economica, 1995) 409

Crook, John (ed), 'Contemporary Practice of the United States Relating to International Law. State Diplomatic and Consular Relations. China Protests U.S. Embassy's and Consulates' Dissemination of Local Air Quality Data in China' (2012) 106 *American Journal of International Law* 851

Cuzán, Alfred G, 'Fidel Castro: A Machiavellian Prince?' in Jorge F Pérez-López and José F Alonso (eds), *Cuba in Transition, Volume 9* (1999) 178, 185, http://uwf.edu/media/university-of-west-florida/colleges/cassh/departments/government/cdocs/III.A.4-Cuzan-1999-Fidel-CastroA-Machiavellian-Prince.pdf, accessed 14 March 2015

D'Amato, Anthony, 'It's a Bird, it's a Plane, it's Jus Cogens!' (1990) 6 *Connecticut Journal of International Law* 1

Danilenko, Gennady M, 'Relevance of Humanitarian and Diplomatic Law to the Conflict in the Gulf' (1991) 1 *Duke Journal of Comparative and International Law* 125

De Brabandere, Eric, 'Propaganda' in Rüdiger Wolfrum (ed), *Max Planck Encyclopedia of Public International Law* (November 2012), http://opil.ouplaw.com.ezproxy.is.ed.ac.uk/view/10.1093/law:epil/9780199231690/law-9780199231690-e978?rskey=MHLaNf&result=1&prd=EPIL, accessed 29 April 2015

Dembinski, Ludwik, *The Modern Law of Diplomacy: External Missions of States and International Organizations* (Dordrecht; London, Nijhoff, 1988)

Den Heijer, Maarten, 'Diplomatic Asylum and the Assange Case' (2013) 26 *Leiden Journal of International Law* 399

Denza, Eileen, *Diplomatic Law. Commentary on the Vienna Convention on Diplomatic Relations* (Oxford, Oxford University Press, 2008)

Dickinson, Rob, 'Twenty-First Century Self-Determination: Implications of the Kosovo Status Settlement for Tibet' (2009) *Arizona Journal of International and Comparative Law* 547

Dimitrijevic, Vojin, 'The Role of Reporting Procedures in Monitoring Violations of Human Rights' (1994) 6 *Sri Lanka Journal of International Law* 55–72

Do Nascimento e Silva, Geraldo Eulálio, *Diplomacy in International Law* (Leiden, AW Sijthoff, 1972) [Do Nascimento e Silva (1972)]

——, 'Diplomacy' in Rudolf Bernhardt (ed), *Encyclopedia of Public International Law, Volume 1* (Amsterdam; London; New York; Tokyo, Max-Planck-Institut für ausländisches öffentliches Recht und Völkerrecht, 1992) 1024 [Do Nascimento e Silva (1992a)]

——, 'Secret Diplomacy' in Rudolf Bernhardt (ed), *Encyclopedia of Public International Law, Volume 1* (Amsterdam; London; New York; Tokyo, Max-Planck-Institut für ausländisches öffentliches Recht und Völkerrecht, 1992) 1034 [Do Nascimento e Silva (1992b)]

Eick, Christophe, 'Protest' in Rüdiger Wolfrum (ed), *Max Planck Encyclopedia of Public International Law* (July 2006), http://opil.ouplaw.com.ezproxy.is.ed.ac.uk/view/10.1093/law:epil/9780199231690/law-9780199231690-e1460?rskey=0DEIfB&result=1&prd=EPIL, accessed 29 April 2015

Falk, Richard A, 'The United States and the Doctrine of Non-Intervention in the Internal Affairs of Independent States' (1959) 5 *Howard Law Journal* 163

Faundez, Julio, 'International Law and Wars of National Liberation: Use of Force and Intervention' (1989) 1 *African Journal of International and Comparative Law* 85

Fédération Internationale des Ligues des Droits de l'Homme; Euro-Mediterranean Human Rights Network *Freedom of Association and Human Rights Organisations in Egypt* (Copenhagen, May 1999) 19, http://www.euromedrights.org/files/emhrn-publications/Freedom-of-Association-and-Human-Rights-Organisations-in-Egypt.pdf, accessed 30 December 2014 [FIDH (1999)]

Field, Jeannie Rose, 'Bridging the Gap between Refugee Rights and Reality: A Proposal for Developing International Duties in the Refugee Context' (2010) 22 *International Journal of Refugee Law* 512

Fiore, Pasquale, 'International Law Codified and its Legal Sanction or The Legal Organization of the Society of States [extract] [EM Borchard tr]' (1932) 26 *American Journal of International Law Supplement* 153

Fischer, Horst, 'Diplomatische und konsularische Beziehungen' in Knut Ipsen (ed), *Völkerrecht* (Munich, CH Beck, 1984) 553

Focarelli, Carlo, 'Common Article 1 of the 1949 Geneva Conventions: A Soap Bubble?' (2010) 21 *European Journal of International Law* 125 [Focarelli (2010)]

——, 'The Responsibility to Protect Doctrine and Humanitarian Intervention: Too Many Ambiguities for a Working Doctrine' (2008) 13 *Journal of Conflict & Security Law* 193 [Focarelli (2008)]

Francis, Samuel, 'Critical Issues. The Soviet Strategy of Terror' (Washington DC, Heritage Foundation Reports, 1985)

Franck, Thomas M, 'On Proportionality of Countermeasures in International Law' (2008) 102 *American Journal of International Law* 715

Frank, Andrew U, 'Tiers of Ontology and Consistency Constraints in Geographical Information Systems' (2001) 15(7) *International Journal of Geographical Information Science* 667

Fruchterman, Richard L, 'Asylum: Theory and Practice' (1971–1972) 26 *Judge Advocate General Journal* 169

Fuhrmann, Gy, '"Prototypes" And "Fuzziness" In The Logic Of Concepts' (1988) 75(3) *Synthese* 317

García Barrón, Carlos, 'Enrique Dupuy de Lôme and the Spanish American War' (1979) 36(1) *The Americas* 39

Gardam, Judith Gail, 'Proportionality and Force in International Law' (1993) 87 *American Journal of International Law* 391

Gaxotte, Pierre, *Friedrich der Große* (Frankfurt etc, Ullstein, 1977)

Gelbard, Robert S, 'Respecting the Rule of Law and Human Rights in Indonesia' Speech delivered at the Trisakti University, Jakarta, 29 June 2000), http://www.hamline.edu/apakabar/basisdata/2000/07/02/0025.html [Gelbard (2000)]

Gentili, Alberico, *De Legationibus Libri Tres* (1594) (Gordon Laing tr, New York, 1924)

Gentzler, J Mason, *Changing China: Readings in the History of China from the Opium War to the Present* (New York, Praeger, 1977)

Giannakopoulou, Anastasia, 'Prototype Theory: An Evaluation,' (2003) 3 ECLOGA Working Papers, http://www.strath.ac.uk/ecloga/archive/2003/ecloga2003contents/, accessed 29 April 2015

Glahn, Gerhard von, *Law Among Nations* 1st edn (New York, Macmillan, 1965) [Glahn (1965)]

——, *Law Among Nations* 5th edn (New York, Macmillan; London, Collier Macmillan, 1986) [Glahn (1986)]

——, *Law Among Nations* 6th edn (New York, Macmillan; Toronto, Maxwell Macmillan, 1992) [Glahn (1992)]

—— and Taulbee, James Larry, *Law Among Nations* 8th edn (New York; London, Pearson Longman, 2007)

Gordon, Gregory S, 'Formulating a New Atrocity Speech Offense: Incitement To Commit War Crimes' (2012) 43 *Loyola University Chicago Law Journal* 281

Gore-Booth, Paul (ed), *Satow's Guide to Diplomatic Practice* 5th edn (London, Longman, 1979) [Satow (1979)]

Grant, Ulysses S, 'State of the Union Address, 4 December 1871' in John Y Simon (ed), *The Papers of Ulysses S Grant, Volume 22: June 1, 1871–January 31, 1872* (Carbondale, Southern Illinois University Press, 1998) 268

Green, Leslie C, 'Trends in the Law Concerning Diplomats' (1981) *The Canadian Yearbook of International Law* 132–57

Han, Xiuli, 'The Application of the Principle of Proportionality in Tecmed v Mexico' (2007) 6 *Chinese Journal of International Law* 635

Hardy, Michael, *Modern Diplomatic Law* (Manchester, Manchester University Press; New York, Oceana Publications, 1968)

Harkavy, Rachel, 'Picking our Battles: A Strategy for the United States in the Wake of Mexico's Becoming a State Party to the International Criminal Court' (2006) 40 *Georgia Law Review* 915.

Harrison, Graham, 'Democracy in Mozambique: The Significance of Multi-Party Elections' (1996) 23(67) *Review of African Political Economy* 19

Harvey, Philip, 'Human Rights and Economic Policy Discourse: Taking Economic and Social Rights Seriously' (2002) 33 *Columbia Human Rights Law Review* 363

Heintschel von Heinegg, Wolff, 'Die weiteren Quellen des Völkerrechts' in Knut Ipsen (ed), *Völkerrecht* (München, CH Beck, 2004)

Helms, Jesse, 'Remarks by Senator Jesse Helms to the US Security Council', 20 January 2000, http://www.fas.org/news/usa/2000/000120-un-usia1.htm, accessed 29 April 2015

Herbert, Alan Patrick, *Independent Member* (London, Howard Baker, 1970)

Herdegen, Matthias, 'The Abuse of Diplomatic Privileges and Countermeasures not Covered by the Vienna Convention on Diplomatic Relations' (1986) 46 *Zeitschrift für ausländisches öffentliches Recht und Völkerrecht* 734–57

Higgins, Pearce (ed), *Hall's International Law* (Oxford, Clarendon Press, 1924) [Hall (1924)]

Higgins, Rosalyn, 'Editorial Comments. The Abuse of Diplomatic Privileges and Immunities: Recent United Kingdom Experience' (1985) 79 *American Journal of International Law* 642 [Higgins (1985)]

Hill, Chesney, 'Sanctions Constraining Diplomatic Representatives to Abide by the Local Law' (1931) 25 *American Journal of International Law* 252–69

Hinckley, Ted C, 'George Osgoodby and the Murchison Letter' (1958) 27(4) *Pacific Historical Review* 359

Hoffman, Daniel N, 'Contempt of the United States: The Political Crime That Wasn't' (1981) 25 *American Journal of Legal History* 343–60

Human Rights and Equal Opportunities Commission (Australia), *A Last Resort? National Inquiry into Children in Immigration Detention* (Sydney, Australia 2004)

Human Rights Watch, 'Malaysia' in Human Rights Watch, *World Report 2009* (January 2009), http://www.hrw.org/world-report/2009/malaysia, accessed 8 December 2012

Hyde, Charles Cheney, *International Law Chiefly as Interpreted and Applied by the United States* (Boston, Little, Brown and Company, 1922)

ICISS Report: See International Commission on Intervention and State Sovereignty

ICRC Commentary: See Sandoz, Yves

ICRC State Parties: See International Committee of the Red Cross

Institute of International Law, *Resolution. Obligations and Rights Erga Omnes in International Law* (Krakow Session, 2005), http://www.idi-iil.org/idiE/resolutionsE/2005_kra_01_en.pdf, accessed 29 April 2015 [Institute of International Law (2005)]

——, *The Protection of Human Rights and the Principle of Non-Intervention in the Internal Affairs of States* (Session of Santiago de Compostella, 1989), http://www.idi-iil.org/idiE/resolutionsE/1989_comp_03_en.PDF, accessed 29 April 2015 [Institute of International Law (1989)]

International Commission on Intervention and State Sovereignty, *The Responsibility to Protect. Report* (Ottawa, December 2001), http://responsibilitytoprotect.org/ICISS%20Report.pdf, accessed 29 April 2015 [ICISS Report]

International Committee of the Red Cross, 'States Parties to the Following International Humanitarian Law and Other Related Treaties as of 13 April 2015' (13 April 2015), http://www.icrc.org/applic/ihl/dihl_setup.nsf/xsp/.ibmmodres/domino/OpenAttachment/applic/ihl/dihl_setup.nsf/6A9E93D954458967C1257DF100397C0C/%24File/IHL_and_other_related_Treaties.pdf?Open, accessed 29 April 2015 [ICRC State Parties]

International Detention Coalition, 'Captured Childhood' (Melbourne, Australia, 2012), http://idcoalition.org/wp-content/uploads/2012/03/Captured-Childhood-FINAL-June-2012.pdf, accessed 29 April 2015

Ioannou, Krateros, 'Propaganda' in Rudolf Bernhardt (ed), *Encyclopedia of Public International Law, Volume 3* (Amsterdam; Lausanne; New York; Oxford; Shannon; Singapore; Tokyo, Max-Planck-Institut für ausländisches öffentliches Recht und Völkerrecht, 1997) 1135

Ipsen, Knut (ed), *Völkerrecht* (Munich, CH Beck, 2004)

Jacobs, Francis G, Ovey, Clare, White, Robin, *Jacobs and White: European Convention on Human Rights* 3rd edn (Oxford, Oxford University Press, 2002)

Jeffery, Anthea J, 'Diplomatic Asylum: Its Problems and Potential as a Means of Protecting Human Rights' (1985) 1 *South African Journal on Human Rights* 10

Jenks, Wilfred, 'The Conflict of Law-Making Treaties' (1953) 30 *British Yearbook of International Law* 401

Jennings, Robert and Watts, Arthur (eds), *Oppenheim's International Law* (Harlow, Longman, 1992) [Oppenheim (1992)]

Johnson, RK, 'Prototype Theory, Cognitive Linguistics and Pedagogical Grammar' (1985) 8 *Working Papers in Linguistics and Language Training* 12

Karmon, Ely, 'The Demise of Radical Islam in Turkey' (International Policy Institute for Counter-Terrorism, 3 June 2000), http://www.ict.org.il/articles/articledet.cfm?articleid=130 [Karmon (2000)]

Kästner, Erich, 'Fabian. Die Geschichte eines Moralisten' in Franz Josef Görtz (ed), *Erich Kästner. Werke, Band III, Romane I,* (Munich; Vienna, Carl Hanser, 1998) 7

Kearney, Michael G, 'Propaganda for War' in Rüdiger Wolfrum (ed), *Max Planck Encyclopedia of Public International Law* (May 2009), http://opil.ouplaw.com.ezproxy.is.ed.ac.uk/view/10.1093/law:epil/9780199231690/law-9780199231690-

e384?rskey=qY5cdy&result=2&prd=EPIL, accessed 30 April 2015 [Kearney (2009)]

——, *The Prohibition of Propaganda for War in International Law* (Oxford, Oxford University Press, 2007) [Kearney (2007)]

Kielsgard, Mark D, 'War on the International Criminal Court' (2005) 8 *New York City Law Review* 1

Kim, Paul, 'Between Principles and Absolutes: Non-Lethal Weapons and the Law of Armed Conflict' in Fraunhofer Institute for Chemical Technology (ed), *Non-Lethal Capabilities Facing Emerging Threats* (Pfinztal, 2003) 2-1

King, Toby, 'Human Rights in European Foreign Policy: Success or Failure for Post-modern Diplomacy?' (1999) 10(2) *European Journal of International Law* 313

Ko, Swan Sik, 'Netherlands State Practice for the Parliamentary Year 1969–1970. Functions of a Diplomatic Mission' (1971) 2 *Netherlands Yearbook of International Law*

Kornbluh, Peter, 'Chile 1964: CIA cover support in Frei election detailed; operational and policy records released for first time', *George Washington University, The National Security Archive* (25 September 2004, updated 27 September 2004), http://www2.gwu.edu/~nsarchiv/news/20040925/, accessed 30 April 2015

Kunig, Philip, 'Intervention, Prohibition of' in Rüdiger Wolfrum (ed), *Max Planck Encyclopedia of Public International Law* (April 2008), http://opil.ouplaw.com.ezproxy.is.ed.ac.uk/view/10.1093/law:epil/9780199231690/law-9780199231690-e1434?rskey=3WJI2y&result=1&prd=EPIL, accessed 30 April 2015

Labov, William 'The Boundaries of Words and their Meanings' in Charles James Nice Bailey and Roger W Shuy (eds), *New Ways of Analyzing Variation in English* (Washington, Georgetown University Press, 1973) 340

Laplante, Lisa J, 'The Domestication of International Criminal Law: A Proposal for Expanding the International Criminal Court's Sphere of Influence' (2010) 43 *The John Marshall Law Review* 635

LaRousse Dictionnaire Français Online (online version 2014), http://www.larousse.com/en/dictionaries/french/s_immiscer/41709?q=immiscer#41614, accessed 28 December 2014

Lauterpacht, Hersch, *International Law and Human Rights* (London, Stevens, 1950) [Lauterpacht (1950)]

—— (ed), *Oppenheim's International Law [International Law. A Treatise. Vol 1: Peace]* (8th edn (London, Longmans, 1967) [Oppenheim (1967)]

LeCarré, John, *The Honourable Schoolboy* (London, Hodder and Stoughton, 1994)

Lillich, Richard, 'Civil Rights' in Theodor Meron (ed), *Human Rights in International Law: Legal and Policy Issues* (Oxford, Clarendon Press, 1984) 115

Linderfalk, Ulf, 'The Effect of Jus Cogens Norms: Whoever Opened Pandora's Box, Did You Ever Think about the Consequences?' (2007) 18 *European Journal of International Law* 853

Linton, Suzannah and Tiba, Firew Kebede, 'The International Judge in an Age of Multiple International Courts and Tribunals' (2009) 9 *Chicago Journal of International Law* 407

Lorek, Ann; Ehntholt, Kimberly; Nesbitt, Anne; Wey, Emmanuel; Githinji, Chipo; Rossor, Eve and Wickramasinghe, Rush, 'The Mental and Physical Health Difficulties of Children Held within a British Immigration Detention Center: A Pilot Study' (2009) 33 *Child Abuse and Neglect* 573

Lowitt, Richard, 'Activities of Citizen Genet in Kentucky, 1793–1794' (1948) 22 *Filson Historical Club Quarterly* 252

MacGibbon, Iain C, 'Some Observations on the Part of Protest in International Law' (1953) 30 *British Yearbook of International Law* 293

Magalonna, Merlin M, 'The Concept of Jus Cogens in the Vienna Convention on the Law of the Treaties' (1976) 51 *Philippine Law Journal* 521–42

Magnuson, William, 'The Responsibility to Protect and the Decline of Sovereignty: Free Speech Protection under International Law' (2010) 43 *Vanderbilt Journal of Transnational Law* 255

Mahoney, Liam and Eguren, Luis Enrique, 'International Accompaniment for the Protection of Human Rights: Scenarios, Objectives and Strategies' (1996) 11 *Institute for Conflict Analysis and Resolution, George Mason University, Working Paper* 43

Matheson, Michael J, 'The Fifty-Eighth Session of the International Law Commission' (2007) 101 *American Journal of International Law* 407

Mazzeschi, Riccardo Pisillo, 'Enzo Cannizzaro, Il principio della proporzionalità nell'ordinamento internazionale [The principle of proportionality in international Law, Giuffrè 2000]' (2002) 13 *European Journal of International Law* 1031

Mendelson, Maurice H, 'The Formation of Customary International Law' (1998) 272 *Recueil des Cours* 155 (Reprint, The Hague, Boston, London, Martinus Nijhoff, 1999) [Mendelson (1998)]

Menge, Hermann, *Menge-Güthling. Langenscheidts Großwörterbuch der lateinischen und deutschen Sprache* (Berlin; München; Zürich, Langenscheidt, 1967)

Merriam Webster (online version 2014), http://www.merriam-webster.com/

Merriman, Roger Bigelow, 'The Spanish Embassy in Tudor England' (1932–1936) 65 *Proceedings of the Massachusetts Historical* Society 391

Milanović, Marko, 'Norm Conflict in International Law: Whither Human Rights?' (2009) 20 *Duke Journal of Comparative and International Law* 69

Miller, Robert Hopkins, 'Gathering Political Information' in Miller, Robert Hopkins (ed), *Inside an Embassy: The Political Role of Diplomats Abroad* (Washington DC, CQ Press, 1992) 16

Mookerjee, Girija Kanta, *Diplomacy: Theory and History, Vol I* (New Delhi, Trimurti Publications, 1973)

Moore, John Bassett, *A Digest of International Law, Vol IV* (Washington DC, United States Government Printing Office, 1906)

Mukharji, Prasanta Bihari, *The Modern Trends of Diplomatic Law* (Calcutta, Eastern Law House, 1973)

Murray, Craig, *Murder in Samarkand* (Edinburgh, Mainstream, 2006)

Murty, Bhagevatula Satyanarayana, *The International Law of Diplomacy. The Diplomatic Instrument and Public World Order* (New Haven; Dordrecht; Boston; London, Martinus Nijhoff, 1989)

Musgrave, Thomas D, *Self-Determination and National Minorities* (Oxford, Clarendon Press, 1997)

Nash, Marian Leigh, *Digest of United States Practice in International Law* (Washington DC, United States Government Printing Office, 1980)

Ni, Kuei-Jung, 'Third-State Countermeasures for Enforcing International Common Environmental Interests: The Implication and Inspiration of the ILC's Articles on State Responsibility' (2004) 22 *Chinese (Taiwan) Yearbook of International Law and Affairs* 1

Offner, John, 'Why Did the United States Fight Spain in 1898?' (1998) 12(3) *Organization of American Historians Magazine of History* 19

Ohman, Magnus 'Political Finance Regulations Around the World. An Overview of the International IDEA Database', International Institute for Democracy and Electoral Assistance (IDEA) (Stockholm, 2012), http://www.idea.int/publications/political-finance-regulations/upload/Political-Finance-Regulations-Overview-of-IDEA-database.pdf, accessed 29 April 2015

Okoronkwo, Pius L, 'Self-Determination and the Legality of Biafra's Secession under International Law' (2002) 25 *Loyola of Los Angeles International and Comparative Law Review* 63

Oxford English Dictionary (Oxford University Press, online version 2014), http://www.oed.com [OED]

Oppenheim (1967): See Lauterpacht, Hersch (ed)

Oppenheim (1992): See Jennings, Robert; Watts, Arthur (eds)

Packham, Eric S, *Freedom and Anarchy* (Commack, New York, Nova Science Publishers, 1996)

Palmer, Gary B, '"Where There Are Muskrats": The Semantic Structure of Coeur d'Alene Place Names' (1990) 32 (3/4) *Anthropological Linguistics* 263

Pan American Union, 'Codification of American International Law: Projects of Conventions prepared at the request on January 2, 1924, of the Governing Board of the Pan American Union for the consideration of the International Commission of Jurists, and submitted by the American Institute of International Law to the Governing Board of the Pan American Union, March 2, 1925' (1932) 26 *American Journal of International Law Supplement* 168

Panhuys, Haro Frederik van; Heere, Wybo P; Jitta, JW Josephus; Ko, Swan Sik, and Stuyt, Alexander M, *International Law in the Netherlands, Volume 3* (Alphen aan den Rijn, Sijthoff & Noordhoff, 1980)

Parker, Karen and Neylon, Lyn Beth, '*Jus Cogens*: Compelling the Law of Human Rights' (1988–1989) 12 *Hastings International & Comparative Law Review* 411

Parkerson, John Embry, 'United States Compliance with Humanitarian Law Respecting Civilians During Operation Just Cause' (1991) 133 *Military Law Review* 31

Parris, Matthew and Bryson, Andrew, *Parting Shots* (London, Viking, 2011)

Pavel, Carmen, 'Normative Conflict in International Law' (2009) 46 *San Diego Law Review* 883

Pfister, Roger, 'Gateway to International Victory: The Diplomacy of the African National Congress in Africa, 1960–1994' (2003) 41(1) *The Journal of Modern African Studies* 51

Phillimore, Walter, 'Proposed Codification of the Law Regarding the Representation of States [extract] [1926]' (1932) 26 *American Journal of International Law Supplement* 177

Plischke, Elmer, *Conduct of American Diplomacy* (Princeton NJ, Van Nostrand, 1967)

Porcino, Peter, 'Toward Codification of Diplomatic Asylum' (1975–1976) 8 *New York University Journal of International Law and Politics* 435

Przetacznik, Franciszek, 'Les dévoirs de l'agent diplomatique à l'égard de l'état accréditaire' (1975) 53 *Revue de droit international de sciences diplomatiques et politiques* 291 [Przetacznik (1975)]

——, 'Les dévoirs de l'agent diplomatique à l'égard de l'état accréditaire' (1976) 54 *Revue de droit international de sciences diplomatiques et politiques* 57 [Przetacznik (1976)]

Reeves, Jesse S (Reporter), 'Diplomatic Privileges and Immunities' (1932) 26 *American Journal of International Law Supplement* 15

Regala, Roberto, *The Trends in Modern Diplomatic Practice* (Milan, A Giuffré; New York, Oceana Publications, 1959)

Reisman, W Michael, 'The Resistance in Afghanistan is Engaged in a War of National Liberation' (1987) 81 *American Journal of International Law* 906

Reitano, Joanne R, *The Tariff Question in the Gilded Age: The Great Debate of 1888* (University Park, The Pennsylvania State University, 1994)

Reiter, Randy B; Zunzunegui, MV, and Quiroga, Jose, 'Guidelines for Field Reporting of Basic Human Rights Violations' (1986) 8 *Human Rights Quarterly* 628

Revue belge de droit international, 'La pratique du pouvoir executif et le contrôle des chambres legislatives en matière de droit international' (1969) (1976) [*RBDI*, 'La pratique belge']

Revue générale de droit international public, 'Chronique des faits internationaux' (1963), (1964), (1965), (1968), (1969), (1973), (1976), (1977), (1978), (1984) [RGDIP]

Richtsteig, Michael, *Wiener Übereinkommen über diplomatische und konsularische Beziehungen. Entstehungsgeschichte, Kommentierung, Praxis* (Baden-Baden, Nomos, 1994)

Riveles, Susanne 'Diplomatic Asylum as a Human Right: The Case of the Durban Six' (1989) 11 *Human Rights Quarterly* 139

Roberts, Ivor (ed), *Satow's Diplomatic Practice* (Oxford; New York, Oxford University Press, 2009) [Satow (2009)]

Rosch, Eleanor, 'Cognitive Representations of Semantic Categories' (1975) 104(3) *Journal of Experimental Psychology. General* 192

Rousseau, Charles, *Droit International Public. Tome IV. Les relations internationales* (Paris, Sirey, 1980)

Rummel, Rudolph J, 'Statistics of Democide: Genocide and Mass Murder since 1900' (Münster, Lit Verlag, 1998)

Sadat-Akhavi, Seyed Ali, *Methods of Resolving Conflicts between Treaties* (Leiden; Boston, Martinus Nijhoff, 2003)

Salmon, Jean, *Fonctions diplomatiques, consulaires et internationales. Tome I* (Brussels, Presses universitaires de Bruxelles, 1976) [Salmon (1976)]

——, 'Internal Aspects of the Right to Self-Determination: Towards a Democratic Legitimacy Principle?' in Christian Tomuschat (ed), *Modern Law of Self-Determination* (Dordrecht; Boston; London; Martinus Nijhoff, 1993) 253 [Salmon (1993)]

——, *Manuel de Droit Diplomatique* (Brussels, Edition Delta, 1996) [Salmon (1996)]

Sandoz, Yves; Swinarski, Christophe and Zimmermann, Bruno, *Commentary on the Additional Protocols of 8 June 1977 to the Geneva Conventions of 12 August 1949* (Geneva, Martinus Nijhoff, 1987) [ICRC Commentary]

Sanei, Faraz, 'The Caspian Sea Legal Regime, Pipeline Diplomacy and the Prospects for Iran's Isolation from the Oil and Gas Frenzy: Reconciling Tehran's Legal Options with its Geopolitical Realities' (2001) 34 *Vanderbilt Journal of Transnational Law* 681

Sarkissian, Raffi, 'The Armenian Genocide: A Contextual View of the Crime and Politics of Denial' in Ralph Henham and Paul Behrens (eds), *The Criminal Law of Genocide* (Aldershot, Ashgate, 2007) 3

Satow (1917): See Satow, Ernest

Satow (1964): See Bland, Nevile (ed)

Satow (1979): See Gore-Booth, Paul (ed)

Satow (2009): See Roberts, Ivor (ed)

Satow, Ernest, *A Guide to Diplomatic Practice, Volume 1* (London, New York, Bombay, Calcutta; Longmans, Green, 1917) [Satow (1917)]

Saul, Ben, *Defining Terrorism in International Law* (Oxford, Oxford University Press, 2010)

Schröder, Meinhard, 'Nonintervention, Principle of' in Rudolf Bernhardt (ed), *Encyclopedia of Public International Law, Volume 3* (Amsterdam; Lausanne; New York; Oxford; Shannon; Singapore; Tokyo, Max-Planck-Institut für ausländisches öffentliches Recht und Völkerrecht, 1997) 619

Seidmann, Gay W, 'Blurred Lines: Nonviolence in South Africa' (2000) 33(2) *PS: Political Science and Politics* 161

Sen, Biswanath, *A Diplomat's Handbook of International Law and Practice* (The Hague, Martinus Nijhoff, 1965) [Sen (1965)]

——, *A Diplomat's Handbook of International Law and Practice* (Dordrecht; London, Martinus Nijhoff) 1988 [Sen (1988)]

Sforza, Julie M, 'The Timor Gap Dispute: The Validity of the Timor Gap Treaty, Self-Determination and Decolonization' (1999) 22 *Suffolk Transnational Law Review* 481

Shaw, Malcolm, *International Law* (Cambridge, Cambridge University Press, 2008)

Shelton, Dinah, 'Normative Hierarchy in International Law' (2006) 100 *American Journal of International Law* 291 [Shelton (2006)]

Shewmaker, Kenneth E; Stevens, Kenneth R and Berolzheimer, Alan R (eds), *The Papers of Daniel Webster. Diplomatic Papers, Vol 2 1850–1852* (London, University Press of New England, 1987)

Shurshalov, Vladimir Mikhailovich, *Osnovaniia deistvitel'nosti mezhdunarodnykh dogovorov* (Moscow, Izd-vo Akademii Nauk SSSR, 1957)

Simon, Sheldon W, 'The United States and Southeast Asia: Blowing Hot and Cold', (Center for Strategic and International Studies, issue December 2000), http://www.csis.org/pacfor/cc/004Qus_asean.html [Simon (2000)]

Sinha, S Prakash, *Asylum and International Law* (The Hague, Martinus Nijhoff, 1971)

Skogly, Sigrun I, 'Human Rights Reporting: The 'Nordic' Experience' (1990) 12 *Human Rights Quarterly* 513

Sloane, Robert D, 'The Policies of State Succession: Harmonizing Self-Determination and Global Order in the Twenty-First Century. Review of Tai-Heng Cheng, State Succession and Commercial Obligations' (2007) 30 *Fordham International Law Journal* 1288

Smith, Frederick E, Earl of Birkenhead (Ronw Moelwyn-Hughes, ed), *International Law* (London; Toronto, J.M Dent, 1927)

Sohn, Louis B, 'The New International Law: Protection of the Rights of Individuals rather than States' (1982) 32 *American University Law Review* 1

Stowell, Ellery Cory, *Intervention in International Law* (Washington DC, J Bryne, 1921)

Strupp, Karl, 'Les règles générales du droit de la paix' (1934) 47 *Recueil des cours* 259 [Strupp (1934)]

——, *Urkunden zur Geschichte des Völkerrechts. Band I. Bis zum Berliner Kongreß (1878)* (Gotha, FA Perthes, 1911) [Strupp (1911)]

—— and Schlochauer, Hans Jürgen, *Wörterbuch des Völkerrechts, Band 2* (Berlin, De Gruyter, 1960–1962) [Strupp and Schlochauer]

Sudan Divestment Task Force, *PetroChina, CNPC, and Sudan: Perpetuating Genocide* (15 April 2007), http://home.comcast.net/~berkshire_hathaway/reports/PetroChina_CNPC_Sudan.pdf, accessed 23 December 2011

Szilassy, Julius, *Traité pratique de diplomatie moderne* (Paris, Peyot, 1928)

Taylor, John R, 'Prototype Theory' in Maienborn, Claudia; Leusinger, Klaus von, and Pornter, Paul H (eds), *Semantics: An International Handbook of Natural Language Meaning, Vol 1* (Berlin, DeGruyter, 2011) 643–64

Thornberry, Patrick, 'The Democratic or Internal Aspect of Self-Determination with some remarks on Federalism' in Christian Tomuschat (ed), *Modern Law of Self-Determination* (Dordrecht; Boston; London, Martinus Nijhoff, 1993) 101

Thürer, Daniel, 'Self-Determination' in Rudolf Bernhardt (ed), *Encyclopedia of Public International Law, Volume 4* (Amsterdam; London; New York; Oxford; Paris; Shannon; Tokyo, Max-Planck-Institut für ausländisches öffentliches Recht und Völkerrecht, 2000) 364

Triska, Jan F and Slusser, Robert M, 'Treaties and Other Sources of Order in International Relations: The Soviet View' (1958) 52 *American Journal of International Law* 699

Tröndle, Herbert, *Strafgesetzbuch und Nebengesetze* (Munich, CH Beck, 1997)

Tsevelekos, Vassilis P, 'The Use of Article 31(3)(c) of the VCLT in the Case Law of the ECtHR: An Effective Anti-Fragmentation Tool or a Selective Loophole for the Reinforcement of Human Rights Teleology?' (2010) 31 *Michigan Journal of International Law* 621

Udombana, Nsongurua J, 'Toward the African Court on Human and Peoples' Rights: Better Late Than Never' (2000) 3 *Yale Human Rights and Development Law Journal* 45

Van den Herik, Larissa, 'A Quest for Jurisdiction and an Appropriate Definition of Crime. Mpambara before the Dutch Courts' (2009) 7 *Journal of International Criminal Justice* 1117

Van der Vyver, Johan D, 'Self-Determination of the Peoples of Quebec under International Law' (2000) 10 *Journal of Transnational Law and Policy* 1

Värk, René, 'Diplomatic Asylum and the Assange Case' (2012) 11 *Proceedings of the Estonian Academy of Security Sciences* 240

——, 'Personal Inviolability and Diplomatic Immunity in Respect of Serious Crimes' (2003) VIII *Juridica International* 110

Verdross, Alfred and Simma, Bruno, *Universelles Völkerrecht. Theorie und Praxis* (Berlin, Duncker & Humblot, 1984)

Wagner, Niklas; Raasch, Holger and Pröpstl, Thomas, *Wiener Übereinkommen über diplomatische Beziehungen vom 18 April 1961. Kommentar für die Praxis* (Berlin, Berliner Wissenschafts-Verlag, 2007)

Wall, Ashley C, 'The Money of Politics: Financing American and British Elections' (1997) 5 *Tulane Journal of International and Comparative Law* 489–519

Wheatley, Steven, 'Democracy in International Law: A European Perspective' (2002) 51 *International and Comparative Law Quarterly* 225

Whiteman, Marjorie M, *Digest of International Law, Vol 6* (Washington DC, United States Government Printing Office, 1968) [Whiteman (1968)]

——, *Digest of International Law, Vol 7* (Washington DC, United States Government Printing Office, 1970) [Whiteman (1970)]

Wolff, Christian, *Jus Gentium Methodo Scientifica Pertractatum* (1764) (Joseph H Drake tr, Oxford, Clarendon Press, 1934)

Woodward, Bob, *Plan of Attack* (New York; London; Toronto; Sydney, Simon and Schuster, 2004)

Wright, Quincy, 'Intervention and Cuba in 1961' (1961) 55 *American Society of International Law Proceedings* 2 [Q Wright]

Yakembe, Yoko, *Traité de droit diplomatique* (Kinshasa, Presses Universitaires du Zaire, 1983)

Young, Eileen, 'The Development of the Law of Diplomatic Relations' (1964) 40 *British Yearbook of International Law* 141

Zeitschrift für ausländisches öffentliches Recht und Völkerrecht, 'Berichte und Urkunden. Völkerrechtliche Praxis der Bundesrepublik Deutschland in den Jahren 1967 und 1968' (1970), 651 [ZaöRV, 'Berichte und Urkunden']

Zelniker, Lindsay, 'Towards a Functional International Criminal Court: An Argument in Favour of a Strong Privileges and Immunities Agreement' (2001) 24 *Fordham International Law Journal* 988

Zemanek, Karl, 'The Legal Foundations of the International System. General course on Public International Law' (1997) 266 *Recueil des Cours* 9 [Zemanek (1997)]

NEWS MEDIA

AAP Newsfeed, 'Fed: Downer Tips Change in Region's Attitude to Zimbabwe', 21 March 2007

——, 'Vic: Melbourne Man Injured in Violent Bangkok Demonstrations', 23 April 2010

Accra Mail, 'Ghana; Government Asked to Privatise GCB And GCAA', 16 April 2001

Advertiser, The, 'Fiji tells Indian Envoys to Leave', 24 May 1990

Afghan Islamic Press (AIP), 'Poll Candidates Warn against "Political Deal"', 2 August 2011

Age, The, 'Argentina May Expel U.S. Envoy', 3 August 1973

Agence France Presse, 'Une expulsion d'ambassadeurs isolerait davantage le Zimbabwe (Paris)', 22 March 2007

Agence France Presse—English, 'Angry Kenya Lashes out at EU Aid Cut Threat', 26 October 2005

——, 'Bahrain Seeks to End US Envoy "Interference"', 5 May 2013

——, 'Britain Backs Envoy over Iran Remarks', 13 December 2010

——, 'British Envoy Embroiled in Sri Lanka Media Crisis', 19 April 2007

——, 'Canada Warns Iran Diplomats Against Recruiting Expats', 11 July 2012

——, 'Chief Legislator Accuses Washington of Meddling in Indonesian Politics', 29 October 1999

——, 'EU set to Punish Ivory Coast', 13 December 2010

——, 'Expelled British Envoy to Leave within 10 Days', 31 May 1991
——, 'Foreigners behind Afghan Parliament Crisis: Karzai', 25 January 2011
——, 'Germany Rankled by US Ambassador Nominee's Comments on Defense: Report', 3 August 2001
——, 'Ghana Warns against Foreign Interference in Elections', 28 November 2000
——, 'Indonesia Probes Foreign Involvement in Unrest', 17 October 2000
——, 'Kenyan President Accuses Britain of Interference', 4 October 2002
——, 'Kenya's Moi Accuses Germany of Interference in Domestic Affairs', 26 October 2002
——, 'Kenya's Moi tells British Envoy to "Keep Off" Reform Process', 15 April 2001
——, 'Lithuania Expels Russian Diplomat', 11 October 2006
——, 'Lula urges African Union to Denounce Honduras Coup', 1 July 2009
——, 'Mahathir Blasts Opposition for Allegedly Seeking Foreign Aid in Election', 26 November 1999
——, 'Malawi Agrees to Allow British Envoy to Return', 14 October 2011
——, 'Malawi Court Re-instates Diplomat Sacked OverAnti-Mugabe Remarks', 25 May 2001
——, 'Minister says Indonesia Caught US "Inflitrator" in Troubled Irian Jaya', 23 October 2000
——, 'Namibian Government Admits Atrocities in Caprivi', 12 August 1999
——, 'Newly Appointed Honduras Leader Orders 48-hour Curfew', 29 June 2009
——, 'Saudi Official says London Envoy caused no trouble, may be further promoted', 19 September 2002
——, 'Spanish Embassy, Under Siege, Vows Business as Usual in Cuba', 27 November 1996
——, 'Sri Lanka Editor Faces Death Threat', 18 April 2007
——, 'Sri Lanka Threatens to Expel Diplomats', 18 April 2007
——, 'Sri Lanka Warns US Over Allegations in WikiLeaks Cables', 21 December 2010
——, 'Stand-off Continues in Bangkok as FM Offers Olive Branch', 12 April 2010
——, 'State Department and D'Amato Denounce Swiss Ambassador's Comments', 27 January 1997
——, 'Stop the Insults, Jordan Warns Syria Envoy', 6 June 2013
——, 'Tanzania Government Issues Formal Protest to US Envoy', 9 June 2000
——, 'Thai Authorities say One Dead in Grenade Blasts', 23 April 2010
——, 'Thai FM Draws Fence around "Internal Affair"', 29 April 2010
——, 'Turkey tells US Envoy to Stop Meddling in its Affairs', 7 February 2013
——, 'Uganda, Rwanda Expel Low-ranking Diplomats', 26 November 2004
——, '"Unacceptable" Overseas Interference Over Expelled Envoy: Gambia', 30 August 2001
——, 'UN Security Council Delegation to Visit Indonesia', 25 September 2000
——, 'US Ambassador Accused of Meddling in Kenya's Internal Affairs', 16 February 1995
——, 'US Envoy Intervenes to Try to Save Syrian Peace Talks', 26 July 1995
——, 'US Envoy Sets Economic Targets for Post-election Bangladesh', 16 May 2001
——, 'US Envoy to Lebanon Summoned over "Interference"', 17 January 2011
——, 'US Rejects Charges of Meddling in Burma', 2 October 1996
——, 'WikiLeaks says Published all US Cables on Internet', 2 September 2011

——, 'Zimbabwe's Australia Ambassador Unrepentant over Howard Dictator Remarks', 11 December 2003

Agence France Presse—German, '"Spiegel": Zwei Bundespolizisten zur Sicherheit aus Iran abgezogen; Nach Berichten über angebliche Festnahme deutscher Diplomaten', 31 January 2010

Akinterinwa, Bola A, 'Nigeria, Cote d'Ivoire. Tango over Asylum-seekers', *This Day, (Lagos)*, 8 October 2000

Al-Ahram Weekly, 'Lawyer Sues Welch', 12–18 June 2003, http://weekly.ahram.org.eg/2003/642/eg2.htm

AlArabiya.net, 'US Rejects Syrian Allegation that Ambassador Incited Hama Protests', 8 July 2011

Aleman, Filadelfo, 'U.S. Ambassador to Nicaragua Defends his Right to Weigh in on Country's Politics', *The Associated Press*, 21 April 2006

——, 'U.S. official: Nicaraguan Voters Face Stark Choices in November Election', *The Associated Press*, 27 April 2006

Alexander, Cathy, 'FED: Gillard Protests Fiji Envoy's Expulsion', *AAP Newsfeed*, 13 July 2010

Allen, Robin, 'More Detained in Bahrain Unrest: Crackdown on Shia Dissidents Leads to 41 Further Arrests', *Financial Times* (London), 5 February 1996

Alleyne, Richard, 'WikiLeaks: Julian Assange will take Britain to the "World Court" if it does not Allow him to Travel to Ecuador', *Daily Telegraph*, 17 August 2012

Amiel, Barbara, 'Islamists Overplay their Hand but London Salons don't See it', *The Daily Telegraph* (London), 17 December 2001

Anadolu Agency (AA), 'Jordan to Expel Syrian Ambassador within Days, MP tells AA', 16 January 2014

Antara—The Indonesian National News Agency, 'House Commission urges Foreign Ministry to Summon US Envoy', 28 September 2000

——, 'Indonesia: Foreign Ministry asks US Envoy to Clarify his Statements', 8 September 2000

——, 'Indonesia: US Embassy Denies American Arrested in Irian Jaya was Spy', 23 October 2000

Arnold, Michael, 'US Envoy Hit Over Remarks On Jerusalem. Indyk: No Solution But To Share City', *Forward*, c 22 September 2000, http://www.forward.com/issues/2000/00.09.22/news3.html

Arostegui, Martin, 'Morales puts U.S. Diplomat in Sights; Says Envoy Funds Rivals', *The Washington Times*, 28 November 2007

Asian News International (ANI), '"Racist" US Diplomat Expelled from India in Devyani Row called "Vegetarians Rapists"', 16 January 2014

Associated Press Online, 'Iraqi PM says he won't Allow US to Meddle in Vote', 5 February 2010

——, 'Myanmar Accuses West of Instigating', 5 September 2000

Associated Press, The, 'China Lashes Out at Britain for "Interfering" in Hong Kong', 7 May 1998

——, 'Egyptian Paper says US Ambassador "Influenced by Jewish Notions"', 16 January 1998

——, 'Envoy Goes Home to Havana At Request of New Leader', 3 November 1980

——, 'Ex-Duvalier Police Chief Granted Asylum in Brazil', 24 February 1986

——, 'Fiji Expels Australia's Top Diplomat', 13 July 2010

——, 'International News', 16 September 1998

——, 'International News. San Jose, Costa Rica', 20 August 1979

——, 'New Zealand Boots Soviet Ambassador', 23 January 1980

——, 'Outgoing U.S. Ambassador in Bahamas Urges Island Chain to Sign Treaty to Protect Americans from Hague-based Court', 10 June 2003

——, 'Report: CIA Funded Chilean Parties', 13 November 2000

——, 'Romania, Hungary Feud Over Diplomat's Detention', 18 November 1988

——, 'Section: International News', 9 December 1995

——, 'Tunisia Breaks Relations With Iran', 26 March 1987

——, 'U.S. Ambassador in Controversy Over Irish Elections', 27 May 1981

——, 'US Ambassador to Mexico Quits amid WikiLeaks Furor', 20 March 2011

——, 'U.S. Envoy Irks Kenya's President With Calls for Political Change', 5 May 1990

——, 'US Envoy Recalled to Consult on Diplomat's Expulsion', 30 May 1982

——, 'U.S. Expels Libyan Diplomats', 5 May 1980

——, 'US Rejects Burmese Charges of Interference', 2 October 1996

Associated Press—German, The, 'Peruanischer Praesident Fujimori muss sich Stichwahl stellen', 13 April 2000

Atkinson, P, 'Vanuatu Dumps Aussie', *Sunday Mail (Australia)*, 5 July 1992

Australian Associated Press, 'Fed: Aust Diplomat Expelled from Solomons', 13 September 2006

——, 'Fed: Govt Must Quickly Investigate Solomon Expulsion: Greens', 13 September 2006

Australian Broadcasting Corporation, '"... About Woomera", Four Corners Programme', 19 May 2003, http://www.abc.net.au/4corners/content/2003/transcripts/s858341.htm, accessed 30 April 2015

——, '"The Guard's Story", Four Corners Programme', 15 September 2008, http://www.abc.net.au/4corners/content/2008/s2365139.htm, accessed 30 April 2015

Australian, The, 'Cubans Expel Czech "for Spying"', 17 April 2006

Azeri Press Agency (APA), 'Cambodian Gov't Warns Foreign Diplomats not to Interfer [sic] in Internal Affairs over Election Dispute', 25 September 2013

Bahrain News Agency (BNA), 'Foreign Minister Holds Meeting with Parliament's Foreign Affairs, Defence and National Security Committee', 19 July 2012

——, 'US Ambassador to Harare seized by security forces', 14 October 2005

Balouny, Lisette, 'Section: International News', *The Associated Press*, 16 September 1981

Baltic News Service, 'Russian Embassy in Tallinn Denies Giving Instructions to Extremists', 18 May 2007

Ball, James, 'UK Blocked $60m Arms Deal over Fears of Iran Link: Firm Refused Licence for Sale to Swaziland in 2008 WikilLeaks Cable Spells Out Possible Destinations', *The Guardian*, 24 February 2011

Balz, Dan, 'A Lengthy Stay for 2 Chinese Dissidents?', *The Washington Post*, 13 June 1989

Barasa, Lucas, 'Criticism That Rubbed Officials The Wrong Way', *The Nation (Kenya)*, 3 February 2005

Barber, Lionel and Coone, Tim, 'Washington Expels Nicaraguan Ambassador In Retaliatory Move', *Financial Times* (London), 13 July 1988

Barkham, Patrick, 'PM Calls Asylum Protest Blackmail: Aborigines Throw their Weight behind Afghan Hunger Strikers', *The Guardian* (London), 26 January 2002

Barriaux, Marianne, 'China Dissident Jailed for 11 years for Subversion', *Agence France Presse—English*, 25 December 2009

BBC Monitoring Africa—Political (Financial Gazette, Zimbabwe, 22 March 2007), 'Foreign Diplomats in Zimbabwe said "Unfazed" by Expulsion Threats', 22 March 2007

——, (*MBC Radio, Malawi, 29 March 2006*), 'Malawi Cautions Diplomats to Follow "Established Channels"', 29 March 2006

——, (*Media Monitoring Project Zimbabwe, Harare, 17 November 2005*), 'Zimbabwe Media Watchdog's Weekly Report for 10–17 November', 18 November 2005.

——, (*Radio France Internationale, Paris, 13 December 2010*), 'French Minister Denies Interference in Cote d'Ivoire's Affairs', 13 December 2010

——, (*Sunday Standard web site, Nairobi,* 2 December 2001), 'Kenya: Paper Analyses why British Envoy was Rebuked by President Moi', 2 December 2001

——, (*The Guardian, Dar es Salaam, Tanzania, 17 September 2013*), 'Tanzania's Opposition Raps Chinese Envoy for Attending Ruling Party's Rally', 17 September 2013

——, (*The People, Kenya, 5 September 2007*), 'Britain to Remain Impartial in Kenya's General Elections—Envoy', 5 September 2007

——, (*The Post website, Lusaka, Zambia, 10 May 2012*), 'Zambian Leader Raps Diplomats' "Interference" in Country's Internal Affairs', 11 May 2012

——, (*Zambia Daily Mail, Lusaka, Zambia, 11 May 2012*), 'Sata asks Foreign Diplomats to "Re-evaluate" Ties with Zambia Opposition Parties', 12 May 2012

——, (*Zim Online website, South Africa, 24 June 2008*), 'Zimbabwe: Police Chief Accuses Tsvangirai of "Stunt" to Harm Country's Image', 24 June 2008

——, (*ZimOnline website, South Africa, 21 December 2010*), 'Zimbabwe Ruling Party Threatens to Expel "Interfering" Western Diplomats', 21 December 2010

BBC Monitoring Asia Pacific—Political (Myanmar Information Committee website, Rangoon, 25 September 2000), 'Burmese Ruling Council uses British PM's Words to Defend Treatment of Suu Kyi', 26 September 2000

BBC Monitoring Europe—Political (Czech News Agency CTK, Prague, 23 February 2006), 'Czech Minister Rejects Belarusia's Allegation of Interference in Internal Affairs', 23 February 2006.

——, (*Rompres, Romania, 14 December 2007*), 'Romania Expresses Regret over expulsion of envoys from Moldova', 15 December 2007

——, (*Sme website, Slovakia, 21 December 2010*), 'Outgoing UK Envoy Criticizes Corruption, Judiciary, Human Rights in Slovakia', 26 December 2010

BBC Monitoring Former Soviet Union—Political (Nezavisimaya Gazeta, Russia, 31 July 2009), 'Russian Newspaper Examines Escalating Diplomatic Row with Ukraine', 3 August 2009

——, (*RTR Russia TV, Moscow, 31 January 2006*), 'Putin says Spy Scandal will not Harm Relations with UK', 31 January 2006

BBC Monitoring International Reports (2000, Kiev, Ukraine, 11 June 2004), 'Ukrainian Weekly Dubs US Ambassador Undiplomatic, Ill-mannered', 12 June 2004

——, (*Infotag, Romania, 14 December 2007*), 'Moldova Says Romanian Diplomats Banned Over "Political Activities"', 14 December 2007

——, (*Kayhan, Iran*), 'BBC Monitoring Quotes from the Iranian Press', 7 March 2004

——, (*Radio Metropole, Port-au-Prince, 22 April 2002*), 'Haitian Minister to Question French Ambassador Over "Inappropriate" Remarks', 22 April 2002

——, (*Radio Metropole, Port-au-Prince, 22 April 2002*), 'Highlights of Radio Metropole News 1145 GMT 22 APR 02', 24 April 2002

——, (*Radio Metropole, Port-au-Prince, 29 April 2002*), 'Foreign Minister on Prime Minister's Meeting', 30 April 2002

——, (*The People, Kenya, 4 February 2005*), 'British Envoy Congenital Liar—Kenyan Foreign Minister', 4 February 2005

BBC Monitoring Kiev Unit (Interfax-Ukraine News Agency, Kiev, Ukraine, 13 February 2014), 'Ukrainian Foreign Ministry Calls in Russian Diplomat over Federalization Remarks', 13 February 2014

BBC Monitoring Latin America—Political (Los Tiempos website, Bolivia, 16 October 2007), 'Bolivian Presidency Minister Considers making US Envoy "Persona Non Grata"', 18 October 2007

——, (*Ecuadoran CRE Satelital radio web site, Guayaquil, 22 April 2005*), 'Ecuador's Gutierrez makes First Statements since Taking Shelter in Embassy', 23 April 2005

BBC Monitoring Middle East—Political (Al-Dustur, Jordan, 14 August 2011), 'Jordanian Paper Slams Act of Giving Information to Foreign Embassies', 16 August 2011

——, (*Al-Sharq al-Awsat, Saudi Arabia, 21 March 2011*), 'Pan-Arab Daily Reports on Downturn in Bahrain-Iran Relations', 29 March 2011

——, (*Daily Star, Lebanon, 18 January 2011*), 'Lebanese Minister Summons US Envoy Over "Interference" in Internal Affairs', 18 January 2011

——, (*Gulf News, Dubai, 7 May 2013*), 'Bahrain Denies Reports of "Strained" Ties with USA', 8 May 2013

——, (*Gulf News, Dubai, 19 October 2012*), 'Bahraini MPs Urge Government to End "Interference" by US Ambassador', 21 October 2012

——, (*Liberte website, Algeria, 3 March 2008*), 'Algerian Premier Criticizes US Ambassador's Interference in Internal Affair', 4 March 2008

——, (*Gulf Daily News, Bahrain, 16 March 2010*), 'Bahraini Petition Reiterates Call for Expulsion of British Envoy', 16 March 2010

——, (*Vision of the Islamic Republic of Iran Network 2, Tehran, 9 August 2009*), 'Iran TV Airs Discussion on Detainees' Confessions, Reactions by West', 9 August 2009.

BBC Monitoring South Asia—Political (Ariana TV, Kabul, Afghanistan, 18 December 2012), 'Afghan Senators Call Paris Conference Against Diplomatic Principles', 19 December 2012

——, (*Arzu TV, Mazar-e-Sharif, Afghanistan, 25 December 2012*), 'Afghan Minister Rejects "Occupied Country" Remark by Iran Officials', 26 December 2012

——, (*Daily Mirror, Sri Lanka, 29 May 2012*), 'Sri Lankan Minister Criticises UK Envoy over Comments on Army Presence in North', 29 May 2012

——, (*The Daily Star website, Dhaka, Bangladesh, 17 February 2014*), 'MP Asks Foreign Diplomats not to Interfere in Bangladesh's "Internal Affairs"', 17 February 2014

——, (*The Daily Star website, Dhaka, Bangladesh, 16 July 2008*), 'US Envoy Discusses Emergency with Bangladesh Leaders', 16 July 2008

——, (*The Daily Star website, Dhaka, Bangladesh, 23 March 2008*), 'US Envoy Refutes "Claims of Interference" in Bangladesh Affairs', 24 March 2008

——, (*Nepalnews.com, Kathmandu, 31 August 2010*), 'Nepal Parliament Body Asks Indian Envoy to Explain Media Remarks', 31 August 2010

——, (*New Age, Bangladesh, 3 June 2008*), 'Bangladesh Asks Foreign Envoys to Refrain from "Interference"', 3 June 2008

——, (*New Age, Bangladesh, 21 March 2008*), 'Bangladesh Urges Diplomats to Stop "Interference"—Paper', 21 March 2008

——, (*New Age, Bangladesh, 2 July 2009*), 'Indian Envoy Perhaps Breached Norms: Bangladesh Foreign Minister', 2 July 2009

BBC Online, '"Anti-Semitic" French Envoy Under Fire', 20 December 2001, http://news.bbc.co.uk/1/hi/world/europe/1721172.stm, accessed 3 May 2015

——, 'Bangladesh War Crimes Trial: Key Defendants', 17 July 2013, http://www.bbc.co.uk/news/world-asia-20970123, accessed 3 May 2015

——, 'Diplomat Censured over Bomb Poem', 18 April 2002, http://news.bbc.co.uk/1/hi/uk/1937696.stm, accessed 3 May 2015

——, 'Eritrea Expels Italian Ambassador', 1 October 2001, http://news.bbc.co.uk/1/hi/world/africa/1572517.stm, accessed 3 May 2015

——, 'European haven for Iraq envoys', 21 March 2003, http://news.bbc.co.uk/1/hi/world/europe/2872995.stm, accessed 3 May 2015

——, 'Fiji expels New Zealand diplomat', 14 June 2007, http://news.bbc.co.uk/1/hi/world/asia-pacific/6751133.stm, accessed 3 May 2015

——, 'Italy Expels Eritrea's Ambassador', 2 October 2001, http://news.bbc.co.uk/1/hi/world/africa/1575814.stm, accessed 3 May 2015

——, 'Julian Assange Security "Sucking Met Police Resources"', 10 February 2015, http://www.bbc.co.uk/news/uk-31356912, accessed 3 May 2015

——, 'Malaysia Accuses Diplomats', 24 November 1999, http://news.bbc.co.uk/1/hi/world/asia-pacific/534847.stm, accessed 3 May 2015

——, 'Pakistan Recalls Dhaka Diplomat', 30 November 2000, http://news.bbc.co.uk/1/hi/world/south_asia/1048296.stm, accessed 3 May 2015

——, 'Profile: Libya's Moussa Koussa', 31 March 2011, http://www.bbc.co.uk/news/world-africa-12915987, accessed 3 May 2015

——, 'Taleban Accuse Iran', 13 September 1998, http://news.bbc.co.uk/1/hi/world/south_asia/169901.stm, accessed 3 May 2015

——, 'US Denies Interfering in Indonesia', 16 October 2000, http://news.bbc.co.uk/1/hi/world/asia-pacific/974694.stm, accessed 3 May 2015

——, 'Zimbabwe "Tracking" British Diplomat', 15 June 2002, http://news.bbc.co.uk/1/hi/world/africa/2046602.stm, accessed 3 May 2015

BBC Summary of World Broadcasts (Agence France-Presse, France, 22 October 1993), 'Western Diplomats Accused of Interference', 25 October 1993

——, (*Anatolia in English, Turkey, 3 April 1989*), 'Iran Links Diplomatic Row with Turkey to Salman Rushdie Affair', 5 April 1989

——, (*Hungarian Telegraph Agency, Hungary; Bucharest Home Service, Romania, 24 November 1988*), 'Hungarian Romanian Relations; Hungarian Expulsion of Romanian Diplomat and Romanian Protest', 28 November 1988

——, (*Iranian radio and agency, Iran, 25 May 1983*), 'Expulsion of Iranian Diplomats from the USSR', 27 May 1983

——, (*Johannesburg Home Service in English, 29 March 1983*), 'Pik Botha's Response to Australian Criticism', 30 March 1983

——, (*Kenya News Agency, Nairobi, 16 February 1995*), 'Kenya; Minister Criticizes US Ambassador's Reported Remarks on Liberalization of Media', 20 February 1995

——, (*KBC Radio, Kenya, 17 February 1995*, 'Kenya; US Ambassador Denies Giving Deadline for Media Liberalization', 20 February 1995

——, (*Managua Home Service, Nicaragua, 11 July 1988 and 12 July 1988*), 'Nicaraguan President, Foreign Minister on Expulsion of US Ambassador', 13 July 1988

——, (*Radio Vilnius, Lithuania, 19 August 1992*), 'Other Reports; Polish Ambassador Accused of Interfering in Lithuanian Internal Affairs', 25 August 1992

——, (*Santiago Home Service, Chile, 2 December 1985*), 'Pinochet on US Relations, Democracy and "Meddling Ambassadors"', 5 December 1985

——, (*SAPA in English, South Africa, 30 January 1989*), 'South and Southern Africa in Brief. S African Envoy Denies Claim of "Hit Team" Attack on Home of ANC Representative in Sydney', 1 February 1989

——, (*Telam, Argentina*), 'Peronist Deputy to Seek Expulsion of Israeli Ambassador', 11 March 1985

——, (*Turkish National News Agency, Turkey, 3 January 1979*), 'British Ambassador Accused of Interfering in Turkey's Internal Affairs', 5 January 1979

——, (*Turkish National News Agency, Turkey, 4 January 1979*), 'British Ambassador Accused of Interfering in Turkey's Internal Affairs (ME/6008/C/1)', 6 January 1979

——, (*TV Myanmar, Myanmar, 1 October 1996*), 'Ruling Council Explains Actions against Opposition at News Briefing', 4 October 1996

——, (*Voice of Israel, Jerusalem, 5 September 1995*), 'Issue of Jerusalem 3000', 7 September 1995

BBC Worldwide Monitoring (Myanmar Alin, Myanmar), 'Paper Attacks Foreign Media, Diplomats', 19 September 1998

——, (*NTV television, Turkey, 16 August 2005*), 'Turkey says Iranian Foreign Minister-Designate not Persona Non Grata in 1989', 16 August 2005

——, (*Polish Radio 1, Warsaw, Poland, 15 July 2005*), 'Polish Consul Expelled from Belarus', 15 July 2005

——, (*RTR Russia TV, Russia, 31 January 2006*), 'Putin Comments on Spy Allegations—Clarification', 31 January 2006

——, (*The News web site, Islamabad*), 'Pakistani Premier says Interference in Pakistani Affairs not to be Allowed', 26 January 2003

——, (*ZTV1, Harare, Zimbabwe, 9 November 2005*), 'Zimbabwean Dons say US Envoy "Main Agent for Political Upheaval"', 10 November 2005

Beard, David, 'Haitians Explode With Joy, Some Clash With Police', *The Associated Press*, 24 September 1994

——, 'In Land Of Calypso, Crime Hits A Sour Note', *The Associated Press*, 1 March 1994

Beaulieu, S, 'Former Duvalier Supporters said to Flee Haiti', *United Press International*, 24 February 1986

Beeston, Richard, 'Occupation "Worse than Nazis"', *The Times*, 10 July 2002

——, 'UK Envoy Expelled by The Gambia', *The Times*, 24 August 2001

Behrens, Paul, 'Stochern im Wespennest', *Süddeutsche Zeitung*, 6 March 2009

Bell, Alex, 'More Calls for Early MDC-T Congress', *SW Radio Africa*, 24 February 2014

Beltrame, Julian, 'Malaysian Politician's Trial Starts Under Cloud: The Judge Rules that International Observers will not be Given Observer Status at the Former Deputy PM's Trial', *The Vancouver Sun*, 3 November 1998

Blanchfield, Mike, 'Alliance will Americanize Canada: Chretien: The Prime Minister's America-bashing, which Helped him in his First Election in 1993, could Backfire on him this Time', *Welland Tribune*, 25 October 2000

Blitz, James; 'Old Nationalist Tensions Lead To Hungary-Romania Discord', *Financial Times*, 26 November 1988

Blitzer, Wolf; Malveaux, Suzanne; Clancy, Jim and Quijano, Elaine, 'CNN Late Edition With Wolf Blitzer 12:00. Interview with Prince Bandar Bin Sultan; Interview with Karen Hughes', 25 April 2004

Bloomfield, Douglas, 'No Different Standards for Jewish Envoys', *Washington Jewish Week*, 17 January 2002

Boak, Josh, 'Karzai Opens Afghan Parliament with Accusations, Call for Unity', *The Washington Post*, 27 January 2011

Bobinski, Christopher, 'Poland Warns U.S. over "Interference Attempt"', *Financial Times*, 8 May 1985

Booth, William and Forero, Juan, 'New Honduran Leadership Flouts Worldwide Censure', *The Washington Post*, 30 June 2009

Boskovic, Boris, '[Yugoslavian Relations with the United States are Cooling]', *The Associated Press*, 11 July 1976

Bourke, Gerald, 'Pakistan Shuts Indian Mission', *The Guardian* (London), 27 December 1994

Brace, Matthew, 'British Diplomats Turn Away Boys Claiming Asylum', *The Times* (London), 19 July 2002

Brooks, David, 'Fiji Expels NZealand ambassador', *Agence France Presse—English*, 14 June 2007

Bulletin, The, 'Ex-ambassador Draws French Ire', 18 July 1985.

Buncombe, Andrew, 'Sri Lankan Army "Victory" is Marred by Editor's Killing; Journalist Accuses Government of Murdering him in Posthumous Essay', *The Independent* (London), 15 January 2009

Caldwell, Alison, 'Expelled Australian Diplomat Leaves Fiji', *ABC Premium News*, 14 July 2010

Calgary Herald, 'Expulsion of Diplomat Demanded', 4 August 1973

CANA News, 'Suriname-Politics-President Bouterse Threatens to Expel US Ambassador', 27 February 2014

Capital, The (Annapolis, USA), 'AP News in Brief at 5:58 p.m. EST', 11 January 2014

Carroll, Raymond and Goldschlager, Seth S; Bureau Reports, 'All Roads Lead to Paris', *Newsweek*, 21 July 1975

Carroll, Rory, 'Cuban Sting shows US Diplomat Handing over Cash to Dissidents', *The Guardian* (London), 24 May 2008

——, 'Manuel Zelaya Refuses to Leave Honduras as Asylum Seeker', *The Guardian* (London), 10 December 2009

——, 'Security Forces Clash with Protestors in Honduras as Tensions Rise after Zelaya's Return', *The Guardian* (London), 23 September 2009

CBS, 'US Diplomat Kicked Out Of Sudan', 7 December 2000, http://www.cbsnews.com/stories/2000/12/07/world/main255471.shtml, accessed 3 May 2015

Cerkez-Robinson, Aida, 'Bosnian Presidency Considers Expelling US Ambassador', *The Associated Press*, 6 February 2001

Channel News Asia, 'Singapore Dismisses Malaysian Media Allegations of Interference in Politics', 22 June 2012

——, 'Sweden and Israel in Furious Diplomatic Row over Art Scandal', 18 January 2004

Chen, Melody, 'Taiwan: AIT Denies Director Leaving for White House', *World News Connection (Source: Taipei Times)*, 9 September 2003

China Business News, 'China Strongly Dissatisfied with Japanese Official's Remarks', 10 December 2013

China Post, 'MOFA Dismisses Interference Charge by Nauru President', 20 August 2002

CNN, 'British, French Embassy Workers on Trial over Iran Protests', 9 August 2009, http://edition.cnn.com/2009/WORLD/meast/08/08/iran.detainee.trials/, accessed 3 May 2015

——, 'Ecuador says WikiLeaks Founder Assange is Seeking Asylum', 19 June 2012, http://www.cnn.com/2012/06/19/world/europe/ecuador-assange-asylum/, accessed 3 May 2015

——, 'Malaysia's Anwar Returns to Court for Closely Watched Trial', 3 November 1998, http://www.cnn.com/WORLD/asiapcf/9811/03/anwar.trial.day.two.01/

——, 'U.S. Diplomat Expelled from Sudan', 7 December 2000, http://www.cnn.com/2000/WORLD/africa/12/07/sudan.diplomat.03/

——, 'U.S. Diplomat Leaving Belarus', 23 March 1997, http://www.cnn.com/WORLD/9703/23/briefs.pm/belarus/index.html, accessed 3 May 2015

——, 'Zimbabwe's President Threatens "Revenge" Against Western Companies', 17 December 2010 accessed 3 May 2015

Cohen, Andrew, 'Regional News. Ottawa', *United Press International*, 13 May 1982

Cohn, Martin Regg, 'Dirty Tricks Accusations Fly as Malaysians Head to Polls', *The Toronto Star*, 27 November 1999.

Colombo Gazette, 'Case Filed against Kariyawasam', 20 November 2013

Crabb, Annabel, 'Howard Carpets Chinese Envoy', *The Age*, 28 April 2001.

CTK National News Wire, 'Czech Embassy in Minsk Probably Damaged by Vandals', 5 February 2008

——, 'Czechs Provide 4 Million Crowns to Support Democracy in Belarus', 23 February 2006

Cumming-Bruce, Nick, 'Expelled Envoy in New Row', *The Guardian* (London), 21 May 1988

Daily Guide (Ghana), 'Troops Hunt for Tsvangirai', 25 June 2008

Daily Herald (Chicago), 'Bouterse Threatens to Boot US Ambassador', 25 February 2014

Daily News, The (New Plymouth, New Zealand), 'Expulsion is Revenge, says Commissioner', 29 December 2008

Daily Telegraph, The (Australia), 'Diplomat Expelled', 13 September 2006

Daily Telegraph, The (London) (Passed to the Telegraph by WikiLeaks), 'Libya's Berber Minority Still out in the Cold', 31 January 2011

Daily the Pak Banker, 'Sri Lanka Warns US over Leaked Cables', 22 December 2010

Daily Tribune, 'Envoy Denies Interference in Internal Affairs', 4 December 2012

Dan, Uri and Eisenberg, Dennis, 'An American Vassal?', *The Jerusalem Post*, 10 July 1997

De Cordoba, José, 'Crisis in Honduras: What was Really Behind the Removal of President Manuel Zelaya, and is he Likely to be Reinstated?', *Inside Costa Rica*,

10 October 2009, http://insidecostarica.com/special_reports/2009/2009-10/honduras_zelaya.htm, accessed 3 May 2015

DefenceWeb (Reuters), 'UK, Malawi Expel Each Other's Diplomats', 28 April 2011

De Onis, Juan, 'Russians Ask 69 Exit Visas in Bolivia', *The New York Times*, 8 April 1972

De Silva, Nilika, 'UN Envoy wants CJ to Step Aside', *Sunday Times (Sri Lanka)*, 19 August 2001, http://sundaytimes.lk/010819/frontm.html, accessed 3 May 2015

Deutsche Presse-Agentur, '2nd Lead: Problems Hit Kenyan Vote-counting; Impatience Sets In', 6 March 2013

——, 'Australia Reprimands Zimbabwe Diplomat over 'Dictator' Jibe', 11 December 2003

——, 'Background: WikiLeaks Documents in Public Interest, Newspapers Say', 28 November 2010.

——, 'U.S. Defends Envoy Against Bosnian Presidency Charges', 6 February 2001

——, 'U.S. Government says it Stands by its Zimbabwe Envoy', 8 November 2005

——, 'Western Ambassadors Rebuked for Walking Out of Mugabe Speech', 3 August 2010

Deutsche Welle Europe, 'Yanukovych Criticizes West for Meddling in Ukrainian Political Crisis', 19 December 2013

Deutsche Welle World, 'Kenyans in Suspense over Poll Outcome', 6 March 2013

Dhaka Courier, 'Pinak Overstepping the Bounds of Diplomatic Norms', 26 June 2009

Dingake, Oagile Key, 'Botswana: Political Party Funding Helps Level Playing Field', *Mmegi/The Reporter*, 15 December 2006

Dispatch, The (Accra), 'Ghana; Government To Deport Diplomat?', 5 September 2000

Doyon, Richard, 'Regional News', *United Press International*, 25 February 1981

Duboudin, Tony, 'Australian Embassies on Terror Alert after Hawke Cuts Libya Ties', *The Times* (London), 20 May 1987

Dummett, Mark, 'Bangladesh War: The Article that Changed History', BBC Online, 16 December 2011, http://www.bbc.co.uk/news/world-asia-16207201, accessed 3 May 2015

Economist, The, 'Jugoslavia; Neutral on whose Side?', 2 April 1977

——, 'Latin America; Goodbye Che', 26 July 1975

EKantipur.com, 'Embassy Statement Row', 30 August 2010

El Universal, 'FCH: estados eluden lucha contra crimen', 22 February 2011, http://www.eluniversal.com.mx/notas/746815.html, accessed 3 May 2015

E-mela, 'Pakistan Regrets over Controversial Remark and Recalls Deputy High Commisioner' (c December 2000), http://web.archive.org/web/20010617072434/http://e-mela.com/Bangladesh/, accessed 3 May 2015

Enders, John, 'Official Accused Of Drug Trafficking Removed As Military Academy Head', *The Associated Press*, 30 March 1981

Eyal, Jonathan, 'Pushing the Limits of Diplomatic Immunity', *The Straits Times* (Singapore), 5 July 2008.

Facts on File World News Digest, '3 Soviet Envoys Expelled During Strike', 7 September 1979

——, 'Ghana', 3 November 1978

——, 'Giscard Scores U.S. Talks with Left', 9 April 1977
——, 'Jailed American Freed', 31 July 1976
——, 'Kyrgyzstan; U.S. Air Base Agreement Signed', 24 August 2006
——, 'Libyan Diplomats Expelled', 22 May 1987
——, 'Mbeki Restricted', 31 December 1987
——, 'Moderate, Rightist, both Claim Salvador Election Victory; d'Aubuisson Charges "Irregularities"', 11 May 1984
——, 'Nicaragua, U.S. Trade Diplomatic Expulsions; U.S. Said to Meddle in Internal Affairs', 15 July 1988.
——, 'Parliamentary Boycott Ended', 8 April 1983
——, 'Schaufele Rejected as U.S, Envoy', 6 August 1977
——, 'Soviet Ambassador Expelled', 8 February 1980
——, 'Tito Attacks U.S. Envoy', 14 August 1976
——, 'Uruguay', 23 July 1982
——, 'U.S. Ambassador Barred', 8 June 1979
——, 'U.S. Backs Off from Envoy's Remarks', 19 November 1982
——, 'U.S. Envoy Expelled; Other Developments', 27 March 1997
——, 'U.S., Israel dispute aid', 17 April 1976
——, 'U.S.S.R. Severs Diplomatic Relations', 15 November 1975
——, 'Venezuela; Chavez Expels U.S. Ambassador; Other Developments', 18 September 2008
——, 'Vietnamese Diplomat Expelled', 13 April 1979
Federal News Service, 'Remarks of Sir Nicholas Henderson, Former British Ambassador, at the Georgetown University School of Foreign Service Seminar "Perspectives on US Diplomacy", Georgetown University, Washington D.C.', 17 November 1988.
——, 'State Department Regular Briefing. Briefer: Charles Redman', 17 November 1988
——, 'State Department Regular Briefing. Briefer: Richard Boucher', 25 September 1990
——, 'United States Institute of Peace. Subject: The Upcoming National Elections in Iraq And The Prospects For Peace And Stability. Speaker: Christopher Hill', 17 February 2010
Fenton, Tom, 'U.S. Ambassador Accused of Send Newspaper Story on Embassy Telex', *The Associated Press*, 4 August 1980
Fenzi, Jewell, Interview with Elizabeth Lewis Cabot, *The Association for Diplomatic Studies and Training, Foreign Affairs Oral History Project, Foreign Service Spouse Series*, 28 April 1987, http://memory.loc.gov/service/mss/mssmisc/mfdip/2005%20txt%20files/2004cab01.txt, accessed 3 May 2015
Fiji Times (Australia), 'NZ Unfair, Cries Voreqe', 16 June 2007
——, 'Voice of the People', 24 May 2008
Financial Times, 'Observer: Speak low. Observer Column', 3 October 2000
——, 'Pakistan Daily Outlines "Bitter" Diplomatic Relations Between Pakistan, India', 10 February 2003
Finke, Nikki, 'British Expel Libyan Diplomat', *The Associated Press*, 13 June 1980.
Finn, Peter, 'Russia Says British Used Rock to Spy; Security Service Accuses Four Diplomats', *The Washington Post*, 24 January 2006.
Fleming, Neil, 'Police Shoot Two Amid Fresh Unrest', *United Press International*, 11 July 1990

Fletcher, Pascal, 'Expulsions Cast Cold War Shadow over U.S.–Cuban ties', *Reuters*, 24 December 1998

Flynn, Anne-Gerard, 'Irish Laud Diplomat called Home by U.S.', *The New York Times*, 8 February 1981

Focus on Israel, 'Disabled Protesters Making Most Noise In This Year's Budget Battle', 10 January 2002

Fofana, Lansana, 'Sierra Leone—Politics: German Diplomat Ordered to Leave', *Inter Press Service*, 9 April 1994

Forward, The, 'New French Ambassador's Remarks Strike Sour Note', 5 September 2003

Frazier, Joseph, 'Helms, Candidate Charge U.S. Interference As Campaign Winds Down', *The Associated Press*, 3 May 1984

Frei, Matt; Willis, David and Ingram, Simon, 'Anwar Upbeat as Trial Opens', *BBC Online*, 2 November 1998, http://news.bbc.co.uk/1/hi/world/asia-pacific/205764.stm, accessed 3 May 2015

Frontrunner, The, ' Diplomatic Row Escalates In South America', 12 September 2008.

Froomkin, Dan, 'No Saudi Oil "Deal", Woodward Says', *The Washington Post*, 20 April 2004

Galpin, Richard, 'Wahid Urged to Remove US Ambassador', *BBC Online*, 2 November 2000, http://news.bbc.co.uk/1/hi/world/asia-pacific/1003746.stm, accessed 3 May 2015

Gannon, Kathy, 'Disappointed Diplomats to Leave Afghanistan—Without Seeing Detained Nationals', *The Associated Press*, 20 August 2001

Gass, Simon, 'International Human Rights Day', *UK Embassy in Iran*, 9 December 2010, http://ukiniran.fco.gov.uk/en/news/?view=News&id=353368682, accessed 31 March 2012

Gavshon, Arthur, 'Ambassador Retired in Midst of Controversy', *The Associated Press*, 10 February 1981

Gedda, George, 'Washington. The Carter Administration has Expelled a Taiwanese Official', *The Associated Press*, 30 January 1979

——, 'U.S. Expels Cuban Diplomat, Accusing him of Associating with Criminal Elements', *The Associated Press*, 3 January 2004

——, 'US Sees Sharp Leftward Drift in Surinam', *The Associated Press*, 5 January 1983

Gehlen, Martin, 'Yogi und Ingo belasten Beziehungen zu Teheran', *Stuttgarter Zeitung*, 28 January 2010

Gentleman's Magazine, The, vol XVI (June 1746), 304–19.

Gibson, John and McDowell, Dagen, 'Government Cracking Down on Indecency; Interview Kerry Senior Advisor Jamie Rubin', *Fox News Network*, 19 April 2004

Gittings, Danny, 'Beijing Offers a Blast from the Past', *South China Morning Post*, 10 May 1998

Gonda, Violet, Interview with US Ambassador Christopher Dell, *SW Radio Africa*, 20 March 2007, http://www.zimbabwesituation.com/old/mar21a_2007.html#Z15, accessed 3 May 2015

Gottlieb, Henry, 'Helms Asks Reagan To Fire Ambassador To El Salvador', *The Associated Press*, 2 May 1984

Government of Hungary, 'International Conference and Exhibition on Cardinal József Mindszenty', *Website of the Prime Minister's Office, Hungary,* 21 September 2012, http://www.kormany.hu/en/prime-minister-s-office/news/international-conference-and-exhibition-on-cardinal-jozsef-mindszenty [Government of Hungary, Mindszenty Conference (2012)]

Graham, Bradley, 'Suriname's Military Rulers Firm Up Libyan Ties; Former Links to Cuba Lapse but New Venture Raises Questions in Eastern Caribbean', *The Washington Post,* 24 February 1987

Graham, John, 'Undiplomatic Activity' *The Times,* 30 December 1989

Greenpeace, 'Edison Out. The Struggle to Stop Coal-Fired Power Plants in Bo Nok and Ban Krut, Thailand', 2002, http://www.greenpeace.org/raw/content/usa/press/reports/edison-out-the-struggle-to-st.pdf>

Guindi, Maurice, 'Egypt-Soviet Relations Close to Total Break', *United Press International,* 16 September 1981

Habib, Haroon, 'Bangla Opposition Alliance Faces Split', *The Hindu,* 28 March 2001, http://www.hinduonnet.com/thehindu/2001/03/28/stories/0328000e.htm, accessed 3 May 2015

——, 'U.S. Envoy's Remarks Raise Hackles in Dhaka', *The Hindu,* 16 June 2001, http://www.hinduonnet.com/thehindu/2001/06/16/stories/0316000j.htm, accessed 3 May 2015

Hanley, Charles, 'An AP News Special', *The Associated Press,* 15 February 1981

Harel, Yisrael, 'Like a Viceroy', *The Jerusalem Post,* 21 March 1997

Hargrove, Charles, 'French Leftist Views Put Across to US Diplomats', *The Times,* 6 April 1977

Harpweek, '1888. Harrison v Cleveland', 3, http://elections.harpweek.com/1888/Overview-1888-3.htm, accessed 3 May 2015

Harris, Leon; Collins, Heidi; Robertson, Nic and Roth, Richard, 'Chief Weapons Inspectors Give Another Update on Iraq to U.N. Tomorrow', *CNN,* 13 February 2003

Harris, Paul, 'Saudi Envoy Praises Bombers', *The Observer,* 14 April 2002

Hartman, Carl, 'Expelled Libyans Refusing to Leave U.S.', *The Associated Press,* 7 May 1980

Hayes, Monte, 'Peru's Presidential Race will Require a Run-off', *The Associated Press,* 13 April 2000

Helmer, Roger, 'Estonia Faces the EU Propaganda Barrage as Expansion Takes Hold', *Lincolnshire Echo,* 2 September 2003

Henderson, Simon, 'The West Must Stop Kidding Itself About Saudi Arabia', *The Daily Telegraph* (London), 11 July 2002

Henry, Neil, 'Kenya Levels Broadside at U.S. Ambassador', *The Washington Post,* 19 November 1991

Herald, The, 'Zimbabwe; Govt Summons, Warns U.S. Ambassador McGee', 17 May 2008

Hindu, The, 'Sri Lanka Sends a Signal', 28 May 2012

Hindustan Times, 'British Ambassador to Harare Placed Under Surveillance', 15 June 2002, http://www.zimbabwesituation.com/june16_2002.html#link13, accessed 3 May 2015

——, 'Devyani Home, Indo-US Diplomatic Row Flares Up', 11 January 2014

——, 'Pacific Tit-for-Tat on Cards After Fiji Expels Diplomats', 4 November 2009

Hoagland, Jim, 'U.S. Rebuffs Iran over Rejection of Envoy-Designate; Iran Rebuffed Over Rejection of Envoy', *The Washington Post*, 5 June 1979

Hobart Mercury, 'Mr Eddie Funde[;] Pretoria Uses Hitmen ANC Warns', 31 January 1989

Hong, Zhang, 'West Still Pushing Democracy in Former Soviet Republics', *Global Times* (China), 17 December 2013

Horsnell, Michael, 'Gaddafi Men Sentence to Death Two Libyan Exiles in London Threat to Link with IRA', *The Times*, 13 June 1980

Hornsby, Michael and Kennedy, Ray, 'Fugitives Shelter in British Consulate', *The Times*, 14 September 1984.

Hossain, Moazzem and Price, Susannah, 'Dhaka Expels Pakistani Diplomat', *BBC Online*, 15 December 2000, http://news.bbc.co.uk/1/low/world/south_asia/1072262.stm, accessed 3 May 2015

Hui, Sylvia and Solano, Gonzalo, 'Ecuador says WikiLeaks Founder Seeking Asylum', *Associated Press Online*, 19 June 2012

Hussain, Thomas, 'Bahrain Orders Iranian Diplomat Out', *United Press International*, 1 February 1996

Hussein, Zahid and Boyes, Roger, 'Taleban Tell Diplomats to Leave Country', *The Times*, 17 August 2001

Hutton, Andrew, 'Section: Regional News', *United Press International*, 16 February 1981

The Independent (Banjul, Gambia), 'Gambia; As US Ultimatum Over Immunity Pact Expires, Gambia, Others Escape Punitive Net', 4 July 2003

Independent, The (Kampala, Uganda), 'South Sudan Conflicts Blamed On Selfish and Opportunistic Politicians', 22 January 2014

Independent, The, (London), 'Law Report: Scope of Duty to Provide Diplomatic Asylum', 10 November 2004

Independent on Sunday, 'Diplomats Expelled', 9 February 2003

India Blooms News Service, 'Julian Assange: OAS Partially Supports Ecuador', 25 August 2012.

Indo-Asian News Service, 'Karzai Protests US Diplomat's Presence at Rival's Meeting', 29 June 2009

——, 'War Crimes Trial Not Closed, Dhaka tells Islamabad', 28 February 2010

Insana, Ron; Mitchell, Andrea; Gregory, David; Press, Bill; Buchanan, Pat; Trainor, Bernard and Cummins, Jim, 'The News on CNBC (20:00)', *CNBC*, 19 April 2004

Integrated Regional Information Network, 'Eritrea: Italian Community Worried By Expulsion of Ambassador', 9 October 2001

Interfax News Agency, 'Polish Diplomat Expelled for Attempts to Destabilize Belarus', 19 May 2005

Intelligence Research Ltd, Caribbean & Central America Report, 'US Takes Active Role in Nicaraguan Elections', 25 April 2006

Intelligence Research Ltd, Latin America, 'News in Brief: Mexico', 2 April 1976

Inter Press Service, 'Nicaragua: U.S. Ambassador Accused of Interfering in Domestic Affairs', 25 October 1984

——, 'Romania: A Fleeing Dictator Reported Captured', 22 December 1989

——, 'United States: Defends Expulsion of Nicaraguan Ambassador', 13 July 1988

Iqbal, Anwar, 'Pakistan Closes Indian Consulate', *United Press International*, 26 December 1994

Iran Brief, The, 'Bahrain and Iran Expel Diplomats', 5 February 1996

Iranian Students News Agency (ISNA), 'Iran's Deputy Minister: German Diplomats have Interfered in Ashura Events', 27 January 2010

Irish Times, The, 'US Penalises States for Refusing to Toe Line on International Court', 2 July 2003

Isachenkov, Vladimir, 'Report: Russia's Spymaster says Moscow won't Expel British Diplomats Accused of Spying', *The Associated Press*, 21 February 2006

Jakarta Post, 'U.S. Ambassador in Jakarta Ruffles Feathers Again', 4 September 2000

James, Ian, 'Nicaragua's Ortega Accuses U.S. of Interfering in Country's Presidential Race', *The Associated Press*, 23 April 2006

——, 'US, Venezuela Increasingly at Odds on Drugs', *The Associated Press*, 2 September 2008

Jansz, Frederica, 'Diplomatic Row over Wayamba', *The Sunday Times* (Sri Lanka), 7 February 1999, http://www.sundaytimes.lk/990207/frontm.html#LABEL3, accessed 3 May 2015

Japan Economic Newswire, 'Asian News—Philippines; U.S. Diplomat Accused of Interfering in August Philippine Coup', 22 October 1987

——, 'Myanmar Accuses British Envoy of having Secret Meetings with NLD', 25 August 2006

——, 'Pakistan Summons U.S. Charge d'Affaires', 16 September 1990

——, 'U.S. Diplomat Breaches Norms of Diplomacy, Myanmar says', 1 October 1996

Javorčíková, Katarina and Gavalec, Miroslav, '13 Disciplinary Actions Against Judges—13 Questionmarks', *Za Otvorenú Justíciu*, 4 May 2010, http://www.zoj.sk/sk/component/content/article?id=252, accessed 3 May 2015

Jayasinghe, Amal, 'Sri Lankan Govt Under Intense Fire as Slain Editor Buried', *Agence France Presse—English*, 12 January 2009

——, 'US Intervention gets Cold Shoulder in Sri Lanka Crisis', *Agence France Presse—English*, 24 August 2001

Jennings, Peter, 'World News Tonight', *American Broadcasting Companies News Transcripts*, 29 January 1981

Jerusalem Post, The, 'Indyk's Absence from Opening of Jerusalem 3000 Ires Government', 6 September 1995.

Jewish Bulletin News of Northern Carolina, 'Drama Erupts in the Knesset: Ambassador Slurred as "Jew-boy"', 11 January 2002

Johnson, Andrew, 'Miliband's Fury as Iranian Embassy Worker is Charged with Spying; Appearance of Senior Staff Member in a Mass Trial in Tehran is Condemned as "an Outrage"', *The Independent on Sunday*, 9 August 2009

Johnston, Cynthia, 'Activists Condemn UK Interference in Bahrain Political Row', *The Scotsman*, 18 March 2010

Jones, David, 'Security Increased for Aquino's Davao Visit', *United Press International*, 22 October 1987

Jones, Jim, 'Botha Threat To Curb Diplomats', *Financial Times* (London), 14 August 1987

Joynes, Kate, 'U.S. Holds Talks with Nicaragua's Splintered Right', *Global Insight*, 19 April 2006

Joyo Indonesian News, 'Syahnakri Plays Down Spat with US Ambassador Gelbard', 28 September 2000, http://www.malaysia.net/lists/sangkancil/2000-09/msg00544.html

Kamm, Henry, 'Malta Takes on the World in Diplomatic War', *The New York Times*, 20 February 1983

Kandell, Jonathan, 'Argentines Given Embassy Refuge', *The New York Times*, 25 September 1974

Kasturi, Charu, 'Tit-for-Tat Kick as Bitterness Lingers US Diplomat Tied to Tickets Told to Leave', *The Telegraph (India)*, 1 January 2014

Keller, Bill, 'Mozambican Elections Thrown in Doubt', 28 October 1994.

Key-young, Son, 'China Envoy Angers Koreans Again', *The Korea Times*, 17 November 2000

Kiel, Frederick, 'U.S. Ambassador to Mexico Embroiled in Dispute', *United Press International*, 24 September 1984

Kilborn, Robert; Hanson, Cynthia, and Hodges, Debbie, 'The News in Brief', *The Christian Science Monitor* (Boston), 28 March 1997

Koh, Tommy, 'The Conduct of a Diplomat in Singapore (Letter)', *The Washington Post*, 14 June 1988

Konglang, Anusak, 'State of Emergency in Bangkok After Parliament Stormed', *Sydney Morning Herald* (Australia), 8 April 2010.

Korea Times, The, 'Dalai Lama's Future Trip to Strain Sino-Korean Ties', 9 September 2000

——, 'Seoul Protesteds [sic] China Envoy's Inappropriate' Remarks', 23 November 2000

Kozak, Michael, 'Letter: Belarus and the Balkans', *The Guardian* (London), 25 August 2001

Kumar, Palash, 'AFP: India, Pakistan Ties Sink Further as Top Diplomats Expelled', *World News Connection*, 8 February 2003

Kurdish Globe, The, 'Barred Candidates Allowed to Stand March Polls', 7 February 2010

Kuttler, Hillel, 'Christopher: Indyk didn't Snub Jerusalem 3000', *The Jerusalem Post*, 11 September 1995

La Guardia, Anton, 'Saudi Arabia Recalls Renegade Ambassador', *Daily Telegraph* (London), 19 September 2002

Lama, Abraham, 'Peru—Politics: U.S. Ambassador Sparks Political Uproar', *Inter Press Service*, 4 July 1997

Langeveldt, Dan, 'Zimbabwe Expels Foul-mouthed Malawian Diplomat', *African Eye News Service* (South Africa), 19 October 1999

Last, Alex, 'Eritrea Plays Down Diplomatic Row', *BBC Online*, 2 October 2001, http://news.bbc.co.uk/1/hi/world/africa/1574910.stm, accessed 3 May 2015

——, 'Fifteen Years Holed up in an Embassy', *BBC Online*, 6 September 2012, http://www.bbc.co.uk/news/magazine-19470470, accessed 3 May 2015

Latinnews Daily, 'Nicaragua: Montealegre Leads Polls', 20 April 2006

Lawless, Jill, 'UK: Assange is Beyond our Reach in Ecuador Embassy', *Associated Press Online*, 20 June 2012

Lee, Matthew, 'On Sri Lanka, ICC Prosecution Could Be an Option for State Party Nationals, Butenis WikiLeaks Fall Out', *InnerCityPress*, 11 December 2010

Lehrer, Jim; Woodruff, Judy; Solman, Paul; Beardon, Tom and Mudd, Roger, 'Raging Bull; Worth the Risk; Mea Culpa; Fair Air?', *Educational Broadcasting and GWETA; The MacNeil/Lehrer NewsHour*, 13 August 1987

Leon, Tony, 'Attitude for Gifts', *Business Day (South Africa)*, 10 October 2005

Ligaiula, Pita, 'Fiji Expels Top New Zealand Diplomat, Claiming he was Involved in Mutiny Plot', *The Associated Press*, 14 June 2007

——, 'US Envoy Criticized by Fiji Military Ruler', *The Associated Press State & Local Wire*, 11 July 2007

Lindgren, April, 'Diplomat Resigns Post: Canada's Ambassador to Mexico Made "Inappropriate" Remarks', *The Ottawa Citizen*, 7 October 1997

Lindsey, Daryl, 'US Ambassador Starts Off on Stern Foot with Germany', *The Christian Science Monitor* (Boston), 6 August 2001

Lippman, Thomas, 'Surviving a Nightmare Inside Castro's Cuba. Expelled Foreign Service Officer Details Harassment During Human Rights Mission in Havana', *The Washington Post*, 1 November 1996

Lopez, Edison, 'Venezuela Threatens To Expel US Embassy Official As Referendum Nears', *The Associated Press*, 29 November 2007

Lopez, Juan and Shoichet, Catherine, 'U.S. Expels 2 Venezuelan Diplomats', *CNN*, 11 March 2013

Los Angeles Times, 'Mugabe Rival Takes Refuge in Embassy', 24 June 2008

MacAskill, Ewen, 'Israel Seeks Head of French Envoy: Foreign Ministry Said to be "Incandescent" after Ambassador Allegedly Speaks of "Shitty Little Country"', *The Guardian* (London), 20 December 2001

McCarthy, Shawn, 'Ottawa Recalls Envoy to Sudan', *Globe and Mail, The (Canada)*, 27 August 2007

McDowell, Robin, 'UN: Myanmar Buddhists Killed More Than 40 Muslims', *The Associated Press*, 24 January 2014

McFadden, Cynthia, Interview with Secretary of Defense Robert Gates and Secretary of State Hillary Rodham Clinton, *ABC News*, 9 November 2010, http://abcnews.go.com/Nightline/transcript-sec-state-hillary-clinton-sec-defense-robert/story?id=12095970&singlePage=true, accessed 3 May 2015

McGrory, Mary 'Italians have Doubts about Golden Uncle', *Sarasota Herald-Tribune*, 16 November 1974.

MacLeod, Alexander, 'Malta's Democracy is Cast in Doubt', *Christian Science Monitor*, 1 March 1983

McVeigh, Tracy, 'Tsvangirai Ready to Take On Mugabe in Election Run-off', *The Observer* (London), 11 May 2008

Mail & Guardian (South Africa), 'Mugabe Tells US Envoy to "Go to Hell"', 8 November 2005

Mainville, Michael, 'Between a Rock and a Spy Case', *The Toronto Star*, 24 January 2006

Malaysia General News, 'Meddling Diplomats can be Ordered to Leave', 6 April 2001

Maletsky, Christof, 'US Remarks Over Abuse Rile Namibia', *Business Day (South Africa)*, 20 August 1999.

Mapondera, Godfrey and Smith, David, 'Malawi Declares Envoy "Persona Non Grata"', *The Guardian*, 20 April 2011

Marcus, David L, 'Saying No to Fidel: Cuban Dissidents Push for Revolution, but they Know Chances are Dim', *The Gazette (Montreal, Quebec)*, 12 October 1996.
Martin, Douglas, 'Move by Uruguay worries U.S. Aides', *The New York Times*, 3 June 1982
Matthews, Roger, 'Singapore Slaps The Hand That Feeds It', *Financial Times* (London), 23 May 1988
Mbao, Elias, 'Banda Tells Off Diplomats Pushing for Regime Change', *The Nation (Nairobi)*, 27 August 2010
Mbitiru, Chege, 'Opposition Leader Ordered Released After Suffering Stroke', *The Associated Press*, 9 June 1991
Mehta, Harish, 'Anti-foreign Feeling Resurging in Thailand', *Business Times (Singapore)*, 1 December 1999.
Melnichuk, Anna, 'Ukrainian Authorities Criticize Western Governments for Pressure Ahead of Presidential Vote', *The Associated Press*, 23 September 2004
Merritt, Chris and Walters, Patrick, 'Fiji Expels High Commissioner', *The Australian*, 4 November 2009
Meyer, Karl E, 'The Diplomat's Tightrope', *The New York Times*, 26 July 1988
Miami Herald, The, 'Claims of Drug Ties in Envoy's Expulsion Rejected; Cuba', 9 January 2004
——, 'Cuba Accuses U.S. Diplomat of Meddling, Sowing Dissent', 19 September 1998, http://www.fiu.edu/~fcf/cubaaccuses.html
——, 'Rebel Ambush Kills 16 from Military Convoy', 22 April 2006
——, 'Soviets Rap Israel Envoy', 1 June 1965
Mideast Mirror, 'Jerusalem 3000 Celebrations Prompt Palestinian Call on Israel to Review its Policy on the City', 5 September 1995
Milwaukee Journal, 'Amin Shifts on Break With Russia', 12 November 1975
Milwaukee Sentinel, 'Russ Break Ties With Uganda', 12 November 1975
Moment, The (London), 'Nigeria; U.S. Wades Into Bayelsa Governorship Battle', 5 November 2011
Morgan, Dan, 'Taiwan Recalls Diplomat Who Scored U.S. Policy', *The Washington Post*, 30 January 1979
Morrison, James, 'Blaming Egypt', *The Washington Times*, 16 January 1998
——, 'Diplomatic Flap', *The Washington Times*, 18 February 2011
——, 'Diplomats expelled', *The Washington Times*, 23 August 2000
——, 'Indyk on the Spot', *The Washington Times*, 27 July 1995
——, 'Ivry discovers America', *The Washington Times*, 27 September 2000
——, 'Making a Name', *The Washington Times*, 27 June 1997
——, 'Mr Ponce Packs Up', *The Washington Times*, 26 August 1996
Mottalebi, Hamed, 'Tehran-Ankara Ties revived', *Echo of Islam*, April 1998, http://www.netiran.com/Htdocs/Clippings/FPolitics/980400XXFP01.html
Moyo, Tabby, 'Namibia; Government Lashes out at Foreign Missions', *The Namibian* (Windhoek), 20 August 1999
Nation, The (Thailand), 'Diplomats Chafe at Rebukes over Meeting with Red-shirt Leaders', 13 May 2010
Nation, The (Kenya), 'Kenya: How Nation Rejected America's ICC Plot', 7 March 2011
——, 'Kenya: Kibaki's Men Furious Over "Clay's Insults"', 4 February 2005.
National Post (Canada), 'Diplomat Hurt by Anti-Israel Remark', 4 May 2004

National Public Radio, 'Show: All Things Considered', 1 June 1992

Neimat, Khaled, 'House Speaker wants Gov't to Look into "Syrian Insults" Against MP', *Jordan Times* (Amman), 16 January 2014

——, 'Syrian Envoy's Remarks to Dominate Sunday's Session', *Jordan Times* (Amman), 9 June 2013

Nepali Times, 'Money for Rights', 5–11 July 2002, issue 101, http://nepalitimes.com/~nepalitimes/news.php?id=5310#.VKP398km4qE, accessed 3 May 2015

New Age, The (Bangladesh), 'Foreign Interference in Local Politics Condemned', 17 July 2008, http://www.bangladesh-web.com/view.php?hidRecord=210546, accessed 3 May 2015

New Nation, The, 'Khaleda Blasts Diplomats Visit to Central Jail', 20 March 2001.

News Bulletin (Interfax-Ukraine), 'Canadian Ambassador to Ukraine Reprimanded for Criticism', 22 September 2004

Newsweek, 'An Envoy's Faux Pas', 13 February 1984

——, 'Canada: The Bitter Truth', 29 December 1975

New York Times, The, 'Iranians Dissolve Communist Party', 5 May 1983

——, 'Bolivia Is Ousting 112 Soviet Aides', 30 March 1972

——, 'Bolivia Military Chiefs Call for Postponement of National Elections', 10 June 1980

——, 'Congo Expels Soviet Aides', 29 July 1971

——, 'Israelis Rebuke U.S. Ambassador', 10 April 1976

——, 'Mozambique Leader Wins Multiparty Vote', 20 November 1994

——, 'Mr Catacazy', 23 October 1871

——, 'Skeptical and Confused, Mozambicans Prepare to Vote', 27 September 1994

——, 'Straight Talk on Pakistan', 24 September 1990

——, 'Suriname Asks Dutch To Withdraw Envoy', 12 January 1987

——, 'The Catacazy Case', 21 March 1895

——, 'The Catacazy Letters', 8 December 1871 (reproducing letter by the US Secretary of State, to the US Minister to Russia)

——, 'Washington Denies "Campaign"', 1 August 1976

New Zealand Herald, The, 'Acting High Commissioner Home from Fiji Today', 28 December 2008

——, 'Calderon Ejects US Diplomat', 22 March 2011

——, 'US Getting Wrong Information about Fiji—Bainimarama', 11 July 2007

——, 'We're not Planning a Sporting Boycott Against Fiji, Says Australia', 6 March 2008.

New Zealand Press Association, 'Fiji Denies Backdown Over McDonald Expulsion', 23 December 2008

Nirumand, Bahman, 'Rüffel aus Teheran', *taz (Die Tageszeitung)*, 9 March 2004

Novak, Robert, 'Critics are Distorting Bob Woodward's Book', *The Augusta Chronicle* (Georgia, USA) 29 April 2004

O'Clery, Connor, 'WikiLeaks: Recalling an Earlier State Department Leak', *Global Post*, 29 November 2010.

Official Kremlin International News Broadcast, 'Press Briefing by Russian Federation Foreign Ministry Spokesman', 11 April 1995.

——, 'Press Conference with President of the Russian Federation Vladimir Putin. The Kremlin, 12:00, January 31, 2006', 31 January 2006.

Olson, Alexandra, 'US Diplomat in Mexico is 1st Casualty of WikiLeaks', *The Associated Press*, 24 March 2011.

——, 'US Ambassador to Mexico Quits Amid WikiLeaks Furor', *The Associated Press*, 20 March 2011.

ONASA News Agency, 'Israeli Ambassador Kicked Out Of Swedish Museum After Vandalizing Art', 17 January 2004

Organization of American States, 'OAS Permanent Council Condemns Coup d'État in Honduras, Calls Meeting of Ministers and Entrusts Secretary General With Carrying Out Consultations', *OAS Press Release E-214*, 28 June 2009, http://www.oas.org/en/media_center/press_release.asp?sCodigo=E-214/09, accessed 3 May 2015

Ottawa Citizen, The, 'I Thought I Knew Everything About Corruption ...', 7 October 1997

——, 'U.S. Replaces Brazil Envoy', 2 August 1961

Ottawa Sun, The, 'World Sunflashes Column. Alleged Spy Tossed', 9 October 2006

Ottaway, David, 'Iraq Said to Have Expelled High-Level U.S. Diplomat', *The Washington Post*, 17 November 1988

PACNEWS, 'Keep Out of Our Affairs: PNG Attorney General', 15 October 2013

Page, Campbell, 'Paris Raps US Over Terrorist Trial Comments/France Attacks American Embassy Statement on Abdallah Sentencing', *The Guardian* (London), 14 July 1986

Pajhwork Afghan News, 'Meet Poll Contenders Thru Govt, US Envoy Told', 23 June 2009

Pakistan Newswire, The, 'Nancy Visits FO to Clarify her Remarks', 24 January 2003

Palencia, Gustavo, 'Honduras Police Break Up Pro-Zelaya Protest', *Reuters*, 22 September 2009.

Palm Beach Post, The, 'Diplomat Has Irish Stewing', 29 January 1981

Panafrican News Agency, 'Namibia; US Expresses Concern Over Human Rights Abuse In Caprivi', 18 August 1999

Park, Nicky, 'PAC: Fiji Not Keen to Replace Aust Diplomat', *AAP Newsfeed*, 16 July 2010

Parr, Henry, 'Politics: Deposed Honduran President Speaks at U.N.', *Inter Press Service*, 30 June 2009

Parthasarathy, G, 'Our Leaders Must Be Cautious', *The New Indian Express*, 3 April 2011, http://newindianexpress.com/magazine/voices/article371102.ece?service=print, accessed 3 May 2015

Paterson, Tony, 'Four Soviets Exposed as Spies', *United Press International*, 18 May 1983

——, 'West German Magazine Tabs Four Soviets as Spies', *United Press International*, 19 May 1983

Payk Net, 'Bahrein Expels Iranian Diplomat', 1 February 1996, http://www.payk.net/mailingLists/iran-news/html/1996/msg00133.html

——, 'Jordan Expels Diplomat, Iran Retaliates', 13 December 1995, http://www.payk.net/mailingLists/iran-news/html/1995/msg00313.html

Peck, Grant, 'Demands for Martial Law to End Red Shirt Protest', *The Scotsman*, 30 April 2010.

Peck, Tom and Buncombe, Andrew, 'David Miliband Called for Sri Lanka Aid "To Win Votes"', *The Independent* (London), 2 December 2010

Penketh, Anne, 'US Ambassador Is Held At Gunpoint Over Mugabe "Plot"', *The Independent* (London), 15 October 2005

People's Daily, 'Barak Urged to Declare U.S. Ambassador "Persona Non Grata"', 18 September 2000, http://english.peopledaily.com.cn/200009/18/eng20000918_50724.html, accessed 3 May 2015

Pereira, Brendan, 'Diplomats "Giving Money to Opposition"', *The Straits Times* (Singapore), 25 November 1999

Peta, Basildon, 'Zimbabwe Threatens Diplomats with Expulsion', *The Independent* (London), 20 March 2007

Peterson, Scott, 'US Spends Millions to Bolster Belarus Opposition. Authoritarian President Lukashenko Headed Toward a Reelection Win Yesterday', *The Christian Science Monitor* (Boston), 10 September 2001

Philippines News Agency, 'U.S. Ambassador Under Fire for Comment on Slovenia's Independence War', 18 January 2014

Phnom Penh Post, The, 'Foreign Envoys Turn Out in Force', 24 September 2013

Pilarte, Doralisa, 'Nicaragua Expels Two US Diplomats, Accuses Them of Instigating Strikes', *The Associated Press*, 25 May 1989

PNG Post-Courier (Australia), 'Kua Blasts EU Envoys', 15 October 2013

Post and Courier, The (Charleston, USA), 'Terrorism Advances and Warnings', 5 March 2003

Pravda Online, 'Lukashenko: "Yugoslav Scenario Won't Materialize"', 5 September 2001, http://web.archive.org/web/20010915005615/http://english.pravda.ru/cis/2001/09/05/14255.html, accessed 3 May 2015

Press-Courier, The, 'Jamaica Demands Envoy Recall; U.S. Apparently Set To Comply', 22 July 1973

Press Trust of India, The, 'Foreign Plot Against Gulf Foiled: Bahrain King', 21 March 2011

——, 'Nancy Powell asks Pak to End Infiltration, Proposes Cease', 23 January 2003

Pringle, James, 'Invitation by British Angers Beijing', *The Times*, 8 May 1998

Radio Free Europe/Radio Liberty, 'Macedonian Presidential Candidate rejects U.S., EU Calls for Participation in Elections', 26 April 2004, http://www.rferl.org/newsline/2004/04/4-SEE/see-260404.asp?po=y

Rahman, Atiqur, 'RAW Hand' in Bid to Break up Alliance', *Tribune News Service*, 21 March 2001, http://web.archive.org/web/20060516102410/http://www.tribuneindia.com/2001/20010321/world.htm, accessed 3 May 2015

Rajghatta, Chidanand, 'Wayne's World: Was Expelled US Official a Bleeding Heart or an Ugly American?', *The Times of India*, 13 January 2014

Ramzy, Austin, 'Conflict in the Air: U.S. Vows to Keep Reporting on Pollution in China', *Time*, 6 June 2012

Reuters, 'U.S. Denies Burma Interference Charges', 2 October 1996, http://web.archive.org/web/20020901171244/http://www.burmanet.org/burmanet/1996/bnn1096n531.txt, accessed 3 May 2015

RIA Novosti, 'An In-depth Look at the Russian Press, July 27', 27 July 2009

——, 'Bulgaria Identifies Expelled Russian Diplomats', 19 March 2001

Right Vision News, 'Govt-opposition Warming in NA; Some Allies Pacified', 22 December 2010

Ritchie, Joe, 'U.S. Expels 4 More Libyan Diplomats', *The Washington Post*, 4 May 1980

Roberts, Andrew, 'Mozambique Pique', *The American Spectator*, March 1992

Rodriguez, Olga, 'Cuba Says Expelled Czech Diplomat is Spy for U.S.', *The Associated Press*, 14 April 2006

Rosenberg, Göran, 'Das Meer der Wölfe; Israels Botschafter und das Kunstwerk', *Süddeutsche Zeitung*, 24 January 2004

Rosenblum, Mort, 'International News (Bucharest, Romania)', *The Associated Press*, 22 December 1989

Raidió Teilifís Éireann News, 'Curfew Imposed in Honduras', 30 June 2009

Russow, Joan, 'US Intervention in Nicaragua Election: Should US Citizens Not be Outraged?', *PEJ News*, 4 November 2006, http://www.pej.org/html/print.php?sid=5916

Rwakaringi, Mugume, 'Govt Demands Apology Over Western Diplomats' Letter', *Voice of America*, 3 April 2014

Sadeh, Sharon, 'Saying as he Pleases, Wishing to do More', *Ha'aretz*, 14 July 2002

St Louis Post-Dispatch, 'World Briefs', 25 January 2014

St Petersburg Times, 'Bolivia Breaks Ties With Cuba', 22 August 1964

——, 'U.S. Envoy Will Leave Brazil Post', 1 August 1961

Samber, Sharon, 'Roller Coaster Diplomat Career of Ambassador Martin Indyk Plummets Again', *Jewish Telegraphic Agency*, c 29 September 1996, http://web.archive.org/web/20070814021454/http://www.ijn.com/archive/2000%20arch/092900.htm, accessed 3 May 2015

Santini, Maureen, 'Shultz Tells Envoy to "Tie his Tongue" on Diplomatic Corps', *Gainesville Sun*, 14 February 1985

Scislowska, Monika, 'Poland Says it will Expel Belarusian Diplomat in Tit-for-Tat Move', *The Associated Press*, 18 May 2005

Shaw, Angus, 'Report: Mugabe to Summon U.S. Ambassador in Zimbabwe", *The Associated Press*, 6 November 2005

——, 'Zimbabwe Threatens to Expel Foreign Diplomats', *The Associated Press*, 19 March 2007

——, 'Zimbabwe Warns Envoys of Expulsions', *Associated Press Online*, 19 March 2007

Shu-ling, Ko, 'Denials: Taiwan's Foreign Ministry Denied the South American Country Wanted to Sever Ties and that a Taiwanese Diplomat had Interfered in the Affairs of Nauru's Government', *Taipei Times*, 20 August 2002

——, 'Paraguay Reaffirms Relations with Taiwan', *Taipei Times*, 20 August 2002, http://www.taipeitimes.com/News/archives/2002/08/20/0000164880

Sibanda, Tichaona, 'Attempts to Oust Tsvangirai Claims Scalps of Two Provincial Leaders', *SW Radio Africa*, 5 March 2014

Simuchoba, Arthur, 'Diplomatic Row Brewing. Zambian Fury at Remarks about Democracy by US Ambassador', *Sunday Times (South Africa)*, 20 March 2011

Simons, Marlise, 'Salvador Aid: US Resolve is Questioned', *The New York Times*, 22 November 1982

Slovak Spectator, The, 'Diplomats Observe Disciplinary Case', 22 March 2010

——, 'LGBT Police Readied For March', 6 June 2011

——, 'Pride—An Open Letter', 24 May 2010

——, 'Pride Diplomats React', 13 June 2011

——, 'The Diplomats' Day in Court', 22 March 2010.

Smith, James, 'International News', *The Associated Press*, 13 September 1984

Snow, Anita, 'Cuba Defends Diplomat Expelled from US, Denies American Accusations', *The Associated Press*, 8 January 2004

——, 'U.S. Forces Begin Dismantling Heart of Haiti's Former Military Power', *The Associated Press*, 22 September 1994

Solberg, Monte, 'Time to Stop Shooting from the Hip, Canada Needs a New Approach', *The Hill Times*, 12 February 2001

Spencer, Geoff, 'Diplomat Denies Claims; Fiji', *Sydney Morning Herald*, 3 November 1989

——, 'US Support for Indonesia Declines Amid Anti-Americanism', *Joyo Indonesian News*, 30 October 2000, http://www.malaysia.net/lists/sangkancil/2000-10/msg01084.html

Stacey, Robin, 'British Envoys Joined Revolt; Romania', *The Times*, 27 December 1989

Star Phoenix, The (Saskatoon, Canada), 'Canada Right to Back Envoy in Sudan Case', 29 August 2007

States News Service, 'U.S.-Bolivian Relations: Halting An Avalanche', 15 June 2009

Straits Times, The (Singapore), 'Pals Again', 6 November 1999

Sudan Tribune, 'S. Sudan Accuses Western Diplomats of Interference, Violating Global Laws', 4 April 2014

Süddeutsche Zeitung, 'Deutscher Diplomat kritisiert. Nach Äusserung zur Kurdenfrage. Ankara warnt vor Einmischung in innere Angelegenheiten', 14 December 1998

——, 'Moi erneuert Angriffe auf deutschen Botschafter', 18 July 1995

——, 'Sierra Leone weist deutschen Botschafter aus', 11 April 1994

Sukin, Kamol, 'US Envoy Accused of Meddling', *The Nation* (Thailand), 29 September 1999

Sunday Mail (Queensland, Australia), 'Diplomat Expelled', 9 February 2003

Swazi Media Commentary (Gaborone, Botswana), 'Govt and Secret Arms Deal', 4 March 2013

Tagliabue, John, 'US Diplomats Accused of Meddling in Campaign', *Sydney Morning Herald*, 1 June 1989

Taipei Times, 'China Rebukes Australian PM over Taiwan', 28 April 2001.

Tanzania Daily News, 'Ministry Cautions Envoys On Politics', 18 September 2013

Tapsfield, James, 'UK Embassy Staff Arrested for "Role" in Iranian Unrest', *Belfast Telegraph*, 29 June 2009

Telegraph & Argus, The, 'Foreign Office Probes Commissioner's Visit', 5 June 2001

Tendler, Stewart; Ford, Richard; Horsnell, Michael and Gibb, Frances, 'Head of Libyan Mission is Expelled After Death Threats', *The Times*, 14 June 1980

Thai News Service, 'Embassy Dismisses Report about Recruiting Iranian-Canadians as "Baseless"', 12 July 2012

——, 'Honduras/Brazil: Honduras Presses Brazil Over Refuge to Ousted President', 30 September 2009

——, 'Pime [sic] Minister Tells Foreign Countries Not to Meddle in Thailand's Internal Affairs', 14 May 2010

——, 'Press Freedom in Turkey Criticized Again', 21 February 2011

——, 'Thailand: Foreign Diplomats Explain Why they Met with Anti-government Protesters', 14 May 2010

Thai Press Reports, 'Iran/United Kingdom Iranian Lawmaker Urges "Immediate" Expulsion Of British Envoy', 21 December 2010
Theodoulou, Michael, 'Tehran puts Military on War Alert', *The Times* (London), 16 September 1998
Thomas, Christopher, 'Iran Reinforces Border as Battle of Words Grows', *The Times* (London), 18 September 1998
Thomas, Jo, 'Jamaican Campaign Going On Amid Rising Violence', *The New York Times*, 12 July 1980
Thompson, Ginger and Lacey, Marc, 'Honduras Gets an Ultimatum After Coup', *The International Herald Tribune*, 2 July 2009
Thomson Financial News Super Focus, 'Venezuela's Chavez Threatens to Expel US Ambassador', 1 September 2008
Thorne, Stephen, 'Clark Slams Gore Endorsement', *Timmins Daily Press* (Ontario), 2 June 2000
Time, 'France: Allies v Soviets', 8 April 1940
——, 'The World: Honorable House Arrest', 24 October 1977
Times of Central Asia, The, 'Kyrgyzstan Expels Two US Diplomats', 13 July 2006
Times of Zambia, The, 'Banda Right On Donors, Says Icoz', 28 August 2010
——, 'Zambia; Don't Meddle in Internal Politics—President Sata', 8 September 2012
——, 'Zambia: Govt to Complain Over Meddling U.S. Envoy', 10 March 2011
Times, The, 'China Condemns Russia for Expulsions. "Manufacturing Split in Communist Movement". Decision to Carry on with Moscow Conference', 1 July 1963
——, 'Col. Perón's Victory Certain', 30 March 1946
——, 'Congo Expels Communist Block Diplomats', 30 July 1971
——, 'Congo Expels United Arab Republic Ambassador', 2 December 1960
——, 'Embassy Denial of Interference', 24 December 1964
——, 'Envoys Return from Panama. Consultation after Stormy Spell', 2 April 1964
——, 'Expulsion of a Papal Official', 12 December 1906
——, 'France And The Soviet. The Recall Of M Suritz', 28 March 1940
——, 'Greek Cabinet Minister Attacks German Envoy', 14 October 1971
——, 'Libya Agrees to Withdraw Four Members of London Mission', 13 May 1980
——, 'Libyan Envoy is Expelled from Egypt', 1 July 1976
——, 'Lord Sackville', 1 November 1888
——, 'Mr Bulwer and the Spanish Government', 26 April 1848
——, 'Political Notes. Debate on Russian Propaganda', 15 May 1931
——, 'Red Propaganda. Commons Debate To-day', Monday 18 May 1931
——, 'Russian Official Leaves Congo', 23 November 1963
——, 'Summoned Home for Consultation', 8 May 1962
——, 'The British Minister at Washington', 25 October 1888
——, 'The Recall of Lord Sackville', 14 January 1889
——, 'The Tunku Wins A Sweeping Victory Party's 89 Seats In Malaya', 27 April 1964
——, 'U.S. "Interference" in Argentina', 14 February 1946.
Tirimizi, Maqsood, 'Nisar Blasts US Pressure', *The Nation (AsiaNet)*, 20 December 2010
Today's Zaman, 'Turkey Warns US Ambassador Over Remarks Criticizing Judiciary', 12 February 2013

Toothaker, Christopher, '2 Arrested in Alleged Assassination Plot', *The Associated Press*, 25 September 2008

Toronto Star, The, 'Fujimori Faces Runoff for Peru's Presidency', 13 April 2000

——, 'Malaysia Tells West to Butt Out', 26 November 1999

——, 'Thai PM Clamps Down on Protests; State of Emergency Imposed in Bangkok After Weeks of Demonstrations', 8 April 2010

Travis, Alan, 'Rebirth of Romania: Thatcher Praises People's Courage', *The Guardian* (London), 28 December 1989

Traynor, Ian, 'Belarussian Foils Dictator-buster ... For Now: Tested US Foreign Election Strategy Fails Against Lukashenko', *The Guardian* (London), 14 September 2001

Treuthardt, Paul, 'New Row Between Paris and Washington', *The Associated Press*, 12 July 1986

Trickey, Mike, 'Ottawa Denies Funding Opposition: Official Says Canada Wants to Depose Ruling Coalition', *Calgary Herald*, 25 November 1999

Ukraine General News Service, 'Russia Sees Nothing Subversive About its Diplomat's Statements in Kyiv', 14 February 2014

——, 'European Diplomats Attending Court Hearings on Gas Case, Says Tymoshenko's Press Service', 4 August 2011

United Nations News Centre, 'General Assembly Condemns Coup in Honduras', 30 June 2009, http://www.un.org/apps/news/story.asp?NewsID=31314&Cr=honduras#.UfDapKxt774., accessed 3 May 2015

Ungoed-Thomas, Jonathan and Franchetti, Mark, 'The British Ambassador Says his Hosts are Boiling People to Death...', *Sunday Times*, 26 October 2003

United Kingdom High Commission in New Delhi, 'Britain's Measures Following Expulsion Of British Diplomat', 1 October 2001, http://web.archive.org/web/20040101165515/http://www.ukinindia.org/press/general/gen_266.asp, accessed 3 May 2015

United News of Bangladesh, 'Bangladesh-India-Pakistan Simla Treaty No Bar to Trying Bangladesh's War Criminals, Law Minister Says About Pak Envoy's View', 27 February 2010

——, 'Selim Asks US Diplomats to Follow Norms', 16 February 2014

United News of India, 'Indian Ambassador has Broken Diplomatic Norms: Nepal Foreign Min', 22 December 2008

United Press International, 'Former Noriega Associates Allowed to Leave Country', 11 May 1991

——, 'Indian Diplomats Ordered Out of Fiji', 23 May 1990

——, 'Leftist Parties Want Gavin Expelled; He Says Accusations Absurd', 26 October 1984

——, 'Libya: Australia Involved in Campaign Against the Arab Nation', 21 May 1987

——, 'Thai Court Hands Down 34-year Jail Terms', 26 August 2011

——, 'U.S. Troubled by Ambassador's Memo', 27 Jan 1997

United States Information Agency, The, 'State Department Report', 2 October 1996, http://web.archive.org/web/20000612055514/ http://www.hri.org/docs/statedep/96-10-02.std.html, accessed 3 May 2015

US Fed News, 'VOA News: Diplomatic Relations Between Harare, West Plumb New Lows', 20 March 2007

Valdivieso, Jeanneth, 'Ecuador Expels US Embassy Official for "Meddling"', *The Associated Press*, 18 February 2009

Vallely, Paul, 'Moi Expels Uganda Envoy and Closes Gadaffi's Embassy: Cross-border Tension in East Africa', *The Times* (London), 19 December 1987

Varlamov, Igor 'Cuban Minisrty [sic] Scolds US Diplomat who Attended Procession', *ITAR-TASS News Agency*, 19 September 1998

Vasagar, Jeevan, 'Kenyan President Faces Rebellion on Sleaze', *The Guardian* (London), 24 February 2005.

Vestergaard, Tanja, 'Sri Lankan Government Threatens to Expel Diplomats Following International Criticism', *Global Insight*, 19 April 2007

Vita, Matthew, 'International News', *The Associated Press*, 3 May 1985

Volkel, Christian, 'Ecuador Expels Another U.S. Diplomat for Alleged "Meddling"', *Global Insight*, 19 February 2009

Walsh, Nick Paton, 'Ambassador Defends Diplomat in Spying Row: British Envoy Hits Back Over Moscow Transmitter: Putin to Raise Russian Allegations with Blair', *The Guardian* (London), 1 February 2006

Walsh, Sarah, 'Foreign Office Probes Commissioner's Visit', *This is Bradford*, 6 June 2001

Walters, Stephanie, 'Kinshasa Expels US Diplomats', *BBC Online*, 19 August 2000, http://news.bbc.co.uk/1/hi/world/africa/888131.stm, accessed 3 May 2015

Washington Post, The, 'Another Libyan Exile Assassinated in London', 26 April 1980

——, 'Libya Recalls 4 Envoys Under British Pressure', 13 May 1980

——, 'Peruvian President Sets October Election For Constituent Body', 2 June 1992

——, 'Undiplomatic Relations In Kenya', 24 November 1991

——, 'U.S. Envoy to Ireland Criticized', 28 May 1981

Webster, Paul, 'US Envoy Makes French See Red', *Manchester Guardian Weekly*, 12 February 1984

Wee, Teo Cheng, 'Other Foreign Envoys at Bersih Rally Too; Diplomats Say it is Part of their Job; Some Surprised at Criticism of S'pore', *Straits Times*, 27 June 2012

Weissert, Will, 'Cuba Demands U.S. Answer Charges that Top Diplomat Carried Funds to Havana Dissidents', *The Associated Press*, 22 May 2008

—— and Cuevas, Freddy, 'Honduran Military Ousts President Ahead of Vote', *The Associated Press*, 29 June 2009

Welt, Die, 'Iran; Gerüchte um Ausweisung des deutschen Botschafters', 8 March 2004

West Africa.net, 'The Joshi Case—Jammeh's Latest Blunder', 24 August 2001, http://www.west-africa.net/jammeh/wwwboard/messages/1479.html

White, Martin, 'Why We Joined Student Protests, by Britons', *Press Association*, 26 December 1989

Wigg, Richard, 'Expulsion of Cubans in Paris "Jackal" Case', *The Times*, 11 July 1975

——, 'Soviet Poet "Expelled" After Visit to Bolivia', *The Times*, 1 April 1972

Wilson, Peter, 'Envoy's Absence Angers Israel', *The Australian*, 7 September 1995

Wong, Gillian, 'China Blasts Diplomats Over Dissident's Trial', *The Associated Press*, 24 December 2009

Woodhouse, Craig, '"Velvet Revolution" Plan Denied By Britain', *Press Association Mediapoint*, 11 August 2009

Xinhua General News Service, 'American Ambassador Criticized for Interference in Slovenia's Coalition Talks', 5 January 2012
——, 'Bangladeshi Leftist Party Blasts U.S. Ambassador in Dhaka', 17 May 2001
——, 'Bolivia Accepts U.S. Ambassador's Apologies for Inappropriate Remarks', 23 October 2007
——, 'Bolivia's Armed Forces Call for Delaying of General Elections', 11 June 1980
——, 'China Upset with Japanese Diplomat's Remarks', 9 December 2013
——, 'Cuba Refutes US Accusation Against its Diplomat', 9 January 2004
——, 'EU Apologizes for Mistakes Made by Envoy in Khartoum: Report', 25 August 2007.
——, 'Expelled Iraqi Diplomat Leaves Philippines', 14 February 2003
——, 'Mexican Public Blasts U.S. Ambassador', 16 March 1984
——, 'Roundup: Kenyan Officials Angered by British Envoy's Graft Allegations', 4 February 2005
——, 'Slovenia-U.S. Disputes Over Alleged Interference Continue', 10 January 2012
——, 'Syria Summons U.S., France Ambassadors to Protest Unauthorized Activities', 10 July 2011
——, 'U.S. Ambassador Under Fire for Comment on Slovenia's Independence War', 17 January 2014
——, 'Venezuela Threatens to Expel U.S. Diplomat Over Referendum Suspicions', 29 November 2007
——, 'Venezuelan President Chavez Admonishes U.S. Ambassador', 31 August 2008.
——, 'Vietnamese Ambassador to Sweden Rebuked', 20 May 1979
——, 'Xinhua World News Summary at 0800 GMT, Sept 1', 1 September 2008.
——, 'Zambian Leader Threatens to Expel "Nosy" Diplomats', 7 September 2012
Xinhua General Overseas News Service, 'Costa Rica Not to Allow Moscow to Replace Expelled Diplomats', 10 September 1979
——, 'Four Soviet Diplomats Expelled from Ghana', 11 September 1978
——, 'Kenyan Paper Exposes Soviet Spying Activities', 4 October 1978
——, 'Libyan Embassy In Kenya Closed', 18 December 1987
——, 'Roundup: Australia-Vanuatu Ties Strained Over Diplomatic Bicker', 6 July 1992
——, 'Soviet Ambassador Attacks Australian Government', 22 November 1980
——, 'Tunisia Asks Iran to Withdraw Diplomats in Three Days', 26 March 1987
——, 'Tunisia Breaks Diplomatic Relations With Iran', 26 March 1987
——, 'U.S. Expels Iraqi Diplomat for Retaliation', 17 November 1988
Xinhua News Agency, 'Cuba to Revoke Approval to Spanish Ambassador', 26 November 1996
——, 'German Ambassador Accused of Interfering in Kenyan Internal Affairs', 13 July 1995
——, 'Jordan Expels Iranian Diplomat', 10 December 1995
——, 'Namibia Unhappy with U.S. Comments on Caprivi', 20 August 1999
——, 'US Ambassador Accused of Meddling with Mozambican Internal Affairs', 15 September 1998
——, 'US Ambassador Under Fire For Interfering Kenyan Affairs [sic]', 16 February 1995

Yanquoi, Orando, 'NDC Accuses British Diplomat Of Political Interference', *Expo Times*, 11–24 April 2001

Zionist Organization of America, The, 'Ambassador Indyk Reportedly Interfered in Latest Israeli Cabinet Appointments', 9 July 1997, http://web.archive.org/web/20050123022753/http://www.zoa.org/pressrel/19970709b.htm, accessed 3 May 2015

Zubeiri, Sami, 'Pakistan Accuses India of Terrorism, Closes Consulate, Expels Diplomat', *Agence France Presse—English*, 26 December 1994

Zygel, Philippe, 'US Ambassador Warns of "Serious Consequences" for Bolivia', *Agence France Presse—English*, 14 September 2008

Index

C

I

N

Y

Z

www.ingramcontent.com/pod-product-compliance
Lightning Source LLC
LaVergne TN
LVHW052211200926
848481LV00001B/80

* 9 7 8 1 5 0 9 9 2 4 5 9 2 *